HISTORY & IMAGINATION

HISTORY
&
IMAGINATION

Essays in honour of
H. R. Trevor-Roper

edited by
Hugh Lloyd-Jones
Valerie Pearl
& Blair Worden

gaudet anas
Duckworth

First published in 1981 by
Gerald Duckworth & Co. Ltd
The Old Piano Factory
43 Gloucester Crescent, London NW1

The editors are indebted to Oxford University Press for kindly
permitting republication of Hugh Trevor-Roper's inaugural and
valedictory lectures. Four other essays in the volume first appeared
as lectures. Those by Charles Stuart on Lord Shelburne and
William Thomas on Lord Holland, which have been slightly
amended for publication, were contributions to a series of lectures
given in Hugh Trevor-Roper's honour by senior members of Christ
Church in the autumn of 1977. Valerie Pearl's essay is a revised
version of her Special Ford's Lecture at Oxford in May 1980.
Michael Howard's is based on the Callendar Memorial Lectures
delivered in the University of Aberdeen in November 1979.

ISBN 0 7156 1570 X

British Library Cataloguing in Publication Data

History and imagination.
 1. Trevor-Roper, Hugh
 2. History – Addresses, essays, lectures
 I. Lloyd-Jones, Hugh   II. Pearl, Valerie
 III. Worden, Blair IV. Trevor-Roper, Hugh
 900   D5.5

ISBN 0-7156-1570-X

Photoset by
The Allen Lithographic Co. Ltd
Kirkcaldy
and printed by
Unwin Brothers Limited
Old Woking

Foreword

In this volume a number of colleagues, pupils and friends offer to Hugh Trevor-Roper, Lord Dacre of Glanton, a collection of essays which, while they could not represent all his historical interests, will give an indication of their range. The book was originally meant to appear at the moment of his retirement from the Regius Chair of Modern History at Oxford, to which he was appointed in 1957 and which he was due to vacate under the age limit in 1981; but his election to be Master of Peterhouse caused him to resign his chair a year earlier than had been expected. His inaugural lecture is republished at the beginning of the volume, his valedictory lecture at the end; and we thank him for allowing them to be included. We wish to record our gratitude and admiration for the way in which he carried out the duties of his chair; for his brilliant lectures, always polished to a high degree; for the stimulating effect he exercised both on pupils and on colleagues, including many outside the Faculty of Modern History; and for the kindness with which he helped and guided many younger scholars, among whom he is always quick to detect unusual promise, and to whom he has devoted seemingly bottomless reserves of time, patience and encouragement. Above all, we wish to express our high regard for him as an historian and a writer of altogether exceptional qualities and achievements.

Hugh Trevor-Roper began his scholarly career as an historian of the seventeenth century, especially in England. His biography of Archbishop Laud established him as one of the leading experts in that difficult and dangerous field; after the war his study of the early seventeenth-century gentry started a long and fruitful controversy; and in the masterly essays collected under the title *Religion, the Reformation and Social Change* (1967) he placed seventeenth-century England, as he insists that the history of England must be placed, in its British and its European contexts. A collection of the essays which he has published since 1967 would reveal the diversity, in time, in place, and in subject-matter, of the interests which he has developed.

History, to Hugh Trevor-Roper, has never been a self-contained or conveniently divisible academic discipline. He started as a classical scholar, and his historical scholarship is rooted in the literary tastes and in the linguistic skills which he then acquired; unlike many English historians, he is at home in many different languages. Logan Pearsall Smith ended his appreciative review of his life of Laud by begging its author to sacrifice to the Graces; instead of being offended, Hugh Trevor-Roper took the hint, and with remarkable effect. At the end of the war he seized upon the opportunity offered by the commission to investigate the circumstances of Hitler's death not only to resolve the immediate problem but to write a study of the

National Socialists that remains unsurpassed, and to give the work a form that makes it a delight to read. The style of *The Last Days of Hitler* has a rhetorical element that recalls Macaulay; since then its author's manner has become less rhetorical, showing more clearly the effect of his close familiarity with the writing of the period – the period of the Authorised Version, of Browne, of Milton – when English prose was at its best. Hugh Trevor-Roper writes not in sentences but in periods, as a reading aloud from any of his writings will reveal: few living authors have a more felicitous ear for the rhythms of the language.

Since the war he has illuminated a wide variety of subjects and problems not merely for his fellow-scholars but for the public reader. Only those who regard breadth as incompatible with depth, or who like to see learning heavily paraded, will fail to recognise the profound and careful scholarship that lies beneath the surface of his work. Only narrow specialists could maintain that the time spent upon his many contributions to magazines and newspapers has been wasted; they have been of untold benefit to the general reader, and unlike most writings of this kind are well able to stand the test of time. The collection called *Historical Essays*, published as long ago as 1957, contains much evidence of this; like *Religion, the Reformation and Social Change* it deserves a sequel, which would be larger and even more interesting.

None of the *Historical Essays* is more remarkable than one devoted to Erasmus, which is most characteristic of its author's aims and attitudes. Hugh Trevor-Roper has never been afraid of controversy, and his courage in challenging established opinions and established reputations which he thought harmful gave him when young the reputation of an *enfant terrible*; nor has increasing age made him more tolerant of cant. That may have made it harder for some people to perceive the firm belief in reason and moderation which lies at the heart of his attitude to history. In an age dominated by collectivism and dogmatism he has never ceased to fight for liberal values, from whatever political corner he has felt them to be threatened; and he has always subjected contemporary opinions, however powerful or widespread their expression, to a calm and judicious scrutiny. He shows a special sympathy for men of intellect who have tried by the use of rational methods to resolve the conflicts of unenlightened partisans. Hugh Trevor-Roper is a descendant of Sir Thomas More; and while he would not have agreed with his ancestor on every subject, it is appropriate that he should trace his descent from the chief English friend and follower of Erasmus.

Hugh Lloyd-Jones

Authors

T. C. Barnard is Fellow in Modern History at Hertford College, Oxford
Robert Blake is Provost of The Queen's College, Oxford
Fernand Braudel is Honorary Professor of the Collège de France
Jeremy J. Cater is Lecturer in History at Royal Holloway College, London
Jeremy Catto is Fellow in Modern History at Oriel College, Oxford
John Clive is William R. Kenan, Jr. Professor of History and Literature at
   Harvard
Richard Cobb is Professor of Modern History at Oxford
J. H. Elliott is Professor in the School of Historical Studies, Institute for
   Advanced Studies, Princeton
G. R. Elton is Professor of Constitutional History at Cambridge
Michael Howard has succeeded Hugh Trevor-Roper as Regius Professor of
   Modern History at Oxford
David S. Katz is Lecturer in Early Modern History at the University of
   Tel-Aviv
Hugh Lloyd-Jones is Regius Professor of Greek at Oxford
Robert S. Lopez is Professor Emeritus of History at Yale
James McConica is a Fellow of All Souls, Oxford, and a Fellow of the
   Pontifical Institute of Mediaeval Studies at Toronto
Arnaldo Momigliano is Alexander White Professor in the University of
   Chicago and Professor in the Scuola Normale Superiore of Pisa
Dimitri Obolensky is Professor of Russian and Balkan History at Oxford
Walter Pagel is Emeritus Professor of the History of Medicine at the University
   of Heidelberg
Valerie Pearl is President of New Hall, Cambridge
P. M. Rattansi is Professor of the History and Philosophy of Science at
   University College, London
Kevin Sharpe is Lecturer in History at the University of Southampton
Charles Stuart is Student in Modern History at Christ Church, Oxford
William Thomas is Student in Modern History at Christ Church, Oxford
Blair Worden is Fellow in Modern History at St. Edmund Hall, Oxford
Frances Yates is an Honorary Fellow of the Warburg Institute

Contents

History:
Professional and Lay*

Hugh Trevor-Roper

Mr Vice-Chancellor,† it is no new experience for me to read to you, my former tutor, an imprudent historical essay, though it is a new experience to do so before this formidable public audience. I can only hope that that audience will be as indulgent to my indiscretions as you have always been since you first interested me in this huge subject of human history. Certainly I shall need their indulgence. For I am, I fear, a somewhat eccentric occupant of this chair. It is now thirty-two years since it was last occupied by anyone whose main interest was not medieval, whose Oxford education had not been at Balliol College, and whose historical training had not been at Manchester: three virtues which in my immediate predecessor, Vivian Galbraith, had achieved so pure and concentrated a form that their continuation after him, at the same rate of progressive refinement, was supposed by some to be essential, by others impossible. Since I have been appointed to succeed him I assume that in the end it was found impossible. The force of Nature could no farther go: the dynasty, after the classic term of three generations, is closed; and in saluting him, as I do, across the temporarily intervening Atlantic, I must reflect on the difficulty of succeeding not only him, but a whole tradition – a tradition of which he was the latest representative, and which is still personified here in that Nestor of our school, Sir Maurice Powicke.

For an inaugural lecture, even at the best of times, is a risky undertaking. When I recall the fate of Nicolas Cop, who had to flee for his life after his inaugural lecture at the University of Paris, or of Ernest Renan, who was suspended permanently from his chair after the lecture with which he had fondly believed himself to be inaugurating a long tenure of it, or even of my own predecessor Sir Charles Firth, who suffered a twenty years' boycott through his incautious utterance on such an occasion – though admittedly all these men courted their fate by suggesting some possible reform of their school – I confess I feel some sympathy with those sage, non-committal

*An Inaugural Lecture delivered before the University of Oxford on 12 November 1957.
†J. C. Masterman, who had been a Student of Christ Church from 1919 to 1946 (eds).

professors who, observing that there is no statutory obligation to deliver this customary oration, slide without a squeak into their chairs. Nevertheless, I believe that a man who undertakes to profess even some scattered parts of a great subject ought at some time to have considered the whole of it and should be prepared on some occasion to express his thoughts. I am therefore going to speak about the professional and the lay attitude towards history; and I have chosen this topic partly because I believe that in it lies one of the essential problems facing the teachers of any humane subject, and partly also because that problem has recurred particularly in the history of this regius chair in which I now find myself enthroned.

For when this chair was founded by King George I in 1724, it was founded with a purpose. It was a Whig chair founded in Tory Oxford. It was the culmination of a determined effort, by those enlightened Whig statesmen who had finally disembarrassed this country of its least successful dynasty, to carry the Glorious Revolution into learning, education, and manners. First, they sought 'to ease the present disaffection of the universities', to capture the education of those men who, they hoped, would serve the state from the entrenched forces of the Jacobites. That was why they created 'regius' chairs – chairs not subject to election by the Tory inhabitants of the place but filled by the direct power of the Whig crown. Secondly, they sought to consolidate the victory of the Moderns, those lay precursors of the eighteenth-century Enlightenment, in their long battle against the Ancients, the crusted clerical Tories of the college common-rooms. They wished to provide for English public servants, and particularly for English diplomatists, a school of modern subjects fit for the modern world. That is why they created chairs not of Greek and Latin or Hebrew or divinity but of history – or rather, as they then were, of history and modern languages. When we put the foundation of these two chairs, the regius chairs of modern history in Oxford and Cambridge, in their perspective – when we remember not only the act of their foundation but the other acts which form the background to their foundation: Lord Macclesfield's scheme for university reform in 1718, his plan for a chair of the Law of Nature and Nations, and the new chairs of history, both lay and ecclesiastical, in the Scottish universities – then we must see it, I think, as part of a large design, a design to make the study of history, as it ought always to be, both useful and controversial.[1]

For these, it seems to me, are two essential functions of history. History that is not useful, that has not some lay appeal, is mere antiquarianism; history that is not controversial is dead history; and neither dead history nor antiquarianism deserves a regius chair. This was well known to our ancestors in the reign of George I. Why should they not know it? All the past century had taught that lesson. Modern history, in the seventeenth century, had come very close to living politics. 'Whosoever, in writing a modern history, shall follow truth too near the heels', wrote Sir Walter Ralegh, who lived to bear painful testimony to his own veracity, 'it may haply strike out his teeth.' Nor

[1]For the origin of the chairs, see Norman Sykes, *Edmund Gibson* (1926), 94–7. Lord Macclesfield's scheme is printed in J. Gutch, *Collectanea Curiosa* (1781), II, 53–75, no. IX.

was it only modern history which had proved so dangerous: one lecture on Tacitus had been enough to ruin Dr Dorislaus at Cambridge. The great lay bible of the country opposition to King Charles I had been a work of history, Ralegh's *History of the World*; and the great lay bible of the Tory supporters of the Stuarts under George I was another work of history, Clarendon's great *History of the Rebellion*, newly published by the press, and to the profit, of Tory Oxford. It was perhaps with some hope of capturing from Clarendon the domination of modern historical doctrine that the Hanoverian ministers planted in Oxford their new Whig professors.

Alas, how can a mere ministerial act compete with a work of genius supported by that most powerful of human forces, and especially of Oxford forces, *vis inertiae*? After the hopes of its founding fathers, the first age of the Oxford history professors must seem a sad anticlimax. As so often, what we complacently call 'the genius of the place' quickly absorbed its would-be reformers; and on its side the government, as it gained in stability, quickly forgot its brief flash of intellectual purpose. Oxford disdained the gift of 'the Duke of Brunswick, commonly styled King George I', sent a curmudgeonly acknowledgment through its beadle, and saw to it that while edition after edition of Clarendon's great work issued profitably from its press, no 'Whig' history was heard within its walls.

As for the new professors, they were good Hanoverians all right; they were modern, urbane, enlightened men; but they were not historians. The first of them, to whom Christ Church owes Rysbrack's elegant busts of the first two Georges, was remembered by Lord Shelburne as 'a gentleman though not a scholar', and his inaugural lecture, 'in commendation of Lord Clarendon's *History*', was described (by Tories) as 'a strange medley of stuff without any method or connexion, and in a most wretched barbarous Latin style'. His successor, the first Hanoverian President of St. John's College, was remembered by his colleagues only for having disgracefully allowed 'one Handel, a foreigner, who they say was born in Hanover', to bring his 'lousy crew' of 'fiddlers' to play in the Sheldonian. The third holder, 'a man', as Dr Johnson described him, 'whose learning was not very great and whose mind was not very powerful', is included in the *Dictionary of National Biography* not as a historian but as 'anecdotist and friend of Pope'; and of the Cornish gentleman who followed him I can discover no record, save that after his death King George III wrote to Lord North that it was high time such places, 'having been instituted for promoting learning in the universities', were awarded to merit, not favour;[2] whereupon he nominated to the chair a sound champion of the royal prerogative memorable only by the sermon which he preached to parliament soon after his nomination: a sermon for which that body unanimously expunged the vote of thanks it had prematurely recorded, and whose text one member would have had burnt by the common hangman. Such was the record of this chair in the eighteenth century, the *siècle des lumières*, the century of the Enlightenment. The irony is that in that century

[2] *Correspondence of George III and Lord North*, I, 62-3. Six years earlier the Crown had declared 'that the Royal Professorships will not for the future be given as sinecures', and hoped, by its example, to shame the university into adopting the same principles in its election of professors. (Letter of Earl of Mansfield to George Greville, 13 Feb. 1765, sold at Sotheby's 11 May 1970, item 213.)

the 'moderns', the laymen, were in fact creating that kind of history which the founders of the chair had perhaps envisaged but had failed to implant in Oxford or even Cambridge. It was the century of Robertson, Hume, and Adam Smith, and of that greatest of historians who called Hume his master, Edward Gibbon. But their spirit, the spirit of civilised lay history, like Gibbon himself, had found life impossible in comfortable clerical Tory Oxford and had chosen to lodge in Calvinist severity elsewhere: among the bare unpromising mountains of Switzerland and Scotland.

How different from this is the second age of Oxford historiography, that great age in the middle and later nineteenth century, the age of Mark Pattison and Thorold Rogers and, if we confine ourselves to regius professors, of Goldwin Smith and Stubbs, Freeman, and Froude! No one could think of them, as we must think of their eighteenth-century predecessors, as sinecurists or *dilettanti*. Their age was one of mountainous labours, heroic controversies, and blood-bespattered gaiters: a great homeric *titanomachia* of which we, an astonished posterity, can still point out the irremovable relics in our midst. Behold yon ancient footprint burnt into the ground of west Oxford, with a dark stain of old blood between the toes and a still perceptible mound of repudiated English dust behind it! That is the last footstep in Oxford of my predecessor Goldwin Smith, summarily described in the *Dictionary of National Biography* as 'controversialist' (and, less objectively, by Disraeli as 'an itinerant spouter of stale sedition'), as he left Oxford and his chair, not, like his great contemporary Thorold Rogers, to return in triumph to it twenty years later, but to spend the last forty-one years of his life in the more congenial atmosphere of radical North America. And this huge rock, now grass-grown where it fell, surely must be one of those boulders which, flying from the powerful hand of Freeman, missed the nimble head of his destined successor Froude: a boulder which ten men could not lift, such as men are now, but he easily lifted and threw it. And here, in Ruskin's Museum in the Parks, between the dusty skeletons of those dinosaurs which seem to us relics of the same remote age, do we not see, reconstructed by the patient skill of modern technicians (aided by a liberal grant from United Dairies), one of those two famous butter-tubs from which those allies in the fray, Freeman and Stubbs, alternately ladled their mutually emollient butter?[3] What splendid days those were! If Goldwin Smith, in his last years, ever looked back from Toronto to consider the record of the six regius professors who had succeeded him in his abandoned chair, even he might have admitted that his resignation had not closed but opened the field of historical controversy in Oxford.

To what can we ascribe this sudden recrudescence of historical zeal in nineteenth-century Oxford? Of course it was part of the general intellectual ferment of those days; but it also sprang, in part, from new problems of organisation, caused in turn by the immense enlargement of historical evidence. In the nineteenth century the archives of European states were opened as they had never been before and the available materials of history

[3] See, ladling butter from alternate tubs,
Stubbs butters Freeman, Freeman butters Stubbs.   Anon.

began that terrifying expansion which, since then, has never ceased. Such an expansion, in its early days, whetted the appetites of historians – and not only of historians: for political and religious controversialists also found, in this new matter, ammunition for those enjoyable private wars which are so necessary not only in order to arrive at truth but also to keep up the blood-circulation in this cold climate. But how was this vast new material to be conquered, organised, digested? If the conquest of the whole Mediterranean world had convulsed and permanently changed the government and economy of ancient Rome, must not the old universities of England also adjust their constitutions to absorb this great new empire of parchment and paper, hieroglyphs and statistics? Ambitious spirits, like Leopold von Ranke, might hope, thanks to all this new evidence, to establish with finality the facts of history; but even to envisage such a task required a robust mind and ample resources. How could it be envisaged by engaging dilettante professors such as had held the chair since 1724, anecdotists, gentlemen if not scholars, memorable only for having improved the graceful manners of Lord Shelburne and enraged the sullen old codgers of St. John's College? How could it be done without some such apparatus of power, discipline, and research as was enjoyed by an authoritarian professor in Berlin?

So, in the middle nineteenth century, there arose in Oxford the demand not merely for more 'professional' historians but also for a German 'professoriate': a bureaucracy of intellectual government and organised research. The great historians who were then appointed to this chair were men of energy, modern in their outlook, professional in their methods, Germanic, often, in their vocabulary and style. All around them, like the German emperors whom they studied and admired, they saw the entrenched particularism of petty princes and encrusted oligarchies. But since university reform was in the air, and royal commissions were on the move, they did not despair. They prepared and mounted a formidable attack upon those citadels of conservatism, the colleges, and the guardians of those citadels, the heads and tutors. The trumpet was sounded by my predecessor Henry Vaughan in 1850, in his proposals to the royal commission, and again, four years later, in his pamphlet *Oxford Reform and Oxford Professors*. Professors, said Vaughan, should have 'a superintendence of some kind' over the history school; perhaps they should even select the examiners and thus determine the standards of that school; there should be organisation, intellectual discipline: history should be a modern science, not merely, as the tutors maintained, 'an easy school for rich men', and one which did not make unreasonable demands on those 'decent easy men', the college tutors.

Oh how glorious is the battle for ancient freedom! Two centuries before, a similar attempt had been made to invade the liberties, the exemptions, the fundamental rights of Englishmen. The Stuart kings, with their tyrannical bureaucracies, their Star Chambers, their High Commission Courts, had sought, through 'mean instruments', officials 'raised from the lees of the people', to impose upon Englishmen a continental despotism. Happily they had been resisted, defeated, and, in the end, destroyed, so that the blessed reign of liberty might return. But now, it seemed, all was once again to be put in jeopardy. Royal tyranny, royal bureaucracy had been driven back; but professorial tyranny, professorial bureaucracy was creeping in. At once the great peers of the University, the Heads of Houses, with their splendid equipages, grave titles, and lavish hospitality, and its substantial gentry, the college tutors with their parliament in common-room, resolved to resist this usurpation of their rights by a 'body of men raised from a comparatively unimportant position'. So from their plentiful tables the college Hampdens arose and, like their predecessors, appealed to ancient rights. Vaughan himself was boycotted in Oxford, cut off, if not from tonnage and poundage, at least from college snuff and college port. Foremost among the champions of 'liberty' was that formidable assertor of ancient tradition, Dr Pusey, who, in a powerful pamphlet, described as 'a treatise against professors', proved to his own satisfaction that the infidelity and immorality which were such a deplorable feature of liberal Germany were the direct result of the professorial system established in its universities.

For fifty years the battle raged. The professors fought hard; they appealed to reason, efficiency, sense; but the eternal vigilance of the tutors never allowed them to prevail, until they either resigned in disgust, like Vaughan and Goldwin Smith, or broke, like Froude, under the strain. Finally, economic facts came to the rescue of the tutors. For just as it is supposed by some historians that the resistance of the English gentry in the seventeenth century was in some way sharpened by a decline in agricultural prosperity, so – according to Sir Charles Firth – the resistance of the Oxford tutors was braced to the last successful effort by the great agricultural depression of the 1880s and 1890s. In the twenty years between 1883 and 1903, he tells us, Oxford colleges lost between a quarter and a third of their agricultural revenues. In such circumstances, argued the tutors, how could they be expected to sustain such expensive luxuries as historical research?[4]

It seems a pity that Sir Charles Firth, that great expert on the seventeenth century, did not himself consider this parallel (which I may perhaps have strained) between the resistance against seventeenth-century royal and nineteenth-century professorial tyranny; for in that case he might have saved himself an unfortunate experience. He might then have noticed that fifty years after the original challenge, when the forces of resistance had acquired strength, not weakness, from the struggle, King James II had rashly sought to reopen the issue, only to be, in such circumstances, almost effortlessly defeated. Unfortunately, Firth omitted to consider this precedent and, in 1904, fifty years after the original challenge, having himself been raised to this throne, he rashly imitated James II and reopened the battle. In his inaugural lecture he suggested that the function of a university was the advancement of learning, the promotion of research. This time, as in 1688, there was no need of a long or bitter struggle. A secret circular letter from the Whig peers had been enough to send King James to exile in France. A printed circular letter from the college tutors was enough to send Firth to his long exile in north

[4]C. H. Firth, *Modern History at Oxford 1841-1918* (Oxford 1920).

Oxford. If King George I had founded the regius chair to demonstrate Whig history, by 1904 it had demonstrated it in the most effective way: by imitation. The Hanoverian professor had become like the Hanoverian king. Just as King George I, though exalted to a royal throne, looked enviously abroad to the streamlined courts of inferior German princes, so his professor in Oxford, though sitting in a regius chair, would look enviously at those less exalted professors in the provinces who could rule their faculties with despotic power, having never known challenge and defeat at the hands of a Whig aristocracy, a *szláchta*, a *plèbe nobiliaire* entrenched in the colleges.

That battle was decided fifty years ago, and now, living as we do in the third age of Oxford historical study, we can afford to look dispassionately back on it, as part of our history. And what, we ask, has been the ultimate result of that struggle? It is, as Montesquieu observed in eighteenth-century England, a separation – at least a theoretical separation – of powers. The threatened flood of professional research has been first dammed, then diverted from the main stream of university life and from the colleges which dominate that stream; but it has not been forbidden. Once safely diverted, it has been left as a private and indeed ever-expanding backwater in which those who have a taste for it may harmlessly fish, and to which they may invite other fishermen who – so long as the colleges do not have to provide them with picnic-baskets – may share in the sport. It is true, the bank of this backwater has become rather congested of late, as the taste for fishing has spread, and even some college-tutors, slipping out of their back-doors at night, surreptitiously engage in the sport; but skilful riparian subdivision, devised by the genius of Manchester, to which we all owe so much and where so many of our professors throughout the country have bought their fishing tackle, has ensured that every man, within his narrowing reach, has the opportunity – without any tiresome controversy with his neighbour or exasperating entanglement of lines – to extract from the swollen stream of historical evidence some small conclusion which, though perhaps not very tasty to the lay palate, may yet be pickled in a thesis or potted in the transactions of a provincial learned society.

Mr Vice-Chancellor, I am one of those who have changed tutorial for professorial status, and as such I ought perhaps to be echoing the views of my predecessors from Henry Vaughan to Sir Charles Firth. In fact I do not. Although reason, sense, logic (as it seems to me) were on their side in their time, human experience forces me to take a somewhat different view; and the view which I wish to express springs from the conviction that history is a humane study and that the study of the humanities requires a different method from the study of the sciences. It may be that human history will one day be reduced to an exact science; but at present, although scientific laws are relevant to it and condition its course, these laws are the laws of other sciences – of economics or geography or statistics – they are not the laws of history. Indeed, if history ever should become an exact science, with established laws of its own, we should then cease to study it as we do: we should apply it, as a form of engineering, and its study as a 'humanity' would be left to those heretics who, still believing in the freedom of the human will, might hope to disprove that grim conclusion. This being so, I am obliged to ask what is the difference in method between the study of humane subjects like history and exact sciences like engineering, and I conclude that this difference can be expressed, and I shall therefore try to express it, very simply.

The difference, as it seems to me, essentially concerns the position of the laity. Exact sciences require specialisation and all the apparatus of speciali-sation, even if such specialisation carries them beyond the bounds of human interest or lay understanding. The fact that a branch of physics or mathe-matics may be quite beyond the interest or comprehension of an educated layman in no way invalidates it, because the validity of such subjects does not depend on lay interest or lay comprehension. Even if no layman can under-stand them, they will still be taught by professionals to professionals from generation to generation. The exact scientists are a kind of pre-Reformation clergy, and their function is to perform their miracles, to continue their Church, not to make themselves intelligible to laymen: for their control of the means of salvation and damnation makes the lay world so dependent on them that it will tolerate and subsidise them even without understanding.

But the humane subjects are quite different from this. They have no direct scientific use; they owe their title to existence to the interest and comprehen-sion of the laity; they exist primarily not for the training of professionals but for the education of laymen; and therefore if they once lose touch with the lay mind, they are rightly condemned to perish. I know it will be answered that all knowledge, including humane knowledge, advances by means of tech-nical specialisation. I do not dispute this answer; for I do not dispute that exact sciences contribute to humane subjects. But since they merely contribute to humane subjects and have not yet absorbed them, it follows that such technical specialisation in respect of them has no value in itself; it owes whatever value it has entirely to that degree to which it makes those subjects clearer, more comprehensible, and more interesting to the intelligent laity. I do not dispute that by a completer professionalism we may arrive at a more perfect knowledge of history or literature: I merely state that that perfect knowledge may be so fine and so uninteresting that nobody, except its discoverers, will wish to possess it. If we believe, as I do, that a knowledge of history and literature is essential to a civilised society, this would be a great loss.

Consider the case of classical studies. A century ago our ancestors knew far less than we can know (if we want to know) about the civilisation of Greece and Rome; and yet somehow, in spite of the more copious fountains which now break out before our feet, we seem strangely exempt from thirst. The study of the classics is now described as 'too narrow'. I do not believe that a study which was wide enough to educate Gladstone and Derby and Asquith and Curzon is too narrow for us. What has happened is not that the subject has lost its value but that a humane subject has been treated as an exact science: professional classical scholars have assumed that they are teaching only other professional classical scholars; consequently they have killed the classics. When I see a Greek tragedy, one of the greatest works of human literature, a tragedy no longer than a single book of *Paradise Lost*, put out into the world with a commentary of three large octavo volumes round its neck, weighing in all nearly half a stone, I fear the poor thing will not get far: it will languish and die, die of strangulation and neglect in some corner of a forgotten bookshelf. If an interest in the classics survives today, apart from the subsidies which they enjoy from the past, that may well be due rather to the enterprise of Sir Allen Lane and his Pelican Books, where they appear, purged of otiose learning, reanimated by lay interest, than to the heavy cossetting of professional scholars.

Similarly, unless we take heed, there is a danger that philosophers may kill philosophy, philologists literature, and historians history. Armies of research students, organised by a general staff of professors, may in time have mapped out the entire history of the world. We may know, or be able to know, what every unimportant minor official in a government office did every hour of his day, what every peasant paid for his plot in a long extinct village, how every backbencher voted on a private bill in an eighteenth-century parliament. Our libraries may groan beneath volumes on medieval chamber administration and bed-chamber administration. But to what end? Just as the layman now turns aside from the great civilised nations of antiquity whose living literature has been stifled with dead learning, and goes a-whoring after the barbarous despotisms of ancient Assyria or the savage empires of pre-Columbian America – peoples of bloody history and no literature at all – so he will turn aside from us and seek interest and enlightenment elsewhere. He may not seek it in such edifying sources; but it will not be for us to complain, who will have driven him away.

This, after all, is what happened in the sixteenth century to the Church which presumed too much on its monopoly of what is supposed an exact magical science. Its endowments were fat as never before; the material for study was growing with the passage of time and the elongation of tradition; and armies of disciplined theologians, fondling their subject with minute expertise, had encrusted it with a rich commentary of scholasticism. And yet somehow the laity would not take it. They declared that religion too was a humane subject, that the laity, not the clergy, are the measure of the Church, and that experts exist to serve others, not themselves. So all that great weight of tradition and scholasticism which clogged and cluttered the free spaces of the intellectual world was suddenly found to be otiose, and the lay spirit of man, the spirit that sought not a self-perpetuating apostolic succession of warranted experts but guidance and education for the lay mind, freedom to move in a present which had become overcharged with the cumber of the past, a clear path back to the pure sources of truth which had since been choked with learned rubbish, turned aside from that tradition, rejected that scholasticism, and, by emancipation from it, enabled the world's great age to begin anew.

For every enlightenment entails a certain disposal of waste learning, and the study of history can sometimes progress as well by forgetting as by remembering the past. Just as, in economic life, societies advance by gradual inflation which frees the present from some part of the burden it has inherited, even if it also mortifies those who have invested their savings in such dwindling securities, so, in historical study, we march similarly forward, constantly devaluing some of our own pious savings, even if that process is also mortifying to those who have invested too heavily in them. At every onward stage there is a cry from the backwoods: from the annuitants who are landed with Dalton's 2½%'s and from the antiquaries who have locked up their intellectual capital in depreciated scholiasts. But somehow these plaintive voices are soon forgotten. Duns, in the sixteenth century, is put unlamented in Bocardo; in the seventeenth century we find ourselves agreeing with Milton's summary dismissal of the early Fathers as 'marginal stuffings'; and in the eighteenth with Goldsmith, who watched the advance of polite learning at the expense of those who had vainly absorbed 'Metrodorus, Valerius Probus, Aulus Gellius, Pedianus, Boethius and a hundred others, to be acquainted with whom might show much reading but little judgment'.

This is the lesson which we must always remember when we demand, as we so often do, more and more research, more and more funds for research, more and more professionalism and specialisation in humane subjects. For humane subjects, called into being ultimately to serve the laity, not to discover some recondite but unimportant truth, can only bear a limited amount of specialisation. They need professional methods, but always for the pursuit of lay ends.

Of course, in the great battles between tutors and professors which ended fifty years ago, I do not believe that Dr Pusey and his allies were fighting to keep humane subjects from professionalisation. Far from it. They were fighting, or some of them were fighting, and he certainly was fighting, to defend clerical monopoly, clerical privilege, clerical bigotry, against the humane, liberal, 'infidel' state. They were resisting the reforms of a progressive government in the same spirit of stagnant reaction in which their predecessors had resisted the gifts of the Whig monarchy. They were the heirs of Gibbon's tutors, those immortal 'monks of Magdalen', 'sunk in prejudice and port', whose 'dull and deep potations excused the brisk intemperance of youth' and whose 'constitutional toasts were not expressive of the most lively loyalty for the house of Hanover'. And on the other hand the intruded professors often represented, even from the beginning, even in the eighteenth century, some trace at least of the enlightenment, the urbanity, the cosmopolitanism of the Whig world against the clerical incivility of Tory common-rooms. Who would not prefer the friends and patrons of Pope, Handel, and Rysbrack to snarling old antiquaries like Antony Wood and Thomas Hearne, the hermit-crabs of Merton College and St. Edmund Hall? Nevertheless, the wars which are ultimately decided are seldom the same wars which were first declared, and the long struggle which the heads and tutors fought in the last century to preserve their sacred college arks against an infidel, upstart professoriate has led to a result very different from their aims. By keeping the direction of historical and all other humane studies in the hands of those responsible for teaching, not research, it has provided at least the machinery whereby the creeping paralysis of professionalism can be kept at bay. Time has shown that the real danger of a German professoriate is not 'infidelity': it is the removal of humane studies into a specialisation so remote that they cease to have that lay interest which is their sole ultimate justification.

But if we have the machinery, have we, what is equally necessary, the spirit to drive that machinery in that direction? That spirit, I venture to suggest, must still be a spirit of research. Since I have spoken against professionalism – or rather, against independent professionalism, professionalism for its own sake – allow me to say a word in favour of research – genuine, productive research. For although I believe that history, unless it is taught by men ever conscious of the lay interest, loses its title to be taught at all, equally I believe that it cannot capture that lay interest unless it is perpetually refreshed from outside, by research. Research is not the same as professionalism. Professionalism is that private expertise which carries the details of a subject progressively farther away from lay comprehension; research (as I am using the term) is the digging of new channels whereby fresh and refreshing matter flows into old courses. For even the purest water, if it remains stagnant for long, loses its taste, nor can it be revived merely by being stirred or analysed or distilled. What is needed is a new body of water flowing into it. It is not enough merely to be rejoined, at intervals, by its own temporarily separated backwaters: the water must be fresh, cold, stimulating. It must flow in from outside sources, and its impact must be perceptible, causing sudden shock, gradual adjustment, and the pleasant gurgle of controversy.

Whence shall such tributary streams come? At different times they have come from different sources, and sometimes, of course, from very slender sources. Refreshment has drained silently in through the spongy earth as well as rattled noisily in through wide, pebbled streams. But I wish to make one general point, and that is, that the greatest refreshment has always been brought in by the laity. I do not mean the laity absolutely, but the laity in respect of purely historical studies: for a man is a layman in respect of those studies even if he is a professional in some other branch of learning. The clergy, in any subject, by a kind of natural law, tend to bury themselves deeper and deeper in the *minutiae* of their own dogma; thus buried, they tend to forget the outer world which may be radically changing around them; and often it takes the less concentrated mind of the layman, who is more aware of these changes, sometimes even his impatient boot, to bring them up to date. The lay spirit not only forces the unwilling professional to jettison, at intervals, his past accumulations; it also poses new problems and suggests new methods and new purposes derived from other disciplines, other sciences.

Consider biblical studies. What advance was made by any of those numerous professional theologians of the early sixteenth century, those monks and canons and apologists and 'Obscure Men' with their portentous learning, comparable with that of Erasmus? They accused him of levity, flippancy, irreverence (today they would accuse him of 'journalism'); they denounced as cowardly and indecent the nimble strategy with which he circumvented and destroyed their floundering monkish cataphracts. In fact

he used professional methods – more professional than theirs – but directed
by a lay spirit. A century later that great lay scholar John Selden was able to
say that 'laymen have best interpreted the hard places in the Bible', and he
listed their names: Pico della Mirandola, Scaliger, Grotius, Salmasius,
Heinsius. Later centuries only illustrate the same point. The study of the
Bible and of Christian antiquities owed more, in the eighteenth century, to
Porson and Gibbon than to Chelsum and Travis, and, in the nineteenth, to
Darwin and Lyell than to Pusey and that Theban Legion of eleven thousand
clergymen who, with him, sought government sanction for the threatened
doctrine of everlasting damnation. If we turn to our own subject, it is the
same. Conceive, if you can, modern history without the contributions of
economists like Adam Smith, Simiand, and Keynes, sociologists like Marx,
Weber, and Sombart, philosophers like Hume and Hegel, scholars of culture
and art-history like Burckhardt and Mâle, even anthropologists and
psychologists like Frazer and Freud. None of these were professional
historians. And yet but for their work the study of history would have dried
up and perished long ago.

For it is the essence of humane studies, since their central object is the study
of man, that they all flow down towards that centre, even though the
professionals in each of them have a natural tendency to move upstream in
search of distant sources and sometimes to get lost on the way. And many
exact sciences too flow in to refresh that same stream. The sciences of
population, of epidemics, of climate, and of price-history are now recognised
to be essential to the understanding of history, and of course the enthusiastic
experts in these subjects often seek to lead us up these tempting tributaries
which they have explored. But we must be firm. We may send surveying
parties up them, we may make brief journeys up them ourselves, but we
must remember that our ultimate purpose is to contine downstream, taking
note of these new waters which are constantly supplying us, but never
forgetting the main direction in which we are going, or ought to be going: the
study not of circumstances, but of man in circumstances.

How far have we remembered this in our last fifty years? My own belief is
that we have sometimes forgotten it. The great influx of tributary knowledge
came in at the end of the last century and the beginning of this, at the time
when we were locked in our academic civil wars. The character of our
research was then determined by the 'German' professional standards of that
time, and its scope was narrowed by the defeat of the professorial party who
had defined it. In consequence, Oxford historical research has tended to be
less a cutting of new channels in order to utilise tributary streams than a
burrowing ever deeper in the old river-bed in order to add to our already rich
collection of historical fossils and caddis-worms. The immense contributions
of a Sombart or a Keynes, which have so reinvigorated the historical studies
of France and America, have so far added little to ours. We may have rejected
them because we think them erroneous. I myself believe that the historical
contributions of both Sombart and Keynes are erroneous. I do not believe in
the demiurgic 'spirit of capitalism', nor do I believe that profit-inflation

caused the expansion of sixteenth-century Europe and that we had Shake-speare when we could afford him. But what of that? These great tributaries which we have ignored have caused tremendous historical developments in other countries, and if we exclude them, we impoverish our own studies. They may be erroneous, but the mere correction of error involves first a new study then a new interest which that error has created. In humane studies there are times when a new error is more life-giving than an old truth, a fertile error than a sterile accuracy.

Think of the great controversies launched by Henri Pirenne's famous thesis on Mohammed and Charlemagne. No one now accepts it in the form in which he published it. But how the living interest in Europe's dark ages was re-created by the challenge which he uttered and the controversy which he engendered! Think too of Max Weber's famous thesis on the Protestant ethic: a thesis of startling simplicity and – in my opinion – demonstrable error. But how much poorer our understanding of the Reformation, how much feebler our interest in it would be today, if that challenge had not been thrown down, and taken up! The greatest professional historians of our century – a Bloch, a Rostovtzeff, a Namier – have always been those who have applied to historical study not merely the exact, professional discipline they have learned within it but also the sciences, the hypotheses, the human interests which – however intermixed with human error – have been brought into it by the lay world outside. I should like to think that in our historical research at Oxford we might pay a little more attention to fertile error, even at the expense of our zeal for unimportant truth.

Mr Vice-Chancellor, I see I am in danger of becoming controversial: and this, I am told, is a grave error – though it may sometimes be one of those useful errors of which I have spoken. Therefore let me conclude; and let me conclude by repairing an omission. In this lecture I have mentioned many of my predecessors, but I have made no mention of one – the one who, to me, is the most attractive of them all. Frederick York Powell, a member of your former college and mine, occupied this chair between Froude and Firth, and his chief fame seems to be that he left the Prime Minister's offer, owing to its external similarity to an income-tax demand, unopened in an old boot, until discreet inquiries from Downing Street led to its rediscovery. During his ten years' tenure of this chair York Powell may have neglected some of those trumpery duties which have interfered with so much good work in the past; but he was the father of Icelandic studies here, the friend of Mallarmé and Rodin and J. B. Yeats and Verlaine, a universal man accidentally thrown up among our grim specialists. How he lives in everything that has been written about him by those who knew him! He contributed impartially to the *Encyclopaedia Britannica* and the *Sporting Times*, was 'as well acquainted with the boxing reports in the *Licensed Victuallers' Gazette* as with the *Kalevala* or *Beowulf*', and dedicated one of his works jointly to the Dean of Christ Church and an old fisherman at Sandgate. How I would like to have known him, that 'infinite spirit prisoned in a finite mind – a winged and aspiring Celt captured and put into the cage of an Oxford donship', that 'Nile seeking to fertilise the adjacent desert', that man who, by his enjoyment of life, seemed, here in Oxford, 'like a sailor fresh from many voyages who has come to see his cousin the church-sexton'.[5] It is true, his inaugural lecture was judged unsatisfactory by his colleagues: it stopped suddenly after half an hour; at least, as I slip away from this ordeal, I know that I am not liable to that imputation.

---

[5] The quotations are from J. B. Yeats. See Oliver Elton, *Frederick York Powell,* I, 439–41; J. B. Yeats, *Letters to his son W. B. Yeats* (1944), 84–5.

1

Remarks on the Homeric Question

Hugh Lloyd-Jones

About the turn of the seventeenth century the great debate between the champions of the ancients and the champions of the moderns that is known as the Battle of the Books marks the moment when the French decided that they could now manage without the ancient writers, and turned their backs upon the study of antiquity. The Abbé d'Aubignac[1] undertook the task of exploding the reputation of Homer; Homer, he claimed, was an inferior poet, whose theology was deplorable, and whose poems were in any case nothing but a collection of old rhapsodies patched together and handed down under his name. Having failed to be elected to the Academy, D'Aubignac had to found one of his own; his dissertation on the *Iliad* was not published until 1715, nearly forty years after his death. Still, it expressed an attitude by no means uncommon at that place and time, and the theory of a collection of rhapsodies pointed in a direction soon to be followed by a person eminently fitted to discuss Greek poetry.

In the reply to the deist Anthony Collins which he published in 1713, Richard Bentley[2] took exception to the trite and empty assertion that 'Homer designed his poems for eternity, to please and instruct mankind'. 'Take my word for it,' he wrote, 'poor Homer in those circumstances and early time had never such aspiring thoughts. He wrote a sequel of Songs and Rhapsodies, to be sung by himself for small earnings and good cheer, at Festivals and other days of merriment; the Ilias he made for the men, and Odysseis for the other sex. These loose songs were not connected together in the form of an epic poem till Pisistratus' time nearly 500 years after.' Unlike D'Aubignac, Bentley did not venture to dispute the very existence of Homer; but to his rigorous eighteenth-century logic the poems seemed deficient in unity and organisation. Even in the great epic of Milton, composed during the preceding century, Bentley found an absence of these qualities; his new edition

---

[1] François Hédelin, Abbé d'Aubignac et de Meimec, *Conjectures Académiques, ou Dissertation sur l'Iliade*, ed. V. Magnien (1925). For eighteenth-century views of Homer, see most recently K. Simonsuuri, *Homer's Original Genius* (1979).

[2] *Remarks upon a Late Discourse of Freethinking* (*Works*, ed. A. Dyce (1838, reprinted 1966), 241ff.).

was based on the hypothesis that the blind poet had dictated the poem to an amanuensis who had taken advantage of its author's blindness to abuse his trust. Bentley dated Homer as early as the eleventh century B.C.; only some five hundred years later, he thought, following an assertion of Cicero,[3] did the Athenian tyrant Pisistratus arrange the poems as we now have them.

Giambattista Vico in his essay on universal law of 1722[4] argued, much as Bentley had done, that the Homeric poems were not a conscious effort of profound philosophy, but the mirror of a simple age. In the second *Scienza Nuova*, which appeared in 1730, he followed D'Aubignac in taking 'Homer' to be simply a collective name and Bentley in arguing that the Homeric poems came together only when collected by Pisistratus; but his judgment of the poems was more sympathetic, and in claiming that they were a collective work of the Greek people he anticipated a notion which later in the century was to be made highly fashionable by the work of Herder. Thomas Blackwell in his *Enquiry into the Life and Writings of Homer* (1735) represented Homer as a primitive bard, whose gifts uniquely fitted the society into which he had been born. Among his pupils at Marischal College, Aberdeen, was James Macpherson; the belief that early epic poems emanate from the people certainly contributed to the vast popularity of Macpherson's *Ossian*.

Not long after the appearance of that fraudulent best-seller, Robert Wood privately circulated the first edition of his *Essay on the Original Genius of Homer* (1767).[5] While accepting the existence of Homer, whom he placed at the same early date as Bentley, Wood explained the phenomena which had led Bentley to suppose that the epics consisted of various rhapsodies which were put together by Pisistratus by means of a different theory. He suggested that they had been composed orally, and were written down only centuries afterwards by Pisistratus or Solon or the Spartan legislator Lycurgus. The guess that Homer was an oral poet is as old as Josephus, who threw it out in the course of an attempt to prove the superiority of Hebrew literature over Greek; but Wood was the first to make a serious case on its behalf.

During the eighties of the eighteenth century Herder made the educated public familiar with the distinctive characteristics of ancient folk poetry, as it was represented by Homer, early Hebrew poetry and German folksong. In 1788 the French scholar Villoison published for the first time the detailed commentary on the *Iliad* contained in the tenth-century manuscript of Homer known as Venetus A, so throwing much light upon the treatment of

---

[3] Cicero, *De oratore*, III, 34, 1.137: 'Quis doctior eisdem temporibus illis aut cuius eloquentia litteris instructior fuisse traditur quam Pisistrati? qui primus Homeri libros confusos antea sic disposuisse dicitur ut nunc habemus?' For a view not unlike Bentley's, see R. Merkelbach, *Rheinisches Museum*, XC (1952), 23ff., and D. L. Page, *The Homeric Odyssey* (1955), 143ff.; for a sceptical reaction, see J. A. Davison, *Transactions of the American Philological Association*, LXXXVI (1955), 1ff. (or in *A Companion to Homer*, ed. A. J. B. Wace and F. H. Stubbings (1962), 219ff.); cf. A. Lesky, *Homeros* (*Sonderausgabe der Paulyschen Realencyclopädie der cl. Altertumswissenschaft*) (1967), 146.

[4] *Il diritto universale* (in *Opere*, ed. F. Niccolini (1931–40)); see J. L. Myres, *Homer and his Critics* (1958), 57.

[5] The work was not published until 1775, four years after its author's death. Josephus: see *Contra Apionem* I, 12, 1.2.

the text and its problems by the scholars of the Hellenistic age, and upon the difficulty of tracing its history back before that time.[6] This publication led directly to the working out of a systematic theory of oral composition and transmission by one of the best-equipped scholars of the time; Friedrich August Wolf published his *Prolegomena ad Homerum* in 1795.

Wolf's theory had obvious weaknesses. He placed the introduction of the Greek alphabet far too late; he was unaware, though he could have learned it from Wood, that a long poem can be transmitted orally; in taking up Josephus' suggestion that Homer was an oral poet he failed to bear in mind that no such idea had occurred to any of the Hellenistic scholars whose opinions were recorded in the scholia. But his theory seemed to many to give the best explanation of the facts, and it was congenial to the spirit of the time; Goethe, then working at *Hermann und Dorothea*, accepted it with enthusiasm, though thirty years later he was to change his view. Wolf had posed a problem that was endlessly debated, with great learning and assiduity, throughout the great age of German scholarship that followed.

Gottfried Hermann[7] in 1832 argued for an original nucleus by a single poet, which had later undergone successive additions and alterations. For the remainder of the nineteenth century this continued to be the most popular kind of view; it was made familiar to the English public by Grote in the second volume of his *History of Greece*, published in 1846. Wilamowitz in his book *Die Ilias und Homer*, published in 1916, placed Homer not at the beginning but in the middle of the Homeric tradition; Homer, he thought, had made use of various early poems, and later poets in their turn had added to or changed his work. This became the most popular type of view, especially in Germany, and continued to be so until recent times. But in England and America certain scholars argued for a unitarian view, sometimes under the influence of anti-German prejudice, but not without putting forward arguments that deserved serious consideration.

This was the situation in 1928, when Milman Parry published his two major contributions to Homeric scholarship.[8] Using and carrying further work on Homer's language and dialect by other scholars which indicated that they were artificial constructions called into being by the requirements of the epic form itself, he was able to give substance to the notion of oral composition by showing in detail that many features of the style, language and dialect of the poems can only be explained by the assumption that they were dictated by its needs. Parry went on to strengthen the proof by examining other traditions of oral poetry, thus creating a whole new science of the comparative study of this kind of composition. But for many years German and other continental scholars clung to their established methods of analysis,

---

[6] For the impact of the scholia upon Wolf, see H. Erbse, 'F. A. Wolf e gli scoli all'Iliade', *Annali della Scuola Normale Superiore di Pisa*, serie 3, IX (i) (1979), 39ff. Wolf's *Prolegomena ad Homerum, sive de operum Homericorum prisca et genuina forma variisque mutationibus et probabili ratione emendandi* appeared in 1795 (3rd edn by R. Peppmüller, Halle 1884).

[7] *Opuscula* V (1834), 52ff.

[8] *L'epithète traditionelle dans Homère* and *Les formules et la métrique d'Homère* were both published at Paris in 1928; for English versions, see *The Making of Homeric Verse*, ed. Adam Parry (Oxford 1971).

taking no notice of this American innovation.

Parry certainly proved that the tradition to which the Homeric poems belonged must have been for many centuries an oral one. But did he prove, as > many scholars have assumed, that they themselves were composed without the aid of writing?[9]

During the last years before his death at the age of thirty-three, Parry was occupied in studying and recording the last phases of the Serbo-Croatian poetic tradition which was the last in Europe to retain its oral character. After his death this work was continued by his assistant A. B. Lord, now Professor > of Slavic and Comparative Literature at Harvard. Lord in his book *The Singer of Tales* (1960) and in many other writings has contended that the Homeric epics must have been composed orally. He has argued that the techniques of written and of oral composition exclude each other; he has maintained, at least until recently, that the coming of literacy brings immediate death to any oral tradition. Like Parry and most other modern scholars, Lord puts Homer at the end of the tradition, in that eighth century to which our earliest specimens of Greek alphabetic writing belong. He thinks Homer must have dictated his poems to someone else who wrote them down.

The late Sir Denys Page was an enthusiastic advocate of the belief that Homer's epics were composed orally. He placed their authors, whom he held to be two different people, in the late ninth or early eighth century. Homer, he thought, adapting the already well-established nucleus theory, 'developed, expanded, transmuted' earlier poems; the structure of his epics was 'loosely knit' and 'the connexions between the chief structural features are usually rather loose and sometimes very weak'.[10] Page accounts for these features, which had been the subject of complaint as early as the time of D'Aubignac, by arguing that the poems were not written down before the sixth century. That is not very different from the view of Wolf. G. S. Kirk in *The Songs of Homer* (1962) took a similar view. At that time he accepted from Lord the proposition, which both have now abandoned, that literacy is at once fatal to any oral tradition; but since unlike Lord he held that a poem could be transmitted orally over a long period without substantial alteration, he believed that two generations had elapsed between the composition of the poems and the time when they were written down. It was during this period, he argued, that they had added to them certain parts commonly held to be later than the time of Homer, such as the lay of Dolon in the tenth book of the *Iliad*, the visit of Odysseus to the underworld in the eleventh book of the *Odyssey*, and the conclusion of that poem.

Although these writers have had great influence, especially in England and America, their view that the epics were composed without the aid of writing is by no means universally accepted, and is now more than ever under attack. > In *Heroic Poetry* (1952) Sir Maurice Bowra offered the results of a study not

[9] This has been alleged by many scholars, including M. P. Nilsson, *Homer and Mycenae* (1933), 179, and E. R. Dodds, 'Homer as oral poetry', in *Fifty Years of Classical Scholarship*, ed. M. Platnauer (1950); (2nd edn as *Fifty Years (and Twelve) of Classical Scholarship* (1962), 13ff.). See Parry (ed.), *The Making of Homeric Verse*, liff.

[10] See *History and the Homeric Iliad* (1959), 259ff., and *The Homeric Odyssey* (1955), 142.

merely of Serbo-Croatian epic but of material supplied by many different epic traditions; he argued that Homer had indeed many centuries of oral tradition behind him, but that he himself composed his epics with the aid of writing. In the same year H. T. Wade-Gery brought out a small, learned and ingenious book called *The Poet of the Iliad*. He suggested that the alphabet which the Greeks adapted from that of the Phoenicians was invented for the express purpose of recording the great epics, which he believed were intended from the first for continuous recitation by relays of performers. Such continuous performance is known to have taken place at the Panathenaic festival in Athens, founded during the sixth century, the occasion for which Pisistratus is alleged to have arranged the works of Homer. Wade-Gery conjectured that the poet might have composed his poems for continuous recitation at the common festival of the Ionian Greeks known as the Panionion, which took place at Mount Mycale in Asia Minor, just opposite the island of Samos.

Bowra's book seems to have led directly to the writing of an important article, in which for the first time a leading German-speaking scholar took account of the importance of Parry's work; this was Albin Lesky in his 'Mundlichkeit and Schriftlichkeit' (1954).[11] Like Bowra, Lesky held that Homer had composed his epics with the aid of writing; and he developed this view in the successive editions of his history of Greek literature (from 1957) and in his article *Homeros* in Pauly-Wissowa's *Real-Encyclopädie* (1967). In 1966[12] Adam Parry, the son of Milman Parry, strongly argued that Homer had used writing; his article drew a reply from Kirk in 1970.[13] In 1971[14] Adam Parry brought out a collection of his father's writings, including English versions of the two important works that had originally appeared in French. He prefaced to the book what seems to me still the best general account of the current state of the Homeric Question. Like Bowra and Lesky, Adam Parry argued that though the Homeric epics bore many signs of belonging to a poetic tradition that had for many centuries been oral they could not have been composed without the aid of writing.

Kirk in replying to Adam Parry[15] abandons the proposition, which he had formerly taken over from Lord, that literacy must at once be fatal to any oral poetic tradition; even Lord now seems to have changed his mind about this matter. Since then such material that makes against this opinion has been accumulated; much of it is conveniently collected in Ruth Finnegan's *Oral Poetry* (1977). First Miss Finnegan points out that several early English poems which contain repeated formulas and other features associated with an oral technique are known to have been composed with the aid of writing; some have even turned out to have been translated from the Latin. Next she mentions living Bantu poets who write their poems in a formulaic style

[11] *Festschrift für Dietrich Kralik* (1954), 1ff. (or in *Gesammelte Schriften* (1966), 63ff.).
[12] 'Have we Homer's *Iliad*?', *Yale Classical Studies*, XX (1966), 175ff.
[13] 'Homer's *Iliad* and ours', *Proceedings of the Cambridge Philological Society*, CXCVI (1970), 48ff. (reprinted in Kirk's book *Homer and the Oral Tradition* (1976), 129ff.).
[14] See n.8, above.
[15] See n.13, above.

elaborated from their originally oral poetic tradition. 'In practice,' writes Miss Finnegan, 'interaction between oral and written forms is extremely common, and the idea that the use of writing automatically deals a death-blow to oral literary forms has nothing to support it.' Miss Finnegan can have no axe to grind, for her book shows no sign of acquaintance with the most recent developments in Homeric scholarship; she never mentions Adam Parry. That makes it all the more significant that her study of a large body of material derived from various epic traditions makes strongly against a dogma that was once one of the main props of belief in the oral composition of the Homeric epics.[16]

Adam Parry affirmed against Kirk Lord's other central proposition, that a poem must continue to suffer 'fundamental change' so long as it continues to be transmitted orally. Kirk in his reply to him claims that if as he thinks the poems were not written down until two generations after their author's death it is easy to understand how those parts of them commonly thought to have been late additions came to be added to the poem. But one can hardly be certain that the existence of written copies must have protected the poems against change and interpolation; written copies would soon have multiplied, and the text would have been subject to alteration.[17]

But if scholars cling to the opinion that the epics were composed orally they do so above all because they hold that, as Kirk puts it, 'a large number of crystallised formulas are employed with an astonishing economy and lack of unnecessary variation' (*Homer and the Oral Tradition*, 115–16). He holds that this 'suggests strongly, and indeed imperatively, that the oral technique was used in full and undiminished degree for the final main act of composition of each of the two monumental poems'. But each of the scholars who have examined the 'formula' in all possible senses of that elusive term[18] has ended by stressing, more strongly than his predecessors, its extreme flexibility and adaptability. The extensive and economical system of formulas revealed by Milman Parry has proved, after close testing, a good deal less tight than people had supposed.

[16] See also Miss Finnegan's paper in *Oral Literature and the Formula*, ed. B. A. Stolz and R. S. Shannon (1977), 127ff. In replying to it, Lord (op. cit., 175) claims that he did not say 'in exactly those terms' that once a singer learned to write he lost the ability to compose orally, while acknowledging that this is how his meaning has been interpreted. He makes it clear that he does not now maintain this view.

[17] Miss Finnegan cites L. D. Benson, 'The literary character of Anglo-Saxon formulaic poetry', *Publications of the Modern Language Association* (1966), 81, and J. Opland, 'Praise poems as historical sources', in *Beyond the Cape Frontier: Studies in the History of the Transkei and the Ciskei*, ed. C. Saunders and R. Derricourt (1974). The third, fourth and fifth chapters of her book deserve the close attention of Homeric scholars.

[18] See, e.g., A. Hoekstra, *Homeric Modifications of Formulaic Prototypes* (1965); J. B. Hainsworth, *The Flexibility of the Homeric Formula* (1968); M. Nagler, *Spontaneity and Tradition* (1975). J. A. Russo in his valuable contribution to Stolz and Shannon (eds), *Oral Literature and the Formula*, 31ff., argues convincingly that a formulaic style is not necessarily oral. In reply Lord (p.67) can only reiterate his conviction that without 'really knowing' an 'oral model' like that furnished by the Serbo-Croatian poems to which he has devoted so much labour 'one is in a rather shaky position for saying that Homer is or is not' an oral poet. It also helps to know some Greek, and to know something about poetry.

Lord's interdiction of what he has called 'the subjective interpretation and appreciation of the Homeric poems' would seem to deny to Homer any power to adapt his style and language to the requirements of an individual context. Not surprisingly it has incurred severe criticism, notably from the late Anne Amory Parry.[19] Lord is not a professional Hellenist; but the paradoxical consequences for literary appreciation that result from belief in such theories as his may be amply illustrated from the work of Greek scholars of great eminence. 'Subtlety of soul, complexity of character, true portrayal of personality,' wrote Page (*The Homeric Odyssey*, 142-3), 'for these we must wait until the practice of the art of writing affords the poet the necessary leisure and the necessary means for reflexion for planning the future in some detail, and for correcting the past.' 'Intricacy of design and subtleties of soul', he added later, 'wholly alien to the oral technique of composition have been sought (and found) in him.'

Bentley, whom Sir Denys Page in many ways resembled, was led by the irregularities of the Homeric epics to embrace the theory of a Homer whose loose songs were not put together to form continuous wholes before the age of Pisistratus. Page's words take us back to the perennial question: do the many occurrences in Homer of what by the standards of much later poetry seem to be inconsistencies, inconcinnities and irrelevances constitute a proof of multiple authorship, or at least of large-scale revision and interpolation? The old controversy between unitarians and analysts returns in a new form.

English-speaking followers of Parry justifiably complain of his neglect by continental scholars; but they themselves have unjustifiably neglected some important continental writings about Homer. Wolfgang Schadewaldt in his *Iliasstudien* of 1938 drew attention to the presence of elaborate links between different sections of the *Iliad* – the working out of pervasive motives, and the presence of an unmistakable unity despite all diversity. Karl Reinhardt[20] in his posthumous book *Die Ilias und ihr Dichter* carried this kind of study further. Hartmut Erbse in his *Beiträge zum Verständnis der Odyssee* (1972) has effectively criticised arguments supposed to prove multiple authorship which had long remained unquestioned; he has even defended the authenticity of the conclusion of the *Odyssey* in a fashion which commands respect. I cannot here deal adequately with the complex problems which the mention of this topic brings to mind; but I will offer a few examples of cases that seem to me to reveal weaknesses in the arguments of those who believe in multiple authorship.

Let me take first Page's treatment of the episode from the nineteenth book of the *Iliad*. 'The start is unpromising,' he writes (*History and the Homeric Iliad*, 313). 'Achilles has lost his friend; he is distraught with grief and rage; Hephaestus has made him a suit of Olympian armour; his mother Thetis brings it to him. Now surely he will rush into battle intent upon the killing of Hector? And so he might; only his mother unexpectedly and very abruptly tells him that he must first make friends with Agamemnon – though she does

[19] 'Homer as artist', *Classical Quarterly*, XXI (1971), 1ff.
[20] For an account of Karl Reinhardt, see my introduction to the translation of his *Sophocles* by Hazel and David Harvey, reprinted in my *Blood for the Ghosts* (1981).

not explain (and we cannot guess) why he must do so at this time or indeed at any time.' The reason is that since Agamemnon is the commander of the army, and Achilles now wants to fight, they have to fight together. Achilles now has ample assurance that Agamemnon will speak and act so as to give him full satisfaction, and so he does. Agamemnon in his speech in the assembly (78f.) saves face by blaming Zeus and his portion and the Erinys for his rash behaviour in provoking Achilles; but in Homer human beings always have to take responsibility for their actions, even though a god has suggested them, and Agamemnon never thinks of withholding the vast indemnity that he has already offered to Achilles.

Achilles replies briefly to Agamemnon's speech, saying that he is eager to go into battle. 'Now, at last,' writes Page (p.314), 'let us hope, the action will begin. But hope is to be long deferred, and the heart to be made moderately sick. Odysseus has a word to say, indeed he has a great many words to say, about food. You cannot expect the army to fight before breakfast; no doubt Achilles is in a hurry, but the men must have their meal.' Meanwhile the indemnity is paid over. 'More than 180 lines have passed,' Page complains, 'since luncheon stole the limelight, and nothing has been achieved.' The gifts are taken to Achilles' tent, Patroclus is again lamented, and in the end Zeus sends Athene to drip nectar and ambrosia into Achilles so that his strength shall not fail. Page remarks that the story 'is none the better for being padded as it is with lecture after lecture about food'.

To me the discussion about food seems to be wholly to the point.[21] Achilles in his grief for his friend can ignore the ordinary processes of life; but Odysseus, always a realist, acts wholly in character in politely reminding Achilles that an army fights better on a full stomach. Agamemnon accepts his suggestion, and also agrees to send at once for the indemnity and to swear that he has laid no finger on Briseis. Achilles protests that he cannot think of eating at such a time; but in a second speech (216f.) Odysseus tells him that though Achilles is the greater warrior he himself is older and has more experience. 'So,' says he, 'let your heart bear with what I say. Men soon grow weary of battle; in battle the bronze strews many a stalk upon the ground, but the harvest reaped is scanty, when Zeus the master of war inclines his scales. The Achaeans cannot mourn for the dead man with their bellies. All day men are falling thick and fast; if we did so, when could we have respite from labour? Those who die we must bury, keeping in check our pity, shedding the tears the day demands; and those who survive hateful war must think of food and drink so that we may the better fight unremittingly against our enemies . . .' It is important to remember that the technique of epic is not the same as that of tragedy; we must learn the technique of epic by patient study of the texts, pausing to ask ourselves whether difficulties may be explained by other means before putting them down to assumed multiple authorship. In a tragedy food would not be likely to find mention at such a moment; but epic presents a broader canvas, on which men of different natures are portrayed, and many actions, arousing different feelings in different persons, are

[21] The same point has now been made by Jasper Griffin, *Homer on Life and Death* (1980), 15ff.

presented. Achilles may grieve passionately for Patroclus and live only for revenge on Hector. But the army must still eat; ordinary life has to go on. The epic has room for Achilles and also for Odysseus; nowhere is the contrast between their characters more clearly drawn. Provided the reader is willing and able to read the text in accordance with the proper canons of the epic poet's art, the value of this episode as a proof of multiple authorship amounts to nothing.

In the fifteenth book of the *Odyssey* Telemachus, who has set out on a journey to ask Nestor and Menelaus if they have news of his absent father, is about to embark on the ship that will carry him back from Sparta to Ithaca when he is accosted by a stranger (223). This man has killed an enemy in Argos and is on the run, with powerful pursuers on his track. He is most ceremoniously introduced, for thirty lines are devoted to his genealogy; his name is Theoclymenus, and he comes of one of the most distinguished families of prophets in the epic world. 'It is natural to presume,' writes Page (*The Homeric Odyssey*, 84), 'that a person whose introduction is so long and loudly trumpeted will do or say something of importance; but the truth turns out to be the reverse. His part is very small, and wonderfully unimportant.' Let us see what part he plays and consider whether we agree.

Theoclymenus accosts Telemachus, imploring him to rescue him from certain death by taking him aboard his ship. His words, Page complains, are 'offensive to the custom of the Greek Epic; they are offensive because ancient custom would frown upon a suppliant who began his prayer by asking the name and address of his protector; it is for Telemachus to ask Theoclymenus not *vice versa*.' It seems to me doubtful whether a man in peril of his life would worry about such niceties before accosting a potential saviour; and I should expect an epic poet to be cognisant of this.

Theoclymenus is taken on board, and when they reach Ithaca (502f.) and are about to land, he asks Telemachus where he can find a lodging. Telemachus replies that ordinarily he would be glad to accommodate him himself, but that as things are he cannot allow him to enter the house without being present himself to ensure that his guest comes to no harm. Since Telemachus plans not to return home before visiting Eumaeus, he will not be able to accompany his guest; and as he points out Penelope seldom enters the hall while the suitors are present, so that she will be unable to protect him. Eurymachus, Telemachus says, is a man greatly respected, and he advises Theoclymenus to go to his house and ask for his protection. Eurymachus is of course one of the most formidable and one of the most offensive of the suitors, being second only to Antinous in those respects.

At that moment a hawk flies by holding a pigeon in its claws and stripping off its feathers. Theoclymenus beckons Telemachus to come aside out of earshot of the rest, takes his hand, and tells him that this is an omen sent by a god; it means that the house of Telemachus and his family is the one royal house of Ithaca, and that its members will always rule. Telemachus thanks him, and instructs Peiraeus, one of his closest friends, to take him to his house and entertain him.

'There is no need to dwell on this,' says Page (p.85); 'one moment Telemachus proposes that his friend shall stay with his arch-enemy Eurymachus; the next moment, without another word about that fantastic proposal, he commits him to the hospitality of his most loyal companion, Peiraeus. What the poet has in mind is beyond our comprehension.' It seems to me obvious that the prediction, though Page dismisses it as 'a drab *non sequitur*', has shown Telemachus that the stranger is indeed a genuine prophet, acquainted by supernatural means with the situation in Ithaca. That is surely enough to explain why he revokes his decision to send him to Eurymachus, and instead sends him to a house where he can count on suitable entertainment.

In the seventeenth book Telemachus returns to the palace of Odysseus and is greeted by Penelope, who is immensely relieved to see him, knowing as she does that the suitors have been plotting against his life. She asks him to tell her what people she has seen (44), but Telemachus defers complying with her request, because he must go to the market-place to pick up Theoclymenus. When he finally comes back and tells his mother what has happened on the journey, he can tell her no more than that Menelaus has been told by Proteus in Egypt that he is with Calypso. But Theoclymenus insists that he himself has more important information than that, and swears a solemn oath that he is not mistaken (155f.). Odysseus, he declares, is already in Ithaca; he knows about the conduct of the suitors, and is planning their destruction. All this, Theoclymenus explains, he has learned from the portent he observed during the conversation with Telemachus described earlier. Penelope replies to him with courtesy, wishing that his prophecy may be fulfilled and promising him rich presents if it is. But it is clear that she does not allow herself to place much hope in its fulfilment, and we know that she has previously been approached by many strangers claiming to have news of her husband whose claims have afterwards come to nothing. So when she hears a true prophecy from a prophet of impeccable credentials, she pays no attention to it, although it is vastly more significant than anything Telemachus has brought back from his long and perilous journey. The irony lends the episode an extra point, which Page has not observed.

In the twentieth book the suitors sit feasting in the hall for the last time, just before the trial of the bow with its terrible consequences for all of them. As they eat and drink, their insolence rises; Ctesippus hurls the hoof of a cow at the disguised Odysseus. Telemachus remonstrates with indignation; in response, Agelaus tells his comrades to restrain themselves, but insists that Odysseus must now be presumed dead and that Penelope must put an end to the uncertainty by choosing a new husband. Telemachus replies by saying, as he has said earlier, that he would be glad if his mother did remarry, but that he cannot turn her out; the situation could hardly be explained more clearly.

At this climactic moment, the suitors break into mad laughter; Athene has turned aside their wits. They are laughing 'with other men's jaws'; that means 'involuntarily', and indicates the mirthlessness of hysterical laughter. The meat they are eating is flecked with blood, and their eyes fill with tears. Theoclymenus now addresses the company. 'Wretches!' he cries out (XX,

351). 'What is the matter with you? Your heads and faces and limbs are shrouded in darkness; a groan is heard; your cheeks are wet with tears; the walls and roof beams are splashed with blood; the porch and courtyard are full of ghosts hurrying to Erebus in the dark; the sun has vanished from the sky, and an evil darkness covers it.' The suitors burst into laughter, and Eurymachus exclaims that the stranger had better leave, since he is talking nonsense. Theoclymenus walks out, not without prophesying that disaster will presently come upon all the suitors. The suitors remark to Telemachus that he is unfortunate in his choice of guests. He sits waiting for his father to make a move; and Athene prompts Penelope to fetch the great bow, so that the suitors can try to string it.

Even Page concedes (p.86) that the speech of Theoclymenus among the suitors is 'brief but memorable'. It is indeed memorable; it brings the whole preceding narrative to the point of climax. In early Greek literature we often encounter the figure of the warner, the man who plainly advises the person or persons who are bent on a disastrous course of the dangers which they are incurring; they pay no attention, since delusion sent by the gods has robbed them of their wits. Often the warner is a prophet; early Greek literature is pervaded by the belief in prophecy, and many of its legends feature members of the great families in which the gift was hereditary, as it was in certain families in historical times. Theoclymenus belongs to such a family. I find that the part he plays in the *Odyssey* fully justifies his ceremonious introduction, and see no need for Page's conjecture that there must have been an earlier version of the story in which Theoclymenus turned out to be the disguised Odysseus.[22]

Now let us consider a problem that affects the central plot of the *Iliad*. In the ninth book Agamemnon sends an embassy to Achilles, offering him a huge compensation if he will return to battle; after a long scene in which the ambassadors implore him to relent, Achilles refuses to yield to their solicitations. Page complains that the rest of the *Iliad* reveals no awareness that this celebrated episode ever occurred, and holds that after the embassy Achilles seems twice to deny that any approach has been made to him by Agamemnon.

The fatal decision of Achilles to compromise by allowing his friend Patroclus to put on his armour and enter the battle in his place is led up to in a series of passages that are subtly linked together in a way I find hard to reconcile with the idea that the *Iliad* is solely a product of oral composition. In the eleventh book Nestor takes out of the battle in his chariot the doctor Machaon, who has been wounded in the shoulder by an arrow. Achilles, standing on his ship where it lies on the beach, notices this, but cannot identify the wounded man. 'Now,' he exclaims to Patroclus (609), 'I think the Achaeans will soon stand about my knees and implore me; for a need that is no longer bearable has come upon them.' Then he sends Patroclus to Nestor's tent to learn the identity of the wounded hero.

'It seems very obvious,' Page writes (*History and the Homeric Iliad*, 305), 'that these words were not spoken by Achilles about whose knees the

---

[22] Page's treatment of the Theoclymenus episode has already been refuted by Erbse, *Beiträge zum Verständnis der Odyssee*, 42ff.

Achaeans were in fact standing in supplication on the previous evening; an Achilles who had rejected their prayers, who had made it clear that he would never accept apology or compensation, but would wait till Hector was killing the Greeks in their tents and burning their ships.' But do Achilles' words really imply that no attempt to persuade him to return to the battle has yet been made? The ambassadors of the ninth book do not actually clasp his knees in supplication; neither do they frankly admit the high-handedness of Agamemnon's behaviour and signify his willingness to express regret.

Nestor seizes the opportunity furnished by Patroclus' visit to talk seriously with him about the situation, using all his considerable powers of persuasion to try to ensure that Patroclus will put the case for reconsidering his attitude to his friend Achilles. On the way back Patroclus meets another wounded Achaean hero, Eurypylus, takes him back to his tent, and tends his wound.

From Eurypylus' tent, Patroclus hears the noise of the Trojan attack on the ships and sets off on his way to Achilles (XV, 390). When he arrives he is in tears, and Achilles inquires the reason for his distress. In reply, Patroclus enumerates the Achaean heroes who are now incapacitated by wounds. 'You are impossible, Achilles,' he says (XVI, 29), 'may I never be overcome by such wrath as that which you guard! You are no son of Peleus and Thetis; your parents are the grey sea and the steep rocks, so unyielding is your purpose. If you are afraid of some prophecy from Zeus which your mother has warned you of, send me!' Here Patroclus is carrying out the instructions given him by Nestor; at least scholars are now less quick to assume that repetition is necessarily the result of interpolation.

Replying, Achilles denies that he fears any prophecy; he feels bitter pain, he says, at the thought that a man should wish to deprive his peer of his prize; he repeats these words with intense emotion. In the ninth book the third of the ambassadors, Ajax, has made the briefest speech, but the one that has come nearest to moving Achilles; he has reproached him with his inflexibility, and his indifference to the plight of his fellow-warriors. 'Ajax,' says Achilles in reply (IX, 644), 'I think all you say is right; but my heart swells with anger, when I remember how Agamemnon treated me injuriously, as though I were an immigrant without honour.' In his speech in the sixteenth book (59), Achilles again says that Agamemnon treated him 'like an immigrant without honour'; and it is hard to resist the impression that he is echoing his speech to Ajax here. In that speech, he has said that he will not fight until Hector threatens his own ships (IX, 650f.); now he alludes to that statement, but so far modifies it as to permit Patroclus to take the field. The view that whoever wrote the speech of Achilles in the sixteenth book takes no account of the ninth book seems to me hardly tenable.

The Trojans, Achilles continues, are now filled with confidence; 'they would soon be filling the ditches with their dead, if Agamemnon were to feel kindly towards me' (71f.). Page complains that Agamemnon must have felt kindly when he sent the embassy; but the offer sent through the ambassadors was accompanied by no adequate apology, nor has any been offered since. Achilles tells Patroclus to go, so that the Greeks may bring back the girl, and noble gifts in addition. This, Page complains, is what has been offered by the embassy, only to be rejected. But now the situation is different; the Greek predicament has become critical, and if Patroclus succeeds Achilles will get Briseis back, and the gifts into the bargain, without having had to fight himself. The supposed proof that the poet of the sixteenth book had no knowledge of the embassy in the ninth has not a leg to stand on.

The discussion of these problems has revealed some of the links between the episodes of the poem which seem to me to indicate that it can hardly have been composed without the aid of writing. 'Delicate and subtle preparations for what will follow, in five hundred lines' time,' writes Page (*The Homeric Odyssey*, 142), 'veiled and indirect allusion now to what happened five hundred lines ago – such artifice lies beyond his power, even supposing that it lay within the bounds of his imagination.' References back and forward (over more than a short space) will be more or less explicit, and limited to the broad outlines of the story. I have space only for these few examples; but I leave it to anyone who has leisure to work through the works of Schadewaldt and Reinhardt to determine whether this is the right way to deal with Homer. If one insists on applying modern standards of strict consistency, at the same time refusing to learn from the patient study of the poems the canons which the poets have observed in their practice, then it is easy to accumulate evidence of multiple authorship. But the underlying unity of both great epics can be discerned, as it was discerned by Aristotle. The human memory is capable of amazing feats, and in theory the poems, with all the links between their various parts, could have been composed without the aid of writing. Only so far no example of anything comparable having been achieved has been adduced; and no one able and willing to perceive the unity of the epics is likely to believe it possible.

If the Homeric poems were indeed composed with the aid of writing as early as the eighth century, the fact is only a little less astonishing than if they were composed orally. Our earliest specimens of Greek alphabetic writing date from the third quarter of that century.[23] More than half consist, like the Homeric poems, of hexameter verse, so that the connection between such verse and writing at that time is not a matter of conjecture. A word for writing material found in Homer is derived from the name of the Syrian town of Byblos; Egypt was open to the Greeks as early as the seventh century, so that papyrus may have been available; but we know that in early times the Greeks used some form of parchment as writing material. The writing of the great book will have been a most laborious business; but in view of the immense value it will have had for the author and his dependants, the effort will have been worth while. Wade-Gery's suggestion that the alphabet was actually introduced in order for the epics to be written down seems to me unlikely; more probably it was invented for practical reasons by merchants trading with those Phoenicians from whose alphabet it was adapted.[24] Kirk

[23] They are conveniently collected by L. H. Jeffery, *The Local Scripts of Archaic Greece* (1961); on 'Nestor's Cup', see R. Meiggs and D. M. Lewis, *A Selection of Greek Historical Inscriptions* (1969), 1ff., and M. L. West, *Zeitschrift für Papyrologie und Epigraphik*, VI (1970), 171ff.

[24] See A. Heubeck, *Schrift* (ch. 10 of *Archaeologica Homerica* (1979)), 151ff.

writes (*Homer and the Oral Tradition*, 130) that 'the agents of traditional culture are normally the last, not the first, to make use of radically new techniques'. That may be true in our day, but it was not necessarily true in Homer's. The early Greeks were nothing if not enterprising, and the value of writing to professional poets will have been immediately apparent.

Wade-Gery believed that the great epics were designed for continuous recitation at a festival, as they were recited at the Athenian festival of the Panathenaea from the sixth century on; he thought of the joint festival of the Ionian Greeks at Mycale. Poetry was in those days designed for recitation, epic poetry being accompanied on the lyre; and though extracts from the great epics were no doubt recited in early, as they were in later, times, their authors surely envisaged at least continuous performances. The tradition must have started centuries earlier, doubtless with the composition of lays as inferior in quality as most of the Yugoslav material[25] which Professor Lord thinks so important for the understanding of Homer; it must have culminated with the creation of the two extensive masterpieces, designed to be appreciated as wholes. For a long time the text will have enjoyed no protection, and addition and interpolation will have occurred easily. It may well be that large sections of the epics, such as the lay of Dolon, the visit of Odysseus to the underworld and perhaps the final episode of the Odyssey entered the poems in this fashion.

Our lack of information about Homer as a person is not necessarily an indication that he lived at a very early date. The ancients on the whole thought that he and Hesiod were contemporary, or very near each other in time; rather more of them made Hesiod the older than made Homer.[26] We know a fair amount about Hesiod as a person, as we know a fair amount about the rather later Archilochus, because he himself has told us something of himself. But poets whose work belonged to a genre which did not allow them to write about themselves left no materials for biography; of Stesichorus and Tyrtaeus, who wrote later still, we know virtually nothing.[27] Certain authors allege that there were people living on Chios and calling themselves Homeridae, 'sons of Homer', who gave recitations and were regarded as authorities on the poems; but we must be wary of Wade-Gery's suggestion that they may have preserved an ancient tradition, for Detler Fehling has lately argued that the whole story depends on a misunderstanding by Hellanicus (4 FGrH 20) of the opening words of Pindar's second Nemean ode, and he may well be right.[28]

We have seen that in the great age of analysis one group of scholars followed Hermann in placing Homer at the beginning of his tradition, and another followed Wilamowitz in placing him at the end.[29] The modern

[25] Specimens are given by F. Dirlmeier, *Sitzungsberichte der Heidelberger Akademie*, Ph.-hist. Klasse (1971), Abh. 1.

[26] See M. L. West, *Hesiod, Theogeny* (1966), 40ff.

[27] See M. R. Lefkowitz, 'The poet as hero: fifth-century autobiography and subsequent biographical fiction', *Classical Quarterly*, N.S., XXVIII (1978), 459ff.; also *The Lives of the Greek Poets* (1981).

[28] See Wade-Gery, *The Poet of the Iliad*, 19ff.; T. W. Allen, *Homer: Origins and Transmission* (1924), 42ff.; D. Fehling, *Rheinisches Museum*, CXXII (1979), 193ff.

[29] See Dodds, 'Homer as oral poetry' (cited in n.9 above).

scholars whose views I have discussed all place him at the end. Mysterious as Homer is and is likely to remain, I feel a good deal more confident that he existed and that we know certain things about him than I did thirty years ago. Without a detailed reexamination of the text of the two great poems, summary treatments of the complicated problems of Homeric scholarship are of very limited value. Such a study, based on the results of the most recent scholarship, is an urgent need; and it will offer a release from the rigours of the period of Homeric investigation which I like to think is now drawing to an end. For far too long Homeric scholars have seemed to be bogged down in a kind of Passchendaele, from which the generals have seen no way out but a minute analysis of formulas, an excessive preoccupation with material objects, an exaggerated confidence in positive historical conclusions based upon the poems.[30] That work has not been futile, but it has gone on long enough, and it is time we took advantage of its results in returning to a detailed study of the poems. We should do so not in a spirit of positivist reductionism, but in that of scholars who while remembering that no labour is too arduous if it will throw light on Homer realise that they are dealing not simply with documents, but with documents that contain great poetry.[31]

---

[30] As to this, see M. I. Finley, 'Homer and Mycenae: property and tenure', *Historia*, VI (1957), 133ff., or in G. S. Kirk (ed.), *Language and Background of Homer*, 191ff.; 'The Trojan War', *Journal of Hellenic Studies*, LXXXIV (1964), 1ff. (where I think Finley has the best of his exchange with G. S. Kirk and J. L. Caskey); 'Schliemann's Troy: one hundred years after', *Proceedings of the British Academy*, LX (1974), 393ff.

[31] The modern literature about the topic is vast; for intelligent surveys of modern Homeric criticism with a bibliography, see James Holoka, *Homer and Modern Literary Critical Discourse*, Diss. Michigan, 1974; 'Homer originality: a survey', *Classical World*, LXVI (1973), 257ff.; 'Homer studies, 1971-7', *Classical World*, LXXIII (1979), no.2. See L. E. Rossi, 'I poemi homerici come testimonianza di poesia orale', in *Storia e civiltà dei Greci*, ed. R. Biachi Bandinelli, I (1978), 73ff. for the view that the Homeric poems are partly oral and partly literary compositions, a view developed earlier by A. Dihle, *Homer-probleme* (1970).

I am grateful to J. Griffin, C. W. Macleod and O. P. Taplin for discussing these questions with me; and particularly to Professor G. S. Kirk, who with characteristic kindness has done so much to improve the statement of a point of view decidedly different from his own. 'Many learned readers of Homer,' he wrote in 1970 (*Homer and the Oral Tradition*, 129), 'evidently have little patience for inevitably arid surveys of the formular language and schematic structure of the great poems; they will gratefully accept the simple picture of Homeric composition that Adam Parry has unfashionably and even daringly revived.' Like Adam Parry, whose position I feel special pleasure in defending, I admit that I have little patience left for the dryness of much modern Homeric scholarship. Griffin, in the book cited in n.21 and in *Homer* (in the O.U.P.'s *Past Masters* series), and Macleod, in his forthcoming commentary on *Iliad* XXIV, write from a standpoint with which I feel much sympathy.

2

A Medieval
Jewish Autobiography

Arnaldo Momigliano

Hugh Trevor-Roper and I have for a long time shared interests both in Jewish history and in the history of historiography. An unusual text by a German Jew has attracted my attention on both accounts. I would like to offer some remarks on it to Hugh Trevor-Roper as a token of gratitude for all that I have learned from him.

Medieval autobiographies are a relatively rare commodity, and this one – by a German Jew telling of his conversion to Christianity (and of becoming a White Canon) – is in no danger of being forgotten. The *Opusculum de conversione sua* by Hermannus quondam Judaeus, who lived from *c.* 1107 to *c.* 1181, was written about the middle of the twelfth century. The text was re-edited with great care on behalf of the *Monumenta Germaniae Historica* by Gerlinde Niemeyer as recently as 1963. A few years earlier it had been given eighteen pages in the *Geschichte der Autobiographie* by G. Misch (III (2), 1 (1959), 505-22). Even better, it has been placed in its Jewish-Christian context with unique authority by B. Blumenkranz in his paper 'Jüdische und christliche Konvertiten im jüdisch-christlichen Religionsgespräch des Mittelalters' which is included in the collective volume *Judentum im Mittelalter* (ed. P. Wilpert, Berlin 1966).

As the Middle Ages are admittedly *terra incognita* to me, my readers may well ask what I am doing there. The answer is that one needs help precisely when one is *in terra incognita*. Having read this text on more than one occasion as evidence for the history of Jewish institutions and for the history of biography, I have been left with two or three puzzles, none of which seems to have been solved – or even noticed – by the modern scholars whom I have consulted. In any case the text as a whole provides food for thought to anyone concerned with the modes and limits of the expression of individuality in autobiography.[1]

[1] G. Niemeyer's edition of Hermannus' *Opusculum* was reviewed by F. J. Schmale, *Hist. Zeitschr.*, CC (1965), 114-20. Previous bibliography in P. Browe, S. J., *Die Judenmission im Mittelalter und die Päpste* (Roma 1973), 62. The text, it seems to me, is basically misunderstood by

The basic facts are well known and easy to summarise. At the age of twenty Judas Levi, son of David, acting as the representative of his father, lent a large sum of money to bishop Ekbert of Münster without asking for security. The father, alarmed, sent Judas back from Cologne to Münster with instructions to remain there until the loan had been repaid. It took Judas twenty weeks to recover the money, and he filled the time in friendly contacts with the bishop's retinue and apparently with the bishop himself. He explored local churches and had the opportunity of accompanying the bishop on a visit to the recent Premonstratensian foundation of Cappenberg. He was not reluctant to dispute with Christians, but above all he was impressed by what he saw. He began to think of the possibility of conversion. Months of doubts and of family tension followed. His inclinations had not escaped notice in his Jewish circle. He tried to postpone marriage with the girl to whom he was engaged. The marriage, however, took place: later it appeared to the writer as the Devil's supreme trick. 'Decursis autem tribus mensibus, ex quo letargico hoc anime mee morbo ceperam laborare' (ch.11), young Judas was again ready to contact Christian priests, monks and nuns, both in Cologne and in the neighbourhood. He soon decided to run away from home and to kidnap a seven-year-old stepbrother who for unknown reasons lived with his mother in Mainz. Having succeeded in both operations, he took refuge in an Augustinian establishment near Mainz. There he left his stepbrother, who was more or less forcibly baptised and consequently never returned to the family. Judas himself entered as a catechumen another Augustinian foundation at Ravengiersburg. He was solemnly baptised in Cologne in November 1129 under the name of Hermannus and soon afterwards admitted as a novice at Cappenberg, the Premonstratensian place he had visited and loved not long before. There he learned Latin. He took holy orders perhaps about 1137, as apparently he had to be thirty years old before he could be ordained. The autobiography ends at this point, but we know from documentary evidence that Hermannus quondam Judaeus was Provost of Scheda in 1170. Two years later he moved to a canonry in the Church of Maria ad Gradus in Cologne. He was still alive in 1181. The title 'primus abbas ecclesiae Scheidensis' given to him by some recent manuscripts of the *Opusculum* seems to be due to confusion. What happened to Hermannus' wife after he left her is of course no part of his story: this 'vita nuova' was without a Beatrice.

Hermannus' autobiography, like all autobiographies by converts, raises the problem of the way in which conversion affected the perception of pre-conversion events. A man who changes his own name because he has become another man has to define the borders between his present and his

---

W. P. Eckert, in *Monumenta Judaica. 2000 Jahre Geschichte und Kultur der Juden am Rhein*, ed. K. Schilling (Köln 1963), 150–51. For background see in the same *Monumenta Judaica* the section by E. Roth, pp.60–130. Cf. furthermore G. Kisch, *The Jews in Medieval Germany* (Chicago 1949; second edn, New York 1970) and the two papers by H. Liebeschütz, *Journal of Jewish Studies*, X (1959), 97–111; XVI (1965), 35–46. For medieval biography in general, see K. J. Weintraub, *The Value of the Individual* (Chicago 1978), 18–114 (on Hermannus and the Premonstratensians, p.63). Cf. also Pl. F. Lefèvre and W. M. Grauwen, *Les statuts de Prémontré au milieu du XIIe siècle* (Averbode 1978).

previous self. Hermannus makes it clear that he writes for Christians, not for Jews. At the same time he projects back into his Jewish past his activities as a controversialist on behalf both of the Jewish and of the Christian faith. In other words, he recognises that these activities did not lead to anything. This point – which has already been duly emphasised by B. Blumenkranz – deserves some further clarification because it is central to Hermannus' view of his own conversion. Born in an age of religious controversies, young Judas Levi had obviously been trained to dispute and, as I have already mentioned, had relished open disputations. In that journey to Münster which proved decisive for his future life, the twenty-year-old moneylender had managed to enter into a (public?) debate with no less a person than the redoubtable abbot Rupert of Deutz, whose *Annulus sive Dialogus inter Christianum et Judaeum* was written just in those years between 1126 and 1128. During the following months, while still searching for an answer, Judas had numerous discussions 'opportune importune' with Christian clergymen (ch.9). On his own showing he had never yielded his ground: in fact he had come out of these disputations rather well, especially in that with Rupert of Deutz. Seen from the Christian point of view, these controversies had contributed nothing to his conversion. By implication his Christian opponents were involved in the failure: they had been unable to enlighten a man who wanted to be en-lightened. What is more remarkable, almost on the eve of his conversion Hermannus attempted a disputation inside a synagogue – this time as the champion of Christianity. But he ended by disavowing what he had said. To be more precise, when he was already on his way to being converted he visited an older brother in Worms and went to synagogue with him. As an opportunity was offered, he produced arguments in support of Christianity. As soon as his brother and other listeners began to be alarmed he blandly assured them that he had intended only to show to the Jews which arguments they should expect from Christian controversialists: 'quam illi responsionem gratanter acceperunt' (ch.16). Perhaps he had no choice but retreat, as he wanted to conceal his intention to become a convert himself. All the same, objectively, he had failed as a champion of Christianity, while before he had succeeded only too well as a Jewish apologist against his Christian opponents.

Hermannus, therefore, pointedly opposes the barrenness of his controversy with Rupert of Deutz (which is also the barrenness of Rupert's controversy with him) to the spiritual fruitfulness of the kind concern shown to him by a domestic of bishop Ekbert. If the bishop had allowed it, that domestic would have submitted himself to an ordeal for the sake of the Jew's soul.

In the sole digression in his story, which he appends to this episode, Hermannus emphasises that love is the only way to convert the Jews: 'Con-firment igitur ad illos caritatem eorum, quantum valent, necessitatibus com-municando ac totius eis forma pietatis existendo, quatenus quos verbo non possunt, lucrentur exemplo' (ch.5). Hermannus must have known that his famous older contemporary and fellow-convert Petrus Alfonsi (alias Moses Sephardi from Huesca) had championed a more aggressive controversial style with Jews and exploited his knowledge of rabbinical literature to reinforce traditional Christian arguments against Judaism. Whether Hermannus had Petrus Alfonsi in mind or not, his words by implication declared disagreement. He had been converted, not by such arguments, but by the benevolence and affection with which he had been received in the bishop's palace, by the discovery of claustral life at Cappenberg, and finally by the prayers of two ascetic women, Berta and Glismut, to whom he had recommended himself (cf. especially ch.5 and ch.12). These women had procured for him that gift of grace which he had been unable to obtain by commending himself to St. Paul and then to the Cross ('frequenter cor meum signo eiusdem crucis consignabam') – no mean steps for a man who was still a Jew (cf. 6 and 11). Paradoxically, but coherently, the only time in which Hermannus presents himself as successful for the right cause in a dispute is on the very eve of baptism, but this happens in a dream, and his defeated opponents are apparently already dead. He dreams of meeting two relatives in the other world and reproaches them for not having understood that Isaiah 9, 6 had alluded to the Cross. The poor relatives can produce no objection. They know by now for themselves that they are damned: 'eterne destinati sumus gehenne' (18).

In the language of the Psalms with which he had been familiar since his early childhood, Hermannus could claim that God 'de stercore pauperem erexit et eum cum principus populi sui collocavit' (cf. Ps. 112, 7-8). In this perspective a dream he had had in his thirteenth year acquired capital importance in his eyes. It determined the structure of his biography and, in some sense, constitutes the first of my puzzles.

The account of the conversion which I have so far summarised and commented upon is sandwiched between the description of this dream and its true interpretation. In other words, the autobiography is presented as the evidence required to explain the dream. The thirteen-year-old boy dreamt that he received a visit from the Emperor Henry V who gave him a white horse and a purse with seven coins in it, hanging from a glamorous belt: furthermore, the Emperor promised to give him the entire property of a prince who had just died. The boy was then asked to accompany the Emperor to his palace and to take part in a banquet. Apparently Jewish dietary rules were observed at the feast, for the Emperor shared with him a dish of herbs. The boy had more or less dreamt of himself as a new Mordecai after the death of Haman. A learned relative to whom he turned for the interpretation of the dream confirmed him in his expectations of honours and wealth: he specified that the white horse was the promise of a beautiful and noble wife (cf. Babyl. Talmud, *Berakhot* 56*b*; *Sanhedrin*, 93*a*). But, to use Dante's language which is here relevant, 'lo verace giudicio del detto sogno non fue veduto allora per alcuno, ma ora è manifestissimo a li più semplici'. Reflecting on this dream after his conversion Hermannus was in a position to give its true explanation: the Emperor stood for God; the horse, perhaps less conventionally, for baptism; the seven coins for the seven gifts of the Spirit; and so on.

What I do not know – and should like to know – is whether there are other

(medieval) autobiographies so neatly constructed to explain a dream. Hermannus places the whole of his autobiographical data between the account of
the dream and its interpretation. Dreams of course play an important part in
autobiographies, though it does not seem to have occurred to any of the
commentators of Dante's *Vita Nuova* whom I have consulted that the *Opusculum* by Hermannus Judaeus might be a useful text to compare.[2] Dreams
occur prominently in documents of two conversions of Christians to Judaism
in the late eleventh and early twelfth centuries, though even these do not offer
the exact parallel I am seeking. The Cairo Geniza has preserved at least two
autobiographical accounts in Hebrew by converts to Judaism; one is anonymous (but by a former priest), the other is by a Norman aristocrat of
Southern Italy (almost certainly also a former priest), Johannes of Oppido,
who in 1102 on conversion took the name of Obadiah.[3] The anonymous
account has been attributed by B. Blumenkranz to Andreas, the archbishop
of Bari whom we know from Obadiah to have preceded him in the conversion by several decades; but the attribution is not cogent, and the story of
Andreas' conversion is a problem in itself into which I do not intend to enter.
The anonymous writer who speaks in the first person tells in a letter of a
dream which persuaded one of his gaolers to allow him to escape. More
relevant to Hermannus' story is the account by the other convert. Johannes-
Obadiah, who speaks in the third person in a fairly lengthy personal memoir,
of which several fragments are preserved, states that he was inspired to
become a convert not only by the example of Andreas, but also by a dream

[2] Cf. M. Pazzaglia in *Enciclopedia Dantesca*, v (1976), 1086-96. For medieval theories on
dreams, F. X. Newman, *Somnium* (Princeton 1962). Cf. also A. Löwinger, *Der Traum in der
jüdischen Literatur* (Leipzig 1908).

[3] A critical edition is about to be published under the title 'Megillat Obadiah hager' with a
discussion in Hebrew by N. Golb in *S. D. Goitein Festschrift* (Jerusalem 1980), making all these
fragments available together. The bibliography provided by *Encyclopaedia Judaica*, s.v. 'Obadiah
the Norman Proselyte', xii (1971), 1306-8, is supplemented by A. Scheiber, 'Der Lebenslauf des
Johannes-Obadja aus Oppido', in P. Borraro (ed.), *Antiche Civiltà Lucane* (Galatina 1975),
240-44. The most recent contribution, of great importance, is by J. Prawer, *Studies in Medieval
Jewish History and Literature*, edited by I. Twersky (Cambridge, Mass. 1979), 110-34. I indicate
here only the previous editions of texts and the discussions relevant to my argument. The
anonymous text published by S. Assaf in *Zion*, v (1940), 118-19 (and also in the volume *Meqoroth
u-mehqarim* (Jerusalem 1946), 143: corrections to this edition by N. Golb, *Journ. Jewish Studies*,
xvi (1965), 71) was attributed to Andreas, archbishop of Bari, by B. Blumenkranz, *Journ. Jewish
Studies*, xiv (1963), 33-6, whereas S. D. Goitein, *Journ. Jewish Studies*, iv (1953), 74-84 had
preferred the identification, already hinted at by Assaf, with Obadiah. Neither suggestion is
cogent, as N. Golb remarks, *Journ. Jewish Studies*, xvi (1965), 69-74. The main fragments of
Obadiah's autobiographical text in the third person were published by E.-N. Adler, *Rev. Ét.
Juives*, lxix (1919), 129-34; J. Mann, *Rev. Ét. Juives*, lxxxix (1930), 245-59; S. D. Goitein, *Journ.
Jewish Studies*, iv (1953), 74-84 (English transl. only); A. Scheiber, *Acta Orientalia Hungarica*, iv
(1954), 271-96 (basically repeated in *Kiryath Sefer*, xxx (1954-55), 73-98 and *Journ. Jewish Studies*,
v (1954), 32-7); A. Scheiber, *Hebrew Union College Annual*, xxxix (1968), 168-72 (text already
translated by Goitein in *Journ. Jewish Studies*, iv (1953), but Scheiber publishes also a letter in
verse concerning another convert to Judaism of about 1100). Relevant also is the paper in
Hebrew by N. Golb, 'A study of a proselyte to Judaism who fled to Egypt at the beginning of the
eleventh century', *Sefer Zikkaron le-I. Ben-Zwi* (Jerusalem 1964), 87-104 (especially 102-4).
Essential for the background is S. D. Goitein, *A Mediterranean Society. The Jewish Communities of
the Arab World*, ii (Berkeley 1971), especially 308-11. It is to be hoped that all the evidence about
Obadiah will be translated and commented upon with due consideration of the traditions of
Norman historiography.

which he had had in his youth when he was still in the house of his father and in some situation of impurity. He dreamt of being in a cathedral and of receiving some message or warning from a man (angel?) who stood near him by the altar. A probable interpretation of the text is as follows: 'Now in the first year in which Johannes was initially defiled in the night in the house of Dreux, his father, in that year he had a dream. He was officiating in the Cathedral of Oppido . . . when he looked up and beheld a man standing to his right, opposite the altar. The man said to him: Johannes.' The content of the message is not preserved; and the situation of impurity in which the dream developed is obscurely described and has been variously interpreted (as its meaning is irrelevant to my argument I refrain from comment).[4]

Obadiah wrote his autobiography after 1121; Hermannus, as I said, became a Christian in 1129. The fragments we have of Obadiah's autobiography come from more than one copy of the text; some are vocalised. A Bible quotation from Joel (3, 4) is in Latin, though written in Hebrew characters. The text was therefore meant for wide diffusion, even to those who needed vocalised Hebrew and could appreciate a biblical text in the Vulgate. Obadiah was by then in Eastern Islamic countries where he met at least one self-proclaimed Messiah, but needed to maintain contacts with the West – if for no other reason, at least to produce evidence for his previous life. In any case his text would be in demand among Jews; it was of obvious interest. One wonders whether Hermannus knew Obadiah's text. It contained a decisive dream in a decisive situation which seems to be the nearest parallel to Hermannus' dream at the age of thirteen. Both converts considered themselves summoned to conversion in a dream which they had had in adolescence.

The natural assumption is that Hermannus had his dream at thirteen, when a Bar Mizvah. The assumption, however natural, is not without difficulties. The age of thirteen is recognised in Talmudic texts as the beginning of full religious duty and responsibility. Though difficult to date, these texts are unambiguous in their contents. A 'Saying of the Fathers' (5, 21) attributes to either Samuel the Small (first century A.D.) or the perhaps later R. Jehudah ben Tema a definition of the fourteen stages of human life: one of the stages is 'at thirteen for the commandments (*Mizvot*)'. A minor Talmudic treatise, *Masseket Soferim*, which is usually dated in the eighth century, is even more definite (18, 5): 'There was likewise a beautiful custom in Jerusalem to train the young sons and daughters to afflict themselves on a fast day . . . and at the age of thirteen [the boy] was taken round and presented to every elder to bless him and to pray for him that he may be worthy to study the Torah and engage in good deeds' (transl. A. Cohen). Furthermore, *Bereshit Rabbah*, a homiletic commentary on Genesis, usually dated in the fifth century, attributes (63, 10) to R. Eleazar b. Simeon, the controversial rabbi of the second century A.D, a saying destined to great fortune in later Judaism: 'A man is responsible for his

---

[4] For the more probable interpretation see N. Golb, *Sefer Zikkaron le-I. Ben Zwi*, 102-3 and *Journ. Jewish Studies*, XVIII (1967), 43-63. For dreams of another convert, A. Scheiber, *Tarbiz*, XXXIV (1964-65), 367.

son until the age of thirteen; thereafter he must say: "Blessed is He who has now freed me from the responsibility of this boy"' (transl. H. Freedman). Notwithstanding these and other pieces of evidence (for which cf. *Jewish Encyclopaedia*, s.v. Bar Mizvah), specialists, as far as I know, still seem to accept as valid the demonstration given in 1875 by Leopold Löw in his classic book *Die Lebensalter in der jüdischen Literatur* (210-17) that the Bar Mizvah ritual as we know it originated in Germany about the fourteenth century. S. B. Freehof ('Ceremonial creativity among the Ashkenazim', *Jewish Quarterly Review*, LXXV (1967), 217-21) substantially confirms this date and origin. Indeed the use of the expression Bar Mizvah, to indicate a boy exactly at the stage of initiation, does not seem to occur earlier. According to Löw's account, in the fourteenth century it became a custom among Ashkenazi Jews that a boy should be called for the first time to read at least a chapter from the weekly portion of the Law on the first Sabbath after he has entered his fourteenth year. On that occasion his father recites the blessing attributed to R. Eleazar b. Simeon. The festivity included, and still includes, presents to the Bar Mizvah, a banquet, and, if the child is gifted, a learned speech by him to the guests. Concurrently he assumes the duty of wearing phylacteries, *Tefillin*, at least during morning prayers except on Sabbaths and holy days.

Now if we go back to the dream which Hermannus had at the age of thirteen we find the banquet, the presents and, maybe, even the speech ('tum ego regali munificentiae debitas rependens gratias'), though admittedly before the banquet. The boy's age and the nature of the dream invite the conclusion that as early as 1120 the Ashkenazim of Cologne had already something like a Bar Mizvah ceremonial. The Mordecai pattern of the dream as a whole would not represent an objection. But how legitimate is the conclusion itself?

Whether the *Opusculum de conversione sua* by Hermannus quondam Judaeus offers a unique example of autobiography inserted between the account of a dream and its explanation; whether the *Opusculum* was written with some knowledge of Obadiah's autobiography; and whether this initial dream is the earliest evidence for the Bar Mizvah ceremony in Germany – these are the questions I ask but cannot answer. The text remains a very telling document of conversion in an age of controversy, because the man who loved controversies before conversion virtually recognised their inanity after it. The relation between this autobiography and the spirituality of the Premonstratensian order to which Hermannus belonged would deserve special study. But if we want to know too much about Hermannus' identity we shall of course end by knowing nothing.[5]

[5] I am deeply indebted to my colleague Professor N. Golb of the University of Chicago who allowed me to use his critical text of Obadiah's fragments before publication and discussed with me their interpretation. I owe other information to Dr B. Smalley, to my daughter A. L. Lepschy, to Rabbi L. Jacobs and to Joanna Weinberg.

3

Dante, Salvation and the Layman

Robert S. Lopez

'Dante, because of his learning, was rather conceited and aloof and disdainful, and – almost like an ill-mannered philosopher – was not good at talking to laymen': with these pungent remarks Giovanni Villani, his younger contemporary and fellow-citizen, winds up an otherwise admiring profile of the poet and laudatory analysis of his works (*Cronica*, IX, 136).[1] Considering that Dante had been a militant leader of the White party, whereas Villani sided with the Blacks who had sentenced him to death, one can hardly blame the Florentine chronicler for qualifying his warm tribute to the 'virtues, knowledge and worthiness of such a great citizen' with a touch of personality criticism. Historian by avocation but merchant by profession, Villani was by no means uncultivated or philistine, but held dear the patriotic, religious and literary beliefs of the middle class to which he belonged. He obviously felt ill at ease with Dante's intemperate invectives ('perhaps immoderately strident, but prompted perhaps by his being an exile') and wilful obscurities ('intelligible to those who have a subtle intellect'). More, there may have been unpleasant recollections: around 1300, when Dante held high positions in the government, Villani, then a beginning apprentice in the Peruzzi company of merchant bankers, may have met or heard him and found him arrogant.[2]

The important question, however, is not whether Villani's comments were dispassionate, but whether they corresponded to fact. 'Conceited, aloof and disdainful', yes, that is the image Dante consciously projected of himself

[1] No Dante specialist can any longer claim full command of the overgrown and controversial bibliography of his field. A mere tourist like me has to ask for expert advice (I am most thankful to Jacques Le Goff, Jaroslav Pelikan, Edward Peters, Riccardo Picchio and Maria Picchio Simonelli), then plunge into the 'selva oscura' with fingers crossed. The bibliographic suggestions that follow are only meant as hints to laymen for further reading.

[2] Compare, for instance, the resentful words of a Cremonese poet and diplomat almost a hundred years older than Villani, Ugo di Persio: 'La maggior noi' m'è quand' a pena – me digna aldire bacalaro' (The greatest annoyance to me is when a scholar hardly deigns to listen to me). Giovanni Villani has earned a solid reputation among historians as a remarkably alert, conscientious and well-rounded observer; he is sometimes slighted for not being the philosopher, political scientist and artistic writer he never aspired to be. E. Mehl, *Die Weltanschauung des Giovanni Villani* (Leipzig 1927) is the only attempt to show his personality in full relief; there would be room for a new and better biography.

in all of his writings and deeds; he was so perceived by his contemporaries and all succeeding generations; one should excuse him by reversing a well-known Churchillian expression, to wit, he had a lot of things to be immodest about. 'Not good at talking to laymen' may seem inappropriate for the poet whose Comedy still speaks to people of all classes throughout the world and the author of a pathfinding essay on the 'vulgar' language and dialects of Italy (written, it is true, in Latin). A conservative, an intellectual aristocrat who registered as a guild member and joined the White party of the nouveaux riches and petty bourgeois but had little sympathy for the newcomers, the merchants and the ignoramuses, Dante was nevertheless a prodigious observer of the people, the animals, the environment, the whole world around him. He certainly could and did talk to the laymen, that is, to the men in the street. But did he listen to what they said? Two connected test cases may, I hope, provide the beginning of an answer: his luminous vision of Purgatory, and his frustrated view of salvation for the virtuous infidel. They are, in fact, two facets of the same problem.

I submit that the structure of Purgatory is Dante's greatest and most original contribution to the geography and theology of the Otherworld. By 'original' I do not mean, of course, entirely unprecedented or unparalleled. Though unmentioned in Scripture and rejected by many medieval and nearly all Protestant denominations, belief in a middle ground between immediate beatification and eternal damnation is virtually as old as Christianity. Long before Christ, it existed in Zoroastrianism and other faiths; Islamic tradition took it over, but tended to reduce the intermediate stage to a bare minimum, the time it took a penitent soul to cross a narrow bridge, confess his faith in God and Mohammed, and proceed to salvation. To the Catholic Church, the last-minute contrition of the soul is in most cases a mere beginning; purgation requires a term of suffering measurable in years and days, but susceptible of being abridged by the prayers and alms of survivors. How and where the penitent soul pays his residual debt, however, was and still is murky. One of Pope John Paul II's latest pronouncements, while reaffirming the need of a trying purification for all souls who have escaped Hell but not fully earned Paradise, does not encourage speculation on the nature and locale of atonement. 'Curiosity', that is, prying into the hidden designs of God, remains a sin in the definition of the Catholic Encyclopaedia, based on that of Aquinas.[3]

Speculation was neverthless bound to grow as hope in and fear of a waiting and probation stage gained ground with the implicit approval of the Catholic Church. When, at long last, Purgatory received official recognition – first inconspicuously, in a letter of Pope Innocent IV in 1254, then more loudly in the Second Council of Lyon twenty years later – it had made its informal appearance in a large number of apocalyptic pieces and purported visions of saints or ordinary people. But most of these accounts, some of which stemmed

---

[3] While waiting for a book on 'curiosity' now being prepared by Edward Peters, one may read on that subject the short remarks and bibliography of my paper, 'Wisdom, science and mechanics: the three tiers of medieval knowledge and the forbidden fourth', in A. Markovits and K. Deutsch (eds), *Fear of Science, Trust in Science* (Cambridge, Mass. 1980).

from early Christian or non-Christian sources, concentrated their attention on Paradise (including the Earthly Paradise) and Hell. Purgatory proper, whether located in a cave or somewhere along the way ascending to the Earthly Paradise, had no well-defined characteristics of its own. Its trials were borrowed from those traditionally associated with Hell: above all the fire of Gehenna, straight from the Gospels, often accompanied by or alternating with icy storms (and, consequently, gnawing of teeth), and sometimes compounded with obscurity and stench. More conservative than literature, the figurative arts clung to their representations of Final Judgments with devils on one side, angels on the other, and no gimmick whatever to introduce middling souls to Heaven through a purgatorial waiting room. Such dualism sharply contrasted with the trinitarian conception of God, Creation and the human society that dominated the thought of the Middle Ages. With reason, Jacques Le Goff links with trinitarianism the efforts of Caesarius of Heisterbach, in the early thirteenth century, to replace 'the double house of eternity' with a 'new triple abode for awaiting the Last Judgment'; but even Caesarius stopped short of figuring out in full detail a space and set of penalties especially designed for the intermediary stage.[4]

The papal and conciliar recognitions of 1254 opened a loophole, if not quite a window, for further characterisation of Purgatory, but there was no rush of onlookers. Two Italian contemporaries of Dante, Giacomino da Verona and Bonvesin della Riva, who described the homes of the dead in some detail, confined themselves to the damned and the saved. The case of Bonvesin della Riva is particularly striking, for he did not compose two separate poems like Giacomino's *Celestial Jerusalem* and *Babylon Infernal City*, but a single *Book of the Three Scriptures*, two of which depicted Paradise and Hell. One might have expected Purgatory in the middle, but the central 'scripture' was devoted to the Passion of Christ.[5] Similarly, Giles of Rome in his learned treatise *De Praedestinatione, Praescientia, Paradiso et Inferno* included only a meagre paragraph mentioning 'besides Paradise and Hell . . . Purgatory and the Limbo of infants.' Dante alone had the imagination and the daring (for a 'curiosity' of this kind could pass Inquisition only if presented as a 'poetical'

[4] The early development of the Catholic conception of Purgatory has been recently examined in a stimulating paper of J. Le Goff, 'The usurer and Purgatory', in the cooperative book *The Dawn of Modern Banking* (New Haven, Conn. 1979); its tight chronologic approach, stressing the decisive two centuries (twelfth and thirteenth), seems to me more useful than the looser search for remote 'forerunners of Dante' in three nevertheless valuable books by that title, respectively by A. D'Ancona, M. Dods and F. Torraca (Florence 1874; Edinburgh 1903; Florence 1906). Nobody exactly foreruns another, and indirect influences are hard to pin down and prove. Even when a direct borrowing is documentable, as shown in the interesting paper of Giosuè Musca, 'Dante e Beda', reprinted in his *Il Venerabile Beda storico dell'Alto Medioevo* (Bari 1973), its impact is more operative on Dante's Hell and Paradise than on his Purgatory, from which the poet separated the Limbo of children and virtuous infidels in order to make its structure independent from and symmetrically comfortable to the structures of the other two houses of the dead.

[5] A short but useful introduction to Giacomino da Verona and Bonvesin della Riva and their bibliography is provided by Aldo Rossi, 'Poesia didattica e poesia popolare del Nord', in E. Cecchi and N. Sapegno (eds), *Storia della Letteratura Italiana*, I (Milan 1965). The far-fetched theory that Bonvesin della Riva had omitted Purgatory because he was a crypto-Cathar is unproved and improbable, though G. Contini still makes a discouraged allusion to it in his edition of *Poeti del Duecento*, I (Milan–Naples 1960).

allegory, not as a 'theological' one) to construct a third Otherworld house that stood comparison to the other two in moral and material stature. Symmetrically designed as a reverse counterpart of his Hell, his Purgatory owed very little to outside sources. Dante leaned somewhat on Aquinas for the pairing of penances with sins, and occasionally found usable scraps of lore in his religious readings, which probably ranged from Bede and the legend of St. Patrick's Purgatory to lecture notes of Brunetto Latini, his teacher, and possibly some translated Arabic text. He needed not and could not draw any profit from conversation with laymen, whose ideas on the subject were hazy. Nobody after him – not even the Roman Church – has undertaken to offer another image of Purgatory. His vision, which inspired a few successive figurative representations and is almost entirely his own brainchild, still is the only one we possess.[6]

Conceived in an ivory tower by a lonesome genius, Dante's middle house of the dead had a room missing. The poet knew it and struggled with the problem throughout his 'poema sacro', but could find no solution without falling into what was, in his time at least, patent heresy. Banished from his city for crimes he had not committed, Dante was profoundly troubled by the fate of the guiltless infidel, perpetually exiled from Paradise because he had not atoned for an original sin of whose existence he might have been totally unaware. Limbo, theologically unimpeachable, was not a sufficient justi-fication for the apparent injustice of the divine judgment, though Dante tried the lame excuse of suggesting that the Greek philosophers had lost their chance through their speculative 'curiosity' (*Purgatory*, III). He contrived reasons for moving as far up as the entrance to Purgatory the most righteous Roman figure (Cato) and promoting to the glory of Paradise three exemplary infidels (famous Trajan, undistinguished Ripheus and providential Raab). There still remained the mass of unbaptised just who in Dante's own time lived a virtuous life in remote countries where the Christian revelation was wholly unknown; what was the just reason for their exclusion? Already brought up in *De Monarchia*, this haunting question comes back in *Paradise*, XIX, the only one in the Comedy that Dante cannot even partially answer except by bowing to the inscrutable designs of God. But his explanation clearly does not appease him: playing on ambiguity, he adds that in the Final Judgment many such infidels will receive a higher seat than certain sancti-monious Christians – and in the following canto he parades Trajan and

[6]This does not mean, of course, that comparative studies of purgatorial conceptions of different ages and cultures have no interest, regardless of any actual interaction between them. H. R. Patch, *The Other World according to Descriptions in Medieval Literature* (Cambridge, Mass. 1950), a somewhat rambling but informative repertory of sources and bibliography, is most helpful for the whole of Europe, including Celtic and Scandinavian traditions as well as some accounts earlier than the middle ages or later than Dante's. Curiously it is weakest on Italian sources and bibliography, on which one must consult the books of D'Ancona, Dods and Torraca previously cited. For Islamic sources, too, it should be integrated with M. Asin Palacios' *Islam and the Divine Comedy* (preferably not the abridged English version but the Spanish original) and with the more moderate claims of E. Cerulli, *Il Libro della Scala* (Vatican City 1949) and G. Levi della Vida, 'Dante e l'Islam secondo nuovi documenti', reprinted in his *Aneddoti e Svaghi Arabi e Non Arabi* (Milan-Naples 1959).

Ripheus, raised to Paradise by divine grace.[7]

It is here, I believe, that Villani's criticism of Dante finds its best substantiation. By paying no attention to the accounts of men in the street, the poet passed by precious information concerning his argument. The virtuous infidels without access to Christian preaching he alluded to lived along the Indus river; next to them Dante mentioned in passing the Ethiopians. Both locations were singled out not only on account of their extreme remoteness, but also because an unbroken tradition reaching as far back as classic Greece endowed their inhabitants with extraordinary and indeed utopian virtues. Unfortunately that bookish lore was stale (as everything else Dante said about India) and could have been easily contradicted by the numerous clergymen and lay merchants who were at that time plying the routes of the Mongol empire and the sultanate of Delhi. Ethiopia was a Christian country, though not a Catholic one. India was widely exposed to the active propaganda of Catholic missionaries who had operated many conversions, built churches and established missions at Cambay near the Indus river and Quilon in southern Dekkan (to say nothing of the legendary 'Christians of St. Thomas' supposedly converted by the doubting apostle). China, too, had a Catholic archdiocese in Peking and suffragan bishops, plus an authentic and ancient Nestorian community; but it might have been a more striking example of guiltless infidelity on account of its much greater remoteness than India's.[8]

Why did Dante, whose knowledge of the political and religious geography of the West was almost impeccable, bungle so badly over the East? So far as the Byzantino-Slav community is concerned, which is not misrepresented but totally ignored, Riccardo Picchio has the perfect answer: he drew an 'ideological iron curtain' between the Latin Christianity and the schismatic. Not one emperor in Constantinople is mentioned in the Commedia after Justinian, not one Slav kingdom beyond Catholic Bohemia and wavering Rascia.[9] The argument, however, cannot apply to the lands of the virtuous infidels, whom Dante desperately wanted to rescue. He could easily have read or heard about Friar Giovanni del Piano del Carpine, the first papal ambassador to the Grand Khan, who as early as 1248 had reached and broadcast on his return the erroneous but encouraging news that the Chinese honoured Jesus, had both the Old and the New Testament and lacked nothing

[7] On the much debated problem of salvation for the virtuous infidel – a problem still haunting the Catholic conscience – one may consult R. W. Chambers, 'Long will, Dante and the righteous heathen', in *Essays and Studies of the English Association*, IX (Oxford 1924), and L. Capéran, *Le Problème du salut des infidèles* (Toulouse 1934).

[8] Utopian literature on India has been recently re-examined by T. Hahn, 'The Indian tradition in Western medieval intellectual history', *Viator*, IX (1978) and by J. Le Goff, 'L'Occident médiéval et l'Océan Indien: un horizon onirique', reprinted in his *Pour un autre Moyen Age* (Paris 1977); on medieval Christian missions in India I have come across no recent survey that can parallel P. Demiéville's masterly 'La situation religieuse en Chine au temps de Marco Polo', in the cooperative *Oriente Poliano* (Rome 1957), but the basic information is easily obtainable from G. Golubovich, *Biblioteca Bio-Bibliografica della Terra Santa e dell'Oriente Francescano* (Florence 1919); on the Christians of St. Thomas one can see the recent paper of B. J. Lamers, 'Der Apostel Thomas in Südindien', *Neue Zeitschrift für Missionswissenschaft*, XIV (1958).

[9] To the best of my knowledge, Riccardo Picchio is the first and only scholar who has noticed and pointed out Dante's 'iron curtain', in a few terse sentences of his *Etudes Littéraires Slavo-Romanes* (Florence 1978), 25-6. The subject deserves fuller treatment, preferably by him.

except baptism – an ideal test case for Dante's query. Less easily, he could have drawn from William of Rubruc's later report the tantalising statements of Mangu Khan, that there was only one God, that the different religions were like fingers of his hand, and that the Christians had the Scripture but did not live by it. Above all, he could have learned a good deal from the merchants. It is unthinkable that Dante had no access to Marco Polo, whose comments on Buddha were so much more helpful than the obsolete legends about India's Brahmins; he might even have corresponded with him, for Polo was one of Venice's leading experts on salt trade and Dante was charged with negotiating an agreement about salt trade between Ravenna and Venice. A detailed, most accurate instruction on travel to China, probably compiled in Genoa, was inserted by Florentine Pegolotti in his manual of commercial practice, perhaps a few years after Dante's death; but other copies must have circulated, for the same instruction with significant variants appears in another Florentine manuscript. Indeed, China and India were the talk of every Italian city when Paradise was written. Why did Dante not leave his ivory tower and listen to the man of the street?[10]

Perhaps he did, but he drew a totally different conclusion. In 1291 two Genoese brothers, Ugolino and Vadino Vivaldi, sailed through the strait of Gibraltar with the intention of reaching India by a western route, converting its people and loading on board its precious wares. It is generally believed, though it cannot be definitely proved, that the unlucky courage of the Genoese brothers (who disappeared at sea) supplied the inspiration for Dante's Ulysses. The moral was, as in *Paradise*, XIX and XX, that no man should be 'curious', and that you cannot reach Purgatory without the will of God.

[10] On the commercial relations between medieval Italy, India and China, and their cultural background, full information and bibliography can be found in a number of papers I have published intermittently over the last forty years. The latest are 'L'importance de la Mer Noire dans l'histoire de Gênes', *Colocviul Romano-Italian, Academia Republicii Socialiste Romania* (Bucarest 1977), and 'Nouveaux documents sur les marchands italiens en Chine à l'époque mongole', *Comptes-rendus, Académie des Inscriptions et Belles-Lettres* (Paris 1977); most of the earlier ones are reprinted in my *Su e Giù per la Storia di Genova* (Genoa 1975); I am preparing a book on the subject.

4

Religion and the English Nobility in the Later Fourteenth Century

Jeremy Catto

What was the contribution of the English nobility to the religious manifestations of the later fourteenth century? The question must be asked by the
historian of religion because the one unifying characteristic of the diverse,
individual and sometimes eccentric novelties of devotion and belief is the
growing participation of laymen: men who, as *The Cloud of Unknowing* puts
it, 'stand in activity by outward form of living, nevertheless yet by inward
steering after the privy spirit of God', and who, not being professed to the
religious life, could still be 'then and then . . . partners in the highest point of
this contemplative act.'[1] Laymen such as the author of the *Cloud* had in mind,
moreover, were men of education and sensibility, the intellectual equals of
the clergy: and the new contemplative literature in the vernacular is matched
in sophistication and learning by the General Prologue to the Lollard Bible
and the works of the 'learned' poets, Chaucer and Gower. At the head of this
educated public were the nobility in whose households civilised manners or
'courtesy' could be learnt, and where, increasingly, there were books;[2] and
their connections with some of the devotional novelties of the age are not
difficult to trace. Their interest is visible behind some of the new liturgical
feasts and devotions, and their personal prayers can occasionally be retrieved
from books of hours or other personal manuscripts.[3] Their support was
fundamental in the astonishing expansion of the Carthusian Order after 1340,
as would be their successors' patronage of the Bridgettine foundation at
Sheen; and evidence has been assembled to show that circles at court lent their
patronage for some years to the band of Lollard preachers and publicists.
Some at least of the nobility, therefore, must have held independent views on

[1] *The Cloud of Unknowing*, ed. Phyllis Hodgson (London, EETS, 1944), 3.
[2] A. R. Myers, *The Household of Edward IV* (Manchester 1959), 2-3; K. B. McFarlane, *The Nobility of Later Mediaeval England* (Oxford 1973), 105.
[3] R. W. Pfaff, *New Liturgical Feasts in Later Mediaeval England* (Oxford 1970), 66; Cambridge University Library Add. MS 451,ff.258v-261v; Oxford, Bodleian Library MS Auct.D.4.4., f.iii; Bodleian Library MS Digby 41, f.91v; for a fifteenth-century example, see W. A. Pantin, 'Instructions for a devout and literate layman', in J. J. G. Alexander and M. T. Gibson (eds), *Mediaeval Learning and Literature, Essays presented to Richard William Hunt* (Oxford 1976), 398-422.

religious as on political issues. In the absence as yet of any general study of lay religious practice and belief in the age of Wyclif, there is room for a survey of the evidence provided by the nobility. This evidence is of course very patchy: some household accounts of variable interest for the present purpose, a few inventories and a considerable number of wills, documents on noble religious foundations, personal liturgical and devotional manuscripts, and a small amount of written material from noble pens. It is enough, however, to suggest that substantial changes were taking place in the religious attitude of the lay upper classes.[4]

No precise definition of the fourteenth-century nobility can be satisfactory; the contemporary conception of nobility could embrace any of the '3,000 or so armigerous families'.[5] If between 100 and 150 secular persons received personal writs of summons to the parliaments of the late fourteenth century, many of them were surpassed in wealth and influence by others who received none. At the most, some notion of peerage may have begun to form at the end of the century, as the hesitant conferment of baronies by patent, marquessates and dukedoms by Richard II suggests. The 'peerage' of Richard II merely confirmed the eminence of families whose fortune was the result of participation in the wars of his grandfather, and it is reasonable, therefore, to see a distinct phase in the emergence of a coherent noble order in the service exacted by Edward III from old families and new men alike. The first phase of the French wars had created a core of professional captains which included on terms of practical equality such established houses as Bohun, Fitzalan and Beauchamp with newly fortunate lineages like Moleyns, Holland, Montagu and Scrope. They shared the experience of war, divided its spoils, and joined in the life of Edward's court; and equality of service was emphasised by new chivalric orders like the Garter, which set before the captains of war a hierarchy of honour unrelated to blood, and indeed a kind of code of professional ethics. The values and experiences which they shared gave at least some unity to the nobility of the late fourteenth century, and allow us to treat them as a more or less homogeneous group in spite of their varied origin. It would, however, be unwise to assume that either the experience or the attitudes which the group engendered were limited to the recipients of a particular, arbitrarily chosen degree of royal favour; a society in which noble households, headed by the king's court, played such an important part in the advancement of lesser men was anything but exclusive.

Like other professional occupations, that of war creates its own conventions and develops broader skills than a strong right arm. The private letters sent back to England and the innumerable captains' accounts tendered at the Exchequer during the reign of Edward III are witness of the new nobility's familiarity with the written word as an essential part of its business; while the maintenance of the lands and fortunes which were the rewards of war depended upon a command of documentation of which a number of

---

[4] I am grateful to Mr James Campbell and Mr Gerald Harriss for allowing me access to the transcripts of a number of household accounts made by the late K. B. McFarlane. Except in one case cited below I have consulted the originals.
[5] McFarlane, *Nobility*, 6–10.

private cartularies and a mass of estate papers, headed by the voluminous Lancaster records, are the remains.[6] Like other trained men of the fourteenth century, moreover, they seem to have been expected to attain some degree of general culture as well, and where evidence survives of the education of their children, it is clear that literary attainments were integral to their training.[7] Inventories of the property of Thomas of Woodstock, Duke of Gloucester, in 1397 and of Henry, Lord Scrope, in 1415 allow a fortuitous glimpse of two noble book collections, too individual not to reflect the owners' taste; they are unlikely to have been unique.[8] For the first time, too, a number of works survive from the pens of the lay nobility: Thomas, Duke of Gloucester's *Ordenaunce and Fourme of Fighting within Lists*, a businesslike but accomplished tract; Edward, Duke of York's *The Master of Game*, his translation and amplification of Gaston, Count of Foix's *Livre de la Chasse*; Henry, Duke of Lancaster's devotional work the *Livre de Seyntz Medicines*, the lost poems of John Montagu, Earl of Salisbury and the surviving *Book of Cupid* and *The Two Ways* of his friend Sir John Clanvowe may be added.[9] Finally, attention has recently been drawn to the role of the nobility as patrons of the literary revival of the late fourteenth century. The variety of texts and manuscripts made for them again betrays the individuality of their taste: it could embrace French romances such as *Floriant et Florete* in the luxurious manuscript of the Marquess of Lothian, which in its surviving form may have been written for Ralph, Lord Neville at Raby Castle; Gower's *Confessio Amantis*, in the more serious vein of court English, which was probably recast for Henry of Lancaster, Earl of Derby; perhaps also the pious 'library' of the Simeon manuscript, which may have been in the possession of Joan, Countess of Hereford.[10] But beyond any individual patronage the creation of a court ambience in the later years of Edward III, and its continuance in the succeeding reigns, encouraged the production of the sophisticated and indeed erudite poetry of Chaucer, Thomas Usk, Gower and Hoccleve, and provided a ready market for art and craftsmanship of a high order.[11] As the patrons of both literature and art the new nobility, in its broadest sense, showed a level of sophistication measurably higher than that of its predecessors.

This nobility, then, was an accomplished as well as a privileged group, and its religion was not that of passive or disinterested observers in matters essentially ecclesiastical. Its members had universally been brought up to

[6] Robert Somerville, *History of the Duchy of Lancaster*, I, 1265-1603 (London 1953), 90-133; Robert Avesbury, *De Gestis Mirabilibus Edwardi Tertii*, ed. E. Maunde Thompson (London, RS, 1889), 372-4, 416-17, 434-7, 439-43, 445-7; H. J. Hewitt, *The Organisation of War under Edward III* (Manchester 1966); McFarlane, *Nobility*, 33, 44-50.

[7] McFarlane, *Nobility*, 243-6, and *Lancastrian Kings and Lollard Knights* (Oxford 1972), 115-17.

[8] Ed. Viscount Dillon and W. St. John Hope-Dillon, *Archaeological Journal*, LIV (1897), 275-308; and C. L. Kingsford, *Archaeologia*, LXX (1920), 90-8.

[9] Sir Travers Twiss (ed.), *The Black Book of the Admiralty* (London, RS, 1871-6), I, 300-28 (Gloucester's treatise); W. A. and F. Baillie-Graham (eds), *The Master of Game* (London 1904); for Henry of Lancaster's work see below, n.37; *The Works of Sir John Clanvowe*, ed. V. J. Scattergood (Cambridge 1975); see McFarlane, *Lancastrian Kings*, 201-4.

[10] Gervase Mathew, *The Court of Richard II* (London 1968), 78, 107-8, and see below, n.33.

[11] Mathew, *Court of Richard II*, 38-52; Maud Clarke, *Fourteenth Century Studies* (Oxford 1937), 115-23.

a number of conventional observances and practices, and the stamp of personality will not be evident before these conventions have been established. Considerable evidence of these observances is scattered among their household accounts, inventories, and wills, which show that noble piety embraced both good works, ranging from alms-giving to the foundation of hospitals, and the more personal solicitation of supernatural help, whether through prayer, the performance of vows, trust in talismans or recourse to holy men or astrologers. The private chapel was probably the centre of most noblemen's devotions, as it had been for centuries; like other aspects of the fourteenth-century household, it was probably becoming more elaborate. It is likely that it was also beginning to reflect personal taste, as separate chapels for husband and wife are often mentioned in wills after 1350. Catherine, Countess of Warwick was able to bequeath a cross from her own altar when she predeceased her husband in 1369.[12] Many of them certainly had choirs and singing masters. Chapel furniture was part of the treasure of captains of war to be bequeathed in their wills; the furniture of a great nobleman's chapel was a notable part of his fortune, as can be seen in the plate, books and vestments in the inventory of Thomas of Woodstock, Duke of Gloucester, in 1397. The size of the équipe can be determined from the mass-books – nearly forty missals, antiphons, psalters, and others. Probably he had his own choir and staff of chaplains as did his brother John of Gaunt. The combination of religious symbols with the marks of rank is shown in the vestments which combine the Name of Jesus and imagery of the Nativity and Salutation with the Duke's arms and badge, those of the English crown, and the insignia of the Garter. Undoubtedly Thomas of Woodstock's sense of his social position was reinforced by the ceremonies in his chapel.

Inevitably, the point at which conventional religion had its greatest effect on the life of the nobility was the point of death. In the fourteenth century, the necessity of laying up treasure in heaven by ensuring the prayers of future generations found expression in foundations and benefactions and above all in chantries. Rosenthal found that 85 noble families of the fourteenth and fifteenth centuries – virtually all the higher nobility – founded chantries whose priests would be endowed to pray for their souls for ever.[13] Prayers for the dead were the most common single concern of noble wills of the later fourteenth century. Joan, Lady Cobham paid for 7,000 masses to be said by canons and friars; Richard II, Earl of Arundel, one of the richest captains of Edward III's reign, left 1,000 marks for lands to maintain six priests and three choristers to celebrate mass each day in the chapel of Arundel castle.[14] It was usual for a founder of a hospital or college to make prayers for his soul a perpetual obligation. The obligation was taken seriously; Chacumbe Priory, for instance, kept careful records of the anniversaries of its patrons the Segrave family, as the accounts of Margaret Marshal, Countess of Norfolk,

[12] Worcestershire Record Office, Worcester Diocesan Records, Reg. Lynne, ff.52v-53, abstracted by N. H. Nicolas, *Testamenta Vetusta* (London 1826), I, 78.
[13] J. T. Rosenthal, *The Purchase of Paradise* (London 1972), 34-5.
[14] Joan Cobham's will in Lambeth Palace, Reg. Whittlesey, ff.114v-115v (*Test. Vet.*, I, 81-2); the Earl of Arundel's, ibid., Reg. Sudbury, ff.92v-95v. (*Test. Vet.*, I, 94-6).

reveal.[15] Royal prayers for the dead set an example. Two accounts of expenses for the anniversaries of the deceased Queens Isabella, widow of Edward II, and Philippa, wife of Edward III, as observed in 1372 and 1373 survive among the records of the Exchequer: the hundred pounds of wax for candles, the cloth of gold imported from Italy, the poor men who bore torches on the vigil and the anniversary day, the offering for the dead queens' souls, the distribution of alms, the free wine served from a barrel, and the donations to the sisters of a London hospital, to three London hermits and to the prisoners of Newgate prison – these arrangements are a model commemoration of the fourteenth-century dead. Many of the nobility were equally punctilious in observing anniversaries. Henry, Earl of Derby, gave two pieces of fine cloth for a dirge on the obit of his cousin the Countess of Saint-Pol, and another payment for a requiem mass for the Earl of Kent.[16] Prayer for the dead was a solemn obligation of blood and friendship.

Charity, too, was a customary part of court and noble piety, though the evidence of it in household accounts does not suggest that it was notably systematic or extensive. It could be ostentatious: and great funerals were universally a time for the occasional doles of which Professor Jordan has disapproved on large economic grounds.[17] Most of the great charitable foundations for the poor and the diseased originated in a later period, but it is significant that the fourteenth-century founders of hospitals were soldiers close to the court: Henry, Earl of Lancaster and his son the first Duke; Sir Michael de la Pole; and Sir Robert Knolles. Others ignored charity altogether. The ministers' accounts of Sir John Dinham the younger record his expenses in minute detail; the only reference to a charitable gift is of fivepence to some labouring men, given by a servant who hastened to assure his master that it was 'more out of fear than charity'.[18] Henry, Earl of Derby's household accounts show that as early as 1381, when he was 15, he made an offering at mass of one penny; in 1398, with far more cash to dispose of, his accounts record exactly the same sum, invariable throughout the year. An additional fourpence was placed upon the altar on feast days, or when he visited a notable shrine or religious house. On Maundy Thursday, he washed the feet of poor men and gave away one gown for each year of his age; and on Easter Sunday he distributed alms in the villages through which he passed.[19] Charity was an aspect of the Earl's state; the sums expended on it, and there is little reason to suppose that much has gone unrecorded, were minute compared to his bills for clothes and horses. The record, so far as it goes, is not impressive.

By the late fourteenth century, then, there seems to have been a conventional if flexible pattern to the religious practices of noblemen, though elements in the pattern were traditional. What is perhaps new is the increasing personal recourse to supernatural help, which took many forms. The circle of

[15] College of Arms MS Arundel 49, ff.29v-30v.
[16] PRO, E 101/397/1; E 101/397/7; DL 28/1/3 f.5; DL 28/1/6 f.8.
[17] W. K. Jordan, *Philanthropy in England, 1480-1660* (London 1959), 146-7.
[18] Formerly Wardour Castle, Ministers' Accounts, 414 (Dinham Mss); Magdalen College, Oxford, McFarlane transcripts, Ser. III, vol. LXXIII, p.2. I have not seen the original account.
[19] PRO, DL 28/1/1 ff.4-5; DL 28/1/10, f.32.

Richard II, it is evident, paid much attention to astrological predictions, as can be seen by the popularity of Father John Somer's astrological tables made for the Princess of Wales, and by Chaucer's allusions to the influence of the stars in the *Knight's Tale*. His *Treatise on the Astrolabe* would presumably have been used, had it been completed, for predictive purposes, as would the *Equatorie of the Planetis* whether or not Chaucer was the author. The proliferation in the later fourteenth century of carefully executed astrological manuscripts such as Oxford, Bodleian Library MS Digby 41 suggests that there was a steady market for such material, and the most spectacular of all, Bodleian Library MS Bodley 581, was intended for the personal use of Richard II. Its combination of injunctions on kingship with the art of geomancy and instructions for ascertaining such delicate political matters as the fidelity of friends may throw light, it has been suggested, on some of Richard's apparently wayward actions. His dependence on the 'judicial of astronomy' is confirmed by the highly wrought horary quadrant made for him in 1399, now in the British Museum. But the underlying interest in the supernatural arts was certainly not peculiar to him.[20]

Moralists complained of the influence of astrologers and it was perhaps more conventionally pious, in time of uncertainty, to consult hermits; one remarkable anchorite, John of London at Westminster Abbey, seems to have had a thriving practice in the court circle. Richard II had sought his advice before he confronted the rebels at Smithfield in 1381, and Thomas IV, Earl of Warwick, attributed his acts to the hermit's advice in his confession of treason in 1397. These aspersions do not seem to have ruined John's credit, since he survived to offer advice to Henry V at the moment of his accession in 1413.[21] There is also evidence in wills and household accounts of the accumulation by noblemen of religious objects of value whose purpose, beyond that of investment, was presumably to be talismans. They were acceptable enough as New Year presents, like the gold tablets with an image of the Virgin, given by Henry of Derby to his Countess. They can be found among the valuables in a number of noble wills, such as those of Elizabeth, Countess of Northampton and William, Lord Ferrers. So far as I know, none of them still exists. The most interesting talismans widely spread among the nobility were relics of the True Cross. They were prized enough to be singled out in wills, and surprisingly many of the nobility possessed them, among them Elizabeth, Countess of Northampton; Thomas, Earl of Warwick; Thomas, Earl of Oxford; Edmund, Earl of March; and William, Lord Bardolf.[22] The

---

[20] Bodleian Library MS Bodley 581 (see Mathew, *Court of Richard II*, 40-1, and J. P. Genet, *Four English Political Tracts of the Later Middle Ages* (London, RHS, 1977), 22-30); D. J. Price (ed.), *The Equatorie of the Planetis* (Cambridge 1955); for the quadrant see British Museum, *A Guide to the Mediaeval Antiquities and Objects of Later Date* (London 1924), 222.

[21] R. M. Clay, *Hermits and Anchorites of England* (London 1914), 153-4.

[22] PRO, DL 28/1/4, f.16v; Countess of Northampton's will in Lambeth Palace, Reg. Islip, f.122r-v (*Test. Vet.*, I, 60-1); Lord Ferrers's, ibid., Reg. Whittlesey, ff.124v-125 (*Test. Vet.*, I, 76); Earl of Warwick's, ibid., Reg. Whittlesey, f.110r-v (*Test. Vet.*, I, 79-80); Earl of Oxford's in *Registrum Simonis de Sudburia* (London), ed. R. C. Fowler (London, CYS, 1927-38), I, 4-6; Earl of March's in Lambeth Palace, Reg. Courtenay, ff.188-189v (*Test. Vet.*, I, 110-13); Lord Bardolf's, ibid., Reg. Courtenay, f.215v (*Test. Vet.*, I, 116).

Countess of Northampton was probably typical in carrying her relic about with her as a charm.

None of these forms of religion and superstition necessarily implies religious sensibility on the part of the court circle. But the religious observance of the nobility was essentially personal, and could take the stamp of individual character. The majority of cases for which there is evidence from service books, inventories or household accounts naturally show little sign of individuality. Nevertheless, there is an increasing tendency to diversification among surviving books of devotion, and some evidence to suggest that new liturgical feasts may have been first celebrated in private chapels. For instance, a missal belonging to Sir William Beauchamp, Lord Bergavenny, is the first English liturgical book to contain, before 1388, the mass of the Holy Name, which would be widely observed in the fifteenth century.[23] Missals in private hands in the late fourteenth century often contain additional prayers suggestive of private devotions: a prayer for St. Teilo, another for the blessing of the bread at Easter, and other prayers were added to the missal of the Braybrooke family, now in the University Library at Cambridge.[24] But the characteristic instrument of noble piety was coming to be the book of hours, a set of devotions originating in the twelfth century but common among the upper classes only from the late fourteenth. It originated as an elaborated psalter; the psalter had been the customary book of lay devotion in the early fourteenth century, and in books of hours variable material, the Litany, canticles, the Office of the Dead, the short Office of the Virgin, and prayers, was added; finally the psalms themselves were often omitted.[25] The liturgical chanting of the psalter gradually gave way therefore to a more individual, humanised and intimate expression of religious sentiment, in the Cult of the Virgin, and the prayers for particular saints and occasions. The process can be seen in the household of the last Bohun Earl of Hereford and his daughters, who married respectively Thomas of Woodstock and Henry, Earl of Derby. The Bohun liturgical manuscripts, the illumination of which suggests that they were made to order in London, begin with the Earl's psalter, made before 1373, with additions of the Litany and other material. Mary Bohun, Countess of Derby, seems to have introduced into her father's psalter, which she inherited, some personal prayers which show that while the recital of the psalms was an intercession for the dead, it aimed to 'inspire [her] heart with an intense sweetness': a phrase which shows the influence of Richard Rolle. This more intimate and personal sentiment can be seen again in the prayer-book she evidently ordered for herself, which contained the Hours of the Virgin, the penitential psalms and the Office of the Dead.[26] Personal religion appears once again in private devotions which had

[23] Trinity College, Oxford MS 8, f.286; Pfaff, *New Liturgical Feasts*, 65-6.
[24] See n.3 above.
[25] L. M. J. Delaissé, 'The importance of books of hours for the history of the mediaeval book', in *Gatherings in Honor of Dorothy E. Miner* (Baltimore 1974), 203-25, esp. pp.204-7.
[26] Bodleian Library MS Auct. D.4.4; Vienna, Österreichische Nationalbibliothek MS 1826*. See M. R. James, *The Bohun Manuscripts* (Oxford 1936); Margaret Rickert, *The Reconstructed Carmelite Missal* (London 1952), 73-5.

nothing to do with local or dynastic loyalties, such as that of Thomas Mowbray, Earl of Nottingham, to the Visitation, or of Thomas of Woodstock to St. Mary Magdalen. Individuality in devotions and the idea of a personal relation between supplicant and saint is at least consonant with the growing taste in noble households for romances whose plot turned on human relationships.

Such observances must often have been influenced by private confessors. The development of the practice of personal confession, stimulated by the friars in the thirteenth century, is an obscure but probably fundamental aspect of later medieval religion. Perhaps by 1300, certainly by 1350, it had become customary for noble families to be advised by their own confessors, usually friars, who were trusted intimates of the household, and often executors of their wills. If some, like John of Gaunt's confessor John Kenningham, prior-provincial of the Carmelites, can hardly have 'lived in', Margaret Marshal retained William Woodford, O.F.M. at Framlingham Castle. Woodford's writings show that he was an authority on the proper practice of confession, and by a curious chance we know that some of the Countess's charities originated in penances set by her confessor, for in one of his works Woodford defended the social utility of the friars by revealing this secret of the confessional. The penances consisted mostly of the repair of bridges and roads near Framlingham, and Margaret Marshal's surviving account book includes an outlay for precisely that purpose.[27] It is likely that by drawing attention to the individual conscience, the practice of confession altered the whole scope of moral life. There is evidence that some of the high nobility took practical steps to examine their consciences systematically. One of the psalters ordered by Humphrey de Bohun, Earl of Hereford, contained a French translation of Grosseteste's *Confession*, a simple guide arranged round the seven deadly sins; and Henry of Lancaster's *Livre de Seyntz Medicines*, which is a kind of confession itself, shows the influence of current aids to penitence.[28]

The reading of the book of hours implies, and the searching of conscience demands, privacy and solitude. Even conventional observances, then, had a new, inward-looking aspect, and this was the aspect which came to the surface, above all, in the ceremonies surrounding death. Funerals, in an age of elaborate cult of the dead, were preeminently an occasion to display a nobleman's state, as can be seen in a number of wills of the early fourteenth century. But shortly after the middle of the century, the number of wills enjoining splendour and pomp at the funeral diminishes sharply, and for the first time wills specifying plainness can be found. The first I have identified is that of Humphrey V, Earl of Hereford, in 1361: he wished to be buried without pomp with no great men present, only one bishop, and 'common people'.[29] Sir Walter Manny, the patron of Froissart and second husband of Margaret Marshal, Richard II, Earl of

---

[27] College of Arms MS Arundel 49, f.38; see Woodford, *Defensorium Mendicitatis*, Cambridge University Library MS Ff.1.21, f.120.
[28] London, British Library MS Egerton 3277, ff.166-168v; and see below n.37.
[29] Lambeth Palace, Reg. Islip, ff.178v-179v (*Test. Vet.*, I, 66-8).

Arundel, and Guichard d'Angle, Earl of Huntingdon, all of them among the most distinguished soldiers of the time, were conspicuous in their rejection of the military accoutrements which would have been appropriate. They are in strong contrast to the warlike caparisons asked for by William Beauchamp, ancestor of the Earls of Warwick, 1268, or for that matter to the blaze of light in which Elizabeth de Burgh, Countess of Ulster, illuminated by two hundred pounds of candles, arranged to lie in state in her will of 1355.[30] Few mourners, no feast, immediate burial in no particular place, no arms or banners and no more than two tapers are increasingly common instructions in the wills of the nobility. They are a pointer to the group of much more forthright wills at the turn of the century, which have provided ambiguous evidence of Lollard sympathies in the court circle. In these later wills, the testator castigates himself as false traitor or stinking carrion, and demands to be laid in a cheap russet cloth. But as these features were shared by the wills of Henry IV and Archbishop Arundel, they cannot be a peculiarity of the small circle of Lollard knights.[31] Rather, there was a gradual development: the tendency to funerary austerity which began in the court circle of Edward III's later years had engendered, by the last years of the century, a penitential rhetoric which could make the will a personal cri-de-coeur as much as a legal instrument.

An enhanced interest in contemplative life seems to be a consistent feature of the religion of the educated laity in the fourteenth century. The library of one nobleman, Henry, Lord Scrope of Masham, played an important part in the transmission of the text of several works of Rolle, his copies of which passed into the hands of his brother-in-law, Henry, Lord Fitzhugh; Scrope's will, with its long series of benefactions to recluses and anchorites, shows the close relation between his personal piety and the established masters of the contemplative art.[32] Interest such as Scrope's must have encouraged the production of mystical writings in the vernacular which is such a pronounced feature of the age. It is paralleled by that of the captain of Calais, Sir William Beauchamp, Lord Bergavenny, whose library presumably contained the exemplar of University College, Oxford MS 97, or at least of the works of Rolle and of his friend Sir John Clanvowe contained in it; and perhaps by that of Joan Bohun, Countess of Hereford, who may have been the owner of the Simeon manuscript with its careful directions for personal spiritual exercises.[33] Respect for contemplatives must also be the explanation for the extraordinary interest in the Carthusian way of life evinced in the court circle.

[30] Sir Walter Manny's will in Lambeth Palace, Reg. Whittlesey, ff.120v–121v (*Test. Vet.*, I, 85–6); Guichard d'Angle's, ibid., Reg. Sudbury; f.104r–v (*Test. Vet.*, I, 179); William Beauchamp's in J. W. Willis-Bund (ed.), *Register of Bishop Godfrey Giffard* (Worcestershire Historical Society, 1902), I, 7–9; Countess of Ulster's in Lambeth Palace, Reg. Islip, ff.164v–166v (*Test. Vet.*, I, 56–9).

[31] McFarlane, *Lancastrian Kings*, 218–20.

[32] H. E. Allen, *Writings Ascribed to Richard Rolle* (London 1927), 29–30; Scrope's will is in Rymer, *Foedera* (London 1704–35), IX, 272–80; and for his inventory see above, n.8.

[33] On the University College MS see E. Wilson, 'A critical text, with commentary, of MS English Theology f.39 in the Bodleian Library', Oxford B.Litt. thesis (1968), II, 30–8, and A. I. Doyle, 'The shaping of the Vernon and Simeon Manuscripts' in *Chaucer and Middle English Studies in Honour of Rossell Hope Robbins* (London 1974), 328–41. I am grateful to Mr Doyle for information on the ownership of the Simeon MS.

Both Edward III and Richard II singled out the Carthusian houses in their annual private charities;[34] and the founders of new houses, who raised the total number in England from two to nine in eighty years, are an interesting group of royal intimates. The series begins with Sir Nicholas Cantelupe, one of the older captains of Edward III and the founder of Beauvale in 1343; then follow the great Hainaulter, Sir Walter Manny the patron of Froissart, founder of the London Charterhouse adumbrated in 1361 and established in 1371; Sir Michael de la Pole, later Earl of Suffolk, founder of the Hull Charterhouse in 1378-9; William, Lord Zouche, whose Coventry Charterhouse was established, with royal patronage, by 1382; Thomas Mowbray, Earl of Nottingham, the admittedly dilatory founder of the Axholme Charterhouse in 1395; and Thomas Holland, Duke of Surrey, founder of Mountgrace in 1397-8. It is clear that the impetus came from the court circle, and the series would culminate in 1415 with the foundation of the Charterhouse at Sheen by Henry V.[35] By then new currents of devotion from the Netherlands and Sweden would swell the contemplative stream flowing from the English Carthusians.[36] It is difficult to avoid the conclusion that the lead was taken, under Edward III as well as Henry V, by the soldiers and courtiers of the intimate royal circle.

All the clues to personal religion among the nobility, therefore, seem to lead to the paradoxical conclusion that the pace was set by the careerist soldiers. It happens that a devotional work written by one of the most successful captains of the early campaigns of the French war, Henry, Duke of Lancaster's *Livre de Seyntz Medicines*, survives in two manuscripts. This unique work, which carries all the signs of personal authorship, provides a glimpse of the inner thoughts of an otherwise conventional nobleman.[37] It is a penitential exercise: a painful examination of conscience, with an allegorical recital of spiritual remedies. The structure is derived from the popular penitential literature of the time, but the allegory is taken from his own experience: of children, of the farmyard, of fox hunting, siege warfare, seafaring, country markets and especially the surgery and medicine of the battlefield. His plainness is reminiscent of contemporary funeral directions; his realism, which makes the skills and experience of a professional soldier a mirror of the life of the spirit, shows that he saw his active life in intimate relation with his 'inward' thoughts, and anticipated Walter Hilton's precept to 'take these two lives active and contemplative since God has set them both, the one and the other'.[38] If the *Livre* is an early hint of the military puritanism

---

[34] PRO, E 101/396/2, f.30v; E 101/397/5, f.35; E 101/401/2, f.37.

[35] E. M. Thompson, *The Carthusian Order in England* (London 1930), 158-9, 167-73, 199-203, 207-10, 218-22, 229-31, 238-41.

[36] Roger Lovatt, 'The *Imitation of Christ* in late mediaeval England', *T.R.H.S.*, 5th series, XVIII (1968), 97-121; and on the Bridgettines see now M. B. Tait, 'The Brigittine Monastery of Syon', Oxford D.Phil. thesis (1975).

[37] E. J. F. Arnould (ed.), *Le Livre de Seyntz Medicines* (Oxford, Anglo-Norman Texts, 1940); see Arnould, *Etude sur le livre des Saintes Médécines du duc Henri de Lancastre* (Paris 1948) lxxx - lxxxvii, and Kenneth Fowler, *The King's Lieutenant* (London 1969), 193-6.

[38] Hilton, *Epistle on Mixed Life*, ed. G. G. Perry, *English Prose Treatises of Richard Rolle de Hampole* (London, EETS, 1866), 19-42; see p.30.

of Ignatius Loyola or the New Model Army, it is also an example of the domestic, intimate imagery in which man's relation to God was coming to be defined: reversing the patriarchal language of earlier devotion, the Duke compared Christ to a child longing for the red apple of the human heart.[39] Noblemen's admiration for the contemplative life, therefore, need not have been only passive: as mystical writers were beginning to envisage, secular business could and should be coloured by private religious experience in the 'mixed life'.

The case of Henry of Lancaster shows that the religion of the fourteenth-century nobility could be something more than the ethical code of the older romances or the obligations and conventions of chivalry. His book survives by chance because it circulated in a restricted circle of the nobility; and however elaborate the manners, however exquisite the taste of the Edwardian and Riccardian courts, we cannot be certain that even the most conforming or worldly courtiers did not harbour similar introspective thoughts, undetectable in the record of their piety. The point is driven home by the relations between the nobility and the radical preachers from Oxford in the 1380s and 1390s, the Lollards. It is now clear that a distinct group of noblemen and courtiers, mostly knights of Richard II's chamber, extended protection to the preachers.[40] Walsingham's list of seven knights has been shown to be substantially accurate, though they evidently had august precedents in the protection extended to Wyclif by John of Gaunt and by their own former mistress, Joan Princess of Wales; and there are other figures on the fringes of the group, notably Sir William Beauchamp, who had their own connections with the Lollards. Evidence of the ambitious scale on which the Lollard Bible and sermon cycle were translated and circulated has recently been brought together, and such enterprises could hardly have been carried through without substantial backing: whether it came from the 'Lollard knights' or from others now unknown, the case for lay patronage of their literary labours is overwhelming.[41] But the other evidence which has been collected on the character of this group of knights makes it clear that in every other respect, including their discernible religious practices, they conformed to convention. They sought, in their wills, prayers for the dead and the intercession of saints; Sir Lewis Clifford had a mass-book and portiforium as well as a more suspicious-sounding 'book of tribulation'; several were crusaders. The one direction in which they perhaps differed from others of their class was in constituting a literary clique: most of them were intimates of Chaucer, and Clifford and Salisbury were friends respectively of Christine de Pisan and Eustache Deschamps. Sir John Clanvowe was almost certainly the author of the exquisite love poem *The Cuckoo and the Nightingale* (or *Book of Cupid*). Yet Clanvowe was the author of a devotional tract which, though rather commonplace, is at least forthright in contempt for the knightly ideal and for

[39] *Livre*, 34.
[40] McFarlane, *Lancastrian Kings*, 148. The knights were Sir Richard Stury, Sir Thomas Latimer, John Montagu Earl of Salisbury, Sir William Neville, Sir John Clanvowe, Sir Lewis Clifford and Sir John Cheyne.
[41] Anne Hudson, 'A Lollard sermon-cycle and its implications', *Medium Aevum*, XL (1971), 142-56.

men who made profit out of war. In fact, like Henry of Lancaster, Clanvowe accused himself, and his tract, written on the eve of his last crusade, may be read as a kind of confession.[42] The knights, then, in whose hearts and hands and purses the fortunes of the Lollards reposed were in every other respect hardbitten careerists and courtiers.

It is probable that sympathy for the ideals of the Lollards was spread among the nobility much more widely than this small clique of courtiers, and merged with their responses to the serious call to inner devotion and self-knowledge made by Richard Rolle and the other mystical writers of the age. The distinction between the attitudes of the conventionally pious and those of critics like the Lollard knights hardly survives analysis. What are we to make, for instance, of Sir William Beauchamp of Bergavenny, intimate of the Lollard knights, in whose library could be found not only devotional tracts like Clanvowe's, but the Latin works of Wyclif (whence Czech scholars copied them), and who yet seems to have been a pioneer of devotion to the Holy Name of Jesus?[43] What, for that matter, should we make of Thomas of Woodstock, who is often portrayed, on Froissart's authority, as the rough soldierly antithesis of the aesthetes of his nephew's court? He was nevertheless open-minded enough about the Lollards they patronised to stage a public debate between Lollard spokesmen and their opponents; and his library, with its magnificent English Bible in the Lollard translation, books of prayers and meditations and theological works, is that of a man of intellectual tastes and probably independent views.[44]

The incidence of radical sympathies transcends political, cultural and social groups. But at least it can be said that the new sensibility of a privileged circle, the close companions of Edward III and Richard II, had a serious religious side which must be somehow reconciled with their wholehearted pursuit of wealth and standing. If they had wealth, they also had experience, broadened by war, crusade, pilgrimage, diplomacy, even exile. More important, they had leisure: and the surviving art and literature of the court shows that however frivolous their amusements, they were not crude. More significant still, leisure afforded them the opportunity of inner reflection, which naturally led to widely different religious sentiments. The clearest examples of these sentiments come not from the pious dowagers of the age but from men of action; and there seems no escaping the conclusion that the religious sensibility of men such as Henry of Lancaster and Sir William Beauchamp was a facet of their intellectual sophistication, and that both were sharpened in the hard schools of foreign war and survival at court. 'Temporal men which have sovereignty with much possession of worldly goods . . . ' they could 'have also received of our Lord's gift grace of devotion, and in party savour of ghostly occupation'.[45] If they failed to respond decisively to

[42] See above, n.9.
[43] Anne Hudson, 'The debate on Bible translation, Oxford 1401', *EHR* (1975), 1-18 (see p.12).
[44] Trinity College, Dublin, MS C.III.12, ff. 212v-219; see above, n.8.
[45] Hilton, *Epistle on Mixed Life*, 24.

Wyclif's call for action, their doubts and ambivalance were probably more attuned than his forthrightness to the promptings of a private and personal religion; and were certainly less naïve.

5

The Patrimony of
Thomas More

James McConica ^

'Our story begins with a fifteenth-century Londoner,' said R. W. Chamber
in his life of More.[1] The remark points in a direction which has been followed
less than one might wish. Like his earlier biographers, More's recen
advocates and critics have had little to say about More's family and youth
Yet there is much that we can learn from them about his ideals, his manner o
life, and the particular character of his humanism.

Thomas More was descended on both sides from enterprising and 'risen
men' from the adjacent counties of Cambridgeshire and Hertfordshire. His
father, Sir John, a judge of Common Pleas and King's Bench, was the eldes
son of William More, citizen and baker of London, who had married ;
Johanna Joye. It was from this marriage that John More's fortune came. He
appears to have been heir to a considerable estate from – remarkably – his
maternal great-grandfather, John Leycester, a clerk of the Chancery and
gentleman of London. Leycester, who died in 1455, married his eldes
daughter, the first Johanna, to John Joye, a prosperous London brewer. She
was mother to William More's wife, outlived both her husband and son-in
law, and through careful management saw to the scrupulous execution of he
father's intentions, so that the great part of John Leycester's wealth, including
his City properties and the estate of North Mimms, descended to he
grandson, the future Sir John More, who was an infant of four when hi
great-grandfather died.[2] As for the family of Thomas More's mother, we
have recently learned that the arms Sir Thomas quartered with those of More
were not, as might be expected, from the Leycester descent, but came from
her. Judge More's first wife, and mother of all his children, was Agnes
daughter of Thomas Graunger, citizen and Sheriff of London. It was probably
after this maternal grandfather that Thomas More was named, and it was to
Thomas Graunger and his brothers 'of the county of Cambridge borne' tha

[1] R. W. Chambers, *Thomas More* (1935), 48.
[2] Margaret Hastings, 'The ancestry of Sir Thomas More', *The Guildhall Miscellany*, II (1961)
reprinted in R. S. Sylvester and G. P. Marc'hadour (eds), *Essential Articles for the Study of Thoma
More* (Hamden, Connecticut 1977), 92–103.

he arms in question were granted, apparently in the 1460s.[3]

Judge More's children, then, were deeply rooted by their descent in the London merchant community and, we must assume, very conscious of their wealth, position and lineage. Their prominence is clearly and perhaps deliberately understated in More's epitaph, with his phrase 'urbe Londinensi familia non celebri sed honesta natus'.

Miss Thrupp long ago informed us of the professional ambitions nurtured in the London mercantile community. Barely two-thirds of the aldermen's sons followed their fathers into trade. Their most evident ambition was to acquire gentility and, therefore, land. What appears to be unusual in the More family is the choice of law as the family profession in two successive generations. Although Miss Thrupp asserted that wealthy citizens' sons were coming to be fascinated by the law in the later fifteenth century, she cites only four examples, all of which can be linked with ambition for landed status.[4] More recently, Mr Ives has pointed out that the legal profession was 'tailored for the landed newcomer; law terms occupied less than half the year, while social connections would introduce him to an inn and to clients.' By contrast, law did not attract many townsmen. No Londoners are known among the barristers of Edward IV's reign; Thomas More was the only Londoner in a list of the forty-nine practising in 1518.[5]

It is not at all fanciful, then, to see in John More's selection of the profession of law an unusual mark of confidence among his peers, the act rather of the hereditary proprietor of North Mimms than of a baker's son. It lifted him into that national community of common lawyers who were widely involved in the life of the nation as members of county society. They were the nucleus of a 'new professional managerial class' for whom, by the late fifteenth century, the highest counsels of the realm were opening up. Thirty-seven per cent of the commoners among the recorded Councillors of Henry VII were lawyers,[6] and they were the largest single group among the Councillors of Henry VIII in the early years of his reign. Erasmus' comment that the profession of law was held in high esteem in England certainly represents the view of More's family and circle. It is to Erasmus' testimony also that we owe the information that when Judge More thought his son's studies were taking him away from the profession, he almost disinherited him.[7]

Sir John, let us remember, reached the dignity of sergeant-at-law in 1503 at the age of 52. He became a judge of Common Pleas and of the King's Bench. When he died in 1530, he left maintenance at Oxford and Cambridge for a student priest, who was to pray for Edward IV, along with members of John More's family. Whatever the service or debt that this commemorated, it

[3] A. Colin Cole, Windsor Herald of Arms, 'Sir Thomas More's quartering and a new "old coat"', *The Coat of Arms*, I, part 93 (1975), 126–31.
[4] S. L. Thrupp, *The Merchant Class of Medieval London* (Chicago 1948), 205, 225.
[5] E. W. Ives, 'The common lawyers in pre-Reformation England', *Transactions of the Royal Historical Society*, 5th series, XVIII (1968), 160.
[6] The others were gentry, knights and esquires, ecclesiastics and peers; Ives, op. cit., 154 n.2, and works cited there.
[7] Ep. 999 in P. S. Allen (ed.), *Opus epistolarum Des. Erasmi Roterodami*, IV (Oxford 1922), 17.

marked the old man's sense of family achievement. His arms had been granted by a King of Arms in the reign of Edward IV.

The education he provided for his eldest son reflects the privilege and confidence of this background. Thomas was sent to St. Anthony's Thread-needle Street, the leading school in London. He then joined the household of John Morton, Archbishop of Canterbury and Lord Chancellor of England, soon to be made Cardinal by Alexander VI at the King's request. Morton had been an executor of Edward IV, an opponent of Richard III and one of the architects of the Tudor accession; this was Judge More's climactic provision for his son's education. It was through Morton's patronage, of course, that More spent the better part of two years at Oxford, before enrolling at the New Inn to begin his legal studies in 1494. On 12 February 1496, aged about eighteen, he was admitted to Lincoln's Inn. This is the first certain date in the story of his life.

More's famous aptitude as an impromptu player in the Christmas festivities of Morton's Lambeth household points to the blend of urbanity and ready wit which was so much the mark of the mature man. It also shows that he had already developed an easy familiarity with the privileged and powerful. His early court poetry shows the same confidence. When he was only twenty-one, and a student at Lincoln's Inn, he was able casually to introduce his newly-discovered friend, Erasmus, to the children of the royal family at Eltham Palace. It seems that within two years of that event he found himself in a lengthy vocational crisis that lasted about four years. Recently, much has been made of the dramatic hesitation in the most sensitive and decisive years of early manhood, when this poised, privileged and infinitely promising young man debated his own future against the background of the cloister and the city of London.[8] What can we learn from it of the spiritual side of More's patrimony?

For information about this we rely on More's early biographers and on Erasmus; nothing about it survives from More's own hand.[9] The circumstances seem to be as follows. More apparently qualified for the bar in 1501. Soon afterwards he began lecturing on Augustine's *City of God* in the church of St. Lawrence Jewry where, incidentally, his father later willed to be buried. He was made a reader in Furnivall's Inn to instruct junior candidates in the law. According to Roper, this appointment lasted 'by the space of three yeares and more'. He continued the humanistic studies already begun, and added to the Greek he was learning with Grocyn the study of Aristotle's *Meterologica* with Thomas Linacre. He practised Greek by competition with William Lily in translating part of the Greek Anthology into Latin. This was the time, again according to Roper, that More 'gave himselfe to devotion and prayer in the Charter house of London, religiously lyvinge there, without vowe, about iiij^{er} yeares'. Both Roper and Harpsfield say that this association

---

[8] Notably by Professor Elton, in P. N. Brooks (ed.), *Reformation Principles and Practice: Essays in Honour of A. G. Dickens* (1980), ch.2. I am not concerned here with the psychological dimension, but with the implications for More's intellectual and spiritual formation.

[9] There is a résumé in E. E. Reynolds, *The Field is Won* (1968), 32–4; Erasmus's account in Ep 999 of August 1519 is the earliest testimony. Roper's version is in E. V. Hitchcock (ed.), *The Lyfe of Sir Thomas Moore, knighte. E.E.T.S.*, CXCVII (1935), 6.

with the Carthusians lasted until More decided to marry at the end of 1504 or, at the latest, in January 1505.

Work since the war on the archaeology and records of the London Charterhouse allows conjecture about More's arrangements.[10] Since in 1490 the Carthusian General Chapter gave permission for seculars to live in a house within the precincts, it was canonically allowable for More to do so. Moreover, the location of the London house of the Salutation had from the first exposed it to the demands of local residents for access to the monastic church, as they had had to an earlier cemetery chapel. Consequently, there was greater freedom of association between monks and layfolk than was normally permissible in a Charterhouse.

Despite these exceptional conditions the London Charterhouse remained exemplary in fervour and in conduct. The Carthusians were greatly favoured among the highly-placed *dévots* of London's court and intellectual circles, and their prestige dated from the foundation of the Salutation. The lists of donors of cells and other benefactors show that More's chosen house of retreat associated him with the wealthy and influential of the preceding century. The interior of the Charterhouse church was warm and rich with the gifts of its patrons – alabaster, gilding, silverwork, and hangings of damask and brocade. Two of the chapels were built and endowed by the celebrated soldier Sir John Popham, who was buried in one of them. Soldiers, indeed, were always prominent. They included the founder, Sir Walter Manny, William Ufford, Earl of Suffolk, and the notorious soldier of fortune, Sir Robert Knolles, who scourged France at the head of one of the free companies. He ended his days a great landowner in his native country, founding almshouses at Pontefract, and cell P at the Charterhouse in London.[11]

The nobility had their place, in John Hastings, Earl of Pembroke, the son-in-law of the founder, and William Ufford, already mentioned. Mary de Valence, Countess of Pembroke and widow of Aymer de Valence, was the donor of cell K and an endowment of two hundred pounds. But most conspicuous were the prominent Londoners. There were two mayors, led by Sir William Walworth, stockfishmonger, whose knighthood was a reward for having slain Wat Tyler with his own hand in his last year of office. Adam Fraunceys, citizen and mercer and mayor from 1352 to 1354, founded five cells and the college in the Guildhall chapel. Another such, William Symmer, citizen and grocer, gave cell Y and the sophisticated aqueduct of 1431. There were other benefactors who came from the administrative class of Thomas More's great-great-grandfather, like John Clyderhow, who was Clerk of Chancery as John Leycester had been. And there were three bishops, among them Thomas Hatfield, who also endowed Durham College, Oxford.

As a group, these successful people were the beneficiaries of the war against France. In their spiritual needs they turned to the domestic English version of the *devotio moderna* with its private devotions, private chapels in the houses of

---

[10] David Knowles and W. F. Grimes, *Charterhouse* (1954), esp. 11 n.14.
[11] See Knowles and Grimes; also Sir William St. John Hope, *The History of the London Charterhouse* (1925).

the laity, and emphasis on spiritual direction arranged, often, through the privilege of appointing one's own confessor. Allied with this devotional taste was a solid orthodoxy.[12] The chief propagators of this new devotion were the two houses with which Thomas More was most closely associated, the London Charterhouse, and the Bridgettine monastery of Syon. As we have seen, the Charterhouse took from its benefactors its tithe of tribute from the French wars and the profits of London commerce. What it gave in return was exemplary conduct of a most exacting conventual discipline, combined with the spiritual direction of the prominent and powerful. In particular, the Carthusians offered something which is central to the spirituality of Thomas More: they offered the devotion of the *Imitation of Christ*.

This famous spiritual treatise was not generally circulated in fifteenth-century England.[13] It was known in the devotional circles in London; beyond, it seems to have been almost unknown, even as a source for other compilations. Its English adherents, 'a small, conservative, intellectual and spiritual elite',[14] seemingly valued it in particular for its teachings on the monastic and contemplative vocation, not as an encouragement to new forms of lay organisation or even, to any extent, as an endorsement of the lay vocation as such. No doubt, in this, as in the circulation of scripture in the vernacular, Lollardy had left its legacy of mistrust. The spiritual ideal of the English devotion was monasticism adapted for people living in the world. The Syon library catalogue thus described the *Imitatio Christi* as, simply, 'solitariis et contemplativis utilis'.[15] In a passage at the end of the preface to his *Confutation of Tyndale's Answer*, Thomas More recommended that 'the people unlearned' should not trouble with controversy over heresy, but rather, read 'suche englishe bookes as moste may noryshe and encreace devocion'. And the three examples were Bonaventure's 'of the lyfe of Christe', the *Scala perfectionis*, and the *Imitation*. It is Mr Lovatt's observation that More thus reduced the *Imitation* 'to the pattern of contemporary English piety'.[16]

Among English religious orders, only the Bridgettines of Syon rivalled the Carthusians in their collective enthusiasm for the *Imitation of Christ*. With them, More's links were even more important and lasting than with the London Charterhouse.[17] The royal foundation of Syon at Isleworth, like the Charterhouse, was exemplary in unswerving orthodoxy and irreproachable observance. In Richard Reynolds it produced a martyr for Rome to stand beside More, Fisher and the London Carthusians. It was also a famous centre of learning, and the Syon library shows the range and depth of the studies of the monks.[18] Both the male and female members of this double house were

[12] Cf. Thrupp, op. cit., 180f.
[13] Roger Lovatt, 'The *Imitation of Christ* in late medieval England', *Transactions of the Royal Historical Society*, 5th series, XVIII (1968), 97-121.
[14] Ibid., 114.
[15] Ibid., 117.
[16] Ibid., 97-8, 117.
[17] The abbé Marc'hadour has recently pointed out that there is no evidence in More's spiritual writings of special partiality to the Carthusians; 'Thomas More's spirituality', in R. S. Sylvester (ed.), *St. Thomas More: Action and Contemplation* (New Haven 1972), 156 n.48.
[18] I am greatly indebted to the research of Michael Beckwith Tait, whose Oxford D.Phil. thesis of 1975 on Syon monastery (Bodleian Library MS D.Phil. *c.* 1802) was drawn to my attention by R. I. J. Catto. To Mr Catto I am also indebted for his perceptions and encouragement while this essay was slowly taking shape.

arefully tried before admission, and most unusually (although in full con-
ormity with Bridgettine practice) they were asked to make an external
novitiate of a year. Many of the monks, like Reynolds himself, John
Fewterer, or Richard Whitford, were university men, and made their
novitiates while still fully engaged at the university. This convention places
More's four-year vigil at the Charterhouse, while he was pursuing his studies
and legal training, in a rather different light. It is probable that he contemplated more than one form of religious life, including that of Syon.
Certainly, among his intellectual peers, the vocation was hardly unusual;
Syon had strong links with Cambridge, and the Charterhouse too had its
share of graduates among the monks. In the spiritual circles of More's
immediate acquaintance the blend of semi-seclusion with the simultaneous if
tentative pursuit of a secular vocation would not have seemed as remarkable
as it has seemed since to all of More's biographers.

At Syon, as at the Charterhouse, there was great experience in the spiritual
direction of the laity, among whom the Queen was the most notable adherent.
There was more time for and emphasis on study, and the monastery was the
chief centre for the production of English works of devotion, especially from
the pens of Richard Whitford, William Bonde, Thomas Betson and John
Fewterer. Of these Whitford was the chief, and it was to him that Erasmus
dedicated his declamation in reply to Lucian's *Tyrannicida*. The library, rich
in theology, sermons and devotional literature, was notably strong in biblical
and patristic texts. Thomas Aquinas, More's favourite scholastic, was the
most popular theological writer, and his works and those of other leading
scholastics rested side by side with the Greek and Latin Fathers, whose
writings comprised almost one quarter of the whole collection. In the
sixteenth century there was a conspicuous increase in the resources of
humanism: classics, grammar, philosophy and theology. The best-
represented Renaissance theologians were Lefèvre d'Etaples and the two
Picos. There were the biblical commentaries of Erasmus and Lefèvre,
Oecolampadius' translation of Theophylact's commentary on the Gospels,
Reuchlin's *Breviloquus vocabularius*, a Hebrew concordance, and from the
donation of Fewterer, a strong section on the Cappadocian Fathers. There
were literary works by Aeneas Sylvius and Valla and the letters of Ficino,
while Gian Francesco Pico was one of the thirteen authors represented by ten
or more works, along with Cicero, Cyprian, and Hugh of St. Victor.[19]

The library of Syon defines the framework of More's religious culture, as
the writings of its monks echo his spirituality. Theirs was a practical, not
mystical, devotion. Whitford's *A werke for householders* (1530) was written for
them that have gydyng and governaunce of any company'. It began: 'In al
thy werkes remembre thyne endynge daye.' This was the theme of More's
Four Last Things, written in 1522 just when his secular career was firmly
launched. Increasingly thereafter it was the theme of his meditation. Like his

[19] The list is headed, not surprisingly, by Aquinas and Augustine. See M. Bateson, *Catalogue of
the Library of Syon Monastery, Isleworth* (Cambridge 1898). Tait, whose analysis I am following,
made important modifications to her conclusions in ch.8 of his thesis.

colleague John Fewterer, whose *Mirror of Christ's Passion* (1534) is considerably more fervent, Whitford adapted a conventual spirituality for lay
use. Behind all these writings lay the magisterial *Orcherd of Syon*, held in high
regard in the fifteenth century and printed in 1519 by Wynkyn de Worde at
the instance of Syon Abbey's steward, Sir Richard Sutton, the co-founder of
Brasenose College, Oxford. The *Orcherd* contained the dictated revelations
of Catherine of Siena, and the prologue to the work says explicitly that the
Middle English version was prepared for the benefit of the Bridgettine nuns
of Syon Abbey. Phyllis Hodgson points out one marked characteristic of the
treatise that is striking to a student of the spirituality of Thomas More.[20]
Where other late medieval treatises dwelt at length on the Passion of Christ,
often in lugubrious detail, the *Orcherd* resembles the writings of the great
English mystics in its intellectual rigour and emotional restraint. St.
Catherine's controlling image is the spiritual cell of self-knowledge which the
aspirant must enter and never leave. There is marked concentration on the
eternal redemptive function of the Trinity in the Incarnation, with the person
of Christ at the centre as the Bridge of God's mercy. The actual shedding of
Christ's blood is given only the barest reference, but it is identified 'in the
sacraments, in Baptism, in Confession, but most often in the Sacrament of
the Altar'. Clearly, More imbibed early on a deep devotion to the Eucharist,
and his spirit is entirely in harmony with that of the *Orcherd*. In the words of
Miss Hodgson, 'May we not see in the *Orcherd* a forerunner in England of
such later devotional writers as Sir Thomas More who explicitly integrated
their devotion to the Person of our Lord with the Mass, and were constantly
aware of the mystical Body of the Church?'[21]

The spiritual world of the young Thomas More, then, was not mysterious.
Its debt to the conventual piety of the most expert and informed writers and
directors of late medieval England is eloquent on every page of his own
treatises, in his concern with the Passion of Christ, with the impermanence of
this world and with the 'four last things', in his sense of the unity of the
Mystical Body, and in his devotion to the Eucharist as the bond between the
world of appearances and the world of everlasting life. His was a highly
sacramental and interiorised religion which, in its modes of expression, was
quite unlike that of his admired friend, Erasmus. More's spiritual peers were
to be found among the monk-graduates at Syon and Charterhouse, who
were fully acquainted with the taste for the sources of Christianity, and who
moved familiarly among the Schoolmen and pre-scholastics alike. And as the
additions to the Syon library after 1500 showed, their erudite and traditional
spirituality could' also be perfectly receptive to the humanist revival of
theology and devotion through philology and *bonae litterae*. However, their
spiritual programme was simply adapted from monastic ideals, and was
marked by an intimate relation between clerical professionals and a coterie of
educated and influential laymen. To this inheritance Thomas More brought

[20] '*The Orcherd of Syon* and the English mystical tradition', *Proceedings of the British Academy*, L
(1964); see 240-1, 243 and passim for what follows.
[21] Ibid., 242.

not only an extraordinary intellect, but a far better education in the classics and the achievements of continental humanism than any of his contemporaries. His long drawn-out interior debate about the direction of his life must therefore have had a deep intellectual dimension. What can we deduce about his sense of lay vocation?

The Thomas More who chose the secular career of a lawyer against the religious life was a confident, urban patrician, accustomed to the world of power, and entitled by his birthright to expect a place in it. This is the man characterised in Holbein's portrait. Some may search there for the lineaments of a saint; at the very least, we can find the burgher aristocrat. I have noticed that a career in law was apparently an unusual choice for a Londoner. It seems to reflect the tradition of the family seen through the eyes of More's father, a family accustomed to measure itself by the standards of the established gentry. More's first wife, Jane Colt, came not surprisingly from just such a background. Her father was a prosperous gentleman whose residence in Essex was near Judge More's manor of Gobions at North Mimms in Hertfordshire; her grandfather had been Chancellor of the Exchequer to Edward IV.

As a vocational choice the law was a definite commitment to secular service, but More's friends of whom we know were not so much the lawyers as the grammarians. Most were priests as well: Whitford, Erasmus, Grocyn and Linacre, William Lily, Andrea Ammonio, Colet, Tunstall and John Holt. More's legal career was conceived in a community dedicated to humane letters. If we accept the tradition of his four years of reflection in the Charterhouse, we might suppose that he entered his new life as a married layman with deeply-considered ideals of a devout and Christian humanism. That Erasmus saw him in this light we know from the influential and famous sketch penned for Ulrich von Hutten,[22] but we must allow for the possibility that, at least by 1519, he was viewing More rather distantly, and that the orphaned, illegitimate scholar idealised the married More's lay vocation. At all accounts, we must confront the question of More's humanism and its place in his chosen life.

Renaissance humanism was, first and foremost, an educational ideal whose proponents wished to recover and propagate the texts of Greek and Latin civilisation. We must add, as a matter of course, the Greek and Latin texts of the Patristic age, which was a part of the Antiquity of those with whom we are concerned. Patristic Christianity was blended with the chief humanist endeavour, the moral and intellectual formation of the *doctus orator*, for whom the scholarly disciplines of grammar and rhetoric, history, poetry and moral philosophy were the heartland of education. For the vast majority, instructed by Quintilian and Cicero, antique culture contained within it the presumption that the man soundly educated would employ his learning in the public forum, for the common good.

More did not belong among the textual scholars and learned printers, who were the familiars of Erasmus. He made his apprenticeship in the related and

[22] See n.7, above.

secondary industry of propagating texts by translation, with many of his epigrams, the life of Pico, and above all, the translations from Lucian. But these, although they had their interest, were journeyman pieces, as perhaps was the *History of Richard III*, which stands alone among his works – unfinished as it is – as an example of humanist history. Although scholarly, More was not a scholar. But we might expect that with his background, his education, and his sense of vocation, he would exemplify the humanist man of affairs, and be a model proponent in the northern world of the *vita civile*, committed to the service of the state, and sanguine about the promise of his fellow man.

It is here that we encounter the difficulty. The blend of Christianity and antique culture raised problems that were experienced as much by sixteenth-century humanists as they had been by Jerome and Augustine. More's laicism was a far cry from the unfettered, unsacramental and Pauline piety found in Erasmus' *Enchiridion* and its introductory letter to Paul Volz. More's letter 'to a monk', published in 1520, defended Erasmus in wholly Erasmian terms, to be sure: he deplored the ignorance and presumption of some monks, their neglect of the common standards of Christian behaviour through undue pride in the man-made rules of a religious order, and the danger offered by the ideals of religion to any who forget their total dependence on the grace and mercy of God. Yet even here, More acknowledged the superiority of the life of vows in ways that Erasmus would have found uncongenial: the layman, 'tossed on the waves of an unhappy world', should be able to look in admiration at the angelic life led by those who have taken religious vows, so that his life 'might seem all the more worthless'.[23] The point is orthodox, but it is not Erasmian.

While debating his vocation, apparently, More wrote a letter to Colet which (albeit indirectly) forms the only likely clue from his own pen to the issues that beset his mind.[24] He asked what there is 'in the city' to move one to live well, and concluded that the city is a place of a thousand evil devices and distracting enticements. Colet was hardly the director to bolster More's esteem for life in the world. We have lately been reminded[25] that his famed sermon to Convocation in 1512 was far from the liberal, anti-clerical tract it was long held to be. Colet argued for the liberty of the Church and the obedience of the laity to their spiritual superiors. If he was unsparing in his attack on clerical slackness, it was because he truly saw the priesthood as mediating between God and man. He resented the appointment of bishops by the prince, and with respect to the Hunne case, affirmed the right of clerics not to be drawn before secular judges. His commentary on the Hierarchies of Dionysius paints a gloomy picture of a kind often echoed by More: 'In this world the seal of Christ, which he stamped upon it, has been almost effaced

[23] E. F. Rogers (ed.), *St. Thomas More: Selected Letters* (New Haven 1961), 140; *The Correspondence of Sir Thomas More* (Princeton 1947), 203, ll. 1434-7: 'nostra nobis vita vilescat impensius'. These two editions will be cited hereafter as *Selected Letters* and *Correspondence* respectively.
[24] *Selected Letters*, Letter 2; *Correspondence*, Ep. 3.
[25] H. C. Porter, 'The gloomy dean and the law: John Colet, 1466-1519', in G. V. Bennett and J. D. Walsh (eds), *Essays in Modern Church History In Memory of Norman Sykes* (1966), 18-43.

and destroyed by the promiscuous jostling of mankind in the universal disorder.' Colet's view of human nature was nominalist or proto-Lutheran: all human practical laws are *calamitosae*.[26] More's comparable scepticism about the powerlessness of laws and ordinances to ameliorate the lot of man runs through the *Utopia*, and his emphasis on the worthlessness of all human endeavour apart from the grace of God is theologically closer to Ockham than to Erasmus. In his letter 'to a monk', he compares even the just acts of man to a 'soiled menstrual cloth'.[27]

The question of More's laicism, like that of his Platonism, is inextricably tied to his translation of the *Life of John Picus* by Gian Francesco Pico, the elder Pico's nephew. According to Cresacre More, when More determined to marry, 'he propounded to himself as a pattern of life a singular layman, John Picus, Earl of Mirandula'.[28] This must carry authority, as family tradition, but is also suggestive of the hagiographic concerns of More's descendants. The *Life* cannot be taken in any obvious way as a pattern for More, since, as is evident, Pico made the contrary decision to that made by More. It was a better model for the person to whom it was dedicated, the family friend who entered the Poor Clares, than it was for a married layman. At the end of the *Life*, Pico was a man who had wrongly resisted a religious vocation, for which (in the judgment of Savonarola) he would suffer in Purgatory. Perhaps more significantly, More shows no interest in Pico's view of man as the only privileged creature: what interests him is Pico's irreproachable morality and his devotional absorption.[29]

More's assimilation of Pico's character to the spiritual traditions with which he was most at home is evident both in his modifications of the *Life* itself, and in the selection of Pico's works which it introduces. His personal introduction of the biography dispenses with the account of Pico's family with the observation that honour and family reputation are derived only from virtue, of which Pico the Elder is a model. Gone from the text is Pico's interest in the Cabbala and in neo-Platonism, along with most of the discussion of Pico's philosophical writings and studies. Everything foreign to More's thoroughly orthodox outlook is eliminated; of all the sources for Pico's thought in the original version, only Thomas Aquinas is singled out for mention. While some of this alteration could be explained as appropriate in a work intended for a nun, we should remark on More's rendering of the phrase accounting for Pico's erudition, that he was inspired by 'vi ingenii et veritatis amore'. In More's rendering, it appeared as, 'love of God and profit of his Church'.[30]

The selections from Pico's writings that follow continue this theme. As abbé Marc'hadour has pointed out, the woodcut of Christ Crucified with the

[26] Ibid., 42.
[27] Quoting Isaiah 64:6; *Correspondence*, Epp. 83, 203, ll.1447-8: 'sed quoniam omnis iusticia mortalium velut pannus est menstruatae'.
[28] W. E. Campbell (ed.), *The English Works of Sir Thomas More*, I (1931), introduction by A. W. Reed, 18.
[29] See V. Gabrieli, 'Giovanni Pico and Thomas More', *Moreana*, IV (1967), and S. E. Lehmberg, 'More's life of Pico della Mirandola', *Studies in the Renaissance*, III (1956).
[30] Lehmberg, op. cit., 73.

instruments of the Passion on the title-page of the book characterises the whole.[31] The theme continues even in the three letters selected by More from the fifty or so printed in Pico's *Opera*: one warns Gian Francesco against court life, a second defends Pico's refusal to use his learning to serve a prince,[32] and the third is a warning to Gian Francesco to avoid the enticements of the flesh, lest he deform the image of God in his soul. It seems reasonable to suggest that among Italian humanists of the previous century, More could scarcely have found one less representative of the commitments of civic humanism.

Is More's humanism then merely a veneer? Nothing could be further from the truth. His rich personal appropriation of the sources of antique civilisation is evident in almost every work that came from his pen, as it is in his intimate and personal style of address. Nor is this humanism merely literary; it is the inspiration of a very precise educational programme for the renewal of the Christian commonweal, a programme which was entirely shared with Erasmus. Apart from the references to it in such major works as *Utopia*, its tenets can be gleaned from three long letters, that 'to a monk' (1519–20) already referred to, to the University of Oxford in defence of the study of Greek (1518), and, earliest of the three, to Martin Dorp in defence of Erasmus' *Praise of Folly* and *New Testament* (1515).[33] More's belief in the recovery of the texts at the fountainhead of the civilisation of Christian Europe is instinct in each of these. So is his advocacy of a secular, humanistic education for the layman as well as for the preacher who needs training in the arts of eloquence to reach the ordinary man. His insistence on knowledge of the relevant ancient languages and their literatures for the progress of theology is too familiar to need rehearsal here. A passage of less obvious but more profound importance occurs in the letter to Dorp, an important statement of More's humanism in itself. At the outset of the letter, More praises Erasmus specifically as a theologian who is a grammarian in the ancient sense, hence a truly learned man, familiar with all branches of knowledge. Such belief in the encyclopaedic learning of the grammarian, which would allow him to penetrate the letter of the text to discover the whole truth that it embodied, was at the root of the humanists' displacement of systematic theology, and was the very nexus between their study of the Christian texts and the renewal of piety.[34] But More's total adherence to this and the other tenets of evangelical humanism never disturbed the traditional Catholic anthropology he imbibed in his youth.

Another light is shed on More's sense of vocation in his attitude to the prevailing political order. His epigrams were first published in 1518. In many ways they were the conventional exercises of a youthful humanist, indebted to a number of identifiable sources and inspired chiefly by his reading of the Greek Anthology. With a few exceptions they seem to have been written

[31] 'Thomas More's spirituality', 128.
[32] Lehmberg, op. cit., 65–6.
[33] *Correspondence*, Epp. 83, 60, 15; see also the discussion by J. H. Hexter in his introduction to the *Utopia* in Edward Surtz, S. J. and J. H. Hexter (eds), *The Yale Edition of the Complete Works of St. Thomas More*, IV (New Haven 1965), lxxivf., hereafter cited as *Utopia*.
[34] This point is developed in J. Coppens (ed.), *Scrinium Erasmianum*, II (Leiden 1969), 77–99.

between 1509, when he first published a small offering in honour of the coronation of Henry VIII, and 1516. They thus represent that phase of More's life when he was most open to the influences of the new learning, after his decision to leave the Charterhouse and take up the life of the married layman.

As his editors have observed, More's differ from the usual run of humanist collections, including those of Erasmus, in their reflection of practical life. Of all More's topics, however, the most original was that of kingship: no other sixteenth-century poet used the theme for short poems.[35] And within the theme of kingship, More's preoccupation is the contrast between the good king and the tyrant. While his observations express the commonplaces of classical and medieval political theory, they are of great interest when placed alongside his next writings, *Richard III* and *Utopia*.

Initially, we notice echoes of the Charterhouse. Epigram 57, from Theophrastus, deals with the immanence of Death, the hidden presence in our bodies, advancing by identical steps with life itself. Epigram 101 recalls the *Phaedo* and announces a theme heard at critical moments throughout the later years: we are all of us shut up in the prison of this world under sentence of death. Yet the inmates struggle for position, as if this prison were a kingdom, loving it as no prison should be loved. Such reflections might be dismissed as showing only a young's man's inclination to romantic solemnity if it were not for the background we have described and the spiritual writings yet to come. This is the authentic More, quite capable of enjoying the resources of classical letters, but far less optimistic, far less committed to the promise of the secular order than were such as Ficino and Erasmus.

In the realm of government, his concerns are announced in a startling poem of dedication, commemorating the coronation of the young king. He hails the youthful Henry VIII with an unsparing reproof of the rule of his late father. The coronation day is the end of slavery and sadness, the beginning of new freedom and joy. The nobility can at last lift its head; laws will once more be enforced; the new reign will be an end to informers and fear.

It would be interesting, to say the least, to know what the new King made of this compliment. It is hard to believe that anything so audacious could have come from another pen than that of an obscure pamphleteer, or of someone with the confidence and sense of command that, I suggest, was part of More's personality and habitual tone. His concern with tyranny continues in a way that makes it impossible to dismiss as a rhetorical commonplace, especially after this highly conspicuous characterisation of the rule of Henry VII. Epigram 14 talks of the love that unites men, not to be found 'in the castles of proud kings' – a phrase missing from the Greek original. Epigram 185 approves the wisdom of a rustic who sees a king only as a man in an embroidered garment: Epigram 227, on the lust for power, deplores kingly greed and misrule. Epigram 182, on the best form of government, prefers the rule of a senate to monarchy. One reason for this is that a senate is elected by the people, while a king is chosen by the 'blind chance' of birth – and his

[35] L. Bradner and C. A. Lynch (eds), *The Latin Epigrams of Thomas More* (Chicago 1953), xxvii and note on Ep. 62.

qualification makes him feel that his subjects were created for him to rule.

It is this last and characteristic twist, the pessimism about the institution in itself, that is More's signature. Erasmus' remark that More had always a special loathing of tyranny has not been lost on More's biographers. Its true ground would seem to have been a sympathy, shared by Erasmus, with local rule; and a hostility, also shared, to the traditional chivalric culture in which both kings and nobles were brought up. In his *Institutio principis Christiani*, Erasmus' elaboration on the medieval Mirror of Princes, hereditary monarchy is described as only the best of the available polities. It is elective monarchy that is first discussed and implicitly preferred. More's *Richard III* can be seen as, in part, a simple illustration of that theme: the commons are the witnesses, the victims and also the judges of Richard's tyranny, as well as the repository of political conscience and moral order.

Such ideas could have been drawn from native sources as old at least as John of Salisbury's *Policraticus* or as recent as Fortescue, or from ancient authors ranging from Suetonius and Tacitus to Augustine, with all of whom More was thoroughly familiar. It is impossible not to relate it also to the burgher aristocratic world of his youth. On 31 October 1516, writing to Erasmus about the reception of his *Utopia* in the Low Countries, More remarked that rulers there did not have under them 'many subjects, as the term is now used by kings to refer to their people, who are really worse off than slaves'. As J. H. Hexter pointed out, the ruling class in Utopia would have been made up entirely of men like Peter Giles, Jerome Busleiden and Jean Le Sauvage, the Chancellor of Brabant.[36]

Utopia, More's treatise on 'the Best State of a Commonwealth', is indeed the culmination of all these views. It was written while More was actively involved in royal service, and while he was contemplating a very serious further commitment. There is no reason to suppose that this was a time of anguished reappraisal of his lay vocation; on the other hand, it is natural that his earlier debate at the Charterhouse should now come to mind, recollected in tranquillity. We might therefore reasonably expect that *Utopia* would contain More's ripe reflection on his settled and prominent service to the secular commonweal.

That is indeed what we find. Utopia is a self-sufficient society entirely dedicated to the humanist ideals of the common good. It is not only the best commonwealth, but the only true commonwealth, because it is only there that men concern themselves seriously with public affairs – *publicum negotium*.[37] There is only one difficulty – the existence of this truly just and moral society is pointedly postulated on a condition impossible of attainment: it is the symbolically difficult abolition of private property, which exists (we are told) in only one place – Nowhere.

Utopia is not an optimistic work. It reveals a profound and startling pessimism, not only about traditional military and aristocratic culture, but about the true state of affairs in the world with which More was most familiar

[36] Hexter, *Utopia*, lxxxi.
[37] *Utopia*, 237-9; 238, l.2.

and from which he came – the world of property, law, and public service. Communism – recalling apostolic Christianity, religious communities and man's pre-lapsarian perfection – can only remind the instructed reader of Original Sin (whatever he knew already of Plato) and therefore of an insurmountable barrier to humanist programmes of reform founded on education and amity alone. All of More's scholarly and rhetorical skills are employed to point the contrast between Utopian society, so close in practice to Christian ideals, and the failures of a society that is More's own. *Utopia* is not a philosophical treatise but a parable, in which More's deep scepticism about traditional institutions and the established social order is extended even to secular positive law and to courtly society. More's perfect and static world was the fruit of a self-examination designed to arouse the conscience of Christian Europe as well as his own. As such, it was entirely in harmony with what his editor has called, 'the central problem of the Christian humanists, "What, truly, is it to be a Christian?" '[38]

If we add to this, ' . . . in the city', we are back to More's question for Colet. More's final answer to it is the dramatic climax of *Utopia* at the end of Book 1, where the debate between Morus and Hythlodaeus reaches a peak of intensity. The 'indirect approach' recommended by Morus is to enter the service of the Prince to do what one can, 'for it is impossible that all should be well unless all men were good . . .' But Hythlodaeus, the prophetic figure, dismisses all these reasonable counsels with a trenchant denunciation of compromise. The whole of the concluding declamation is given to him, and the force of this in the structure of the Book must be acknowledged. He repudiates the reasonable observation of Morus that 'Life cannot be satisfactory where all things are common' with the stark reply that objectors must contemplate the model of Utopia. This is the dramatic setting for the start of the discourse on the ideal Commonweal.

Utopia's credentials as a treatise on the responsible role of the Christian in the service of the secular prince are therefore most ambivalent. In this respect alone the contrast between it and Machiavelli's famous treatise could not be greater: it is anything but a 'how to' book, and is neither a guide nor an exhortation to others. It paints a dark and threatening picture of the world of affairs, and reminds the reader, with eloquence, brilliant invention and moral passion, of the ideals for which he should strive. But beyond that it gives no hint of what should be done. It throws the reader back on himself in a world whose conduct, he is warned, is deeply hostile to the Christian vocation. If he should venture and fail, what is more, he will lose not only his goals, but his integrity.[39] *Utopia* is thus as Augustinian as the spiritual climate in which More's early conscience was formed; in a world of uncertainties, a man must rely on his inner resources.

While we can agree, therefore, that in 1515-16 More and Erasmus 'stood in complete agreement on precisely those matters which at the time both regarded as of primary importance',[40] there is an underlying divergence in

[38] Ibid., lxxv.
[39] Ibid., xci.
[40] Ibid., lxxiv.

their attitudes to the lay vocation. This stems in turn from differing evaluations of the worth of human institutions and the capacity of human nature to improve through education. Although Erasmus disapproved of More's entry into royal service, he did not see the issue in More's terms. He was usually pleased when a friend won a place in influential councils, although (as with More) he might regret the loss to letters.[41] He was shy of involvement himself, but accepted a place as Councillor in the Netherlands to Prince Charles. Admittedly this was not a taxing post, but his innumerable letters of advice to princes and other notables show that he took the role seriously. There is no trace of More's deep apprehension of moral corruption from such involvement, nor did he share More's preoccupation with the sinfulness of mankind. He saw human nature rather through the eyes of the Greek Fathers, as above all, *capax Dei*. The two views are theologically harmonious, but temperamentally worlds apart.

The author of *Utopia* could not be a committed careerist, and now we know that More was not.[42] He was always ready to stand outside himself to assess his actions, a habit that must go back to his early spiritual discipline, and that found brilliant literary expression in dialogues like *Utopia*, in which he appears as one of the protagonists. More was a philosopher and man of letters who from personal conviction, but without much expectation of success, worked hard and brilliantly at his profession and the particular tasks set for him by the King. As Henry's trusted friend he hoped for an opportunity to affect one of the two polar extremes of English society where he thought change might be wrought – the court and the commons. Essential to the evangelical education of the latter, of course, were peace and sound doctrine. It is suitable that More should have found his role in government in the services of private counsel to the King at home, of diplomatic negotiation abroad, and finally, in the exhausting office of official controversialist against what he saw as the devastating threat to public conscience posed by Lutheran heresy. More lived in a spirit of Christian hope, and he was an ironist, but his view of human nature was far less sanguine than that of most of his humanist associates. The hair shirt, the private austerities, the life in the household at Chelsea with daily mass, the reading of scripture at meals, household prayer at night, private study and devotion in the early hours of the morning, midnight office at the great feasts, and, in the garden, a retreat where he spent each Friday in reading and prayer – all of this, despite the humanist *paideia*, the sociability and the legal career, has, finally, less in common with the religion of the *Enchiridion* than it has with the religion of Syon and the Charterhouse.

A set of 'instructions for a devout and literate layman', written in the early fifteenth century and only recently discovered and published, seems to be an aide-memoire for an earlier citizen of (probably) London, quite possibly a lawyer, probably of the Throckmorton family, and written by a priest who was an Oxford graduate. Its recipient reads Latin, owns his own house, and is the head of a family for whose spiritual edification he is held responsible by

[41] See n.39.
[42] G. R. Elton, 'Thomas More, Councillor', in Sylvester, *Action and Contemplation*.

his director. At a lower social level it echoes the world of the devout magnate Henry of Lancaster, or Cicely Duchess of York, or Richard Beauchamp, Earl of Warwick. It envisages a rigorous spiritual discipline each day, starting with prayers and mass, and aiming above all at a constant state of recollection on certain appointed themes. Mental prayer is urged even at table, where spiritual reading is done by members of the family, including the children, taking turns. The recipient of this instruction is expected to expound spiritual matters to his wife and dependents, to withdraw to 'that secret place' (*locum illum secretum*) after dinner to confer with devout friends until Vespers, and to examine his conscience daily. He is constantly to bear in mind his final end. His temporal duties and obligations are not so much as mentioned. The world of the Lady Margaret Beaufort, of John Fisher and John Colet, was such a world. So too, at heart, was the world of Thomas More.[43]

To conclude from this simply that More was 'medieval' would be a crude evasion, obscuring the life of his mentality and spirit. His differences with Erasmus cannot be explained by a comparison of their ages – Erasmus was the older man by a decade – or by attempts to distinguish degrees of commitment to the formal disciplines of European humanism. They rest on philosophical attitudes which transcend the tenets of humanism as such, although the two men were nurtured by the same general religious and literary culture, and were equally concerned for the welfare of their fellow men and the renewal of the Christian spirit. In the subtle but momentous differences of inflection in their common language we find foreshadowed not only their very different fates, but also the coming divergences between evangelical humanism on the one hand, and on the other, the main religious debate over the issues of sin, grace and salvation.

[43] W. A. Pantin, 'Instructions for a devout and literate layman', in J. J. G. Alexander and M. T. Gibson (eds), *Medieval Learning and Literature. Essays Presented to Richard William Hunt* (Oxford 1976), 398–420; Latin text, 420–2.

6

The Rejection of the Reformation in France

*Fernand Braudel**

The following brief essay will argue an unaccustomed case: this has its advantages – those of a fresh point of view – and its drawbacks; for pleading a case can only claim to open a debate, not to close it. It is only too likely to be one-sided.

Before embarking upon this course, it would, I think, be helpful to take a few precautions and to specify the theoretical framework of my approach. All the elements that go to make up the 'religious' phenomenon, since they lie at the very heart of the cultural domain, inevitably obey the simplifying rules of a universe (that of culture and civilisation) which is sufficiently original to possess if not its own *laws* – that would be too much to expect – at least its *regularities*. Civilisations and cultures, like all human history, have a life spanning the short and the long, or very long, term. In the following pages, I shall try to move away from the short-term history which has been so much studied, and to pay special attention to the long term, *la longue durée*. This will oblige us to pass by or ignore events, episodes, circumstances and dramatic moments (which I leave, I may say, with some reluctance).

The long term has obvious claims: the Reformation did not begin on All Hallows' Eve, 31 October 1517, when Luther nailed his theses to the door of the *Schlosskirche* in Wittenberg. Nor did it end, in France that is, either with the promulgation (1598) or with the Revocation (1685) of the Edict of Nantes. For many years before 1517 there had been signs of the powerful currents of the *Pre-Reformation*. Incidentally I do not greatly care for this expression. Is the name not misleading since there followed both the Protestant Reformation and the Catholic Counter-Reformation? In a book which he never had time to write, Lucien Fèbvre proposed to replace the term *Pre-Reformation* with that of *The Restless Years* (*Les Temps Inquiets*), of which he dated the first stirrings about 1450. I like this expression, which I have used a great deal. But were restlessness and anguish really the dominant influences over the second half of the fifteenth century, at a time when western Europe, after the disturbances, crises and disasters of the Hundred Years' War, was

*Translated by Sian Reynolds.

experiencing a prolonged revival, a truly biological renaissance, a renewed and undeniable sense of *joie de vivre*, as if it were being washed by a springtime flood of religious waters? In fact, the Reformation was already potentially in existence, in gestation, more than half a century before Luther. And turning now to France, could one say that the fate of the Reformation was sealed there in 1598? Or in 1685? Or even in 1735, when the last man sentenced to the galleys for Protestantism was freed? Or in 1787, when Louis XVI granted civil rights to the Protestants who had not possessed them until then? Or even in 1980, when it is estimated that there are about two million practising Protestants in France?

In the short term, civilisations, whose appetite is limitless, are almost constantly accepting all the 'goods', one after another, that their neighbours have to offer or which come within their grasp. In the long term, there is usually some form of adaptation: definite acceptances or categorical refusals are rare – not to say very rare. Whenever this happens, when a wholesale acceptance or rejection is made, a culture is defining its own identity, from top to bottom. Conquered Gaul accepted Rome and was thereby transformed for centuries to come; but modern France rejected the Reformation, and thus defined and affirmed her own existence. This much is agreed: but for what reasons and in what circumstances?

Since this refusal came from deep down, we shall not be able to establish it unless we first cut away the glittering surfaces of history as the textbooks tell it; this may be a lengthy operation. But perhaps, by carefully choosing the points of incision, the samples to be taken, we may be able to move comparatively quickly. To help us, we can make use of what Charles Rémusat in 1876 called *l'uchronie* (never-never-time). It may be a bad habit to rewrite history as it never was, to alter the course of major events so as to imagine what might have happened. But although a sleight-of-hand like this may be an illusion, it is not pointless. In its own way, it measures the weight of events, episodes and actors who were believed, or believed themselves, to be responsible for the entire course of history. Could they have been different or not?

The dramatic event that took place at Wittenberg on 31 October 1517, then, striking though it was, only set in motion the vast process of the Reformation to the extent that Pope Leo X excommunicated the monk Luther. It is not too far-fetched to imagine that the Pope might have sought a compromise with him: Church tradition was not hostile to such things – indeed it was itself troubled by a perpetual need for *aggiornamento*, an insistent *reformatio ecclesiae* constantly renewed. The Church could answer yes or no to the call for innovation, accommodation, creative imagination. After all, it said yes to St. Francis of Assisi and the mendicant orders. Today's historians, all passion spent, recognise that 'the embattled brothers were sometimes closer to each other in attitudes, methods and even doctrines than they themselves imagined' (Jean Delumeau). If the Protestant revolt tore apart 'the seamless mantle of the Church', it did not challenge the kingdom of Christ, of God made man: the essential message of Christianity was surely thus preserved. In any case, Luther's real break with Rome was not fully accomplished until

1520, after a long series of negotiations. From that point on, there was no turning back: in April 1521, at the Diet of Worms, Luther appeared before Emperor Charles V, at the time only a young man; but a young man who was already – and always would be afterward – a prince of tradition, respectful of all that had been done or thought before him. How can one imagine him letting himself be seduced by the dramatic wind of change, by a future already discernible?

In France, the moment of truth came even later. The first revolutionary shock of the Reformation was felt outside the frontiers of France and penetrated the huge kingdom only slowly. Not until about 1534-5, long after the drama at Wittenberg, can France be said to have been touched in its entirety by the new ideas, as a careful drawing of the religious map incontestably shows: Lutheran ideas travelled down the major axes of communication in France, above all the Seine and the Rhône valley; for to the east, Picardy, Champagne, Lorraine (which was not yet French) and Burgundy formed a huge hostile block, faithful to tradition and difficult to leap across. Did Protestantism reach France by way of the North Sea and the English Channel, capturing the barrier zones in the east from the rear? By 1534-5 at any rate, there was not a town, village or road in France where Protestantism had not passed by. Not everywhere had been conquered by any means; but everywhere had been touched, illuminated by its passing.

But these were the years when two clear camps had not yet unequivocally formed. In this vast kingdom, where the old life pursued its accustomed course, where the dominant force was that of inertia, individuals found themselves in a twilight zone (*Zwielicht* in German, in French *demi-jour* or, even more picturesquely, *entre chien et loup*). All thinking society was tempted, interested and hesitant. François I, whom we usually think of as bathed in the golden light of the Renaissance, was a living and in a way terrifying example of this hesitation and uncertainty. He did it is true have at his side his sister, the adorable and admirable Marguerite, who had been since 1526 in touch with humanists and men of the Reformation. In her circle, men talked of projects, '*nouvelletez*' and the opening of new doors and vistas. It was of some moment, then, when her marriage in 1527 to the King of Navarre took her away from the Court, which was thus effectively deprived of her influence. But the King was not in any case free to act; neither in heart nor in mind was he fully committed to change. When he was freed from his Spanish prison in 1526, he left behind his two sons as hostages to the enemy. He would not be safe from that direction until after the Paix des Dames (1529). Besides, how could he have moved forward? It would have meant refusing to listen to a 'reactionary' old counsellor like Chancellor Duprat (who did not die until 1535), ignoring the vigilant and venomous hostility of the Sorbonne, running against the machine of monarchy, forgetting that the Concordat of 1516 had delivered over to him the Church of France, which, tit-for-tat, made the Most Christian King the prisoner or virtual prisoner of the upper clergy.

All the same, Protestantism had not yet taken on the implacable countenance of Calvin, who was not to be undisputed master of Geneva until after 1538. In 1530, there were other well-known and more reassuring faces: the generous Zwingli, the 'amiable and pious' Melanchthon. What was more, in 1532, Henry VIII of England offered François I a 'virtually Protestant' alliance, designed to come to the aid of the reformed church princes of the Schmalkalden League. Caught 'between left and right', in Michelet's words, François I hesitated, wavered and did not commit himself. Perhaps because choosing, or appearing to choose, the Reformation would have meant immediately losing Italy, indeed having Italy against him? It would have meant giving up his plans and visions – pipe-dreams perhaps but pipe-dreams can be important. 'The common people,' wrote a contemporary, 'do not understand the reasons for the King's conduct. To me it is clear that he is not ill-disposed towards the Reformation. If he conceals it, that is because he cannot do otherwise because of the Clergy of his Kingdom. Only wait until he has acquired the parts of Italy he desires and then see how much remains of his friendship with the Pope and the Papists.' Was this contemporary right? Did François I, like his predecessors, have his eyes fixed on Italy to this extent? It is possible; but the *idée fixe* of his life was his struggle with the Emperor –with *Cesare* as the ambassadors of the Italian cities said. To slip for a moment into the effortless speculation of never-never-time, how extraordinary it would have been, how heavy with consequences directly touching the Emperor himself, if François I had rallied or made concessions to the Reformed religion! If one could begin history all over again, as one can an experiment in a laboratory, what food for thought there would be in a France embracing Protestantism without a war, almost amicably, at the whim of a king. After a volte-face of this order, the history of France would have been completely different, and with it the history of Europe as a whole.

However, I doubt whether, either before or after the Wars of Religion, the Monarchy was really calling the tune. Even during what I consider to be the easy, early years, the King would have required a will power he did not possess to prevent the machinery of repression from lumbering into action. The wheels of violence were already beginning to turn of themselves. In the night of 17 – 18 October 1534, the famous placards were posted up in Paris, Orleans, Blois; and in Amboise, where François was himself, one was posted on the very door of his bedchamber. The placards were extremely strongly worded: they denounced 'the pompous and arrogant papal mass', all 'the time spent on ringing bells, dressing-up and other kinds of sorcery'. How can one believe in transubstantiation, the incendiary text continues, as if Jesus Christ was 'hidden and wrapped up under the accidental covering of bread and wine'? Before Calvin, here is violence erupting on to the stage. How could the vacillating policy of François I fail to be influenced, diverted or indeed completely stopped in its tracks, by this event, at a time when violence was already raging across Christian Europe, violence which reached a peak in the apocalypse of the Anabaptist troubles in Münster (1534-5)?

After the affair of the placards, the repression got under way, martyrs were burnt at the stake, and threatened Protestants began to take precautions and leave the kingdom. Among the fugitives was Marot, who had already been arrested in 1521 and 1532, and who fled to the Court of Navarre and then to Ferrara, where he met Calvin who was also in flight.

Was this the point of no return? No, because in 1535, the Latin edition of Calvin's *Institution chrétienne*, published in Basle, was preceded by a dedication to the King of France. But in 1562 began the drama of the long Wars of Religion. If I had the talents of Claude Manceron, and his gift for making a counterpoint of the biographies of contemporary individuals, the first picture in my series would be François I taking part in an expiatory procession after the affair of the placards, the second Calvin and Marot meeting in Ferrara. But I shall not pursue this familiar sequence of brightly-coloured images, over the necessary chronological span, down to Henri IV, Louis XIII, Louis XIV or even Louis XVI: it is only too easy to imagine, for we have heard it many times before. The narrator changes but the narrative remains, like Ariadne's thread. I do not say that history of this kind, micro-observation, is not important. It can teach us plenty of things on the way, bringing new facts or previously unrecorded details to our attention. But the big questions raised by the fate of the Reformation in France are not adequately posed or sufficiently developed in this perspective. What was really going on behind the King's policy?

No one these days still subscribes to Engels's hasty judgment that the Reformation was in part a 'bourgeois revolution', one that is on a secondary plane and in some sense a consequence, after 1450–1500, of the establishment of the new structures of capitalism. This explanation has been easy to contradict, but that is not to say that economic history and social history did not have a part to play in the many-sided destiny of the Reformation.

In France, the long period of the Wars of Religion (1562–1598) coincided on the whole with a period of economic health, thanks to which France was able to finance these endless conflicts and support the destruction and expense they clearly brought. France, like Germany during the Thirty Years' War, became a rendezvous for all the mercenaries of Europe, who came mainly from the Swiss cantons and from Germany. The Peace of Augsburg in 1555, an earlier version of the Edict of Nantes, brought calm to the German interior, while on the far-off Hungarian frontier the truce concluded in 1568, and later renewed, left only sporadic fighting going on; hostilities did not break out again until 1593 and ended again in 1606. These dates are important: they explain the large numbers of unemployed German mercenaries who regularly passed through Lorraine and Champagne and were constantly engaged in the French wars. This continued until at least 1593, when there was something of a downturn in the economic situation, as the lean years began; and at about the same time soldiers became harder to recruit in Germany. These were important factors – certainly more important than Spanish subsidies. I have written elsewhere and repeat here, no doubt unnecessarily, that the St. Bartholomew Massacre (24 August 1572) was not provoked by the intrigues of the southern enemy. Nor were the Ligueurs of later years in the pay of Spain (we have records of the meagreness of Spanish subsidies): they were obeying their own passions. This explanation, which is firmly established by the documents at Simancas, and which ought after all to satisfy French retrospective pride, has yet to succeed in reaching and convincing most traditional historians.

Another aspect of the European conjuncture, and probably the most important, is to be found in the repercussions of the Treaty of Cateau-Cambrésis, by which Henri II in 1559 turned away from his Italian conquests to devote his efforts to fighting the Reformation at home. During this period, as the historian Lucien Romier has written, the true 'Catholic King' was not Philip II in Spain, but the King of France. Abandoning Italy led to extremely bitter protests from the French troops and their commanders in Piedmont. Clearly by 1559, the French crown was no longer hesitating, above the *mêlée*. With Henri II, it took sides. But the important thing is that the return of peace led to the demobilisation of the nobility from the King's military service. Until then, the pattern had been to spend the winter on one's estates and the summer campaigning in Italy. This demobilisation brought about a social crisis of sufficient gravity for the petty nobles, now left idle, to provide military leadership for the Protestant revolt.

As for the bourgeoisie, if it is hard to believe in its revolutionary rise which is supposed to have got the first wave of capitalism off the ground, it can at least be said that the lower clergy, in the first half of the sixteenth century, gave a fairly wide welcome to the new ideas, just as in 1789 the lower clergy welcomed the coming Revolution; by the end of the century, by contrast, the same lower clergy had declared itself against the Reformation, in Paris for instance between 1588 and 1594, as we can see from Arlette Lebigre's most recent book describing the 'Revolution of the Priests': a fierce revolution directed against the King and the Huguenots.

Even more significant is the attitude of the extremely brilliant intellectual elite – neither nobility nor bourgeoisie strictly speaking – which had dominated France socially and politically throughout the sixteenth century, which had professed on all counts an enlightened tolerance and scepticism *à la* Montaigne, and which renewed the educational system from top to bottom by ousting the Church in favour of lay schoolmasters. These men, who are described in George Huppert's most recent book (*Les Bourgeois Gentils-hommes*, 1977) were the successors and inheritors of the earlier humanist currents. All of them were sympathetic to the evangelical reforms. And yet the great majority of them moved away from Protestantism as it gradually became identified with civil war and with the destruction of the State and the Church as an institution – that is of the public order, which they regarded as indispensable. Accused of opportunism by Calvin, denounced by the Jesuits as false Catholics, these were the people who formed the active ranks of those known as the *politiques*: they were to contribute to the ending of the religious wars, fighting the troops 'of psalm-singing shop clerks who were prepared to kill and burn in the name of the Lord' as George Huppert writes. They nevertheless remained faithful to their ideal, on the margins of the reaction which became widespread during the *Grand Siècle*, and were to find themselves excluded from the centres of power, whether they liked it or not.

In other words, underneath the surface of events great social forces were at work. They nourished the French Wars of Religion. And they also worked towards their extinction and eventually to the failure of the Reformation in France.

Why, though, did France, intellectuals included, reject Protestantism? The whole problem clearly needs looking at afresh.

A secular movement back towards religious faith had overwhelmed Europe in its entirety towards the middle of the fifteenth century, propelling it out of its indifference and ignorance. This was a movement present everywhere and no doubt at all levels in society. I would imagine that even the rise of popular 'superstition' which was to lead to the outbreak of witchcraft had its origins in the same general movement. France, the rendezvous and crossroads of Europe, participated fully in this mighty transformation. Paris moreover was undeniably one of the capitals of humanism, and France had its Latinists and its Greek and Hebrew scholars who discovered new Promised Lands: Rome, Greece, Judea – a discovery which amounted to implanting, at the very heart of a Christian civilisation, a pagan civilisation which, say what one will, contrasted with it. To the Christianity built up over the centuries since the Fathers of the Church was now opposed a Christianity which had returned to its evangelical sources, since to revive it was to place oneself in the shadow of the living example of Jesus Christ. If the Reformation had not burst brutally upon the world in Germany, a different less violent 'reformation' would probably have been formulated in France. There is nothing to stop us imagining for a moment the possible consequences of the preaching of a Lefèvre d'Etaples (1455-1536). But the noisiest formulation of the Reformation occurred in Germany, which was almost entirely swept up by it, from the Netherlands of Erasmus to the Swiss Cantons of Zwingli. France came only in second place; and although it was affected, disturbed even, it was never conquered in the full sense of the term.

Perhaps it was protected by its very size, its inertia, the heavy weight holding it down in traditional habits. At any rate, from the time of the first war (1562-1563) it was clear that if the Huguenots were an active and thriving minority in France, they were still a minority. They lacked troops. The great majority of the population remained faithful to Rome, to the old religion. It is characteristic that the Protestants succeeded neither in taking Paris nor in capturing the King. The last word went to the Catholic majority in the country, which was, like all majorities, slow to mobilise and to gather impetus. I believe that 'number' decided the outcome of the interminable conflicts. In other words, without denying their role altogether, I am inclined to minimise the action of even the most resolute Catholic leaders, whether the men of the first 'triumvirate' – François de Guise, Montmorency, the Maréchal de Saint-André – or the party of the Guises as a whole. 'The Guises,' wrote Lucien Romier (who was I may say a good historian), 'were arrogance itself, with intelligence, savoir-faire and a passionate belief in the good cause of the Church, *which owed in part to them the safeguarding of Catholicism in France.*' I do not find the italicised words altogether convincing. If causes are won, it is often because they are already won in advance. It was the Catholic majority in the country that provided the support for these conspicuous, passionate and dramatic characters who moved on the floodlit centre of the stage. The assassination of the Duc de Guise at Blois on 23 December 1588, on the orders of Henri III (which made it an execution, since the King was the source of all justice), resounded throughout the whole of France, because the victim had been so prominent in the events of that tragic year. An obscure diarist in Bar-sur-Seine in Champagne expressed his alarm at the explosion of quarrels that were political as much as religious and which spread through France like wildfire. 'From this time,' he wrote, 'sons were set against fathers, brothers, uncles and nephews . . . This evil was so contagious that it spread even to women, setting mother against daughter, and sisters would go to war, sometimes tearing each other's hair out.' This text is not sufficient evidence on its own, but it does point to the activity of the majority. It was the multitude which swayed the course of history. The Church was saved by the Paris of the Ligues, the Paris of barricades and passionate preachers. It is true that the Paris of the Ligues appeared to lose the struggle, gave every sign of being defeated. When Henri IV entered the capital on 22 March 1594, the Ligueurs, too heavily compromised, left the city by the Porte Saint-Denis to the north, along with the Spanish troops. They went into exile, and we can find abundant mention of them in the Spanish documents, in Brussels or in other towns in the Low Countries. And yet after a fashion they were the winners. For the essential thing was the Catholic cause – and it triumphed. Henri IV, the Huguenot, had to embrace the Catholic Church. 'Paris is worth a mass': he ought to have said 'France is worth a mass'. For it was the French, the party of the majority, who forced the mass upon him. And Catholicism also triumphed in the unparalleled surge of religious fervour which was to mark the first half of the seventeenth century, the '*Grand Siècle*'.

Thereafter, the vigilance of the French monarchy did not relax for an instant. The capture of La Rochelle (1628) and the Peace of Alais (1629) finally eliminated the State's fear of the Protestants, who were suspected of establishing enclaves in their strongholds, like the United Provinces in the Netherlands. In the end, just as Spain under Philip II had expelled the Moriscoes (1610-1614), France expelled her Protestants in 1685, with the Revocation of the Edict of Nantes. One can just possibly exonerate Louis XIV himself: the King may have believed in good faith in the massive conversion of his Protestant subjects; but one must in passing accuse Catholic France, the France of the majority, which had not laid down its arms. It is clearly revealing that for years after the Revocation, the King's government had a comparatively smooth passage, whereas the first twenty years of Louis XIV's reign had been stormy ones on the domestic front. The country showed its appreciation to the government for this measure of intolerance which we, historians and citizens of the twentieth century, find and continue to find distressing in retrospect.

But the French determination not to leave the Catholic fold presents us in turn with a problem – indeed the problem of problems. And one which is not limited to the French 'situation'. The Catholicism that emerged from the conflicts of the sixteenth and seventeenth centuries was not confined to France, but was also that of Italy, southern Germany, the Rhineland, Portugal and Spain. If one draws a map of these unambiguous manifestations, one finds that the old West, not to say Old Europe, remained on the whole loyal to Rome. Broadly speaking, on the European mainland, the frontiers of Catholicism were the Rhine and the Danube. Unmistakably, these were the former frontiers of the Roman Empire. So perhaps we should invoke what might be called an extraordinary accumulation of history, remote-controlled from the distant past. There was already in existence a cultural and material privileged zone, favouring what would later be European Catholicism, a previously constructed coherent universe, beside which the new Europe, beyond the Rhine and the Danube, was made to feel inferior, subordinate and, vis-à-vis Rome, in a near-colonial situation. The Reformation meant both a break with the Roman Church, and a break with the dominant Europe of the south: a new country was taking the place at the head of the European 'world-economy' of an old country that had long been privileged. The centre of this economic world had long lain in Venice: by the beginning of the sixteenth century, it had moved to Antwerp, and eventually, after some hesitation, it became fixed in Amsterdam by the end of the century. The fortune of Europe was changing hands.

In this connection, as I have frequently argued, I do not accept the tortuous explanation put forward by Max Weber: nothing could have been more natural than the transfer of power from a country of ancient wealth to a country of recent wealth: northern capitalism would essentially take over the practices and instruments of Mediterranean capitalism, which had blazed the trail. Protestantism did not invent capitalism: the north was an inheritor not an original creator.

But to return to France; her position at the meeting point of these two Europes meant that France always managed to look both ways. However, having been for centuries enmeshed in the very ancient network of Romance civilisation, she remained lodged there. Perhaps it was impossible for France ever really to break free from it.

It so happens that at two periods of my own life, in 1925 and again in 1940–42, I have lived at Mayence (Mainz), on that frontier, the Rhine, which the Counter-Reformation reoccupied in force, with the Jesuits, from the end of the sixteenth century. Evidence of the reconquest is to be found in the Baroque churches with their cupolas and *accolades*. Built much later, some-times even in the eighteenth century, do they bear witness, as I thought then and still think, to the inertia and religious loyalties of France stretching away into the distance? They were and are a line of defence.

7

The Smiling Spleen

Walter Pagel

> . . . man, proud man,
> Drest in a little brief authority . . .
> His glassy essence, like an angry ape,
> Plays such fantastic tricks before high heaven
> As makes the angels weep; who, with our spleens,
> Would all themselves laugh mortal.
>
> *Measure for Measure*, II,ii.117-23.

Reading Shakespeare today we may be puzzled at the very different functions ascribed to the spleen. Manly courage and youthful impetuosity have their origin in the spleen. Worcester says of a nephew's wrongdoings, 'It hath the excuse of youth and heat of blood . . . A hare-brain'd Hotspur, governed by a spleen.' But so, too, does laughter. 'If you desire the spleen, and will laugh yourselves into stitches,' says Maria to Sir Toby, 'follow me.' Enjoying Patroclus' mimicry, Achilles cries out: 'O enough . . . Or give me ribs of steel! I shall split all In pleasure of my spleen.'[1]

'By the spleene we are moued to laughter',[2] is a doctrine which bears the hallmark of ancient humoralism, the theory by which health, disease, and the basic character-types had been understood since ancient times. The vicissitudes of the association made between spleen and laughter, and its unexpected survival in the work of van Helmont, the sworn seventeenth-century enemy of humoralism, are an interesting chapter in the history of ideas.

We search in vain in the ancient medical classics for any statement of the association between spleen and laughter. Only in the satirist Persius do we encounter a character 'laughing by virtue of a wanton spleen' (*sum petulante splene cachinno*).[3] Pliny associated laughter and intemperance with a large spleen.[4] Late in the third century Quintus Serenus Samonicus described a man whose 'inept laughter' reputedly disappeared and gave way

[1] In translating 'spleen' as 'gelaunt' (in a mood) in the lines from *Measure for Measure*, A. W. von Schlegel and Ludwig Tieck missed the point: *Shakespeare's Dramatische Werke ubersetzt*, I, 200; *Henry IV Pt. 1*, V,ii.17-19; *Twelfth Night*, III,ii.63-4; *Troilus and Cressida*, I,iii.176-8.
[2] *Batmas vppon Bartholome his Booke de Proprietatibus rerum* (London 1582), Bk. V, Cap.41.
[3] Persius, Aulus Flaccus, *Satirae*, I, 12.
[4] Plinius, Caius Secundus, *Naturalis historia*, XI, 80, ed. C. Mayhoff (Lips. 1875), II, 258.

ever after to a severe countenance when his swollen spleen had been removed.[5]

The belief in an association between spleen and laughter was part of the medieval tradition. The Persius quotation seems to have disappeared, but the late-Roman lore was reflected in the *Talmud*, compiled in the early Christian centuries, where the spleen was called the origin of laughter.[6] For the medieval tradition proper, Isidorus (*Splene ridemus*),[7] and the *Viaticum* of ibn-al-Jazzar[8] (*splen est instrumentum risus*) in Constantinus Africanus' translation, have pride of place. The tradition was popularised through the famous Salernitan 'boke teachinge all people to gouerne them in helthe': *splen ridere facit.*[9] In this form it was repeated again and again, notably in the *Lilium medicinae* of Bernard Gordon (*c.* 1285)[10] and the encyclopaedic *De Proprietatibus rerum* of Bartholomaeus Anglicus.[11] The matter is briefly mentioned – or, rather, dismissed – in Konrad von Megenburg's *Buch der Natur* (1309-74):[12] some believe, he says, that laughter increases and decreases with the size of the spleen.

Medieval authors tried persistently to explain and provide a rationale for the association. Bernard Gordon said it was *per accidens*: a side-effect of the purging of the 'melancholic humour' by the organ.[13] The *Problemata* (citing Isidorus and Ebardus of Bethun for the fact) held it to be quite 'natural', due to attraction by the spleen which was the proper domicile for black bile (*melancholia*).[14] Basing himself on Galen, Ali Abbas (*c.* 1000) had already likened the spleen to a sponge, swelling and contracting, receiving humoral impurities and hence producing such a thick humour as black bile.[15]

The belief retained its place in the anatomical textbooks of the sixteenth century. The Persius quotation, absent from the medieval tradition, was revived in Jerome Cardan[16] and in Bauhinus' *Theatrum Anatomicum*.[17] Since Bauhinus was the main source of traditional anatomical data for William Harvey, it is scarcely surprising that it resurfaces in his Lumleian *Lectures on the Whole of Anatomy* in 1616.[18]

[5] Samonicus, Quintus Serenus, *Medicinae praecepta*, XXIII, 25. Julius Preuss, *Biblisch-Talmudische Medisin* (Berlin 1911), 112.

[6] *Berakoth* 61b. Preuss, op. cit., 112, not necessarily the source for the poet-philosopher Jehudah ha-Levi, *Das Buch Kusari*, IV, 25, ed. David Cassel (Leipzig 1853), 351.

[7] Isidorus Hispaliensis, *Etymologiae*, XI, I, ed. W. M. Lindsay (Oxford 1911), vol. II.

[8] Ibn al-Jazzar (ascribed to Constantinus Africanus), *Viaticum*, in *Opera Ysaac* (Lugduni 1515), II, f.162r; M. Steinschneider, 'Constantinus Africanus und seine arabischen Quellen', *Virchows Archiv f. path. Anat.*, XXXVII (1866), 351–410, at p.372.

[9] S. de Renzi, B. de Balzac and C. Daremberg (eds), *Flos medicinae Scholae Salerni*, IV, 3, art. 5, vv.1784–5; Brian Lawn, *The Prose Salernitan Questions* (Oxford 1979), 71-2.

[10] Bernardi Gordoni, *Opus Lilium medicinae*, VI, 7 (Lugduni 1550), p.560.

[11] Bartholomaeus Anglicus, *De proprietatibus rerum*, V, 41 (Argentor. 1491), sig. f3v.

[12] Konrad von Megenberg, *Buch der Natur*, I, 37 (ed. Fr. Pfeiffer, Stuttgart 1861), 30-1.

[13] *Opus Lilium medicinae*, VI, 7, pp.563-4.

[14] *Problemata Aristotelis* (incipit: 'omnes homines') (Cologne 1571), f.57r. Ebardus Bethuniensis, *Graecismus*, XII, 1.107, ed. J. Wrobel (Bratislaviae 1887), 186.

[15] Haly, Abbas, *Liber totius medicinae* (Lugduni 1523), f.40r; *Liber Pantegni*, theorice, III, 30, in *Opere Ysaac*, f.13v.

[16] Hieronymus Cardanus, *Synesiorum somniorum omnis generis insomnia explicantes*, I, 14 (Basil. 1585), 27.

[17] Caspar Bauhinus, *Theatrum anatomicum auctum ad morbes accommodatum*, I, 43 (Francof. 1621), 141.

[18] William Harvey, *Praelectiones anatomiae universalis*, 1616 seq. (London 1886), f.33v; G. Whitteridge, *The Anatomical Lectures of William Harvey* (Edinburgh and London 1964), 126-7.

In the anatomies of Columbus (1559)[19] and Sal. Alberti (1589),[20] the comparison of the spleen with a sponge continued. Already in 1543, Andreas Vesalius had pointed to the eminently absorptive function of the spleen, attributable to its rich endowment with vessels. He thought that could explain the popular belief that the spleen was the 'author of laughter'. By attracting away thick, faeculent, and sordid blood, it left the rest of the blood more agile, as if it were gladdened, 'as universally believed'.[21] Thomas Bartholinus' anatomical textbook summarised the matter thus in 1641: the spleen attracted the thick parts of the chyle, and rendered blood pure and lustrous. Hence it was possible to concede the ancient opinion that the spleen was the seat of laughter. Animals with large spleens were cheerful.[22]

It was not directly, but through a side-effect, then, that 'the spleen laughs'. Gordon had already noted that in this it differed from the heart, from which issued wrath, superiority, and wisdom in direct fashion. The *Problemata* held the effect of the spleen to be *valde naturaliter* although indirect. The anatomist Laurentius compared it in 1600 to wheat emerging sweeter and 'happier' from fertile crops surrounded by lupines, which attracted away the bitterness of the soil. The spleen similarly rendered the blood purer and brighter, replacing melancholia by a happy mood and laughter.[23]

The attitude of Paracelsus (1493-1541) is of particular interest. One would hardly expect him to have missed the 'laughing spleen' as a tempting humoralist target, to be demolished by abuse and derision. In fact, in an early treatise he adopted a humoralist stance, although he stood the traditional doctrine on its head: the spleen is concerned not with laughter, but with weeping. Weeping, he says, is 'constipation of the spleen' (*weinen ist ein constipaz in milz*).[24] He argued, moreover, against distinct location of an emotion in the spleen, finding 'spleenishness' (*miltikeit*), which is expressed in cheerfulness, or sorrow, or wrath, as being present 'materially throughout the body'.[25]

Apparently in his later writings Paracelsus had rejected the humoralistic designation of the spleen as the 'chair' (*stuhl*) of black bile.[26] He did not consider the spleen an essential organ, since he stated that it could surgically be removed with impunity. He followed tradition in this opinion. Pliny had mentioned animals which survived spleenless.[27] Caelius Aurelianus (4th century) spoke of surgical removal of the spleen, but doubted it had

[19] Realdus Columbus, *De re anatomica* (1559), XI, 7 (Francof. 1593), 425.
[20] Salomon Alberti, *Historia plerarumque partium humani corporis* (Vitebergae 1585).
[21] Andreas Vesalius, *De corporis humani fabrica*, V, 9 (Basil. 1543), 514.
[22] *Caspari Bartholini Institutiones anatomicae auctae a Thoma Bartholino* (Lugduni Bat. 1641), 100; Thomas Bartholinus, *Anatomia reformata* (Hagae Comit. 1655), 109; Vopiscus Fortunatus Plempius, *Fundamenta medicinae*. Ed. altera (Lovanii 1644), II, 133.
[23] Andreas Laurentius, *Historia anatomica* (1600), VI, 21 (Francof. 1602), 480, 487.
[24] Paracelsus, *Buch der Geberung der empfintlichen Dinge in der Vernunft*, 4, *Samtl. Werke*, I, Abteilg. ed. K. Sudhoff (München 1922-33), I, 280.
[25] Paracelsus, *Drei Bücher der Wundarznei Bertheonei*, II, Vorrede, ed. Sudhoff, VI, 107.
[26] Paracelsus, *Praelectiones chirurgicae de vulneribus*, ed. Sudhoff, V, 346.
[27] Plinius, *Naturalis historia*, XI, 80 – possibly the basis for *Talmud*, Chulin III, 2 and Sanhedrin 21b: sprinting improved after splenectomy; Preuss, *Biblisch-Talmudische Medisin*, 249.

ever been performed.[28] By the seventeenth century, splenectomy was a standard item in medical literature. Riolan (1618, 1626),[29] Harvey,[30] Fludd (1623),[31] and George Thomson (1656)[32] thus discussed it. Riolan denied the traditional role of the spleen in melancholia, and its production of black bile or any other acid juice. He did not believe that splenectomy had ever been performed. The most trustworthy report of such an operation seems to be that of Rousset (1590): no doubt was possible, he said, as to the performance of successful splenectomy in animals.[33]

It was a root and branch destruction of ancient and contemporary humoralism that was intended by Jean Baptist van Helmont (1579-1644). His work marks a water-shed in the story of the 'laughing spleen'. In fact, the spleen smiles on van Helmont, too – but how different is his conception from the classical one! The spleen is for him the *Duumvir* who, together with the stomach, enshrines the vital principle, the *Archeus* of the organism. It provides the acid juice, the ferment, that enables the stomach to take the initial and final decisions in digesting and admitting what is wholesome and rejecting what is not. This decision is a matter of life and death for the organism. It is the spleen that is highly vascularised. It bears that miraculous network of vessels (*rete mirabile*) which Galen had wrongly located at the base of the brain, and gives the brain superiority over other organs. Vesalius had pointed out Galen's error, and van Helmont now claimed for the spleen that which Galen had claimed for the brain. The brain received impulses from the spleen, conferring upon it the power of associating percepts through imagination and fantasy. That constituted the intuitive and subconscious 'knowledge' which underlay reflex action and the promptness and accuracy of the lutanist's instrumental play. The spleen actively 'creates' sleep – sleep is not privation of wakefulness, but a real and positive state. Indeed, all our subconscious dream-life and psychic activity derive from the vital principle in the *Duumvirate* of spleen and stomach. Those functions were not due to vapours or humours, nor did impulses of this kind travel through preformed anatomical canals. They took place by 'Nod of Command' or 'Word of Power', or a 'mere look' (*solo aspectu*). No explanation involving a quality, such as cold or warm, or humoral mixture, could ever approach the mystery of 'Action by Regimen'.[34]

Van Helmont advanced the most extreme claims for the spleen. He seems alone in the history of physiological doctrine in enthroning it as the central authority in the organism. Yet it is possible to find a precedent. The *Talmud* was referred to earlier in this paper, and we must revert to it. In a Mishnaic

[28] Caelius Aurelianus, *On Acute Diseases and on Chronic Diseases*, III, 61 (in chronic diseases), ed. I. E. Drabkin (Chicago 1950), 150.
[29] Joh. Riolanus, *Anthropographia et osteologia*, II (Paris 1618), 229-30; ibid. (Paris 1626), 217.
[30] Harvey, *Praelectiones anatomiae universalis*, f.35r.
[31] Robert Fludd, *Anatomiae amphitheatrum* (Francof. 1623), 101 – in a dog.
[32] Charles Webster, 'The Helmontian George Thomson and William Harvey. The application of splenectomy to physiological research', *Medical History*, XV (1971), 154–67.
[33] Franciscus Roussetus, *Hysterotomotokias i.e. Caesarii partus assertio historiologica* (Paris 1590), 153–4; E. Gurlt, *Geschichte der Chirurgie*, III (Berlin 1898), 722-3.
[34] Joh. Bapt. Van Helmont, *Jus duumviratus*, I, *Opera* (Francof. 1682), 285, and ibid., XXXII, 292.

microcosmic schedule, the spleen is presented as the central regulator in the human body, the *nemosin*, i.e. corresponding to what the laws (*nomoi*) are in the greater world.[35] The ancients had held no such exalted conceptions of the spleen. They relegated that organ to the position of a garbage-bin. Plato had already assigned to the spleen the task of purging impurities arising in the region of the liver. Its loose texture allows it to form cavities that contain no blood. Hence, when filled with impure residues, it swells. When the body is purged, the spleen subsides again to its original size.[36] Galen proceeds further along the same lines. The spleen produces black bile and removes a surplus of that acid excremental humour which can interfere with gastric digestion. Just as the kidney has the inborn power to attract urine, so the spleen is endowed with a force drawing black bile (*helktikē dynamis symphytos melancholikēs*), a *vis insita*. When the organ attracts less melancholic humour than normal, and the blood waxes impure, the entire body assumes an unhealthy colour, the blood thickening and growing darker.[37]

Van Helmont was angrily scornful of Galen's black bile. It was a humoralist fiction, or, at best, a base excremental residue incapable of any function, let alone a process of such dignity and significance as gastric digestion.[38] In van Helmont's opinion, and that of other advocates of acid digestion such as the experimentalist J. Walaeus (1645), the stomach receives acid from the spleen.[39] To van Helmont, this was a vital 'ferment' of high spiritual rank, added to the acid generated in the stomach-wall. It was the true digestive agent. Galen, by contrast, had claimed that function for heat and gave an auxiliary and often harmful role to his 'excremental' black bile from the spleen.[40]

Apart from its physiological functions, the singularly elevated position given to the spleen in van Helmont's philosophy is due to his location therein of the site at which the divine in man, his mind (*mens*), communicates with the vital principle, the *Archeus*.[41] The principle was bound up with matter, that is, with 'empty' water, from which all things were generated. It gave a specific 'disposition' to water. It made possible the emergence from it of individual objects and persons, and accounted for their specific differences. It is active-matter with a psychic and a somatic aspect that is integral and not an addition of one to the other – a monistic (Leibnizian) rather than a dualistic (Cartesian) conception. Although a product of creation, it is far removed from the Creator. That He, the Father of Lights, should send His light directly into the lower soul (*Archeus*) signals beatific joy and heavenly bliss (*risus ex nexu duplicis animae*). The light is received in the spleen, where the

[35] Aboth R. Nathan, 31, 3; Preuss, *Biblisch-Talmudische Medisin*, 112.
[36] Plato, *Timaeus*, 72c.
[37] Galen, *De naturalibus facultat.*, II, 9, ed. Kuhn, II, 132-3.
[38] Van Helmont, *Scholarum humorist. passiva deceptio*, I, 78; II, 169-70.
[39] Van Helmont, *Jus duumviratus*, VIII, 286; W. Pagel, 'Van Helmont's ideas on gastric digestion and the gastric acid', *Bulletin of the History of Medicine*, XXX (1956), 524-36; Joh. Walaeus, 'Epistolae duae de motu chyli et sanguinis', in T. Bartholinus, *Institutiones anatomicae* (Lugd. Bat. 1645), 446. W. Pagel, *New Light on William Harvey* (Basel 1976), 115-17.
[40] Van Helmont, *Jus duumviratus*, VIII, 286.
[41] Ibid., LX, 296.

vital principle is sited.[42] That is why it is to man alone that laughter is given. It furnishes another weighty reason for denying the description of man as merely an *animal rationale*. In promulgating that conception the heathen schools failed to understand the true and divine *intellectus*, the *spiritus abstractus*, of which man partakes. He partakes in it since his is a *spiritus concretus*, and this sets him apart from other creatures. Unlike them, he is not to be ranged in the category of bodies; he derives his denomination and definition from the divine Spirit and Light of the Intellect.[43]

There is, then, a place in van Helmont's philosophy for the 'laughing spleen'. The spleen smiles upon him from the most exalted possible position. He is the recipient of divine illumination. It is the purely spiritual *intellectus*, which has no dealings with *ratio* – with the operations of Peripatetic syllogism and lower reasoning which could admirably be performed by many animals such as foxes and bees.[44] The old adage, *splen ridere facit*, is placed in a totally new perspective by van Helmont. For more than a millennium it formed an article of the humoralist creed and system. Now it was formulated in a theosophic version. Its 'materialistic' explanation in terms of humours, qualities and complexion is replaced by the quest for the invisible spirit, for the 'Inner man', for what was divine in man. That was typical of the way in which van Helmont transformed topics of natural philosophy, of science and medicine, into theosophical speculation; and it explains why it is difficult to find a clear historical precedent for his novel conception. He could not have known the Gnostic lore enshrined in the alchemical-hermetic Leyden Papyrus: God, the Creator, 'laughed' seven times, 'cha-cha', at successive stages of the creation.[45]

In van Helmont's time and even more after him the spleen came to be divested of its humoralist attributes. Black bile was regarded with scepticism, especially its supposed origin in and transmission from liver to spleen. Harvey's long-standing adversary, Jean Riolan the younger (1577-1657), had judiciously and persistently denied the sponge-like anatomical form ascribed to the spleen as an organ eminently fitted to absorb black bile. He stated that the spleen could not be the seat and container of the 'melancholic humour' (1618, 1626).[46] He also doubted the production and conveyance of acid to the stomach by the spleen. That was, on the other hand, firmly believed by van Helmont[47] and even by Johannes Walaeus (1604-49),[48] the first to confirm experimentally the circulation of the blood. Nevertheless, it was Walaeus' experiments with vascular ligatures that enabled him definitively to dispose of all theories based on transmission of humours, blood, or chyle, from liver to spleen. That applied particularly to 'atrabilious excrement'. Nor was it

[42] Ibid.
[43] *Venatio scientiarum* (ibid., LXIV, 31).
[44] Ibid., XXIV, 34.
[45] M P. E. Berthelot, *Collection des ancients Alchemistes Grecs* (Paris 1887), I, 19; Albert Dietrich, *Abraxas* (Leipzig 1891), 23.
[46] Joh. Riolanus, *Anthropographia et osteologia*, II, 21 (1618), 229-30; (1626), 217.
[47] J. B. Van Helmont, *Jus duumviratus*, VIII, 286.
[48] Walaeus, 'Epistolae duae', 446.

true that blood was formed in the spleen from black bile and chyle. Experimental evidence showed that all blood came to the spleen through the splenetic artery, not by the portal vein, the reputed carrier of black bile from the liver. The blood was, rather, drained away through the portal vein. However, the spleen *was* 'black and acid'. It was responsible for the provision of gastric acid and likely to extract it from the heart-blood transmitted by the arteries. Apart from being a receptacle, similar to the gall-bladder, the spleen acted like a chemist who separated acid spirits from solid material.[49]

Walaeus published these findings when van Helmont had been dead for over a year (1645), and three years before the first printing of his works (1648). There was a distinct anti-humoralist tenor to Walaeus' work and an appreciation of the spleen which rescued it from its traditional humiliating position as a garbage-bin (*cloaca*). Though far removed from van Helmont's theosophical restatement of the splenetic problem and its smiling aspect, Walaeus' sober and progressive account has important features in common with the equally sober observational and chemical knowledge which van Helmont's religious and theosophical 'liabilities' did not prevent him from contributing.[50]

The 'smiling spleen' epitomises ancient and traditional humoralism. Our expectations of its demolition by the most implacable adversary of humoralism, van Helmont, are disappointed. Yet it is by no means as a relic of tradition that the idea retains its place in van Helmont's work. It is utterly transformed in accordance with his programme for reforming medicine. The spleen is raised from its Cinderella-status to the position of equal sharer, as *Duumvir* together with the stomach, of central authority in the organism. Nexus of his two souls, *mens* and *Archeus*, the 'smiling spleen' now became the supreme symbol of the joy vouchsafed to man alone among creatures, enshrining the light that comes to him from the Father of Lights.

---

[49] Ibid., 447-8, 459-60, 470.

[50] Those wishing to pursue our subject further might consult Nicander Jossius Venafranus, *On Pleasure and Pain, On Laughter and Weeping, On Sleep and Wakefulnes, On Hunger and Thirst* (Rome 1580), a lone protest against the Renaissance orthodoxy, and a work published in the second edition of Jossius' work (Frankfurt 1603): the 'Most Elegant and Useful Dialogue on Laughter, its Causes and Effects', by Antonius Laurentius Politianus (on whom see Jöcher, *Gelehrten-Lexicon*, III (1751), 1663).

8

Arthur Hall, Lord Burghley and the Antiquity of Parliament

G. R. Elton

The sad story of the conflicts, in 1576 and 1581, between Arthur Hall, burgess in Parliament for the Lincolnshire borough of Grantham, and the House of Commons is not unfamiliar, but especially Hall's downfall on the second occasion has not yet been properly investigated. At first sight it might seem to be no more than the minor tale of personal misfortune and thin-skinned members of the House which has been told before.[1] However, as one looks more closely, some hitherto unnoticed details emerge which by throwing light on Elizabethan politics and political notions justify another account of the case.

Hall first drew adverse attention to himself in the session of 1572 when, contrary to the temper of the House, he opposed the petition for the execution of the Duke of Norfolk and thus became something of a marked man, especially for that busy parliamentary hand, Thomas Norton. In the next session (1576) he added to his offence by trying to use the parliamentary privilege of freedom from arrest for his private advantage. An old quarrel between himself and one Melchisedech Mallory had involved an assault as a result of which his servant Edward Smalley was assessed for damages, to the tune of £100, in the court of London's Recorder, William Fleetwood. To escape payment, Smalley got himself arrested and then released by privilege, in order to bar the judgment. The House outmanoeuvred Hall by recommitting Smalley to the Tower, an action which protected the privilege but nullified its effect. In the end Hall had to find the £100 to free Smalley and, furiously angry at what he regarded as biased proceedings, put the whole affair on record in a tract written some time after the end of the 1576 session and sent to the printer. It was this product of let-off steam that provoked the troubles of 1581.

Hall's pamphlet[2] consisted of two really separate pieces:

[1] H. G. Wright, *The Life and Works of Arthur Hall of Grantham, Member of Parliament, Courtier and first Translator of Homer into English* (1919), 68–75; J. E. Neale, *Elizabeth I and Her Parliaments, 1559-1581* (1953), 407–10; S. E. Lehmberg, *Sir Walter Mildmay and Tudor Government* (1964), 183–5.

[2] Only one copy survives, in the Grenville Library now in the British Library (G.5524). The tract was reprinted in *Miscellanea Antiqua Anglicana* (for Richard Triphook, 1816), and since this reprint is more readily available it will here be used for the text. In all subsequent citations of this or any other document I have modernised the spelling.

A letter sent by F.A. touching the proceedings in a priuate quarrel and vnkindnesse, betweene Arthur Hall and Melchisedeche Mallerie Gentlemen, to his very friende L.B. being in Italy. VVith an admonition to[3] the Father of F.A. to him being a Burgess of the Parliament, for his better behauiour therin.

Though the two parts were signed through separately, there is no doubt that they were printed and published together, as contemporary comment, for instance in the rebuttal drafted in the circle of Sir Walter Mildmay,[4] confirms. Yet the two 'letters' concerned themselves with very different issues. The first is an account – vigorous and fascinating, with much splendid use of language – of the whole Mallory-Smalley affair: Hall's side of the story, though not quite as partisan as this sounds. The second essay contains reflections on the nature and antiquity of Parliament, with a long and not always courteous analysis of the qualities requisite in a member of the House of Commons. It makes no reference at all to the business of 1576.

As the Commons later pointed out, the book carries the name of neither author nor printer. The printer, in fact, was one Henry Bynneman, a member of the Stationers' Company who held various printing privileges.[5] The book also bears no date, but the first part, pretending to be a real letter, is dated 19 May 1576, two months after the end of the session it describes. This therefore will be the genuine date for the composition of part one, the other being written later; and there is no doubt that the pamphlet was printed later still. In his testimony before the Commons' committee Bynneman mentioned that Hall had received six copies of it in the last Michaelmas term (1580) and six in the Michaelmas term before that,[6] but those copies of 1579 were produced only after Hall had told his printer that the Privy Council raised no objection to the copies already printed.[7] Hall engaged the Council's attention in September-November 1579, and although the matter then at issue arose out of a different quarrel (with the Bishop of Lincoln) mention was made of a book of Hall's on which a little earlier the Council had pronounced.[8] Thus most probably the Council had the *Letter to F.A.* before them in the middle of 1579, and most probably it was printed in the spring of that year.

The Parliament, of course, could not turn its attention to the affair until it met again, on 16 January 1581, and even then it took more than two weeks before the blow fell. On 2 February, Thomas Norton reported the allegedly libellous book to the House and offered the conjecture that it had been written by Hall. Two Councillors joined in. Mr Secretary Wilson conveyed the information that Hall had admitted his authorship before the Council, and Sir Walter Mildmay, Chancellor of the Exchequer, described the book's

---

[3] *Sic.* The reprint silently and convincingly emends to 'by'.

[4] Northamptonshire Record Office, MS.F(M)P.112; see below, p.92.

[5] W. W. Greg (ed.), *A Companion to Arbor* (1967), 22, 26, 34, 44. Bynneman's responsibility was discovered by the House of Commons (*Commons Journals*, hereafter *C.J.*, I, 122-3).

[6] Thomas Cromwell's Parliamentary Diary (Trinity College Dublin, MS.N.2.12; hereafter Cromwell Diary), f.104. The testimony of the scrivener and his man (*C.J.*, I, 122-3) throws light on the complex processes involved in book production.

[7] *C.J.*, I, 125.

[8] *Acts of the Privy Council*, XI, 293, 306, 313, 326-7.

contents as 'dangerous and lewd'. It was resolved that the Serjeant-at-Arms should arrest Hall, and a committee was appointed to examine the printer.[9] On the 6th, when both the printer and Hall were examined at the bar, Hall's behaviour was insufficiently subdued to please his adversaries. The Commons greatly enlarged the committee of enquiry which sat on the 13th; on the 14th, its chairman, Sir Christopher Hatton, Vice-chamberlain, reported its findings. Hall was declared guilty of a serious breach of both privilege and decorum, and his punishment was pronounced in several resolutions. He was to be imprisoned in the Tower for at least six months until he had made a full and acceptable submission to the House, was to be fined 500 marks (the money going to the Queen), and was to be expelled the House for the duration of the present Parliament. Hall appeared once more in the record: on 18 March, the day of the prorogation, it was agreed that, since Hall had not yet submitted, further action should be left to a committee of Privy Councillors who were to report in the next session.[10]

On the face of it, therefore, the case appears to be precisely what it has usually been taken to be. Angered by a publication which had revealed the secret proceedings of Parliament, had criticised a number of members (especially Speaker Bell, since dead) for their activities in 1576, had questioned the antiquity of the Commons' share in the authority of Parliament, and had by implication suggested that many members were less than fit to sit in the House, the Commons had spontaneously and unanimously quashed the offender, creating in the process some valuable precedents for their own juridical power over their members. The lead had been taken by that notoriously independent, indeed oppositionist, burgess, Thomas Norton, who disliked Hall on grounds of religion, but even some who in 1572 had stood up for Hall now joined in the hunt against him. Few cases in the reign of Elizabeth display a more unitedly affronted and determined House of Commons, acting by its own will and from within its own precinct: and that is the impression left by Neale's account.

Yet there are some fairly obvious puzzles in it all. If Norton really felt that the dignity of the House had been so badly affronted by a book published nearly two years earlier (if indeed it was ever actually published in more than a technical sense), why did he allow more than two weeks to elapse before he raised the matter? This delay contradicts Neale's conviction that both Norton and the Commons were anxious to get at Hall. Those two weeks witnessed a quarrel with the Queen over the Commons' proposal for a political fast,[11] and it would have been well in accord with Tudor managerial practices if Arthur Hall had been used tactically to take the House's mind off its defeat in that business. If this is what happened, the appearance of spontaneous anger becomes less convincing.

The record in the Commons Journal also raises difficulties. The entry on 14 February narrates the day's proceedings, from Hatton's speech to the last

---

[9] None of the committees appointed in this affair appears to reflect any significant selection or bias.
[10] C.J., I, 122-3, 125-7, 136; Cromwell Diary, f.104.
[11] Neale, 378-82.

esolution of the House, ending with the words: 'And so it was afterwards drawn into form, read to the House, and entered by the clerk, in haec verba, viz.'[12] There follows exactly the same matter once more, in the form of a report (the information laid before the House, the details of the investigation, finally the resolutions) which repeats much of the first part verbatim. Probably this formal record, though placed on the right day in the fair copy of the Journal, was not put before the House until the last day of the session (18 March) when a member recorded that 'this day was an order penned read in the House concerning Mr Arthur Hall and allowed of the House'.[13] To judge by appearances, therefore, the House on 14 February arrived unprompted at the orders for Hall's conviction and punishment, the Clerk then drawing up the record and presenting it for approval at a later date. However, there exists a perfect draft of that record, now found among the Burghley papers and headed with the date 13 February, the day on which the committee investigated Hall.[14] Who then drew up the decisions of the House? Did the resolutions of the 14th first get formulated that day or were they in fact produced in the committee? Burghley's possession of the draft, while it does not necessarily indicate any responsibility in the Lord Treasurer himself, assuredly implies an involvement of the Privy Council. Thus the location of the draft tentatively suggests that the Councillors on the committee rather than the Commons as a House were responsible for the decisions taken, while its date strongly suggests that on the 14th the House received not only a report on what had happened but also in effect instructions on what to do about it. Who was after Hall?

The Council's activity throughout the business calls for investigation. As we have seen, they had probably examined the book in the summer of 1579 but the order then issued cannot have been hostile to it. After it had been made, Hall told his printer that he could go ahead, and copies were produced about which no one troubled himself for some eighteen months. Bynneman printed a small stock and distributed some of it, before stopping because he wanted to see payment first.[15] Thus, whatever may have been said at the Council Table when Hall admitted his authorship, and despite the fact that the investigation by itself proves some objections to book and author, no action resulted: in 1579 the Council did not home in on Hall. Yet when the matter came up in Parliament in 1581, Councillors quickly took the lead, with Wilson in effect putting the case against Hall, Mildmay backing him up, and Hatton chairing the committee which attended to him. Were these Councillors acting simply as conscientious members of the House?

There was certainly some personal animus involved. According to Hall himself, he and Wilson had at one time been on good terms, but this ended

[12] *C.J.*, I, 125–7.
[13] Cromwell Diary, f.114v.
[14] British Library, Lansdowne MS.31, ff41v–52r. The date as given reads Tuesday, 13 February, though the day was actually a Monday.
[15] *C.J.*, I, 122–3. There was some conflict over numbers printed. Bynneman said that he produced some eighty or a hundred of which twelve had been sent to Hall; Hall claimed that he had only ever received one, knew nothing of the stock, but was willing to have it destroyed if the House demanded that.

in 1576 when Wilson voted for Smalley's committal to the Tower.[16] Mildmay, so far as the evidence goes, took the most trouble over the affair. Among his papers there survives a long analysis and confutation of Hall's discourse on the antiquity of Parliament, written in the hand of his secretary (his son–in–law William Fitzwilliam).[17] It is most unlikely that this paper could have been produced in the middle of a busy session; surely it was written earlier, probably when Mildmay first encountered Hall's pamphlet during the Council's investigation of 1579. The dating is supported by the fact that Mildmay's counterblast ignored those offensive revelations about the 1576 session which became the burden of the charge against Hall in the Commons. Apparently, therefore, he had at once, in 1579, taken exception to Hall's scepticism touching the antiquity of Parliament, but, finding himself frustrated by the Council's unwillingness to take action, had to wait until the next Parliament to demonstrate his disgust.

However, Wilson and Mildmay had not been the first movers: that role belonged to Thomas Norton. Norton and Hall were certainly enemies: even the *Letter to F.A.* makes this plain. It may be (as has been held) that Norton, supposedly a puritan, resented one who according to himself respected the old religion,[18] but this would not appear to have been the reason most obvious to Hall himself. As he told the story, he discovered during Smalley's troubles that he had run foul of a much more easily identified interest: after the jury's verdict against his man he used strong language 'of his trusty and well spoken friends the Londoners' and regretted 'the defences to his ability he hath made in all places where anything was spoken to their rebuke'.[19] It is certainly the case that right through these conflicts he found himself running up against Norton, the Lord Mayor's Remembrancer, and Fleetwood, the City's Recorder in whose court Smalley had been tried. When first the possibility was mentioned that Smalley had behaved deviously, Norton started hot on the trail and Fleetwood promptly joined in; and it was Fleet–wood who in 1576 introduced an abortive bill to confirm the judgment against Smalley and to expel Hall from the House for his share in the deceit – five years before this was actually done.[20] Thus there are some broad hints that the hunting of Arthur Hall sprang from motives linked to the obscure politics of the City.

City politics, however, do not adequately explain Norton's role, any more than does his personal dislike of one who perhaps leant to Rome. In Neale's picture of these Parliaments, Norton appeared as an independent, a puritan, and a frequent leader of opposition to Queen and Council. However, we now

[16] *Letter to F.A.*, 34–5.

[17] Northants Record Office, MS.F(M)P.112 (unfoliated). For Fitzwilliam's role see Lehmberg, *Mildmay*, 313.

[18] Norton was passionately anti-papist, whether or not that makes him the puritan partisan Neale held him to be. As for Hall, he explained that his enemy Mallory died 'leaning to the old father of Rome, a dad whom I have heard some say Mr. Hall doth not hate'; he also admitted to liking Father William Peto, that implacable opponent of Henry VIII's Divorce and later cardinal, though, as he put it, he doubted his cloth (*Letter to F.A.*, 21, 105).

[19] Ibid., 19.

[20] Ibid., 31, 41.

know that he was really one of the Council's most important men of business in the House and that his initiatives are always likely to have reflected the desires of the Council.[21] Thus his behaviour again draws attention to the reality behind the pretence. The whole affair was set up in the Commons by three interventions: Norton's first report of the book opened the campaign, Wilson's lengthy description firmly tied Hall into the story, and Mildmay's measured indignation defined the tone of the attack. This looks like the execution of a well-rehearsed plan. Hall's troubles must now look to have been manufactured for him in the Council, with his enemies there using the Commons against him after the Privy Council itself had failed to act on first seeing the book.

One further puzzle turns up a significant answer when resolved. Even though at the start of the Commons' investigation Hall shared the stage with Henry Bynneman, the printer, with Henry Shurland, the scrivener responsible for writing the fair copy delivered to the printer, and with one Welles, Shurland's man, who had scurried about between the other three, thereafter nothing more is heard of anyone except Hall himself. In the conditions of Elizabethan pamphleteering, a determined pursuit of an author which absolutely ignored his printer strikes one as very surprising. However: Norton, as counsel to the Stationers' Company and employed against unlicensed printers, had long been well versed in the politics of the printing trade. While the whole complex story is still being unravelled, a few relevant points have already emerged.[22] Thus in October 1582, in the course of his activities against John Wolf, a member of the Fishmongers' Company who was moonlighting as a printer, Norton included Bynneman in a list of those properly licensed to print.[23] He was unlikely to persecute a member of the trade of whom he expressly approved. More revealing still is a letter of the following January, from Norton to Hatton, in which Bynneman is described as Hatton's servant.[24] If the printer was a protégé of the chairman of the committee which dealt with Hall, his disappearance from the action becomes very explicable. The difference of treatment meted out also puts Hatton, with Wilson and Mildmay, among Hall's enemies on the Council, while the whole tenor of these proceedings confirms that we should look to Council politics if we wish to understand the truth about the assault on Hall.

Thus the Privy Council appears to have contained influential men who took the first opportunity to raise the Commons' hackles against Hall, yet it had done nothing itself in 1579. For Hall had his friend on the Council too, and that no less a person than Lord Treasurer Burghley. Their association went back to 1552 when William Cecil acquired the wardship of young Arthur Hall,[25] and true to his conscientious style he seems thereafter to have kept a

[21] M. A. R. Graves, 'Thomas Norton the Parliament Man: an Elizabethan M.P., 1559-1581', *Historical Journal*, XXIII (1980), 17-35.

[22] I am most grateful to M. A. R. Graves, who is investigating these matters as part of his study of Thomas Norton, for drawing my attention to this side of the story.

[23] Greg, *Companion to Arbor*, 24.

[24] British Library, Add. MS.15891, f.42. I owe this reference to Mr Graves.

[25] Hall was described as Cecil's ward as early as October 1552 (*Calendar of State Papers Domestic 1547-1580*, 46), though the patent did not issue until 12 May 1553 (*Calendar of Patent Rolls, Edward VI*, V, 136-7). The wardship yielded Cecil an annuity of £50.

soft spot in his heart for his difficult ward and a protective eye on his doings. Burghley's friendship is quite enough to account for Hall's immunity in the investigation of 1579, but the behaviour of those other Councillors in 1581 – in the Commons, where Burghley no longer sat – calls for a look at their relations with the Lord Treasurer. Wilson, an older man who was to die soon after the end of the 1581 session, belonged to the Earl of Leicester's faction on the Council and favoured the Earl's forward Protestant policy in the Low Countries, against Burghley.[26] Mildmay, the Lord Treasurer's professional assistant in Exchequer matters and his loyal ally in the faction struggles of the 1560s, had yet risen in office under Burghley's predecessor, was never really a Cecilian, and because of his puritan sympathies came to oppose the Alençon match, the chief issue dividing the Council in the years under consideration. Thus he stood with Leicester against Burghley.[27] Hatton, whose rise at court had not been exactly agreeable to the Lord Treasurer though their relations usually remained amicable on the surface, in 1579-81 also resented the Queen's dalliance with French suitors and favoured an aggressive foreign policy;[28] whether of Leicester's faction or not, he certainly at this time strengthened it on the Council. That is to say, all these three Councillors at this juncture opposed Burghley's support of the Queen's policy. As for Norton, who ordinarily had good relations with several Councillors, his closest tie at this point was to Hatton: unlike his formal letters to Burghley, his correspondence with the Vicechamberlain breathes an air of familiar friendship.[29] On the other hand Fleetwood, so eagerly active against Hall in 1576, took no part in the campaign of 1581 – and Fleetwood was very definitely Burghley's man. This would seem to clinch it: the real target for the Council group in pursuit of Hall was Hall's sole friend in high places, Burghley himself.

Burghley's friendly assistance came into the open in the later stages of the affair. The attack on Hall through the Commons had been sufficiently successful to get him imprisoned in the Tower and condemned to severe penalties. However, Parliaments came and went, and (as we have seen) the impending prorogation caused the enforcement of the condemnation to be remitted to a committee of all the Privy Councillors in the House. When they were appointed the Parliament was about to be prorogued, so that the demand for a report back made sense, but since that Parliament never met again, being after eighteen more prorogations finally dissolved in April 1583,[30] it proved easy to substitute for that committee of Councillors the Council itself in full session – with Burghley at the head of it. On 10 March 1581, after four weeks in the Tower, Hall decided to mobilise his patron.[31] Opening with the characteristic reflection that 'to the afflicted and wronged

[26] Thomas Wilson, *A Discourse upon Usury*, ed. R. H. Tawney (1925), 8-9.
[27] Lehmberg, *Mildmay*, esp. pp.157ff. For earlier relations see Wallace T. MacCaffrey, *The Shaping of the Elizabethan Regime* (1968), esp. pp.182, 200.
[28] E. St. J. Brooks, *Sir Christopher Hatton* (1946), 167ff. Cf. esp. Hatton's letter to Burghley, 26 Sept. 1580: H. Nicolas, *Memoirs of the Life and Times of Sir Christopher Hatton K.G.* (1847), 158-61.
[29] Cf. e.g., ibid., 161-2, 234-5, 242-3.
[30] Symonds D'Ewes, *The Journals of all the Parliaments during the Reign of Queen Elizabeth* (1682), 310.
[31] Lansdowne MS.31, f.114.

mind without remedy, complaint is some ease', he explained he was writing because he understood that Burghley was to be 'judge between the late dealings of the Lower House of Parliament and me'. Thus he knew of the remission to the Council eight days before the Commons formally ordered it, a detail which once again indicates who was really running things there. The chances are that it was Burghley himself who had decided to get the case thus transferred once the inconvenient Parliament was out of the way; certainly no one would have known the date of the coming prorogation sooner than he.

It would seem that Burghley had first hoped for an accommodation with the House, but this had proved impossible. In his letter, Hall related that after his imprisonment he had with difficulty obtained from the Speaker a copy of the articles compiled against himself and had at first intended to answer them in writing, no doubt in his customary unrepentant spirit. Reflecting, however, 'how my answers, my excuses and submission hath been always hitherto accepted of the House', he decided to wait 'till I might be heard by a more favourable judge'. Nevertheless, on the advice of 'my great and good friends (of the which your lordship is chief)', he had against his better judgment written 'a few lines' to the Speaker to test the opinion of the House, 'whether it remained as hardly bent towards me as it began'. That note the Speaker had on the 8th read to the House, at which point (so Hall had heard) 'there was some appearance of favour'. The House appointed a committee who, as he understood it, were to come to discuss those articles with him, though according to the Journal this new committee was left entirely free to do as they pleased about Hall's letter.[32] The message that in the end reached the prisoner testified to no relaxation of hostility: the House 'willed me to look to myself, for I should receive no such favour [of an interview to explain and answer the articles], and that I that made the book might find out what urged against me'. He felt sure that he could show that his alleged offence did not merit 'any such censure as they lay on me', but Burghley could see 'what profit I should have reaped if I had liberally submitted myself to them in writing when upon such a preparative as I have written so small fruit follows'. With this letter he sent a draft to the articles which does not survive.

So Hall would have to make his explanation to the Council, at which point Burghley took over: it was now he who guided Hall's mind, and indeed his pen, in preparing his submission. The draft, in Hall's own hand, was plentifully corrected and enlarged by Burghley in person, and the fair copy accepted all his emendations.[33] Many of these represented only verbal improvements, several of them tending to make Hall sound a little more respectful than at first he appeared. For instance, he had admitted that 'I did, being in some passion for mine own private cause, touch the Speaker and some other parties

---

[32] *C.J.*, I, 132.
[33] The draft is Lansdowne MS.31, ff.54–55v; the fair copy (ibid., ff.56–7) was written out by Hall's secretary (the scribe of the letter of 10 March). The interesting drafting history of the document was inexplicably muddled by Wright who claimed that Hall's draft had 'corrections in another hand' and that the copy was 'in Burghley's own handwriting' (Wright, *Arthur Hall*, 190, n.1). Perhaps he misread his own notes.

by name'; after Burghley's revision this emerged as 'use some speeches of the Speaker, whom otherwise I reverenced, and some other persons by name to whom I have no malice, though I was somewhat offended'. There are several such mollifying additions, but it is not they that mark the interest of Burghley's recension.

For what must strike one on reading the draft is that in effect Burghley made no real attempt to alter Hall's tone and general stance – the tone of an honest man carried by justified grievance into slightly over-hasty and un-fortunate speech and action, and the stance of one whose very particular allegations and complaints, arising out of his private affairs, had been unfairly interpreted as a general attack on the claims and doings of the Commons, or even on the validity of the law made in Parliament. On the contrary (Burghley's additions in brackets):

> I do from the bottom of my heart reverence the laws and proceedings in the Parliament (in both Houses and Council) and do allow of the ancient authority of that (Common) House wherein the third estate of the (whole) realm is duly represented.

Thus Burghley fully agreed with Hall that the Commons had exaggerated what had happened, an opinion supported by an actual reading of the pamphlet which is nothing like as provocative as had been pretended. The Lord Treasurer's longer additions enlarge rather than diminish Hall's claims to righteousness and show clearly on whose side Burghley was. One such inserted passage explains that Hall's mistakes were entirely venial: Hall was made to confess his fault only 'as far forth as in my conscience any ways I can be moved, knowing that to be true that the wisest may say, *hominis est errare*'. And where Hall had ended by asking that his words be ascribed 'rather to the passion of myself being grieved than to any intent of slander or infamy to any of them all', Burghley added a long and powerful peroration:

> And I require them and every of them to consider how easily many very wise men, yea men of age and experience, may err in speeches and writings uttered whilst their minds are grieved with their particular conceits touching themselves in credit and profit. Aye, though I know that my coming hither is not to pronounce anything against any person but against myself, yet in acknowledging mine own faults I do hope that some others, though very few, will not so condemn me as that they will not be content to enter into their own hearts or conscience to consider whether by some sharp speeches against me, as I did take them, I had not some cause to think hardly of them. But yet, howsoever any other might so seem to give me cause, yet I confess that I did not well in such a public sort to tax any for the same, but I know I ought to remember the saying of Almighty God, which says, *Mihi vindiciam*.

Thus the most defiant words in the submission as prepared came from Burghley, not from Hall, and it may not be fanciful to read in them the Lord Treasurer's answer to those fellow Councillors who had used Hall against him. However, further thoughts seem to have counselled caution: before the Council saw the document the whole passage after 'credit or profit' had disappeared, to be replaced by a few colourlessly conventional phrases:

By him who is most willingly ready to spend his ability and life in her majesty's service, and to his uttermost to maintain and pray for the prosperity of all her Highness' most honourable councillors and others the makers and judges of the laws of this realm.[34]

These words, too, have more of a ring of Burghley than of Hall.

The Council accepted the submission on 2 April, and Hall went free, long before the six months' minimum imposed by the House had elapsed. His fine, too, was remitted by the Queen, and since that Parliament never met again his expulsion had no consequences. Indeed, he was again elected for Grantham to the next Parliament, in 1584, though he delayed turning up (if ever in the end he came) and grew apprehensive that his enemies might reopen the whole affair by enquiring whether the earlier sentence had been carried out – and if not, why not.[35] No such move was made, and if it had been it would have failed, as one of Hall's enemies noted in due course – Thomas Cromwell the diarist, a member of every committee appointed in the business and chairman of the one which returned so dusty an answer to Hall's attempt to make peace. In 1587, collecting precedents for the arrest and release of members of the House, Cromwell listed 'Mr. Hall, committed to the Tower by order of the House and delivered by force of the general pardon'.[36] That is to say, Hall was allowed the benefit of the statute 23 Elizabeth I, c. 16, a benefit which effectively barred any further action against him for any alleged offence committed before the date of his pardon. We may well suppose that Burghley had procured this for him.

The Council had been the first to see the offending pamphlet; Councillors and their chief assistant had led the hunt in the Commons; the Council brought the affair to an end, and factious favour there rescued Hall, even as factious hostility had first got him into trouble. Even though obscure conflicts within the city of London and the readily roused *amour propre* of the House of Commons played their undoubted part in the story, the real origin of Hall's troubles evidently lay in the Privy Council. Like so many other parliamentary events in the reign of Elizabeth, the demolition and restoration of Arthur Hall reflected the politics of Council factions rather than strictly House of Commons matters. In the rash folly of Burghley's client, his opponents in the Council saw an opportunity to get at Burghley himself, for if Hall had had to suffer the punishment imposed by the House the loss of face would certainly have extended to his patron. Very possibly the fact that by attacking Hall the conciliar managers of the Commons got themselves out of an awkward situation at the start of a session which looked likely to turn difficult gave them their chance: Burghley could not well oppose a move, however tiresome to himself, which might bring peace between Queen and Commons. With admirable dexterity he had then saved Hall without causing positive offence in the Commons or exacerbating the feelings of his conciliar opponents.

[34] *Acts of the Privy Council*, XIII, 8–11.
[35] Hall to Burghley, 13 Dec. 1584 (Wright, op. cit., 193–4).
[36] P. L. Ward (ed.), *William Lambarde's Notes on the Procedures and Privileges of the House of Commons, 1584* (House of Commons Library Document no. 10), 90.

The Councillors got their chance also because the anger excited by Hall's book was not unreal. In 1601, Francis Bacon recalled that Hall was sent to the Tower because he had alleged 'that the Lower House was a new person in the Trinity',[37] and that vivid phrase – which was indeed Hall's[38] – has stuck in the memory. Neale held that of all the counts against Hall this was the one 'that stung deepest'.[39] Perhaps it did, and it is certainly true that when Norton opened the attack he complained not only of animadversions on individual members (which are to be found in the first part of Hall's pamphlet) but of general doubts cast on the authority of the House, a theme of the second part.[40] However, it looks as though he emphasised the former far more, and the articles which Hall extracted from the Speaker, as well as the formal record entered in the Journal, also concentrate on the offence committed in revealing the secrets of Parliament and in making personal attacks on members there. What therefore really stirred things up was Hall's reckless (though at this distance rather delightful) description of all that had happened over Smalley's Case in 1576. In his hostile analysis, Mildmay disallowed Hall's professions of good intent and concluded that it was the denial of antiquity to the Commons that constituted 'this lewd purpose and perilous practice thus maliciously published in print',[41] words which he repeated in the House; but in actual fact the attack concentrated more on the personal issues.

That first part of the book does indeed include a certain amount of angry disrespect directed at personal enemies, though – contrary to the allegations – it is hard to see that Hall had been particularly cutting about Robert Bell who at worst emerges as a man capable of bungling and changing his mind: a bit inefficient in executing his managerial role. Norton and Wilson come in for worse swipes. What that section does not display is enmity to the Parliament as such. Hall knew himself well enough and was capable of admitting his faults. The device of a fictitious author permitted a description of the real one: Hall, we are told, was possessed of 'a sensible tongue at will to utter his mind, no want of audacity, of sufficient courage, well disposed to liberality, loving and sure to his friend, secret where he is trusted', but also 'overweening of himself . . . furious when he is contraried, without patience to take time to judge or doubt the danger of the sequel . . . so implacable if he conceive an injury'.[42] His enemies might have wished to adjust the balance of this appraisal, but it was not a bemused one, nor does the tale of the quarrel with Mallory disguise the absurdities and follies of Hall's own behaviour. The tone of the pamphlet inclines one to its author – a frank and rather wry tone. As for Parliament, Hall opens with an earnest avowal of his pride in his place in the House ('I am a member of the grave, great and considerate council of the Parliament') and concludes with a special complaint that Mallory's

---

[37] *The Letters and Life of Francis Bacon*, III, ed. J. Spedding (1868), 37.
[38] *Letter to F.A.*, 78: a study of past legislation 'will dissuade the antiquity of our third voices, which many defend, and also will show a light of the admitting the third person in this trinity'.
[39] Neale, 407.
[40] *C.J.*, I, 122a.
[41] Northants. Record Office, MS.F(M)P.112, at end.
[42] *Letter to F.A.*, 3.

behaviour had contemptuously impeded 'the judgment of that High Court of Parliament': and both points were sincerely made.[43]

Hall thus did not despise Parliament; the charge was false. That makes the second part of his book, in some ways the less entrancing, the more profoundly important one. In it he considered the institution, its history and authority. In form an address of advice to a new member of the House – 'Son, forasmuch as I now have obtained for you my place in the Common House of Parliament' – it professes to teach him his proper bearing there and introduces that subject quite logically with a discussion of the kind of institution of which this tyro has now become a member. Whatever hidden purposes may be read into the analysis, the writer appears only anxious to understand the reasons for certain claims to political power which he himself accepts as rightly maintained in his own day, and he therefore considers the antiquity of Parliament's authority and the date from which he can demonstrate the Commons' share in it. With a precision exceptional in these debates, Hall had seized on the crucial point: he defined Parliament as a body that makes laws, and in tracking its antiquity he thus pursued the making of laws through English history. A survey of that history from Brutus to Henry III firmly disposes of any notion that something properly called a Parliament existed before the thirteenth century. While Hall admits to finding the term used in the chronicles, he rightly points out that these 'do rather use the word (as indeed it is proper where any conference is) than that it carries with it, where it comes, the same to be understood to be the great court of Parliament' as it has existed from Henry III's day to the present.[44] Such laws as were made before that time were made by kings, and if they took advice they got it from assemblies very different from genuine Parliaments. Even the assembly at Merton (1236), which he recognises as 'the first Parliament of name and record', should not be regarded as identical with 'a Parliament as now we use ours'.[45]

Hall thus evinced a grasp of historical context unusual among Elizabethan historians, let alone parliamentarians. Moreover, even after something really to be called a Parliament can at last be found, distinctions, he insists, must not be fudged. Though he accepts the existence of the institution from the reign of Henry III, he points out (correctly) that throughout the thirteenth century all laws continued to be enacted by the king's authority alone.[46] Like others since his time, he finds the presence of the commonalty first properly documented in the Statute of York (1322). Again in tune with more recent research, he emphasises that under Edward III parliamentary consent applied more particularly to taxation, but he is perhaps a little more strict than some modern successors when he argues that, whatever may be said about request or consent or advice, the documents clearly show that the law-making authority remained with the king alone. While he agrees that the authority of the whole Parliament is recorded by the time of Henry VII, he maintains that

[43] Ibid., 2, 45.
[44] Ibid., 61.
[45] Ibid., 63.
[46] Ibid., 63-7.

a real change to the present condition came only with the assembly of the Reformation Parliament in 1529; from that point he has no difficulty in recognising his own kind of Parliament 'held of the three estates, wherein the Commons were one'.[47]

Hall's history was really very good. He was right in holding that the making of laws 'by the authority of this present Parliament' (instead of by the king's authority, though made in the present Parliament) came about during the fifteenth century, though he postdated the event a little;[48] and he was right about the change which came over the institution in the 1530s when it assumed its Elizabethan – indeed, its modern – guise. Standing so near to the event, he could not properly work out what had happened under Henry VIII, but he pinpointed the critical date with surprising accuracy.

The rest of this second part of the pamphlet discusses the function of the Commons in a modern Parliament and deduces the qualities required for service in the House. In both respects Hall could hardly be faulted. He firmly rejected the possible charge that his historical review intended 'to disgrace that noble, grave and necessary third state of Parliament (which if I were so lewdly disposed I never were able to touch)', and he took care to demonstrate his loyalty to the Queen by praising her regard for Parliament. One of his most perceptive remarks touched the policy of the Tudors in this respect: 'What contented minds of late ages the kings and queens of this realm have carried in matters of Parliament, when things have not fallen out current to their expectations, I think not only all Parliament-men but the whole country knows.'[49] He demanded exceptional qualities in a member of the House, though his violent onslaught on any willing to serve outside interests there for a fee set standards of austerity beyond the possibilities of the scene.[50] No doubt it caused offence where it was intended to.[51] Otherwise, however, nothing that he said about the nature of the Elizabethan Parliament and the Commons' function in it could possibly distress the most slavish admirer of the institution. This song of praise sufficiently accounts for the fact that in trying to convict him of contempt his enemies had to concentrate on his report of Smalley's Case and exaggerate the offensiveness of his remarks there. Still, none of that praise could disguise the manner in which he had denied remote antiquity to the Parliament (dating it from about 1250 instead of the mists of time) and had reassessed the Commons' share in the legislative process (refusing to accept it as surely proven before the reign of Henry VII).

With these arguments Hall had entered into a current debate among scholars which had important meaning for the sense of self-importance

[47] Ibid., 74.

[48] Cf. my '"The body of the whole realm": Parliament and representation in medieval and Tudor England,' *Studies in Tudor and Stuart Politics and Government*, II, 19ff. (esp. p.29) for an analysis of these problems written long before I had occasion to read *Letter to F.A.* and based on the same principle that the constitutional position of Parliament needs to be assessed from an analysis of its law-making power.

[49] *Letter to F.A.*, 78-9.

[50] Ibid., 93-4.

[51] Mr Graves has rightly pointed out to me that in 1572 Norton was much attacked in the House precisely over this issue. Hall had his wicked moments.

common in Parliament, not to mention practical implications for anyone wanting to use the institution as an instrument for political action. The history of Parliament could not be confined to the concerns of pedants, and the debate about 'origins', active in Elizabeth's reign, was to endure for some time. Most contributors professed to find something justly called a Parliament almost as far back as they could reach. They usually achieved this by looking for assemblies called to give advice and naming every such meeting, however selective, a Parliament; what they entirely ignored was Hall's important emphasis on the making of laws and the authority behind them.[52] Hall was aware of the antiquaries: 'In reading, I have gathered many flowers out of Mr William Lambarde's garden, a gentleman, after my verdict, though unknown to me, for his painful, rare and learned collection worthy to be known.'[53] It is interesting that he should have seen Lambarde's notes on Parliament, which later appeared in his *Archeion* (1591), before 1579; since he had no acquaintance with the author and advised readers to look for themselves at what Lambarde had to say, we must suppose that those collections were generally available much earlier than is usually thought.[54]

Mildmay knew them too: he used them in trying to demolish Hall's attack on the ancient authority of Parliament. In the main his treatise was a point-by-point refutation of Hall's texts and arguments from the reign of Henry III onwards.[55] He convicted Hall of some over-rapid citation and of occasional tendentious compression; but because of his refusal to give weight to Hall's discovery of a principled line of argument (the authority by which laws are made), his attack missed its target and testified more to the rage of injured pride than the disagreements of scholars. Though he promised to consider the chronicle evidence for the existence of Parliament before the beginning of the statute book, evidence which Hall had comprehensively discarded, he never did so, contenting himself with a few rude remarks to the effect that Hall's analysis was too vague to merit examination. Mildmay added a hint that Hall's authority, Lambarde, in fact did not support him. Up to a point, this was true: in the *Archeion* Lambarde allows various pre-Conquest assemblies back to the days of Ine to have been law-making parliaments.[56] On the other hand, being an honest antiquary, he could not discover any indication of the three estates before the days of King John and felt much happier once he could rely on the statute book; it was manifestly this section,

---

[52] Cf. the essays printed in T. Hearne, *Curious Discourses* (1771), I, 281-309, which shows such views being expressed by eminent antiquaries like Francis Tate, Arthur Agard, and even William Camden. John Hooker, in 1572, reprinted the medieval *Modus Tenendi Parliamentum* under the impression that it described Parliament in the days of Edward the Confessor: *Parliament in Elizabethan England: John Hooker's 'Order and Usage'*, ed. Vernon F. Snow (1977), 125.

[53] *Letter to F.A.*, 75.

[54] His biographer, citing no evidence, says that Lambarde began to work on the *Archeion* 'at least as early as 1579' (Retha M. Warnicke, *William Lambarde – Elizabethan Antiquary* (1973), 84). Hall's testimony would support this conjecture and even permit thoughts of a markedly earlier date since by 1579 at the latest Lambarde's notes on Parliament must have been circulating in a reasonably finished form.

[55] Northants. Record Office, MS.F(M)P.112.

[56] William Lambarde, *Archeion*, ed. C. H. McIlwain and P. L. Ward (1957), 129-33.

from the Statute of Merton onwards, that was used by Hall.[57]

Hall's achievement, hidden because buried in a virtually vanished polemical tract, must be accounted notable. Rather than piling up cases of general assemblies back to Lucius or even Brutus in a desire to give the Parliament the desirable accolade of immemorial existence, he endeavoured to establish criteria by which to define the institution and then to trace back their historical existence; and he set them out. Perhaps he was moved by consider-ations less worthy than scholarly truth – a mischievous desire to puncture the pretensions of self-important men who had ill-treated him – but this hardly matters, except to show that dubious motives can produce good learning. As he saw it, the Parliament of his day was to be defined by three characteristics. It consisted of the three estates of prince, lords and commons – a very important definition which had only recently displaced the opinion that the king was no part of Parliament whose three estates comprised the spirituality, the nobility and the commons.[58] Secondly, only Parliament had

> power to deprive the subjects of this land of life, lawful inheritance, or goods. The authority thereof doth stretch to them all, to take away life, inheritance, yea of the crown of this realm, and every man's chattels, and hath full power to make and alter laws.

Thirdly, therefore, the authority of Parliament consists in its exclusive power to make law.[59] By tracing back these characteristics – the three estates, omnicompetence, and the authority behind the laws made – the proper antiquity of Parliament could be discovered.

That still remains the sole sound method for solving this particular his-torical question, and it still produces very much the answer pronounced by Hall. He made his mistakes: even allowing for the limited materials available to him – chronicles and the statutes from Magna Carta onwards – one may accuse him of hasty and sometimes slipshod research, though one must be impressed by the consistency with which he applied his defined criteria to the evidence he used. In the result, he dated both the parliamentary authority of law-making and the arrival of the Commons' House a little too late, as Mildmay was not slow to point out, though Hall certainly came much nearer the truth than did Mildmay and all the other believers in immemorial antiquity. Hall made his minor mistakes partly, no doubt, because they suited his polemical purpose, but partly because he so well realised the importance of the ultimate emergence, in the reign of Henry VIII, of the kind of Parliament familiar to him at first hand that he discounted partial moves in that direction during the previous century and a half. Conscious of a revolu-tionary moment in the 1530s, he underplayed the prehistory of the revolution.

[57] Ibid, 136–40.
[58] Cf. my *Studies*, II, 32-5. This opinion, the modern commonplace, was accepted by Mildmay in F(M)P.112, at the start ('our Parliament is a public assembly of the three estates, viz. the prince, nobility and commons of the realm') and endorsed in 1584 by Burghley who declared that the Commons and Lords were two members of the Parliament, and the Queen, its head, the third: 'of these three estates doth consist the whole body of the Parliament able to make laws' (D'Ewes, *Journals*, 350).
[59] *Letter to F.A.*, 80-1.

Well, that can happen to us all, and in all essentials Hall was right.

Thus Arthur Hall, difficult, choleric and often tiresome, was not just an 'egregious' person given to wonted pigheadedness – a man (it has been claimed) who, even though his history may have been better than his opponents', deserved his fate because he crossed the men whose devotion to Parliament heralded the future.[60] He did get into trouble with needless ease and, as he himself recognised, once in it would not again extricate himself while any sense of grievance remained. Like others of Burghley's wards he must have been a sore trial to that father of his country. At a later date, further soured by his experiences in a truly ridiculous pursuit of the widowed Countess of Sussex, Hall was to turn against his patron,[61] but in 1581 he relied on him and had cause to thank him. In his conflicts with the House of Commons, the most important of which originated in conflicts quite extraneous to the House, Hall had much justice on his side, and as an historian of Parliament he stood high above his contemporaries because he understood the need to allow for change through time. For an Elizabethan, he avoided anachronism with exceptional success. It is good to know that Lord Burghley, engaged in once more saving him from the consequences of his ready temper, agreed with him about the antiquity as well as the current authority of Parliament.

[60] Cf. esp. Neale, *Elizabeth I and her Parliaments*, I, 253, 408. See also ibid., II, 437-8, for the apostolic succession of 'great parliamentarians'.
[61] Wright, *Arthur Hall*, 88-9.

9

Renaissance Philosophers in Elizabethan England: John Dee and Giordano Bruno

Frances Yates

There were two major philosophers of the Renaissance whose lives and work impinged upon Elizabethan England; one was John Dee; the other was Giordano Bruno. Both were 'occult' philosophers, ultimately descending from the Hermetic-Cabalist core of Renaissance Neoplatonism; both were admirers of Pico della Mirandola and Marsilio Ficino, the Italian founders of the movement; both were also profoundly affected by the German continuers of the movement, particularly by Henry Cornelius Agrippa.

I have often asked myself whether the Elizabethans were able to absorb easily the influences of both Dee and Bruno; whether they saw them as fundamentally opposed, or whether they were able to combine the Bruno influence with that of Dee in some satisfactory general solution. I do not think that anyone has as yet asked this question. The present essay is a first attempt at looking at Dee and Bruno together, as both, in their separate ways, in contact with Elizabethan England.

Bruno was in England for only two years (1583–5); yet during that lightning visit he published dialogues in Italian reflecting the religious and political situation in England and designed to attract the attention of leading Elizabethan personalities. Bruno passed like a comet over the Elizabethan scene, but his influence may well have been profound owing to the brilliance of his personality and powers of expression.

Dee was a native of England (or rather of Wales) who lived in the British Isles during the whole of his life (1527–1608), except for very extensive travels abroad. He was firmly based on the English court, with its knights, scientists, politicians and poets. Yet Dee was far from stationary: a much travelled man, he was at home in Europe, at the centre of an important network of philosophers and thinkers with enthusiastic politico-religious aspirations. Bruno also was an international philosopher, an enthusiastic missionary of some kind, having no settled base like Dee, but with wide European contacts. For Bruno, his visit to Elizabethan England was but one episode in a far-flung career. For Dee, the Elizabethan court was his spiritual home but seen in a wide continental setting – Italy, France, Germany – which was also the setting for Bruno's mind. Both these philosophers were at home in the large world of European politico-religious movements of the latter part of the sixteenth century, but the one had a fixed base in England, the other was a temporary visitor who yet seemed to find in Elizabethan England an atmosphere congenial to his outlook.

This pattern of congruence and yet of contrast comes out in the details of the careers of the two men, the curious way in which they seem to overlap without coalescing. Bruno was present at the debates organised at Oxford in June 1583, for the entertainment of the Polish Prince Alasco, then on a visit to England. After the Oxford visit, Philip Sidney brought Alasco to call on Dee at Mortlake,[1] a visit which highly gratified Dee as a mark of particular favour and recognition of his learning and scholarship.

As regards 'the Sidney circle', it is clear that the circle, in the person of Sidney himself, recognised Dee as the important Elizabethan philosopher to present to the visiting Polish prince. As regards Bruno, it would seem from his own works, published in England, that he regarded himself, hopefully, as belonging to the Sidney circle. But what actually was the attitude of the circle is a little ambiguous.

Almost immediately after the momentous visit of Sidney to Dee at Mortlake, Dee left England for his continental mission, which included a visit to Alasco in Poland. During the whole two years of Bruno's time in England, Dee was absent abroad.

Thus Dee and Bruno are moving rather close to one another in England in 1583, but there is no record that they met. Bruno pursues his mission in England in the following years while Dee is absent abroad, pursuing his own mission. What was the relation between the two men and their missions? Why did Dee leave England immediately after Bruno's arrival? The possibility cannot be entirely ruled out – though there is no evidence for it – that Dee might have been avoiding Bruno.

Bruno finally left England for France in October 1585, thereafter continuing his travels in Germany, and arriving early in 1588 at Prague,[2] hoping to attract the notice of the occultist Emperor, Rudolf II. Meanwhile Dee had been in Poland with Alasco, and had reached Prague, accompanied by Kelley in 1586.[3] Thus both Bruno and Dee visited Prague on their travels, both intense occultist missionaries, both hoping to find favour with the imperial patron of the occult, Rudolf II. Well-informed circles in Prague were certainly aware of the nature of the missions of Bruno and Dee. Flattering offers were made to entice Dee to Rome, which he cautiously avoided.[4] Bruno, however, was to fall into the trap of Mocenigo's invitation.[5] He returned to Italy in 1592, and met his death at the stake in Rome in

---

[1] *The Private Diary of Dr John Dee*, ed. J. O. Halliwell (Camden Society 1842), 20; F. A. Yates, *Giordano Bruno and the Hermetic Tradition* (London 1964), 206.
[2] Yates, *Bruno*, 313ff.; R. J. W. Evans, *Rudolf II and his World* (Oxford 1973), 228ff.
[3] Evans, *Rudolf,* 225ff.
[4] Peter French, *John Dee* (London 1972), 122-5.
[5] Yates, *Bruno*, 338ff.

1600, a martyr for something – shall we say for Renaissance occult philosophy and magic?

The Prague situation repeats, though in a more menacing form, the situation of Bruno and Dee in England in 1583. Both these Elizabethan occult philosophers were pursuing continental missions which involved visits to Prague, though apparently they did not amalgamate in any way. Dee was to continue his mission until his return to England in 1589, where he was put under a cloud but not burned at the stake. Bruno went on, eventually to Italy where mortal danger awaited him.

During these last decades of the sixteenth century there was going on, both an intensification of the movement of Renaissance occult philosophy (included within Renaissance Neoplatonism), and an intensification of the reaction against it. Platonism became suspect particularly in its association with Cabala.[6] The movement set in motion by Ficino and Pico had developed in ways considered dangerously heretical by the Council of Trent and the Catholic reaction. (There had, of course, been orthodox opposition to the movement from its inception.) Francesco Patrizzi, a late Renaissance Neoplatonist, discovered to his surprise that Neoplatonism could not be admitted as a Christian philosophy in Rome. Giordano Bruno had hoped that even his extreme version of occult philosophy could be combined with an ostensibly Catholic version of reform, only to be even more fatally disappointed in Rome. And even in Protestant England the spirit of reaction overtook Dee. The philosopher who had inspired the Sidney circle, the centre of the science of the Elizabethan age, found himself on his return to England in 1589 no longer at the centre of Elizabethan movements, but somewhat ostracised, relegated to Manchester under suspicion, his former friends afraid to consult him openly.[7] What happened to Patrizzi, Bruno and Dee in the late sixteenth century was symptomatic of the age. The burning of Bruno was a symbol of the reaction against the daring spiritual adventures of the Renaissance.

This reaction was not confined to the hardening of opinion against the occult in post-Tridentine Catholicism. It was also strongly present among reformed theologians, and particularly in Lutheran Germany. The Hermetic-Cabalist influences from Italy had powerful repercussions in Germany, as recent research is bringing to light. The Abbot Trithemius was a major exponent of these influences in Germany. Trithemius was an ardent admirer of 'Hermes Trismegistus', of Ficino, and, above all, of Pico della Mirandola.[8] Trithemius developed Pico's Cabalism in an extremely magical direction; the fifth book of his *Steganographia* teaches the techniques of angel-conjuring. Cornelius Agrippa was the disciple of Trithemius and became the chief German exponent of Magia and Cabala in his influential text-book on these subjects, the *De occulta philosophia*. The strong reactions of Martin Luther against what he believed to be invocations of the devil became involved, in ways recently studied by Frank Baron, with the historical Faust, and with

---

[6] F. A. Yates, *The Occult Philosophy in the Elizabethan Age* (London 1979), 61ff.
[7] Ibid., 89ff.
[8] Frank Baron, *Doctor Faustus from History to Legend* (Munich 1978), 3ff.

Agrippa as a supposed disciple of Faust.[9]

It is important to remember that both Dee and Bruno were influenced, not only by Ficino and Pico, but also by Agrippa, their German disciple. This is one of the many complex strands in the situation which have to be borne in mind as we try to think about Dee and Bruno in relation to Elizabethan England. The occult philosophy, Italian in origin, had been coloured by its passage through Germany, and by the reactions, both Catholic and Protestant, against it.

In what follows, I make a preliminary attempt at comparing the ideas of Dee and Bruno, trying to determine where they agree or differ, as a necessary preliminary to trying to assess their influence in England.

An important line of approach is through a comparison of the attitudes of Dee and Bruno to the *De occulta philosophia* of Agrippa, that handbook of occult philosophy which combines the natural magic of Ficino with the Cabalist magic of Pico in one daring statement. Agrippa and his work, as an extreme example of the movement, became the chief target of the reaction both Catholic and Protestant. Though Agrippa believed, with all Christian Cabalists, that Cabala had confirmed the truth of Christianity, yet he was to incur the violent disapproval of the reaction as the Faust figure, exhibiting the damnation which threatened students of the occult philosophy. His *De occulta philosophia* can thus be used as a kind of touchstone or test of the positions of philosophers like Dee and Bruno.

Agrippa's book, like his philosophy, is divided into three worlds: the elemental world of terrestrial nature; the celestial world of the stars; and the supercelestial world of spirits, or intelligences or angels.[10] Through all three worlds there ran, as the connecting link, number. In the lower elemental world Agrippa studied number as technology or applied science (or magic). In the celestial world, his study of number was related to astronomy, astrology, optics and the mathematical sciences generally. In the supercelestial world, he believed that he knew the secret of conjuring angels by numerical formulations in the tradition of Pico, and of Trithemius his teacher.

Thus this fantastic outlook could include intensified cultivation of the mathematical sciences (genuine mathematical sciences) and intensified superstition as to the possibility of extending science to the supercelestial world and thereby conjuring angels – the spirits who after all knew at first hand how the universe works and whose assistance would confer on the scientist-magus wonderful power for effecting some total scientific-religious reform.

This is the outlook into which Dee fitted his scientific and mathematical studies.[11] In his Preface to the English translation of Euclid, he speaks of all things being divided into things Supernatural, things Natural, and a third or middle kind called things Mathematical. These are Agrippa's three worlds; Dee is following Agrippa's classification. And he followed Agrippa by attempting to conjure angels in the supercelestial world. Agrippa's book was

[9] Ibid., 70ff.
[10] Yates, *Occult Philosophy*, 37ff.
[11] Ibid., 81ff.

used by Dee and Kelley in their elaborate Cabalistic calculations.

It must be emphasised that Dee believed himself to be an ardent Christian, and was extremely shocked and hurt when contemporaries refused to believe in the angelic nature of the spirits he consulted. Dee's Christianity (as I have discussed elsewhere) was based on the traditions of Christian Cabala.[12] The Christian Cabalists, from Pico della Mirandola onwards, all believed that Cabala could confirm the truth of Christianity,[13] that Cabalistic manipulations of Hebrew letters in the Divine Name could confirm that Jesus is the name of the Messiah. This belief is implied in the third book of Agrippa's *De occulta philosophia* which shows that Agrippa, like Dee, believed himself to be a Christian Cabalist.[14] Hence followers of Agrippa, like Dee, could feel themselves justified in calling themselves Christians.

If we now turn to Giordano Bruno, the philosopher whose career runs so strangely close to that of Dee, we find that Bruno, too, was an Agrippan, a deep student of Agrippa's magic, his mind and outlook impregnated with the Agrippan magical philosophy – that extreme expression of the Renaissance occult philosophy descending from Pico and Ficino.

That there is an influence of Agrippa on Bruno was suggested as long ago as 1903 by Lewis McIntyre,[15] to mention one of the writers on Bruno who have made this point. The most recent study of Agrippa, the valuable book by Charles Nauert,[16] discusses at some length Agrippa's influence on Bruno. He points out, as McIntyre has also done, that Bruno's *De monade* is heavily influenced by Agrippa's *De occulta philosophia*. He argues that Agrippa's exposition of a magical world view, intimately connected by occult bonds, is profoundly consistent with Bruno's outlook.

Nauert's book was published in 1965, one year after my *Giordano Bruno and the Hermetic Tradition* (1964) which he had not seen. Neither had I, of course, seen Nauert's book. My arguments strongly support his view of a deep influence of Agrippa on Bruno, not only in a general way but in a quite precise way. I showed by exact quotation that Bruno was taking the details of his magic from Agrippa, copying his magic images and repeating his incantations. In the *Explicatio triginta sigillorum* there is a defence of 'good' magical religion which is based on Agrippa.[17] In the *Cena de le ceneri* the description of the ascent of the magus through the spheres of the universe is based on Agrippa's passage on the ascent.[18] One could go on in this way (as I have done

[12] Ibid., 79ff.

[13] Ibid., Part 1. For recent studies in French on Christian Cabala see *Kabbalistes Chrétiens* (in the series *Cahiers de l'Hermétisme*), edited by Antoine Faivre and Frédérick Tristan (Paris 1979). This volume includes a French translation of Gershom Scholem's study of the beginning of Christian Cabala, a note on the forthcoming study of Pico and Christian Cabala by Chaim Wirszubski, and essays on Christian Cabalists of Germany, France, England, including one on Agrippa.

[14] Yates, *Occult Philosophy*, 46.

[15] J. Lewis McIntyre, *Giordano Bruno* (London 1903); Yates, *Bruno*, 131, 148–9. The similarity between the world views of Agrippa and Bruno was noted by Ernst Cassirer.

[16] Charles Nauert, *Agrippa and the Crisis of Renaissance Thought* (Urbana 1965), 194ff.

[17] Bruno, *Opera latine*, ed. F. Fiorentino *et al*, II(ii), 180ff. Compare Agrippa, *De occulta philosophia*, ed. K. A. Nowotny (Graz 1967), I, 4–5; Yates, *Bruno*, 271–3.

[18] Bruno, *Cena de le ceneri*, dialogue 1; translated by E. A. Gosselin and Lawrence S. Lerner as *The Ash Wednesday Supper* (Archon Books 1977), 90.

in *Giordano Bruno*) looking to Agrippa as a source for Bruno's major themes, of universal animation, of magical correspondence, and showing that the actual magic – the magic images and incantations – which go with this philosophy in Agrippa is present in Bruno, who copies the magic images and the magical recipes.[19] Of course such themes and such images could have reached Bruno from the general Hermetic tradition, but it would seem that Bruno tended to rely on Agrippa, as the easily accessible printed handbook.

So then – returning to our comparison of Dee and Bruno – both these Elizabethan magi were profoundly influenced by Agrippa. Was their outlook, then, the same? Would Dee, his pupils and his disciples, have immediately recognised Bruno as entirely congenial, as a foreign visitor whose philosophy and outlook were entirely compatible with their own?

Though both could be called occult philosophers, there were certain basic differences between the attitudes to Christianity of Agrippa and Bruno. Agrippa believed that Cabala confirmed the truth of Christianity. Bruno was not a Christian; he believed that the 'Egyptian' religion, supposedly taught by Hermes Trismegistus, was superior to both Judaism and Christianity. This basic difference was related to the different interpretations given by Bruno and Agrippa of the Hermetic-Cabalist tradition. Let me try to put this problem in as simple terms as possible.

That Agrippa was a *Christian* Cabalist is clear, not only in the Cabalist section of the *De occulta philosophia* but also in the *De vanitate*, that strange work in which Agrippa rejects all knowledge as vain in an apparently complete scepticism. But if the work is read carefully to the end it will be found that Agrippa accepts one kind of knowledge as not vain, and that is knowledge of the Christian gospels.[20]

I believe that Philip Sidney, Dee's most eminent disciple, has understood and approved Agrippa's meaning in the *De vanitate* when, in the *Defence of Poetry*, he makes the remark that 'Agrippa will be as merry in showing the vanity of science as Erasmus was in commending Folly'. And Sidney goes on to say that beyond the sceptical merriment of the two scholars there was something else; 'But for Erasmus and Agrippa, they had another foundation than the superficial part would promise.'[21] I interpret this to mean that this 'other foundation' would be the Gospel, alone exempt from scepticism according to both Erasmus and Agrippa.[22]

Far more detailed investigation of the important problem of the influence of Agrippa in England is needed than I can indicate here. But the suggestion is that Sidney would have seen Agrippa as a *Christian* Cabalist, whose sceptical mysticism led him to acceptance of Christianity, a position comparable to the mystical scepticism and the Christian humanism of Erasmus.

This attitude may have emanated from Dee's teaching. For Dee was a

---

[19] The magic images in Bruno's *De umbris idearum* (*Op. Lat.*, II(i)), 133ff., are copied from Agrippa, *De occ. phil.*, II, 37ff.: see Yates, *Bruno*, 193ff. Other references for Bruno's use of Agrippa's magic are given in Yates, *Bruno*, 201, 239–40, 243, 250ff., etc.

[20] Yates, *Occult Philosophy*, 42–3.

[21] Philip Sidney, *A Defence of Poetry*, ed. J. A. Van Dorsten (Oxford 1966), 49–50.

[22] Yates, *Occult Philosophy*, 44.

follower of Agrippa, not only in his pursuit of the occult sciences but also in his Christianity. Dee always firmly believed that he was a Christian, that his angel-summoning was a pious activity. For Christian Cabalists, their daring ventures into the occult sciences were protected by the holy Cabalist side of their activities. This protection shielded them, they believed, from the dangers of magic.[23]

Now Giordano Bruno's non-Christian beliefs constitute a basic difference between Dee's occult philosophy and that of Bruno. By a curious switch of the religious outlook of more orthodox occult philosophers like Agrippa and Dee, Bruno believed that the ancient 'Egyptian' religion descending from the ancient Egyptian sage, Hermes Trismegistus, was superior to Judaism and Christianity, that the ancient Egyptian truth had been corrupted by both Jews and Christians, and that the true universal reform expected by occult philosophers, like himself, consisted in a return to Egyptianism, to the ancient Egyptian magical religion described in the Hermetic *Asclepius*.[24] This was a daring and, one must think, shocking alteration of the orthodox history of occult philosophy, according to which Hermes Trismegistus and his 'Egyptian' religion were prophetic of Christianity, and could be easily combined with Christian Cabala. One cannot but think that, if the Elizabethan disciples of Dee had grasped the drift of Bruno's teaching, they would have been alarmed. For though Bruno quotes at length from Agrippa's Cabalist arguments he is not using his Cabalism as holy protection against this darker 'Egyptian' magic.[25] Bruno's Cabalism is merely an adjunct to his wholesale acceptance of Hermetic or Egyptian magic. This outlook may well have seemed alarming to Christian occult philosophers of the Agrippa-Dee type as they listened to, or read, the brilliant harangues of the strange foreign philosopher who had landed on their shore.

Another rather pronounced difference from Dee's teaching is Bruno's distrust of 'mathematics'. As we saw, Dee formulated within his version of occult philosophy an intensive cultivation of mathematical sciences, of all the mathematical disciplines. Dee's knowledge of mathematics was part of his equipment as a professional astrologer, but expanded, in ways not yet clearly understood, by his Cabalist studies. Bruno, on the contrary, proclaimed himself to be 'against' mathematicians. What this meant exactly, is far from clear. Bruno's little book 'against mathematicians' was published at Prague in

[23] Ibid., 24, 47, etc.

[24] On Bruno's preference for 'Egyptian' (i.e. Hermetic) wisdom rather than Jewish or Christian, see *Lo spaccio della bestia trionfante*, dialogue 3 (*Dialoghi Italiani*, ed. G. Aquilecchia (Florence 1958)), 799–800; *De umbris idearum* (*Op. Lat.*, ii(i)), 1ff.; *Cabala del Cavallo Pegaseo* and *L'Asino Cillenico* (*Dial. Ital.*), 865ff.; *De magia* and *De vinculis in genere* (*Op. Lat.*, iii), 395ff., 633ff.; Yates, *Bruno*, 192–5, 223, 258–66, etc.

These attitudes are also clearly discernible in the *Cena de le ceneri* in which the rising Copernican sun becomes emblematic of the new dawn of Egyptian Truth. Yates, *Bruno*, 238ff.; Gosselin and Lerner's introduction to *The Ash Wednesday Supper*, 50–1.

[25] On Agrippa's aim of using Cabala as protection for Hermetic magic, Yates, *Occult Philosophy*, 46–7. Agrippa was following Pico and Reuchlin in this Christianised use of Cabala. Bruno, by rejecting the Christian Cabalist protection, could lay himself open to the charge of being a 'black' magician. Yates, *Bruno*, 322–4.

1588,[26] two years after Dee, the astrologer and mathematician, had visited that city. Possibly he meant by this publication to dissociate himself from the mathematical Elizabethan magus and astrologer. However that may be, Bruno's slant 'against mathematics', is curiously at variance with Dee's insistence on the sciences of number as of fundamental importance.

We thus have the situation that Bruno the extreme 'Egyptian' occultist who relegates Judaism and Cabala to second place is less scientifically advanced than Dee the mathematician and Cabalist. Dee's version of occult philosophy with its mathematical slant was moving more in the direction of Isaac Newton than was Bruno's thought. Dee's firm grounding in astrology, underlying his developments of Cabala and other occult interests, gave definition to his emphasis on mathematics. Dee really was a mathematician, which Bruno was not.

There is another important difference between Agrippa and Bruno. Agrippa, like Reuchlin his teacher, totally rejected scholasticism. He wished to provide a philosophy more powerful than outworn scholasticism – namely the occult philosophy – to take the place of scholasticism as the philosophy compatible with Christianity.[27] Bruno, with his Dominican training, still respects Thomas Aquinas, though his world view is not that of an Aristotelian but that of a magical animist. Bruno as it were formulates magical animism as a philosophy in such a way as to make him a kind of magical scholastic (like Campanella).

This side of Bruno might well have looked suspicious in Elizabethan England as verging too much in a Catholic direction, an impression which would have been strengthened by Bruno's attack on Protestant Oxford, though with some aspects of this attack members of the Sidney circle would have been in agreement, particularly Dee himself. For Dee admired and studied the works of pre-Reformation Oxford scientists and philosophers and deplored their neglect. Bruno's defence of the thinkers of pre-Reformation Oxford[28] might well have been approved by the Sidney circle who would have been taught by Dee to honour Roger Bacon and his school.

To return to the influence of Agrippa on Dee and Bruno. One may perhaps see the Agrippa influence as operating in different directions on the two philosophers. Dee absorbs the mathematical Cabalism which he believed protected by Judaic influences, which he deeply respected. Bruno is a Catholic (though non-Christian) occultist, preferring Egyptianism to Judaism and using his scholastic training towards the formulation of daring philosophical hypotheses, heliocentricity and earth movement, which he

[26] Yates, *Bruno*, 313ff.
[27] On Reuchlin's aim of providing a more 'powerful' philosophy to replace scholasticism, see the article by Charles Zika, 'Reuchlin's *De verbo mirifico* and the Magic Debate of the late fifteenth century', *Journal of the Warburg and Cortauld Institutes*, XXIX (1976), 104–38. Agrippa's *De occulta philosophia* endeavours to provide the guide to such a philosophy.
[28] On Bruno's defence of the learning of medieval Oxford, and the appeal of this attitude for Dee and the Sidney circle, see my 'Giordano Bruno's conflict with Oxford', *Journal of the Warburg Institute*, II (1939), 234ff. Nicholas Clulee has recently emphasised the importance of the medieval influence on Dee's science; see Nicholas Clulee, 'Astrology, magic and optics: facets of John Dee's early natural philosophy', *Renaissance Quarterly*, XXX (1977), 632–80.

interpreted as expressive of a magical animism. Though Dee was interested in Copernicanism,[29] he never proclaimed himself a philosopher of heliocentricity, nor used the sun-centred universe as a symbol of Hermetic reform, as did Bruno.

Though Dee was abroad while Bruno was in England, there is a curious account, written by Bruno himself, which is something like a confrontation between Dee's disciples and Bruno. This is the famous *Cena de le ceneri*, or *Ash Wednesday Supper*, published in England in 1585, which describes a debate on the subject of the Copernican theory.[30] Two Oxford doctors had been invited by Fulke Greville to meet and argue with Bruno on this subject. Greville himself was present at the debate and probably also another English knight and courtier, Philip Sidney. Both Greville and Sidney had been taught by John Dee. Bruno ran into difficulties with the Oxford doctors over his exposition of the Copernican theory. 'The gentlemen who were present' demanded that the book of Copernicus should be brought to check Bruno's statements. Bruno claimed that the book proved him right but he was really quite wrong in reporting Copernicus as having said, not that the moon revolves round the earth, but that both revolve on the circumference of the same epicycle. Bruno claimed that the point at the centre of the epicycle on the diagram was not the earth but the point made by the foot of the compass in describing the epicycle. Those present at the debate, dissatisfied by Bruno's confidence in his error, 'went back to mumbling in their own language'.[31] Among these dissatisfied mumblers would presumably have been, not only the Oxford doctors, but Greville and Sidney. It would appear therefore that the disciples of Dee may not have been favourably impressed by Bruno's astronomical science.

But, as I have argued and has now been admirably expounded by Gosselin and Lerner in their English edition of *The Ash Wednesday Supper*, the whole debate about a sun-centred cosmology was a metaphor for Bruno's religious teachings, for his 'Hermetic' religious mission. The rise of the Copernican sun heralded the rise of a sun of magical religion which should solve all the problems of the age by its illumination. Another account of Bruno's debate at Oxford states that it was about Marsilio Ficino's magical philosophy, and that the book sent for at the debate was Ficino's *De vita coelitus comparanda*.[32] The sun-centred universe was the symbol of Bruno's vision of a universal magical religion, inspired by the works of 'Hermes Trismegistus'. This revived 'Egyptian' religion was, for Bruno, somehow compatible with a Catholicism reformed in a magical direction. The leader proclaimed by Bruno of this Hermetic-Catholic reform was Henri III of France, on whose behalf he was appealing to Elizabethan Englishmen.

[29] Dee had a copy of the book of Copernicus in his library. F. A. Yates, *Theatre of the World* (London 1969), 17.

[30] The problems about Bruno's Copernicanism, which I raised in *Bruno*, 241ff., have now been admirably discussed and clarified by Gosselin and Lerner, *The Ash Wednesday Supper*. This is, so far, the best and most understanding English translation of one of Bruno's Italian works.

[31] Gosselin and Lerner, *The Ash Wednesday Supper*, 175-93. Bruno would have despised their objections as 'merely mathematical'; Yates, *Bruno*, 241ff.

[32] Yates, *Bruno*, 207ff.; *The Ash Wednesday Supper*, 197.

How does Bruno's mission in England compare with the Hermetic mission which Dee was preaching on the Continent? I do not think anyone has as yet tried to think seriously about this. I hazard a few suggestions.

The religious centre of Dee's mission was the mysterious *monas hiero-glyphica*, an emblem of unification and return to the One, which contained strong Cabalist, alchemical, mathematical ingredients but which, as a whole, must have been seen by Dee as fully compatible with Christian Cabala, in which he profoundly believed. It was more compatible with a reforming Puritan slant on the situation than was Bruno's deeply 'Egyptianised' Catholicism. Dee's mission encouraged the 'mathematical' outlook; the *monas hieroglyphica* would lead more in that direction than the 'Egyptian' sun of Bruno's revelation. Dee's heroine was the reformed Elizabeth of England; Bruno's the obscurely Catholic King of France. And yet, the whole object of both Hermetic missions was to dissolve differences; Bruno's 'Egyptianism' is aimed at drawing together Elizabeth and Henri in an occultism which should go deeper than doctrinal differences. Dee's cabalistic *monas* also contained within it politico-religious aims of unification.

It does seem to me, however, that Dee's *Christian* Cabalist movement would have been less alarming to Elizabethans than the non-Christian 'Egyptianised' Catholicism of Bruno.

Where Bruno and Dee influences would coalesce in Elizabethan England would be in the politico-religious sphere. Both these representatives of Renaissance occult philosophy were against the Spanish-Habsburg version of Counter-Reformation, against the reaction which was suppressing Renaissance philosophy and magic, or – to use that vague term – Renaissance Neoplatonism in Europe. Dee's vision of an extended influence for Queen Elizabeth I in an imperial theme, as Dee and Edmund Spenser built it up, stood for the support of magical Neoplatonism, a late stand for the Renaissance against the reaction.

With this politico-religious orientation of Elizabethan England, Bruno was in entire agreement, as a continental magus opposed to the Spanish-Habsburg version of Counter-Reform. Hence Bruno's vast vision in the *Spaccio della bestia trionfante* of the expulsion from the constellations of tyrannical influences and their replacement by the liberalism of reform was a vision with which the Sidney circle could be in agreement, and it was, in fact, dedicated to Sidney. Bruno echoes, both here and in other works published in England, the chivalrous cult of the Queen and the presentation of her as a messianic figure. In this politico-religious sphere, the Bruno and Dee versions of occult philosophy should have been able to fuse in support of a movement standing for Renaissance tradition against the forces of reaction.

It is indeed in the poetic expression of this outlook that Bruno draws closest to the Elizabethans. The 'heroic enthusiasms' which he expressed in Italian poetry when he was in England have a tantalising affinity with some of Sidney's sonnets. I explored some of these resemblances in an article published many years ago.[33]

Yet the whole question of Bruno's influence in England, and on Sidney, still presents puzzling unsolved problems. I now feel that the main occult influence on Elizabethan England was the Dee influence, and that the Bruno influence would have been subsidiary to that. Or perhaps one should look at the question, not as an *influence* of Bruno on Elizabethan poets but as a *reflection* by Bruno of the imagery of the Elizabeth cult.[34] When in the *Eroici furori* the enthusiasts come in bearing *impress* shields with mystical devices, this is a reflection of the Accession Day Tilts. As I have suggested elsewhere, Bruno was linking the *Eroici furori* dialogues with the chivalrous romance woven around the Virgin Queen and echoing the imagery of the Elizabeth cult. Since it was Dee who had done so much to build up the Hermetic cult of Elizabeth, Bruno by adopting its imagery was acting in consonance with Dee's mission, or rather expanding it to include his master the French King.

The present essay has made yet another attempt at tackling these problems from the new aspect of comparison between Dee and Bruno as both Elizabethan magi. It is a first attempt at such a comparison; the results are inconclusive. The point which I would wish to emphasise in conclusion is the importance of Agrippa as an influence on both Dee and Bruno. The extraordinary strength of the influence of Agrippa's *De occulta philosophia* has not yet been fully realised. It was an influence which operated in diverse ways with differing results. It encouraged Dee's Cabalistical angel-conjuring. It encouraged Bruno's magical mnemonics. It was central not only to the spread of Renaissance magic but also to the reaction against it.

---

[33] 'The emblematic conceit in Giordano Bruno's *De gli eroici furori* and in the Elizabethan sonnet sequences', *Journal of the Warburg and Cortauld Institutes*, VI (1943). Bruno's use of Petrarchan conceits as emblems with profoundly religious meanings (such as the Cabalistic 'death of the kiss') is one of the most striking of his insights. It connects with his emblematic use of heliocentricity.

[34] F. A. Yates, *Astraea: The Imperial Theme in the Sixteenth Century* (London 1975), 110.

10

Social Policy in Early Modern London

Valerie Pearl

Restriction, our text-books tell us, was the keynote of economic and social policy in the sixteenth and seventeenth centuries. In the 'dark ages' of our economy, we learn, concern for stability outweighed concern for economic growth. Policy under Elizabeth and James I, wrote George Unwin in a famous essay, insofar as it consisted in strengthening monopolies and excluding foreign merchants, was conducted 'at the expense of national commerce and industry'. Its results were, he thought, not economic growth but prolonged slump and depression.[1] Unwin's extreme view, never wholly accepted, nevertheless influenced later work. F. J. Fisher, in a seminal article published in 1940, seemed, but for different reasons, to take almost as gloomy a view of economic and social policy-making after 1550: governments, he wrote, were dominated by vested interests, by urgent social and financial pressures, and by conservatism.[2] According to R. H. Tawney, state intervention at this time was invariably ineffective: at best it was 'irregular and capricious'.[3] Most text-books tell us that industrial policy was restrictionist, and emphasise the failures of government in theory, policy and practice.

Each generation writes its own history. The *laissez-faire* views of George Unwin reflected the free trade battles of the 1920s. His successors believed in state-directed or guided economies. For such schools, government action fell short, being neither 'free' in Unwin's sense nor inspired by the long-term goals approved by the Webbs and Tawney. Lately, some of our urban historians, perhaps also inspired by the spirit of the times, have discerned a connection between restrictionist economics and elitist politics. Economic conservatism has been linked with a contraction of the political base in Tudor and Stuart towns. Urban life, it is said, was dominated by a series of ever more powerful oligarchies. Some have even seen London, however populous

[1] R. H. Tawney (ed.), *Studies in Economic History: the collected papers of George Unwin* (repr. 1966), 168–86.
[2] F. J. Fisher, 'Commercial trends and policy in sixteenth-century England', *Economic History Review* (hereafter *Ec.H.R.*), x, no.2 (1940), 95–6; cf. 'Some experiments in company organisation', *Ec.H.R.*, IV (1933), 185, where Fisher saw signs of more positive attitudes towards industrial development.
[3] T. Wilson, *Discourse upon Usury* (ed. R. H. Tawney, 1925), 165.

and pluralistic it is admitted to have been, as bound by the same fetters.[4]

In some respects, the gloom has lifted a little recently. Joan Thirsk has reconsidered industrial growth. She has shown how both policy and tempo changed under the inspiration of the so-called 'Commonwealth party' until cheap mass goods of home manufacture transformed the domestic market by providing employment and consumer goods for some of the poorer classes of society.[5] Meanwhile a number of excellent recent local histories has revised our view both of the scope and of the achievements of sixteenth-century government. We are now aware that from the early sixteenth century the development of government commissions and of special and petty sessions enabled J.P.s to carry far greater burdens of administration created by an expanding range of social legislation, even if that legislation was not always translated into local action. As the temporal power of the Church declined, the activities of the secular courts and lay magistrates expanded, particularly in towns. Magistrates also grew more sensitive to public opinion. By the early seventeenth century Quarter Sessions had increasingly assumed the role of county forum where views could be expressed not only by members of the gentry, but also by men outside their ranks; some of these lesser families would rise to office after 1642. While some economic regulation met with neglect and certain centralising policies with strong opposition, social welfare measures like the marketing of grain and poor relief were usually promoted energetically until the 1650s, and sometimes well beyond. Ancient institutions, such as the hundred and manorial courts, tried, at least under Elizabeth and James, to preserve communal obligations and customs. Local officials lacked neither authority nor status in the eyes of the public; even the lowly constable, the 'dull wit' of literature, the comic Dogberry, proves to be neither so lowly, stupid nor ineffective as he was once painted.[6]

If some of the gloom has lifted from the provinces, it is time it was lifted from London too. London (that is, the area within the jurisdiction of the Lord Mayor) was probably unique in Europe in the high number, proportionate to population, of elected and appointed officials chosen to represent the 26 wards, 242 precincts and 111 parishes of which it was composed. Perhaps one in ten householders held annually some office or other. Something like 3,000 officers were elected to 25 wards regularly within the City's square mile.[7]

[4] P. Clark and P. Slack, *Crisis and Order in English Towns 1500-1700* (1972), 37.

[5] J. Thirsk, *Economic Policy and Projects* (Oxford 1978), passim.

[6] A. Hassell Smith, *County and Court: Government and Politics in Norfolk 1558-1603* (Oxford 1974), 88, 90, 93, 102-11; J. S. Cockburn, *A History of English Assizes 1558-1714* (Oxford 1972), 8, 113-8, and ch.8, passim; J. S. Morrill, *Cheshire 1630-1660* (Oxford 1974), 248-53; A. Fletcher, *A County Community in Peace and War: Sussex 1600-1660* (1975), 218-27; M. G. Davies, *The Enforcement of English Apprenticeship 1563-1642* (Cambridge, Mass. 1956), 190, 198, 231-4; R. W. Heinze, *The Proclamations of the Tudor Kings* (Cambridge 1976), 99-101, 228; F. G. Emmison, *Elizabethan Life: Home, Work and Land* (Chelmsford 1976), 197-203; T. G. Barnes, *The Clerk of the Peace in Caroline Somerset* (Leicester 1961: Department of English Local History Occasional Papers no.14), 21-9, 35-47. For a different view of the effectiveness of the *Book of Orders* and social policy, see P. Clark, *English Provincial Society from the Reformation to the Revolution* (1977), 350-6.

[7] Figures compiled from numbers of ward officers given in J. Stow, *A Survey of London*, ed. C. L. Kingsford (2 vols, Oxford 1908), passim; J. Strype, *A Survey of the Cities of London and Westminster* (2 vols, 1720), passim; and from various wardmote inquest books in the Guildhall Library.

Around 1640, when the population (excluding the suburbs) was roughly 180,000, perhaps another 1,400 officers, nearly half as many again, were responsible for organising relief of the poor in the parishes.[8] Then there were also the wardens of the yeomanries in the City companies (one of whose tasks was to collect and to allocate the quarterage fees for the relief of poverty), other gild officers and the governors of hospitals, most of whom owed their positions to some system of direct or indirect election. In some ways, sixteenth-century London suffered not from too little government but from too much.

The elaborate collection of courts and assemblies with their hosts of unpaid officials which had characterised the late medieval City continued to flourish in the early modern period. The intensity of activity by the local wardmote (the City equivalent of the hundred court) may have reached an apogee under Elizabeth.[9] A slow decline in communal regulation set in under her successors, most noticeably from the 1650s. Thereafter the community functions of the wardmote also decayed. In its withering away there was silenced a powerful common voice often raised in support of good neighbourliness, church-going, and collective endeavour, effective in its advocacy of the prevailing *mores*. Apart from elections and minor regulation, what was left of its social aspect in the eighteenth century was little more than a select, convivial, clubbish assembly.

We cannot, of course, see London as a government of the market place, a northern *agora*. Here was a hierarchical community in which the degree of participation was nevertheless remarkable. Here at ground level, in wardmote and vestry, it was possible to express something of common aspirations, even if these were limited – as it was naturally assumed by nearly everybody that they ought to be – to parish pump politics and to local poor relief. In the smaller inner parishes, practically all but the lowest and *dependent* classes were brought into some small measure of self-government; even some almsmen were included if they had seen better days. Men voted normally on a prepared panel of names, the precincts and vestries were effectively under the control of substantial and right-thinking citizens, and the agenda were usually limited to parochial subjects. There was not much rope given to the dissident: the 'face-to-face' aspects of popular *mores* can be as intimidating to unconventional individuals as are the decrees of tyrannies. Nevertheless, within these limitations, the collaboration and involvement of ordinary Londoners were of considerable importance in the development of democratic processes.

There is a widely held view, based on a misreading of Unwin, that the majority of Londoners were excluded from the freedom of the City.[10] In fact, the sixteenth century saw a spectacular increase in the number of

[8] Numbers of officers varied from one parish to another. Usually there were two church-wardens, four overseers, six assessors and one beadle. Constables and hospital beadles also played their part. See E. M. Leonard, *The Early History of Poor Relief* (Cambridge 1900), 99.
[9] V. Pearl, 'Change and stability in seventeenth-century London', *The London Journal*, v, no.1 (May 1979), 16, 20, 25.
[10] G. Unwin, *The Gilds and Companies of London* (1908), 224; G. Unwin, *Industrial Organisation in the Sixteenth and Seventeenth Centuries* (Oxford 1904), 61.

freemen who composed the new yeomanry organisations.[11] Before the middle of the fifteenth century, the gilds of London operated very high scales of charges inhibiting all but the well-to-do from taking up the livery or becoming free of the City.[12] The charges began to decline rapidly in the late fifteenth century. The reign of Henry VII saw a dramatic drop: the current fee for becoming free of the gild was halved from 13s. 4d. to 6s. 8d. In 1529, Acts of Common Council preserved or even reduced these rates for particular trades.[13] An Act of Parliament of 1531 preserved similarly reduced rates for all gilds.[14] Despite an approximately six-fold increase in food prices in the century following the Act of 1531, the fee to most London gilds remained unchanged at 3s. 4d. right down to 1661.[15] Entry into apprenticeship was eased too in this period by the comparatively small sums taken in premiums for entrants into the lesser crafts – except for foundlings who, coming into the world more naked than others, often had a substantial sum paid for them by parish officers. I have calculated that the number of freemen increased at an even faster rate than the population of London: in the order of an eight-fold increase from about 4,000 to more than 30,000 by the middle of the seventeenth century, at which time freemen probably made up perhaps three-quarters of male householders in the City.[16] The term 'elitist', so often used today, is inappropriate for a class consisting of more than half the number of heads of families.

It is possible that the increase in the number of freemen was deliberately encouraged by interested groups in national and City government. We know that in the Elizabethan period some leading politicians, such as Lord Burghley, and some intellectuals, notably Sir Thomas Smith, were concerned to remedy the decay of towns by stimulating new industries, and that a number of towns invited Englishmen and aliens to settle and to bring their trades and skills with them.[17] A significant collaboration (still largely unexplored) emerged in the sixteenth century between governmental and municipal interests. The Act of Parliament of 1531 which held down rates for entry into gilds condemned 'the great hurte' due to excessive fees, and set out maximum charges for the entrance to and expiry of apprenticeships. Although there are no explanatory preambles either to the parliamentary act or to the acts of Common Council which kept fees down, the tenor of national legislation is clear. It speaks of the 'sinister minds' of some of the companies and refers to the 'damage' suffered by the King's subjects because of the

[11] Unwin, rightly in my view, linked the growth in numbers of freemen to the absorption of aliens into the gilds, but did not mention the extent of the expansion: *The Gilds and Companies of London*, 246–51.

[12] Corporation of London Record Office (hereafter CLRO), Letter Book G, f.104; A. H. Johnson, *The History of the Worshipful Company of the Drapers* (Oxford 1915), II, 29 and n.3; G. Unwin, *Industrial Organisation*, 48.

[13] CLRO, Letter Book O, ff.103, 115v, 148v, 258v.

[14] *Statutes of the Realm* (1817), III, 22 Hen. VIII c.iv, 320; G. R. Elton, *Reform and Renewal* (Cambridge 1973), 110.

[15] A. H. Johnson, op. cit., II, 29, 235; C. M. Clode, *Memorials of the Guild of Merchant Taylors* (1875), I, 54.

[16] 'Change and stability in seventeenth-century London', 14–15.

[17] J. Thirsk, op. cit., 28–50, 52–3, 68–9, 78, 86–8.

excessive charge in putting their children to a trade.[18] An Act of 1536 further improved citizens' prospects by forbidding gild officers to take oaths from journeymen that they would not set up as masters.[19] The process was accelerated in 1563 by the exclusion of the metropolis from the clause of the Statute of Artificers which confined admission to apprenticeship to the sons of 40 shilling freeholders. Since the sons of husbandmen and copyholders were thus denied urban apprenticeships other than in London and in Norwich (which was also excepted) they would obviously be propelled towards the rapidly expanding City.[20] So harsh in some respects to the newly arrived countryman, as a popular literature full of references to 'cony catchers' informs us, London, in this respect, invited the ambitious.

The economic privileges of freemen may have become less advantageous in the face of suburban competition, particularly after the middle of the seventeenth century, but their political privileges did not decline. It is a mistake to see the City government as *increasingly* oligarchic. Common Council in early modern London was subordinate to, and closely controlled by, the Court of Aldermen. But from the later years of Elizabeth, when Common Council first won the right to seats on the City Lands Committee[21] (the most powerful of the City committees), its powers gradually and haltingly increased. The power achieved by the Common Council in the eighteenth century was the culmination, not the reversal, of a previous trend. A similar progression can be seen in the parishes. By 1700, in contrast with Middlesex only one quarter of the City parishes were closed, or 'selected'.[22]

In times of political crisis or challenge, the ordinary rate-payer participated in City politics. From the time of Elizabeth there was popular pressure in London for consumer protection and for the extension of relief of the poor. Collectivist policies in that century were not only advocated: they were adopted. Municipal bakeries, corn mills and breweries appeared briefly in London and other towns.[23] Even though they did not establish themselves in the economy for long, we should not underestimate the sense of communal responsibility which prompted these failed enterprises. More significant economically was the provision of buffer stocks of grain against scarcity, another example of consumer protection. These measures are not to be

[18] See n. 14, above.
[19] *Statutes of the Realm*, 27 Hen. VIII c.v, 654. In 1547, the Drapers' Company passed an ordinance fining masters who omitted to make apprentices free of the Company on completion of their term. A. H. Johnson, op. cit., II, 119. Common Council attempted to stem the flood of masters and journeymen by an act of 1556 stipulating that apprentices should not be enrolled as freemen before the age of 24. Journal of Common Council (hereafter J.Co.Co.), XVII, ff.6v-7v.
[20] 'Change and stability in seventeenth-century London', 14. Not all London crafts, however, welcomed additional apprentices at this time. See W. S. Prideaux, *Memorials of the Goldsmiths' Company* (1896), I, 64.
[21] N. R. Shipley, 'The city lands committee, 1592-1642', *Guildhall Studies in History*, II, no.4, 162-5.
[22] S. and B. Webb, *English Local Government . . . The Parishes and the County* (1906), 174 n.i.
[23] CLRO, Repertories of the Aldermanic Bench, XXIV, ff.323, 329; XXV, ff.239v, 346v-347v; S. Thrupp, *A Short History of the Worshipful Company of Bakers of London* (1933), 75-9; 'Change and stability in seventeenth-century London', 25; P. Slack, 'Poverty and politics in Salisbury 1597-1666', in *Crisis and Order in English Towns*, 164-203; Stow (ed. Kingsford), II, 66; CLRO, J.Co.Co., XXVII, f.261.

dismissed as 'simply the expression of a pious opinion', the words used by Tawney to describe some sixteenth-century agrarian legislation.[24] In the early seventeenth century the City (excluding the suburbs) aimed to supply one third of the estimated need for grain in times of shortage, a proportion which the Privy Council in 1632 tried to raise to one half.[25] Price controls of other essential commodities were also evoked, although with less success.

Popular pressure manifested itself also in demands for the enlargement of the political powers of Common Council – a movement which was particularly effective in two radical periods: during the Puritan Revolution between 1649 and 1651, and again between 1688 and 1690.[26] In both periods, radical Common Councillors produced demands for municipal reform which fore-shadowed nineteenth-century programmes. Both periods also saw freer entry into some of the overseas trading companies and into their activities. After 1688, with a small monied group entrenched in the Bank of England and the East India Company, Acts of Parliament threw open most of the older corporations and made them available to a much wider circle of traders than hitherto.[27] Thus the direction of historical change in London in three centuries fits uneasily into simple categories labelled 'restrictionist' and 'elitist'.

Has too much undifferentiated material been stuffed into another pigeon-hole entitled 'poor relief'? I believe that here, too, there has been a failure to recognise the extent of public action. The failure is strikingly shown in received notions about the operation of the poor laws, or, at least, about how they worked in London.

Professor Jordan, in his important volumes on charity, did a disservice to the evidence insofar as it concerned the poor rate imposed by Acts of Parliament. He concluded that 'in no year prior to 1660 was more than 7 per cent of all the vast sums expended on the care of the poor derived from taxation'.[28] Subsequent work on a fair spread of towns and rural areas has

[24] R. H. Tawney, *The Agrarian Problem in the Sixteenth Century* (1912), 377.

[25] In the early seventeenth century, the Lord Mayor estimated the total requirements of corn for the City under his jurisdiction at 70,000 quarters per year. The amount stored in times of dearth may have varied from between one-sixth and one-third of this sum: in 1594, for example, between 11,000 and 12,000 quarters were stored (British Library, Harleian MS.6850, f.266; W. H. and H. C. Overall (eds), *Analytical Index to the Remembrancia* (1878), 387, 389, 390-1; CLRO, J.Co.Co., XXXI, f.324v). According to Gras, the amount of cereals required for all purposes, including bread, would have exceeded the Lord Mayor's estimate: N. S. B. Gras, *The Evolution of the English Corn Market* (1926), 77. An Act of Common Council in 1631 suggested the establishment of a separate magazine for 10,000 quarters of corn in addition to the 20,000 quarters stored (or meant to be stored) by the companies with the intention of serving the whole population, not just the needy: CLRO, J.Co.Co., XXXV, ff.347-8; see also CLRO, Bridgehouse Corn Book 1568-1581. The corn was ground in the mills erected for that purpose by the municipality at the Bridge House. The corn needed for London, the suburbs and 'part adjacent' was said by the Lord Mayor to be between 130,000 and 140,000 quarters: *Remembrancia*, 345.

[26] CLRO, J.Co.Co., XLI, passim. G. de Krey, 'Trade, Religion and Politics in the Reign of William III' (Princeton Univ. Ph.D. thesis, 1978), ch.4. For City radicalism in the early eighteenth century, see N. Rogers, 'Resistance to oligarchy: the City opposition to Walpole and his successors, 1725-47', in J. Stevenson (ed.), *London and the Age of Reform* (Oxford 1977), 1-29.

[27] G. de Krey, op. cit., ch.1; R. P. Brenner, 'Commercial Change and Political Conflict: the Merchant Community in Civil War London' (Princeton Univ. Ph.D. thesis, 1970), passim.

[28] W. K. Jordan, *Philanthropy in England, 1480-1660: A Study of the Changing Pattern of English Social Aspirations* (New York 1959), 140. Jordan stated that 21 parishes in his sample ten counties raised poor rates in 1623. Yet London alone provides evidence for a greater number of parishes raising poor rates in this year. Ibid., 132.

produced results which contradict this view. It has been shown not only that the poor rate accounted for far larger sums than Jordan estimated, but that the public accounts raised from taxation and parish property, together with money from parochial fees and fines, outweighed the sums given by charity.[29] Work on City records (the poorly documented suburbs have not yet been tackled) bears out the importance of public action both by the government and by municipal and parochial authorities. In the City, the exemplar of philanthropic action, public rating and parish rents, augmented by the sums raised from fees and fines, provided the greater share of parochial support for the majority of parishes within the walls. Indeed in the 50 parishes in pre-Fire London for which the appropriate evidence survives, public rates provided the most important single source for funds in as many as 32 parishes.[30] London had pre-empted government action in the matter initially by establishing compulsory taxation for the poor as early as 1547, 25 years before an Act of Parliament imposed national rating.[31]

In many parishes, including some of the poorer ones, and in the wards outside the walls or straddling them, there were systematic attempts by parochial officials from the 1560s, when our records mainly begin, to purchase houses and lands. They were acquired partly out of parish 'stock', partly by public rating and by loans from parishioners, and partly as a result of legacies and donations to the parish. Sometimes, the object was to buy up chantry and fraternity lands which had long since made some contribution to parochial relief but had been confiscated by the government. Local authorities were officially encouraged in such action by the Poor Law Act of 1547. Rightly denounced then and since for its imposition of servile status on vagrants, the

[29] L. Stone, *The Causes of the English Revolution 1529-1642* (1972), 155 n.83; R. W. Herlan, 'London's poor during the Puritan Revolution: the parish of St. Dunstan's in the West', *Guildhall Studies in London History* (1977), III, 1, 13-15; R. W. Herlan, 'Poor relief in the London parish of St. Antholin's Budge Row, 1638-64', ibid. (1977), II, 4; R. W. Herland, 'Social articulation and parochial poverty on the eve of the Restoration', ibid. (1976), II, 2.

[30] Guildhall Library Record Office, Churchwardens' Accounts (hereafter GLMS, C.W.A.), as follows. GLMS 6836:I, C.W.A. St. Helen's Bishopgate; GLMS 3907:1, C.W.A. St. Lawrence Poultney; GLMS 3989:I, Poor's Book, St. Bartholomew the Great; GLMS 1176:1, C.W.A. St. Margaret New Fish Street; GLMS 3556:1, C.W.A. St. Mary Aldermanbury; GLMS 959:1, C.W.A. St. Martin Ongar; GLMS 942A, C.W.A. St. Botolph Billingsgate; GLMS 685:1, Poor's Book, St. George Botolph Lane; GLMS 2596:2, C.W.A. St. Mary Magdalene Milk Street; GLMS 651:1, Poor's Book, St. Thomas Apostle; GLMS 66:1, C.W.A. St. Mary Colechurch; GLMS 1303:1, St. Benet Fink; GLMS 1279:2, C.W.A. St. Andrew Hubbard; GLMS 5018:1, C.W.A. St. Pancras Soper Lane; GLMS 645:2, C.W.A. St. Peter's Westcheap; GLMS 4352:1, Vestry Minute Book, St. Margaret Lothbury; GLMS 4810:2, C.W.A. St. James Garlickhithe; GLMS 4409:1, C.W.A. St. Olave Jewry; GLMS 3891:1, C.W.A. St. Mary Abchurch; GLMS 2895:2, C.W.A. St. Michael Le Quern; GLMS 7674, Poor's Book, St. Alban Wood Street; GLMS 1188:1, C.W.A. St. Michael Crooked Lane; GLMS 4071:2, C.W.A. St. Michael Cornhill; GLMS 2089:1, Poor's Book, St. Andrew Wardrobe; GLMS 5026:1, C.W.A. All Hallows Lane; GLMS 5026:1, C.W.A. All Hallows Honey Lane; GLMS 5090:2, C.W.A. All Hallows London Wall; GLMS 1016:1, C.W.A. St. Matthew Friday Street; GLMS 1542:2, C.W.A. St. Mary Staining; GLMS 5714:1, C.W.A. St. Mary Somerset; GLMS 4383:1, C.W.A. St. Bartholomew Exchange; GLMS 4423:1, C.W.A. St. Christopher Le Stocks; GLMS 1124:1, C.W.A. St. Katherine Coleman. This is a minimum list since a number of Churchwardens' Accounts do not distinguish between the poor stock and the church stock, and therefore cannot be used in such a calculation. With the exception of a few very rich and very poor parishes, all were rated towards the poor.

[31] CLRO, J.Co.Co., XV, f.325v.

Act had at least one far-sighted recommendation. It directed parishes and
J.P.s to buy up local property to house the impotent poor. The recom-
mendation was repeated, moreover, in the great Poor Law Acts of the
Elizabethan period.[32]

The purchase of property was organised so efficiently in London and, it
appears, managed so effectively that in the five largest extra-mural parishes
which contained just over one-sixth of the City's population in 1640, by far
the largest sums at that time supporting the poor came from parish rents.[33] It
is not likely that such publicly owned property was more than about one-
fifteenth of the total housing stock in any parish.[34] Nevertheless the existence
of even this very small degree of publicly owned real estate may have been
significant at a time of great pressure on housing when complaints of slum
conditions and of exploitation by property owners were rife. There is
growing evidence also that from the early seventeenth century City parishes
purchased rack-rented properties and established them as 'poor's houses', as
they were called. The main initial motive of such real estate investment,
however, was not to house the poor but to provide funds for their relief.

Both the credit and the financial acumen of the leaders of the parish as
public landlord are revealed in the records. A deliberate policy of raising loans
from parishioners to purchase property and lands can be discerned even in the
most crowded parish in the City with the largest number of poor: St. Botolph
Aldgate.[35] These 'managers', presumably acting as Parliament had suggested
in buying back the important chantries, went beyond the statute and sought a
good investment. The raising of loans, although they were far from sufficient
for all their parish poor, was an act of foresight, for it took place in the 1560s
during an economic depression – a good time to buy property. Our records
are rarely explicit enough to enable us to discover in each parish how these
considerable rentals were distributed and how the money for the capital
investment was found; but it is plain that the parish stock in hand, carried
forward each year, supplied the basis. Charitable bequests and legacies were
also a very important if sometimes unquantifiable element in these funds.

Local authorities in London implemented national poor law legislation
much more closely than historians have allowed. The early twentieth-
century historians of this subject, Miss Leonard and the Webbs, showed that
the implementation was not uniform, but we need to revise their evaluation
of its effectiveness. They considered that, excellent though the poor law was
in itself, it was 'only well executed for a few years'. 'So far men objected to

---

[32] *Statutes of the Realm*, IV(i), 1 Ed. VI c.iii, cl.xi; IV(ii), 39 Eliz. c.iii, cl.v, and 43 Eliz. c.ii, cl.iv.
[33] GLMS 9237, C.W.A. St. Botolph Aldgate; GLMS 6047:1, C.W.A. St. Giles Cripplegate;
GLMS 6552:1, C.W.A. St. Bride's Fleet Street; GLMS 3146:1, C.W.A. St. Sepulchre's Holborn;
GLMS 4525:2, C.W.A. St. Botolph without Bishopsgate.
[34] For example, in St. Thomas Apostle, eight properties were parish-owned in a parish of 112
houses or householders: GLMS 665:1, passim. For numbers of households, see T. C. Dale, *The
Inhabitants of London in 1638: edited from MS 272 in the Lambeth Palace Library* (1931), 182-3.
[35] GLMS 9235:1, July 1562, list of persons who have given money for a stock for the poor. The
records of St. Botolph Bishopsgate show enormous sums from legacies as well as rents: GLMS
4525:1,2. Here, as in St. Botolph Aldgate, rents and legacies contributed increasingly greater
sums than rates.

pay rates,' Miss Leonard observed, 'they were not firmly convinced of the duty of the state to relieve the poor.'[36] Like Professor Jordan after her, Miss Leonard believed that the law was only carried out efficiently in the years between 1629 and 1640, and only then under monthly exhortation from the Privy Council. The evidence for London contradicts these views. A longer and more consistent administration of the law, down to the smallest details, was shown by the City than has yet been demonstrated in any other locality – even in Norwich. The City's attention to so many aspects of the poor's welfare reinforces the impression that concern for poverty deepened and led to more consistent and more various provision than existed before or later. Wards, parishes and gilds were all mobilised, even more so than in the late medieval period, to judge by the small numbers of poor and sick housed in the hospitals at their dissolution and by recent accounts of the size, personnel and activities of the monasteries in their last years.

The idea still widely held that London relieved only 'freemen' or even only 'householders' belongs to the same group of erroneous conceptions about a largely disadvantaged population to which I have already referred. Acts of Parliament before the Act of Settlement of 1662 had laid down that anyone with a minimum residence qualification was eligible: three years' residence was required until 1598, but no residential qualifications were demanded in the great Acts of 1598 and 1601.[37] There is not an example known to me from more than 150 volumes of records of a person being refused relief on the ground that he was not a freeman. Usually men and women in receipt of the weekly dole were householders – but that is not to say that they *had* to be householders to get relief. Livery companies, parishes and wardmotes paid out considerable sums to many poor folk in need, in their own localities as elsewhere, 'the straggling poor' as they were called. Sometimes, the sums paid over and above doles could amount to as much as one quarter of all monies disbursed.[38]

Some historians have suggested that the poor law was rigid in its operations, unable to adjust to economic crisis or to individual needs. Flexibility is rarely a feature of administrative systems, and the poor law was no exception. Yet the variation in most City parishes in the size of the dole (from 1s. to 6s. monthly, according to discretion, from the 1620s to 1640s and up to 10s. a month by the 1660s) suggests that overseers considered the *need* of the recipient and adjusted pensions accordingly. Poorer parishes were much more restricted, especially in bad times. Here the dole was usually lower on average; the variation was considerably smaller; there were fewer supplementary benefits and payments in kind; and the provision for orphans and foundlings was less vigilant.[39]

[36] E. M. Leonard, *Early History of English Poor Relief*, 94; S. and B. Webb, *English Local Government: English Poor Law History*: Part 1, *The Old Poor Law* (1927), 149.

[37] *Statutes of the Realm*, IV(i), 14 Eliz. 5, cl.xvi; IV(ii), 39 Eliz. c.iii, 43 Eliz, c.ii.

[38] In a poor parish like St. Andrew Wardrobe, nearly 50 per cent of the receipts for the poor were going to casual distributions in the middle of the seventeenth century, and just over 50 per cent to pensioners: GLMS 2089:1, C.W.A. St. Andrew Wardrobe, passim.

[39] See the records of St. Bride's (GLMS 6552:1), St. Sepulchre's (GLMS 3146:1), St. Giles Cripplegate (GLMS 6047:1), St. Botolph Aldgate (GLMS 9237), and St. Botolph without Bishopsgate (GLMS 4525:2). As an example of variations in size of pensions see the records of St. Magnus London Bridge, Poor's Book (GLMS 1186, passim).

Another discretionary feature of the poor law was the large sums which were given in most inner parishes as supplementary payments. Let me illustrate by an example taken from the middle of the century. Peter Hartly, an old man in receipt of the dole in St. Bartholomew Exchange, a well-to-do but not one of the richest parishes, was paid a yearly pension of £2 3s. 4d. In addition, the parish paid his rent which came to £2 a year. When he fell sick an extra £2 10s. was expended on nursing fees and doctor's bills. Shortly after, the parish purchased a shirt for him and two pairs of shoes at a cost of 9s. 2d.: a total of £7 2s. 6d. in one year, a sum roughly equivalent to the wage of a journeyman in one of the poorer trades. In common with all those considered by the overseers to be poor, whether on the dole or not, he would have received, besides gifts of clothing, the annual free distribution made in most London parishes, often endowed by legacies, of cheese, bread and fuel.[40]

The tradition of making extra payments to meet special needs became a notable feature of the City, especially during bad times when churchwardens were ordered to make payments as needed.[41] Christmas bonuses for pensioners must also be added to the total receipts. Voluntary collections in the church and from door to door made an increasing contribution to poor relief in poorer and larger parishes as the century went on: charitable giving was encouraged, not frowned upon, in Protestant and Puritan England. Official special collections and 'briefs' ordered by the Lord Mayor for the poor of the City – and even elsewhere – were more frequent during the seventeenth century, and became a significant element in the total provision after the Fire. More significant earlier, because it raised much more money, was the doubling of the poor rate in crises, as for instance during the bad harvests and the economic and political dislocation of the years 1649-51.[42] Then the City parishes took action which went beyond the explicit terms of national legislation. The great Act of 1598 had laid down a maximum level of tax for ratepayers: no one was to be rated at more than 6d. weekly.[43] By the mid-seventeenth century, the old sixpenny rates in London had risen to nearly 1s. 6d. a week and even doubled further to 3s. in years of particular hardship.[44] (That is not to deny, of course, that there remained great accumulations of individual and parochial wealth in London which could have contributed far more than they did to the welfare of the needy.)

Seventeenth-century reformers such as Sir Matthew Hale charged that poor law rates were levied on rentals only, not on goods.[45] Sixteenth- and seventeenth-century legislation, as well as legal opinion, was explicit that, in towns, goods and personal property were also rateable.[46] In practice, however, Hale was probably right in suggesting that in London too much reliance

[40] E. Freshfield (ed.), *The Account Books of the Parish of St. Bartholomew Exchange in the City of London 1596-1698* (1895), 133.
[41] E. Freshfield (ed.), *The Vestry Minute Books of the Parish of St. Bartholomew Exchange . . . 1567-1676* (1890), vol. 1643-76, p.47.
[42] Ibid., 26, 28. But in some poorer parishes, such as All Hallows the Great, special collections increased at the expense of rates in the total sums collected, after the middle of the seventeenth century.
[43] *Statutes of the Realm*, IV(ii), cl.xii.
[44] Freshfield, *Vestry Minute Books of St. Bartholomew Exchange*, vol. 1643-76, pp.26, 28.
[45] Sir M. Hale, *Discourse Touching Provision for the Poor* (1683), 7-8.
[46] Michael Dalton, *The Countrey Justice* (1655), 115, quoting the resolution of the judges of assize in 1633 that extra sums could be levied from a man 'for his visible ability'.

was put on rental value and not enough on ownership of other kinds of property. Yet the rating was not based solely on rental, as a glance at the parish rating lists will show. Adjustment of rates occurred not only when a new householder moved in, but most noticeably on the death of the head of the household: the widow was normally assessed lower than her husband had been. There are also instances of year-by-year adjustments, presumably corresponding to the varying economic circumstances of the taxpayer. Miss Leonard alleged that the seventeenth-century unwillingness to pay rates was so general as to undermine the system. In London's inner parishes I have found such refusal rare; the small number of ratepayers in arrears was usually carefully noted in the records.[47]

London operated a rate-in-aid scheme in line with the provisions of the Acts of 1555, 1563 and 1598, which enjoined aldermen and J.P.s to levy rates on rich parishes to support poor ones.[48] Thus, 87 of the richer parishes supplemented the other 24 parishes which contained nearly half the population of the City. Guided by rough egalitarian principles, doles were compared and were adjusted when necessary with the aid of a poor's book in each parish inspected annually by the Court of Aldermen. In a poor parish, for example, like St. Andrew Wardrobe, where the mean rent was well below the City average, about one-third of the total expenditure on the poor came from richer parishes.[49] There is evidence that the Aldermen aimed at a rough parity between poorer and richer areas in numbers of pensioners: in one of the largest extra-mural parishes where we have fairly full records, the number of pensioners per head of population was remarkably close to the number in the rich areas[50] – although this was less impressive than it looks, since the number of poor was far greater in the outer parishes.

The fellow-feeling of human beings does not submit easily to quantification and comparison. One eminent historian has recently detected coldness towards children as a typical expression of family feeling in the early modern period.[51] Can his social thermometer be working properly? If there were coldness towards children, we might expect to find positive callousness towards orphans. Yet when we look closely at the inner City in the sixteenth and seventeenth centuries, a different picture emerges. Apart from the parishes, Christ's Hospital catered for about 700 orphans a year.[52] For such a

[47] Freshfield, *Vestry Minute Books . . . St. Bartholomew Exchange*, passim. Occasionally ratepayers offered to pay more than the sum rated: GLMS 4810:2 (n.p.), C.W.A. St. James Garlickhithe. Some parishes included among their books of reference a 'statute' book. See GLMS 1176:1 (n.p.), St. Margaret Fish Street.
[48] *Statutes of the Realm*, IV(ii), 39 Eliz. c.iii, cl.ii. Calculated from the rate equalisation scheme operated by the City and described in the repertories of the aldermanic bench, parish records and Christ's Hospital records.
[49] GLMS 2089:1, passim; D. V. Glass, *London Inhabitants within the Walls 1695* (London Record Society, 1966), xxii, xxiii; T. C. Dale, *Inhabitants of London in 1638*, 27-9.
[50] Cf. St. Bride's Fleet Steet, whose population was about 5,000 in the middle of the seventeenth century, with St. Bartholomew Exchange containing a population of around 800. St. Bride's spent roughly six times as much on the poor as St. Bartholomew Exchange.
[51] L. Stone, *The Family, Sex and Marriage in England 1500-1800* (1977), esp. 99-102.
[52] V. Pearl, 'Puritans and poor relief: the London Workhouse 1649-1660', in D. Pennington and K. Thomas (eds), *Puritans and Revolutionaries. Essays in Seventeenth-Century History presented to Christopher Hill* (Oxford 1978), 211, 212 n.3.

purpose it had been founded, but its gradual transition to a famous school brought more orphans into the care of the localities. As one might expect, the poorest parishes supported fewer of these children than did the richer ones; the great number of unemployed and elderly received priority. The 87 or so moderately rich and rich parishes provide many examples of care and humanity, although we need not swing to the other extreme of imagining the existence in London of Pestalozzian villages for the fatherless young.

National legislation made the charge of poor children one of the special obligations of parochial authorities. But Parliament laid stress on apprenticeship: it made no mention of nursing and caring for the very young. Here, London made a special contribution. The City suffered acutely from the problem of poor, parentless children, an almost universal phenomenon of early modern society caused by low life expectancy and accentuated in the City by recurrent plague. Unexpectedly there is little evidence, in parish records of pre-Fire London, of the common accompaniment – the youthful gangs of homeless street-arabs described in some vagrant literature of the time. London, however, suffered more than rural areas from foundling children left on the doorsteps of wealthier parishes in the hope that responsible citizens would welcome them. Provision for these unfortunate children occupied much of the time of the parish overseers and churchwardens. Indeed, the cost of maintaining foundlings was higher per head and usually higher in total within the parish than the cost of doles or pensions paid out to the elderly, the sick and the unemployed.

Whereas the average dole was about £2 10s. a year in mid-seventeenth-century London, the charges incurred by richer parishes for foundlings ranged between £5 and £11 a year, depending on age and the kind of provision made. A comprehensive study of three parishes ranked among the top third in wealth, St. Bartholomew Exchange, St. Margaret Lothbury and St. Christopher le Stocks, shows that from the later sixteenth century boy and girl foundlings were nursed, cared for and even 'educated'.[53] We know that, in the City, petty schools and some of the grammar schools took poor children either without fees, if very poor, or on payment of a small sum. Even foundlings were educated. Poor's books record expenses for schooling amounting in mid-century to 8s. a year for each orphan. They also record the buying of horn books for them and for children of poor families. Some were supplied with 'books' – the titles unfortunately are not given – and with the Bible.[54] It is not clear how much or how little real education was provided.

[53] Freshfield, *Vestry Minute Books of St. Bartholomew Exchange*, passim; GLMS 4352:1, C.W.A. St. Margaret Lothbury; GLMS 4423:1, C.W.A. St. Christopher Le Stocks; GLMS 6836:1, C.W.A. St. Helen's Bishopgate; GLMS 1455:1, C.W.A. St. Botolph Aldgate; GLMS 645:2, C.W.A. St. Peter Westcheap; GLMS 4887:1,2, C.W.A. St. Dunstan's in the East; GLMS 4071:2, C.W.A. St. Michael Cornhill; GLMS 4570:2, C.W.A. St. Margaret Patten; GLMS 524, C.W.A. St. Michael Wood Street; GLMS 1313:1, C.W.A. St. Martin Ludgate. For radical attitudes to the education of very young children, including girls, see C. Webster, *The Great Instauration: Science, Medicine and Reform* (1975), 103ff., 220.

[54] K. Charlton, *Education in Renaissance England* (1965), 98, 104; S. M. Wide and J. A. Morris, 'The episcopal licensing of schoolmasters in the diocese of London 1627-1685', *Guildhall Miscellany* (1968), 402-6; I. Pinchbeck and M. Hewitt, *Children in English Society* (1969), 36-41; Freshfield, *Vestry Minute Books of St. Bartholomew Exchange*, passim; GLMS 645:2 (n.p.), C.W.A. St. Peter Westcheap; GLMS 1455:1 (n.p.), C.W.A. St. Botolph Aldgate; GLMS 1016:1 (n.p.), C.W.A. St. Matthew Friday Street, f. 102.

Perhaps the foster mother taught the three Rs, or the children attended trade schools: both were necessary and usual preparations for apprenticeship to which by Act of Parliament orphan children were destined. A few references in the records suggest regular school attendance. Girl foundlings[55] were educated as well as boys, perhaps in the belief that children should be given something to do irrespective of their sex, more probably from a Puritan desire to inculcate habits of industry and good order among both sexes. It is likely that girl orphans were mainly taught vocational skills and spent more time knitting than in writing or in casting accounts. That foundlings were educated as well as nursed was not out of period. Such provisions were made in Christ's Hospital. Even the Corporation of the Poor, the London workhouse established under the Commonwealth, devoted two hours a day to the education of its charges.[56] Orphans were destined for apprenticeship, which in most cases involved, theoretically at least, a training in reading, writing and casting accounts: the Goldsmiths, for example, rigorously imposed a writing test on applicants for apprenticeship and ensured that masters taught their apprentices to read and write.[57]

Most parishes sent foundlings out to nurse in the country around London. St. Bartholomew Exchange used nurses in Ware and Hertford, and orphans were sent from other parts of the City to Walthamstow, Hounslow, Brentford, Chelsford in Kent, and Guildford.[58] Perhaps the practice of nursing some distance from the metropolis explains what appears to be the higher survival rate of foundlings in the early modern period. Removal from London no doubt proved a defence against epidemics, although expense may have been uppermost in the minds of the vestry. Having been fostered and educated, orphans and foundlings were apprenticed for longer than usual terms to solidly-based 'mechanical' trades such as silkweaving, shoemaking and tailoring. Apprenticeship, and service in other people's houses, were less traumatic than we might think, for they were normal through all ranks of society. Of course, orphans were always liable to exploitation, but overseers

---

[55] Freshfield, *Vestry Minute Books of St. Bartholomew Exchange*, vol. 1643-76, pp.28, 108; E. Freshfield (ed.), *The Vestry Minute Book of the Parish of St. Margaret Lothbury 1571-1677* (1877), passim; E. Freshfield (ed.), *Minutes of the Vestry Meetings and the Records of the Parish of St. Christopher Le Stocks* (1886), passim. For schooling of orphans, see also GLMS 587:1, C.W.A. St. Anne and St. Agnes; GLMS 66:1, C.W.A. St. Mary Colechurch; GLMS 3146:1, C.W.A. St. Sepulchre; GLMS 7882:1,2, C.W.A. St. Dunstan in the East; GLMS 6836:1, C.W.A. St. Helen's Bishopsgate; GLMS 9237, Poor's Book, St. Botolph without Aldgate; GLMS 645:2, Poor's Book, St. Peter Westcheap; GLMS 818:1, Poor's Book, All Hallows the Great.

[56] V. Pearl, 'Puritans and poor relief', 223.

[57] Goldsmiths' Company MS.1648.13.39, Apprentice Book, 1; Wardens Accounts and Court Minutes, v, E.F. MS.1522 B.39, ff.22 (16 July 1536), 100 (5 April 1538), 27 (25 Aug. 1536); Goldsmith's Hall, Ordinances and Statutes, 1, MS.2524, c.81, f.58v, 1469. See also A. H. Johnson, *History of the . . . Drapers*, II, 28.

[58] Freshfield, *Vestry Minute Books of St. Bartholomew Exchange*, passim; GLMS 3891:1, C.W.A. St. Mary Abchurch; GLMS 9235:2, C.W.A. St. Botolph without Aldgate; GLMS 4570:2, C.W.A. St. Margaret Patten; GLMS 1432:4, C.W.A. St. Alphage London Wall; GLMS 524:1, C.W.A. St. Michael Wood Street; GLMS 2895:2, C.W.A. St. Michael le Querne; GLMS 1016:1, St. Matthew Friday Street; GLMS 7673:1,2, C.W.A. St. Alban Wood Street; GLMS 1188:1, C.W.A. St. Michael Crooked Lane; GLMS 3989:1, Poor's Book, St. Bartholomew the Great. For the practice of wet-nursing by Londoners, see R. A. P. Finlay, 'Population and fertility in London, 1580-1650', *Journal of Family History*, IV(i) (1979), 26-38.

and churchwardens were alive to the danger. Extra payments were made to foster-mothers as rewards for proper care. Modern social workers may find that their activities go back a long way. St. Bartholomew Exchange sent representatives on annual inspections of their charges, and on one occasion a report that the children being nursed at Ware were ill-treated prompted an extra visit.[59]

No system can guarantee humane treatment. Two features of City life provided minor safeguards against abuse: the smallness of City parishes, where everyone knew everyone else,[60] and the practice by which decisions about the poor were frequently made by a general meeting of parishioners. Large boards of governors, elected in Common Council, maintained communal responsibility over most London workhouses and hospitals. The Corporation of the Poor surpassed all of them with its 52 governors elected annually in the City's wardmotes.[61] Even so, we should of course beware of taking too sentimental a view of parochial administration. Unfortunately the sessions records, which present us with the harsher face of poor relief, do not exist in any number for the pre-Restoration City. I have found few *charges* of neglect in the parish records – but churchwardens and overseers are unlikely to have deliberately recorded their own failings and errors. Heavy-handed paternalism by parish officers is suggested by the unhappy custom of naming foundlings, sometimes with Christian as well as surnames, after the parish or alley where they were found. So many poor little Robert Foster Lane le Grands, Thomas Leg Alleys, Sarah Threadneedles, and Margaret Throgmortons: such children, their parents unknown, might bear patronymic witness throughout their lives to their base and obscure births – unless of course they changed their names, as one suspects many of them did: few such names seem to have survived. Badging the poor with tin armlets, making the dole dependent on unpleasant parish tasks, and driving away immigrants (particularly pregnant women who might be a charge on the rates) were other inhumanities of the time.

Although most seventeenth-century pensioners were either orphans or widows, there were also examples of provision for large families – again provision suggested by Act of Parliament. Often, these families were problem ones, partly disadvantaged in one or more ways and often in trouble with the law or with their neighbours. One case particularly illuminates relations within the close-knit community of parish poor and overseers. A

---

[59] Freshfield, *Account Books of St. Bartholomew Exchange,* vol. 1567-1643, pp.163, 167; Freshfield, *Vestry Minute Book of St. Bartholomew Exchange,* vol. 1643-76, p.62. Here, seventeenth-century practice anticipated a reform put forward by later writers. Similarly the eighteenth-century suggestions of James Hanway and others that apprentices should be sent out of the City into the country to be bound, and that a fee of not less than £4 2s. should be given with them, had been met by the seventeenth century in my three parishes and in many others. Freshfield, *Vestry Minute Book of St. Bartholomew Exchange,* passim; Freshfield, *Vestry Minute Book of St. Christopher Le Stocks,* passim; Freshfield, *Vestry Minute Book of St. Margaret Lothbury,* passim; J. Hanway, *An Exact Appeal for Mercy to the Children of the Poor* (1766), 34-6.
[60] 'Change and stability in seventeenth-century London', 15.
[61] V. Pearl, 'Puritans and poor relief', 223.

widow on the dole in the 1630s came to court (perhaps the poor man's court set up in 1516 for low cost suits) to plead her cause. She lost it and found herself in Wood Street Compter. The vestry bought her out and paid her debts. So that she might mend her ways, they insisted that the money be paid back weekly from her dole. But the repayments were beyond her means and she took to selling apples in the parish's main thoroughfare. In doing so she offended again. Hawking, one of the common resorts of the hard-up and unskilled poor, was illegal. Moreover, she compounded her offence by the loud calling-out of her wares. The respectable vestrymen found a solution which may be seen as a triumph of humanity tempered by a respect for private enterprise. Her stock of apples was bought up and the vestry undertook to pay her rent.[62]

The records show a variety of supplementary benefits: payment of the debts of prisoners and of the costs of spells in Ludgate, Newgate and Bridewell; redemption of clothes in pawn; payment of medical fees (a practice enjoined by Act of Parliament and found even in poorer parishes); provision of rent-free accommodation (either out of the parish property devoted to the poor, or by rent to the landlord); and payment of municipal and other taxes of the slightly better off when they fell on hard times.[63] A few parishes made a point of buying out harsh landlords and taking over their property which they managed in a more generous fashion. Rehousing sometimes resulted in early examples of town improvement. When St. Bartholomew Exchange bought up property belonging to rack-renting landlords in Dibbles Alley in 1652, the parish renovated two of the houses for the use of pensioners and laid on piped water.[64] But rehousing could also disregard tenants' rights. John Stow cites an early example of houses being pulled down over people's heads – the inhabitants had refused to go when their houses were to be demolished to make way for the Royal Exchange.[65]

Where there is public or publicly controlled housing one must also expect to find that the relationship between landlord and tenant is not exclusively economic. There is evidence in the sixteenth century of a squatter in the public domain. It is a single case only and we do not know how widespread squatting was. What does emerge is the leniency with which the offence was treated. In 1585 a widow, unable to find a home, barricaded herself in the Vestry House of St. Margaret Lothbury. The Vestry House was not a room in the church as today but a two-storied building adjoining it. She was told by the churchwardens that her pension would be stopped, perhaps in lieu of rent, unless she left. She refused, and continued to occupy the building for two years. On her departure, the Vestry voted to restore her pension.[66] Such

---

[62] Freshfield, *Vestry Minute Book of St. Bartholomew Exchange*, vol. 1567-1643, pp.119, 124.

[63] *Statutes of the Realm*, IV(I), 1 Ed. VI, c.iii, cl.xi.; Freshfield, *Account Books of St. Bartholomew Exchange*, 147ff.; Freshfield, *Vestry Minute Book of St. Bartholomew Exchange*, passim. Freshfield, *Vestry Minute Book of St. Margaret Lothbury*, passim.

[64] Freshfield, *Vestry Minute Books of St. Bartholomew Exchange*, vol. 1643-76, p.42. Freshfield, *Account Books of St. Bartholomew Exchange*, pp.147ff.

[65] Stow (ed. Kingsford), II, 303.

[66] Freshfield, *Vestry Minute Book of St. Margaret Lothbury*, 17, 18. See also a statement in C.W.A. of St. Dunstan's in the East, 1648 (n.p.) 'that all the poor who have parish houses to pay their accustomed rents by which they may acknowledge the parish the owners thereof, and not dispose of the same houses to inmates as of late they have done'.

conciliatory treatment of a clear case of 'direct action' witnesses to a fairly tolerant and reasonably cohesive community, although of course not one without conflict.

It hardly needs saying that this was not 'the welfare state'. We should remember the distinction commonly made between the unfortunate and the wicked pauper, the one deserving of charity, the other of punishment. 'There are God's poor and the Devil's poor,' thundered Thomas Adams in the pulpit in 1628, repeating the common currency of medieval times. But fire in the pulpit and broadsides in the press do not necessarily turn into thunderbolts in the street. There is evidence, especially in the richer parishes, that aid was occasionally given even to transgressors and malefactors. Here, few, except vagrants towards whom harsh measures were usual, were denied relief if their sufferings were known.

Historians have rightly pointed out that the poor law provided a supplementation for inadequate wages arising from widespread under-employment in early modern society. This supplementation has been described in a number of recent histories as too small to be of significance. Are we right to discount it? Although it is difficult to estimate total figures for relief in London, there is no doubt that the amount was considerable. Until the mid-seventeenth century, many gilds raised yearly sums for the poor through quarterage payments of the yeomanry. They also gave generously to the poor even outside their membership, in parishes where they had some association. It is not easy to put a figure on such contributions because of the great number of companies and their disparities in wealth, size and generosity. Nevertheless, quarterage payments alone may have raised £2,000 a year in the mid-seventeenth century, and the total relief payment from the livery companies could have been in the region of £14,000.[67] A second source of aid was the City wardmotes. Although the records for seventeenth-century London are generally too sparse for us to estimate the total contribution of the wardmotes, the evidence does permit an informed guess for the 111 City parishes. I estimate that about £15,000 was raised directly for the poor in these parishes. Quarterage payments and wardmotes together thus provide a possible total of nearly £30,000 a year. The figure receives some support from various contemporary estimates made at the end of the seventeenth century. The most convincing of these gives a total of £40,000 from the City and suburban parishes (the livery companies are excluded).[68] In using this figure we must allow for the relative increase in wealth during the seventeenth century; but even when we allow for it, my £30,000 seems unlikely to be an over-estimate for the earlier part of the century.

An interesting calculation can be made. Contemporaries placed one-fifth

[67] This figure is only a conjecture based on the records of some of the larger companies whose records are in the Guildhall Library.

[68] The Board of Trade in 1697 conjectured that £400,000 was paid in taxes throughout the country towards the poor of which about £40,000 was raised within London and the Bills of Mortality: Jordan, *Philanthropy*, 141; Public Record Office, C.O. 389/14. A year's poor rates towards raising a stock for the Corporation of the Poor in 1697 was assessed at just over £10,000 in December 1698: J.Co.Co., LII, ff.228-230v.

of the City population in the category of 'poor'. Thus around 8,000 house-holders would each be receiving, in money and kind, supplementation to the value of £3 15*s.* a year over and above their earnings, as well as free parish housing where it was provided. Of course, this money was going partly to unproductive non-wage earners; on the other hand something should be allowed for wage earners who would have been called upon to support their aged, orphaned or infirm relatives.

Such supplementation throughout the City buttressed the poor in times of hardship. By maintaining demand it helped also to preserve the small trader and shopkeeper. It allowed perhaps even some small measure of economic growth, particularly in those cheap and new manufactures that Joan Thirsk describes as serving the mass of people through the provision of by-employments and consumer goods. Conceivably, however, it also encouraged a countervailing tendency. Did the alleviation of distress have an important influence on the size of the available labour supply? Did it make labour less amenable and therefore less attractive to entrepreneurs and investors? Have we here a factor in the retardation of capitalist development?

These are large questions which we cannot answer here. The *political* effects of poor relief, however, are plain. The poor laws, as laid down by Acts of Parliament, were administered in London by more than 1,400 elected officials involving one in every 21 householders. Sustaining demand in bad times as well as good, poor relief helped to preserve political stability. In a time of unprecedented but not necessarily unforeseen growth, the operation of the parochial 'poor stock' exemplified the managerial enterprise and energy of hundreds of City and parochial officials. It testified to a growing sense of communal responsibility which increased, rather than diminished, in the century of Puritanism. Poor relief in London was not a cure for poverty. At the same time it was emphatically not the harsh 'new medicine' presented to us by Professor Tawney.

11

The Language of Adam in Seventeenth-Century England

David S. Katz

'There is scarce any subject that hath been more throughly scanned and debated amongst Learned men,' wrote John Wilkins, one of the founders of the Royal Society, 'than the *Original* of *Languages* and *Letters*.'[1] Yet despite this intense study, there was very little that could be thought to be indisputable fact for seventeenth-century linguistic scholars. The identity and nature of mankind's first language were obscure, and simple solutions did not suggest themselves. Until the sixteenth century, most Western thinkers assumed that this first language was Hebrew: this was the belief of Isidore of Seville in the seventh century, and of Dante seven hundred years later.[2] Afterwards, however, Hebrew became merely the leading candidate. The principal problem was that the Old Testament makes no mention of the Hebrew language at all. The closest approach to an identification is Isaiah's reference to 'the language of Canaan'.[3]

In any case, the most pressing aspects of the question were mystical rather than exclusively scholarly. For God created the world through speech: 'And God said, Let there be light: and there was light'; 'In the beginning was the Word, and the Word was with God, and the Word was God.'[4] Since God created the world by speaking the original language, it was argued, then perhaps by following the thread backwards mankind might discover and acquire some of the inner secrets of the universe. It was known that Adam's language precisely expressed things: then there was none of the ambiguity normally associated with language. When he named the animals he chose

[1] John Wilkins, *An Essay Towards a Real Character, And a Philosophical Language* (London 1668), 2.
[2] W. S. Allen, 'Ancient ideas on the origin and development of language', *Transactions of the Philological Society* (1948), 35-60. The classic work on this subject is A. Borst, *Der Turmbau von Babel* (Stuttgart 1957-63), III/1. See also L. Couturat and L. Leau, *Histoire de la Langue Universelle* (Paris 1903); L. Formigari, *Linguistica ed empirismo nel Seicento inglese* (Bari 1970); R. Fraser, *The Language of Adam: On the Limits and Systems of Discourse* (New York 1977); M. Cohen, *Sensible Words* (Baltimore & London 1977). For the medieval Nominalists, Hobbes, and a discussion of the quest for a 'universal grammar' see G. A. Padley, *Grammatical Theory in Western Europe 1500-1700* (Cambridge 1976), 141-3, 154-209.
[3] Isaiah XIX.18.
[4] Genesis I.3; John I.1.

words which mirrored exactly their essential natures. Language was perfectly congruent with reality. If the identity of this Adamic language could be revealed, then mankind would *already* possess the means to uncover more of God's divine plan.

Most scholars rejected the notion, as John Webb the architect put it, 'that the language spoke by our first Parents, admitted any whatever alteration either in the Form or Dialect and pronunciation thereof, before the *Confusion of Tongues* at *Babel*'. This original language, he said, was called '*Lingua humana*, the *Humane Tongue*',[5] whose nature was revealed in the biblical description of Adam's naming of the animals:

> And out of the ground the LORD God formed every beast of the field, and every fowl of the air; and brought *them* unto Adam to see what he would call them: and whatsoever Adam called every living creature, that *was* the name thereof. And Adam gave names to all cattle, and to the fowl of the air, and to every beast of the field . . .[6]

For early modern Englishmen, the tags that Adam gave to God's creatures were not mere arbitrary sounds. 'He came into the World a Philosopher,' explained the churchman Robert South, 'which sufficiently appeared by his writing the Nature of things upon their Names: he could view Essences in themselves, and read Forms without the comment of their respective Properties.'[7] Francis Bacon noted that the 'first acts which man performed in Paradise consisted of the two summary parts of knowledge; the view of creatures, and the imposition of names'. Bacon praised 'that pure and uncorrupted natural knowledge whereby Adam gave names to the creatures according to their propriety'.[8] Milton would make exactly the same point. His Adam talks of how he 'nam'd them, as they pass'd, and understood Thir Nature, with such knowledge God endu'd My sudden apprehension'. 'Moreover,' Milton wrote in his *Christian Doctrine*, 'he could not have given names to the animals in that extempore way, without very great intelligence.'[9]

The names which Adam gave to the creatures thus expressed in some way their essential natures, so that naming was equivalent to knowing. This model condition prevailed until the expulsion from the Garden of Eden, when man began worldly life with a curse both upon his labours and upon his language. It would be 'too-too happy!', lamented Joshua Sylvester in his translation of Du Bartas's scriptural epic, 'had that fall of thine Not cancell'd so the Character divine'.[10] John Donne believed that 'names are to instruct us, and express natures and essences. This *Adam* was able to do.'[11] 'I cannot but

---

[5] John Webb, *An Historical Essay* (London 1669), 16-17.
[6] Genesis II.19-20.
[7] Robert South, *A Sermon Preached At . . . St. Paul, Novemb. 9. 1662* (London 1663), 11.
[8] Francis Bacon, *Works*, ed. J. Spedding *et al.* (London 1857-9), III, 296; IV, 20.
[9] John Milton, *Paradise Lost*, VIII, 352-4; *Complete Prose Works of John Milton*, ed. D. H. Wolfe *et al.* (New Haven 1953), VI, 324 (*Chr. Doc.*, bk. i., ch.vii). See also S. E. Fish, *Surprised by Sin* (Berkeley & London 1971), 107-30.
[10] Joshua Sylvester, *Du Bartas His Diuine Weekes* (London 1641), 57.
[11] John Donne, *Essays in Divinity*, ed. E. M. Simpson (Oxford 1952), 23: written about 1615; first published 1651.

conceive,' John Webster argued, 'that *Adam* did understand both their internal and external signatures, and that the imposition of their names was adaequately agreeing with their natures: otherwise it could not univocally and truely be said to be their names.' For there was an exact correspondence between words and things before the Fall, and if Adam's names did 'not exactly agree in all things, then there is a difference and disparity between them, and in that incongruity lies error and falshood'.[12] Theophilus Gale, formerly a Fellow of Magdalen College, Oxford, noted that we can no longer 'give *names* exactly suited to the natures of things, as *Adam* before them did'.[13]

Although naturally the biblical evidence was always paramount, scholars were aware that classical sources also referred to the question of the original language. Among the most important of these was Plato's *Cratylus*, in which Socrates explained that 'words should as far as possible resemble things . . . if we could always, or almost always, use likenesses which are perfectly appropriate, this would be the most perfect state of language.'[14] Yet the classical testimony that captured the imagination of early modern Europeans dealt with a more thorny question: the exact identity of this original language which mirrored reality so precisely. This was the famous story from Herodotus of Psammetichus, King of Egypt, who 'took two newborn children of common men and gave them to a shepherd to bring up among his flocks. He gave charge that none should speak any word in their hearing.' Psammetichus wanted 'to hear what speech would first break from the children'. They said nothing for two years, but 'one day as he opened the door and entered both the children ran to him stretching out their hands and calling "Bekos"'. The King made enquiries and discovered that 'Bekos' was the Phrygian word signifying bread. 'Reasoning from this fact,' Herodotus concludes, 'the Egyptians confessed that the Phrygians were older than they.'[15]

The experiment of Psammetichus was for most early modern English scholars important but not conclusive empirical evidence. Samuel Purchas the great cataloguer of religions thought that the children's utterance was simply 'the voice that they had heard of their nurses the Goats'. Purchas cited a similar experiment with thirty children, in which the aim was to discover which 'Religion whereto they should addict themselues. But neither could they euer speake', let alone follow a particular rite.[16] Joshua Sylvester expressed the same point in verse:

> Fools which perceiv'd not, that the bleating flocks
> W^ch powl'd the neighbour Mountains motly locks
> Had taught this tearm, and that no tearms of *Rome*,
> *Greece, Egypt, England, France, Troy, Jewry*, come,
> Come born with us: but every Countries tongue
> Is learnt by much use, and frequenting long.[17]

[12] John Webster, *Academiarum Examen* (London 1654), 29–30.
[13] Theophilus Gale, *The Covrt Of The Gentiles* (Oxford 1669–77), II, 7.
[14] *The Dialogues of Plato*, trans. B. Jowett (3rd edn, Oxford 1892), I, 382–3.
[15] Herodotus, II, 2 (ed. Godley, I, 275, 277).
[16] Samuel Purchas, *Pvrchas his Pilgrimage* (2nd edn, London 1614), 46.
[17] Sylvester, *Du Bartas*, 122.

An English report of the 'conferences of the French virtuosi' included a note that 'Women have such a facility of speaking, that if two Children especially of different sexes were bred up together, 'tis likely the female would speak first . . . Which was the reason of the miscarriage of the King of *Egypts* trial, which he made only with Boys.'[18] Still, despite these doubts, this text from Herodotus carried great weight, especially among the seventeenth-century language planners. Nathaniel Smart, in his introductory poem to the linguist-vicar Cave Beck's scheme for a universal character, even said that the children's words were prophetic, as if to say 'to retrive again One common speech should be thy work O *Beck*'.[19]

This testimony from Herodotus was compelling but was far removed from Adam's naming of the animals. One of the most imaginative interpretations of the scriptural evidence came from Johannes Goropius Becanus, the Netherlandish physician and linguist. Goropius Becanus found Dutch equivalents for all of the proper names in Genesis, with the aim of establishing his own mother tongue as the *lingua humana*.[20] The novel and unscriptural hypothesis that Adam spoke Dutch in Paradise provoked great scholarly mirth across Europe, and in England as well. Samuel Purchas was merciless:

> *Goropius* by a few Dutch Etymologies grew into conceit, and would haue the world beleeue him that Dutch was the first language; which if it were, we English should raigne with them as a Colonie of that Dutch Citie, a streame from that fountaine, by commerce and conquests since manifoldly mixed. But his euidence is too weake, his authoritie too new.[21]

Nevertheless, Goropius Becanus did find some supporters, or at least some sympathisers. His fellow countryman Abraham Mylius saw much truth in his theories, and provided several additional arguments.[22] The work of Goropius Becanus was carried forward in the next generation by Adrian van Schriek (Schriekius) who not only posited Dutch as the *lingua humana*, but also sought to prove that Celtic derived from Hebrew, a thesis which was developed by Samuel Bochart and Pierre Borel.[23]

The Dutch challenge for the honour of being the Adamic vernacular was introduced into England by Richard Rowlands, the eccentric Roman Catholic student of Anglo-Saxon from Christ Church, Oxford. Rowlands was London-born, a cooper's son, but when he found himself barred by

[18] G. Havers and J. Davies, *Another Collection Of Philosophical Conferences* (London 1665), 215.
[19] Cave Beck, *The Universal Character* (London 1657), sig. A5v. On early modern language planning see especially J. Knowlson, *Universal Language Schemes* (Toronto & Buffalo 1975); V. Salmon, 'Language planning in seventeenth-century England; its context and aims', in C. E. Bazell *et al.* (eds), *In Memory of J. R. Firth* (London 1966), 370–97; O. Funke, *Zum Weltsprachenproblem in England im 17. Jahrhundert* (Heidelberg 1929).
[20] Johannes Goropius Becanus, *Origines Antwerpianae* (Antwerp 1569), especially pp.539–51; A. Williams, *The Common Expositor* (Chapel Hill 1948), 229.
[21] Purchas, *Pilgrimage*, 46.
[22] G. J. Metcalf, 'Abraham Mylius on historical linguistics', *Proceedings of the Modern Language Association*, LXVIII (1953), 535–54.
[23] G. Dottin, *La Langue Gauloise* (Paris 1920), 6–7; V. Tourneur, *Esquisse d'une Histoire des Etudes Celtiques* (Liège 1905), 191, 195, 197; G. Bonfante, 'Ideas on the kinship of the European languages from 1200 to 1800', *Journal of World History*, I (1953–4), 678–99, especially pp.685 ff.

religion from taking his degree, he emigrated to the Low Countries whence his grandfather had come, and adopted the original family name of Verstegan. Richard Verstegan became a printer in Antwerp, corresponded with Sir Robert Cotton, and even managed to procure an interview with Philip II in 1595.[24] Verstegan was very sympathetic to this new theory, and began to make enquiries. 'In conference one day with *Abraham Ortelius* (who had bin acquainted with *Becanus*)', he recounted,

> I asked him yf hee thought that *Becanus* himself beeing so learned as hee was, did in deed belieue this language to bee the first of all languages of the world, to wit, that which was spoke by *Adam*: he told mee that hee verely thought *Becanus* did so belieue: and added further, that many learned men might peraduenture laugh at that which hee had written, but that none would bee able to confute it.

Whereby, Verstegan concluded, 'I gessed that *Ortelius* did much enclyne vnto *Becanus*'. That Abraham Oertel, the great sixteenth-century Flemish geographer whose atlas was a standard work, should be sympathetic to the idea that Dutch had been spoken in the Garden of Eden, was a powerful recommendation. Verstegan himself rehearsed the etymologies of Goropius Becanus, and concluded that the Dutch language provided 'fit and proper significations for these moste ancient names'. If it was not absolutely clear that Dutch was the Adamic language, then surely 'it cannot bee denied to bee one of the moste ancientest of the world'.[25] Nevertheless, Verstegan's work alone lacked the ability to establish the antiquity of Dutch. Most Englishmen, like Samuel Butler, found it difficult to believe that when Eve was in the Garden 'the Devil tempted her By a *high Dutch* Interpreter'.[26] Ben Jonson's Epicure Mammon thus provided a comic moment when he tried to convince Surly the gambling soldier that Adam wrote a treatise dealing with 'the philosopher's stone, and in High Dutch . . . Which proves it was the primitive tongue.'[27]

In any case, other languages apart from Dutch had supporters who put them forward in the academic controversy which raged on the Continent and eventually drew in many of the great figures of early modern linguistics. In Spain, John Huarte argued that the 'frantike persons speaking of Latine, without that he euer learned the same in his health time' implied not only 'the consonance which the Latin toong holds with the reasonable soule' but quite possibly the identity of the language which Adam used to name the animals.[28] Wolfgang Lazius collected evidence that the French, Spanish and Italians once spoke German dialects in the remote past. Athanasius Kircher, the German Jesuit scholar, not only conducted research into the Chinese language, but also sought to prove that German is a dialect of the language spoken by

[24] *Dictionary of National Biography, s.v.* 'Rowlands'.
[25] Richard Verstegan, *A Restitution of Decayed Intelligence* (Antwerp 1605), sigs. ++r–v; pp.190–3: a second edition appeared at London 35 years after his death, in 1655.
[26] Samuel Butler, *Hudibras*, ed. J. Wilders (Oxford 1967), 6.
[27] Ben Jonson, *The Alchemist*, II, i. 84–6.
[28] John Huarte, *Examen de Jngenios* (London 1594), 46–7. Jourdain Guibelet the French royal physician refuted Huarte's book in his *Examen De L'Examen Des Esprits* (Paris 1631), especially pp.386–92.

Ashkenaz son of Gomer, the ancestor of the Teutonic race. Nicholas Serarius reported that Samaritan was in fact the oldest language, and was fiercely attacked by Kircher and by Brian Walton, the editor of the Polyglot Bible. Perhaps most importantly, the works of Joseph Scaliger were being disseminated and digested by Edward Brerewood and others, along with his classification of European languages into eleven unrelated 'mother tongues'.[29] One of the French 'virtuosi' whose researches were transmitted to England announced that Hebrew, Latin, and Greek were all perfect 'Mother-Languages'.[30] Descartes, reporting on a proposal for a universal 'common writing' sent to him by his friend Marin Mersenne in November 1629, wrote that its author claimed to have discovered the mother tongue from which all other languages are descended. Charles Sorel the historiographer complained that those who put forward such claims were always vague regarding the exact identity of the Adamic tongue, because they wanted others to believe that the language they had discovered was extraordinarily secret and mysterious.[31]

But the most bizarre theory was an English contribution, and came from John Webb, the pupil, relation, and executor of Inigo Jones. Webb was the man whom Christopher Wren defeated for the post of Surveyor of Works after the Restoration. 'When then it is reputed ridiculous to hear that *Adam* spake *Dutch* in Paradice', Webb thought, it might be worthwhile to consider the argument that 'the Language of the Empire of CHINA, is, the PRIMITIVE Tongue, which was common to the whole World before the Flood'. This novel concept could be proved by the fact that the Chinese 'were primitively planted in CHINA, if not by *Noah* himself, by some of the Issue of *Sem*, before the remove of *Nimrod* to *Shinaar*, and the *Confusion* of *Tongues* at *Babel*'. The Chinese language could not have changed because their country had never been conquered 'as could prejudice, but rather dilate their language'. The Chinese had always been isolated from commercial and cultural contacts, lest their language and customs become corrupted. The proper names in the Old Testament were simply translations from the Chinese. Adam quite clearly spoke Chinese in the Garden because language 'was not a studied or artificial speech, nor taught our *First Parents* by Art and by degrees as their Generations have been, but concreated with them'. Despite Webb's unique beliefs on the origin of speech, he joined in the common hope that a universal language might be found so that 'we might no longer complain of

[29] Borst, *Babel*, iii/1; M. T. Hodgen, *Early Anthropology in the Sixteenth and Seventeenth Centuries* (Philadelphia 1964), ch.8; D. C. Allen, 'Some theories of the growth and origin of language in Milton's age', *Philological Quarterly*, xxviii (1949), 5–16; Francis Lodwick, *Works*, ed. V. Salmon (London 1972), ch.3; Bonfante, 'Ideas', 678–99; Knowlson, *Universal language*, ch.1; P. Cornelius, *Languages in Seventeenth- and Early Eighteenth-Century Imaginary Voyages* (Geneva 1965), ch.1; Williams, *Expositor*, ch.11; D. Abercrombie, 'Forgotten phoneticians', *Transactions of the Philological Society* (1948), 1–34.
[30] Havers and Davies, *Conferences*, 304–5. For more on the French view of Hebrew, see D. P. Walker, *The Ancient Theology* (London 1972), 99–101.
[31] In M. Mersenne, *Correspondance*, ed. P. Tannery et al. (Paris 1945), ii, 323–9; Knowlson, *Universal Language*, 44–50, 65–70. For the minority view that the Adamic tongue disappeared entirely at Babel see Thomas Hobbes, *Leviathan*, ed. C. B. Macpherson (Harmondsworth 1968), 101 (ch.4); Havers and Davies, *Conferences*, 214, 304–5; Purchas, *Pilgrimage*, 45; Henry Edmundson, *Lingua Linguarum: The Naturall Language* (London 1655), sig. f3v.

the unhappy consequences that succeeded the *Confusion at Babel*, nor *China* glory that she alone shall evermore triumph in the full fruition of those abundant felicities that attended mankind, whilst one common Language was spoken throughout the World'.[32]

The nature of the Adamic language was thus fairly clear and its essential features were not in doubt even though its identity was the subject of a protracted debate during this period. Psammetichus and the Phrygians notwithstanding, all parties agreed that any conclusions regarding the original language eventually would have to be made to blend with the irrefutable authority of scripture, especially the Hebrew Old Testament. Proponents of tongues other than Hebrew as the Adamic vernacular would have to explain away a very simple but weighty argument in favour of the Jewish language: all of the proper names in Genesis have a particular meaning well-suited to the individual concerned. In other words, when scholars were called upon to demonstrate that Hebrew was the ancient mother of all languages they were driven back upon the etymological proofs they ridiculed in the works of Goropius Becanus. Thus William Robertson the Scottish grammarian proved the antiquity of Hebrew by reciting that the 'name of the first man was אָדָם *Adam*, which signifieth, *earthly man*, So, the name of his wife, the first woman, was חַוָּה *Chavah*, which signifieth, *living*'. Goropius Becanus was able to find Low German equivalents for these scriptural names, despite Robertson's claim that these names 'are acknowledged to signifie thus, in the Hebrew onely, and not in any other Language'.[33] As Edward Leigh exulted, 'How many proper Names in the Scripture are derived from the Hebrew! And how significant are their Etymologies!'[34] On the basis of this evidence, Joshua Sylvester concluded that 'Gods ancient VVILL VVas first enrowled by an *Hebrew* quill'.[35] In spite of various dissenting claims, and the protests of men like John Webb, who believed that 'the *Hebrews* have no surer foundation to erect their Language upon, than only a bare Tradition of their own', most early modern Englishmen came to the conclusion that Adam and Eve spoke Hebrew in the Garden of Eden.[36]

'The common and more receiued opinion is,' wrote Samuel Purchas in the middle of James I's reign, 'that the Hebrew was the first, confirmed also by vniuersalitie, antiquitie, and consent of the Christian Fathers and learned men.'[37] Among these Fathers Purchas cited Augustine, whose testimony on a variety of controversial questions relating to the origin and dispersion of

---

[32] Webb, *Essay*, 42–4, 146, 187–8; S. Ch'en, 'John Webb: A forgotten page in the early history of Sinology in Europe', *Chinese Social and Political Science Review*, XIX (1935), 295–300. For the relationship between Chinese and the search for a universal language see W. W. Appleton, *A Cycle of Cathay* (New York 1951), ch.2; Cornelius, *Languages*, chs 2 & 4; and H. N. Davies, 'Bishop Godwin's "Lunatique Language"', *Journal of the Warburg and Courtauld Institutes*, XXX (1967), 296–316.

[33] William Robertson, *Gate . . . To the Holy Tongue* (London 1654–5), sigs A5v–A6 (2nd Gate).

[34] Edward Leigh, *Critica Sacra* (3rd Hebrew edn, London 1662), sig. A2. The first edition was published in 1641.

[35] Sylvester, *Du Bartas*, 122.

[36] Webb, *Essay*, 42.

[37] Purchas, *Pilgrimage*, 46.

early man would prove so influential in the seventeenth century. Augustine believed that 'the language originally used by men was the one later called Hebrew from the name of Heber, in whose family it stayed unchanged when the diversity of languages began'. Heber, or Eber as he is called in the Authorised Version, was the great-grandson of Noah's son Shem. Augustine cited the 'well-founded tradition', even in his own time, that 'the Hebrews were given his name, being called, as it were, *Heberaei*'. Eber's son was named Peleg, 'which means "Division", namely, because he was born to him at the time when the earth was divided among different languages'.[38] Purchas tinkered with Augustine's analysis, but maintained the belief that 'the puritie of Religion and Language remained in *Hebers* posteritie'. As a result, the 'Nation and Language of Israel borrow their name (Hebrew) of him'.[39]

One finds echoes of these ideas throughout the linguistic writings of the early modern period. Guillaume Postel, the famous sixteenth-century French linguist and translator, rejected the story from Herodotus and claimed Hebrew as the original language, despite some doubts. Conrad Gesner the Swiss naturalist defended Hebrew as well.[40] This was also the view of Pedro Mexia, the popular Spanish encyclopaedist whose works were translated into English as well as other European languages. The Hebrews, he thought, took their name from Heber, and 'neuer loste their firste and aunciente tongue'. Mexia quoted Augustine here for support. In a greatly expanded encyclo-paedia, published in England almost fifty years later, Mexia wrote that Hebrew 'was the first vsuall tongue among men; before the confusion of Tongues'. It was in Hebrew that 'God spake first to his Prophets; as the like our blessed Lord and Sauiour did, when he was conuersant among men.'[41]

Nicholas Gibbens, a Cambridge-educated preacher, published a detailed commentary in the last year of Elizabeth's reign on the first fourteen chapters of Genesis. Gibbens used Jewish sources freely, and his citations indicate that he was familiar with the rabbinical Bibles published during the sixteenth century. What 'language it was y^t men spake,' he asked, 'before this con-fusion of tōgues'? Gibbens refused to credit the story from Herodotus, and proceeded to argue that 'the Hebrue was the originall and mother of all'. Syriac and Chaldee (Aramaic) could be thought of as mere dialects of Hebrew, whose influence was felt closest to Palestine: 'the languages which are farthest disagreeing, are (for the most part) farthest scattered.' The proper names of Genesis could only be Hebrew words, and it is inconceivable that Moses translated these names into the Holy Tongue.[42]

Richard Verstegan, writing about the same time as Gibbens, repeated some of these ideas, despite his devotion to the Dutch theories of Goropius Becanus. All of mankind took part in the building of the Tower, he thought, 'except *Heber* and his family' who gave that name to 'his posteritie, who

[38] Augustine, *The City of God*, XVI, 3, 11 (ed. Sanford and Green, V, 21, 61, 63); Genesis X.
[39] Purchas, *Pilgrimage*, 46.
[40] Allen, 'Some theories', 8.
[41] Pedro Mexia, *The Foreste or Collection of Histories* (London 1571), 106; *Times Store-Hovse* (London 1619), 701.
[42] Nicholas Gibbens, *Qvestions And Dispvtations Concerning The Holy Scriptvre* (London 1602), 429.

there-vpon were called *Hebrewes*'.[43] Joshua Sylvester expressed the same point in rhyme: Hebrew, he said,

> (*Adams* language) pure persisted since,
> Till th'yron Age of that cloud climbing Prince;
> Resounding onely, through all mortall tents,
> The peer-lesse accents of rich eloquence;
> But then (as partiall) it it self retir'd
> To *Hebers* house: whether, of the conspir'd
> Rebels, he were not; but in sober quiet,
> Dwelt far from *Shinar*, and their furious ryot . . .[44]

After careful examination of the evidence, Lord Chief Justice Matthew Hale confirmed that 'it be commonly thought the *Hebrew* Language was the common Language of the *Canaanites*'.[45]

Theophilus Gale, a tutor at Oxford during the Commonwealth and a nonconformist teacher afterwards, identified Hebrew as the original language as a part of a much grander project. It was Gale's life work to prove that all languages, philosophy, and learning derived from the Hebrews and their scriptures. His goal was a sort of reformed Platonism, but of course Plato was 'reported to have lived fourteen years with the *Jews* in *Egypt*; and, we need no way dout, derived the choisest of his contemplations . . . from the Jewish Church'. Heber gave his name to the Hebrew language, which continued in purity from the Garden through the Confusion, until the Babylonian Captivity; all languages, including Greek, derived from the Hebrew. That the ultimate source of all languages was 'the *Hebrew*, or *Jewish* Tongue', he insisted, 'is an *Assertion* generally owned, and maintained by the most learned *Philologists* of this Age, and that not without the consent of some of the *Ancients*, and learned *Heathens*'. Gale quoted Plato's *Cratylus*, the standard Jewish commentaries in the sixteenth-century rabbinical Bibles, and even pointed to some kabbalistic theories. For further information, he advised, one only had to look in 'the six dayes volume of the Book, VVhere *God*, and mighty *Nature* doth appear, VVrot in an *Vniversal Character*'. Hebrew in the Garden of Eden was perfectly expressive of meaning: 'So *pure*, and of so *Vniversal sense*, God thought it best for *Innocence*.'[46]

Others expressed their doubts. Sir Thomas Browne discussed the issue in his 'enquiries into vulgar and common errors'. He wished, he said, that children committed unto the school of Nature would speak Hebrew 'not only for the easie attainment of that useful tongue, but to determine the true and primitive'Hebrew'. But he remained uncertain whether modern-day Hebrew could be the 'unconfounded language of Babel' which had been preserved by the children of Heber. Nevertheless, Browne did believe that 'probability stands fairest' for this theory, rather than that 'the language of

[43] Verstegan, *Restitution*, 7.
[44] Sylvester, *Du Bartas*, 123.
[45] Matthew Hale, *The Primitive Origination of Mankind* (London 1677), 163. Hale also thought that Webb's Chinese theory was 'but a novel Conceit': ibid.
[46] Gale, *Gentiles*, I, sigs *3r-v, **3r-v, ***v; pp.51, 53–4, 59; III, 117-18.

Phaenicia and Canaan' was the original tongue.[47] Brian Walton, the editor of the Polyglot Bible, expressed a similar point of view.[48] Richard Flecknoe the poet was not quite sure either. He wondered whether all languages 'derived from the *Hebrew* or no (as tis most probable)'.[49]

The compilers of the few Hebrew grammars in English were less equivocal in their support for the ultimate antiquity of Hebrew. That of William Robertson, of the University of Edinburgh, was one of the most popular, and the second section was reprinted for general use as late as the nineteenth century. One could read the 'Oracles of God' in Hebrew, which included 'the very first, Primitive, and Originall Words of his own Spirit'. Robertson's grammar was prefaced by a declaration from some of the most influential London ministers and preachers, who encouraged the 'attaining of this Sacred and Original Language'. One of the ministers who signed this statement, Thomas Symson of Tottenham High-Crosse, expressed his feelings in a stronger fashion: 'O Tongue of Tongues! of Languages the *first* . . . Nay, *once* the *only* Language! none beside Was spoken in the world, till *Babels* pride.' Hebrew, the footnote in Robertson's edition explains somewhat superfluously, was spoken, 'as the Learned observe, by *Adam* in Paradise'.[50] These same sentiments were expressed in another Hebrew grammar, published by John Davis the following year. Hebrew, he wrote, 'is the Language of *God's Word*, the Language of *Canaan*'.[51] Grammarian Edward Leigh believed that Hebrew was 'the most ancient and holy Tongue; for Antiquity it is the Tongue of *Adam*, for sanctity the Tongue of God.' It was in Hebrew that 'God spake to the Prophets and Patriarcks, in this Tongue the Angels spake to men, in this Tongue the Prophets wrote the Old Testament'. This statement appeared in all editions of his *Critica Sacra*, both before the Civil War and after the Restoration.[52]

The Hebrew language was glorified in seventeenth-century England as the *lingua humana*, the language spoken by Adam and Eve in the Garden of Eden, by mankind until the Confusion at the Tower of Babel, and by the Jews, the descendants of Heber who, although they took on other vernaculars, still preserved the sacred tongue and the crown of its literature, the Hebrew Old Testament. The 'dictates of right reason and Art', explained the Oxford schoolmaster George Dalgarno, 'certainly have not been followed in the primary Institution of any language unless it be of the Hebrew alone'.[53] William Robertson wrote that the 'usefulnesse' of Hebrew

---

[47] Thomas Browne, *Pseudodoxia Epidemica* (London 1646) in *Works*, ed. G. Keynes (London 1964), II, 393.

[48] Cornelius, *Languages*, 10.

[49] Richard Fleckno, *Miscellania* (London 1653), 109.

[50] Robertson, *Gate*, sigs A1r-v (1st Gate); A5r-v (2nd Gate). Among the group that signed this statement was Joseph Caryl, one of the few members of the Whitehall Conference on Jewish resettlement (December 1655) who supported the unconditional readmission of the Jews. See also G. F. Black, 'The beginnings of the study of Hebrew in Scotland', in L. Ginzberg *et al.* (eds), *Studies in Jewish Bibliography* (New York 1929), 463-80.

[51] John Davis, *A Short Introduction To The Hebrew Tongue* (London 1656), sig. A4v.

[52] Leigh, *Critica Sacra*, sig. A2.

[53] George Dalgarno, *Didascalocophus* (Oxford 1680), 113.

is infinitely to be valued above any thing which is attainable by the Latine; because in these the Oracles of God are delivered to us, in their Originall Purity; and in them, those very words, which were the words of him, who spoke by them as never man spoke . . . the very first, Primitive, and Originall Words of his own Spirit, in the Old and New Testament, which no language in the World besides these can boast of.

More extravagantly, Robertson noted that the 'Learned are verily perswaded, that, without doubt, there shall be a Language spoken in heaven, for ever: and that there shall be one Language: and also, that *this* shall be that very Language.' The four and twenty elders and the four beasts of Revelation, after all, said 'Amen, Allelujah, which are Hebrew words'.[54] Edward Leigh agreed that Hebrew, 'as is thought, shall the Saints speak in Heaven'.[55] If 'we Shall speak this Language to Eternity,' asked Thomas Sympson, the London preacher, 'If so; what paines, what cost should not be given, To learn on earth, what we shal speak in heaven?'[56]

Hebrew became a very fashionable learned language in the seventeenth century, and took its rightful place among Latin and Greek, those languages which, as Richard Flecknoe put it, 'subsist, as it were, upon the stock of their Ancestors'. Flecknoe even complained of 'the *Scripture* style amongst the common *Rabble*, who are our *Rabbies* now, and . . . cant it in the *Hebrew* phrase'.[57] Respect for Hebrew was especially prevalent among sectarian preachers. The seventeenth-century biographer of the New England pioneer John Cotton recounted with pride that when Cotton was examined for a Fellowship at Emmanuel College, Cambridge, the examiner set a particularly difficult translation from Isaiah, but 'though a . . . resolution thereof might have put a good Hebrician to a stand, yet such was his dexterity, as made those difficult words facil, and rendred him a prompt Respondent'.[58] Richard Corbett, the poet of Christ Church, has his 'Distracted Puritane' lament that

> In the holy tongue of Chanaan
> I plac'd my cheifest pleasure:
> Till I prickt my foote
> With an Hebrew roote,
> That I bledd beyond all measure.[59]

When Bunyan's Christian pilgrim passed through Vanity Fair accompanied by his friend Faithful, 'they naturally spoke the language of Canaan'.[60] Of language in the Garden, cried Joshua Sylvester,

> What shall I more say? Then, all spake the speech
> Of God himself: th' old sacred *Idiom* rich,
> Rich perfect language, where's no point, nor signe,
> But hides some rare deep mystery divine . . .

[54] Robertson, *Gate*, sigs A4 (1st Gate); A6 (2nd Gate).
[55] Leigh, *Critica Sacra*, sig. A2.
[56] In Robertson, *Gate*, sig. A5 (2nd Gate).
[57] Fleckno, *Miscellania*, 77, 80.
[58] John Norton, *Abel being Dead yet speaketh . . . Life . . . Of . . . John Cotton* (London 1658), 10
[59] *The Poems of Richard Corbett*, ed. J. A. W. Bennett and H. R. Trevor-Roper (Oxford 1955), 56-9
[60] John Bunyan, *The Pilgrim's Progress* (Harmondsworth 1965), 126.

For Sylvester, and for most seventeenth-century English language theorists, the very words of Hebrew were divinely significant. Hebrew had 'no word but weighs, whose Elements Flow with hid sense, thy points with Sacraments'.[61] Some observers thought that this fascination with Hebrew was getting out of hand. The introduction to the Bay Psalm Book praised the English Bibles which 'used the Idioms of our owne tongue in stead of Hebraismes, lest they might seeme english barbarismes'.[62] Samuel Butler's Hudibras was well equipped with

> *Hebrew* Roots, although th' are found
> To flourish most in barren ground,
> He had such plenty, as suffic'd
> To make some think him circumcis'd
> And truly so perhaps, he was
> 'Tis many a Pious Christians case.[63]

Others were unhappy because the renewed interest in the biblical languages seemed to throw doubt on the accepted translations of scripture and thereby emphasised unduly the letter rather than the spirit of the text.

John Webster thought that 'while men trust to their skill in the understanding of the original tongues, they become utterly ignorant of the true original tongue . . . which no man can understand or speak, but he that is . . . taught the language of the holy Ghost'.[64] Thomas Hobbes was even more emphatic about the subject: Latin, Greek, and Hebrew were once 'very profitable, or rather necessary,' he wrote, 'but now that is done, and we have the Scripture in English, and preaching in English, I see no great need'. Hobbes saw more purpose to devoting one's efforts towards 'understanding well the languages of our neighbours, French, Dutch, and Spanish'. Furthermore, he warned, 'A minister ought not to think that his skill in the Latin, Greek, or Hebrew tongues, if he have any, gives him a privilege to impose upon all his fellow subjects his own sense, or what he pretends to be his sense, of every obscure place of Scripture.'[65]

But the utility of Hebrew was more than simply linguistic, as Hobbes no doubt understood. Augustine, so influential among early modern linguistic thinkers, here too set the stage for further discussion. 'This Hebrew tongue,' he wrote, 'is the exclusive possession of the people of Israel, among whom the city of God has passed its pilgrimage as well as among the saints, while it has been less perfectly represented by its mysteries among all men.'[66] Pedro Mexia brought up the same point, saying that Hebrew was 'particular to the Iewes, and the mysteries and prophecies (as also the coming of Christ) being concealed therein: it was very requisite, that such mysteries should bee written in a tong more common then the Hebrue.'[67] It was these 'mysteries'

---

[61] Sylvester, *Du Bartas*, 121-2.
[62] *The VVhole Booke of Psalmes* ([Cambridge, Mass.] 1640), sig. **3.
[63] Butler, *Hudibras*, 3.
[64] Webster, *Academiarum Examen*, 8.
[65] Thomas Hobbes, *Behemoth*, ed. F. Tönnies (London 1889), 53, 90.
[66] Augustine, *The City of God*, XVI, 3 (ed. Sanford and Green, V, 21).
[67] Mexia, *Store-Hovse*, 701.

that contemporaries hoped to uncover. Sir Thomas Urquhart the colourful Cavalier translator therefore chided those who refused to comprehend the deepest significance of the Confusion at Babel, even though they had wisely 'perused the interpretation of the Rabbies on that text', because of pre-conceived notions about the nature of speech and the Adamic first language.[68]

The figure of Adam before the Fall was a popular and powerful one in seventeenth-century England. 'The end then of learning,' wrote Milton to Samuel Hartlib in 1641, 'is to repair the ruins of our first parents by regaining to know God aright, and out of that knowledge to love him, to imitate him, to be like him.'[69] This utopian image was very influential for both Christians and Jews in the seventeenth century: if the perfect language which Adam and Eve spoke in the Garden of Eden was Hebrew, then help from contemporary Jews became correspondingly more important. Doll Common noted in her millennial ravings that the English were accustomed to 'call the Rabbins, and the heathen Greeks to come from [Jeru]Salem, and from Athens, and teach the people of Great Britain to speak the tongue of Eber, and Javan'.[70] Contacts with Jews were renewed in England as early as the 1590s in response to the interest in instruction in the Hebrew language and Jewish biblical exegesis, as Jewish converts to Christianity such as Philip Ferdinand and John Immanuel Tremellius began to make their way to the land from which the Jews had been expelled in 1290.[71]

Sir Thomas Urquhart was correct: linguistic thinkers and planners did turn towards the rabbis in their search for knowledge, for as astronomer Seth Ward noted, the Adamic tongue would have to be a 'naturall Language, and would afford that which the *Cabalists* and *Rosycrucians* have vainely sought for in the Hebrew'.[72] The Kabbalists, as John Donne put it, who 'are the Anatomists of words, and have a Theologicall Alchimy to draw soveraigne tinctures and spirits from plain and grosse literall matter, observe in every variety some great mystick signification'.[73] This is what John Wilkins meant when he wrote that 'if you will beeleeve the Jews, the Holy spirit hath purposely involved in the words of Scripture, every secret that belongs to any Art or Science, under such Cabalisms as these'. More importantly, he thought, 'if a man were but expert in unfolding of them, it were easie for him

---

[68] Thomas Urquhart, *Logopandecteision* (London 1653), 8. Urquhart's published views on language were often more satirical than serious: see his *Works* (Edinburgh 1834), especially *The Discovery of A most exquisite Jewel* (London 1652).
[69] Milton, *Complete Prose Works*, II, 366–7 (*Of Education*).
[70] Jonson, *Alchemist*, IV, v.13–16: punctuation altered here. Javan was the son of Noah's son Japheth; 'Javan' in Hebrew means 'Greece'. See Genesis IX–X.
[71] S. Stein, 'Phillipus Ferdinandus Polonus: A sixteenth-century Hebraist in England', in I. Epstein (ed.), *Essays in honour of . . . J. H. Hertz* (London 1944), 397–412; C. Roth, 'Jews in Oxford after 1290', *Oxoniensia*, XV (1950), 64–8. See generally D. S. Katz, *Philo-Semitism and the Readmission of the Jews to England, 1603-1655* (forthcoming, Oxford Historical Monographs).
[72] [Seth Ward and John Wilkins], *Vindiciae Academiarum* (Oxford 1654), 22. On the mystical interest in Jews among seventeenth-century English scientists, see H. R. Trevor-Roper, 'Three foreigners: the philosophers of the Puritan Revolution', in his *Religion, the Reformation and Social Change* (London 1967), 237–93. He has written perceptively elsewhere regarding the role of the Jews in England during the Civil War period. See especially his *Historical Essays* (London 1957), 146–60; and 'Europe's brief flood tide of philo-semitism', *Horizon*, II, 4 (March 1960), 100-3, 124-5.
[73] Donne, *Essays*, 48.

to get as much knowledge as *Adam* had in his innocencie, or human nature is capable of'.[74]

The study of the Hebrew language in seventeenth-century England was therefore more than a linguistic exercise, more even than a tool towards understanding more clearly the word of God as revealed in the Old Testament. The scholarly revival of Hebrew studies in England is well-known.[75] But the perception of Hebrew as the language spoken by Adam in the Garden of Eden raised it to an entirely different plane. Hebrew was a tongue which stood apart from common languages, even New Testament Greek. 'All's heathen, but the Hebrew', Ben Jonson's Amsterdam deacon reminded the alchemist, even 'Heathen Greek'.[76] The significance of the Hebrew language was thus far broader than its obvious position of honour as the language in which the Old Testament was written. Yet even after scholarly investigations revealed that the first man spoke Hebrew, what was most compelling about this original language was that it was the repository of the divine secrets, and that once deciphered Hebrew might provide a ready and easy way to mystical knowledge. God created the world by speaking Hebrew. The very essence of Creation was somehow locked within: 'where's no point, nor signe, But hides some rare deep mystery divine.'[77] Even though some Hebrew instruction was available at Oxford and Cambridge, attention was inevitably focused on European Jews, who understood her secrets and significances. 'And it is observed,' Izaak Walton's angler said of the Jews, 'that many of those people have many secrets yet unknown to Christians; secrets that have never yet been written, but have been since the days of their Solomon . . . delivered by tradition, from the father to the son.'[78] For only this ancient people with its kabbalistic mysteries might help Gentiles to overcome the 'ruines of *Babell*' and so to marvel at the linguistic perfection in the Garden of Eden, when Adam named the animals and understood the nature of the universe.[79]

[74] I. W[ilkins], *Mercvry* (London 1641), '83' = 101. For other examples of Wilkins's interest in Hebrew, Kabbalah, and the Adamic tongue, see ibid., 19, 68-71, 78-9, 82-3, '81-2' = 99-100, 105-6, 109; *Essay*, sig. B2, pp.5, 11, 19; *Vindiciae*, 5. The English understanding of Kabbalah was confused at best before the publication of Christian Knorr von Rosenroth's *Kabbala Denudata* in 1677. For the early modern Jewish kabbalistic view of the Hebrew language, see especially the following works by Professor Gershom Scholem: *Major Trends in Jewish Mysticism* (Jerusalem 1941), 202-82; *On the Kabbalah and Its Symbolism* (New York 1969), 32-86; *Sabbatai Sevi* (London 1973), 1-102; *Kabbalah* (Jerusalem 1974), 87-203. On the Christian use of Kabbalah in the seventeenth century see J. L. Blau, *The Christian Interpretation of the Cabala in the Renaissance* (New York 1944); F. Secret, *Les Kabbalistes Chrétiens de la Renaissance* (Paris 1964); and F. A. Yates, *The Occult Philosophy in the Elizabethan Age* (London 1979).
[75] See éspecially I. Baroway, 'Toward understanding Tudor-Jacobean Hebrew studies', *Jewish Social Studies*, XVIII (1956), 3-24; E. I. J. Rosenthal, 'Edward Lively: Cambridge Hebraist', in D. W. Thomas (ed.), *Essays . . . Presented to S. A. Cook* (London 1950), 95-112; A. C. Partridge, *English Biblical Translation* (London 1973), 33-138; C. Roth, *A History of the Jews in England* (3rd edn, Oxford 1964), 145-6.
[76] Jonson, *Alchemist*, II, v.16-17.
[77] Sylvester, *Du Bartas*, 121.
[78] Izaak Walton, *The Compleat Angler* (Everyman edn, London, 1906), 148-9.
[79] Webster, *Academiarum Examen*, 25.

12

Archbishop Laud and the University of Oxford

Kevin Sharpe

In April 1630 William Laud was appointed Chancellor of the University of Oxford. He regarded it as his first duty to reform the university 'which was extremely sunk from all discipline'. From the outset he addressed himself vigorously to the task. He sent frequent letters and injunctions to the university designed to prevent the accumulation of degrees, to end disorders at disputations, to enforce the wearing of proper academic dress and in short to maintain, in all aspects of university life, order, decency and formality 'which are in a sort the outward and visible face of the university'. The outstanding result of his effort to reform was the new code of statutes which Strickland Gibson, that eminent Oxford scholar and Keeper of University Archives, described as 'perhaps the greatest piece of university legislation ever successfully brought to completion'.[1] Few would argue with that verdict. Even more than for his generous gifts of coins and manuscripts, more than for his establishment of lectureships in Arabic and Hebrew, Archbishop Laud, as Chancellor of Oxford, is most remembered for the code of statutes which bears his name.

The process of compiling the new statutes was long and laborious. Laud's involvement began before his appointment as Chancellor when he urged William, third Earl of Pembroke, then Chancellor of Oxford, to instigate a complete reformation of the university statutes.[2] It ended seven years later in June 1636 when Secretary Sir John Coke delivered to the university a book of statutes signed by Laud and sealed by Charles I as the official volume to be lodged in the university archives.[3] During the intervening years Laud participated energetically in the compilation of the new code.[4] The bulk of the labour

[1] W. Scott and J. Bliss (eds), *The Works of the Most Reverend Father in God William Laud* (7 vols, 1847-60), v, 13, 16, 26-8, 82; Oxford University Archives, Convocation Register (hereafter Convoc. Reg.) R 24, f.44ᵛ; S. Gibson, 'Brian Twyne', *Oxoniensa*, v, 106.
[2] Convoc. Reg. R 24, f.12; *Works of Laud*, v, 14; S. Gibson, *Statuta Antiqua Universitatis Oxoniensis* (1931), xlviii.
[3] *Works of Laud*, v, 126-32; *Historical Manuscripts Commission Reports, Cowper* (hereafter *H.M.C.R. Cowper*), II, 121; Convoc. Reg. R 24, ff.125-9.
[4] Laud helped devise the statutes which enacted the new collegiate cycle for electing proctors and those which governed appeals: Bodleian Library, Twyne MS. XVII, p.65; *Calendar of State Papers Domestic* (hereafter *C.S.P.D.*) 1628-9, pp.341, 361, 398, 408, 414, and 1631-3, p.134; Convoc. Reg. R 24, f.37ᵛ; *Works of Laud*, v, 56, 59. For other matters referred to him see Twyne MS. XVII, p.65.

of collating and correcting old statutes was borne initially by the delegates appointed by Pembroke – most notably by Brian Twyne the antiquarian scholar and Fellow of Corpus. But after August 1633 when Convocation, the governing body of the university, sent the draft of the new statutes for his consideration,[5] the directing hand was that of Laud himself.[6] It was he who now composed the final version and arranged for the new statute book to be printed in 1634. Nor did Laud confine himself, in reviewing the delegates' draft, to mere forms or trifles. When the new statutes, now printed, were presented to Convocation in July 1634 – almost a year since his draft had been submitted – Twyne complained that not only by the delegates who compiled them, but also by the heads of colleges who attended the weekly meetings at which the draft statutes were read, 'there were many alterations perceived and discovered in diverse passages and particulars both in phrases and substance'. Indeed 'there were many innovations discovered which we thought not of and many things hooked in and left out'.[7]

These innovations and alterations were again Laud's own. For though in revising the delegates' draft he continued to call upon the assistance of one of their number – Peter Turner of Merton – Laud tells us that he reserved to himself 'the last consideration of all'.[8] After 1633 there was no consultation. Laud's statute book was delivered to the university as a *fait accompli* – to be obeyed, not discussed, to be received by Convocation not voted on by it. He intended it to be received by the university as royal legislation.[9] Even when the statutes were printed, however, Laud's labour was not ended. He announced to Convocation that the new code was to hold authority for only a trial period ending in September 1635 after which he would himself finally settle the statutes 'reserving to myselfe power . . . to adde that which shall be fit and alter or take away from those statutes that which shall be found to be either unnecessary or incommodious'.[10] The final version, in which manuscript emendations and additions were entered into the printed book, was not ready until the summer of 1636.[11] On June 22 Secretary Sir John Coke

[5] Convoc. Reg. R 24, f.67; Twyne MS. XVII, p.66. Laud endorsed the university's letter 'The submission of Oxford statutes to me and my ordering of them': *C.S.P.D.* 1633–4, p.189.

[6] For a general history of the delegates' work see Gibson, 'Brian Twyne'; C. E. Mallet, *A History of the University of Oxford*, II: *The Sixteenth and Seventeenth Centuries* (1924), ch.17; Gibson, *Statuta Antiqua*, x–lxix; J. Griffiths (ed.), *Statutes of the University of Oxford* (1888), preface; G. R. M. Ward (ed.), *Oxford University Statutes*, I: *The Caroline Code* (1845), preface. All the above underestimate Laud's role which emerges clearly in Twyne MS. XVII. I shall be developing this argument more fully in the seventeenth-century volume of the History of Oxford University.

[7] Convoc. Reg. R 24, f.91; *Works of Laud*, V, 101; Twyne MS. XVII, p.72. Twyne was not given time to make a copy of his draft: ibid., p.67.

[8] Gibson, 'Twyne', 103, and *Statuta Antiqua*, lxiii; *Works of Laud*, V, 99.

[9] 'A Remonstrance', in Bodleian Library, Bodleian MS. 594, f.140, complained that the book was imposed on the university. Twyne refers to widespread opinions that the statutes were invalid because 'not expressly and openly read in Convocation': Twyne MS. XVII, p.79. See H. R. Trevor-Roper, *Archbishop Laud* (1962 edn), 279.

[10] Convoc. Reg. R 24, f.91.

[11] No modern edition of the statutes distinguishes the 1634 code from the revised version of 1636. The emendations and additions can be clearly read in the original books in the Bodleian, N.I. Jur. Seld., Arch. Bodl. B 120 E. See S. Gibson, 'The collation of the Corpus Statutorum Univ. Oxon', *Bodleian Quarterly Record* (1925), 271–4.

addressed the Convocation which was held to receive the new constitution of the university, and a commission, appointed by the King, took acknowledgment from the heads of houses that they accepted the statutes as the laws by which they would govern and be governed.[12]

It was three years since Laud had taken personal charge of the task – years during which he had been not only elevated to the see of Canterbury, but also appointed to committees of the Council for Ireland and the Treasury, for foreign affairs and finance. Why in the midst of his public business had Laud devoted so much time to the government of Oxford? What did he set out to achieve by the new statutes? How readily were they obeyed, how effectively enforced? Finally, what may we learn from Laud's activities as Chancellor about his wider aims and ideals for the governance of church and state? Such questions lead us to consider the nature and reception of the new statutes which enshrined Laud's policy for the university and, perhaps, his hopes for the future of the commonwealth.

The amended statute book of 1636 saw a myriad of revisions – most of them intended to explain the statutes more precisely and to plug the loopholes through which miscreants had escaped during the probationary year. They are testimony to Laud's concern for detail and the care and attention which he had brought to the task. Tutors were now admonished to supervise the behaviour and appearance as well as the studies of their students; provisions were made to ensure that lectures took place, lasted the specified hour and made an original contribution to the subject; fines were imposed on those who failed to attend at disputations; residence qualifications for degrees were defined more strictly; and, in general, more checks and severer punishments were decreed in matters of discipline. The statute book was supplemented too by an epinomis – an addition or appendix after Plato – which declared that those who offended against the statutes were not guilty of that crime alone. Because the statutes enjoined the taking of oaths, breach of them was also perjury. The new code not only prescribed in detail what was expected and required. It also invested wide powers in the university officers responsible for discipline. In particular, the authority of the Chancellor and Vice-Chancellor was increased so that all lapses not covered by the letter of the law might yet be caught in the web of a discretionary power vested in the magistrate.

As defined by the statutes of 1636, the powers of the Chancellor were extensive. In matters of discipline, authority was given him 'to punish offenders against the statute of the university with corporal chastisement, money-fine, imprisonment, degradation, suspension from degrees, discommoning, proscription, banishment or expulsion from the university, censures ecclesiastical, or in any other reasonable manner . . .' In addition a discretionary power was given him to punish all offenders where no provision was made for it in the statutes. As opponents of the statutes complained, the authority of the Chancellor was universal and unbounded.[13]

[12] Convoc. Reg. R 24, ff.123[V], 125; *H.M.C.R. Cowper*, II, 121.
[13] Bodl. MS. 594, f.140: 'all other statutes which gave any limitation to the Chancellour's power are in the said late book of statutes quite removed and taken away, as impediments to his absolute government.'

Effective authority within the university lay not with the Chancellor but with the Vice-Chancellor – who was resident. The 1636 code endowed him with jurisdiction over 'all which conduces to the honour of the university and the safety and welfare of one and all'. No less emphasis was placed on his duties: to see that offenders were not only punished but detected; 'to make diligent search not only during day, but also by night after such delinquents; and also to take care that heretics, schismatics and all other persons who think otherwise than aright of the Catholic faith, and the doctrine and discipline of the Church of England are exiled . . .' The Vice-Chancellor's principal weapon in the enforcement of order and discipline was the Chancellor's Court of the university. Title XXI of the Laudian code stipulated that the court was to hold session every Friday in the North Chapel of St. Mary's, with the Vice-Chancellor and two proctors presiding and an under-bedell of the law attending. Its procedure closely resembled that of church courts;[14] its jurisdiction ranged over all matters in which members of the university were a party. Much of the business of the court concerned actions for debt, but it dealt too with '*reformatio morum*' and specifically with '*transgressi statuti*'.[15] Under these heads the records of the court reveal the examination of offenders charged with night walking, prostitution, slander and assault.[16] Defendants who failed to attend were automatically banished the university and, at least on paper, penalties and sanctions (imprisonment and excommunication) were severe. Appeals were heard on Wednesdays but were to be refused 'to certain persons sometimes out of hatred to the offences which have been committed and sometimes to rebuke the audacity of persons who in the midst of popular disturbances . . . screen themselves'.[17] The statutes expressly precluded appeals by those contumacious of the court.

Then as now the principal disciplinary officers of the university were the proctors. Among other tasks it was their prescribed duty to attend frequently at university exercises, sessions and disputations to ensure that all was done in accordance with the statutes. The proctors also patrolled the city by night with powers to fine instantly. By statute they received half the fine. The revisions of 1636 empowered each of them to appoint two assistants among whose duties it was 'to range the streets, lanes, eating houses and wine shops during sermon time'.

However, the central institutions in Laud's quest for order and discipline were the colleges and halls. This was both necessary and convenient. As Mr Curtis has shown, the sixteenth and seventeenth centuries had seen the emergence of the colleges as the most important and autonomous academic communities: heads of colleges had the right to dispense their members from

---

[14] For procedure in the sixteenth century see 'Praxis iudicaria in Curis Cancelarii Oxoniensis', Lambeth Palace MS. 2085; cf. 'Praxis Curia Academicae' (*c.* 1770), Oxford University Archives, CC/131/1/3. See also M. Underwood, 'The structure and operation of the Oxford Chancellor's Court from the sixteenth to the early eighteenth century', *Journal of the Society of Archivists*, VI (1978), 18–27.

[15] Oxford University Archives, Chancellor's Court MS. (hereafter Chancellor's Court MS.) 27/6; Underwood, op. cit., 25.

[16] E.g. Chanc. Court MSS. 18/15, 18/19, 18/89.

[17] Griffiths, *Statutes*, 221, 226–7; Underwood, op. cit., 24–5; Bodl. MS. 597, f.141.

any of the new statutes which conflicted with their own.[18] It was within these smaller communities of residential colleges that Laud hoped discipline would be most effectively enforced. At the heart of the statutes were orders to ensure that students came up to colleges, were matriculated from colleges, resided only in colleges and returned to colleges each evening by nine o'clock sharp. Tutors in colleges were expected to supervise discipline as well as study and Laud looked to the heads of colleges to ensure the conformity of their members to the code. Attempts were made to bring the heads of colleges more under the Chancellor's scrutiny. The statutes of 1636 invested the Chancellor with authority to nominate the principals of halls;[19] it also established the Hebdomadal Council, ordered by Charles I at the instigation of Laud in 1631, as a permanent assembly.[20] Critics of this innovation accused Laud of expanding the powers of the assembly beyond those envisaged by Charles I in his letter of 1631. The Hebdomadal Council with the Chancellor and Vice-Chancellor sat as a court, passed censures on delinquents and issued decrees on matters of discipline. In short it was to be employed as another agency for enforcing the letter and spirit of the statutes.[21]

These then were the offices and institutions through which Laud hoped to reduce the university to 'piety and sobriety', to 'peace and unity'. On 22 June 1636, the day the statutes signed and sealed were delivered, Secretary Coke praised the improvements already witnessed during the years of probation: students were no longer to be found in taverns or brothels, 'nor seen loitering in the streets or other places of idleness or ill example but all contain themselves within the walls of their colleges . . . And if those temporary and imperfect orders produced so good effect what may now be expected from this body of laws and statutes so complete and so digested . . .'[22] The university, Coke told them, might now become the perfect model for the commonweal, an academy from which those nurtured through discipline to virtue might emerge as governors of a well-ordered nation.

Later in the summer, at the end of August, Charles I came to visit his seminary of virtue and learning. The royal visitation of August 1636 is an important chapter in the history of the university and of the personal rule of Charles I. By it the students and governors of Oxford University would behold the 'royal Justinian', the author of their new law, the symbol of all authority.[23] And there at Oxford Charles could see a utopia of order and sobriety, the promise of a perfect commonweal in the future. The royal visit was the enactment in image and ceremony of the spirit and body of the statutes. As the King approached from Woodstock, the governors and students,

[18] M. Curtis, *Oxford and Cambridge in Transition 1558-1642* (1959); Mallet, *History of the University*, II, 331; Griffiths, *Statutes*, 138.
[19] The complaint (in Bodl. MS. 594, f.141) that this was an unfounded innovation is substantiated by a report sent to Laud in ?1633 that there was 'No evidence for it in any record of the university': *C.S.P.D.* 1633-4, p.386.
[20] *C.S.P.D.* 1631-3, pp.135-6.
[21] Bodl. MS. 594, ff.143-4^V. Laud thought it crucial: *Works of Laud*, V, 82.
[22] *Works of Laud*, V, 12, 130.
[23] Ibid., V, 129.

correctly attired and ranked according to their degrees, lined the royal path to Laud's own college, St. John's, and thence to Carfax.[24] The royal entertainments carefully devised by the university mirrored the royal hopes and expectations for the realm.

On 29 August, in Christ Church Hall, William Strode, the Public Orator of the university, presented his play *The Floating Island*, which was written at Laud's instigation.[25] The Floating Island was a kingdom distracted by dissenting passions and on the verge of anarchy. The monarch, King Prudentius, and his minister, Intellectus Agens, in vain attempt to bridle their licence; and the passions, led by Audax, Irato, Desperato, Sir Amorous and Hilario, break out into rebellion and plot to murder the King. Prudentius, hearing of their conspiracy, retires to safety, leaving them to govern. The passions elect Fancie as their queen, but soon become dissatisfied with her fickle rule and, quarrelling among themselves, bring her reign to an end and the realm near to ruin. Prudentius returns to save the kingdom and the passions willingly submit to restraints which they now understand to be necessary. Reason rules over passion, order over chaos. In accordance with the conventions of the masques, with the Topos of Caroline iconography, and perhaps with academic taste, the characters of the play are Platonic 'essences'. But the immediate relevance of the moral both for the kingdom and for Oxford in 1636 becomes clear in the epilogue:

> The isle is setled; Rage of Passions laid
> Phancy to Prudence bowes. Let all be staid
> In your Acceptance too, and then each breast
> Will cease its floating . . .

Strode's play, however, did not meet with unqualified acceptance. Though the King expressed his approval, many spectators tired of the play, as having too much of morality, too little of wit in it.[26] More successful, because more exotic and colourful in scene and costume, was the next day's production, also arranged by Laud, William Cartwright's *The Royal Slave*.[27] The play, set in Persia, centred on the Persian custom of elevating a captive slave to be King for three days before being offered as a sacrifice to the Gods. Cratander, the slave chosen, displays not the libertinism typically exhibited by those enjoying such short rule, but a truly regal disposition. By his beauty and countenance, by his wisdom and discretion, by his condemnation of unnecessary luxury, by his respect for law and self-restraint in the exercise of authority, by his probity and resistance to the temptations of sensual pleasures, he emerges in the eyes of all the court as the model of monarchy. For Cratander is acquainted with philosophy, the disciple of Socrates: his virtues

[24] Convoc. Reg. R 24, ff.132-4; Twyne MS. XVII, pp.187, 191-5; *Works of Laud*, V, 148-55; J. Taylor, 'The royal visit to Oxford in 1636: a contemporary narrative', *Oxoniensa* (1936), 151-9.
[25] B. Dobell (ed.), *The Poetical Works of William Strode* (1907), 137-240. Strode, Public Orator of the university since 1629, told his audience that he wrote the play 'at the instance of those who might command him' (ibid., 139). Laud paid the expenses and it seems likely that it was penned at his request (ibid., xxvii).
[26] *Works of Laud*, V, 148; *Poetical Works of Strode*, XX. Strode was made a Canon of Christ Church in 1638.
[27] Twyne MS. XVII, f.191; G. Blakemore Evans, *The Plays and Poems of William Cartwright* (1951).

are 'the fruits of learning'. His fellow slaves of baser parts, frustrated that their licence too is bridled by his virtue, complain 'we live not under a King, but a pedagogue'. They plot to kill him and to give vent to their lust upon the ladies of the court. But Cratander saves the Queen and her attendants and wins freedom for himself and good terms of peace for the slaves. A King by nature, he is appointed by the Emperor monarch of the conquered provinces. Cartwright's play was not only a panegyric to the virtues of Charles I. Though the epilogue to the university excused the production as the sport of courtiers not scholars, there was, no less than in Strode's play, a message for the university too. Like Strode's Prudentius (and his minister), Cartwright's Cratander exemplifies the man of learning as the man of virtue; only he who is master of his own passions can rule for the good of others unable to bridle their own. Learning and virtue are the qualities required for government.[28] Charles I had underlined the same message more directly in his letter to Convocation: universities he regarded as 'the seminaries of virtue and learning from whence the better part of our subjects by good education may bee disposed to religion, vertue and obedience of our lawes, and enabled to do service both in church and commonwealth'.[29] The next year, Cartwright was nominated by Laud 'Architypographus', or overseer of the new Oxford press. In 1642, then reader of metaphysic in the university, he lived at Oxford on terms of familiarity with Charles I. His play had been well received: 'His Majesty and all the nobles commended it for the best that was ever acted'; the Queen, acknowledging its wider appeal, requested that it be restaged at court.[30]

But for all its appeal to the court, the students, it seems, preferred more flashy spectacles of lesser substance. When, after the King's departure, such a performance was prepared for the courtiers and others remaining in town, 'Such was the unruliness of the yonge schollars to come in that uppon their breakinge in the strangers [and] others could not be placed doe what the Vice-Chancellor would; and so there was no play at all.'[31] The world of perfect order had departed with the King. Even before there had been bad omens. Only a month after the statutes had been delivered, Laud had thought it necessary, in preparing for the royal visit, to admonish heads of houses that their students be made to wear prescribed academic dress, 'not any long hayre, nor any bootes, nor double stockins rolled downe or hanging loose about their legges as the manner of some slovens is to doe'. Heads of colleges were authorised to name a Fellow with proctorial power for the duration of the visit.[32] Though reason was now embodied in statute, it had not yet mastered the passions of Oxford youth. Indeed, the revisions which were made to the statutes in 1636 were an implicit recognition that the printed book of 1634 had not solved – perhaps could not solve – the problem of discipline. In those revisions it was admitted that scholars often dodged

[28] The plots to kill Prudentius and Cratander as 'heavy philosophical spoil sports who place restrictions upon all the natural passions of man' are strikingly similar: ibid., 599.
[29] Convoc. Reg. R 24, f.125^V.
[30] Blakemore Evans, *Cartwright*, 13–21.
[31] Twyne MS. XVII, f.194^V.
[32] Convoc. Reg. R 24, ff.134, 136; *C.S.P.D.* 1635–6, p.92; Twyne MS. XVII, f.191.

sermons and disputations, paid scant respect to seniors, stayed out of college all night, drank, gambled and debauched themselves. Often it was acknowledged that the problems were beyond the power and diligence of the magistrate: innkeepers were specifically ordered to block all back walls and 'wandering walks', 'through the labyrinths of which the night rakes so often steal away from the magistrates'.[33] Rigorous efforts were made to ensure at least that students could not plead ignorance of the requirements of the statutes.[34] In April 1635 orders were sent to all colleges and posted at Carfax commanding students to attend sermons, present themselves for matriculation, conform in dress and manners and avoid loitering in streets and taverns. The same year the whole text of the statutes was epitomised on one printed sheet – perhaps in the hope that the less there was to read, the more likely it was to be read. In 1638 Thomas Crosfield devised an epitome of the new statutes with a timetable of all compulsory lectures and especially a table of detailed injunctions on discipline. While the statutes were being reduced for the convenience of students, more were added to the full code as new problems arose. In November 1636 Laud ordered that communion services and prayers be in Latin and in the body of St. Mary's rather than the chancel.[35] If the enactment of laws could itself have solved the problem of discipline, the university would have become the ordered commonweal of Laud's dream.

But the reality fell short of the dream. Laws could not crush the young blades of Oxford who flaunted the latest fashions and enjoyed the lifestyle of their class.[36] Ignorance, drunkenness and violence remained features of student life. In 1638 Laud urged the Vice-Chancellor to prevent students loitering in alehouses during the vacation; in 1640 he recommended to Vice-Chancellor Christopher Potter, the Provost of Queen's, 'a more strict watchfulnesse and observance against all haunting of tavernes', for drunkenness was 'the mother or the nurse of almost all other distempers'.[37]

So serious were the complaints about drunkenness that some sent their children to be educated abroad in more sober environments.[38] Charges of violent assaults by student on student occur frequently in the case-books of the Vice-Chancellor's court.[39] But despite the severe sentences listed in the statutes, those convicted were only obliged to acknowledge their guilt in public, and swear not to offend again.[40] Public shame could be effective, but only when reinforced by severer punishment.[41] Greatest success came from

[33] Griffiths, *Statutes*, 160; Convoc. Reg. R 24, f.108.
[34] See Laud's letter of 5 May 1637 to the Vice-Chancellor requiring him to ensure that every college had a correct copy of the statutes: *Works of Laud*, v, 168.
[35] Twyne MS. XVII, f.130 &[V]; Bodleian Library, Wood MS. 423, 15; *Statuta Selecta e Corpore Statutorum Universitatis Oxon.* (1638); F. S. Boas (ed.), *The Diary of Thomas Crosfield* (1935), XV; *Works of Laud*, v, 156-7.
[36] Cf. *Works of Laud*, v, 173, 263.
[37] Ibid., v, 201; Convoc. Reg. R 24, f.180.
[38] *Works of Laud*, v, 258.
[39] Vice-Chanc. Court MSS. 18/15, 18/89.
[40] See for example the acknowledgment of John King of his fault in assaulting one Fisher: Magdalen College Oxford. MS. 281, 'Frewen's book 1628-40', f.10 (I would like to thank Mr Gerald Harriss for permission to cite this MS.).
[41] Laud recommended public whippings: *Works of Laud*, v, 196-7.

the new examination statutes which replaced the submission of theses and participation in demonstrations with formal examinations for degrees.[42] It was a reform considered by all to be a real achievement. But the examination statute, like all the rest, required constant vigilance and the diligent co-operation of the magistrate – and it is significant that even Peter Turner admitted that the new statute had often worked by 'conniving at some defects now and then . . .'.[43]

As Laud himself acknowledged, laws could not cover all contingencies and 'when the laws are silent . . . power must be applied'.[44] In short the success of the statutes was largely dependent on the officers and magistrates who should enforce them. Alarmingly they were often partners in crime. In 1636 it was admitted that proctors made 'idle efforts' to detect students in taverns and failed to exact fines. Tutors were often found in the same alehouses as their charges. The revisions of 1636 made proctors liable to any fines they failed to levy, and the epinomis rendered officers as well as students open to a charge of perjury 'if (which Heaven forbid) they suffer any statutes to grow out of date from lack of use and desuetude'.[45] Unfortunately it was only Heaven that could forbid it. The central problem for Laud, for the statutes, indeed for the policy of 'Thorough' in church and state, was a dependence on per-sonalities – personalities less endowed with a sense of duty than the author of the statutes. The only officer on whom Laud could totally rely was himself. Vice-Chancellor Frewen told him that while he had been present the disputa-tions had been conducted well, but his absence for just a fortnight saw the examinations brought to a 'dead stand'. While Frewen took great pains over the examination statutes, Laud acknowledged 'that the great business would greatly fall to nothing if the Vice-Chancellors for the future did not take that prudent and vigilant care'.[46] Sadly not all of them did. Laud had occasion to complain to Vice-Chancellor Baylie that, unlike his predecessor Pincke, he failed to supervise discipline. And when the Vice-Chancellor failed to be vigilant, the other officers were left to act as it best suited them. In February 1637 Laud complained that he had heard nothing of the success of the statutes all year; he urged special care of the decree against 'noctinavigation', for 'I doubt not the proctors will be negligent enough . . .'.[47]

Indolence and indifference were not the only problems. Direct opposition to Laud, and to the statutes, from the city, and more seriously from within the university, was another. In the case of the city, Laud's chancellorship served only to enflame the long-standing rivalry between town and gown.[48] For as Chancellor, Laud was a fervent champion of the university's rights and privileges over the town, not least because powers of licensing inns and right of search were important to the success of the statutes. In response to a

---

[42] Convoc. Reg. R 24, f. 167 (Laud); *Works of Laud*, v, 212 (Turner), 235 (Frewen), 256-7 (Baylie).
[43] Ibid., v, 212.
[44] Griffiths, *Statutes*, 227.
[45] Ibid., 188; Ward, *Statutes of the University of Oxford*, I, 345.
[46] *Works of Laud*, v, 267-8; cf. *C.S.P.D.* 1637-8, 438.
[47] *Works of Laud*, v, 163-4, 260. Laud required weekly reports.
[48] See e.g. *Works of Laud*, v, 276-8; Queen's College Oxford MS. 378, ff.2ff.

university petition for more authority in matters concerning the reformation of the youth of the university, Laud helped secure a new charter granting the university extended powers to search in the town and suburbs for robbers, gangsters, prostitutes and students lodging outside college.[49] The city was ordered to assist the search. There was no use establishing a perfect commonweal in the university if its enemies could take refuge in the town. But even the charter did not solve the problems. In 1634 Charles I stipulated that there should be but three licensed alehouses in Oxford: by 1639 it was said that there were 300 unlicensed,[50] and Vice-Chancellor Frewen told Laud that at least 100 inns had been licensed by a J.P. who was himself a brewer on condition that the innkeepers buy their beer from him.[51] Here was a symptom of a larger and long-experienced problem: the town refused to comply with university laws about student discipline when the interests of the town were at stake. And drunken students, if poor scholars, made good customers.

Within the university, Laud's authority as Chancellor was compromised from the very day of his appointment. For Laud won the contest for the honour against Philip Herbert, third Earl of Montgomery and later fourth Earl of Pembroke, by only nine votes. Within a week of the election, fifteen members of the university appealed against it to the King, arguing that Frewen, as Vice-Chancellor, had Convocation unconstitutionally summoned. On the death of a chancellor, it was argued, the office of vicechancellor became also automatically void and authority descended to the senior doctor.[52] Secondly, it was alleged, the Convocation was 'surreptitiously held, no competent warning being given . . . the same being begun before the Beadle had fitly warned it'.[53] The election was therefore void. The appeal remained unheard and the suspicion that Laud had not been duly elected was never allayed. It cannot have helped the Chancellor to command the respect and cooperation upon which he depended. In 1641 Laud himself reflected, 'I suffered much by the clamours of the Earl of Pembroke, who thought it long till he had that place, which he had long gaped for.'[54]

Nor were the statutes themselves heralded as a great triumph by all members of the university. That is not surprising for after August 1633 the business was taken out of their hands. Twyne, we recall, reported the dismay of the delegates and heads of houses that the statute book of 1634 was substantially different from that which they had approved; he showed anxiety about the arbitrary power of amendment which the Chancellor reserved to himself and noted that some critics boldly believed 'the said

[49] S. Gibson, *The Great Charter of Charles I to the University of Oxford* (1933), 33. For this clause see Public Record Office (hereafter P.R.O.), SP 16/315/27; for privileges confirmed and extended, see 'Confirmatio generalis omnium veterum chartarum et privilegiorum Almae universitatis Oxon. . . . ', Bodleian Library, Gough Oxford MS. VI, and Bankes MS. 12/7.
[50] *C.S.P.D.* 1633-4, p.386; *Works of Laud*, V, 238. In August 1637 Dean Fell reported 94 unlicensed taverns: ibid., V, 179.
[51] *C.S.P.D.* 1639, pp.372-4.
[52] Mallet, *History*, II, 303-4; *Works of Laud*, V, 4; cf. *Diary of Crosfield*, 42.
[53] Bodl. MS. 594, f.139&[v].
[54] *The History of the Troubles and Tryal of William Laud* (1695), 181.

statutes are not to be obeyed, as being not expressly and openly read in Convocation'. Thomas Crosfield reflected in January 1635 on 'the university statutes and what exceptions could be made against them'. Others in 1641 complained that, like Laud's election, they were illegal because imposed upon the university not voted by it.[55] Their purpose was no other than the removal of all restraints upon the office of Chancellor and an assault upon the liberties of Convocation and Congregation. Through the Hebdomodal Council the Chancellor sought to predetermine all important issues, 'so that when the business comes to be passed in the Convocation, most come pre-engaged'.[56] At his trial Laud was charged with illegal innovations intended to subvert the university's liberties through an absolute power invested in the Chancellor.[57]

These protests and charges are evidence that the effects of the statutes had been felt. But they are evidence too of a faction within the university opposed to the code before it was promulgated and devoted to its destruction after it had passed. To Anthony à Wood and later to Mallet, the explanation for such opposition is again simple: protests about Laud's election and the statutes were Puritan complaints against a new Arminian regime.[58] According to this interpretation, Laud's friends in the colleges were those who, like Juxon at St. John's, Frewen at Magdalen and Jackson at Corpus, shared his religious views. His enemies – Prideaux at Exeter, Brent at Merton, Kettell at Trinity, Hood at Lincoln, Radcliffe at Brasenose – were those for whom those views were anathema. Undoubtedly this analysis contains some truth: in all the complaints against the statutes there are hints of religious grievances, and a university petition to Parliament in 1642 pressed specifically for a new code which would foster 'the true reformed Protestant religion'.[59] There is evidence too of opposition within the university to restrictions on preaching and to a new emphasis on reverence and ceremony.[60] But in general Mallet's picture is over-simplified. For what is striking about the statutes is the *absence* of detailed injunctions on religious matters – beyond a general insistence on subscription and conformity to the Church of England.[61] True it is that in the 1630s there were wildly differing views about that, but, at least as Chancellor of Oxford, Laud was unwilling to place stress on those differences.[62] He rigorously enforced the royal proclamation forbidding public discussion of doctrinal controversies, and barred a proponent of Arminian doctrines no less readily than he punished those who railed against them.[63] He also seemed

[55] Above, p.147 n.9; *Diary of Crosfield*, 77; H.M.C.R. Leybourne-Popham, 4-5; cf. Bodl. MS. 594, ff.139-40.

[56] Bodl. MS. 594, f.144^V.

[57] *History of Troubles and Tryal*, 435; *Works of Laud*, IV, 187-9.

[58] Mallet, *History*, II, 304.

[59] E.g. the complaints against oaths, and especially the oath *ex officio* ('whereby men are enjoyned to . . . accuse others, to detect and accuse themselves') and subscriptions in Bodl. MS. 594, ff.141, 145; H.M.C.R. *Leybourne-Popham*, 4-5.

[60] Bodl. MS. 594, f.144, complains that Hebdomadal Council issued orders to restrain preaching. See *Commons Journal*, II, 191 (petition of 22 June 1642).

[61] Griffiths, *Statutes*, 182. The test of orthodoxy was subscription to the 1562 articles and 1603 canons.

[62] Cf. below, p.160.

[63] W. C. Costin, *William Laud, President of St. John's College and Chancellor of the University of Oxford* (1945), 16.

anxious to avoid confrontation over questions of ceremony. When Proctor Corbet refused to bow at the altar in St. Mary's Laud would 'not give him any command, either to do or desist or to appoint any substitute, but leave him and let him do as it shall please God and himself'.[64] Secondly it is clear that Laud was able to gain the cooperation, at least at times, of those who disagreed with him on points of theology. It was Prideaux, listed by Mallet as an enemy, whom Laud asked to revise Chillingworth's *The Religion of Protestants a Safe Way to Salvation*, and Prideaux who replied that 'no man shall be more ready to execute the Archbishop's commands'. Laud showed similar respect to others, advancing men like Dean Fell irrespective of their religion. [65] When he wrote in 1635 to the Bishop of Winchester with advice on the education of scholars at New College, Laud even agreed that 'Calvin's Institutions may profitably be read, and as one of their first books for divinity . . . '.[66] He wished only that students be grounded first in philosophy and logic – in accordance with the traditional curriculum. On the evidence of his chancellorship at Oxford it is hard not to substantiate Laud's own defence of his actions: 'I have nothing to do to defend Arminianism . . . and yet for the peace of Christendom, and the strengthening of the Reformed Religion, I do heartily wish these differences were not pursued with such heat and animosity . . . '.[67] Within the university, Laud pursued not doctrinal controversy, but a learned ministry.

Opposition on religious grounds was not the principal obstacle. It was but one factor in a myriad of personal relationships, which then, even more than today, formed the hub of the university. Laud centred his hope for discipline on the college and, within the college, the effectiveness of discipline depended on the head. Opposition to Laud and to the statutes from within the colleges took many forms: personal antagonisms and jealousies, reaction against change, internal college politics, localist revolt against central interference – and indolence and ineptitude. As Potter pessimistically told Laud in 1635: 'One main reason of their irregularities is because they have been left every head to his own humour.'[68] Those differing humours did not always owe their differences to religion, but they were responsible for different results. At Queen's, Potter, one brought up in a strong Calvinist tradition, strictly enforced the statutes and all Laud's injunctions.[69] The President of Corpus, Thomas Jackson, reduced all to order and sobriety, winning even the respect of the usually vitriolic Prynne who, though he shared not Jackson's religion, yet regarded him as 'a man otherwise of good abilities, and of plausible, affable, courteous

---

[64] *Works of Laud*, V, 205–6; cf. ibid., IV, 220–1, and *C.S.P.D.* 1638–9, pp.46, 68.
[65] *C.S.P.D.* 1635–6, p.486; *History of Troubles and Tryal*, 369.
[66] *Works of Laud*, V, 118. However, he thought it dangerous to read the works of Calvin too early.
[67] *History of Troubles and Tryal*, 353.
[68] *C.S.P.D.* 1635, p.142.
[69] *Diary of Crosfield*, xix–xxiv. Potter ordered the wearing of round caps on Sundays in accordance with 'the command given by the Chancellor' and the abstention from flesh in Lent 'commanded by the Chancellour'. Whilst remaining a Calvinist, he encouraged bowing and an emphasis on ceremony. (Ibid., 44, 50, 74.)

deportment'.[70] In 1638, by contrast, Laud had occasion to complain about the conduct of disputations at Brasenose: 'I would have you speak with the Principal [ironically the puritan Radcliffe] that he would command their cellar to be better looked to, that no strong and unruly argument be drawn from that topick-place.' By 1640 the Vice-Chancellor protested in his defence that after all his efforts, drunken students had only moved from the streets into the colleges where eyes were less watchful.

We cannot know how watchful they were in every college. But we do have a wealth of evidence for one notorious case – that of Merton College. For here, as well as the formal college registers and reports, we have the private letters to Laud of Peter Turner, a senior master of the college who had been closely involved in the compilation and revision of the statutes, and who now stood high in the Chancellor's esteem. The long saga of Laud's relations with Merton is too detailed to be told in full here. It began in the autumn of 1637 when a serious quarrel between two of the Fellows was referred to Laud's attention.[71] It seems probable that during the winter of the same year information, and complaints about the disorders in the college, reached Laud through Turner, who in March 1638 was advising him how to order a visitation so that it might not appear who had entered the protests. Laud appointed a commission to investigate.[72] On 29 March a detailed question-naire (consisting of thirty articles) was sent to the Warden and Fellows in order to discover whether university and college statutes were correctly observed. It was an extremely thorough document, of inquisitorial detail.[73] At the beginning of April the Visitors appointed to investigate the college (Richard Baylie, John Lambe, Arthur Duck and Gilbert Sheldon) reported on the irregularities complained of or detected: postmasters' places were sold, meals were not attended in the common hall, lectures were not read, nor college records maintained. College properties were corruptly administered, Bible reading and Latin were abandoned, and students often spent the night outside college in the company of whores or lay within it, unable to speak English, let alone Latin, in a befuddled stupor induced by the illegal double-strength beer favoured by the Warden.[74] After this catalogue of sins it seems a mere footnote to add that the statute book was not in the library.[75] So serious were these charges that Sheldon thought Brent would be best advised not to endure a full enquiry, 'but should lay the key under the door and be gone'. In view of this it was surely an excess of academic understatement which prompted

[70] T. Fowler, *The History of Corpus Christi College* (1893), 189-90; *Brasenose Quarter-Centenary Monographs*, II: *The Sixteenth and Seventeenth Centuries* (Oxford Hist. Soc. 1909), 29; *Works of Laud*, v, 261.

[71] *C.S.P.D.* 1637, p.393.

[72] *C.S.P.D.* 1637-8, p.316; Merton College, 'Collegii Mertonensi Registrum 1567-1731' (hereafter Colleg. Mert. Reg.), pp.328-9. I am grateful to Mr Roger Highfield for his permission to see and cite this register.

[73] P.R.O., SP 16/376/68; G. C. Brodrick, *Memorials of Merton College* (Oxford Hist. Soc. 1885), 78.

[74] Brodrick (op. cit., 81-4) summarises the ordinances issued by the commissioners to deal with the grievances pending a full enquiry. See *C.S.P.D.* 1637-8, pp.341-2; cf. 'Colleg. Mert. Reg.', p.330, and *C.S.P.D.* 1637-8, p.453.

[75] 'Colleg. Mert. Reg.', p.331.

Brent's reply and his regret 'that you should conceive amiss of us'.[76]
Laud ordered that the college obey the visitors' injunctions until the formal
hearing in October. Throughout the summer he wrote constantly for further
information and reports. Brent replied that all was enacted according to his
command.[77] And there the historian would have to leave it – were it not for
the secret missives of Peter Turner. For Turner informed Laud of the
evasions and deceit practised by Brent: first the Visitors' orders were ignored;
secondly the three fellows appointed to prosecute the complaints about the
college were dismissed and replaced by more malleable representatives who,
having no objections to the existing administration, replied to all enquiries
'*omnia bene*'.[78] But by August, perhaps because he realised that Laud was well
informed of the real state of affairs, even Brent admitted that all was not well.
Two or three Master-Fellows regularly joined students in the alehouse, 'and
some young women have lately been begotten with child where two of our
masters frequently resort and sometimes lodge'.[79] The final hearing in
October served only to incriminate Brent and others further. The orders sent
by Laud and read by Turner on 15 October catalogued the sins of the college
and the rules by which it was to be governed in future. All too often they only
repeated the very statutes of 1636: students were to live in college and return
by nine o'clock each night; Fellows and students should wear academic dress;
copies of the statutes were to be displayed in the library.[80] Ironically even
these injunctions were enforced but spasmodically and grudgingly.[81] Brent
became Laud's bitter opponent.[82]

Merton is a notorious case of a college where Masters, Fellows, and
students flouted their own and the university statutes. But we should not
assume that because it was notorious, it was exceptional. We should recall
that we are informed of the ills of Merton not through the reports of any
university or college officer, but from the private correspondence of Peter
Turner. What went on within the walls of other colleges where Laud had no
confidant (and where the historian accordingly has no evidence) perhaps best
remains to us, as to him, a mystery. We may only note that in 1640, Brent
admitted that junior masters usually failed to attend early morning prayers,
but yet believed them to be 'frequented as well by us as any other college'.[83]
He may have been right.

By 1636, Laud had succeeded by 'indefatigable industry' in devising a code of
law by which the university of Oxford was to be reduced to order, discipline
and sobriety. When one reviews Laud's labours as Chancellor, when one reads
his painstaking correspondence with the university, it is indeed, as Hugh

[76] *C.S.P.D.* 1637-8, pp.348, 573.
[77] 'Colleg. Mert. Reg.', pp.330-1; *C.S.P.D.* 1637-8, pp.561, 607; *Works of Laud*, VII, 460-2, 478-9.
[78] *C.S.P.D.* 1637-8, p.562. Laud ordered Brent to reappoint the first three: *Works of Laud*, VII,
460-2; cf. Turner's letters of 20 and 26 August: *C.S.P.D.* 1637-8, p.588.
[79] Ibid., 588.
[80] Ibid., 221; 'Colleg. Mert. Reg.', pp.333-6.
[81] *C.S.P.D.* 1638-9, p.174; cf. *C.S.P.D.* 1639-40, p.508.
[82] *History of Troubles and Tryal*, 308, 343; *Works of Laud*, IV, 193-4.
[83] *C.S.P.D.* 1639-40, p.508.

Trevor-Roper put it, 'hard to realise that it was but an item in his vast programme for the reconstruction of the whole basis of secular and ecclesiastical government'. And yet it was more than a mere item. For the university to Laud was like the court to Charles himself – a model for the government of church and state. Universities were in the realm as in the body 'the noble and vital parts, which being vigorous and sound send good blood and active spirits into the veins and arteries . . . '.[84] As Chancellor, Laud hoped to establish at Oxford his ideal commonweal, a seminary for a wider world – a world in which liberty never descended to licence, where order was imposed on anarchy, beauty upon dilapidation, learning upon ignorance, unity upon faction. Because Oxford was his 'seminary',[85] we may learn much from the history of Laud's chancellorship about his ideals for the future governance of the realm and something, too, of the reasons for his failure to enact them.

As Archbishop of Canterbury Laud has been depicted recently as the man who destroyed the Elizabethan compromise by a rigid insistence upon conformity, as the prelate who provoked the rise of revolutionary puritanism by a breach with traditional and orthodox predestinarianism.[86] At first this judgment seems convincing, not least because it is endorsed by many contemporaries. At his trial Laud, as Archbishop and as Chancellor of Oxford, was charged with innovating in matters of doctrine and ceremony, with leading the church via Arminianism to Popery. And the all but universal hostility shown to the Laudian bishops in 1641 is evidence of the conviction those charges then carried. Yet when we turn from the testimony of his accusers and critics to the evidence of his writings and actions, that judgment and those charges seem less persuasive. The Laudian statutes and Laud's correspondence with the university are notable for their *silence* on questions of theological controversy. As Chancellor he rigidly enforced Charles's proclamation forbidding debate – in the universities as well as the pulpit – on questions of salvation and free will.[87] Tooker of Oriel was silenced for his defence of Arminianism no less than were its critics.[88] Laud's correspondence, orders and works as Bishop of London and Archbishop of Canterbury are similarly silent. Commitment to a belief in predestination had never been an official doctrine of the Church of England;[89] and, whatever the fears of his contemporaries, from the evidence of his works and correspondence it is hard not to endorse the view that Laud 'for all his schoolman's outlook allowed that some parts of doctrine were genuinely "indifferent"'.[90] Laud's chaplain and biographer Peter Heylyn tells us that in a sermon preached at Oxford in

[84] *Works of Laud*, V, 129; Trevor-Roper, *Archbishop Laud*, 273; *Works of Laud*, V, 130.
[85] Below, p.162.
[86] N. R. N. Tyacke, 'Puritanism, Arminianism and counter-revolution', in C. Russell (ed.), *The Origins of the English Civil War* (1971),119–43; R. Ashton, *The English Civil War* (1978), ch.5.
[87] S. R. Gardiner (ed.), *The Constitutional Documents of the Puritan Revolution 1625-60* (1906), 75.
[88] *Works of Laud*, V, 15.
[89] Russell modifies Tyacke in stating that predestination was 'the normal though not quite the official doctrine of the Church of England': *Parliaments and English Politics 1621-9* (1979), 29. Cf. the debates in Parliament in 1629 for the uncertainty concerning the articles of the Church of England: W. Notestein and F. Relf (eds), *Commons Debates for 1629* (1921), 23–8, 33–5, 95ff., 119.
[90] Trevor-Roper, *Archbishop Laud*, x; cf. Laud's own remark: 'in and about things not necessary there ought not to be a contention to a separation': *Works of Laud*, II, 218.

1615 he 'insisted on some points which might indifferently be imputed either to Popery or Arminianism . . . '.[91] But the Laud of the 1630s should not be judged by one episode in 1615. Certainly by 1630 Laud told Dr Brooke, Master of Trinity, Cambridge, who was preparing a tract on predestination, ' . . . I am yet where I was that something about these controversies is unmasterable in this life'.[92] If the central tenet of Arminianism was a belief in God's universal grace and the freewill of all men to obtain salvation then Laud's Arminianism, as Prynne discovered in preparing the charges against him, is hard to prove.[93]

What cannot be denied is that during Laud's archiepiscopate there was a greater emphasis on *iure divino* episcopacy, on sacraments and ceremony. This was not, however, novel, nor exclusively Arminian, nor perhaps primarily the work of Laud. Whitgift and Bancroft zealously persecuted puritan non-conformity; in this the laxity of Abbot's long primacy was the exception rather than the rule.[94] And the renewed insistence upon reverence owed as much to the accession of Charles I as to the succession of Laud.[95] It was Charles who ordered the communion table to be placed in the east end of the church.[96] Whatever his own preferences, in his visitation articles and orders to the clergy Laud had insisted only that it be placed in 'convenient sort'.[97] Concerning such questions and rites the revised canons of 1640, as even the nonconformist Gardiner acknowledged, are evidence less of a rigidity which breeds division, more of 'a serious effort to find a broad ground'.[98]

Few of Laud's contemporaries saw him in this light; few understood his ideals. As Clarendon acutely observed, he failed to make 'his designs and purposes appear as candid as they were'.[99] As Chancellor of Oxford and as Archbishop of Canterbury, Laud pursued order and unity, not discord and division. The statutes for Oxford, like the articles of enquiry for his metro-politan visitations, show Laud's primary concern with externals – with the details of conduct and discipline. It is in these that his industry most contrasts with Abbot's indolence, his firmness with Abbot's indulgence.[100] To Carlyle, Laud was 'like a college tutor whose world is forms, college rules'; to Mallet such rules seemed 'disproportionately rigid and minute'.[101] But these writers failed to understand that for Laud uniformity and order in externals were the means toward sound learning in the university and spirituality within the

[91] Cited by Nicholas Tyacke in 'Arminianism and English culture', in A. C. Duke and C. A. Tamse (eds), *Britain and the Netherlands*, VII: *Church and State since the Reformation* (The Hague 1981). I am grateful to Mr Tyacke for allowing me to see a typescript of this essay.
[92] *Works of Laud*, VI(i), 292.
[93] W. Lamont, *Godly Rule* (1969), 65.
[94] Ibid., ch.3.
[95] I shall be developing this argument in a book on the personal rule of Charles I.
[96] P.R.O., P.C. 2/43/304, 3 Nov. 1633; C.S.P.D. 1633–4, p.273.
[97] See Laud's visitation articles as Bishop of London in 1628 and as Archbishop of Canterbury in 1635 in *Works of Laud*, V(ii); cf. ibid., VI(ii), 312, 348–50.
[98] J. P. Kenyon (ed.), *The Stuart Constitution* (1966), 166–71; S. R. Gardiner, *History of England from . . . James I to the . . . Civil War* (10 vols., 1883–4), IX, 143.
[99] Edward Hyde, Earl of Clarendon, *The History of the Rebellion* (ed. W. D. Macray, 6 vols., 1888), I, 125.
[100] Compare Laud's visitation articles with Abbot's less detailed proceedings: *Works of Laud*, V(ii).
[101] W. H. Hutton, *William Laud* (1895), 239; Mallet, *History*, II, 333.

church. The decay of discipline in the universities, he told Gerard Vossius, 'is the cause of all our ills in church and state', for order in the university was 'a thing very necessary in this age both for church and commonwealth since so many young gentlemen and others of all ranks and conditions have their first breeding for the public in that seminary'.[102] In the Church too nothing had more conduced to draw men from piety than 'the want of uniform and decent order'.[103]

Order in the academic world as in church and state required authority – and the recognition of authority. As during his archiepiscopate he stressed the independent authority of the church and the prerogatives of its courts, its bishops and its clergy, so during his chancellorship he emphasised the independent jurisdiction of the university and the powers of its officers – Chancellor, Vice-Chancellor and proctors.[104] An insistence upon order and discipline and an emphasis upon authority were not, however, threads which spun a straitjacket for the conscience. Prideaux remained Professor of Divinity throughout Laud's chancellorship; Proctor Corbet was left undisturbed despite his nonconformity; even William Hodges of Exeter who had offended by his scandalous sermon was restored after submission.[105] Few in the university, and indeed few in the church, were deprived of their positions as a result of differences concerning doctrine or ceremony.[106] Rather Laud (and many Laudian bishops) are remarkable for their patience with the obstinate and their attempts to win over the refractory.[107] And among those whom Laud advanced in the university and the church, we find men like Samuel Fell, Richard Sibbes, and Joseph Hall who differed from him in belief and even practice.

Nor did order and discipline forge chains for the intellect. The Oxford of William Laud was not the Salamanca of Philip II. Rather at Oxford during the 1630s the new learning, and especially the new science, flourished – thanks not least to Laud's donations of manuscripts and mathematical books, and his endowment of a lectureship in Arabic. And at the court of Charles I, as even the critical Lucy Hutchinson acknowledged, 'men of learning and ingenuity in all arts were in esteem and receiv'd encouragement from the King'.[108]

If by a study of Laud's chancellorship we may understand more clearly his ideals and objectives, we may similarly comprehend more easily the obstacles to their fulfilment. We have argued that Laud as jealously guarded the freedom, privileges and jurisdiction of the university within the city, as those of the church within the commonwealth. Maintenance of the privileges of the university (as of the church) was inextricably linked with discipline and order

[102] Trevor-Roper, *Archbishop Laud*, 117; *Works of Laud*, v, 101.
[103] *Works of Laud*, II, xvi.
[104] For Laud's defence of proctorial authority against the Dean of Christ Church, see *Works of Laud*, v, 223.
[105] *Works of Laud*, v, 66.
[106] Evidence of Laud's metropolitan reports; cf. Hutton's comment on the High Commission Act books (*William Laud*, 99).
[107] E.g. *Works of Laud*, v(ii), 318, 335, 340–1, 356.
[108] Nicholas Tyacke, 'Science and religion at Oxford before the Civil War', in D. Pennington and K. Thomas (eds), *Puritans and Revolutionaries* (1978), 73-93, and 'Arminianism and English culture'.

within. Only if it was above reproach could the university, like the church, defend its privileges and jurisdiction. Only if it enjoyed independent jurisdiction could an institution properly reform itself. That is why Laud took pains to secure for the university a new charter of privileges to accompany a new code of discipline, why he pressed for equal representation for gown and town on the commission of the peace. But privileges attracted resentment. The city was as hostile to the favours shown the university as was the laity to the pretensions of the church. Vice-Chancellor Frewen made the identification clearly in a letter to Laud in October 1640. For all the university's efforts towards reform, 'some of our back friends in Parliament will give us but little thanks: some there, perhaps many, rather desiring we should be guilty, that they might with more colour use us as they did the monasteries.'[109]

There were enemies within as well as assaults from without. In the university as in the church and state Laud discovered that 'private ends are such blocks in the public way'.[110] As we have seen the officers of the university responsible for discipline were often negligent: no less remiss were the bishops in the Laudian church, or the justices and deputy lieutenants in the counties. Even diligent officers met with unreliable subordinate officials. In the diocese and the locality, no less than in the case of Merton College, a return of '*omnia bene*' could cover a multitude of sins. Hebdomadal Council may have been instituted as a governing body of the university, but in so far as it consisted of heads of houses, it was also an assembly of representatives from the colleges. Like the gentry governors of the provinces they too often served their private interest first, the demands of the government second. Like those leaders of county society, the heads of colleges jealously guarded their local autonomy against encroachment from above. Some heads of houses objected to the statutes, some opposed any increase of chancellorial power. There was little that Laud, as Chancellor, could do. Potter admitted as much: on hearing of Laud's intent to carry out a visitation of the colleges, he told him that he was 'like to find a great necessity of it'.[111] When he sought the power of Metropolitan visitation, Laud acknowledged his weakness as Chancellor, and though he won the right, he never exercised it in practice. The history of the university shows the limits to the effectiveness of authority: the impossibility of complete supervision.

1636, the year in which the statutes were finally completed and a new charter secured, in which as if by celebration he entertained the royal party at Oxford, was also the year when 'it might well appear to Laud that his policy had triumphed wherever it had been applied'.[112] It soon became clear that this was but an illusion. As the dissensions grew within the realm, Laud clung desperately to the university as the hope for an ordered commonwealth, free from faction and vice in the future. As he told the sons of the Elector Palatine at the degree ceremony in 1636, students in particular must conquer youthful

[109] *Works of Laud*, v, 42, 179, 283, 291.
[110] Ibid., vi(i), 310.
[111] *C.S.P.D.* 1635, p.142.
[112] Trevor-Roper, *Archbishop Laud*, 271.

passions. But that hope depended upon the maintenance of discipline, and when he had perhaps abandoned his most strenuous efforts elsewhere he continued to chivvy the officers of the university. 'There is,' he urged, 'a greater necessity to hold up good order in the brokenness of these times.'[113]

Even within Oxford, however, Laud's triumph was qualified. Few within the university (perhaps in the realm) opposed his ideals when they understood them. Many opposed the means (the scant respect for interests, the extension of authority) and the methods (the detailed enquiry, the persistent hectoring) by which they were translated into practice. What to Laud were efficient procedures were to others arbitrary courses. The unity and cooperation for which he had asked on his appointment as Chancellor were, from the beginning, no more than a dream. Like the realm, the university was *not* just one body ruled by one head, but a series of commonwealths, some governed by reason, some by passion, often contesting with each other, at times divided within themselves. 'Thorough' in Oxford, as in the country at large, depended upon personalities: depended that is on those who governed identifying their local and private interests with the public good. Too few made the identification; too many had a different view of the public good.

But the story of Laud's chancellorship was not one of complete failure. As the troubles of 1640-1 mounted, Laud delayed his resignation as Chancellor because, despite some difficulties, 'I have found so much love from the university that I could not make myselfe willing to leave it'.[114] The Vice-Chancellor reassured him in 1641 that though he vacated the office, his gifts, his endowments, most of all the discipline and reformed manners which were the legacy of his statutes, assured his fame 'howsoever long care is taken for the study of the arts and the honour of letters'.[115]

As his days neared an end Laud feared for the future of the university and the church. One night in November 1642, he records, 'I dreamed that the church was undone and that I went to St. John's in Oxford where I found the roof off some part of the college, and the walls ready to fall down'.[116] Laud's college is still standing, and the statutes which he devised governed the university until the nineteenth century. Nor was the church undone. For in the 1640s Oxford emerged as the stronghold of church and crown. When the Long Parliament divided between Cavaliers and Roundheads, most of those Oxford men who had matriculated during Laud's chancellorship supported the monarchy.[117] When the troubles had passed, it was the zeal of the gentry which secured the restoration of a hierarchical, episcopal church along with the crown. And among the nominees to the vacant bishoprics were many best known for their roles in the university of Laud's chancellorship.

---

[113] *Works of Laud*, V, 149.

[114] *The True Copie of a Letter sent from the Most Reverend William Lord Archbishop of Canterbury to the University of Oxford when He Resign'd his Office as Chancellor June 25, 1641*, 2; cf. *C.S.P.D.* 1640-1, p.253.

[115] *Works of Laud*, V, 302.

[116] *History of Troubles and Tryal*, 197

[117] Of 30 graduates who matriculated between 1628 and 1639, 18-20 can be identified as royalist (biographical information from M. F. Keeler, *The Long Parliament 1640-1641* (1954)). This contrasts with the 169 Oxford graduates of all ages in the Long Parliament who divided into 73 royalists and 91 parliamentarians (D. Brunton and D. H. Pennington, *Members of the Long Parliament* (1954), 7).

13

The Year of the
Three Ambassadors

J. H. Elliott

In the opening days of April 1640 the court of Charles I was startled by the arrival in quick succession of two special envoys from the king of Spain. There was already a resident Spanish agent in London, Don Alonso de Cárdenas, 'a silly, ignorant, odd fellow' in Charles I's opinion.[1] Cárdenas was now joined by Don Antonio Sancho Dávila y Toledo, Marquis of Velada, who arrived from Flanders with all the pomp expected of a Spanish ambassador, including a train of '120 persons, of whom 20 are of note and sit at his own table'.[2] A few days later a third envoy, the Marquis Virgilio Malvezzi, slipped into Plymouth from Spain, and travelled incognito to London. A wraith-like apparition, he vanished into the lodgings of the Marquis of Velada in Chelsea, later to re-emerge in order to make an official entry into the court. 'Here,' the Venetian ambassador reported, 'they are utterly in the dark as to the objects of this sudden mission, and everyone, especially his Majesty, is full of impatient curiosity to learn the particular instructions of this second ambassador extraordinary.'[3]

The activities of these three Spanish envoys in London during the critical months which saw the summoning and dissolution of the Short Parliament and the opening of the Long have not passed unnoticed in historical literature.[4] The ambassadors' propositions have been recorded, although with a becoming brevity, for their mission is well known to have been singularly – and even ludicrously – abortive. In consequence, it figures as little more than a marginal interruption to the grand narrative of events that led by inexorable stages to the collapse of the personal government of Charles I.

But we should not automatically assume that simply because things did not happen, they could not have happened. We, who see a discredited English regime and a Spanish monarchy on the brink of defeat, know that the extra-

[1] *Calendar of State Papers Domestic* (hereafter *C.S.P.D.*) 1639–40, 22.
[2] *C.S.P.D.* 1640, 6.
[3] *C.S.P. Venetian*, 1640–2, 34.
[4] See in particular Samuel R. Gardiner, *History of England from the Accession of James I to the Outbreak of the Civil War*, IX (London 1894), 131 etc., and C. V. Wedgwood, *The King's Peace, 1637-1641* (London 1955), 328-9.

ordinary embassy was condemned to failure from the outset. But let us try for a moment to forget the apparently inevitable dénouement and see the Spanish mission through the eyes of the two statesmen, one Spanish and one English, who, for their own very different reasons, were desperately anxious that it should succeed.

How strangely similar, in their greatness and their defects, are those two towering figures of the 1630s, the Count-Duke of Olivares and the Earl of Strafford. Imperious and self-willed, they stand majestic and alone, obstinately defying men and the elements as the storm clouds gather. Wentworth, 'Black Tom Tyrant', the ruthless apostle of 'thorough'; Don Gaspar, the *Conde-Duque* – born, it was said, in Nero's palace in Rome – constantly proclaiming the virtues of discipline and order. Loyal and inflexible servants of indecisive masters, they were ready to die – as they had lived – for the same guiding principle: that the king's service was paramount, and that, in desperate times, necessity knew no law.

That the times were indeed desperate, neither had any doubt. For Spain, confronted by a Protestant coalition under the leadership of a Catholic France, the fortunes of war hung precariously in the balance. For the government of Charles I, acutely short of money and faced with the rebellion of the Scots, there was little time to lose. By the end of the decade both Olivares and Strafford sensed that disaster was close, and they cast about with a growing desperation for some device by which it might be averted. For a few brief months in the spring of 1640, each saw the other as essential to his own salvation. It soon became clear that both were self-deceived; but even the self-deceptions of statesmen reveal something of importance about the nature of their statesmanship.

'It is wise not to trust the English, who have a reputation for deceit – something which their religion does nothing to discountenance.'[5] Long experience had taught the Count-Duke the value of scepticism when dealing with the inhabitants of that heretical, fog-bound island. How could he forget the duplicity and arrogance of the Duke of Buckingham during the extraordinary visit of the prince of Wales to Madrid in 1623? 'Buckingham and the devil have their seat in England,' records a laconic entry in his register of correspondence.[6] This was the unholy combination that had engineered the attack on Cadiz – happily frustrated by divine intervention and human forethought – within a few months of the breakdown of the negotiations for the English marriage. How could he ignore, too, the bewildering tergiversations of Charles I's foreign policy since the time when Cottington arrived in Madrid in 1630 to bring the Anglo-Spanish hostilities to a close, and returned home with the draft of a secret treaty, never implemented, for an offensive and defensive alliance of the two crowns against their common enemy, the

[5] Archivo General de Simancas (hereafter AGS), Estado, legajo 2520, Olivares in Council of State, 29 December 1635. Spanish documents are cited in these notes by their New Style dates, but all dates given in the *text* of this essay follow the Old Style, except that the new year is taken as starting on 1 January.

[6] Biblioteca del Escorial, MS. K.1.17, f.133.

Dutch? And yet, with a kind of exasperated persistence, Olivares had continued through the 1630s to track down his elusive prey, in the hope that, sooner or later, it might somehow be lured into his capacious net. Unfortunately the English had their memories also, and not least the memory of the lost Palatinate. In any event, Charles I had his own domestic preoccupations, and wanted the benefits, but not the obligations, of continental alliances. Mutual interest, however, had proved sufficiently strong to produce the informal arrangement, misleadingly known as the Cottington Agreement, by which Spanish bullion and supplies were routed by way of Dover and safely convoyed to Flanders in English ships, to the advantage both of English merchants and of royal revenues.[7] But for the Count-Duke this was not enough. As he pored over his maps, anxiously calculating the relative strength of the Habsburgs and their rivals, he could not but cast glances, part anguished, part wistful, at that dangerously volatile neutral waxing fat on the commerce of the warring nations.

'Today,' he told his colleague in March 1638, 'our own forces and those of our enemies are almost equally balanced . . . so that one can clearly appreciate the enormous disequilibrium capable of being produced by the power of the king of England, so formidable on the sea.'[8] If only the Count-Duke could harness that power to the cause of Spain and the Habsburgs, how valuable it could be! How useful, too, a few thousand stalwart Irishmen for replenishing the diminished *tercios* of the Spanish army! The scenario was irresistibly attractive, but each time the Count-Duke was about to get it into focus, an alternative, and much less agreeable, vision would abruptly intrude upon his mind's eye. In this, Charles I, that unreliable monarch, would make common cause with the French and the Dutch, and English forces would march through Germany to restore the Elector Palatine. Of course it would never happen. Even Charles would never be so foolish as to risk the prosperity of his kingdoms for so chimerical a cause. Yet 'the obstinacy of the Calvinists' and the inscrutable ways of God were liable to cast rational calculations to the winds, and made it necessary to give thought to *futuros contingentes* . . .

Within a few months, however, the worst of all such contingencies seemed to have been happily dispelled by Charles's troubles with the Scots. Olivares followed with close attention the course of events in Scotland, not unlike those little local difficulties he had himself faced in Portugal in the preceding year. It was to be expected, he decided in July of 1638, that 'this will calm down, like the Portuguese business'.[9] But not, he hoped, too soon. For, as he advised Cárdenas shortly after his arrival in London, it was in Spain's interest that the rebellion should continue. The more Charles was persuaded of the truth of reports circulating in his capital that the French and the Dutch were covertly helping the Scots, the sooner he would come to realise who his true

[7] For this arrangement and its origins, see Harland Taylor, 'Trade, neutrality and the "English Road", 1630-1648', *The Economic History Review*, xxv (1972), 236-60, and J. S. Kepler, *The Exchange of Christendom* (Leicester 1976).
[8] AGS, Est., leg.2053, *El Conde Duque sobre las materias del Palatinato* (document prepared for meeting of Council of State of 7 March 1638).
[9] AGS, Est., leg.2521, *consulta* of Council of State, 17 July 1638.

friends were.[10]

As the Count-Duke had anticipated, Charles, the eternal wobbler, began veering once again towards the side of Spain, although such desperate swings only intensified the Count-Duke's deep-seated mistrust of wild English responses to the proffered alliance.[11] But mistrust becomes a luxury when hope begins to fade. In December 1638 the fall of Breisach cut Spain's overland corridor to Flanders. 'A great storm threatens us this year,' Olivares warned his colleagues as the first reports of the fate of Breisach reached Madrid.[12] Only a fragile maritime route now linked Spain to the Netherlands, and its very fragility drove home the critical importance of England for the outcome of the international conflict.

Short of persuading the Emperor to launch an invasion of France – a prospect that could only be regarded as remote – Olivares could see only three ways of restoring the European balance before it tipped inexorably in favour of the French and the Dutch. None by itself was likely to prove sufficient, but some combination of the three might yet do the trick. One possibility was that Charles I would yet be persuaded to ally himself with Spain. Even if the alliance proved of little practical benefit as long as Charles was preoccupied with the Scots, the Spanish advisers of the Cardinal Infante in Brussels believed that the formation of a Madrid–London axis would do much to promote the chances of a satisfactory peace settlement.[13] A second possiblity was that Richelieu's policies would drive France to revolt. The climate was propitious, and at this very moment that indefatigable *intrigante*, the Duchess of Chevreuse, was weaving her spider's web of conspiracy in London, along with her fellow-exile, the Duke of La Valette. The third, and most immediate, hope was that a massive Spanish fleet, now being fitted out, would succeed in defeating the Dutch as it forced its way up the Channel, and in disembarking in Flanders the troop reinforcements which the Cardinal Infante so urgently required.

Slender hopes, perhaps, built on slender foundations, and no man was more conscious than Olivares of the fickleness of fortune in politics and war. But his hopes rose as the splendid Armada of a hundred ships moved up the Channel in September 1639. Nothing quite like it had been seen since 1588;

[10] AGS, Est., leg.2575, draft despatch to Cárdenas, 13 September 1638. In view of Olivares's suspicions, which at least in part were justified, of Richelieu's contacts with the Portuguese dissidents during the Evora troubles, the rumours of French intervention in Scotland seemed to him by no means implausible. On 18 February 1639 Cárdenas wrote to Don Miguel de Salamanca in Brussels that he could find no hard and fast evidence of any such intervention; but on 25 March he reported, although on the basis of hearsay, that it was certain that the rebels had been brought some £40,000 by a former servant of the Archbishop of Bordeaux, who had been despatched to Scotland by Richelieu (Archives Génerales du Royaume, Brussels, Secrétairerie d'Etat et de Guerre (hereafter AGR, SEG), Registre 369, ff.59v. and 97). Richelieu's agent was possibly Thomas Chambers, for whom see David Stevenson, *The Scottish Revolution 1637-1644* (Newton Abbot 1973), 186-7, which restates the generally accepted view that Richelieu did not in fact give the Covenanters any assistance. For an earlier attempt by Richelieu to make contact with the Covenanters through Chambers, see Carl J. Burckhardt, *Richelieu and his Age*, III (London 1971), 155-6.
[11] Gardiner, *History*, VIII, 377.
[12] British Library, Egerton MS.2053, f.1, *Papel del Conde Duque sobre una propuesta* . . .
[13] AGS, Est., leg.3860, Cardinal Infante to King, 27 February 1639, and *voto* of Olivares, 29 March.

but unhappily the resemblance held true to the end . 'I cannot deny to your highness,' the Count-Duke wrote to the Cardinal Infante on learning of Tromp's victory at the Battle of the Downs, 'the extreme concern and distress with which the news of the great disaster to our armada has been received. There is indeed nothing we can do but bow our heads to the Lord's commands; and I really believe that our presumption as regards this armada was such as to justify our punishment.'[14] Philip II, it seemed, was still alive and well in Madrid.

But for the Count-Duke, as for Philip II, spiritual resignation did not preclude temporal activity. Orders were at once given for ships, cannon and crews to be brought to Spain from Italy; the Cardinal Infante was instructed to purchase ships wherever he could find them; and the Marquis of Velada, *maestre de campo* of the Spanish army of Flanders, was appointed ambassador extraordinary to the king of England, his mission to secure English protection for the Channel passage, and to persuade Charles to take revenge on the Dutch for their defiance of his authority in attacking the Spanish fleet in British territorial waters.

While he awaited Velada's arrival, Cárdenas found himself unusually busy. Early in December 1639 another of Richelieu's enemies, the Huguenot Duke of Soubise, arrived in London, carrying with him plans for a clandestine operation to seize La Rochelle and launch a Huguenot rebellion. The plans were outlined to Cárdenas by the Duchess of Chevreuse and the Duke of La Valette, who made clear that they were contingent on guarantees of Spanish help. The question of aid to the Huguenots always raised delicate problems of conscience which could only be resolved at the highest theological levels in Madrid; but the Cardinal Infante assured Madrid that, if these could be resolved and the scheme went ahead, it stood every change of bringing about that general peace settlement for which everybody yearned.[15]

The Duchess of Chevreuse and the Duke of La Valette, however, were not the only plotters to pay a visit to Cárdenas that December. On the 18th, a few days after he had written to Madrid to report Charles I's decision to summon parliament, the envoy received a visit from 'a person who is very intimate with the Viceroy of Ireland, the man who today enjoys most authority with this king'.[16] The Lord Deputy's emissary – was it perhaps that arch-contriver, Sir Tobie Matthew, who some months later was acting as a go-between?[17] – came to ask whether Philip IV would be willing to lend Charles 400,000 ducats (£100,000) on 'very favourable conditions'. Cárdenas, who lacked instructions for dealing with this contingency, could only promise to inform Madrid, while suggesting that a levy of Irishmen for the king of Spain's armies would help the negotiations forward.

Although the Lord Deputy's overture found Cárdenas unprepared, it should

[14] Bayerische Staatsbibliothek, Munich, Codex hisp.22, f.117v, 29 November 1639.
[15] Archivo Histórico Nacional (hereafter AHN), Madrid, Est., libro 971, Cárdenas to Miguel de Salamanca, 16 December 1639, and covering letter from Cardinal Infante to King, 30 December.
[16] AGR, SEG, R.370, f.299v, Cárdenas to Miguel de Salamanca, 30 December 1639.
[17] AGR, SEG, R.377, f.71, Ambassadors to King, 9 July 1640.

not have come as a complete surprise. Some four years earlier he had written from Dublin to the then Spanish resident in London, asking for Spain's help in the restitution of the Palatinate.[18] During his time in Ireland he had been an insistent advocate of friendly relations with Spain; and his return to London in September 1639 to assume a dominant position at court was a cause of understandable alarm to the French ambassador, who rightly feared the replacement of a pro-French by a pro-Spanish party in the councils of the king.[19]

Wentworth's hispanophile inclinations were not new, and he was quicker than the majority of his compatriots to appreciate that the United Provinces now represented a greater threat than Spain to England's vital interests.[20] In late 1639 his feud with the Earl of Holland and other members of the Queen's party, notorious for their pro-French inclinations; his suspicions about covert French and Dutch assistance to the rebellious Scots; and his appreciation of the way in which Spain's defeat at the Downs might be turned to Charles I's advantage, all enhanced his predisposition to seek an understanding with the Spaniards. Above all, the king needed money, and he needed it quickly; and who but the king of Spain could provide it on the necessary scale? Charles wanted £300,000 for his war against the Scots, and the city of London was not be to be bullied into offering him a loan.[21]

It is not surprising, then, that the Lord Deputy, in his agonising search for funds before the meeting of parliament, should in due course have beaten a path to the residence of the Spanish envoy. A visit by Cárdenas to congratulate him on his elevation to the earldom of Strafford gave him the pretext for a return call with an interpreter on Sunday 2 February 1640. Through the interpreter he explained to Cárdenas that he was, and always had been, a Spaniard at heart, because he believed that it was in his master's interest to make common cause with Spain.[22] So began a dialogue that was to last into the summer.

Strafford's increasingly urgent interest in Spain was paralleled by that of Olivares in England. The king of England's decision to call parliament into session struck Olivares as extremely unwise; but Charles's very difficulties offered interesting new opportunities for the forging of an Anglo-Spanish alliance.[23] At such a critical moment, however, a mere resident agent hardly seemed a figure of sufficient stature to guide the necessary diplomatic negotiations to a successful conclusion. It was true that the Marquis of Velada was on his way to join Cárdenas in London, but Velada, coming from Brussels, was not fully alive to the latest thinking in Madrid. A personal emissary from the Duchess of Chevreuse made the same point. With her customary brisk-

[18] AGS, Est., leg.2520, Wentworth to Juan de Necolalde, 5 October 1635.
[19] C. V. Wedgwood, *Thomas Wentworth, First Earl of Strafford* (London 1961), 235 and 267.
[20] I am grateful to Professor Nicholas Canny for advice on this point, and for valuable help in elucidating Strafford's motivation in 1639-40.
[21] Robert Ashton, *The Crown and the Money Market, 1603-1640* (Oxford 1960), 176-7, and Valerie Pearl, *London and the Outbreak of the Puritan Revolution* (Oxford 1961), 96-9.
[22] AGR, SEG, R.371, Cárdenas to Miguel de Salamanca, 17 February 1640.
[23] AGS, Est., leg.2521, *consulta* of Council of State, 17 February 1640.

ness, the Duchess had told Charles that it was incumbent upon him to revenge himself on the Dutch for the humiliation he had received at the Battle of the Downs, but he had so far shown a strange disinclination to take her advice. She urged Olivares to appoint a proper ambassador and to arm him with proposals that would strengthen the union of the Spanish and English crowns, like the offer of a marriage between Prince Baltasar Carlos and the Princess Mary. On the other major topic of concern in London – the conspiracy being organised by herself and La Valette – she was equally forthright. Cárdenas had been managing well, but slips had occurred, and it was time for the Count-Duke to send a trusted agent to complete the deal.[24]

Olivares agreed: the Duchess was right. But who could be sent to London? The great generation of Spanish diplomats – men of the stamp of Zúñiga and Gondomar – had passed away, and Olivares found himself as short of ambassadors as he was of generals. Yet he was persuaded that, if only the right man could be found, 'we could expect on this occasion to negotiate a breach between England and Holland, totally restore our fortunes in relation to France, and simultaneously restore the king of England's fortunes in Scotland, without his having to call parliament or break with the French'.[25]

The Count-Duke was never at a loss for long. His thoughts turned to the Marquis Virgilio Malvezzi, whose services in the Council of War had qualified him for more exalted duties.[26] It was, to say the least, a curious selection. Malvezzi was known, and despised, in Madrid, as the house historian of the Olivares regime – an occupation which, in the Count-Duke's opinion, had prepared him admirably for the London embassy, since he possessed 'particular knowledge of the matters to be discussed with that king, as he has been through all the papers for the purpose of writing the history on which he is currently engaged'. This, at least, was all too true. Malvezzi's passage through the archives has left a trail of missing papers which powerfully attests to the diligence of his historical research.[27]

By the late 1630s Malvezzi's credentials as a scholar and historian were somewhat tarnished by the closeness of his relationship to Olivares; but his *Romulus*, published in his native Bologna in 1629, had won him an international reputation. His fame had been enhanced by his *Discourses* on Tacitus, published in 1632, of which Milton was to remark unkindly that Malvezzi 'can cut Tacitus into slivers and steaks'.[28] His unswerving devotion to the cause of Spain had naturally attracted the attention of Olivares, who was the subject of Malvezzi's highly flattering *Portrait of the Politic Christian Favourite*. In 1636, the year after its publication, he received his reward and was

[24] AGS, Est.K, leg.1420, f.19, Duchess of Chevreuse's report.
[25] AGS, Est., leg.2521, *voto* of Olivares in *consulta* of Council of State, 6 March 1640.
[26] AGS, Est., leg.2521, Council of State, 17 February 1640.
[27] AGS, Est., leg.2054, royal order to Andrés de Rojas, 5 June 1639. One of a number of orders for the transfer of recent state papers to Malvezzi to assist him with his history.
[28] *The Works of John Milton*, III (New York 1931), 39.

summoned to Madrid to record the triumphs of the regime. This he did in works of exquisitely convoluted prose which reveal him as a master of verbal prestidigitation. Even the Battle of the Downs was transformed from defeat into victory, thanks to a little skilful although not entirely unjustified play with the fact that the majority of the soldiers on board the Spanish ships did eventually make the crossing from England into Flanders. The Spanish fleet, we are told, 'fighting with such disadvantage, wonne more than it lost. Victories being not measured by the losses in a mighty Monarch who wants no money; But onely by the glory, which consists in obtaining his end, and the meanes of obtaining it.'[29]

Such sleight of hand would certainly stand him in good stead if and when he reached London – for Olivares had some doubts whether it was right to send the marquis on so exacting a mission. 'His weakness is so great, his parsimony in eating so extreme, his tendency to sea-sickness so acute, that it would not seem reasonable to expose him to the risk of losing a life so utterly dedicated to Your Majesty's service.' The marquis, it was true, was a lean and hungry man, whose poignant account of his exiguous diet indicates that he took his meat, like his Tacitus, in slivers.[30] But he unhesitatingly offered to die, as he had lived, in the service of Spain and its king.

Some time in March Malvezzi received his instructions.[31] He was to slip out of Spain unobtrusively and, once in England, was to lodge with his fellow ambassador extraordinary, the Marquis of Velada. His first duty was to assist the Duchess of Chevreuse; his second to negotiate with the French conspirators, for the most effective means of restraining the ambitions of the king of France was to foment civil war in his realms – something which the Duke of La Valette's plans for the seizure of La Rochelle promised to achieve, although regrettably only with the aid of the Huguenots. The Duke of Soubise was a Huguenot, and Philip IV had no intention of abandoning his pledge never to give help to heretics. But Malvezzi was authorised to reach an agreement with La Valette (happily a Catholic), offering him 60,000 ducats a month over four months to put 10,000 infantry and 2,000 cavalry into the field. His employment of Huguenots in his army, although to be deplored, would serve the higher end of saving a Catholic cause imperilled by the union of Catholic France with the heretics.

Malvezzi's final piece of business was with the king of England. Charles must be persuaded that his one hope of salvation lay in alliance with Spain and war with the Dutch. The articles of an alliance had already been negotiated in the secret treaty between Olivares and Cottington of January 1631, and Charles could be assured of territorial satisfaction, either in the Palatinate or

---

[29] The Chiefe Events of the Monarchie of Spaine, in the yeare 1639, trans. Robert Gentilis (London 1647), 130. For Malvezzi's work and career see Rodolfo Brändli, Virgilio Malvezzi, Politico e Moralista (Basle 1964) and D. L. Shaw's excellent introduction to Malvezzi's Historia de los Primeros Años del Reinado de Felipe IV (London 1968).

[30] Biblioteca Apostolica Vaticana, Chigi A.III.53, ff.476-7, Malvezzi to Fabio Chigi (1640?), where he describes his daily diet as limited to 'una minestre di ovo e pane, e 3 oncie o poco più di carne in piccatiglia'.

[31] AHN, Est. leg.3456, no.11, early draft of instructions for Malvezzi's mission to England, 7 March 1640.

in Zealand, subject, of course, to the little matter of its prior reconquest. Malvezzi was to propose that Spain should be allowed to raise 20,000 recruits in the British Isles for the army of Flanders, and in return Philip would lend 8,000 Spanish veterans to help defeat the Scots. Once Charles's authority was restored at home, and his fleet expanded with Spanish financial help, he would be in a position to embark on hostilities against the Dutch and the French. If an extra *douceur* were needed, Malvezzi could hint at the possibility of still closer ties, in the form of an Anglo-Spanish match.

'We are directing all the artillery of our negotiation against England,' the Count-Duke wrote to the Cardinal Infante.[32] But it looks as if Malvezzi, an untried gunner, was being sent into battle armed only with a pea-shooter. The secret Cottington treaty of 1631 was not taken seriously in London, and perhaps least of all by Cottington himself, who explained, a shade too disingenuously, that he had not liked to reject it on the spot when the Count-Duke thrust the draft into his hands.[33] This draft had proposed an Anglo-Spanish 'league of confederacy offensive and defensive' against the United Provinces, with the king of England to receive 100,000 crowns a month from Spain, and, in due course, the island of Zealand. In 1640, as indeed in 1631, the only obvious point of appeal to the English ministers was the offer of a subsidy.

While the draft of the secret treaty might have been used as an opening gambit in the negotiations, the tenor of Malvezzi's instructions suggests that this was not the intention, and that Olivares was hoping to get his treaty implemented. If so, he had not the faintest understanding of the gravity of Charles's situation, or indeed of the temper of British political life. Within his own terms of reference, his proposals made sense. Why should Spain devote its increasingly scarce resources of men and money to baling out the king of England, unless it could secure in return his participation in the war? Seen from Madrid, the logic behind his reasoning was impeccable. But this was not the first time – nor would it be the last – when the Count-Duke's fertility in devising grand designs was matched by no comparable gift for relating them to the local topography.

Olivares proceeded on the assumption that Charles now found himself in such desperate straits that his only salvation lay in alliance with Spain. Ironically this was exactly the conclusion now being reached by Charles's principal minister. The prospect that parliament would vote supplies looked increasingly slight, and the presence of no fewer than three Spanish envoys in London suggested that the king of Spain meant business. Strafford was therefore ready to take the initiative when all three came to see him on 29 April.[34] It is unfortunate that Malvezzi's correspondence with Olivares is not to be

---

[32] BS, Codex hisp.22, f.119v, 24 March 1640.
[33] *State Papers Collected by Edward, Earl of Clarendon*, II (Oxford 1773), appendix, pp.xxxiv-xxxv, Dorchester to Sir Robert Anstruther, 16 October 1631. I am indebted to Professor Albert J. Loomie for advice on Cottington's reaction and on other questions concerning Anglo-Spanish relations discussed in this essay.
[34] AGR, SEG, R.374, ff.172-6, Velada to Cardinal Infante, 11 May 1640.

found. How we should have enjoyed a pen-portrait of Cottington composed, in the Malvezzian manner, of carefully balanced antitheses, or a
glimpse of that skilful dissection of the Earl of Strafford which persuaded the
Count-Duke that he must be 'a man of parts'![35] Instead, we must content
ourselves with the more matter-of-fact reporting of the Marquis of Velada,
who seems to have been the dominant figure in this ill-assorted trio.
Strafford, in Velada's opinion, was a great man, 'who likes to give the
impression that he is in charge. He has a peculiar way of coming right out
with his proposals when you are not expecting them, and gives you no time
to prepare your reply.' It was not a form of negotiation to which Spanish
ambassadors were accustomed. Bluntly, Strafford asked them how much the
king of Spain was prepared to offer, and what instructions they carried about
a royal marriage.

The startled ambassadors were compelled to equivocate, while implying
that everything was negotiable. The discussion then turned to the names of
possible British members of the negotiating party, with Strafford proposing
Cottington, Hamilton and Windebank. Cárdenas objected to Hamilton as a
notorious francophile, and although Strafford came to Hamilton's defence,
the ambassadors were later gratified to learn that his place had been taken by
Northumberland. On 2 May the English commissioners, with the exception
of Windebank, met the ambassadors at Strafford's house. Here the Spaniards
produced the text of the old Cottington treaty, which the commissioners
pondered in an inner room, returning to say that they could proceed no
further without consulting the king. Another meeting took place on 8 May,
this time at Northumberland's house. Although the invitation came too late
for him to attend this meeting, the Spanish ambassadors had dropped their
objection to the inclusion among the commissioners of the Marquis of
Hamilton, at the special request of Strafford, who described him as being his
man, body and soul.[36]

Three days before the meeting of 8 May, the Short Parliament was dissolved. Even before the dissolution, Velada had noted a correspondence
between the fate of parliament and the fate of the Spanish proposals.[37] For the
ambassadors, the dissolution of parliament was Spain's opportunity: now,
more than ever, Charles would need Spanish help. Public opinion in London
also took for granted a reciprocal relationship, although of a very different
kind. It was widely believed that parliament had been dissolved because the
Spanish ambassadors had offered the king large sums of money as the prelude
to an Anglo-Spanish union and the restoration of popery.[38] There is no
evidence that the possibility of Spanish subsidies played any part in the
decision to dissolve, although it is hard to believe that the prospect, however
faint, of an alternative option was not in the minds of some of those who sat at
the Council table that day.

[35] AGS, Est., leg.2521, *voto* of Olivares, 16 June 1640.
[36] AGR, SEG, R.374, ff.201-2v, Velada to Cardinal Infante, 12 May 1640, and ff.210-12v, the
same, 18 May 1640.
[37] Velada's letter of 11 May.
[38] AGR, SEG, R.374, ff.227-9, Velada to Cardinal Infante, 19 May 1640.

If the dissolution of parliament made an understanding with Spain all the more desirable to Strafford and his friends, it also had the effect of reducing the value of such an understanding to Spain. How far would Charles ever be able to deliver his side of the bargain? In particular, what chance was there now of inducing him to make war on the Dutch? At the meeting on 8 May Cottington observed that circumstances had changed since 1631, and drew the ambassadors' attention to the articles which had been discussed with the Spanish resident, Juan de Necolalde, in 1634 – articles for an Anglo-Spanish naval agreement which stopped short of an English commitment to war against the United Provinces. The ambassadors, who were perfectly well aware of the Necolalde proposals, offered to look among their papers to see if they could find any such document.

Velada came away from the meeting convinced that there was no possibility of inducing Charles to declare war on the Dutch, but that there was some hope of obtaining the offer of a fleet to protect the maritime route to Flanders. Cárdenas had already reached the same opinion, but was optimistic about the general course of the negotiations. He was equally optimistic about the other great business, the conspiracy of the Dukes of La Valette and Soubise, and was able to send to Madrid on 8 May the draft of a set of articles agreed by the conspirators.[39] He had glimpsed the glittering possibility of a double *coup* engineered in London: an English alliance and a French revolt. It would certainly earn him his promotion from resident agent to ambassador.

Parliament had been dissolved, but Strafford persuaded his colleagues that the war with the Scots must go on. The city of London, however, was not prepared to offer the £200,000 loan requested by the king. On 10 May the Council committed the recalcitrant aldermen to prison; and on the morning of the 11th Strafford came round, unaccompanied, to Velada's house.[40] As usual, he came immediately to the point. If Spain would lend his master 1,200,000 ducats (£300,000) on the security of English ships and merchandise in Spanish ports, he would enter into commitments which in due course would lead infallibly to war against the Dutch. He was not willing, however, to ratify the secret Cottington Agreement, which stipulated an immediate break with the United Provinces; and the Spanish ambassadors were not empowered to accept anything less. Velada's assessment of this meeting was that the king's need of money was now so acute that he would be prepared to offer Spain better terms than he had ever offered before. While these would fall short of immediate hostilities with the Dutch, they would certainly extend to a squadron of thirty ships for convoy duty and for the defence of Dunkirk in the event of a siege. But he had to admit that the English were asking for a great deal of money, and he begged Madrid for what it was least likely to give him – quick decisions, ready cash, and clear instructions covering all contingencies.

On 13 May Strafford, weakened by dysentery, called the ambassadors to his house, and this time promised that the king would break with the Dutch

[39] AGS, Est., leg.2521, Cárdenas to Olivares, 17 May 1640 and to King, 18 May.
[40] AGS, Est., leg.2521, Velada to King, 21 May 1640; Gardiner, *History*, IX, 131-2.

as soon as Scotland was reduced. In return, he asked for half the £300,000 loan to be paid within a month, and the other half in October. The ambassadors, for their part, requested Irish troops.[41] Two days later they were back again. Strafford, who was confined to bed, swore himself to secrecy on a Bible, and told them that his master had resolved to enter into an offensive and defensive alliance with Spain against the Dutch as soon as the Scots were reduced, an outcome expected by the end of the year. He was also prepared to give immediate orders for the raising of 3,000 men for the Spanish army, in spite of his own need for an army of 10,000 Irish for the war against the Scots. But speed was vital: the king's necessities were so great that any delay in providing the loan would be tantamount to its rejection.[42]

The despatches of the ambassadors reporting these various meetings took nineteen days to reach Madrid by way of Brussels. During the course of those nineteen days the fortunes of the Spanish crown took a dramatic turn for the worse. The tide of insurrection which had been flowing that spring through the countryside of Catalonia swept into the city of Barcelona on Corpus Christi Day, and claimed its most eminent victim in the person of the Viceroy. Philip IV, it appeared, now had a revolt of Scottish proportions on his hands.

The Count-Duke, deeply shaken by the news from Barcelona, saw all his carefully contrived schemes on the verge of collapse. Where now could he find the money, or the troops, to reverse the drift of the war with the Dutch and the French? While the rebellion in Catalonia added to the importance of the negotiations in London, it simultaneously reduced the chances that Madrid could capitalise on any successes the envoys might achieve. In spite of his domestic preoccupations, however, the ambassadors' despatches received Olivares's prompt attention. He was encouraged by their reports on the French Malcontents, and much gratified by the receipt of the draft treaty with La Valette. But he had to admit that he could see no prospect of action before the spring of 1641 – with its present difficulties Spain could not possibly find the troops, and it would be necessary to recruit large numbers in Ireland.[43] Philip IV added his own helpful marginal comment: the recruits could just as well be Scottish or English. The more subtle aspects of British affairs clearly continued to elude Madrid.

The Count-Duke wanted the Council of State to look at once at the ambassadors' reports of their negotiations with Strafford, although it seemed to him that Charles's promise to commit himself to eventual war with the Dutch was quite without substance. He praised the ambassadors for their discretion in handling the question of a possible Anglo-Spanish marriage – the prince was such an 'inestimable jewel' that his future was not to be casually risked. He was persuaded by Malvezzi and Velada that the English had no interest in seeing the war between Spain and the United Provinces brought to an end. But they also persuaded him of something else, which was

---

[41] AGR, SEG, R.374, fs.264-6, Velada to King, 23 May 1640.
[42] AGR, SEG, R.374, fs.252-6, Velada to King, 25 May 1640; Joseph Cuvelier et Joseph Lefèvre, *Correspondance de la Cour d'Espagne sur les Affairs des Pays-Bas*, VI (Brussels 1937), doc.1177.
[43] AGS, Est., leg.2521, undated paper of Olivares on *capitulación asentada con el duque de la Valeta*.

bound to introduce a new element into his calculations – that Charles I might lose his throne. The consequences for Spain of the transformation of England into a republic could prove disastrous. An alliance of Britain and the United Provinces as twin republics would inevitably lead to the loss of the Spanish Netherlands, and would give such strength to heresy as to threaten Europe with a total 'inundation'.[44]

Circumstances, then, had changed dramatically since Olivares had launched his London initiative three months before. Then, he was hoping to swing Charles I into the Habsburg camp. Now, it was a question of keeping Charles on his throne. 'I regard it as supremely important that the king of England should not be lost', even if it entailed 'some, and more than a little, cost' to Spain. But how much was 'more than a little'? Not, it seemed, as much as Strafford requested. Only an outright English declaration of war on the Dutch could justify the kind of sum Strafford had in mind. For a more modest agreement, consisting of a squadron of a dozen or so English ships and 6,000 Irish recruits a year, he felt that a loan for the remainder of the year of between 200,000 and 500,000 *escudos* (£50,000–£125,000), payable on a monthly basis, would be an appropriate sum. A few days later, the king wrote to Malvezzi to that effect,[45] and Olivares himself, after some hesitation about the courtesy titles to be employed, wrote a personal letter to Strafford, replete with high-sounding expressions of regard.[46]

By June of 1640, then, Olivares was prepared to contemplate a more limited agreement of the kind that he was not prepared to envisage when Malvezzi's instructions were drafted in March. It is natural to wonder whether the course of events might have taken a different turn if the ambassadors had been authorised to negotiate from the moment of their arrival an agreement along the lines discussed with Necolalde in 1634, by which Charles would not have been obliged to declare war on the Dutch. Under those conditions a settlement might have been reached. But would it have been worth the paper on which it was written? Could Charles have produced the ships for Spain? Could Spain have produced the money for Charles? By the spring of 1640 Spain's resources were stretched to the limit. With the crown's expenses running at over ten million ducats a year, regular payments of 100,000 ducats a month to Charles I would have imposed a severe additional strain; and if there is any single element of certainty amidst all the uncertainties of the Spanish crown finances, it is that 'regular' payments were never regular.

In any event, £25,000 a month would not have gone far to meet Strafford's needs. He wanted £150,000 to £200,000, cash down, to save the English crown from defeat in its war with the Scots. Olivares himself commented adversely not only on the size of the sum demanded, but also on the character and scale of the advances required. This was tantamount to an admission that

[44] AGS, Est., leg.2521, *voto* of Olivares, 16 June 1640.
[45] Pierpont Morgan Library (hereafter PML), New York, Rulers of Spain: Philip IV, Item 8, King to Malvezzi, 25 June 1640; Cuvelier, *Correspondance*, VI, doc.1182.
[46] AGS, Est., leg.2575, El Conde Duque al Virrey de Irlanda, 25 June 1640.

Strafford's request was beyond Spain's capabilities. If the Count-Duke's requirements of Charles I were hopelessly unrealistic, so also were Strafford's of Philip IV. But then he had never claimed to possess any extensive knowledge or understanding of the continental scene. He had clutched at the hope of salvation from Spain without any real appreciation of Spanish affairs – and also without any real appreciation of the implications of his action for the affairs of his master.

If Strafford had gravely misjudged the situation, and failed to grasp the probable domestic consequences of his attempt at *rapprochement* with Spain, this was partly the result of his remoteness from the English political scene since 1633. He underestimated the strength of feeling against Charles's government, just as he overestimated, on the basis of his Irish experience, his own ability to manipulate men and control the course of events. Again on the basis of his Irish experience he had come to see Catholics as a lesser threat to the established church than the extreme Protestants, and therefore did not share, or fully appreciate, the obsession of his compatriots with the dangers of Spanish power and the restoration of popery.

The results of this miscalculation were disastrous for both himself and his royal master. Considering the temper of the country in the spring of 1640, nothing was better calculated to deepen the prevailing distrust about the intentions of Charles and his principal adviser than the flirtation with Philip IV. And all for what? For the promise of Spanish silver that anyone who knew Spain and its ways of conducting business could confidently have predicted would never be paid. Not for the first time, the king of Spain's reputed treasures were the cause of wildly exaggerated hopes.

They were also the cause of no less exaggerated fears. Strafford's negotiations with the Spanish ambassadors made him dangerously vulnerable to the attacks of his enemies, who played with success on the popular obsession with Spain and popery. While he lay on his sick bed, the Dutch and French envoys too were busily at work disparaging the Spanish connection.[47] The results of their activities were reflected at the various meetings held in June between the three ambassadors and the English commissioners. To the ambassadors' surprise, Cottington and Windebank returned with stiffer terms, and Strafford told them that an Anglo-Spanish alliance would take time to arrange, whereas his master needed the money now. On 16 June, at a session attended by Cottington and Windebank in Strafford's house, Strafford, still sickly and very weak, warned them that, if the king's request went unanswered by Spain, he would have no alternative but to turn to the Dutch.[48]

Although the talks continued, there now seems to have been no conviction on either side that they could succeed. When Cárdenas was at last raised by Madrid to ambassadorial rank in July in recognition of his labours, Windebank commented to Viscount Conway: ' . . . so we shall have three ambassadors from that King, and a huge pair of spectacles, and yet we cannot see business enough for one.'[49] Cottington and Windebank knew that the game was up;

[47] Wedgwood, *Strafford*, 289.
[48] AGR, SEG, R.377, ff.59-65v, Ambassadors to King, 9 July 1640.
[49] *C.S.P.D.* 1640, 496, 21 July 1640.

but Strafford had nowhere else to turn. Hoping against hope he drafted on 18 July a reply to the personal letter he had received from Olivares. In this draft, translated into careful Spanish, he applauded the Count-Duke's celebrated wisdom, and assured him that his letter would take its place among the treasures that he bequeathed to his descendants. He had been working, he wrote, for a lasting alliance of the crowns of England and Spain. Once this alliance was achieved, nothing could prevent their two kings from dividing the world between them. 'Let us set ourselves then, to do this great work . . . and let us not miss this great opportunity . . . We for our part will press ahead with the Irish levies requested by the Catholic King, while Your Excellency (assuming that the money cannot be sent from Flanders as we should prefer) sends from Spain a loan of 400,000 *escudos* [£100,000], in conformity with my proposals to His Catholic Majesty's ambassadors to this court. And let the loan be sent with all speed, or else the season will be gone . . .'[50] The letter was duly received by Olivares, but the draft translation fell into the hands of Pym and his friends,[51] who can only have seen it as further proof that the Earl of Strafford was far too dangerous to be allowed to live.

Characteristically, when Madrid at last decided to act, it was much too late. Towards the end of July the ambassadors decided that Charles's position could not be worse, and that it would pay Spain in the long run to accede to Strafford's request, even if in the short run it brought little in the way of tangible benefits.[52] The Count-Duke – his prospects almost as dark as those of Strafford, since the outbreak of the Catalan revolt – was inclined to agree, and orders were sent to Italy to release money for use in Flanders and England. 'So as not to fall into despair,' wrote Olivares to the governor of Milan, 'we are playing all the cards we can.'[53] These cards consisted of four alternative versions of a letter to be forwarded from Brussels to the ambassadors in London explaining that, in the present state of the crown's finances, it was possible to provide them with a maximum of one (two, three or four) hundred thousand ducats (£25,000 to £100,000).[54] But even this last gamble was frustrated. The money was never sent on from Flanders, where the Cardinal Infante was acutely short of funds; and early in 1641 Velada wrote that 'the state of the kingdom is not such as to make us think that it would be advisable to lend the sum of money authorised by His Majesty; and we would not have given it, even if it had been to hand'.[55]

He was, of course, right. In November, Strafford had been arrested; in

[50] House of Lords Record Office, Nalson XII, ff.1-7. I am extremely grateful to Professor Conrad Russell for informing me about this letter, and making available a transcript. I am also much indebted to him for frequent discussions over a number of years about the relationship of British and continental politics in the years before the Civil War.
[51] A note from Olivares to his secretary Carnero, dated 17 September 1640 (AGS, Est., leg.2575), refers to 'this letter from the viceroy of Ireland', but there is no sign of the letter itself. For Pym's possession of a draft of the letter, see Conrad Russell, *The Crisis of Parliaments* (Oxford 1971), 327-8.
[52] AGR, SEG, R.377, ff.38-45v, Ambassadors to King, 2 August 1640.
[53] AGS, Est., leg.2521, Olivares to Francisco de Melo, 9 September 1640.
[54] AGS, Est., leg.2575, draft letters (four different formats), 11 September 1640, with accompanying secretarial note that 'these are the cards to which the Count refers'.
[55] AGR, SEG, R.378, ff.256-7, Velada to Miguel de Salamanca, 1 February 1641.

December, Charles announced his intention of marrying his daughter to prince William of Orange. The Spanish negotiations were not only dead but buried. Instructions were now on their way from Madrid ordering Velada and Malvezzi to proceed to Flanders, where Malvezzi was to continue his negotiations with the French Malcontents. Cárdenas, who seemed set to become a permanent fixture on the London scene, was to remain behind in charge of embassy business.[56] In February 1641, Velada, who was as dilatory in leaving as he had been in coming, received a final letter from Philip IV. There was, the king wrote, nothing more to be said for the time being about Charles's request for money, nor about Strafford's offer to fit out a squadron of twenty ships, 'because, with his imprisonment, the question has assumed a different complexion'.[57]

A futile end to a futile affair . . . But the study of the past is, or should be, something more than the study of successful men and successful designs. Failures have their histories, no less than successes, and they can tell us at least as much, and sometimes more, about that strange blend of circumstance, intention and personality of which the course of events is fashioned.

When considered in the harsh light of the political and financial realities of the 1630s, the efforts of both Olivares and Strafford seem to have stood not the remotest chance of success. The benevolent neutrality of the England of Charles I in the European conflict was one thing; its active participation on the side of Spain was another, and a very different one. The only effective contribution from the British Isles that Madrid could reasonably expect consisted of Irish recruits for the army; and the quest for Irish levies was indeed a continuing and major element in its dealings with Charles I. But Olivares was aiming at much more than this, although nothing in the reports of Spain's envoys in London suggested that he had any serious chance of achieving his ambition.

Strafford, for his part, was harbouring expectations of Spain which Sir Arthur Hopton, the English ambassador in Madrid, knew to be totally unrealistic. 'As for these here,' he wrote to Windebank in June 1640, 'it is very little, or nothing, they can avail us: For ships they have few, mariners fewer, landsmen not so many as they need, and, by all signs, money none at all that can be spared. So as, if we should be brought into a war, the whole weight therefore must light upon us . . . I will not deny but that, for the balance of Christendom, some league with Spain were not unfit; but it is more certain that reason of state begins at home.'[58]

Since the men on the spot offered no serious encouragement to either Olivares or Strafford, the two ministers must be regarded as the true authors of their own designs. How, then, are we to explain such a remoteness from reality? Strafford in Ireland had shown a unique determination to disregard all the rules, and his very successes during his period of Irish government can

[56] PML, Philip IV, King to Velada, 17 December 1640.
[57] PML, Philip IV, King to Velada, 10 February 1641.
[58] *State Papers . . . Clarendon*, II, 86, Hopton to Windebank, 15/25 June 1640.

only have encouraged him to think that he could do the same in England. Like Strafford, Olivares was a lone player, and one who played for high stakes. Endlessly resourceful in constructing grand designs, he could pride himself on achieving the near-miraculous feat, year after year, of saving Spain from collapse. Each year the task grew harder, and the ingenious political projections more dependent on a conjunction of improbable events. As with Strafford, there was now a measure of desperation in the Count-Duke's grand designs; but also, as with Strafford, there remained a lingering conviction that somehow the world might yet be conformed to the dictates of an over-mastering will.

The capacity for self-delusion, which had been nurtured by long years of a political isolation all the more dangerous for being voluntarily imposed, was finally to prove the undoing of them both. In seventeenth-century conditions the ruthless determination of an energetic first minister could at times move mountains. But men were a different matter, and it was always dangerous to ignore the resulting hatred and mistrust. So it was with Strafford and Olivares. Unwilling or unable to heed the warning signals, both of them had become incapable of moving outside the bounds of the world which over many years and with much ingenuity they had fashioned for themselves.

It was a world in which success or failure would alike be written large. In 1625 Olivares had told the Count of Gondomar: 'As the minister with paramount obligations, it is for me to die unprotesting, chained to my oar, until not a fragment is left in my hands.'[59] Seven years later, Wentworth wrote to Carlisle in a similar vein: 'Let the tempest be never so great, I will much rather put forth to sea, work forth the storm, or at least be found dead with the rudder in my hands.'[60] The two ministers had cast themselves in the same heroic mould, both anticipating in the event of failure a last dramatic gesture and a watery grave. Now, as the seas closed over them, they struggled vainly towards each other like drowning companions. But the waves were too high, the distance too great, and neither stood any real chance of reaching the shore.

---

[59] John H. Elliott and José F. De La Peña, *Memoriales y Cartas del Conde Duque de Olivares*, I Madrid 1978), doc.v, 112.
[60] Wedgwood, *Strafford*, 263.

14

Classical Republicanism and the Puritan Revolution

Blair Worden

The civilisation of seventeenth-century England rests, we may broadly say, on two intellectual pillars: the Bible, and the literature of classical antiquity. Historians of politics have given more attention to the former than to the latter. The relationship between puritan theology and puritan politics has been debated by many scholars. But who has investigated Thomas Hobbes's claim that the Civil War was largely caused by 'the reading of the books of policy and histories of the ancient Greeks and Romans'? Perhaps, it might be argued, Hobbes's statement does not deserve serious consideration. The constitutional claims of the Long Parliament reveal, after all, a conspicuous insularity and a conspicuous mistrust of abstract political theory. In any case, the Puritan Revolution does not at first sight appear the most promising territory in which to seek classical political influences. The celebration of reason and human dignity in classical literature seems hard to reconcile with the puritan emphasis on man's helplessness and depravity. Half a century earlier, Protestant and classical ideals had coexisted with little difficulty. That had been an intellectually more open period, when Tacitus had been the hero of the *avant-garde*, when Shakespeare and Ben Jonson had explored universal problems of political behaviour in the setting of ancient Rome, and when, in country houses, Plutarch had lain beside the Bible as a source of moral instruction. But what room was left for pagan thought by the uncompromising demands which the apocalyptic puritan eschatology of the Civil War made on the loyalties and enthusiasms of its adherents?

If paganism was challenged in mid-seventeenth-century England, however, no reader of Milton or Marvell could suppose that it was suppressed. We shall find that the classical legacy endured in politics as in literature. Excellent books by Zera Fink, Caroline Robbins, Felix Raab and John Pocock have familiarised us with a tradition of seventeenth-century classical republicanism which, guided by the writings of Machiavelli, sought to revive the virtues, and to learn from the achievements and the mistakes, of ancient Rome.[1] The Machiavellian tradition, in England as elsewhere, merged

[1] Z. S. Fink, *The Classical Republicans* (1945); C. Robbins, *The Eighteenth-Century Commonwealthsman* (1959); F. Raab, *The English Face of Machiavelli* (1964); J. G. A. Pocock, *The Machiavellian Moment* (1975).

with ideas of native and medieval origin; but it owed most to classical historians and their Renaissance interpreters. Pointing back to Livy, Machiavellianism celebrated the glories of the early Roman republic and lamented the erosion of the civic virtue and the manly independence which were held to have flourished in the classical and late medieval city-states. Pointing back to Polybius, Machiavellianism propounded the cyclical view of history and examined the problem of the balanced constitution. Pointing back to Tacitus, it explored the techniques, and revelled in the fascination, of power. Seventeenth-century Machiavellianism was not, as some writing on the subject might lead us to suspect, a mere intellectual parlour-game. I have suggested elsewhere that it found practical application in the politics of William III's reign.[2] Here I shall argue that it affected political developments of the Puritan Revolution.

The term 'Machiavellian', admittedly, needs to be used with caution. Many-faceted as the Machiavellian tradition is, it does not contain all the ingredients of classical republicanism. 'Machiavellian' is clearly too narrow an adjective to convey the influence of the two authors on whose works Hobbes especially blamed the collapse of the early Stuart monarchy, Aristotle and Cicero. It cannot altogether accommodate the influence of Seneca, whose writings did so much to inspire the 'neo-stoicism' of the 'Silver Age of the European Renaissance'.[3] In much seventeenth-century classical republican writing, indeed, a Machiavellian enthusiasm for *virtù* and civic action is tempered by a melancholy stoic detachment. Classical literature, like the Bible, offered a variety of inspirations. It also offered a variety of political lessons. To suggest that republicanism was the only conclusion which could be reached by a study of classical political literature would be as misleading as to argue that a study of classical political literature was the only route by which men could become republicans. There were royalists who derived instruction and comfort from Tacitus and Machiavelli.[4] There were parliamentary soldiers and saints unacquainted with the classics who called for the abolition of monarchy.

There were also, however, republican politicians of the Interregnum whose beliefs were steeped in classical and Machiavellian literature. If we look in particular at the four years between the execution of Charles I in January 1649 and the dissolution of the Long Parliament in April 1653, we discover that those men cooperated remarkably closely and to remarkable effect. Of course, the influence of political philosophies on the actions of hard-pressed politicians is never easy to trace exactly. The relationship between ideas and events is likely to prove as vexing a problem to the student of seventeenth-century classical politics as it has been to historians of puritan politics. We must be careful not to claim too much. But it would be a pity to claim too little.

[2] In an edition of part 5 of Edmund Ludlow's *A Voice from the Watch Tower* (Camden Society 1978).
[3] H. R. Trevor-Roper, *Princes and Artists* (1976), ch.4. Hobbes's suggestions are in *Leviathan*, chs 21, 29.
[4] For Tacitus, see e.g. the English publications of the works of Virgilio Malvezzi in the 1640s; for Machiavelli, see e.g. Raab, *English Face of Machiavelli*, 146-54 (on Clarendon).

Who were the classical republicans (as we shall call them) who achieved most influence in the later stages of the Long Parliament? Perhaps the most prominent of all were those named by the correspondent of Oliver Cromwell in 1650 who referred disapprovingly to 'Tom Chaloner, Harry Nevile and those wits'. Thomas Chaloner was a Yorkshireman. In his youth he had visited Florence, the shrine of Machiavellianism, and had reputedly imbibed his republican principles there. Henry Nevile of Berkshire was in Florence in 1643–4 and again in the 1660s. He had lifelong contacts and friendships at the Tuscan court. He was a lifelong friend too of James Harrington, the most distinguished thinker of English Machiavellianism. Nevile and Harrington may well have been in Italy together in 1636.[5] Later they became close literary partners. A useful ally of Nevile and Chaloner in Parliament was James Harrington's cousin Sir James Harrington, who seems likely to have secured James's appointment as one of Charles I's attendants in 1647:[6] it would be interesting to know what political company James Harrington kept in the years after the King's execution, when his great work *Oceana* was forming in his mind. Nevile's and Chaloner's closest and most valuable parliamentary associate, however, was Nevile's Berkshire neighbour Henry Marten. Although Marten knew his Machiavelli, his debt to Machiavellianism may have been smaller than that of Nevile and Chaloner; but the difference, if there was one, was scarcely visible to M.P.s who opposed the policies which Nevile, Chaloner and Marten advanced.

After the Restoration Henry Nevile produced a major new translation of Machiavelli's *Works*, and wrote that classic of Machiavellian literature, *Plato Redivivus*.[7] Nevile's career and thought have many parallels with those of another prominent classical republican of the Long Parliament, Algernon Sidney. Like Nevile, Sidney was in Italy in the early 1640s and again in the 1660s.[8] Like Nevile, too, he wrote prolifically after the Restoration on politics and literature, most notably in his *Discourses concerning Government*, a work deeply influenced by Machiavelli. It is in October 1649, when Sidney helped Henry Marten to secure Nevile's election to Parliament, that the classical republican group may be said to have taken shape. In Parliament, on the Council of State, and on council and parliamentary committees it became one of the most tightly knit parties among the rulers of the new republic. We

---

[5] 'The Pilgrim Book of the English College', in H. Foley (ed.), *Records of the English Province of the Society of Jesus* (7 vols, 1877–83), VI, 613. I am indebted to Mr Edward Cheney for this reference. For the survival of Machiavellianism under the Medici, albeit in an emasculated form, see Eric Cochrane, *Florence in the Forgotten Centuries* (1973), 118ff. The most valuable discussions of seventeenth-century Anglo-Tuscan intellectual relations – a subject which might repay fuller investigation – are to be found in the discrete writings of A. M. Crino, especially in her *Fatti e Figure del Seicento Anglo-Toscano* (Florence 1957). Nevile's friendship with Harrington is movingly described by Aubrey.

[6] *Commons Journal* (hereafter *C.J.*), 12 Jan. 1647, 27 Apr. 1649. Sir James and Chaloner provided the Commonwealth's expertise on the Mint.

[7] For Nevile's authorship of the translation see Raab, *English Face of Machiavelli*, appendix B *Plato Redivivus* is reprinted and edited by Caroline Robbins in *Two English Republican Tracts* (1969).

[8] For the earlier visit see Foley, 'Pilgrim Book', 623; A. Collins, *Sidney Papers* (2 vols, 1746) II, 705.

shall see something later of the aims of the classical republicans and of the success with which they pursued them.[9] For the moment it is enough to notice that their policies involved a repudiation of the traditional goals of political puritanism at home and abroad. In domestic affairs, the classical republicans confronted puritan theology and puritan clericalism. In foreign affairs, they reversed the puritan policy of an international Protestant alliance and helped to guide England into war against the Protestant Dutch.

How did the classical republicans acquire the confidence to challenge the orthodoxies of the Puritan Revolution? In this essay we shall propose some lines of enquiry which might repay fuller exploration. Initially we shall try to learn something of the formation of the classical republicans' ideas. We shall then suggest that those ideas, however alien to puritanism they might appear, were reflected in and fortified by the literature which the period of puritan supremacy produced. We shall seek to identify the guiding philosophical principle which animated the opposition of the classical republicans to puritan philosophy. And we shall look at those circumstances of the early 1650s which enabled classical republican ideas to make their political impact.

First, we need to move backward in time from the mid-seventeenth century. As we do so, we begin to notice some family footprints. The transmission of ideas from one generation to the next within noble and gentry households is a subject which deserves more attention than it has received. For the family of one of our classical republicans, Algernon Sidney, there are papers which enable us to follow that transmission surprisingly closely.[10] We shall find cause to suspect that a similar transmission occurred within other families represented among the classical republicans of the Interregnum.

Algernon Sidney, a writer in politics, reminds us so often of an earlier writer in politics, his great-uncle Sir Philip Sidney. Both men have the haughty and inflammable temper of the Sidney family. Both became legends more through their deaths than through their lives: Philip died a martyr to international Protestantism on the field of Zutphen in 1586, Algernon a martyr to the Whig cause on the scaffold in 1683. When Algernon, during his voluntary exile at Rome in 1661, had a portrait of Philip sent to him from Frankfurt,[11] he may have been giving expression to something more profound than mere family piety.

Algernon's paternal grandfather and Philip's younger brother was Robert Sidney, who under James I became first Earl of Leicester of the Sidney descent. From childhood Robert was carefully moulded in his brother's image. After Philip's death Robert took over many of Philip's political and intellectual contacts at home and abroad. The attempt to sustain the influence of the Sidney circle through Robert was not wholly successful, but it left a lasting impression on him. Philip, who cared deeply for his brother's education,

[9] Their cooperation, their allies, their policies, and the evidence from which their activities can be deduced, are discussed in my *The Rump Parliament* (1974).
[10] Those papers are among the De L'Isle MSS. in the Kent County Record Office at Maidstone. I have used them by kind permission of Viscount De L'Isle, V.C., K.G.
[11] Collins, *Sidney Papers*, II, 709.

had urged him to draw up tables in which to record his deductions from his classical and historical reading.[12] The first Earl's surviving commonplace books suggest the influence of that advice. Those commonplace books were inherited and faithfully continued by the second Earl, who succeeded the first Earl in 1626, and of whom Algernon was the second son. A man of prodigious learning, the second Earl was a devoted pupil of the freethinking mathematician Thomas Harriot and a friend of Hugo Grotius.[13] We are able to glimpse, amidst the feuds of a querulous household, the descent of interests and commitments from the first Earl to the second, and from the second Earl to Algernon.

The second Earl built up a notable collection of antique busts at Penshurst, the family seat. He also had a catalogue compiled of the family's marvellous library.[14] Among a remarkable range of interests, the catalogue and the commonplace books reveal a preoccupation with writers in the Machiavellian tradition: Polybius (whom the first Earl read in Latin and German), Livy (of whom the second Earl made a detailed study), Tacitus and Machiavelli himself. Tacitus occupied a special place in the family's interest. One of the first Earl's lifelong friends was the foremost Tacitean scholar in Europe, Justus Lipsius, whose edition of Tacitus' *Works* he heavily annotated, and whose own writings were generously represented in the Sidneys' library.[15] Another was the most influential translator of Tacitus in England, Sir Henry Savile.[16] The second Earl, another student of Tacitus, formed contacts with the family of the Duc de Rohan, who did so much to adapt Tacitean political thought to Protestant ends.[17]

The rage of Tacitism in the Europe of the later sixteenth and earlier seventeenth centuries is a large subject.[18] Any general explanation of it, we may suggest, must take account of the ambivalence towards courtly life, the tension between attraction and repulsion, which is one of the principal intellectual responses to the rise of the Renaissance and baroque monarchies, and which in England comes to characterise both politics and literature in the reign of James I.[19] The Sidneys felt that ambivalence and that tension. The first Earl, who desperately needed courtly employment to ward off chronic indebtedness, became Chamberlain to James's wife Anne of Denmark. With

[12] A. Feuillerat, *The Prose Works of Sir Philip Sidney* (4 vols, repr. 1968), III, 130-3.
[13] Kent County Record Office, De L'Isle MSS. [U1475] ZI/4, pp.477-8; ZI/9, pp.68, 154; Z47. The second Earl appointed Henry Hammond to the living of Penshurst.
[14] For the busts (long disappeared) see A. Michaelis, *Ancient Marbles in Great Britain* (1882), 20n. The library catalogue is De L'Isle MS. Z45/2.
[15] *Historical Manuscripts Commission Reports* (hereafter *H.M.C.R.*), De L'Isle and Dudley, II 562; British Library (hereafter B.L.), classmark C.142e.13. An influential translation of Tacitus *Agricola* was dedicated to the first Earl in 1585.
[16] Feuillerat, *Sidney*, III, 130-3; De Lisle MS. ZI/9, p.191; *Calendar of State Papers Domesti* (hereafter *C.S.P.D.*) 1611-18, p.175.
[17] De Lisle MS. Z9, p.12; Collins, *Sidney Papers*.
[18] For a good introduction to it see Peter Burke, 'Tacitism', in T. A. Dorey (ed.), *Tacitus* (1969)
[19] David Norbrook, 'Panegyric of the Monarch and its Social Contexts under Elizabeth I and James I' (Oxford Univ. D.Phil. thesis, 1978) illuminates this topic. I am grateful to M Norbrook for allowing me to cite his thesis. See too G. K. Hunter, 'A Roman thought Renaissance attitudes to history exemplified in Shakespeare and Ben Jonson', in B. S. Lee (ed.) *An English Miscellany* (1977).

one half of his mind, he loved to dress in 'the bravest cut and fashion', and thrilled to the merest hint of royal favour.[20] The other half prompted him to retreat whenever possible to the estate and the library of Penshurst. There, like a senator of the early Roman empire, he could enjoy the sensation and the forms of independence even as he lost the substance. 'Princes,' he remarked in his notes on Tacitus, 'may please the people with some shows of their ancient liberties.'[21] The tone of that observation, as of so many of the first Earl's comments on statecraft, is tantalisingly but revealingly equivocal. Something of the first Earl's ambivalence towards courtly life can be sensed too in that half Arcadian, half ironic poem with which Ben Jonson immortalised a visit to the Sidney seat: 'Thou art not, Penshurst, built to envious show.' A similar ambivalence is to be found in a play of Jonson in which the Sidneys took a special interest, the Roman drama *Sejanus*. By a skilful blend of material drawn from Tacitus, from Machiavelli and from Lipsius, Jonson engages his audience's sympathy for 'the old liberty' of republican Rome, while inviting us to envy the chilling statecraft which defeats it.[22]

By the time of Algernon Sidney's maturity, the great age of Tacitism is over. Tacitus continues to be closely studied, but responses to him display less excitement and less equivocation. No outward reservations qualified the contempt for 'the cruel and filthy Tiberius' which a reading of Tacitus produced in Algernon. But were there inward reservations? To read his manuscript treatise 'Court Maxims', a dialogue in which a courtier and a countryman debate the subtleties of Restoration political manoeuvre, is to sense a side to Algernon which relishes, even as he condemns, the statecraft of the Stuarts.[23] In other respects, too, similarities between Algernon's thought and that of his forebears may be as suggestive as the differences. Neither the first nor the second Earl was a republican. Both men, however, read Buchanan and concerned themselves with the problem of political resistance. Literary critics have detected the influence of Buchanan's radical ideas in Sir Philip Sidney's *Arcadia*:[24] they appear again in the writings of Algernon. The second Earl's remarks on the origins of government and on popular sovereignty might equally well have come from Algernon's pen. Many of the other preoccupations which run through the repetitive illustrations from classical and medieval history in Algernon's *Discourses* are also to be found in the massive historical notes which his grandfather, and still more in those which his father, had compiled: the perils of absolutism; the dominance of worthless favourites at court (favourites, the Earls omitted to add, who were consistently successful in checking the ambitions of the Sidneys); the historical role of the nobility.[25]

[20] *Nugae Antiquae* (1769), 120.
[21] B.L., C.142e.13, p.44.
[22] D. Boughner, *The Devil's Disciple. Ben Jonson's Debt to Machiavelli* (1966), ch.5, and the articles listed on p.242 of that work.
[23] The manuscript is now in the Warwickshire Record Office.
[24] For the bibliography see Roger Howell, *Sir Philip Sidney* (1968), 294. There is perhaps support for the view in references to *Arcadia* in De L'Isle MS.ZI/11.
[25] De Lisle MSS., ZI/1, pp.403, 629-30, 711-12; ZI/9, loose pages 1-4, and in the main volume p.212; Z9, p.251; Z47.

On that last subject, in particular, Algernon Sidney's sentiments betray his lineage. James Harrington clinically attributed the breakdown of the constitution in 1642 to the economic decline of the nobility in the previous century and a half. Algernon, writing under Charles II, injected passionate indignation into Harrington's diagnosis. A Sidney on his father's side, Algernon was a Percy on his mother's. He believed that the 'ancient powerful warlike nobility', who 'by birth and estate enjoyed greater advantages than kings could ever confer upon them for rewards of betraying their country', did 'ever preserve the people's liberties'. In the sixteenth and seventeenth centuries, he asserted, the nobility had been drawn into political and economic dependence on the crown, and had consequently been 'effeminated and corrupted'. The 'modern courtiers' of Restoration England 'by their names and titles oblige us to call to mind such things as are not to be mentioned without blushing. Whatever the ancient noblemen of England were, we may be sure they were not such as these.' To the degrading despotism which Algernon saw in Stuart rule, Tacitus again offered a classical parallel. 'Tacitus,' Algernon remarked, 'is plentiful in showing that the first work of the Roman tyrants was to destroy all virtue in the nobility and people.'[26]

The aristocratic bias of Algernon Sidney's *Discourses* is far removed from the social teaching of the *Discourses* of Machiavelli. Yet if, as Felix Raab implied, Algernon adapted Machiavelli to his own purposes, the influence of Machiavelli and of the classical thought which Machiavelli illuminated is as evident in Algernon's writings as in the compositions of his father and grandfather.[27] The family traditions which can be traced from Sir Philip Sidney to Algernon Sidney may have taken different forms in different generations; but the intellectual and imaginative inheritance which those traditions preserved among the Sidneys was unlikely to yield to the apocalyptic puritanism of the Civil War. We are often reminded of the 'puritanism of the household'. There was a classicism of the household too.

The descent of ideas within individual families is perhaps to be expected. Their descent within groups of families may be more surprising. When Algernon Sidney, Henry Nevile and Thomas Chaloner cooperated in the Long Parliament, they were making their own generation's contribution to a habit of collaboration which can be traced back to the mid-sixteenth century. The three families had risen through the patronage of Protector Somerset. (Is the adoption of the term 'Commonwealthsmen' by Civil War republicans a tribute to that distant genesis?) Subsequently the families had adhered to the factions which successively advocated a forward policy in Europe and the New World: the party of the Elizabethan Earl of Leicester; the party of Essex (with its self-consciously 'Tacitean' political values); the party of Prince Henry; and the party of the third Earl of Pembroke.[28] Relations between the

[26] 'Court Maxims', pp.71, 131–3.
[27] Cf. Fink, *The Classical Republicans*, 144–5.
[28] That lineage is traced by S. L. Adams, 'The Protestant Cause . . . 1585–1630' (Oxford Univ. D.Phil. thesis, 1972). I am grateful to Mr Adams for allowing me to cite his thesis. For the Tacitism of the Essex faction see G. Ungerer, *A Spaniard in Elizabethan England: The Correspondence of Antonio Pérez's Exile* (2 vols, 1974–6), I, 466n., II, 376.

Sidneys and the Neviles were especially close. William Sidney, Algernon's great-great-grandfather, who acquired Penshurst for the family, and Henry Nevile, our Henry's great-grandfather, were political partners who rose together in 1550. A generation later, in 1578, we find their heirs, who were intimate and lifelong friends, commending the youthful friendship which was emerging between their own heirs, the grandfathers of our Algernon Sidney and our Henry Nevile. That youthful friendship, which likewise persisted into maturity, had a Tacitean flavour: the two men travelled in Europe with Sir Henry Savile and became associates of a supreme exemplar of political Tacitism, Antonio Pérez.[29] By 1607 the Sidneys and the Neviles had established shared contacts in Tuscany.[30]

The Sidneys, the Neviles and the Chaloners were all learned families. Our Thomas Chaloner's grandfather, Sir Thomas Chaloner, ambassador to Spain under Elizabeth, translated Erasmus' *Praise of Folly*, wrote a verse work *De Republica Anglorum Instauranda*, and was posthumously praised in Ben Jonson's *Discoveries* as one of the Renaissance writers who 'began eloquence with us'. In the 1590s our Thomas Chaloner's father, also Sir Thomas, the naturalist and experimental philosopher who was befriended by Bacon, was an agent for the Earl of Essex in Florence. In 1612 our Thomas Chaloner, visiting Florence in adolescence, found himself feted there because the Tuscan court 'build upon his father for a chief foundation' of a proposed match between Prince Henry and the sister of the Duke of Tuscany.[31] Thomas's father was Governor of Prince Henry's household, where he tried to find a place for the eldest son of his friend Robert Sidney, Algernon's grandfather.[32] He allied too with our Henry Nevile's grandfather, who, distressed by the neglect of 'merit' at court, was one of James I's boldest critics.[33] His criticisms were to be proudly recalled in his grandson's *Plato Redivivus*.

The grandfather, who had been an ambassador to France in the 1590s, would in turn have doubtless been proud to learn than his grandson was invited (through Algernon Sidney's elder brother) to become the Commonwealth's ambassador to Spain in 1650,[34] just as our Thomas Chaloner's forebears would doubtless have warmed to Thomas's plea in 1648 for a return to the days of 'worthy Hawkins and the famous Drake'.[35] Algernon Sidney's father, an ambassador to Denmark in the 1630s, must have been pleased when Algernon was sent on an important embassy to Copenhagen in 1659. Henry Nevile's grandfather, who had been a rival of Sir Walter Ralegh, might have been less pleased to notice the close alliance which developed in the later

---

[29] Collins, *Sidney Papers*, I, 246-7, 271; Feuillerat, *Sidney*, III, 130-3; De L'Isle MS. ZI/10, p.513; T. Birch, *Memoirs of the Reign of Queen Elizabeth* (2 vols, 1754), I, 25-6; Public Record Office, classmarks P.R.O. 30/50/2, f.70; and 30/50/3, f.7; Ungerer, *Pérez*, II, 219-20, 338-40, 348-50, 371-4.

[30] *H.M.C.R.* De L'Isle and Dudley, III, 372.

[31] T. Birch, *The Life of Henry Prince of Wales* (1760), 322.

[32] Collins, *Sidney Papers*, II, 307-8.

[33] Adams, 'The Protestant Cause', 180-1; *Winwood's Memorials* (3 vols, 1725), II, 198, 211.

[34] *C.S.P.D.* 1649-50, p.465.

[35] The quotation is from Thomas Chaloner's verse preface to Thomas Gage, *The English American* (1648).

stages of the Long Parliament between our Henry Nevile and Sir Walter Ralegh's son Carew Ralegh.[36] Nevertheless Carew's presence in the Commonwealth government, which often paraded him before foreign dignitaries, was an appropriate accompaniment to a cult of Elizabethan and of Jacobean political literature in the early 1650s, when Sir Walter Ralegh's works were in great demand. If the classical republicans had needed reminders of the aspirations of that earlier generation, many publications of the early 1650s would have provided them.[37] Among them was Fulke Greville's *Life* of Sir Philip Sidney, which was first published in 1652, when it was dedicated to Algernon's sister. About the same time, Lely was commissioned by the second Earl of Leicester to paint Algernon's younger brother Henry in a pointedly Arcadian setting.[38]

If the 'Jacobethan' revival of the 1650s is a useful witness to our theme, the literature produced by the Interregnum itself is a more important one. The classical republicanism of the Puritan Revolution is a literary as well as a political phenomenon. As so often in the seventeenth century, the relationship between literature and politics is a matter not only of correspondences and echoes but of the interaction of personalities. It is to the literary republicans that we now turn.

First, and most obviously, there is Milton, apologist for regicide and the Commonwealth's Secretary for Foreign Tongues. Milton, whose own prewar visit to Italy, not least to Florence, had been so formative an experience, looked abroad and to antiquity for political instruction. In 1647-8, as politicians vainly proposed insular and pragmatic solutions to the post-war constitutional crisis, Milton urged a broader perspective. 'Britain (to speak a truth not oft spoken),' he observed, 'as it is a land fruitful enough of men stout and courageous in war, so it is naturally not over fertile of men able to govern justly and prudently in peace . . . For the sun, which we want, ripens wits as well as fruits; and as wine and oil are imported to us from abroad, so must ripe understanding and many civil virtues be imported to us from foreign writings and examples of best ages: we shall else miscarry.' In 1652, when he was struggling to persuade the government to allow the Count of Oldenburgh a pass to visit England, Milton lamented the insularity of most M.P.s, who were 'entirely ignorant of public political matters'. No more than three or four members of the Council of State, he complained, had been abroad. Among that handful he must have had in mind Henry Nevile and Thomas Chaloner, whom he certainly regarded as his warmest allies in the Count's

---

[36] *C.J.*, 27 Dec. 1650, 29 July 1651, 10, 18, 24 Feb. 1653. Ralegh sat on few committees of which Nevile was not a member.

[37] Kevin Sharpe, *Sir Robert Cotton* (1976), 246; *Mercurius Politicus* (repr. 1971), II, 390, IV, 20, 136-7, V, 104-5.

[38] Oliver Millar, *Sir Peter Lely* (1978), 45; and the Lelys at Althorp. The second Earl described his own youthful friendship with the ninth Earl of Northumberland as 'Arcadian' (Collins, *Sidney Papers*, II, 371-2). To the list of those who are known to have plagiarised *Arcadia* during the Puritan Revolution (see Howell, *Sir Philip Sidney*, 165) can be added Bulstrode Whitelocke: see the passage about architecture innocently quoted from his Annals in my *The Rump Parliament*, 132.

cause. There are other indications that Chaloner and Milton were friends.[39] We know of some of Milton's other friendships from his *Second Defence* of 1654, where he risked offending Cromwell by praising three opponents of the Protectorate. One was Algernon Sidney. Another was John Bradshaw, who had been President of the Commonwealth's Council of State and an invaluable ally of the classical republican group. The third was Robert Overton, with whom Milton enjoyed 'similitude of study'. Overton, whom we meet in the textbooks as a disaffected colonel, proves also to have been a poet, a lover of Donne and Herbert, and a devotee of Roman history.[40] We are sometimes too quick to dismiss the Interregnum as a period of philistinism.

Our second literary republican – however gingerly the term republican should be applied to him – is Milton's friend Andrew Marvell, that 'notable English Italo-Machiavellian', who visited Italy in the mid-1640s, and who according to Aubrey was an 'intimate friend' of James Harrington. We shall see more of Marvell. For the moment let us merely hazard the speculation that Milton's association with Thomas Chaloner, and the intimate connections which existed between the Chaloner and the Fairfax families, could help to explain Marvell's surprising appointment by Thomas Fairfax as tutor to his daughter Mary in 1650 or 1651. Thomas Chaloner's younger brother, the antiquary James Chaloner, who had married into the Fairfaxes and who was a consistently dependable supporter of the classical republicans in Parliament, was appointed by Thomas Fairfax to help govern the Isle of Man in 1652. Our third literary republican is Thomas May, the Long Parliament's official historian, whom the Duchess of Newcastle accused of relentlessly comparing Parliament's heroes 'to all the great and most famous heroes, both Greek and Roman'. May had written a translation, with a celebrated 'continuation', of Lucan's *Pharsalia*, and had there explored the great crisis of Roman liberty. May's version was republished, with the support of the classical republicans in Parliament, in 1650, the year in which Marvell borrowed from it for the Horatian Ode.[41] May was a close friend of Thomas Chaloner. When May died in 1650, Chaloner was instructed by the Council of State to see what use Parliament might make of his papers; Chaloner and Henry Marten were put in charge of the arrangements for May's interment in Westminster Abbey; and Chaloner, Marten and Sir James Harrington were asked to find a replacement for May as Parliament's historiographer.[42]

Our fourth literary republican is George Wither. Like May, Wither was a survivor of an earlier literary age. Like many other poets, he had enjoyed the patronage of Algernon Sidney's grandfather Robert, who himself has recently

[39] J. M. French, *Life Records of John Milton* (5 vols, 1949-58), III, 151, 164; W. R. Parker, *Milton. A Biography* (2 vols, 1968), II, 959, 992.
[40] Overton's papers, my knowledge of which I owe to Mrs Barbara Taft, are in the Princeton University Library. His interest in classical history is also evident from his pamphlets of 1649 and 1659.
[41] *Mercurius Politicus*, IV, 5-7, 135-6; H. M. Margoliouth, *The Poems and Letters of Andrew Marvell* (third edn, 2 vols, 1971), I, 378. The conventional attribution of the hostile poem 'On Tom May's Death' to Marvell is doubtful: H. Kelliher, *Andrew Marvell* (1978), 40.
[42] *C.S.P.D.* 1650, p.432.

been discovered to have been a poet of stature.[43] In 1643, according to Peter Heylyn, George Wither and Henry Marten advertised their disrespect for monarchy by disporting themselves among the regalia of which Parliament had taken charge. Wither is a poor man's Milton. There is the Miltonic belief in his role as national prophet; there is the same readiness to project private grievances as burning issues of public morality; there is the same ability to turn with the political tide. Like Milton, too, Wither benefited from the friendship of John Bradshaw.[44] In the 1650s Wither composed a series of elaborate parallels between the histories of the Roman and the English republics.[45] The frequent appearance of such parallels in the literature of the Puritan Revolution is in itself, perhaps, hardly remarkable. Often they are merely ornamental. A dose of the poetry of the hack panegyrist Payne Fisher will dispel any temptation to attach deep cultural significance to classical allusions wherever we find them. Yet it seems fair to suggest that Marvell's Horatian Ode of 1650 and Milton's sonnet to Vane in 1652 –

> Vane, young in years, but in sage counsel old,
> Than whom a better senator ne'er held
> The helm of Rome –

reflect a literary development in which parallels between republican Rome and republican England became a source of imaginative pressure.[46]

Perhaps the most influential (if in literary terms hardly the most distinguished) of those parallels were provided by our fifth and last literary republican, the pamphleteer Marchamont Nedham. A 'great crony' of Milton, Nedham was recruited by John Bradshaw as a government propagandist. From 1650 he edited the Commonwealth's most successful newspaper, *Mercurius Politicus*. Nedham's contacts in Parliament were not confined to the classical republican group, but he supported the group's policies at critical moments and was rewarded with advance indications of government policy. Nedham's editorials were a series of history lessons. Drawing on a wide range of classical and medieval illustrations, he sought to educate a people 'bred up and instructed in the principles of monarchy' to 'learn to be true Commonwealthsmen'. He gave most space to Roman history, and urged the new-born republic to derive instruction both from Rome's splendours and from its shortcomings. In the period of uncertainty which followed the abolition of the English monarchy,

[43] For Robert Sidney's poetry see the articles by Hilton Kelliher and Katherine Duncan-Jones in *British Library Journal*, 1975, and by Miss Duncan-Jones in *English Literary Renaissance*, 1979. For Robert's patronage of Wither see Norbrook, 'Panegyric of the Monarch', 259. In 1620 Sir Thomas Wroth dedicated to the first Earl a translation of Book II of the Aeneid: in 1648, now a parliamentary colleague of Algernon, Sir Thomas demanded 'any government rather than that of kings . . . from devils and kings good Lord deliver me'.

[44] The regalia episode is discussed by P. B. Anderson in *Philological Quarterly*, 1935. For Bradshaw see Wither's *Westrow Revived* (1654), 44. Since writing this essay I have discovered that Mr Christopher Hill, in his contribution to J. Carey (ed.), *English Renaissance Studies presented to Dame Helen Gardner*, has devoted to the similarities between Wither and Milton a more detailed, and more sympathetic, comparison.

[45] Wither, *The Modern Statesman* (1654), 56ff.

[46] For the Machiavellian content of Milton's sonnet see J. Carey and A. Fowler (eds), *The Poems of John Milton* (1968), 326n.

and amidst the continuing war against Charles II – 'young Tarquin', as Nedham always calls him – *Mercurius Politicus* sought to instil an awareness that England was engaged in a historical epic as decisive as, and in many ways directly parallel to, the conflict between liberty and tyranny which in Nedham's eyes had been the central theme of Roman history.

Seventeenth-century classical republicanism, it has been well said, was a language, not a programme. We have seen that it found inspiration in family traditions and was given expression in literature. But it was not a philosophy likely to produce a united political platform.[47] The affinities which classical republicans discerned between the Roman and the English commonwealths were spiritual, not constitutional ones. Proudly independent, the classical republicans offered automatic support neither to the event – regicide – nor to the institution – the purged Long Parliament – which gave them power. There was one principle, however, behind which republicans in Parliament could unite. Like the theorists of the social contract and of resistance rights, on whose arguments they frequently drew, they believed that all power derived originally from the people and could be resumed by the people. That belief was affronted by what the classical republicans saw as the major political problem of their time, hereditary monarchy. On the subject of medieval hereditary monarchy the classical republicans were not at one. They were agreed, however, that since the accession of Henry VII hereditary monarchy had (except perhaps in the reign of Elizabeth, whose posthumous popularity gave the classical republicans considerable trouble) been disastrous to England.

Their chief objection to hereditary monarchy was that it was irrational. Politics were a conflict between reason on the one hand and passion and will on the other. Popular sovereignty answered to reason: the hereditary principle embodied passion and will. The faith of the classical republicans in reason – a word they so often used but rarely if ever defined – is central to their political creed. Like so much else in the writings of the classical republicans, the faith was hardly novel. Their rationalism sets them in an old and broad tradition of Renaissance humanism; and it separates them from many, perhaps most, of their fellow politicians. Reason, the classical republicans held, instructed men to pursue the common good: passion and will drew them to the pursuit of sectional concerns. 'If we have anything of piety or of prudence,' urged James Harrington, 'let us raise ourselves out of the mire of private interest unto the contemplation of virtue.'[48] Harrington's association of virtue with civic unity recalls Machiavelli's *virtù* and the belief, to which the classical republicans enthusiastically subscribed, that societies flourish

---

[47] The prose writings of the classical republicans of which I have made most use in this essay are: Sidney's *Discourses*, which I have read in the 1772 edition of Sidney's *Works*; Sidney's 'Court Maxims'; Milton's pamphlets of 1649-60; Harrington's *Oceana*, which I have studied in J. G. A. Pocock (ed.), *The Political Works of James Harrington* (1977); Nevile's *Plato Redivivus*; *Mercurius Politicus*; and Wither's *The Modern Statesman*. By treating the authors of those works as a group, and by seeking common denominators among them, I shall inevitably give an inadequate impression of the subtlety, the distinctiveness, and the development of their various ideas.
[48] Pocock, *Harrington*, 169.

when citizens take responsibility for their own defence and proudly involve themselves in their own government. We are far removed here from the pessimistic theology of the Calvinists (to whom government, a necessary consequence of the Fall, was nothing to be proud of), from the pessimistic psychology of Hobbes (to whom men are 'subjects', not 'citizens') – and, perhaps, from the dislike of government implicit in the demands for de-centralisation advanced by M.P.s in 1640–2 and by Levellers in 1647–9.

The rationalism which informs the classical republicans' approach to politics is evident too in their study of history. Like the great Roman historians themselves, they saw the past as a storehouse of political lessons, applicable to the present because the laws of political behaviour, although manifested in different forms in different societies, were constant. Machiavelli had written that 'in all . . . peoples there are the same desires and the same passions as there always were. So that if one examines the past with diligence, it is easy to foresee the future of any commonwealth, and to apply those remedies which were used of old.' The historian was thus a political scientist, whose office was to identify the universal, rational principles beneath the varieties and the changes of the past. James Harrington thought that the 'ancient prudence' which he wished to recreate in seventeenth-century England had been 'first discoverd unto mankind by God himself in the fabric of the Commonwealth of Israel, and afterwards picked out in his footsteps in nature and followed unanimously by the Greeks and Romans'. Nedham, in the history lessons of *Mercurius Politicus*, repeatedly stressed that his temporal 'examples' illustrated eternal principles of 'reason'.[49]

Nedham was a learned man; but his editorials did not so much explore Roman history as raid it. His readers were not encouraged to examine too closely the contexts of the events he described. History, the classical republicans knew, was a two-edged sword. They insistently contrasted the discipline, the austerity and the virtue of the Roman republic with the effeminacy, the luxury and the corruption of the empire which had succeeded it. They knew, however, that other writers could effectively portray the republic as a shambles from which Rome had been rescued by imperial peace and stability.[50] Unreliable as evidence of the superiority of republican principles, history proved untrustworthy as a sanction for their implementation. Nedham and others liked to suggest that England had been a republic 'till the Romans yoked it', but it was not a point they sought to press.[51] Reason was always the ultimate authority. If English kings had acquired excessive constitutional privileges, then history, which was a process of trial and error, had sinned against reason, which should learn from history's mistakes. Similarly it was reason, not research, that explained the origins of political authority. That sovereignty derived from the people seemed to Algernon Sidney 'common sense'. 'It cannot be imagined,' wrote Sidney; 'it seems very improbable, not

[49] Machiavelli, *Discourses*, I, ch.39; Pocock, *Harrington*, 161; *Mercurius Politicus*, e.g. IV, 101–4, 133–5, 165–8, 294.

[50] See e.g. Clement Walker, *The History of Independency* (1660), part 2, pp.145–6. For the restored Charles II as Augustus Caesar see H. D. Weinbrot, *Augustus Caesar in 'Augustan' England* (1978).

[51] *Mercurius Politicus*, III, 278, IV, 357–60,; John Sadler, *The Rights of the Kingdom* (1649), 26ff.; Sidney, *Discourses*, 402.

o say impossible,' argued Nevile; 'nor is it credible,' echoed Milton, that the people would ever have renounced their sovereignty or entrusted kings with powers which exceeded the people's needs.[52]

Rationalists in their political and historical philosophies, the classical republicans were rationalists too in religion. In politics, they wished to expose the hollow mystery of divine right and hereditary monarchy. In religion, they challenged the mystery of the Trinity. Like most anti-Trinitarians (Socinians) they were also Arminians, opponents of the Calvinist doctrine of predestination; and opponents too of religious intolerance and of the political and intellectual pretensions of the clergy. Milton's Arminianism and his Socinianism will be well known to readers of his *De Doctrina Christiana*. Professor Pocock had detected a 'Socinian streak' in James Harrington.[53] The Socinianism of Thomas Chaloner and Thomas May was notorious. George Wither rejected predestination.[54] Marvell, when he argued for toleration in *The Rehearsal Transpros'd*, turned for support to such Arminians as Grotius, John Hales and William Chillingworth. Thomas Chaloner, Henry Marten and Henry Nevile were all cheerfully anti-clerical. Chaloner, wrote Aubrey, was 'as far from being a puritan as the east from the west'. In 1657 he teased the clergy with a hoax involving the supposed discovery of Moses' tomb. Marten thought theology 'a matter for a university, perhaps, not for a kingdom'.[55] In 1659, Nevile's reputed 'atheism' was debated by Parliament for five hours after he had declared, in the company of three clergymen, that 'he was more affected by reading Cicero than the Bible'.[56] To classical republicans, the Bible was a political manual: a history book, comparable to the great histories of Greece and Rome. It is instructive to contrast Nevile's remark about Cicero and the Bible with the shocked response of the puritan republican Edmund Ludlow, who was appalled by Arminianism and Socinianism, to the suggestion 'that we are to take the history of the holy scriptures as those of Titus Livius or Polybius'.[57]

A fuller study of the classical republicans would dwell on the limits, as well as on the extent, of their rationalism. Within the Puritan Revolution, however, that rationalism is a secularising force. In the winter of 1650-1 we can, I believe, discern a change in the prevailing mood at Westminster: a shift from the apocalyptic vocabulary of the previous two years to the more worldly calculation of the two which followed. During that winter, our classical republicans significantly broaden the base of their parliamentary support. As they do so, their eyes are chiefly on foreign and on commercial affairs.[58]

The early 1650s brought a revolution in English diplomacy. England, which under the early Stuarts had cut a pitiful figure on the Continent,

---

[52] Sidney, *Discourses*, 25, 55; Robbins, *Two English Republican Tracts*, 84-5; *The Works of John Milton* (Columbia edn), VII, 361.
[53] Pocock, *Harrington*, 109.
[54] C. H. Hensley, *The Later Career of George Wither* (1969), 64-5.
[55] Marten, *The Independency of England Endeavoured to be Maintained* (1648), 12.
[56] Robbins, *Two English Republican Tracts*, 9n.
[57] Ludlow, *Voice* (Camden Soc.), 9.
[58] These brief statements are, I hope, given some substance in my *The Rump Parliament*, 261-72.

became, thanks to Cromwell's army and Blake's navy, the envy and the arbiter of Europe. France and Spain competed for England's favour. Ireland and Scotland were conquered and incorporated. The commercial and maritime supremacy of the Dutch was ended by the Navigation Act of 1651 and by the Anglo-Dutch war of 1652-4. In the evolution of the Commonwealth's foreign policy the classical republicans played a critical part. They fostered ambitious programmes for the encouragement of trade and sea-power. They figured prominently in negotiations with foreign ambassadors. England's relations with Tuscany, although hardly their main diplomatic concern, were normally regarded as their special preserve. So were relations with Venice, a state which they saw as in many ways the modern embodiment of ancient political wisdom. They received deputations from trading companies. They were heavily involved in the formation of English policy towards Ireland and Scotland. In the summer of 1652, when their cohesion was perhaps at its most impressive, they ensured that the government remained committed to its anti-Dutch policy.

The classical republicans were hardly the first seventeenth-century politicians to press for an ambitious foreign policy. There was, after all, a strong tradition of Protestant and anti-Spanish imperialism. Strident exponents of that tradition saw the Puritan Revolution as the first act of a drama of European liberation. Even in the most secular celebrations of the Commonwealth's diplomacy we often find a messianic strain. But that diplomacy was not a Protestant one. From an early stage the Commonwealth sought to 'preserve the balance of the two crowns of France and Spain' by 'a bending towards Spain'.[59] In the 1640s Parliament had repeatedly beseeched the King to 'enter into a more strict alliance' with the United Provinces, while the courts of France and Spain had feared that a parliamentary victory in the Civil War would be followed by an Anglo-Dutch crusade against monarchy and Catholicism.[60] Yet in the early 1650s Commonwealth propaganda came to describe the United Provinces not as the bastion of Protestantism, but as Carthage.[61]

In one sense, the abandonment of Protestant goals in Europe by the classical republicans was a break not only with puritan politics but with family ones. The Sidneys, the Neviles and the Chaloners had long concerned themselves with overseas trade and colonisation and with England's relations with Ireland and Scotland. Until the Civil War, however, the families were consistent advocates of a vigorous Protestant diplomacy. Their representatives in the 1650s retained the vigour but shed the Protestantism. Yet that departure was less profound than it may seem. Even in their most fulsome Protestant enthusiasms the families had always displayed a hard-headed respect for diplomatic and economic realities. In the later sixteenth and earlier seventeenth centuries, considerations of religion had for the most

[59] [Slingsby Bethel,] *The World's Mistake in Oliver Cromwell* (1668), 11.
[60] Gardiner's *Constitutional Documents*, 253, 266; H. J. Smith, 'The English Republic and the Fronde' (Oxford Univ. B.Litt. thesis, 1958), 7, 25-6; above, p.177.
[61] *Mercurius Politicus*, III, 113; cf. Marvell's 'The Character of Holland', l.141.

part seemed, to the supporters of a forward Protestant policy, to point in the same direction as considerations of security and wealth. By the middle of the seventeenth century, the weakening of Spain and the attainment of independence by the United Provinces had altered the diplomatic map. It was the achievement of Algernon Sidney, Henry Nevile, Thomas Chaloner and their allies to recognise that change and to adjust England's diplomatic sights accordingly.

Under their guidance England became, in Machiavelli's terms, a 'commonwealth for expansion'. Of course, the new diplomacy is not to be explained solely by the influence of Machiavelli. The Dutch had long been hated economic rivals, and the motives of many advocates of an anti-Dutch policy were primarily if not exclusively economic. None of the classical republicans, however, had discernible stakes in the commercial interests which may have profited from the Commonwealth's diplomacy. Certainly they concerned themselves with national economic considerations. Even so, the adoption of a courageous and revolutionary foreign policy, whatever its economic or territorial aims, is unlikely to be accomplished without ideological inspiration, especially if it breaks with the prevailing ideology of its time.

The classical republicans found that inspiration in classical example. England, they argued, would be a new Rome, with a civilising international mission. In 1656 James Harrington reminded his readers 'that if we have given over running up and down naked and with dappled hides, learned to write and read, for all these we are beholding to the Romans'. So 'to ask whether it be lawful for a commonwealth to aspire unto the empire of the world is to ask whether it be lawful for her to do her duty, or to put the world into a better condition than it was before . . . What can you think but if the world should see the Roman eagle again, she would renew her age and her flight?'[62] Marvell's Horatian Ode caught a new mood in the summer of 1650 with its tribute to Cromwell's victories in Ireland (whether or not that tribute is ironic):

> What may not then our isle presume
> While victory his crest does plume!
> What may not others fear
> If thus he crown each year!
> A Caesar he ere long to Gaul,
> To Italy an Hannibal,
> And to all states not free
> Shall climacteric be.

Marvell's Cromwell, a prince who liberates the republic, is a supremely Machiavellian figure.[63] About the time that Marvell was writing the poem, *Mercurius Politicus* described Cromwell as 'the only *Novus Princeps* that ever I met with in all the confines of history', and remarked that 'this brave Scipio, my Lord General Cromwell, after he hath wholly subdued Ireland and Scotland to the Commonwealth of England, ought to do the like elsewhere,

[62] Pocock, *Harrington*, 192, 328-9.
[63] See the essay by J. A. Mazzeo in the *Journal of the History of Ideas*, XXI (1960). Mazzeo's central point seems to me to survive the assault on it by Hans Baron in the same volume.

that so our domineering and insolent neighbours may be brought under'. In February 1651 Nedham, borrowing from the Duc de Rohan, proclaimed that England was 'a mighty animal indeed, if it knew its own strength; and such a one as might make itself (if not master, yet) arbiter of affairs in Europe.'[64]

Classical republicans strove to emulate Rome's triumphs. Did they also seek, when they formulated their diplomacy, to imitate the policies by which Rome's greatness had been achieved and her civilising mission accomplished? The point would be hard to prove. As in political theory, so in foreign policy, the language of classical republicanism is easier to identify than the programme. The evidence concerning political decision-making in the early 1650s is dry and institutional. It tells us of decisions, not of motives.[65] Nevertheless, speculation may prove worthwhile. Here let us briefly speculate in one area: the common aim of incorporation and union which guided the Common-wealth's policies towards Ireland, Scotland and the United Provinces.[66]

Early in January 1651 *Mercurius Politicus* floated one of the most remarkable diplomatic initiatives in English history. This was the scheme, which the government was to urge on the Dutch a few months later, for a complete integration of the two commonwealths. In the same issue of the newspaper, Nedham gave the first indication of the government's intention to annex Scotland.[67] The proposal for Anglo-Dutch union no doubt had its roots in the traditional Protestant aim of establishing over the Netherlands the sovereignty which had been offered to Queen Elizabeth. In the early 1650s there seemed a possibility that the federation of the United Provinces would dissolve, and the Commonwealth perhaps hoped to detach and absorb those maritime provinces which welcomed English friendship. Other thoughts, however, may also have lain behind the initiative. It was about this time that Milton, whose friendship with Nedham was probably at its closest in the early 1650s, confided to his commonplace book: 'That a federation or league formed with a republic can be trusted more than one formed with a prince is shown by Machiavelli.'[68] Relations between the Romans and states which they had

---

[64] *Mercurius Politicus*, I, 29, 277-8, II, 213-4; Rohan, *A Treatise of the Interest of the Princes and States of Christendom* (1641), 53-5. Perhaps students of Marvell could profitably look more closely at Nedham than they have done. In 1649 Marvell and Nedham had been fellow contributors to the royalist collection *Lachrymae Musarum*. For the jingoism of 1650-1 see also *Memoirs of the Life of A. Sydney*, in Sydney's *Works* (1772), 18ff.; Oliver Cromwell's letter of 4 September 1650; C. Hill, *Puritanism and Revolution* (1958), 131-2.

[65] We should add that not all admirers of Machiavelli thought his lessons applicable to the England of the 1650s. There were those who argued that continental adventure had always damaged England's interests, or who questioned the morality of foreign aggression. In the precarious political circumstances of the early 1650s, too, there was a mixed reception for Machiavelli's claim that domestic social conflict, which renewed and sustained *virtù*, was essential to territorial expansion. Machiavelli's argument was adopted by Sidney after the Restoration (*Discourses*, e.g. 131, 172ff.; cf. Robbins, *Two English Republican Tracts*, 90-1), but we do not know whether (like the brave spirit John Hall in 1650-1) he would have professed it earlier. The fact remains that the Commonwealth government, whose domestic policies were predominantly directed to the attainment of social and political stability, was persuaded to jeopardise that stability by embarking upon the expensive and unpopular Dutch war.

[66] For the anticipation of that aim by Bacon see C. Hill, *Intellectual Origins of the English Revolution* (1965), 98.

[67] *Mercurius Politicus*, II, 90, 94.

[68] *Complete Prose Works of John Milton* (Yale edn), I, 504.

conquered or with which they allied were a source of continual interest to England's classical republicans. The subject acquired a pressing interest with the final defeat of the Scots in September 1651. At first the government proposed merely to absorb Scotland as a subordinate province. In the following months, however, that unadventurous policy was dropped in favour of a programme of complete political and economic integration, with representation for Scotland at Westminster. The classical republicans played an important part in the evolution of the new policy,[69] which was warmly supported by *Mercurius Politicus*. 'In old Rome,' Nedham explained at length, 'it was their custom to admit such as they conquered into the privileges of their city, making them free denizens.'[70]

In April 1653, when the Commonwealth's foreign exploits were at their peak, Cromwell dissolved the Long Parliament by force. Some classical republicans, like James Harrington and George Wither, continued to exult in England's imperial role. Marvell celebrated England's foreign triumphs under the Protectorate; so did the poet Edmund Waller. As a political force, however, classical republicanism was broken. Many of its exponents, implacably opposed to the Protectorate, retreated into nostalgia. Algernon Sidney was among them. He recalled of the Commonwealth period that 'neither the Romans, nor Grecians, in the time of their liberty, ever performed any actions more glorious than freeing the country from a civil war which had raged in every part, the conquest of two such kingdoms as Scotland and Ireland, and crushing the formidable power of the Hollanders by sea; nor ever produced more examples of valour, industry, integrity, and in all respects complete, disinterested, unmoveable, and incorruptible virtue, than were at that time seen in our own nation.'[71]

Such retrospective glorification of the Long Parliament was widespread. It produced many comparisons between the English and the Roman republics. Although not wholly without justification, it rarely descended to supporting detail; and by the late seventeenth century it had produced a comfortable myth. The numbing influence of that myth in the eighteenth and nineteenth centuries did as much to impede exploration of the impact of classical republicanism on puritan politics as has the decline of classical education in the twentieth century. In 1742 Bishop Warburton could remark, in an influential footnote in his edition of Pope's *Essay on Man* (IV, 133), that 'when Cromwell subdued his country' in April 1653 'the spirit of liberty was at its height, and its interests were conducted by a set of the greatest geniuses for government that the world ever saw embarked together in one·common cause'. The revival of radical aspirations in the late eighteenth and early

[69] *C.J.*, 9 Sept. 1651, 13 Apr., 7, 8 Oct. 1652; P.R.O., SP25/138.
[70] *Mercurius Politicus*, IV, 231. The newspaper also reflected the policy of the Cromwellian army: see F. D. Dow, *Cromwellian Scotland* (1979), 30-1. Nedham, whose editorials frequently illustrated arguments for radical social change by appeals to Roman example, was anxious to attract the soldiery to Roman history (e.g. V, 37-41).
[71] Sidney, *Works*, 184-5, 328. Sidney's panegyric may have been heightened by his editor (see Ludlow, *Voice*, 69-71), but is likely to have reflected his own sentiments: see 'Court Maxims', pp. 15-16, 129-30.

nineteenth centuries inspired a band of scholars – William Godwin, Francis Maseres, J. T. Rutt, John Forster – to exalt the Long Parliament's reputation. While the Parliament was eulogised, the classical republicans of the Puritan Revolution became plaster saints. In 1726 the most influential of Marvell's early biographers aimed 'to draw a model for all free-born Englishmen, in the life of a worthy patriot, whose every action has truly merited to him, with Aristides, the surname of the just'. He succeeded only too well. Marvell's 'Roman virtue' became legendary while his poetry remained unread.[72] As for Algernon Sidney, a nineteenth-century biographer legitimately complained that 'it has been the fashion to represent him as a kind of melodramatic republican, clothed in the toga of antiquity, regarding with fierce and scowling eye the details of modern constitutions, and anxious to erect an impossible sort of commonwealth'.[73] Wordsworth's

> Sydney, Marvel, Harrington,
> Young Vane, and others who called Milton friend

echoes a tired litany.

Whig historiography kept republican names alive; but Whig mythology was vulnerable to scholarship and to changing intellectual priorities and fashions. Roman virtue is a dead cult, and the cult of the Long Parliament has died with it. Yet if we can reach behind the mythology, there is a historical problem to be grasped: the existence, at the climax of the Puritan Revolution, of a group of able and influential politicians whose idealism was fuelled, and whose policies were influenced, by their interest in and admiration for classical antiquity. It may have been a slightly unfair question, but it was not a wholly unfair one, that Milton asked his countrymen on the eve of the Restoration, as the Revolution collapsed about him: 'Where is this goodly tower of a Commonwealth, which the English boasted they would build to overshadow kings, and be another Rome in the west?'

---

[72] E. S. Donno, *Andrew Marvell: The Critical Heritage* (1978).
[73] A. C. Ewald, *The Life and Times of the Hon. Algernon Sydney* (2 vols, 1873), I, 265.

15

Sir William Petty, Irish Landowner

T. C. Barnard

Throughout the seventeenth century Ireland was regarded as a stock from which enterprising and ruthless Englishmen might enrich themselves. The career of the first Earl of Cork, an English younger son who by 1640 had an annual Irish rental of some £20,000, was simply the most spectacular use of the opportunities offered by Ireland. The fame and fortune of Sir William Petty, the indigent son of a Hampshire clothier, who had arrived in Dublin in 1652 with less than £500 and whose annual income by 1685 was £6,700, suggested that Ireland after 1660 still offered an easy ascent to riches. Seventeenth-century Irish land settlements which had systematically transferred estates from Catholic to Protestant ownership were essential to these quickly made fortunes. In this essay I shall examine Ireland's place in Petty's career, and the uses to which he put his wealth. I shall suggest that official policy after 1660 was less uniformly favourable to Protestants than has sometimes been argued, and that many of the obstacles with which Petty grappled were erected by the government.

I shall also be concerned with a less familiar side of Petty's activities. The man who was a founder member of the Royal Society, who worked to revive its ailing fortunes in the 1680s and who later presided over the Dublin Philosophical Society, was constantly distracted from his scientific work by his Irish property. His intention had been very different. He had hoped to demonstrate sensationally on his newly acquired and remote lands the utility of his learning and techniques. He believed he had the method to assess accurately and then develop Ireland's resources. Yet after 1660 he failed to turn his colony into a showcase for rational procedures and, as the difficulties multiplied, he restricted himself to the mundane tasks of peopling the lands and providing his tenants with a sufficient livelihood to pay their rents. Even the connection between Petty's experiences as an Irish landowner and his writings and experiments was more tenuous than has sometimes been supposed. Government service in Ireland in the 1650s had undoubtedly focussed his attention more closely on demography, political statistics and technological improvement. But on his estates he generally contented himself with solving basic problems by rudimentary methods, with the result that he seldom tested his ideas on his lands or drew general conclusions from his own experiences in Ireland.

Petty came to Ireland at a time when the land market was particularly brisk. The Catholic rising of 1641 and the unsuccessful war which followed doomed the Catholics to a general expropriation, the result of which was to reduce the Catholic share of Irish land from 60 per cent to 22 per cent. As this policy had been instituted by the Long Parliament and implemented by the usurper Cromwell it was hoped that the restored Charles II would reverse it. However confiscation followed by Protestant plantation belonged to a pattern of stabilising and anglicising Ireland which was too well established to be abandoned lightly. Irish policy was invariably decided in London and there in 1660–3 rival groups competed for the King's ear. Those interested in maintaining the recent land transfers – the Protestants settled in Ireland before 1641 who had increased their holdings, and the English soldiers and investors whose contributions to the state had been repaid in Irish land – resisted a lobby of Irish Catholics. Some Catholics could argue that they had never participated in the 1641 massacres or that they had fought on behalf of both Charles I and Charles II, even sharing exile with the latter. Charles II wanted to please all. Favoured Catholics were immediately restored to their hereditary estates; at the same time prominent Irish Protestants, usually those with access to the court or important in the Restoration, were pardoned and had their new lands confirmed. The King had hoped a similar generosity might inform the general settlement. The very idea angered the Protestants, who had no wish to lose so quickly their monopoly over office, power and the lushest lands. They argued that Ireland would never be secure so long as the Catholic Irish owned sizeable estates; they also pointed out that Ireland lacked enough acres to satisfy all claimants.

The settlement enacted allowed those Catholics who could prove their innocence of any part in the 1641 risings or their subsequent good behaviour to regain their possessions. Where these claims conflicted with those of recently established proprietors, the newcomers would be compensated with land elsewhere. Also, in order to provide a sufficient stock of land to meet claims, the soldiers and adventurers had to disgorge one-third of their grants. The stages by which these arrangements had evolved – discussion at court and in the English Privy Council, more talks and drafting in the Irish Council, debate and passage in the Irish Parliament – had been attended by well-organised political pressure and intrigue in which the Protestants had shown themselves superior. Controversy did not end with the passing of the acts by the Dublin Parliament in 1662 and 1665. A court, staffed by English commissioners, sat in Dublin to adjudicate the claims to innocence. Thereafter lands had to be apportioned, compensation decided for the displaced Protestants, and possession secured by the legal owner.

These processes further embittered and disappointed many Catholics and Protestants, who refused to accept the settlement (formally completed in 1669) as definitive. Loss of records, unclear boundaries, and the underdeveloped and extremely confused Irish land law occasioned proliferating wrangles over ownership. Protestants found themselves kept from estates in remoter regions by the former Catholic proprietors. Individual Catholics were hindered in their efforts to repossess their lands by partisan Protestant officials. But more generally many Catholics felt that they had received scant justice from a Court of Claims that was short-lived and staffed by Englishmen, and from a settlement whose authors were Protestants. The Catholics' agents, notably Richard Talbot (later to be Earl of Tyrconnell), intrigued at court to reopen the question. Charles II's willingness to listen to these complaints, to appoint special commissioners to review the matter, and by virtue of his prerogative to reinstate some Irish Catholics made Irish Protestants intensely uneasy and willing to associate with English critics of the later Stuarts.[1]

Irish Catholics had long realised that no English parliament would improve their lot. Instead they looked to the monarch to use his prerogative on their behalf. Not only did they lobby assiduously, they also fluently defended the royal prerogative. One Irish Catholic assured James II that Ireland 'by the King's prerogative is at his disposal independently of the Parliament of England', and insisted that if only Catholics were returned to power in Ireland 'they would make you [James II] as absolute in Ireland as your heart could wish'. Protestants naturally seized upon such Catholic utterances to show the danger of leniency towards the papists, and questioned both the Catholics' constitutional arguments and Charles II's and James II's actions in undermining the acts of 1662 and 1665. Protestants asserted that the King could not dispose of confiscated Irish lands without parliamentary consent, that those lands had merely been vested in the King as Parliament's trustee, and that any letters patent or grants by made royal commissioners were invalid until confirmed by the Irish Parliament.[2]

Thus after 1660 there was much Protestant unease about the monarch's intentions towards the settlement. What so far had been achieved had resulted from and must be maintained by intense lobbying. Yet fears for the future could not be allowed to let the Protestants neglect their estates. Although they had had to struggle to retain them or wrest them away from Catholics, and although they feared they might again be overrun or repossessed legally by those same Catholics, the new owners exploited what they occupied. The Protestants prospered as years of peace, a growing population and buoyant trade increased demand for Irish foodstuffs, and they displayed their wealth self-confidently in modish new houses, embowered in deer parks and gardens, and crammed with pictures and furniture shipped from London and the Continent. Petty grew rich with them, and yet was less fortunate than this stereotype suggests. Indeed when we see how much less lucky we may have

[1] The settlement is best described by J. G. Simms in T. W. Moody *et al.* (eds), *A New History of Ireland*, III (Oxford 1976), ch.17; and K. S. Bottigheimer, 'The restoration land settlement: a structural view', *Irish Historical Studies*, XVIII (1972).

[2] 'A series of eight anonymous and confidential letters to James II about the state of Ireland', *Notes and Queries*, CXXIV (1882), 361, 401; Bodleian Library, Oxford, Carte MS. XXXIX, ff.681v-2; M. F. Bond (ed.), *The Diaries and Papers of Sir Edward Dering* (London 1976), 147-8.

to question the stereotype.

Most who obtained lands in the 1650s did so through either military service in Ireland or investing money in the island's reconquest. Petty, however, acquired his as recompense for government service. He belonged to a group whose importance in building a strong Protestant presence in Ireland has been neglected. Attention has focussed mainly on those who participated in the government-sponsored schemes of plantation. As important in creating a solid Protestant interest in Ireland were those who came under their own auspices. Ireland by the seventeenth century was a part, though perhaps not a very welcome one, of the usual career pattern in the army, government service and the Protestant church. Many (especially those graduates denied appropriate openings in England) accepted Irish posts in the hope of stepping from them into something better in England. Most found themselves marooned in Ireland, but since lands there were cheap they could console themselves by becoming landed gentlemen and the founders of dynasties.

Deft use of his wits and of his talent for self-promotion enabled Petty to profit from the opportunities in England after the Civil Wars. He accumulated jobs both at Oxford and at Gresham's College before accepting in 1652 a posting to Ireland as physician to the army. Other offices came his way from a regime desperately needing, but short of, able administrators. What lifted Petty from the ranks and income of a successful bureaucrat was his success in planning and executing the surveys of the confiscated Catholic lands in Ireland. He gained at least £9,000 and an unrivalled knowledge of Ireland's topography. He invested some of his earnings in London property, but much was paid in or spent on Irish lands. By 1660 Petty was a substantial landowner, and though this was not yet his principal interest, concern for his estates governed his activities. Like so many other recipients of Irish land he watched apprehensively to see what character the new settlement would take. As one high in favour during the Interregnum, especially with Ireland's governor Henry Cromwell, he had to explain away the past and ingratiate himself with the returned royalists.

Petty's decision in 1659 to return to London and pay court was wise. The talents which had originally brought Petty employment again assisted him. Charles II, delighting in Petty's conversation, pardoned and knighted him and confirmed and increased his Irish lands by letters patent.[3] Petty had surmounted the first hurdle, but others remained. In common with most men interested in the Irish land settlement, Petty moved to Dublin in 1663 as the scene shifted there. He enlisted the aid of the two chief controllers of Irish affairs, Ormonde and Orrery, both of whom he had helped in the 1650s to preserve or extend their estates. He paid the Irish Lord Chancellor £100 in order to have inserted into the bills special clauses to confirm his

[3] Carte MS. xlii, f.492; Historical Manuscripts Commission (hereafter H.M.C.). *Ormonde MSS.*, i, 70; *Calendar of State Papers relating to Ireland* (hereafter *C.S.P. Ireland*), *1660-2*, 180, 277, 280, 307, 316, 502-3; ibid., *1663-5*, 603.

lands.[4] Aware of the need of his presence where claims could be decided and lands set out, Petty returned to Dublin in 1666.

Petty's behaviour between 1660 and 1666 was not exclusively defensive. He knew there were pickings to be had while men were uncertain what belonged to whom. He tried to buy up, cheaply and secretly, dilapidated property in Dublin. He negotiated to develop housing and to introduce brick building into the city of Limerick. Knowing that the soldiers who had received or awaited payment in land would grow impatient and impecunious as their acquisition of secure titles was further delayed, he bought up their claims contained in debentures. By grants and purchases, he secured lands scattered through five Irish counties. To these, marriage to a Munster baronet's widow in 1667 added estates (mainly in County Cork) worth £1,000 annually.[5] All posed problems – of waiting to see which rival claims from innocents would be upheld or which royal grants would encroach on them, of gaining possession, of extinguishing the former owners' influence and of finding satisfactory tenants and agents. All gave Petty reason to watch with trepidation the variations in royal policy. However, one part of his estates excited Petty's most extravagant hopes and involved him in continuous trouble. That part, his holding in the inaccessible western county of Kerry, was regarded by contemporaries as the chief source of his wealth, and his own obsession with it seemed to confirm that opinion. The truth was different. Petty calculated that £4,800 of his annual income of £6,700 derived from Ireland. Of that £4,800 no more than £1,100 was expected from Kerry, and for much of his lifetime it never yielded that sum.[6]

In 1657 Petty had accepted lands in Kerry, at the mouth of the Kenmare River, because no one else wanted them. The region was remote, English influence was slight and Protestants were rare. Moreover much of the land was either bog or mountain. A range of mountains isolated it from the rest of Ireland, and even the sea journey around Mizen Head was perilous. It was the contrast between what the region appeared to be and what Petty believed it might be made which beguiled him into adding to his holdings there at every opportunity after 1660. Here was a region overdue for assimilation to English ways. It cried out to Petty for planting with industrious Protestants and for economic exploitation. Petty, having surveyed much of Ireland, detected or suspected rich natural resources. The pasture was fertile, the seas and rivers

[4] Bowood House, Wiltshire, Petty Papers, XVIII, 4 Aug. 1688. This study is mainly based on the unpublished Petty Papers which were in the Austin Cooper collection in the early nineteenth century and which have subsequently been divided between Bowood and the Osler collection in McGill University Library at Montreal. The only studies of Petty to make use of these sources are: Lord Edmond Fitzmaurice, *The Life of Sir William Petty* (London 1895), and Lindsay Sharp, 'Sir William Petty and some aspects of seventeenth-century natural philosophy', D.Phil. thesis, Oxford 1976). I am most grateful to the Marquess of Landsdowne and the Earl of Shelburne for permission to use their manuscripts, and to Lord Dacre of Glanton for his good offices in this matter.
[5] Petty Papers, VI, series I, 13 Nov. 1660, 4 Dec. 1660, 15 Dec. 1660, 9 Jan. 1660/1, 26 March 1661; McGill University Library, Osler MS. 7612, 18 April 1668, 13 May 1668, 23 June 1668.
[6] Petty Papers, V, 4 Dec. 1683; Fitzmaurice, *Petty*, 320-3; J. Aubrey, *Brief Lives*, ed. A. Clark (Oxford 1898), II, 142.

teemed with fish or glistened with pearls. Trees clad the hill-slopes and could easily be shipped away as timber. Iron-ore, lead and silver were thought to lie in the hills, and marble might be quarried. Even the inhabitants were said to be industrious if only they could be freed from the oppressive heads of their septs. In Kerry, Petty planned to enrich himself, assist the government by pacifying and improving an intractable area, and set an example to others in 'the terrible work' of planting Kerry. He would also demonstrate the utility of his scientific method by applying it to the essential tasks of colonising and improving the region.[7]

Petty's hopes of enlarging his Kerry estates depended on what the Court of Claims in Dublin decided. Two of the leading Catholic landowners displaced from those lands enjoyed the sympathy of the King and Ormonde, having soldiered with them.[8] A further complication was a claim to Kerry, dating back to the 1580s, of Ormonde himself, who was eager to uphold it and use the lands to endow his younger son.[9] Petty, aware of these interests, nervously watched the Court of Claims' deliberations, and intrigued to influence them. The question gave him an interest opposed to Ormonde's, and started a process of estrangement which would have serious results. Ormonde's influence over Irish affairs was enormous. Petty had not contented himself with working to defeat Ormonde's claim to Kerry. He aspersed Ormonde's honesty, emphasising how greatly he had profited from the land settlement, and belittled his administration. This hostility towards Ormonde showed itself in Petty first attaching himself to and then forwarding the campaign to have him removed from the Irish Lord Lieutenancy.[10] Petty succeeded in his immediate objects: Ormonde's claim over Kerry was rejected and in 1669 he was dismissed as Lord Lieutenant. But in the longer term Petty lost, for Ormonde henceforward suspected him, and while conventionally praising Petty's talents, kept him from important office or favour.

The Court of Claims in denying Ormonde's title upheld the grant of much of south Kerry to satisfy three regiments' arrears of pay. The decision was the cue for Petty to act. Previous dealings with the soldiers given Irish land had convinced him that they could not tell 'what to do with this body nor have they stock or brains to manage it'. Although they had apparently spent £12,000 proving their title in Kerry, Petty believed they were willing to sell. £36,000 would buy them out. Prosperous as he was, Petty did not command sums of such magnitude. Tantalised by the prospects just beyond his grasp, he confided: 'Lord, what might one do now with ready money in Ireland.'[11]

[7] Osler MS. 7612, letter to J. Rutter, May 1668.

[8] They were Donogh McFinin, generally regarded as reliable, and the more troublesome Col Donogh McGillicuddy. Carte MS. XXXII, f.17; XXXVI, f.565; XXXVIII, f.181&v; XLII, f.190; XLIV ff.72&v, 479; XLVIII,ff.116, 120-1; CCXIX, f.135; National Library of Ireland, Dublin, D.10,000 Petty Papers, XIX, 29 Oct. 1672; *C.S.P. Ireland, 1669-70,* 678-9.

[9] Osler MS. 7612, 16 Oct. 1666, 26 Oct. 1666, 8 Aug. 1667; Petty Papers, IX, 9 Aug. 1670; XIII 25 July 1671; Carte MS. XXXV, f.80; XL, ff.645, 647; CXLIV, f.50; CXLV, f.146&v; H.M.C. *Ormonde MSS.,* N.S., II, 173.

[10] Carte MS. XLVIII, f.221; CCXX, ff.290v, 431. On the general campaign to remove Ormonde see J. I. McGuire, 'Why was Ormonde dismissed in 1669?', *Irish Historical Studies,* XVIII (1973)

[11] Osler MS. 7612, 26 Oct. 1666, 30 March 1667.

This chance came at a particularly awkward time for Petty. He faced the loss of rents from, and the costs of rebuilding, his London houses destroyed by the Fire. His marriage had also burdened him with the debts inherited by Lady Petty from her first husband.[12] Credit facilities in Ireland were primitive and those in London apparently closed to Petty. In these circumstances his only course was to seek a partner. He chose Sir George Carteret, newly arrived in Dublin to occupy his office of Vice-Treasurer. Carteret engaged in actual and projected colonisation, both in North America and in Ireland.[13] His known interest and the possibility that he might persuade settlers from the Channel Islands (where he had been Governor) to migrate to Kerry attracted Petty to him. But above all Petty needed cash. He proposed that Carteret put up £8,000, while he contributed £4,000. Even that modest sum would overstretch Petty's resources, and he asked Carteret to lend him £2,000 or £3,000 at 10 per cent interest.[14]

To entrap Carteret, Petty presented an alluring prospectus of the intended colony. The size of the settlement would be such that 'no man in Ireland has so much lands in one spot, nor do I believe many of the sovereign princes in Italy and Germany have so much, perhaps not much more for their dominion, much less for their prosperity'. He emphasised the region's hidden or under-developed assets, and insisted that the investment would soon return £10,000 annually. Carteret was not convinced. If he entered into partnership with Petty, it was short-lived, small-scale and soon dissolved in acrimony. Petty was obliged to scale down his original, grandiose plans. In the end he spent £3,700 on 164,000 acres, as well as receiving some scattered scraps to compensate for lands elsewhere which had been restored to Catholics.[15]

Petty's stake in Kerry, although smaller than he had intended, was nevertheless impressive, and had been acquired thanks to the opportunities of the 1650s and 1660s. Unfortunately his high hopes for the lands were largely unrealised. Petty had originally intended to reside for part of the year on the estate. Instead he paid rare and fleeting visits, and relied on incompetent or dishonest subordinates. One suspects that his more considerable tenants, the Hayes, the Orpens and the Hassets, who combined leases from Petty with local or estate posts, did best from Kerry. Petty had expected to attract as tenants Englishmen and Protestants, who were 'honest, willing to take pains, skilled in their employments, have some stock and . . . do delight in improvement and good husbandry'.[16] He offered preferential terms to such

[12] Osler MS. 7612, 23 June 1667, 14 March 1667/8, 13 May 1668, letter to Lady Petty, June 1668, 23 June 1668, 28 Feb. 1670/1, 18 July 1671; P. E. Jones, *The Fire Court* (London 1970), II, 154–5.

[13] Carte MS. XXXIII, f.237&v; XLIX, f.163; K. G. Davies, *The Royal African Company* (London 1957), 62, 65&n.4; K. H. D. Haley, *The First Earl of Shaftesbury* (Oxford 1968), 186, 231&n.1, 233; D. T. Witcombe, *Charles II and the Cavalier House of Commons* (Manchester 1966), 92–3, 94, 98, 198.

[14] Osler MS. 7612, 16 Oct. 1666, 26 Oct. 1666, 30 March 1667, 9 June 1666/7, 12 Dec. 1668.

[15] Osler MS. 7612, 26 Oct. 1666, 12 Dec. 1668, 26 Aug. 1676, 10 July 1677, 10 April 1683; Petty Papers, box D, items 70 and 98; v, 14 Sept. 1681; H. W. E. Petty-Fitzmaurice, Marquess of Lansdowne (ed.), *The Petty-Southwell Correspondence* (London 1928), 75.

[16] Osler MS. 7612, 18 Feb. 1667/8, 3 March 1667/8, 9 March 1667/8, 18 April 1668, 13 May 1668, 8 June 1668 (two letters), 16 June 1668, 17 Nov. 1668.

men, but few settled there. Soon Petty had to content himself with leasing land to the existing inhabitants, regardless of their religion or the types of agriculture they practised.[17]

Petty's disappointments in Kerry arose from the terrain itself and from shifting government policy. Petty, convinced of the intrinsic worth of Kerry and having spent lavishly to realise it, only to receive a meagre return, blamed all on the government. In doing so he ignored his own chastening experience of trying to develop the region. Even before the state obstructed him, he had seen pet projects founder. He had failed to find partners or enough suitable tenants. Costly projects on which he embarked, such as iron-founding and fishing, disappointed him. If we consider the ironworks which Petty re-established near Kenmare we shall see that he was misled by the seemingly inexhaustible supplies of fuel in the form of timber. Cheap fuel was his only asset. The local ore was of low quality and had to be supplemented with the better ore from the Forest of Dean, which was costly and difficult to obtain. Skilled workmen, essential to the building and running of forge and furnace, were hard to entice to Kerry, and once there either deserted to other works or grew unruly. The iron made in Kerry was poor, lacked buyers and was unwanted locally. Petty summed up the sorry history of his iron-making when he wrote 'our iron it seems is ill-made and but little of that, and what is made is squandered away. It's made at excessive charge and sold at less rates.'[18]

The fisheries did little better than the ironworks. Fishing seemed an obvious industry to encourage. But to succeed, it required a surprising outlay. Although boats might be built cheaply in the locality, nets and other equipment had to be bought at high prices in England. Salt was essential to preserve the fish and that too had to be bought from others. Even when the necessities had been provided (and Petty never procured the proficient fishermen from elsewhere to set an example to his tenants), success depended on the unpredictable movement of the shoals, and on finding regular, accessible markets. At best Petty's fisheries were intermittently profitable, and the great expense, unsatisfactory managers and slack demand several times made him contemplate abandoning the whole venture.[19]

By 1675, Petty, having invested heavily in ironmaking and fishing and having reaped little profit, was disillusioned with Kerry. His other Irish rentals were having to subsidise operations there. He had not abandoned hopes of turning Kerry into a humming colony, and he had learnt from early mistakes how methods could be improved and rationalised. Nevertheless Petty's schemes contracted to the more orthodox activities to employ his tenants and guarantee regular payment of his rents. One result was that the destruction of the woodlands by the use of the timber for pipe and barrelstaves,

[17] Osler MS. 7612, letter to Rutter, May 1668, 16 Jan. 1672/3, 17 Oct. 1677; Bodleian, MS. Eng. Hist. C.266, f.16.

[18] For a fuller account of this venture, see T. C. Barnard, 'Sir William Petty, Kerry ironmaster', *Proceedings of the Royal Irish Academy*, forthcoming.

[19] A detailed account is in T. C. Barnard, 'Fishing in late seventeenth-century Ireland: the experience of Sir William Petty', *Journal of the Kerry Archaeological and Historical Society*, forthcoming.

a short-term expedient which he reprobated in others, was sanctioned.[20]

His failure to make the expected profits had easily identifiable explanations arising from the remoteness and backwardness of Kerry. It was, thanks to its geography, less amenable than almost all other Irish counties to the sort of rapid and spectacular development planned by Petty. Yet by 1675 Petty had another explanation for his poor showing in Kerry which distracted him from the purely economic factors.

In theory at least the English government enthusiastically backed schemes such as Petty's to strengthen the Protestant interest and to pacify and enrich the kingdom. Yet successive generations of English planters had bemoaned the frequently unhelpful behaviour of the authorities. The doubts about the security of the Restoration land settlement inevitably led Irish Protestants to accuse the regime of retarding Ireland's improvement. In practice fears that the settlement might be undermined had not stopped Protestants from behaving as if they were secure for all time. Only in the 1680s were numerous Catholics restored to their estates at the Protestants' expense. Petty himself lost portions of his lands outside Kerry to Catholics. But Petty was not too dismayed to profit from this uneasy situation by buying up more lands cheaply. An inveterate opportunist, he dropped the idea of purchasing an English estate in favour of further Irish investment.[21]

Petty's conventional worries about the government's land policies did not cause him to reduce or shed his Irish interests. There was, however, one aspect of official policy from which he suffered greatly and which, he alleged, retarded his ventures in Kerry. Petty attributed his poor return from Kerry and his retreat from his grand plans to the quit-rents assessed on the lands.

Quit-rents were the rents paid to the crown for the lands granted in the 1660s. Numerous landowners complained that the rents were unrealistically high, sometimes exceeding the lands' annual value. Twice commissioners were empowered to reduce the quit-rents, and the King, the English and Irish councils and the law courts also authorised reductions for Protestant and Catholic proprietors. In Petty's case the quit-rents on the Kerry estates had not only been set too high – at over £1,600 annually – but also based on clerical error. Petty's quit-rents had been calculated on the total acreage and not, as was customary, according to the 'reduced column' of the total profitable acreage, because the columns in the official survey of Kerry had been wrongly labelled.[22]

[20] Osler MS, 7612, 18 Feb. 1667/8; Petty Papers, XVI, 23 May 1674; L. Sharp, 'Timber, science and economic reform in the seventeenth century', Forestry, XLVIII (1975), 69-71.

[21] Petty Papers, V, 4 Dec. 1683, XVII, 18 March 1685/6, 26 June 1686, 3 Aug. 1686, 21 Aug. 1686; XVIII, 15 Jan. 1686/7, 22 Jan. 1686/7, 21 May 1687, 2 July 1687; Petty-Southwell Correspondence, 258, 269; W. J. Smith (ed.), Herbert Correspondence (Cardiff and Dublin 1965), 293.

[22] Much material connected with this controversy is scattered through Petty's papers, the state papers and the surviving records of Ormonde and Essex. Comprehensive statements of the issues and episodes occur in Petty's anonymous and hitherto unattributed tract, The case of the Kerry quit-rent 1681 (n.p., n.d.), and Bodleian, Rawlinson MS. C.439, ff.298-301v; Carte MS. LIV, f.43; LX, ff.602-4; CCXVIII, f.503&v; British Library (hereafter B.L.). Add. MS. 28085, ff.72-73v; Petty Papers, box D, items 1, 69, 79; C.S.P. Domestic, 1676-7, 84-5, 404-6, 499-500.

Petty, the unrivalled master of Irish surveying, was incensed at falling victim to the careless mistake of a clerk recording the results of the survey he himself had supervised. He sought redress through the obvious channels – the commissioners appointed for that purpose, the Irish Viceroy and his Council, the law courts, the Privy Council and the King – and yet received no satisfaction. More than once the Irish Lord Lieutenant and the Irish law officers recommended a dramatic reduction.[23] But Petty was not allowed the benefit of these decisions, and instead faced an alarming bill for arrears of quit-rent. For the period between 1660 and 1668 alone, before he was possessed of the Kerry lands, £20,000 was demanded.

The authorities agreed that so long as the matter was unresolved, English plantation would be hindered. The case seemed clear-cut, the mechanisms for settling it existed and many others in a similar condition had been relieved, so that Petty's failure to receive justice requires explanation. A part of the answer is the haphazard and ill-defined procedures for making decisions in Irish cases. The jurisdiction of the Irish courts over estate and fiscal matters was blurred, and as a result suits might be interrupted by executive action or transferred to England. The decisions of the Dublin government were frequently overturned in England where, in addition, the Privy Council and the Treasury could be bypassed by the King. In the end access to court and royal favour counted for more than a just cause, and Petty lacked that favour.

Another complication was that matters connected with the Irish revenue had become politically sensitive. Charles II hoped that Ireland, after decades of being subsidised by England, would not only pay its own way but supplement the English revenue. He was encouraged in this hope by the powerful syndi- cates of Anglo-Irish politicians and merchants who competed to farm the Irish revenues. Thanks to their useful financial services and their highly-placed connections in England and Ireland, the revenue farmers were formidable opponents. Petty, alas, incurred their enmity. In 1675 he had at first been included among the new farmers, only to be dropped mysteriously from the contract. Immediately Petty railed against the trickery of the successful farmers, and again in 1682, when a new farm was in the offing, he proposed schemes of his own and disparaged his rivals. Also, of course, the farmers wanted to keep the King's Irish revenues at as high a rate as possible, and therefore opposed any suggestion of reducing what was legally owed. Successive farmers defaulted in their payments to the King, leaving office with large arrears unpaid. Since the farmers might well have to find large sums to pay off those debts, they would not willingly forego what Petty owed. Thus, behind the many refusals to abate Petty's rents, we see the hand of the revenue farmers. Petty lacked the court influence to defeat that well-organised gang.[24]

---

[23] Attorney-General Domville's favourable report of 1682 is in Carte MS. LX, ff.621-32. It provoked a dissenting opinion from Solicitor-General Temple, in Rawlinson MS. C. 439, f.301v. See also: *C.S.P. Domestic, 1679-80*, 415; Osler MS. 7612, 21 April 1683, 23 June 1683; Petty Papers, box D, item 79.

[24] Petty Papers, V, 8 May 1680; VI, series II, 24 June 1675; XIX, 23 Oct. 1675; B.L., Stowe MS. CCVI, f.153; Carte MS. XXXIX, f.547; LII, ff.566-7; LIV, ff.197, 242&v; LXX, f.556v; CLXVIII, f.131; CCXVIII, ff.503&v; CCXXXII, f.63; H.M.C., *Ormonde MSS.*, N.S., VI, 367, 411; VII, 150, 162, 174;

Petty's apparent powerlessness at court in this affair contrasts with his high standing there immediately after 1660. The trouble was that his relationships with those in authority, even when they admired his talents, were prickly and ambivalent. His dealings with Ormonde and Essex, the Irish viceroys during much of this period and as such well-placed to assist him, illustrate this. These men, struggling to rule Ireland, wearied of the ambitious projects with which Petty bombarded them, whether for a statistical survey of national resources, the founding of banks or the rebuilding of Dublin Castle. Ormonde, so bewildered by experimental science 'that it is all the most clear demonstrations can do to make me comprehend the necessary consequences and effects of a windmill', was bored by Petty's loquacity. The idea that Petty be added to the Irish council in 1679 was vetoed by Ormonde because 'he will make so many objections and propose so many motions that much of our time will be lost in them'. Ormonde publicly praised Petty's abilities, but privately regarded him as a tedious projector, unsound in religion, a competitor for his Kerry lands and a political opponent who had undermined his standing in London.[25] Civilities were observed, but the two men eyed each other with suspicion. Gifts of venison could not stop Petty cataloguing how Ormonde had profited since the Restoration, and, after dancing attendance at Kilkenny Castle in the futile hope of favours, Petty complained, 'I can't say that I believe the Ormonde family to be our friends beyond fair and civil words, nor do we think they have done for us what we deserved from them.'[26]

Essex, Lord Lieutenant between 1672 and 1677, though closer in politics to Petty and an admirer of Petty's writings, was also alive to his faults. He declared 'that in all His Majesty's three kingdoms there lives not a more grating man than Sir William Petty'. Essex thought that justice required an abatement of Petty's quit-rents, but lacked the control over Irish affairs to enforce such a decision.[27]

Petty's dealings with English politicians whose aid he sought are more obscure. His friends seem generally to have been among the second-rank administrators like Robert Southwell, Joseph Williamson and Samuel Pepys. His omission from the revenue farm in 1675 he attributed to the hostility of the English Lord Chancellor, Heneage Finch.[28] We can also see how the

Petty-Southwell Correspondence, 100; Aubrey, *Brief Lives*, II, 144; *C.S.P. Domestic, 1675-6*, 442; *C.S.P. Domestic, Addenda 1660-85*, 454; *Calendar of Treasury Books*, V, 27. Some implications of the revenue farm are discussed in M. Twomey, 'Charles II, Lord Ranelagh and the Irish finances', *Bulletin of the Irish Committee for Historical Sciences*, LXXXIX (1960), but we must await a new study by Mr Sean Egan of Trinity College Dublin for a full elucidation.

[25] H.M.C., *Ormonde MSS.*, II, 286; N.S., IV, 377, 506, 527; V, 332, 336; Carte MS. CXLIII, f.154.

[26] H.M.C., *Ormonde MSS.*, II, 265, 306; Petty Papers, V, 12 March 1681/2, 10 Sept. 1681, 25 March 1682, 11 April 1682; VII, 23 May 1676; B.L., Add. MS. 21,484, f.64v; *Petty-Southwell Correspondence*, 73, 77, 317, 327.

[27] Petty Papers, box D, item 79; V, 5 June 1675; XIV, 10 Jan. 1673/4; XIX, 3 Nov. 1674; Osler MS. 7612, 13 Jan. 1676/7, 28 Aug. 1677, 18 Sept. 1677, 6 Oct. 1677, 20 Nov. 1677; Carte MS. XXXVIII, f.579; *Petty-Southwell Correspondence*, 33-4; O. Airy (ed.), *Essex Papers, I, 1672-79*, Camden Society (1890), 83; J. C. Beckett, 'The Irish viceroyalty in the restoration period', in Beckett's *Confrontations: Studies in Irish History* (London 1972), 75-80.

[28] Osler MS. 7612, 28 Aug. 1677; Aubrey, *Brief Lives*, II, 144.

King's enjoyment of his company waned, and how Charles derided him for weighing air and scoffed at his double-hulled boat which sank. Perhaps Petty's poor standing in the English court was best indicated by his failure to secure an office appropriate to his talents. His hopes of useful employment actually rose at James II's accession, for he had already benefited from the new King's favour when James had been Duke of York. James's eagerness to adopt an apparently tolerant and broadly-based policy, coupled with his willingness to listen to Petty's schemes for Ireland, endeared him to Petty. In addition Petty knew that the best hope of ending the dispute over the Kerry quit-rents was in the King's exercise of the prerogative on his behalf.[29] All too soon Petty was disillusioned when the King acted only to reinstate Catholics and ignored his quit-rents. Petty then joined other Protestants in criticising royal policy in Ireland.

Petty's failure to secure remission of his quit-rents revealed the feebleness of his support in high places. Denied what he regarded as his rightful place in the Irish council, revenue farm and the bureaucracy, he grew bitter and started to believe that his want of favour alone prevented him from profiting from his extensive Irish estates. The quit-rents obsessed him, and he deployed his great powers to plead for justice in the affair. The trouble was that his combative instincts were aroused, so that venom, spite and ridicule undermined his more reasoned arguments. Those whom he regarded as the authors of his misfortunes retaliated and protected themselves by permanently denying Petty office, influence and redress. Friends begged Petty to prefer diplomacy, but in vain.[30]

Petty justified his absorption in the battle by insisting that until the matter was settled he could not safely continue investing in Kerry. He contended that the revenue farmers' actions after 1675 had obliged him to halt his more costly enterprises, notably the iron manufacture. He alleged that the revenue farmers had entered the land and distrained for arrears in 1676, that they had had him briefly imprisoned for debt and had then granted parts of the Kerry estates to the former Catholic owners. Petty exaggerated the disruption caused by the revenue farmers, for he regained most of the lands when he was granted a custodium over them in 1678. Furthermore he paid neither the annual quit-rents nor the enormous arrears. Nevertheless he had been discouraged, and he feared that his title to Kerry might be revoked if the final decision over the quit-rents went against him.

Other vicissitudes had already persuaded Petty to limit his activities in Kerry before the revenue farmers harrassed him. Yet, though both iron-making and fishing had brought poor returns, Petty believed that reforms would improve the situation. After analysing the accounts of the ironworks in 1675, he identified the problems there as mainly managerial, and ordered rational new procedures to be adopted. With the right method it was worth persevering. Furthermore the experience of other Irish ironfounders was encouraging. Lord Cork and the partners in the contemporary project at

[29] Petty Papers, box D, item 72, p.14; *Petty-Southwell Correspondence*, 213, 233, 283.
[30] Osler MS. 7612, 21 Jan. 1667/8; *Petty-Southwell Correspondence*, 34–5, 108.

Enniscorthy in County Wexford had profited only after overcoming early difficulties very similar to Petty's. But in any case iron-making was the easiest way to benefit from his chief asset, the thick woodlands, and the work of felling and preparing timber usefully added to his tenants' incomes.[31]

The case of the fisheries was similar. Once Petty rid himself of crooked managers and had bought the boats and nets, it was sensible to continue fishing the waters. Obviously profits depended on the presence of fish, but Petty also appreciated the importance of this activity to the economy of many of his parishes. Without seasonal employment in fishing, in curing and packing the catches and in mending the equipment, his tenants would be hard put to pay their rents regularly. Quite deliberately Petty decided to persist in activities from which the direct profit was uncertain, but which indirectly assisted his tenants and in that way benefited his rentals.[32]

Thus by 1675 Petty was prepared to ignore the lessons from his disheartening experience and, more modestly than before, to develop Kerry. He believed that the uncertainty generated by the quit-rents and the revenue farmers' intervention distracted him and prevented him discovering whether his rationalised methods would have improved his colony. Accordingly he staked all on settling the matter as the precondition of the successful implementation of his policies, and retained his belief that if only he could have undisputed possession, have the quit-rents reduced and the arrears cancelled, a flourishing plantation would be created. His will of 1685 testified both to how little had so far been achieved and to Petty's unquenchable confidence. He vowed to devote the remainder of his life to developing the lands, especially by promoting 'the trade of iron, lead, marble, fish and timber, whereof my estate is capable'. Decades of his ownership had so far made little impact, but the potential was there if only it could be realised.[33] It was left to Petty's heirs to appreciate the natural difficulties in the way of success, and to abandon direct supervision of the estates to others.[34]

Petty may have magnified the villainy of the revenue farmers, and underestimated the primitiveness of his lands. But undeniably his income from Kerry was far less than he had expected – at most £1,100, instead of £10,000 – and than contemporaries believed he enjoyed. Popular imagination had been caught by the size of Petty's Kerry estate and his passionate defence of it. The rents from his relatively untroubled and already well-developed and populous lands in the east of Ireland were the corner-stone of his fortune and enabled him to invest heavily in Kerry. Yet for all his reverses in Kerry, he was a rich man who had taken spectacular advantage of the chances afforded by Ireland. He himself admitted to his wife in 1679, 'we are almost as rich as the envious

[31] Barnard, 'Sir William Petty, Kerry ironmaster'.

[32] Barnard, 'Fisheries in late seventeenth-century Ireland'.

[33] Fitzmaurice, *Petty*, 324.

[34] For the later history of the estate: Petty Papers, XVIII, 9 March 1696/7; H. W. E. Petty-Fitzmaurice, Marquess of Lansdowne, *Glanerought and the Petty-Fitzmaurices* (Oxford 1937), ch.5; G. J. Lyne, 'Land tenure in Kenmare and Tuoist, 1696–*c*.1716', *Journal of the Kerry Archaeological and Historical Society*, X (1977).

say we are', adding the vital qualification: 'but are kept out of it by much oppression and some fraud'.[35]

From the foregoing account the place of Ireland in Petty's rise appears obvious. However if we look more closely, we shall find the role of Ireland differed from that which Petty had intended. The career he aimed at was that not of an Irish landowner, constantly preoccupied with his estates, but of an office-holder and scientific innovator in England. He had welcomed the chance to advance his career by accepting government employment in Ireland in 1652, but had seen Irish service as an interlude before he would return to better things in England. He was pleased to have established a sound financial base in Ireland in the 1650s, and intended to use it to launch his public career in England. Such a career seemed within his grasp in 1660, when the new King feted him and smiled on his schemes of technological renovation and experiment. Quickly his plans went awry. The atmosphere in Restoration England was less congenial than he had supposed. The Royal Society failed to bring utilitarian and humanitarian benefits.[36] His own career entered the doldrums. Accustomed to the confidence of Ireland's rulers in the 1650s, he now chafed at being on the edges of influence. Intelligent men still relished his company. Aubrey, for example, admired him as 'an excellent droll' able to 'preach *extempore* incomparably, either the Presbyterian way, Independent, Capuchin friar or Jesuit'.[37] But the dullards who dominated the English and Irish councils suspected his past politics and present scepticism, and were bored by his arrogance, intemperance and endless projects.

Petty's failure to secure public office, for which he angled, both obliged and allowed him to concentrate on Irish affairs, for £4,800 of his annual income of £6,700 was expected to come thence. While the settlement was being hammered out, as we have seen, Petty acted as other Protestants, dividing his time between London and Dublin. Once the Kerry estate was his, Petty thought after a short period of personal oversight he would be able to leave its management to subordinates and to live the life of a rich absentee in England. As early as 1668 he realised his mistake when he protested that 'our estates here [in Ireland] are mere visions and delusions and require more attendance than a retail shop'. He was soon convinced that an Irish estate 'cannot subsist without the owner's daily presence and inspection'. Once the success of the Kerry venture hinged on sorting out the quit-rents, Petty went wherever he thought a decision could be obtained, and fitted his other work, including his writing and experiments, around that. Bit by bit, and much against his will, Petty had been sucked into Irish affairs, so that his estates there were no longer the hidden spring of his fortune but his consuming interest.[38]

---

[35] Petty Papers, V, 18 June 1675, 11 Aug. 1679, 19 Oct. 1681; box D, item 69; XIX, 26 June 1675; Osler MS. 7612, 10 Dec. 1671, 27 March 1677, 20 Nov. 1677; *Petty-Southwell Correspondence*, 58.

[36] M. I'Espinasse, 'The decline and fall of Restoration science', *Past and Present*, XIV (1958); M. Hunter, 'The social basis and changing fortunes of an early scientific institution: an analysis of the membership of the Royal Society, 1660-1685', *Notes and Records of the Royal Society of London*, XXXI (1976); Sharp, 'Sir William Petty', 255-73.

[37] Aubrey, *Brief Lives*, II, 143; *Petty-Southwell Correspondence*, 186.

[38] Osler MS. 7612, 30 June 1668, 21 July 1668, 15 Jan. 1669/70; Petty Papers, V, 18 June 1672, 30 July 1672, 26 July 1679, 22 May 1680, 23 Feb. 1683/4, 19 April 1684, 27 May 1684, 16 May 1685; XIX, 1 Aug. 1674.

Petty's tribulations, connected both with the remoteness and character of Kerry and with his own controversial reputation, were probably unique in Restoration Ireland. Yet some problems he shared with most substantial Irish Protestant landowners. They too posted constantly between Dublin and London, in order to shape and then preserve the general settlement, and to protect individual interests. Like Petty, these other proprietors, though fearful that their lands might be lost to Catholics, went ahead and stocked and settled them. They may also have encountered the same difficulties as Petty over the question how freely Irish profits could be spent.

As Petty intended to pass more time in London than in Dublin and yet relied more on Ireland than England for revenue, he needed to remit his Irish rents into England. This was not easily done. The obvious method was to use bills of exchange. In those Irish ports, mainly on the eastern and southern seaboard, with a regular English trade, such bills were easy to come by. However the premium was high and could fluctuate wildly with the season, the state of the harvest and the hazards to shipping from warfare and piracy. Often the exchange rate rose to 10 per cent. Sometimes it was cheaper to send money from Cork than from Dublin; occasionally no bills were to be had. For Petty the basic problem was worsened by the inaccessibility of Kerry and its meagre trade with other parts of Ireland. He had in fact to pay exchange on money remitted from Kerry to Dublin.[39]

These difficulties may have influenced Petty in two ways. His eagerness that fishing and iron-making continue, notwithstanding early losses, arose in part because of an incidental benefit. If English merchants could be persuaded to buy his goods in Kerry (and Petty devoted great efforts to trying to establish such a trade), he could then be paid in cash in London, as Lord Cork had been before him.[40] In the event English traders were not interested, and Petty was denied the cash payments. Forced to depend on costly or unreliable bills of exchange, Petty may have chosen to spend more time in Ireland in order to consume his income. Certainly he was unable to become an office-holding absentee as he had originally intended.

Some light is cast on Petty's own ambitions by the injunctions for his children's futures contained in his will. He instructed his elder son to buy an English estate and to invest in an English office. He wanted his younger son to live in Ireland and manage the estates there. For his daughter he proposed an Irish match. England was where Petty wanted his heir to flourish, but the Irish foundation of the family fortune could not be neglected. He recognised the vital ties of the Pettys with both England and Ireland, and advised them to go on sailing in 'a double bottom'.[41]

Petty himself had neither obtained valuable office nor set up as an English landed gentleman. The first failure was not his own fault. The decision not to buy an English estate is more curious. A friend enquired of Petty in 1687, 'if it

---

[39] Osler MS. 7612, 17 Oct. 1676 (two letters), 13 Jan. 1676/7, 13 Feb. 1676/7, 6 Oct. 1677; Petty Papers, v, 25 March 1682.
[40] Barnard, 'Sir William Petty, Kerry ironmaster'.
[41] Petty Papers, v, 4 Oct. 1681; Fitzmaurice, *Sir William Petty*, 324.

is true, as the world reports, that you are a great moneyed man, why have you lost all this time to vest it in good land?' In the last decade of his life Petty seemed about to remedy the omission by negotiating successively to buy two west-country estates. Like Ormonde, Orrery and Southwell, he regarded the west country as most convenient as he would have still to divide his time between England and Ireland. Petty contemplated spending £6,000. Ultimately he viewed the purchase as an investment and not as a means of buying social prestige. (Indeed he claimed that he had refused a peerage because he was reluctant to have to live at an appropriately high rate.) In the end he did not buy the estates because he felt he would receive a better return on his money in Ireland, though he may also have had trouble in raising the required cash and transferring it from Ireland to England.[42] As a result Petty ended his days in rented houses in Dublin and London. Although he owned buildings, nowhere was there one in which he and his wife were prepared to reside.

Petty carefully calculated how best to use his money. He concluded that the acquisition of office was to be preferred, and he recommended that course to his heir. In doing so, he was influenced by his own disappointments and by close observation of the career of his great friend Sir Robert Southwell. Southwell, sharing Petty's Anglo-Irish background and scientific tastes, achieved what eluded Petty, lucrative office in England. Southwell's father had used the income from the family's extensive estates around Kinsale in County Cork to start his son on a successful bureaucratic and diplomatic career. At several times Southwell consulted Petty about his plans. In 1663, after continental travels, Southwell weighed the rival attractions of service in England and Ireland. He could see no post in Lord Lieutenant Ormonde's gift 'agreeing with the method of my education'. While he thought his foreign experiences would assist him in England, they would be regarded as irrelevant in Ireland. Furthermore Southwell predicted that if he won fame in England, it would follow automatically in Ireland. Later Petty cited Southwell's example when he argued that the purchase of an office was the best way to provide for a son. Petty alleged that the outlay of £5,000 by Southwell's father had brought Southwell posts worth £1,000 annually. When later taxed by Southwell with not having bought an English estate, Petty answered that office was the better investment.[43] Southwell's was the example which Petty wished his son to emulate. We know too little of the Southwells' financial affairs to decide whether or not Petty was right to suppose the two families' cases were comparable. Southwell had certain obvious advantages. He was well-liked by those in power – he managed, for example, to retain the confidence of both Petty and Ormonde – and did not obtrude his own views. Office usefully supplemented his income from the hereditary Irish estates. Those lands were in any case situated in a well-settled and prosperous part of the island, and it was easier to remit money from them into England via

[42] Osler MS. 7612, 20 Nov. 1677, 27 April 1680; Petty Papers, v, 11 Aug. 1679, 16 Aug. 1681, 14 Sept. 1681, 24 Sept. 1681, 27 Sept. 1681, 4 Oct. 1681, 24 Dec. 1681, 18 Feb. 1681/2, 28 Feb. 1681/2, 25 March 1682, 7 May 1682, 5 June 1682; vii, 26 Sept. 1687, 28 Sept. 1687; *Petty-Southwell Correspondence*, 289, 296-7.

[43] Petty Papers, ix, f.7; xix, 19 Jan. 1674/5; *Petty-Southwell Correspondence*, 296-7.

Bristol or Minehead than to send it from Kerry to London. Southwell's success was crowned when he bought the King's Weston estate near Bristol, where his son would commission Vanbrugh to design a new seat.

The account of Petty offered here may seem perversely one-sided. Petty, while struggling to manage his Irish lands, wrote prolifically and with originality, experimented and participated in the intellectual life of London and Dublin. *Virtuosi* still revered him. His Irish revenues enabled him to buy costly equipment and persevere in elaborate experiments, notably those to prove the sea-worthiness of a double-bottomed boat. Yet his hopes of making the running of the Kerry colony central to his scientific interests by applying and perfecting techniques there and by garnering information came to little.[44]

For all his expertise and self-advertisement, Petty fared worse as a colonist than men with more modest and orthodox aims and methods. In Kerry itself the Herbert estates, until beset by the prevalent uncertainty of the 1680s, prospered modestly, though radical improvements were few. Those lands had the advantage of long ownership in one family, so that efforts to settle them dated back nearly a century. A newer plantation in Kerry, undertaken by Sir Francis Brewster, seems to have attracted more settlers than Petty's. Brewster, an entrepreneur reminiscent of Petty in some of his interests, utilised his widespread commercial contacts in Dublin and London.[45] The contrast between Petty's projects and those of his neighbours was not absolute, but before the 1680s Petty appeared to have unique ambitions and tribulations.

Enmeshed in a net of lawsuits, petitions and applications, Petty loosened his scientific ties with London and postponed his grander schemes. Addicted to applying the principle of reason, and insistent on preferring experience to received authority, he seemed eccentric to cling to his troublesome Kerry estates. He did so because he believed that the setbacks could be explained rationally, and that once the region was rigorously and systematically managed and exploited it would respond as he had predicted. Approaching the district with fixed preconceptions, he could not accept that the allegedly idle life of the Kerryman, traditionally centred on stock-raising, fitted the area's conditions better than the activities on which he lavished money. If Petty died a rich man in 1687 it was despite and not because of his enormous holdings in Kerry. He also went to his grave a disappointed man, for Ireland had not answered his expectations.

[44] T. C. Barnard, 'Sir William Petty, his Kerry estates and Irish population', *Irish Economic and Social History*, VI (1979), 64-7; Charles Webster, *The Great Instauration* (London 1975), 441-6; Sharp, 'Sir William Petty', 210-12, 299, 348-51.
[45] National Library of Ireland, MS. 7861; *Herbert Correspondence*, passim; P. O'Connor, 'The seignory of Castleisland in the seventeenth century', *Journal of the Kerry Archaeological and Historical Society*, III (1970); Carte MS. CCXVII, ff.148-9; F. Brewster, *Essays on Trade and Navigation in Five Parts* (London 1695), 11-20, 116. Also there are numerous passing references to Brewster's colony in Petty's papers.

16

Voltaire and the Enlightenment Image of Newton

P. M. Rattansi

While the publication of the *Principia Mathematica* in 1687 secured almost universal admiration for the scientific and mathematical genius of Sir Isaac Newton, his contemporaries differed widely in their assessments of what he had achieved in his masterpiece. Edmond Halley placed Newton's genius nearest to the gods in the ode he prefixed to that work. One of Newton's greatest scientific contemporaries, Christian Huygens, was astonished, however, that Newton should have chosen to rear his magnificent structure on such a 'manifest absurdity' as the idea of an universal attraction.[1] Leibniz was to accuse Newton of having turned all the operations of nature into a perpetual miracle.[2] Brought up on Cartesian rationalism, Huygens and Leibniz saw in the acceptance of 'unintelligible' attraction a reversion to the 'occult' qualities of the despised scholastics and an abandonment of that luminous clarity the Cartesian revolution had brought into physical thought. It was the combination of 'rational' (a rigorous mathematical-mechanical method) and 'irrational' (the use of a notion of force not reducible to mechanical impact) that they found dismaying and disconcerting in Newton. The first review of the *Principia* in the *Journal des Savants* set the tone for the dominant continental response. The reviewer recognised that Newton had laid claim to the creation of a new 'system of the world'. What he had created, in fact, was a system of mechanics, more perfect than anyone could have dared to imagine, but based on assumptions that were arbitrary and unprovable. Newton wrote as a geometer, not as a physicist. Only when he substituted true motions in place of the ones he had imagined would he succeed in founding a new physics.[3]

Nearly half a century was to pass before Newton found worthy champions in the land of Descartes. Recalling that time, the physicist Maupertuis wrote of the timidity, fear and caution with which, in his earliest work of 1732, he had pleaded with his countrymen not to dismiss Newton's concept of

---

[1] Huygens, *Oeuvres Complètes* (The Hague 1888-1950), IX, 538.
[2] H. G. Alexander (ed.), *The Leibniz-Clarke Correspondence* (Manchester 1956), 11-12.
[3] *Journal* (1688), cited in P. Mouy, *La Devéloppement de la Physique Cartésienne* (Paris 1934), 256.

'attraction' out of hand. According to Maupertuis, the notion remained almost wholly confined to its island home. If it ever chanced to cross the Channel, it was feared as a monstrous apparition. So charmed were those on the Continent with having given a semblance of the mechanical to their explanations of nature, 'that they rejected without hearing true mechanism when it offered itself'.[4] But Maupertuis was not alone. He was soon joined by a populariser of genius, Voltaire. Once he had been reassured by Maupertuis of the scientific worth of Newton's work, Voltaire used all his propagandist skills to familiarise an educated public with Newton's ideas and to persuade it to adopt them. He succeeded in achieving Newton's apotheosis as the founding father of a new age of reason.

Long familiarity has dulled the surprise we ought to feel at Voltaire's taking it upon himself to dethrone Descartes and install Newton as a pioneer of the Enlightenment. To have made the Cartesian mode of explaining nature appear no more than 'a semblance of mechanism', while conferring the status of *la méchanisme veritable* on a system based on attraction, was no mean achievement. Why did that cause enlist Voltaire's passionate interest and how did he help to carry it to victory? Those questions deserve a serious answer since it is Descartes who, at first glance, would seem to be a much more fitting symbol for an age of reason.

Descartes had supplied a philosophical basis for the ancient dream that the lucidity and rigour which seemed uniquely characteristic of mathematical reasoning could be extended to all human knowledge. Aristotle had traced the power of mathematical demonstration to the patterns of reasoning it employed. By formalising it in his logic, he believed he had laid the way open for the attainment of a comparable degree of certainty in other fields of knowledge. For Aristotle such an enterprise by no means demanded that the richness of the sensible world be reduced to the pale abstractions of mathematics, as Plato had attempted in his *Timaeus*. By the sixteenth century, the scholastic–Aristotelian edifice of knowledge aroused in some innovators the same revulsion as the Gothic cathedral. They reverted to the classical ideal of mathematical harmony as articulated by Pythagoreans and Platonists. That ideal inspired and provided the justification for Copernicus' overthrow of ancient cosmology and substitution of a more 'harmonious' system of the world. The appeal of his reform remained largely confined to those who, like Kepler and Galileo, accepted the mathematical ideal. It was Descartes who grasped that their piecemeal attempts to amend the old structure were futile.

In his *Discourse* (1637), Descartes had compared received knowledge to a ruined building, now beyond repair. It must be razed to the ground. A new one was to rise in its place, on new foundations and according to the design of a single architect, Descartes himself. It was to be a classical edifice, not the Gothic monstrosity with which his teachers had familiarised him at La Flèche. Mathematics was again to supply the supreme model for all human knowledge. By accepting that ideal, Descartes was rejecting Aristotle's view of the power and fascination of mathematics.

[4] Cited by P. Brunet, *L'Introduction des Théories de Newton en France au XVIIᵉ siècle* (Paris 1931), 9.

For Aristotle the conviction carried by mathematical demonstration lay in the patterns of reasoning it embodied, not in its use of such specifically mathematical concepts as points, lines, surfaces and solids. Each science had its own appropriate basic concepts and entities, and in each it was possible to arrive at secure knowledge by valid reasoning. The immobile and insensible served the science of the immobile and insensible, that is, of mathematics. It would be quite inappropriate to build up a science of the changing and the sensible realm of physics by using Plato's geometrical atoms. Aristotle's four elements, themselves sensible and changeable, could explain changes in that realm far more adequately.[5]

Descartes insisted that the power of mathematics resided in its indubitable starting-points. Nothing short of the certainty available in arithmetic and geometry was to be aimed at in all human knowledge. That could be attained only by confining attention to questions of order and measure. Our ideas would then carry the hallmarks of truth: clarity and distinctness. Sense-experience was delusive and confused, and sensed qualities were utterly dependent on the more basic mathematical features of matter as it impinged on the senses. The simplest basic concepts for physics were matter and motion.

Voltaire did not deny Descartes' importance as a destroyer of old ideas. He had given sight to the blind.[6] But he had expelled ancient reveries only to introduce novel chimeras.[7] 'A man who disdained experience, never cited Galileo, and ventured to construct without materials, could not but erect an imaginary edifice.'[8] Descartes' system had turned for Voltaire into 'an enchanted castle'.[9] Descartes had achieved results quite contrary to those he had intended because, although one of the greatest geometers of his age, he had soon abandoned geometry and the 'geometric spirit' for the *esprit de système*. His philosophy was an ingenious romance, his physics a tissue of errors. Galileo was greater than Descartes, since he had not tried to create an imaginary universe, but was content to examine that which existed.[10]

Voltaire recognised in Descartes the pioneer of the conception that the *esprit géométrique* need not remain confined to mathematical sciences but could be exended to all knowledge. He had blazed the trail for the *philosophes* by addressing his reform not to the academies but to the educated layman. One of Descartes' early works affirmed that his interest did not lie in 'scholastic type' distinctions but in devising rules to serve the contingencies of decision in everyday life.[11] He had not embellished his work with the names of past thinkers, and he emphasised the distinction between erudition and the search for truth. He thought those who were best acquainted with the thinkers of the past were likely to be most infected with their errors and least

[5] A. Mansion, *Introduction à la Physique Aristotelienne* (Louvain-Paris 1945), 134–8.
[6] 'Lettres philosophiques', in *Oeuvres Complètes* (Paris 1879), XXII, 132.
[7] Letter to Comte des Alleurs, 1736, in ibid., XXXV, 51.
[8] 'Siècle de Louis XIV', in ibid., XIV, 534.
[9] Ibid., XXXV, 51.
[10] Ibid., XXXV, 52.
[11] Descartes, *Philosophical Works*, tr. Haldane & Ross (Cambridge 1931), 'Regulae', I, 2.

fitted to receive his novel ideas.[12]

According to Voltaire Newton was superior to Descartes because his discoveries had been made by experience and then confirmed by geometry. In his early 'Philosophical Letters' (1734), Voltaire attempted a lengthy Plutarchian comparison of the two thinkers. He portrayed a Newton who had quickly detected the falsity of the vortices which Descartes had imagined to explain the motion of the planets round the sun and gravitation on the earth. Newton had exploded the notion of such vortices, to his own satisfaction, by rigorous calculation – that guide which had ceased to keep in check the extravagancies of Descartes' lively imagination. Newton had then despaired of any other way of explaining those phenomena. The sight of a falling apple in the solitude of a garden during the Plague year of 1666 had plunged him into a profound meditation, carefully guided by mathematical reasoning. How scrupulous Newton was in not mistaking conjecture for truth was shown by the fact that he rejected the results of those meditations because they did not accord with the faulty measure of the earth then available. Only the revision of that measure prompted him to take up his former calculations again.

Newton's approach, so different from Descartes', was equally evident in his optics, where he had 'anatomised' a single ray of light with more dexterity than the most skilled dissector of a human body. By 'the bare assistance of a prism'[13] he had demonstrated that light consisted of a mixture of coloured rays. Descartes had gained immortal fame by mathematically explaining the rainbow, but had then committed himself to a fundamentally erroneous conception of the nature of light.

Voltaire was aware that his comparison would shock his countrymen. They had recognised numerous defects in Descartes' philosophical and scientific ideas. They believed those defects could be remedied. Certainly, they were not generally disposed to replace them with Newton's doctrines. Voltaire dated the beginnings of the decline of the 'Chimerical philosophy' of Descartes in France to 1730.[14] His own conversion to Newton's doctrines had begun during his self-imposed exile in England after his second confinement in the Bastille. The fruits of his sojourn were the *Lettres philosophiques* (1734), four of which were devoted to Newton. Voltaire depicted a land where the spirit of toleration, reason and good sense prevailed in every sphere of life. He believed that the same spirit of sanity and modesty was evident in the greatest of English thinkers: Bacon, Locke and Newton.

Voltaire said he had found nothing in English thought comparable to the corroding scepticism of Montaigne, La Rochefoucauld's biting satires on human nature, Pascal's tragic pessimism, Malebranche's 'sublime illusions', or the deeply flawed teaching of Descartes. Instead, the English had given the world Bacon's experimental philosophy, Locke's anatomy of the human mind and Newton's great system of the world. In the four letters on Newton,

[12] 'Principia philosophiae', in ibid., I, 209.
[13] Letter XVI, in *Oeuvres Complètes*, XXII, 141.
[14] 'Ecrivains français du siècle de Louis XIV', in ibid., XIV, 63.

Voltaire described his optical discoveries, explained his ideas of gravitational attraction, assigned to Newton priority in the discovery of the infinitesimal calculus, and had praise even for his Biblical chronology.

The thorniest part of Voltaire's endeavour was the defence of Newtonian attraction. It was precisely in the name of reason that continental thinkers had denounced it. They complained that when Newton and his followers were asked to explain how parts of matter could act on other parts without any material intermediary, they resorted to obscure ideas which involved a continuous divine intervention. 'In the time of Mr. Boyle, nobody would have ventured to publish such chimerical notions,' Leibniz complained to Samuel Clarke in 1716. 'But it is men's misfortune to grow, at last, out of conceit with reason itself, and to be weary of light . . . What has happened in poetry, happens also in the philosophical world. People are grown weary of rational romances . . . and they are become fond again of tales of fairies.'[15]

Voltaire defended Newton against the charge of reviving 'occult' qualities by using arguments that implied a revision of the notion of what constituted a rational explanation. The man who had first traced the ascent of water in a force pump to the pressure of the atmosphere, or of the movement of the arm to muscular contraction, had discovered something new and useful, even if the causes of the elasticity of the air or muscular contraction remained unknown. Newton had shown that the reason why heavy bodies fell towards earth and the planets were retained in their orbits around the sun was a gravitational attraction, and that no subtle matter nor any other force could possibly be involved. It was not necessary for him to have furnished 'the cause of this cause', one of the secrets of God. Voltaire hinted that those who were dissatisfied with Newton's explanations demanded that a rational explanation must be anchored not only in a systematic, but in a *complete* account of nature, and were falling prey, like Descartes, to the *esprit de système*.[16]

One unexpected feature of the *Elémens* is the extent to which Voltaire commended the Newtonian system of thought for its decisive *theological* superiority over those of two other leading thinkers, Descartes and Leibniz – unexpected since the 'rational' God of the continental thinkers may, at first sight, appear more congenial to a champion of Enlightenment rationalism. Voltaire did not doubt Descartes' piety, but pointed out how often Cartesians tended to succumb to atheism. 'Give me matter and motion and I shall build you a universe.' How easily could Descartes' proud boast turn into a denial of God's role in creation, as Spinoza's had done! Newton placed no such confidence in the power of puny human reason to reconstruct even a 'likely story' about the way in which God had put together the universe. He had regarded the universe as expressing not rational necessity or a principle of 'sufficient reason', but God's unfettered and sovereign voluntary choice. Fallen man had access only to the results of that choice, as revealed in the arrangement of the world, in the structure and organisation of living things, and in the motions and processes ruling natural phenomena.

[15] Alexander, *Leibniz-Clarke Correspondence*, 92.
[16] *Oeuvres Complètes*, XXII, 131.

Underlying the contrasting ways in which Descartes and Newton studied nature were, thus, to Voltaire's mind, two different ways of conceiving the relation between God and his creation, emphasising either the 'Hellenic' or 'Hebraic' elements in the Christian conception of God. If the stress was on divine reason, then, as Descartes had affirmed, human reason could be said to participate in it whenever it conceived clear and distinct ideas which could then serve as the first principles of an essentially deductive account of nature. Experience would need to be called upon only to decide between alternate ways in which a particular effect mechanically resulted.[17] On the other hand, if the stress was on the divine will, we would be content to study phenomena through experience and experiment, and trace its causes in so far as we could mathematically prove them. It would lead us to renounce the hope of ever attaining the knowledge of ultimate causes or a complete system of knowledge like that envisaged by Descartes or Leibniz.

It was true that the voluntaristic conception of God had been declared unworthy and favourable to atheism. Was not a God who made planets orbit the sun from west to east, and decided upon a particular number of animal species, planets and stars in His universe, like a capricious artisan? Just before the Hanoverian succession, Leibniz had accused Newton of promoting the decay of religion in England by holding such a view of God. God, surely, always chose the best. When Samuel Clarke, who defended Newton's opinions, replied that there were indifferent states of affairs which offered no 'rational' basis for a choice, Leibniz insisted that nowhere in nature was it possible to find two exactly similar things. If God had made things between which differences were 'indiscernible', He would be deprived of 'sufficient reason' for placing one rather than another in a particular place. Clarke retorted that it was exact similarity which made it possible for two individual rays of light to produce the sensation of redness.[18] For Leibniz 'indiscernibleness' detracted from the rationality of God, while for Clarke it served best to express the power and majesty of God.

Voltaire accepted and repeated Clarke's arguments. His preference for a will-theology was also evident in his defence of Newtonian ideas of space and time. Rationalist thinkers had traditionally rejected the conception of space as a featureless void. Descartes, stripping matter to its bare essence, had finally arrived at the clear and distinct idea of 'extension'. Since extension could hardly be the extension of nothing, he had then proceeded to identify space and matter making the universe a plenum. Leibniz said space was nothing but an order of co-existence among things, as time was an order of succession among events. Newton, by contrast, conceived space and time not merely as states of relations but as absolutes. According to Voltaire, Newton's conception served far better to establish the existence and true attributes of God. If the world was finite and contained a void or empty space, then the existence of matter was not a necessity but a result of divine choice. Once matter existed, it had to be extended. There was no such necessity in its possession of

[17] G. Buchdahl, *Metaphysics and the Philosophy of Science* (Oxford 1969), 79-180.
[18] Alexander, op. cit., esp. 97-101.

powers such as those of gravitational attraction. It had been endowed with them by God's free choice. Newton's world was radically contingent on the divine will. Descartes' world could easily be imagined as self-sufficient. It was 'indefinitely' extended and wholly material, and never ran down because the total quantity of motion in it always remained constant. Newton's conception was therefore far more favourable to establishing the necessity of a divine creator and the utterly dependent nature of matter, and offered the greatest protection against pantheism or materialism.

Why was the Newtonian idea of God as a *dominus* and the absolute disparity between the divine and human intellects more congenial to Voltaire than the rational supreme architect of Descartes and Leibniz? His bitter experience of persecution for his opinions in France and his reflections on the tolerant atmosphere he had breathed in England had led Voltaire to trace the roots of intolerance to the conviction of being in absolute possession of the truth. Descartes and Leibniz overturned the old dogmatism of the schools, only to fall prey to the *esprit de système*. A moderately sceptical view of the limits of human knowledge, such as the one precisely delineated by Locke, was the best guarantee of freedom of thought.

Voltaire was justified in his belief that Newton attached great value to the theological superiority of his own ideas of space and time over those of Descartes and Leibniz. During his years of exile in England, Voltaire had been close to Samuel Clarke. His testimony is an accurate reflection of the indivisibility of scientific and religious concerns in Newton's circle. 'When I wrote my treatise about our Systeme,' Newton had written to Richard Bentley in 1692, 'I had my eye on such Principles as might work with considering men for the beleife of a Deity . . .'[19] The religious ideas appended to the second edition of the *Principia* were not pious afterthoughts tacked on to a scientific treatise to deflect the criticisms of religious zealots. The union of science and religion is evident in Newton's earliest manuscript remains. It determined his initial response to the teachings of Descartes. In a manuscript dating from the 1670s, Newton rejected Cartesian ideas of matter, of motion and of mind or soul.[20]

Newton believed that at the heart of Cartesian philosophy lay a radically defective notion of extension, which offered 'a path to atheism'. It was necessary to 'overthrow' it, for only then would it be possible to lay 'truer foundations of the mechanical sciences'.[21] Descartes had identified extension with matter. But a clear idea of extension revealed it as infinite, uncreated and existing eternally. It was an absolute idea involving no reference to God, and no contradiction was involved when the idea of the existence of matter was combined with that of the non-existence of God. Such an idea of matter paved the way to atheism. The idea of motion which Descartes had adopted (in part to circumvent the Catholic ban on Copernicanism) was purely

[19] Newton, *Correspondence* (Cambridge 1959), III, 233.
[20] 'De gravitatione', in A. R. and M. B. Hall (eds & trs), *Unpublished Scientific Papers of Isaac Newton* (Cambridge 1962), 89–156.
[21] Ibid., 131.

relative, and took no account of the fact that *real* forces were involved in true, as distinct from merely relative, motion. It was necessary to refer motion to 'some motionless thing such as extension alone or space in so far as it is seen to be truly distinct from bodies'. Moreover, by his absolute distinction between thinking and extended body, Descartes had rendered the union of mind and body 'unintelligible'.[22]

All these grave disadvantages could be avoided by sharply distinguishing space from matter. Extension could be 'clearly conceived', as outside of the world and empty of body. The idea was not one of nothing, but rather an 'excessively clear' one.[23] 'Nothing' had no properties, while extension was uniform and unlimited in length, breadth and depth. It could not be imagined, but could certainly be understood. Once space and matter were distinguished, the idea of matter became indissolubly united with that of God. Space was an 'emanent effect of God' and in that sense necessary. 'If ever space had not existed God at that time would have been nowhere.' Matter existed only because God had so willed: God had 'created the world solely by an act of will'.[24]

So intensely did Newton wish to downgrade matter that he suggested that it would be possible entirely to do away with the concept of matter or body. Imagine that God had made a portion of space tangible, impenetrable and mobile. It would then have all the properties of body as known to us. It would excite perceptions in created minds and be capable of being moved by them. Even our own power to move what we took to be our bodies could be conceived as a much weaker analogue of the divine power to make empty space impenetrable. Just as God was not space, but contained it 'eminently', so created mind could then also be said 'eminently' to contain body. Newton believed that such a conception of body or matter would explain and confirm 'the chief truths of metaphysics': that God existed, that He had created the world from nothing, and that bodies differ from minds but can combine with them.[25]

Already in the 1670s Newton was elaborating the array of concepts that he would deploy in the *Principia* and in the 'General Scholium' added to its second edition: the ideas of absolute space and time, of forces as real entities, and of an analogy between God's creative and sustaining activity and the power of human beings to move their bodies by the exercise of the will.

Voltaire believed that a will-theology served to cut down human pretensions to absolute knowledge. By providing the basis for the empirical and experimental approach of Newton and Locke, it had contributed to the spirit of toleration characteristic of English life. The virtues of a distinct English 'experimental philosophy', free from the opposing dogmatisms attributed to scholasticism and Cartesianism, had already been emphasised by the founders and publicists of the Royal Society soon after the Restoration in

[22] Ibid., 143.
[23] Ibid., 132.
[24] Ibid., 141.
[25] Ibid., 142.

1660. They praised it as the best preservative against the 'enthusiasm' or fanaticism which they condemned as the root cause of civil war and regicide in England. By undermining excessive confidence in opinions, the 'experimental philosophy' would make men more obedient to authority. Bishop Sprat, the Royal Society's first historian, remarked that ' . . . the doubtful, the scrupulous, the diligent Observer of Nature, is nearer to make a modest, a severe, a meek, an humble Christian . . . '. The Fellows of the Society met every week to witness experiments. They did not speculate prematurely on the causes involved in them beforehand, since they knew how easy it was to fit experiments to preconceptions. When their interpretations of the experiments diverged, no quarrels arose, since they recognised that 'there may be several Methods of Nature, in producing the same Thing, and all equally good'.[26] Robert Hooke, who as first Curator of the Society was entrusted with presenting a weekly experiment before the Fellows, agreed that scientific knowledge was likely to grow very slowly. Besides the obscurity of things, there was the added difficulty that 'even the forces of our own minds conspire to betray us'. The only safeguard was in 'the real, the mechanical, the experimental Philosophy . . . '.[27]

The myth of an 'experimental philosophy', free from all speculative commitments and presuppositions, deriving theories solely from experiments, was already taking shape in the mid-seventeenth century. It was expressed in a popular and influential form by Sprat. He berated the founders of 'new dogmatisms' who had rejected the ancient varieties of that same distemper, but had then imposed their own theories on men's reason. It reinforced for him the lesson of the English civil war: 'For we also have beheld the Pretenders to publick Liberty, turn the greatest Tyrants themselves.' Sprat obviously included the Cartesians among the new 'dogmatists'. He sharply contrasted the approach of the Royal Society with that of Descartes, who had rejected all he could learn from the senses 'and wholly gave himself over to a reflexion on the naked Ideas of his own mind'. The result was narrow and obscure apprehensions and a wilful ignorance. Very different was the method of the members of the Society, meeting to view experiments, and only then taking it upon themselves to 'judge and resolve upon the matters of fact'. They venerated 'the inartificial process of the Experiment, and not the Acuteness of any Commentary upon it . . . '. If disputes arose, they were never such as to divide them into factions, since they would be based 'not on matters of speculation or opinion, but onely of sence . . . '.[28]

Sprat wished to present the 'experimental philosophy' purely as a method. Like any method claiming to lead to truth, it was really anchored in a metaphysic – a set of assumptions about what the world is like and what constitutes a satisfactory and adequate explanation of change. The myth of the 'experiment' as a quasi-religious act, which permitted the true nature of things to be reflected in the cleansed and polished 'mirror of the human mind',

[26] Sprat, *The History of the Royal Society of London* (London 1702 edn), 92.
[27] Hooke, *Micrographia* (London 1665), Preface.
[28] Sprat, op. cit., 95-7, 91-2.

occasionally broke down in Sprat's treatise. That is evident in Sprat's discussion of the merits of Sir Christopher Wren, whom he chose as exemplifying the Society's ideal. Sprat gave Wren's reformulation of the Cartesian laws of motion precedence above all his other achievements. Descartes had based them only on 'gross Trials' of tennis and billiard balls, while Wren had devised a special instrument for the purpose and had confirmed his conclusions by hundreds of experiments. Why was so much importance to be attached to the laws of motion and why were they to be regarded as the 'Principles of all Demonstrations in Natural Philosophy'? Sprat's answer is revealing: because ' . . . Generation, Corruption, Alteration, and all the Vicissitudes of Nature, are nothing else but the effects arising from the meeting of little Bodies, of differing Figures, Magnitudes, and Velocities'.[29]

Such a conception of what nature is like and how all changes in it are to be explained could scarcely have been derived from experiment. Rather, it provided the *framework* for the interpretation of experiments and, at least in the 'exact sciences' of that time, governed the choice and design of the experiments themselves. The 'mechanical-mathematical' conception of nature which Sprat described had only recently been clearly articulated and no one had contributed more to it than Descartes. It was misleading, therefore, to set up a contrast between a Descartes who began with presuppositions about nature and proceeded to build up a deductive account of natural phenomena, and the English experimental philosophers who were said to have begun with the results of observation and experiment which they then generalised by induction. When discussing the errors of Descartes, Voltaire singled out his laws of motion, his vortices of subtle matter, and his ideas about the nature of light and colour, magnetism and the motion of the heart. It would be difficult to attribute these to a tendency to devise *a priori* explanations in preference to induction from phenomena. Historians today attribute them, rather, to failures of conceptualisation, or mathematisation, or experimental testing of hypotheses.[30] Descartes himself was conscious of many of these deficiencies, but had aimed above all at persuading others that it was possible, in principle, to construct mechanical explanations for all natural phenomena.[31]

The contrast between the English 'experimental philosophy' and the Cartesian philosophy, as propagated by the Royal Society, was accepted fully by Newton in his earliest published work. His paper on light and colours, read before the Society in 1672, seemed like a classic vindication of the 'experimental philosophy'. Wishing to investigate colours, Newton had darkened his chamber and made experiments with a prism. Conclusions 'rigidly' drawn from experimental results were subjected to further experimental tests which culminated in a single 'crucial experiment'. From these experiments, which appeared to have been carried out in a single session, emerged a new theory of colours, overturning all previous ones. Newton had

[29] Ibid., 312.
[30] P. Mouy, op. cit., 1-71; R. S. Westfall, *Force in Newton's Physics* (London-New York, 1971), 56-98; Buchdahl, op. cit., 79-180.
[31] Mouy, *La Développement de la Physique Cartésienne*, 142.

found that each beam of coloured light, as it emerged from the prism on to a screen, had a characteristic index of refraction. He had not been able to change the colour or the degree of refraction by reflection, refraction or other optical means. That was proof, to Newton, that visible 'white' light was a mixture of rays of different colours. A prism separated out the colours, but did not create them by mixing light and shade, as ancient and even contemporary theories held.

Newton's attempt to tailor his account to fit the methodological prescriptions of the dominant 'experimental philosophy' was not entirely successful. Hooke conceded that Newton's discovery of an invariant relation between colour and refrangibility was an important experimental discovery. However, Newton's conclusion that white light was a mixture of colours depended on the hypothesis that light consisted of material particles. Hooke suggested that the experimental results were equally compatible with his own pressure-wave theory. In his reply Newton insisted that he did not need 'to explicate my Doctrine by an *Hypothesis*' at all, and that what he had asserted was 'most rigid consequence', drawn from 'experiments concluding positively and directly'.[32]

Recent historical studies have established that a far longer period of preparation, reflection and trials lay behind the idealised 'historical narration' Newton presented in the paper read before the Society. Only an experimenter with great mathematical competence would have been puzzled, as he said he was, by the fact that an oblong spectrum emerged from the prism instead of the round image of the sun. His experiments were by no means as independent of theories about the nature of light and colours as he maintained.[33] Indeed, theory, experiment and interpretation were so intertwined in his work – as in that of his other great scientific contemporaries – that they could not adequately be restated in terms of either of the two major conceptions of legitimate scientific method which then prevailed.

By Voltaire's time, Newton's redefinition had given a much greater mathematical tone to the 'experimental philosophy'. Newton's disciple, Colin Maclaurin, wrote that experiments and observations alone could not have enabled Newton to explain causes from effects and then effects from those causes: 'a sublime geometry was his guide in this nice and difficult enquiry.'[34] Newton believed that our knowledge is confined to gathering the properties of things from the phenomena, but that we must always seek quantitative laws linking the variations in those properties, because scientific knowledge must assume the form of the most secure knowledge that, besides revelation, we are acquainted with, that of mathematics. The mathematical link between colour and refrangibility of a light ray was an example of such a relationship. 'Hypotheses', to explain why that was so, had an inferior degree of certainty. Similarly, mathematical laws subjecting the motions of gross

[32] I. Bernard Cohen (ed.), *Isaac Newton's Papers and Letters on Natural Philosophy*, second ed. (Cambridge, Mass.-London 1978), 123.

[33] Recent studies are listed in ibid., 499-501.

[34] C. Maclaurin, *An Account of Sir Isaac Newton's Philosophical Discoveries*, second ed. (London 1750), 8.

bodies of the whole *machina mundi* to precise calculation could be formulated on the assumption that bodies behave as if they attract each other, with a force varying in accordance with a universal law, although the nature of the 'attraction' remained a matter for conjecture. Newton had also relaxed the requirement, prominent in the 'experimental philosophy' of the early Royal Society, that any forces involved in natural phenomena must ultimately be reducible to contact of one body with another, since that was the only kind of action that was intelligible. That criterion led the continental *savants* to condemn Newtonian attraction. Newton assigned the assertion that 'all the Phaenomena of Nature are purely mechanical' to the class of 'Hypotheses that can never be established by experiments'.[35]

Newton's modification of the 'experimental philosophy' was grounded in a voluntaristic theology. In the 'General Scholium' added to the *Principia* he rejected the view that the diversity of things in the world was to be attributed to 'Blind metaphysical necessity'; thus he pointedly dissented from Leibniz's views. That diversity depended, rather, on the 'ideas and will of a Being necessarily existing', a 'living, intelligent, and powerful Being'.[36] It is unnecessary to assume that Newton came to favour a voluntaristic conception of God only as the chorus of continental criticisms grew louder. The conception was an important component not only of the 'context of justification' of his gravitational theory, but equally of the 'context of discovery' in which it was formulated. It helped to loosen the tyranny of picturable or 'intelligible' mechanisms upon his conceptual imagination.

What has been said so far may seem to vindicate the historical accuracy of the image of Newton that Voltaire presented in his *Elémens*. There was, nevertheless, a difference of nuance in Voltaire's enthusiastic adoption and advocacy of Newton's 'experimental philosophy' and its associated theological stance. Newton's attitude had been fashioned in the religious and political atmosphere of mid-seventeenth-century England. Like the Cambridge Platonist thinkers whose arguments found many echoes in his early manuscript writing, 'De gravitatione', Newton regarded it as urgently necessary to revise Cartesian conceptions of matter and motion because they unwittingly lent strong support to the menacing forces of materialism and atheism. His God was the God of Abraham and Isaac, not the cold rationalist principle of Deism.[37] In exalting the conception of God as 'pantokrator' in the 'General Scholium' in 1713, he set his face against the temper of a time when the Church of England was relaxing the requirements of belief it demanded from its flock.

Voltaire, on the other hand, was not really aiming to overwhelm the individual consciousness with an image of God of will and power continually and most intimately involved in the universe He had created. Voltaire chose to emphasise human insignificance in the vastness of the universe rather than

[35] A. Koyré and I. B. Cohen, 'Newton and the Leibniz-Clarke correspondence', *Arch. inter. d'Hist. des Sc.*, xv (1962), 114.
[36] A. Motte and F. Cajori (eds & trs), *Mathematical Principles of Natural Philosophy* (New York 1969), II, 546.
[37] Frank E. Manuel, *The Religion of Isaac Newton* (Oxford 1974).

divine immensity.[38] His fervent promotion of the Newtonian God of will and power was not aimed primarily at countering materialism and atheism. Voltaire regarded the greatest threat to freedom of thought as originating in grandiose systems of thought, made binding by authority on pain of persecution. Cartesianism was the latest example of that menace. A repressive church had first unsuccessfully tried to stifle its influence in France, but later came to embrace it as the basis for a new theology. Malebranche had reconciled Descartes with orthodox faith. Arnauld and Bossuet came to see Cartesianism as a new version of the *philosophia perennis* of Plato and St. Augustine. It was the same Bossuet, tutor to the Dauphin, who had condemned scepticism and toleration as twin monsters bred by the Reformation.[39] Traditionally, a will-theology had served to demolish the pretensions of a rational theology. In Voltaire's hands, it was turned against *all* grand systems of thought. The *esprit de système*, most recently expressed by Descartes and Leibniz, must itself be extirpated. The 'experimental philosophy' would make it impossible to set up any new dogma and would fatally weaken the power of authority to suppress free thought and to bar the way to human progress and happiness. Voltaire would enthusiastically have approved Maclaurin's verdict on the Cartesian philosophy: ' . . . the foundation is so faulty, and the whole superstructure so erroneous, that it were much better to abandon the fabrick, and suffer the ruins to remain a memorial, in all time to come, of the folly of philosophical presumption and pride.'[40]

Voltaire had fully recognised the intimate link binding Newton's view of God and his conception of 'experimental philosophy', but he would have found uncongenial some other implications which flowed from Newton's will-theology. Newton believed that God's hidden will was revealed to fallen man not only in the structure and workings of nature, but in the unfolding course of history. By comparing historical events with Biblical prophecy, it was possible to demonstrate that the future had been foretold in minute detail. Newton devoted a great deal of his energy to such an enterprise, with the aims of confuting those who scoffed at religion and of securing the Protestant reliance on the Bible against the Catholic Counter-Reformation onslaught.[41] Knowledge about history was hidden in the Bible but could be seen to be there only retrospectively. So, too, truths about nature were concealed in ancient bodies of wisdom, but their full meaning would become clear only when they had been 'inductively' rediscovered. The Pythagorean 'harmony of the spheres' was really an enigmatic representation of Newton's law of universal gravitation; the literature of alchemy contained hints of the active principles which operated in nature.[42]

With the growing influence of Voltaire's image of Newton as the founder

[38] P. Pomeau, *La Religion de Voltaire* (Paris 1969), 215; J. Erhard, *L'Idée de Nature en France dans la Première Moitié du XVIIe Siècle* (Paris 1963), 133ff.

[39] Bossuet, 'Défense de l'Histoire', in *Oeuvres Choisies* (Nimes 1785), III, 425.

[40] Maclaurin, op. cit., 82.

[41] Frank E. Manuel, *Isaac Newton, Historian* (Cambridge 1963).

[42] J. E. McGuire and P. M. Rattansi, 'Newton and the "Pipes of Pan"', *Notes & Records Roy. Soc. Lond.*, XXI (1966), 108–43; B. J. T. Dobbs, *The Foundations of Newton's Alchemy* (Cambridge 1975).

of a new kind of rationalism, which had supposedly broken free of theology and metaphysics and required nothing but the immediate testimony of the senses to build up its picture of the world, the integration of the religious and the scientific in Newton's thought became increasingly incomprehensible to succeeding generations. To Biot and Laplace, Newton's monumental labours in Biblical prophecy appeared so eccentric that they were tempted to regard them as proof that Newton's famous mental collapse of 1693 had left his intellect gravely impaired. Those charges were refuted by Sir David Brewster, who published the first comprehensive life of Newton in 1855 when the Darwinian storm lay in the future, and the alliance between science and religion in England through natural theology remained intact. But work on Newton's manuscripts shocked Brewster by revealing an aspect of Newton's thought that he, too, found irrational: the study of alchemy to which he had found Newton had devoted a great portion of his most creative years.[43]

The 'Newton industry' of the last few decades has given us much deeper knowledge of many diverse facets of Newton's life and work on the basis of his great manuscript remains, but without fully reconciling what seems 'rational' and 'irrational' to us in Newton's thought.[44] It is only by going beyond Voltaire's image to that seventeenth-century *milieu* in which Newton's intellectual formation took place that we can hope to bring together all that recent scholarship has discovered in a truer likeness of Isaac Newton.

[43] Brewster, *Memoirs of the Life, Writings and Discoveries of Sir Isaac Newton* (Edinburgh 1855), II, 374-5.
[44] R. S. Westfall, 'The changing world of the Newtonian industry', *Journ. Hist. Ideas*, XXXVII (1976), 175-86; Cohen, *Papers*, 498-504.

17

The Varangian–Russian Controversy: the First Round

Dimitri Obolensky

'Where did the land of Russia have its beginning?' *The Russian Primary Chronicle,* c. 1100.

'Scriptorum de origine Ruthenorum varietas plus obnubilat eorum originem quam declarat.' Jan Długosz, *Historia Polonica*, A.D. 1455-80.

For more than two hundred years the 'Varangian question' has been at the heart of every discussion regarding the origins of the medieval Russian state. The meaning and derivation of the term *Rus'*, by which the Eastern Slavs called their country in the early Middle Ages, and which Arabic and Byzantine authors rendered respectively as *Rūs* and *Rhos*; the origin of the people who bore that name; and the role played in the foundation and early history of the Russian state by the Varangians, as the Viking merchants, mercenaries and settlers were known in Eastern Europe: these problems have not ceased to divide historians and philologists who seek an answer to the question first raised at the turn of the eleventh century by one of the authors of the Russian Primary Chronicle: 'Where did the land of Russia have its beginning?'

Two schools of thought have fought over this issue since the mid-eighteenth century. The 'Normanists' trace the name *Rus'* to a Scandinavian root, and hold that it was first used to denote Varangians, before being transferred, in a geographical and political sense, to the territory, inhabited mainly by Eastern Slavs, over which the Viking overlords of Kiev came to rule in the late ninth and tenth centuries. The 'Normanists' have thus tended to regard the Varangians as the founders of the Russian state. In contrast, the 'Anti-Normanists' have usually derived the name *Rus'* from a non-Scandinavian language, have been reluctant to accept that the people who first bore this name were Northmen from Scandinavia, and have argued that the Kievan state could not have been born *ex nihilo* with the advent of the Varangians, since the Eastern Slavs had led a socially organised life in this area for centuries before the Viking era. Recently, too, 'Anti-Normanists' have argued that states are born not of foreign conquest, but of an internal process of social and economic development, and that the Russian state was no exception to this sociological norm.[1]

Today some of the heat has been taken out of the controversy. The gap between the two schools has, on several issues, narrowed significantly and areas of common ground are beginning to emerge. And yet the age-long debate continues: 'Normanists' and 'Anti-Normanists' remain distinct species, recognisable by the importance they attach to this or that piece of evidence in the Varangian dossier. They differ in the emphasis they lay on social and economic factors, in their interest in linguistic problems, and sometimes, it must be admitted, in the extent to which they have allowed non-scholarly considerations to cloud their judgments.

Three principal phases may be distinguished in the history of the Varangian-Russian controversy: during the first hundred years the main protagonists were historians; in the 1840s they were joined by a powerful linguistic team, who subjected the written evidence to minute philological analysis; finally, in the present century, the area of debate has shifted to several hitherto peripheral disciplines, such as archaeology and toponymy. Extraneous factors – ethnic prejudice has been the most blatant, political pressure the most insidious – have at times weighed heavily in the balance. To the student of Russian social and political thought these alien pressures are of considerable interest: thus the debate between the 'Normanists' and the 'Anti-Normanists' was involved in the eighteenth century with the German and the anti-German parties in the Russian Academy of Sciences, in the nineteenth century with the controversy between 'Westerners' and Slavophiles, and most recently with attempts to make the history of the early medieval Russian state conform to the patterns of Marxist sociology.

This essay is not primarily concerned with the scholarly issues of the Varangian-Russian controversy. Its purpose is to describe and assess the significance of the first public debate between the two rival schools, which took place in 1749-50 in St. Petersburg. This opening salvo in what was to prove a long-drawn-out battle is, I believe, of general interest to historians for a variety of reasons. In the first place, the arguments marshalled on both sides were to become staple ammunition in subsequent discussions on the origins of the Russian state, and many of them are still used today. Secondly, the two scholars whose prolonged debate is the subject of this essay represent two contrasting views of the historian's function: the debate was between a professional and dedicated antiquarian, devoted to the meticulous study of documents, persuaded that the historian has no other duty save to discover the truth, and an amateur with an encyclopaedic knowledge and turn of mind, a populariser seeking to reach a wide reading public, a strong believer in the moral, didactic and patriotic purpose of history. Thirdly, their acrimonious battles, fought within the precincts of the Russian Academy of Sciences, afford us a glimpse of the scholarly world of eighteenth-century

[1] The history of the Varangian-Russian controversy is surveyed in the following works: V. Moshin, 'Varyago-russky vopros', *Slavia*, x (1931), 109-36, 343-79, 501-37; I. P. Shaskol'sky, *Normanskaya teoriya v sovremennoy burzhuaznoy nauke* (Moscow-Leningrad 1965); K. Rahbek Schmidt, 'The Varangian problem: A brief history of the controversy', in *Varangian Problems. Scando-Slavica, Supplementum I* (Copenhagen 1970), 7-20.

Russia, with its simultaneous reliance on German academics and its desire to be freed of their dominance, its newly found vitality and monumental quarrels, and its exposure to chauvinism and xenophobia.

It is time to present the two protagonists: Gerhard Friedrich Müller and Mikhail Vasil'yevich Lomonosov.

Müller, a native of Westphalia, was one of the group of German scholars and scientists who were invited to staff the new Russian Academy in St. Petersburg, founded by Peter the Great in 1724, and who, almost until the end of the century, dominated the life of that remarkable institution.[2] Thanks to the efforts of Christian Wolff and his disciples, the Universities of Halle, Marburg and Leipzig became the principal channels for the supply of these German-trained scholars to Russia.[3] It was from Leipzig that Müller, at the age of twenty, arrived in St. Petersburg in 1725, the year of Peter's death. After a spell of teaching and administrative work, he was appointed in 1730 professor of history and member of the Academy. In 1730-1 he travelled on official business to Germany, Holland and England, entrusted with the double task of recruiting foreign scholars and improving the Academy's image, an image tarnished by reports of the constant and unseemly quarrels between the academic and administrative staffs. He spent two and a half months in England and on 10 December 1730 was elected a Fellow of the Royal Society.

On his return to Russia, Müller fell foul of his patron, Johann Schumacher, the Academy's all-powerful secretary, known, on account of his attempts to browbeat the academicians, as 'flagellum professorum'. This was the beginning of his troubles. In order to escape from them he accepted an invitation to accompany Bering on his second expedition to Kamchatka. The rigours of the journey proved too much for him at first: he contracted a disease, which he himself diagnosed as hypochondria. He managed, however, to reach Yakutsk, and for ten years (1733-43) travelled across Siberia, studying mineral resources and local industries, collecting ethnographic, historical and geographical material, and examining some twenty archives in widely scattered areas. The Siberian expedition was a turning point in Müller's life. It anchored him firmly in his adopted country, gave him a solid training in Russian history, and led to the publication of his *History of Siberia*, the first volume of which appeared (in German) in 1750.

On his return to St. Petersburg Müller soon found himself at odds with his chauvinistic colleagues who suspected him, quite unfairly, of denigrating Russia's past. In 1747, however, his position greatly improved: the president

[2] On Müller see: A. F. Büsching, *Beyträge zu der Lebensgeschichte denkwürdiger Personen, insonderheit gelehrter Männer*, III (Halle 1785), 1-160; P. Pekarsky, *Istoriya Imperatorskoy Akademii Nauk v Peterburge*, I (St. Petersburg 1870), 308-430; N. L. Rubinshtein, *Russkaya istoriografiya* (Moscow 1941), 99-115; A. G. Mazour, *Modern Russian Historiography*, second edn (Princeton, N.J. 1958), 16-23; H. Rogger, *National Consciousness in Eighteenth-Century Russia* (Cambridge, Mass. 1960), 202-13; S. L. Peshtich, *Russkaya istoriografiya XVIII veka*, II (Leningrad 1965), 210-31.

[3] See E. Winter, *Halle als Ausgangspunkt der deutschen Russlandkunde im 18. Jahrhundert* (Berlin 1953) (Veröffentlichungen des Instituts für Slawistik, no.2); M. Raeff, 'Les Slaves, les Allemands et les "Lumières"', *Canadian Slavic Studies*, I (1967), 521-51; 'The Enlightenment in Russia and Russian thought in the Enlightenment', in J. G. Garrard (ed.), *The Eighteenth Century in Russia* (Oxford 1973), 30-5.

of the Academy, Count Kiril Razumovsky, appointed him official historio-grapher of the Russian state and rector of the college of higher education attached to the Academy. On 29 January 1748 Müller renounced his Prussian citizenship and became a Russian subject. In due course his German name was russianised to the more homely Feodor Ivanovich Miller. He was about to face the greatest ordeal of his professional life.

A public meeting of the Academy had been arranged for 6 September 1749, at which Müller and Lomonosov were to speak. Müller's paper, entitled *Origines gentis et nominis Russorum*, was to be read by him in a Russian translation. He owed this assignment to Schumacher who, in recommending him, had testified, somewhat unkindly, that he possessed 'quite a good Russian pronunciation, a loud voice and a presence of mind bordering on impudence'.[4] For his part, Lomonosov would deliver a panegyric of the Empress Elizabeth, whose name-day it was the day before. He was soon to launch a fierce attack on Müller's paper: so from the victim we must turn to the assailant.

Michael Lomonosov, on his way to becoming Russia's leading poet of the time, an innovator and law-maker in the fields of grammar, prosody and style, and a scientist of European stature, was then, at the age of thirty-eight, professor of chemistry in the Academy of Sciences.[5] The son of a fisherman of the White Sea coast, he came to Moscow in 1731 and, spurred on by an insatiable thirst for knowledge, got himself admitted as a student of the 'Slavo-Graeco-Latin Academy', an institution of higher education which, somewhat incongruously, then specialised mainly in the teaching of Latin. Five years later, at the age of twenty-five, he was sent in a group of twelve Russian scholars to Germany to complete his education. For three years (1736-9) he studied philosophy, physics and chemistry in Marburg under Christian Wolff. The master's high regard for his pupil's ability was equalled by the extraordinary indulgence with which he viewed the brawls and wild drinking bouts that filled the Russian students' leisure hours in the quiet University town. It speaks for Lomonosov's robust constitution that he was able to combine this riotous activity with a great deal of hard work. A further period of study at Freiberg in Saxony was followed by one of those rum-bustious scrapes which so often enlivened Lomonosov's life. In a tavern one evening he met a Prussian recruiting officer who, observing with satisfaction Lomonosov's size and physical strength, invited him to supper. During the meal he sang the praises of a soldier's life, got his guest drunk and persuaded him to enlist. Lomonosov woke up next morning to find a red tie round his neck – the emblem of a Prussian royal hussar. A few days later, under cover of darkness, he escaped from the fortress in which the recruits were held. He scaled two ramparts, swam two moats and found himself in an open field. At dawn his flight was observed. Pursued by cannon shot and a company of mounted hussars, he out-distanced them all and escaped to the safety of

[4] Pekarsky, op. cit., 359.
[5] The bibliography on Lomonosov is, of course, abundant. A useful biography in English is B. N. Menshutkin, *Russia's Lomonosov. Chemist, Courtier, Physicist, Poet* (Princeton, N.J. 1952).

Westphalia which, fortunately for him, was only a few miles away. By 1741, none the worse for this escapade, he was back in St. Petersburg. Before long he was appointed by the Academy to teach physics, chemistry and poetry.

The accession in November 1741 of the Empress Elizabeth put an end to the ascendancy of the 'German party', which had been a marked and un-popular feature of the government of the Empress Anne (1730–40). The mood of the Academy now began to reflect the prevailing patriotic and anti-German feelings, and Lomonosov expressed them with his customary vigour. Several simultaneous legal actions were brought against him for assault and battery; and when these exploits began to claim victims among Russian academicians, the authorities were forced to intervene. Charged with discourteous behaviour and with interrupting the Academy's meetings by outrageous pranks and general rowdiness, Lomonosov was placed under house arrest (1743–4). Finally he was induced to beg forgiveness in the following terms, no doubt gleefully devised by his former victims: 'I declare that I truthfully abhor, solemnly recant and would like to consider unsaid those abusive words, unreasonable in the highest degree, with which I, being drunk, defamed the gentlemen professors on the 26th day of April of the past year . . . I realise the enormity of my unforgivable misdeed, and promise most sincerely to mend my ways.'

We do not know whether the authorities were more impressed by Lomonosov's repentance or by the thought that his learning and ability made him indispensable. The fact is that, once again, he was forgiven. The year after he signed his abject recantation he was appointed to the chair of chemistry and to full membership of the Academy.

Such was the formidable opponent who faced Müller in 1749. Lomonosov, whose reputation as a scholar, writer and scientist was rapidly rising, now appeared as the chief mouthpiece of the anti-German party in the Academy. In one respect only did Müller enjoy obvious superiority: he was by far the better historian.

The public meeting at which Müller and Lomonosov were to speak was postponed at short notice by the Academy's president, Count Razumovsky. Some academicians, it appeared, had taken exception to several passages in Müller's speech, whose text had been circulated in advance. Lomonosov duly delivered on 26 November 1749 his panegyric of the Empress; but Müller's text, printed both in Latin and in a Russian translation, was sent early in September by the Academy's chancellery to an investigating committee of six members. They were to rule on whether it contained 'anything prejudicial to Russia'. One of the committee's members was Lomonosov. In his separate report, dated 16 September 1749, he concluded that Müller's speech is 'most unworthy, preposterous and vexatious for Russian listeners, and, in my opinion, can in no wise be corrected so as to make it suitable for public delivery'.[6] On 27 September the Academy's chancellery ordered all copies of the speech, printed and manuscript, to be confiscated and confined to the

[6] M. V. Lomonosov, *Polnoe Sobranie Sochineny*, VI (Moscow-Leningrad 1952), 24–5.

archives. Müller wrote to the president complaining that his judges had been biased; Razumovsky then ordered the text of the speech to be re-examined at a special meeting of the Academy.

This new examination lasted from 23 October 1749 to 8 March 1750, and occupied twenty-nine sessions. At first Müller spoke in his own defence. Lomonosov was the most active advocate for the prosecution. He later alleged that the discussions were accompanied by mutual abuse, stopping just short of physical violence; Müller, he said, threatened his opponents with his stick, and banged it against the conference table. In his second and final report to the Academy's chancellery, dated 21 June 1750, Lomonosov restated even more starkly his conviction that Müller's paper should on no account be published, and added that many of his arguments were 'dangerous'.[7] The issue was scarcely in doubt: Müller was almost completely isolated. On 24 September 1750 the chancellery ordered that all copies of his paper be destroyed, on the ground that it was 'prejudicial to Russia'. On 8 October, by the president's command, Müller was stripped of his rank of academician and deprived of his chair.[8]

Along with Lomonosov's two reports to the Academy's chancellery, our knowledge of his debate with Müller comes, in the main, from three sources. First there is Müller's paper *Origines gentis et nominis Russorum*. The order to destroy all the copies was disregarded. In January 1751 the existence was recorded of six manuscript copies, 491 printed Latin copies and 488 printed Russian ones.[9] In 1767 a manuscript copy of the Latin text was sent from St. Petersburg by A. L. Schlözer to J. C. Gatterer in Göttingen, who published it in his *Allgemeine Historische Bibliothek*.[10] Secondly there are detailed criticisms of Müller's paper by Lomonosov, the first written between 25 October and 3 November 1749, the second, composed after 8 March 1750, containing his replies to Müller's counter-arguments.[11] Thirdly there is Müller's own record of the debate, based on the notes he took at the time.[12]

Müller began his paper by refuting a number of current and fallacious theories about the origin of the Russian people. He singled out for special obloquy the belief that the Russians descend from the Roxolani, a Sarmatian tribe which occupied the steppes between the Dnieper and the Don in the second century B.C. This was hardly calculated to please Lomonosov who believed, wrongly, that the Roxolani were Slavs, that they migrated to the

[7] Ibid., 79-80.

[8] For detailed accounts of the 1749-50 affair, see Pekarsky, op. cit., 359-65; Lomonosov, *Polnoe Sobranie Sochineny*, VI, 546-52.

[9] Pekarsky, op. cit., 361, n.1; M. M. Gurevich and K. I. Shafranovsky, 'Ob izdanii 1749 goda rechi G.-F. Millera "Proiskhozhdenie Russkogo naroda i imeni rossiiskogo"', in *Kniga. Issledovaniya i materialy*, VI (Moscow 1962), 284-5.

[10] 'Auszug eines Schreibens aus St. Petersburg vom 2/13 Jun. 1767', in J. C. Gatterer (ed.), *Allgemeine Historische Bibliothek von Mitgliedern des königlichen Instituts der historischen Wissenschaften zu Göttingen*, V (Halle 1768), 280-340. I am indebted to Mr J. S. G. Simmons for his help in tracing this rare publication in the more arcane recesses of the British Library's catalogue of printed books.

[11] Lomonosov, *Polnoe Sobranie Sochineny*, VI, 17-80.

[12] Müller's notes, which are still unpublished, were used by S. L. Peshtich in his account of the 1749-50 affair: *Russkaya istoriografiya XVIII veka*, II, 222-31.

shores of the Baltic and that the Russians derived their name from them.[13]

Müller then turned to the earliest history of the Slavs. These, he argued were not the indigenous inhabitants of present-day Russia. Following the Russian Primary Chronicle, he stated (wrongly) that they were driven out of the Danube region by the Romans and (rightly) that they migrated to the Dnieper valley and then northward, where they encountered the aboriginal Finns. Lomonosov in his reply appealed to the verdict of what a modern historian, in a different context, has called 'ethnic truth':[14] to trace the origins of the Slavs no further back than the time of the Roman occupation of the Danube valley was to detract from 'the glory' of the Russian people; Müller's assertion that the Slavs were 'driven out' of the Danube region was a deplorable example of his penchant for endlessly cataloguing their defeats and disasters; while to date the arrival of the Slavs on the Dnieper in the fifth century of the Christian era was nothing short of an assault on the authority of the Russian church and state. The last statement is supported by two curious arguments: according to the Primary Chronicle, the inhabitants of the Dnieper valley were evangelised by St. Andrew the Apostle; to suggest that the Slavs were not yet there at the time was to impugn the Russian Church's belief in the apostolic origin of its Christianity, and also to show disrespect for the memory of Peter the Great who established the Russian Imperial Order of St. Andrew. Faced with these red herrings, Müller pointed out that a historical dissertation and a panegyrical speech were two different things, that the historian's first duty is to tell the truth, and that the church obliges no one to believe in fables, such as the story of St. Andrew's preaching on the Dnieper. Over the question of the retreat of the Slavs from the Danube, Lomonosov conceded victory to his opponent in the end, though not very gracefully: Müller, he submitted, could at least have expressed himself in more suitable language, by stating, for instance, that they retreated 'impelled by love of freedom'.

From the Slavs Müller turned to the main theme of his paper, the Varangians, whom, following the Primary Chronicle, he identified with the Rus'. Here his views owe a considerable debt, which he acknowledges, to another German expatriate, Gottlieb Siegfried Bayer. A notable philologist, Bayer came from Königsberg to St. Petersburg in 1725 at the invitation of the president of the Russian Academy of Science, L. Blumentrost, and remained in Russia until his death in 1738. He is mainly remembered today for his treatise *De Varagis*, published in 1735, in which, in order to ascertain the origin of the Russian people, he drew on a variety of Greek, Latin and Scandinavian sources, many of which have since figured prominently in the 'Normanist' arsenal.[15]

Bayer was no doubt a better scholar than Müller. Yet Müller had the advantage over his colleague of knowing some Russian, and was thus able –

---

[13] The theory of the derivation of the name Rus'/Rhos from the Roxolani was recently, and unsuccessfully, revived by G. Vernadsky, *Ancient Russia* (New Haven 1943), 97, 129, 147.

[14] R. Jenkins, *The Dilessi Murders* (London 1961), 99–117.

[15] T. S. Bayer, *Opuscula ad historiam antiquam, chronologiam, geographiam, et rem numariam spectantia* (Halle 1770), 339–70. On Bayer, see Mazour, *Modern Russian Historiography*, 14–16.

n support of his contention that the Varangians were not Slavs (as
Lomonosov believed) but Scandinavians – to draw on native sources as well.
Above all he relied on the Primary Chronicle, which provided him with two
key arguments: Ryurik, the earliest known ruler of north Russia, was a
Varangian; and the names of most of the early Russian princes and nobles are
patently Scandinavian. The second of these points appears to have been
conceded by Lomonosov. In his use of non-Slav sources Müller, in the main,
follows Bayer: the 'Russian' names of the Dnieper rapids enumerated in the
ninth chapter of Constantine Porphyrogenitus' *De administrando imperio* are
Scandinavian; the Frankish Bertinian Annals relate that the people called
Rhos, sent in 839 by the Byzantine emperor to Louis the Pious, declared that
they were Swedes; Liutprand of Cremona, in describing his visit to Constantinople in 968, mentions 'Rusios quos alio nomine Nordmannos appel-
amus'; and the Icelandic sagas provide evidence of considerable activity of
Scandinavians in Russia. One of Müller's philological arguments seems to
have been a new one: he was apparently the first to see a connection between
the name *Rus'* and the Finnish name for Swedes, *ruotsi*.

Lomonosov's efforts to counter these arguments were not very impressive. He tried to discredit the authority, and even the scholarly integrity,
of Bayer; restated his conviction that the Varangians were descended from
the Roxolani; and, after vainly attempting to demonstrate that the names of
all the Dnieper rapids were Slavonic, conceded that 'some' of the early rulers
of Russia did have Scandinavian names. One of Lomonosov's arguments,
however, was persuasive: he was able to show that Müller's use of Scandinavian sagas was, at best, uncritical and that the *Heimskringla*, on which he
placed so much reliance, contained 'absurd tales of heroes and wizards'.

On an overall assessment of this debate there can be no doubt that Müller
wins on points.[16] By banning his paper, the Russian authorities were, perhaps
inevitably, swayed by expediency and prejudice. To be sure, Müller's paper
was not free from factual errors, several of which Lomonosov was quick to
point out:[17] some no doubt were due to his imperfect knowledge of the
Russian language. He himself lamented, perhaps with undue modesty, his
'balbutientem linguam et haesitantem in alieno sermone (Russico) vocem'.[18]
He could expose his flank in an unguarded moment;[19] and, at least on one
occasion, Lomonosov scored a good debating point.[20] Several times, goaded

[16] E. Winter (ed.), *Lomonosov, Schlözer, Pallas. Deutsch-Russische Wissenschaftsbeziehungen im
18. Jahrhundert* (Berlin 1962) (Quellen und Studien zur Geschichte Osteuropas, XII) 56–61,
awards the first prize to Lomonosov. We differ.

[17] Müller made an unfortunate attempt to emend the name of the mythical Slavonic prince
Gostomysl, and believed quite wrongly that Askold and Dir, the ninth-century Varangians who
captured Kiev, were one and the same person: *Allgemeine Historische Bibliothek*, V, 331-3, 337-8.
Lomonosov took him severely to task for these blunders: *Polnoe Sobranie Sochineny*, VI, 20, 40, 78.

[18] *Allgemeine Historische Bibliothek*, V, 284. In his autobiography, written in 1775, Müller states
that in 1730 he knew virtually no Russian: 'Opisanie moikh sluzhb', in G. F. Miller, *Istoriya
Sibiri*, I (Moscow-Leningrad 1937), 148. He must have acquired a reasonably good knowledge of
the language during the ten years (1733-43) he spent in Siberia.

[19] See Lomonosov, op. cit., 48-50.

[20] Ibid., 74.

beyond endurance by his opponent's methods of arguing, Müller reacted angrily. In all fairness, however, it must be admitted that he was under severe provocation. Lomonosov had the irritating habit of distorting Müller's views, in order to ridicule them more easily; and he was not above resorting to cheap jibes and ribaldry.

Particularly unfair was Lomonosov's repeated taunt that Müller disparaged native Russian sources, and belittled the great Nestor who was then believed to be the sole author of the Primary Chronicle. In fact, though he does not always follow him uncritically, Müller shows high regard for 'patre historiae Russicae, beato Nestore',[21] and on the whole relies on the evidence of the Primary Chronicle more than Lomonosov does. Furthermore, in his desire to damage his rival, Lomonosov showed a singular lack of scruple. Thus, in his first report to the Academy's chancellery, he warned that Müller's paper, if published, would because of its unpatriotic content bring the Academy into disrepute, and suggested even more insidiously that 'if one were to accept that Ryurik and his descendants, who ruled over Russia, were of Swedish origin', 'dangerous conclusions' might be drawn – an argument calculated to impress the authorities of a country which had been at war with Sweden as recently as 1743. Particularly odious, in the same report, was Lomonosov's feigned astonishment that the author of a work detracting from the antiquity of the Russian people should be enjoying their country's 'great benefits', a charge that ignored the fact that Müller had been a Russian subject for nearly two years.

In the last resort, apart from the personal hostility and national antagonism between the two men, the conflict between Lomonosov and Müller was one between two different types of mind and two contrasting notions of the historian's task. Lomonosov, for whom this debate marked his début as a historian, was an amateur, lacking adequate training in this field. His vocations were literature and science, and in both fields he proved to be a genius. His historical work, as can be seen in his posthumous history of the Russian people 'from the beginning' to the middle of the eleventh century, seldom rises above the level of simple description and rhetoric. And, as his polemic with Müller demonstrated, he regarded the study of history as having above all a didactic and patriotic purpose. His desire to free Russia's cultural life from the influence of German scholars was understandable and, within limits, legitimate. But his judgment of their work was clouded by chauvinism and warped by distrust. The conclusion, to which Müller's paper inescapably led, that Russia owed her state to Scandinavian immigrants, was to him intolerable; and Müller's entire paper consequently became the object of his patriotic wrath.

Müller, by contrast, was a thorough-going professional. A. L. Schlözer, the greatest of all German pioneers of Russian medieval studies, stayed in Müller's house in St. Petersburg in the early 1760s, and left a vivid portrait of his patron, with whom he was later to quarrel.[22] Müller was then, at the age of fifty-six, a tall, good-looking and powerfully built man, hard-working

---

[21] *Allgemeine Historische Bibliothek*, v, 297.
[22] A. L. *Schlözers öffentliches und privat-Leben, von ihm selbst beschrieben* (Göttingen 1802), 28-31.

nd precise in manner, yet capable of gaiety and sallies of wit. Schlözer was
impressed by his strong sense of justice and by his devotion to Russia. Yet he
eemed to him also to be an irascible and opinionated man, embittered by
trife and possessed of an uncommon knack of making enemies in high
places. Among his more attractive features were the kindness and generosity
he showed to numerous young students from Germany who had come to
eek their fortunes in Russia and who, more often than not, landed penniless
on Müller's doorstep.

Müller was no doubt more of a compiler than an original historian. As an
antiquarian his influence was lasting and beneficial. He was one of the first to
how Russian historians the importance of subjecting medieval documents to
a critical examination, thus laying the foundations of a *Quellenkritik* on which
Schlözer was later to build. And, as his debate with Lomonosov shows, he
trongly believed that the historian owes a loyalty that extends beyond the
interests of his own nation, that for him too 'patriotism is not enough'. In one
of his letters he wrote: 'the duty of the historian is difficult to carry out . . . He
must seem to be without a fatherland, without a religion, without a
sovereign.'[23] It would be hard to imagine a greater contrast to Lomonosov's
view of the historian's role. It was almost inevitable that the debate between
the two men over the Varangian-Russian problem came to pose the question
of the historian's primary duty and of the purpose of his craft.

A few words may be said in conclusion about the subsequent fate of our two
protagonists. Lomonosov's life belongs to the history of Russian literature
and Russian science. His connection with the Academy, of which he became
the virtual head in 1760, continued until his death; so did his acrimonious
quarrels with its members. The range of his scholarly activity was astonishing. The subjects in which he was actively engaged included chemistry,
physics, mathematics, the making of mosaics, grammar, poetry and history;
he played a leading part in the foundation of Moscow University (1755);
propounded in his works on stylistics a new and more organic relationship
between Church Slavonic and the spoken vernacular, thus laying the foundation of modern literary Russian; was primarily responsible for introducing
the verse-forms which have dominated Russian poetry ever since; and wrote
odes, sacred and panegyrical, which are still impressive by the clarity of their
diction and their rhetoric. He died in 1765.

Müller, too, retained his links with the Academy which had treated him so
shoddily in 1750. It made amends to him before long. In February 1751 he
was reinstated as an academician, and given back his chair. In 1754 he became
the Academy's secretary, having to correspond, by virtue of his office, with
foreign scholars and writers. One of them was Voltaire. Müller had already
written to him on 14 April 1746, informing him, in his capacity as the senior
academician, that he had been elected an honorary member of the Russian
Academy.[24] Voltaire wrote back to Müller on 28 June, gratefully accepting

[23] Pekarsky, op. cit., 381.
[24] Ibid., 383.

the election (which he had privately solicited through the French envoy to St Petersburg), and assuring him that he would have replied sooner 'si longo e gravi morbo non laboravissem'.[25] Subsequent correspondence between the two men was less happy. In 1757, at the instigation of Ivan Shuvalov, the Francophile favourite of the Empress Elizabeth, Voltaire was invited by the Russian government to write the history of Peter the Great's reign. The early drafts of the *Histoire de l'Empire de Russie sous Pierre le Grand* were sent by Voltaire to St. Petersburg, where they were examined by a committee of experts, who were also expected to supply him with some of the necessary material.[26] The committee comprised Müller and Lomonosov. Both sent in numerous comments (Müller is said to have provided about two hundred) many of which annoyed Voltaire. In a letter to Shuvalov, dated 1761, he complained of the absurd claim made by one of his correspondents (presumably Lomonosov) that the history of the Slavs goes back to the Trojan War, and protested at the efforts (made no doubt by Müller) to persuade him to adopt the Germanic transliteration of Russian proper names. He was particularly incensed by such forms as Woronestsch, Ivanowistch and Waciliewistch, which, he rightly concluded, came from the pen of a German. 'Je souhaite à cet homme,' he retorted, 'plus d'esprit, et moins de consonnes.'[27]

It is pleasant to be able to record that Müller's life eventually entered a more serene phase. In 1765 he moved to Moscow, where he felt sheltered from the squabbles of the Academy and the vexations of Lomonosov. He even basked for a while in the favour of Catherine II. He died on 11 October 1783, after fifty-eight years spent in the service of his adopted country.

[25] Th. Besterman (ed.), *Voltaire's Correspondence*, XV (Geneva 1956), 102-3.

[26] See E. Shmurlo, *Vol'ter i ego kniga o Petre Velikom* (*Voltaire et son oeuvre 'Histoire de l'Empire de Russie sous Pierre le Grand'*) (Prague 1929).

[27] *Voltaire's Correspondence*, XLVI (Geneva 1959), 81-4.

18

Lord Shelburne

Charles Stuart

The active political career of William, Earl of Shelburne, later Marquess of Lansdowne, covered twenty-two years from 1761 to 1783. Within this period he held office for a total of only three and a half years, as President of the Board of Trade between April and September 1763, as Secretary of State for the Southern department between July 1766 and October 1768 and, finally, between March 1782 and February 1783 successively as Secretary of State for three months and then for the remaining eight months as Prime Minister. For the last twenty-five years of his life he was virtually in political retirement.

It is reasonable to ask why a politician with such a brief official career should deserve any detailed consideration. In part this is best answered in terms of his complex and equivocal character and the extraordinary enigma of his overwhelming political unpopularity. But he is also of interest for his original and far-sighted political views which, when taken with his inability to apply them, give to his career an air of unsolved paradox which invites enquiry.

Contemporaries acknowledged his ability, foresight and wisdom. The Marquis of Buckingham, who as Lord Temple had served in his government as Lord Lieutenant of Ireland and who was by no means an admirer, wrote of him as 'one of the quickest and most indefatigable Ministers that this country ever saw'. Wraxall judged that 'in application to business, facility of comprehension and aptitude for affairs' he was the equal both of the younger Pitt and of Charles Fox. Later generations have not changed this judgment. Disraeli wrote in a famous passage that Shelburne was 'the ablest and most accomplished minister of the eighteenth century', while in recent times Sir Keith Feiling judged him to possess 'the most distinguished mind' among ministers of the Hanoverian era.[1]

This distinction of mind can be seen in the positions he adopted in relation to the great issues of his time. Whether he addressed himself to the problems of America or India or Ireland or to the constitutional and administrative problems of Westminster – whatever the issue, he always considered it

[1] Buckingham and Chandos (ed.), *Memoirs of the Courts and Cabinets of George III* (London 1853), I, 302; N. W. Wraxall, *Posthumous Memoirs of his own time* (London 1836), III, 238; Keith Feiling, *A History of England* (London 1966), 721.

without prejudice and made every effort to collect accurate information on which to base his actions. So in the 1760s he was almost alone in seizing the great political truth that the expansion of British power after the Treaty of Paris and the return of the Tories to court had in the one case created a need for more efficient forms of administration, and in the other presented a challenge to the comfortable Whig monopoly of offices of profit under the Crown which had obtained for two generations. Where Newcastle and his political heirs, the Rockingham connection, were simply fighting old battles to recover their lost supremacy, where Bute was striking vain and empty postures, and Pitt, however much he concealed his intentions in clouds of obscure rhetoric, had little positive in mind, Shelburne looked to a new deal. As he wrote in one of his autobiographical fragments:

> the old mode of false government was worn out and seen through. It was proposed no longer to sacrifice all merit and worth in Army, Navy, Church and State to the miserable purpose of corrupting a majority in the House of Commons . . .

Here he expressed a point of view which was only to be generally accepted after the disasters of the American war had demonstrated its validity.

Similarly, in treating the American question Shelburne pointed in the direction of moderation and compromise. He deplored the Declaratory Act not because he dissented from the truth of its assertion of Parliament's sovereignty but because he saw that the only consequence of needlessly raising the question of right would be to arouse 'jealousy and distrust . . . throughout the colonies'. He spoke out in Parliament against 'attaching the name of rebellion and traitors to the Americans' as 'dangerous, imprudent and unjust', and he warned against adopting rash measures before considering whether they could be enforced. 'What can be effected,' he asked prophetically in December 1765, 'against colonies so populous and of such magnitude and extent? The colonies may be ruined first, but the distress will end with ourselves.' The solution which he offered when back in office in 1767 to the vexed problem of raising revenue in America was to develop a system of quit-rents for the new lands as they were occupied. But he recognised that such a system required information to be collected from the colonies before a final judgment could be made on it and so it could not be hurried. When, therefore, Charles Townshend made his fatal boast in the Commons that he could raise an immediate revenue, from which his foolish import duties were developed, Shelburne's own proposals were ruined.

Out of office after 1768 Shelburne continued consistently to oppose the policy of coercing the colonies. It was not simply, he argued, that it was wrong but also that it would not work and further that it would give hostages to France and Spain whose hostility over Corsica and the Falkland Islands was plainly to be seen. He returned more than once to his point that to call the Americans *rebels* was 'idle and wicked' and that any separation from the colonies would harm England far more than it harmed America. In clinging to his hope, even after the surrender at Saratoga, that full independence would not have to be granted to the Americans he may justly be faulted by his

wn test of what could be enforced. And it was an unwise burst of rhetoric
1at led him to say in March 1778 in this context that once independence was
ranted 'the sun of Great Britain is set and we shall no longer be a powerful or
:spectable people'. Three years later, by the summer of 1781, he had
:ccepted that he was wrong and admitted that he 'had waked from his dreams
f British dominion'. Thenceforth, and especially after his return to office, he
)ught to secure out of the peace with America what we would call today a
)ecial relationship. He put this plainly in a letter to his agent negotiating in
aris in July 1782 when he said:

> My private opinion would lead me to go a great way for Federal Union; but is either
> country ripe for it? If not, means must be left to advance it.

'hree months later he returned to the same theme, writing on this occasion:

> If we are to look to regain the affection of America, to reunion in any shape or even
> to commerce and friendship, is it not of the last degree of consequence to retain
> every means to gratify America?

In the outcome Shelburne failed to secure his special relationship with the
)rmer American colonies. Old resentments survived the peace, sources of
·iction remained between the countries and it was to be more than a hundred
ears before the understanding friendship which he sought with statesman-
ke wisdom was finally attained.

Shelburne's views in relation to Ireland were as generous and liberal as his
iews on America. His early upbringing in Ireland at his grandfather's home
1 Kerry and his immense riches as an Irish landlord gave him special
nowledge and understanding of that unhappy country. When Secretary of
tate in 1767 he had endeavoured to make room for the growing Irish
emand for a greater share in their own government without sacrificing the
ountry to the shameless jobbery of the local politicians. His idea was to make
se of the Crown's prerogative to put an end to the wholesale grant of places
nd pensions for life, and to remove the control of appointments exercised by
1e Lords Justices by insisting that the Viceroy, whose powers they exercised
uring his prolonged absences, should be resident throughout his term of
ffice. As events turned out his period of office was too brief for him to
chieve either end, but he continued, while in opposition, to speak for Irish
berties. So when towards the end of 1773 the Irish Parliament proposed a tax
n the incomes of absentee landlords he refused to join with the Rocking-
ams in petitioning against it, notwithstanding his own vast rent-roll which
vould have suffered severely, because he acknowledged the inalienable right
f the Irish Commons to control their own finances. But side by side with
1is liberal and unselfish outlook there went an absolute determination to
1aintain English suzerainty. When in the summer of 1782 the second
\tockingham government, of which he was a member, moved towards a
elaxation of the trade restrictions imposed on Ireland, he was delighted. But
is pleasure in this was combined with a firm declaration of Ireland's sub-
rdinate position. 'Let the two kingdoms be *one*,' he wrote to the then Lord

Lieutenant, 'which can only be by Ireland's *now* acknowledging the super intending power and supremacy in *precise* and *unambiguous* terms to be wher nature has placed it.' Later that same year, when he was Prime Minister, thi anxiety to sustain England's control over Ireland led him to exaggerate th power available for his ends. His policy was not in the end put to the tes because his government fell, but it is only fair to admit that in respect c Ireland he hoped to preserve a position which the ministers he had appointe to deal with the situation saw was inevitably impermanent.[2]

Shelburne's wisdom in respect of India was of slower growth. Early in hi career he had entered the labyrinth of East India Company politics. His initia purpose was political; as Dame Lucy Sutherland has written, he was 'alive t the value to a rising politician of support from interests outside the House'. Subsequently, he allowed himself to be involved in financial speculation through the stock-jobbing manoeuvres of his confidential agent Lauchli Macleane. But by the time he had attained office again in 1766–8 he ha progressed to a more detached and statesmanlike view of the problems of th East India Company. He saw that the Company's territorial power ha vastly extended itself; he wished to distinguish between its profits from trade to which it was wholly entitled and which should, in his words, 'always be it first object', and its new revenues from its conquered territories. He wishe Parliament to take a share from the latter after full allowance of the Com pany's costs of collection and of the maintenance of its army. Above all h wanted the directors in London and their representatives in India to be mad to act honestly. As for the natives of India, he wished those under Compan rule to be reconciled to alien government by its honesty and mildness, whil he wanted the vast numbers who were outside Company control – th 'country powers' as they were known – to be freed 'of any jealousy they ma entertain of our unbounded ambition'.

To all these ends he urged Parliamentary intervention 'on behalf' as he late put it 'of the honest proprietors as well as the public'. When, therefore North's government proposed its Regulating Act for India in 1773, Shel burne, though in opposition, gave it his general support, while urging ye again the importance of distinguishing between the Company's trading profits and its territorial revenues. Insofar, then, as he hoped for the Englis connection with India to be essentially one of trade and for the extension o the Company's political authority to be arrested, his foresight failed him Certainly the Company was to lose its monopoly of trade as he hoped, bu the 'country powers' were not to be sustained, nor perhaps could they hav been. Nevertheless, it is a tribute to Shelburne's intellectual honesty that i retirement he implicitly accepted this; certainly he deplored the shamefu prosecution of Warren Hastings and acknowledged the debt the country owed him for sustaining and extending British rule in India.

There remains to consider one last issue on which Shelburne showe characteristic originality and insight. This was the problem of parliamentary

[2] Buckingham and Chandos, op. cit., I, 69, 74, 81, 83–4.
[3] Lucy S. Sutherland, *The East India Company in Eighteenth-Century Politics* (Oxford 1962), 92

epresentation. He had recognised as early as the 1760s that the old admini-
trative machinery needed reform if it was to control the extended colonial
mpire under British rule. When, many years later, he became Prime
Minister he was true to this political diagnosis and gave the first impetus to
ubstantial administrative reforms which were completed by the younger
Pitt. But this was only one aspect of his analysis of the governmental system
ffecting the executive powers of the Crown and its departments. He wanted
lso to reform the House of Commons itself. His purpose was to broaden its
epresentative basis, not just to weaken the influence of Crown and ministers
ver it – that after all was the cry of every eighteenth-century minister out of
ffice seeking the favour of the backbenchers – but on the wider ground that
uch a broadening would give political influence to new centres of popula-
ion. He was quick to appreciate the growth of the manufacturing class. As
arly as 1766, before he had returned to office and when he was anxious to
give his wife a jaunt, he took her to Birmingham to view the wonders of one
f its newly established button factories. He believed that, in time, this new
manufacturing and middling class would come to exercise great political
nfluence, indeed would govern. At the same time he had no romantic
llusions about the political wisdom of the squirearchy. 'The landed interest,'
he said on one occasion, 'was neither the whole nation nor the most enlightened portion of it'; and he added, at another time, that in his view the
ountry gentry were least open to conviction because both their fortunes and
their understandings were at a stand. In this way Shelburne anticipated the
reat parliamentary reform of 1832 and his reasons for reaching this position
vere purely intellectual. He stated his position clearly in a memorandum he
vrote towards the end of his life:

> As nothing in the world is, or can be in the nature of things fixed, all political
> institutions are perpetually, though insensibly, changing. So it is the business of
> sagacity to foresee and act upon every approaching change.

Why, then, it may be asked, when he was equipped in such large measure
vith the 'sagacity to foresee' was Shelburne virtually unable to secure any
action upon approaching change'? One part of the answer to this question
es in his inability to work with others in a ministerial team. He was touchy
nd interfering as a subordinate, uncooperative as an equal and secretive
vhen in command. At the time of his first period of office at the Board of
Trade he had attempted to make his acceptance conditional on his being
ranted 'equal access to the King with the other ministers'. He only
bandoned this claim when his patron, Bute, persuaded him that, if granted,
: would create what he was pleased to call 'a nest egg of ministerial discord'.
Then, having waived this demand and taken office on the understanding that
e would be subordinate to the Secretary of State, he immediately sought the
ight of direct correspondence with the American Commander-in-Chief.
While this demand is understandable in terms of efficiency it showed little
egard for the feelings of his older and more experienced superior (Egre-
mont), and not surprisingly it was briskly refused. Thereupon Shelburne

demanded the transference to his department of the whole American correspondence. Once again, on grounds of efficiency this was defensible, but as an
act of empire-building by a junior minister it was not. All this was done after
only three months in office, and because his schemes got him nowhere
Shelburne's answer was to talk of resignation which eventually, in spite of the
commonsense advice he rather surprisingly received from Bute to the contrary, he fulfilled two months later.

After three years, in which Shelburne may reasonably be thought to have
grown up, his conduct as Secretary of State showed no better appreciation of
political realities. On this occasion he was blessed with the support of
Chatham, the effective Prime Minister, and he had by reason of his own
office regular access to the King. Yet, when he found himself outvoted in
Cabinet on the policy to be adopted towards America, his answer was to
cease to attend Cabinet meetings. Indeed, his first inclination was to resign
and he only held back from loyalty to his new patron, Chatham, who had by
then been forced by ill-health to withdraw himself. All this was in March
1767. Not surprisingly, after three months of non-cooperation his colleagues
would have been glad to be rid of him and in June of that year the Duke of
Grafton, then acting as Prime Minister, told Chatham so.[4] Nevertheless, at
the end of the year Grafton went out of his way to try to lure Shelburne back
into full cooperation. The death of the neurotic Charles Townshend had
opened the possibility of a more liberal American policy by the government
It was now proposed to hive off all American business and entrust it to a new
third Secretary of State. Grafton, who shared with Shelburne an abhorrence
of the policy of coercion, begged him to transfer to this new office and thus to
give American affairs a fresh direction. Here was all that Shelburne had
wanted in 1763 and more, and yet his answer was to refuse. Moreover, his
refusal was grounded on mere punctilio. The scheme for a third secretary, he
complained, had been discussed without his knowledge – since he had not
attended the Cabinet this is hardly surprising – and on this formal ground of
incivility, he held back. He added that he did not want to take on the burden
of 'framing and modelling' the new office – though this was a task about
which he had already thought deeply. After this second rebuff Grafton
naturally yielded to his colleagues' pleas to be rid of Shelburne. He wrote to
Chatham to propose his dismissal. Chatham, rather than consent, resigned
himself. But Shelburne did not wait for any of this. Instead, on his own
independent decision, he chose once again to resign.

More than thirteen years were to pass before Shelburne returned to power
Then, in March 1782, he joined Rockingham's second ministry holding the
office of Home Secretary which was created by merging the responsibilities
of the old Southern department, shorn of its diplomatic duties, with the
colonial responsibilities of the now suppressed third secretaryship. The administrative uncertainties created by this new arrangement were aggravated
by the bitter personal suspicions of the new Foreign Secretary, Charles James

[4] W. R. Anson (ed.), *Autobiography and Political Correspondence of Augustus Henry, Third Duke of Grafton* (London 1898), 213.

Fox. Thus Shelburne was immediately plunged into disputes with his colleagues. The new ministry was a coalition between Rockingham's group, led in the Commons by Fox, and the talented rump of Chatham's former supporters following Shelburne. It had been formed with the objective of ending the American war. But the war now embraced France, Spain and Holland as active enemies. So Fox, as Foreign Secretary, expected full control of all peace negotiations while Shelburne saw the American side of the war as part of his colonial responsibilities. Friction and mutual suspicion inevitably followed and Rockingham, who was mortally sick, was unable to control his colleagues. When he died the King named Shelburne as his successor and Fox resigned. Now, at last, Shelburne was in a position to lead his government in the direction he thought right. But even as the King's chosen minister he was still unable to generate the vital confidence and cooperation of his colleagues which could have established his ministry. He kept his cabinet unanimous, observed one of its members sarcastically, 'by never meeting them'. The same critic went on to observe that it was 'Lord Shelburne's evident intention to make ciphers of his colleagues'.[5] Shelburne clearly trusted his fellow ministers as little as they trusted him. He believed that if he could negotiate peace he would win the support of a war-weary Commons. But when the Commons judged his peace terms to be inadequate he had no alternative strategy in mind. For the third and final time he resigned.

No statesman can expect to further his views by perpetual resignation. Shelburne's inability to work with others is, then, a substantial explanation of his failure to attain his ends. But it is not a complete answer. Colleagues in all walks of life are often generously indulgent towards their highly talented but difficult fellows, because they are ready to endure their asperities in order to benefit from their talents – in short, because they like them and trust them. Had Shelburne been so liked and trusted his career could well have taken a different path. But he was not. He was widely disliked and distrusted and it was this, as Wraxall stresses, which was his 'greatest political defect'. Against this handicap he could only have attained his ends in conditions of despotism – a point made by Richard Pares when he wrote of him that 'he would have shone as the prime minister of a benevolent despot'.[6]

How, then, did Shelburne win his evil reputation in public life? The fact of it is indisputable but, as Dame Lucy Sutherland has pointed out, 'there is no reason very obvious to posterity' to explain it.[7] Everything that we can learn of Shelburne from his published letters and papers, from his first wife's diary or from his friends shows him to have been, in private life, considerate, unselfish and amiable with, above all else, a wholly disinterested and dedicated regard for truth. Henry Fox and Lord George Germaine were the two contemporary politicians whom he most disapproved; in both, the quality he singled out for his distaste was the same – Fox, he said, 'despised knowledge' and Germaine 'had no desire of searching out truth'. Even his venial prejudice against the

[5] Buckingham and Chandos, op. cit., I, 76, 84.
[6] Wraxall, op. cit., III, 241; Richard Pares, *King George III and the Politicians* (Oxford 1953), 78n.
[7] Sutherland, op. cit., 92.

Scotch (he recalled with pleasure Admiral Boscawen's *mot* that the Scotch made good soles but bad upper leather) is explained in the same terms – 'they had no regard for truth'. The friends he sought were intellectual friends without regard to social distinction. The most famous of them were men such as Adam Smith and the French economist Morellet, whom he praised at the end of his life for 'liberalising' his ideas, and perhaps most of all the three radical thinkers who at different times made their home with him – Price, Priestley and Bentham. Priestley lived seven years with him in London and at Bowood 'nominally' as he later wrote 'as librarian but in fact as a friend'. Bentham's comment on arrival at Bowood in the early 1780s was that Shelburne 'was one of the pleasantest men to live with that God ever put breath into – his whole study is to make all about him happy'. Later he added that Shelburne 'valued himself on his friends and on their mutual fidelity', instancing Dunning, Camden and Alderman Townshend. As a husband and father he showed himself to be equally winning. His first wife's diary reveals him as a loving companion concerned alike for her entertainment and her instruction, prepared to read to her from sermons and to show affectionate interest in the progress of their baby son – a perfect example of the family man.

Notwithstanding the readings from Barrow's sermons it must be admitted that Shelburne was a vigorous anti-clerical. 'Will any reasonable and impartial friend of the Church,' he asked towards the end of his life, 'pretend that the clergy assist progress one hundredth part as much as they impede it?' And he extended this scepticism particularly towards bishops whom he accused of casting their mantle over every proposal for restricting the liberty of the subject. But although anti-clerical he was not hostile to the Christian faith. As a young man at Christ Church he had read and thought about religion for two years. 'I had no enlightened person to give me a lift,' he tells us in his autobiography, 'and I was left to grope my own way . . . at last I made up my own mind and have never since had an anxious thought upon the subject.' Later he explained his attitude. 'I consider man,' he wrote,

> as placed in the midst of a beautiful garden . . . surrounded with great and inaccessible mountains. The wise part of mankind are content to remain in the garden and quickly see that the door beyond is shut; the foolish part are continually struggling against nature and trying to ascend.

Here, then, is Shelburne in his home and at his fireside among his friends – cultivated, generous, amiable, moral. How are we to explain the contrast between this and his public reputation for deceit and dishonesty – between the affection and respect felt for him by his personal friends and the active dislike expressed by George III, who once wrote that he disliked him as much as Wilkes, or the fundamental distrust of other politicians? How was it that he came to be lampooned by the press as ambitious, devious and corrupt? He certainly did not start his political life with such a reputation. When he left active service in the army in 1761 and began his political career as a protégé of Lord Bute he expressed views of a naïve purity such as appealed to his priggish patron. When, at Bute's orders, Shelburne became the intermediary o recruit Henry Fox to government service, the latter was quick to express his friendly disapproval of the young Shelburne's 'puerile notions' and to try to impose some worldly common sense on him. The breach between them did not arise until early in 1763 and this marks the beginning of Shelburne's reputation for deceit. The issue was simple: had Fox agreed to give up the Pay Office on retirement from active government service and in return for a peerage? Bute and Shelburne thought that he had and Bute told the King so. Fox had originally feared that he might have to resign but, on second thoughts, judged he need not. Bute seems not to have known of Fox's change of mind and, when the misunderstanding became clear, cravenly blamed Shelburne for his misinformation. Fox naturally broke out in fury against Shelburne who defended himself with truth and dignity. He had reported to Bute in good faith and simply as a conversation what he had thought would be Fox's conduct. No plan had been built upon this report. But the King was violently hostile to Fox for quite other reasons; Fox had tried to launch his young sister-in-law, Lady Sarah Lennox, as the royal mistress.[8] Bute saw in Shelburne's earlier report of Fox's intentions something that fitted with the King's wishes and used it to try, unsuccessfully as it proved, to fulfil them. Later he defended himself to Fox by calling the whole affair a 'pious fraud' of Shelburne's – though insofar as there was any fraud it was his own. Fox's famous riposte, that he could see the fraud but where was the piety, set the pattern of Whig attitudes towards Shelburne from then on. And as Shelburne attached himself exclusively to the elder Pitt from that date it was inevitable that he should be assailed by the old Whigs.

Five years after this so-called 'pious fraud', on the occasion of Shelburne's resignation from the Grafton government, his reputation for duplicity and treachery was extended from the Whig *salons* to the whole political world. These were the years when he had been involved in the East India Company's affairs, and though he was far from being as corruptly implicated as his enemies alleged, there was enough material and rumour to create the image of him as a jobbing minister using his position for gain. His house in Berkeley Square, bought from the unpopular Bute, was quickly ascribed to improper gains. With journalistic genius Wilkes dubbed him 'Malagrida' after the harmless old Jesuit who had been executed in Lisbon on trumped up charges of encouraging a plot to assassinate the Portuguese King. A year later in one of the earliest *Letters of Junius* this pejorative image was extended and improved. Henceforth Shelburne was to be known as 'Malagrida' or 'the Jesuit of Berkeley Square' and the image was so well established that even George III accepted it. Shelburne could never escape from this. In politics, as George Rose warned the younger Pitt many years later, particularly instancing the case of Shelburne, 'when once an idea of intrigue is established it is not possible to do away with such impressions'.[9]

Yet Shelburne's evil reputation could never have been established in this way if he had not himself contributed to it. Faults of character and manner

---

[8] John Brooke, *King George III* (London 1972), 95-7.
[9] A. Aspinall (ed.), *The Later Correspondence of George III* (Cambridge 1968), IV, 508n.

undoubtedly made his situation worse. His character was contrary, secretive and vengeful. In his autobiography he acknowledged these failings, admitting that he had 'never forgotten a kindness nor an injury', and adding, in defence of his contrariness, 'as I was crossed in everything I was determined to cross in my turn'. His secretiveness was particularly damaging when he got caught up in the East India Company's affairs. His good friends Barré and Dunning begged him not to try to conceal his involvement. 'It should not be attempted to keep it private,' wrote Barré, adding that 'it would only increase suspicion to be too prompt in telling it, but surely it would be wise to meet it when it offers with temper and with truth.'[10] This was what Shelburne could not bring himself to do. His character led him to conceal what was in no way dishonourable, and in concealment he fed malicious rumour. But more than his character, his manner helped to undermine his reputation. He had had no early education in the ways of the world. Until the age of fifteen he was neglected in Ireland. Thereafter he had been 'supposed to go about and pick up what acquaintance offered', as he later described it. Two years at Christ Church did not make up the loss – nor four years of army service. Unpolished in youth he had to teach himself. The result was disastrous. The manner he evolved was unnatural, exaggerated, affected; his great-grandson and biographer writes sadly of his 'overstrained affectation of extreme courtesy and his habit of using unnecessary compliments in conversation'. This factitious, unnatural manner won him the reputation of insincerity wherever he went. His manner thus reinforced the malicious Whig stories of his insincerity and deceit. Even his friend Bentham admitted what he described as 'the prodigious . . . ambiguity of his language' to which he added Shelburne's unfortunate habit of following the same plan of flattery to gain different people which, if not recognised at first, could not fail to be noticed when applied to others.

So, in great measure, Shelburne made his own troubles. He was often suspected unjustly because of the way he behaved in public. It did not help that he was a master of sarcastic invective in public speaking and so by riling his opponents encouraged them to malign him in revenge. No detailed analysis of his political conduct between 1778 and 1783 really stands up to the adverse judgments passed on it by contemporaries and later historians alike. He treated Rockingham with far greater consideration and trust in 1779 and 1782 than Rockingham showed him in 1780. His conduct towards the younger Pitt after the formation of Pitt's government from which he was painfully excluded was a great deal more dignified and more generous than Pitt's was towards him. But all this is of small significance; what counted was what people thought and by 1783 everyone in politics distrusted Shelburne. The weight of his unpopularity, his friend Camden told him, was too great to stand against. And the younger Pitt showed, as always, a cold and accurate judgment when he refused to include him in his government and sought instead to solace him with his elevation as Marquess of Lansdowne.

Must we then leave Shelburne as an interesting but ineffective politician of

[10] Sutherland, op. cit., 211-12.

far-sighted views but no achievement? I think not. For though he was unable to carry his views forward, others did, particularly Pitt in the first ten years of his administration. Nor was Shelburne's influence limited to the party of Mr Pitt – the Tories of the future. He also influenced the Whigs through his younger son, Lord Henry Fitzmaurice, later third Marquess of Lansdowne, who was to sustain the doctrines of moderate Whiggism for more than fifty years after his father's death. As Charles Fox observed when considering the fate of his old enemy at the end of his life:

> Whatever disappointments Lansdowne may have had in public life he must be very unreasonable if he does not consider them all compensated in Lord Henry.[11]

---

[11] This and all other quotations not otherwise indicated are taken from the second and revised edition of Fitzmaurice's *Life of William Earl of Shelburne* (London 1912).

General Oughton *versus* Edinburgh's Enlightenment

Jeremy J. Cater

Between 1770 and 1774 the liberals of Edinburgh faced a serious and protracted challenge to the cultural ascendancy which they had so recently arrived at in the city and its region. The strength of traditionalism in Edinburgh had declined greatly since the failure of its full-scale assault on liberalism in a series of notable battles in the mid-1750s. During the 1760s the liberals had risen into a position of local dominance partly through the exercise of their own abilities, partly through the patronage of powerful allies at court and in parliament, and partly through their ideological and personal connections with the movement of rapid economic development and expansion which was then sweeping the southern lowlands of Scotland. Adam Smith and Adam Ferguson, Lord Kames and William Robertson were among the leaders of this group. By 1770 they and their associates commanded the university, dominated the church, and were highly placed in the machinery of law and local administration. They formed, in fact, a kind of local liberal establishment.

Their objective was a thorough re-ordering of society, so that its moral, economic, and political structures would be characterised respectively by self-control, by growth and by civic participation, instead of by collective pressure, stagnation and hierarchical exclusiveness. They envisaged the release of hitherto untapped psychological and social energies into a future that would be more free, more rational and more expansive than the past. Their method was to apply a sceptical attitude to the whole corpus of culture which they had inherited: not necessarily discarding individual ingredients or conclusions, but sifting, re-combining and re-presenting them all in new ways. In both method and objective they owed much to David Hume, whose intellectual brilliance and whose personal vulnerability had combined to make him a special totem figure for Edinburgh's liberals: often disagreed with, always affectionately admired.

Not all of Scotland, however, responded to the new model now being erected in Edinburgh. In 1770 a strong traditionalist counter-attack was launched from Aberdeen, where the new currents had yet done little more than ripple the surface of a still deeply conservative society. James Beattie, professor of moral philosophy at Aberdeen, published his *Essay on the Nature and Immutability of Truth in opposition to Sophistry and Scepticism*, a vigorous re-assertion of the validity of traditional values, and a vehement exposure of the dangerous moral and social consequences of sceptical thinking. The main thrust of the book was aimed explicitly at Hume's heterodoxy on religion. But Edinburgh's liberals closed ranks around him *en masse*, despite their own disagreements with him on this matter: partly out of pure friendship for the man, whom they conceived to have been grossly maligned in print by an ill-mannered and ignorant stranger; but also, and more profoundly, because they saw in the book, implicitly, a general threat to the future growth, or even present survival, of any liberal culture in Scotland, whether specifically Humean or not.

The fortunes of Beattie's book, and of Beattie himself, thus became, and were to remain for the next four years, a focus for the conflict of Scottish liberals and traditionalists. The *Essay* was admirably designed to provide a rallying point for the scattered forces of traditionalism. It was sufficiently simplified to be readily comprehensible by any educated person; sufficiently conventional to win easy acceptance by the general public; artful enough in style to catch and keep the reader's interest continuously; broad enough in scope to unite many of the variant forms of traditionalism; aggressive enough to promote high morale among its partisans and to drive them forward into battle with renewed appetite for victory. Its partisans in Edinburgh included all those who saw their values threatened by the new modes of thought and behaviour: transplanted Aberdonians; evangelical ministers of the kirk; professors of old and neglected subjects in the university; judges, magistrates and others professionally responsible for the maintenance of law and order; conservative bankers and merchants facing the challenge of more dynamic competitors; the timid and the conventional generally. For two years these forces struggled, revitalised but powerless, against the city's entrenched liberal establishment.

In June 1772 a dramatic reversal of fortunes occurred. The movement of economic development and expansion in the lowlands which had helped the liberals to power in Edinburgh came to an abrupt halt. Over-extended, it collapsed in bank failures, the forced sale of landed estates, mercantile distress, poverty and unemployment. Liberalism suffered a serious crisis of confidence, as well as of credit. It fell back into a defensive position for the next two years, while the ensuing depression lasted. The traditionalists surged forward triumphantly, vindicated in their prophecies of doom to the vices and follies of the age. Their pet project was now to bring Beattie to a chair in the University of Edinburgh. There he might trumpet his message to greater effect than when tucked away in Aberdeen; there he would provide valuable ideological support for his allies' drive to political, ecclesiastical and administrative power. The occasion was heaven-sent. For Adam Ferguson, with atrocious timing and insouciant disregard for consequences, chose now to apply for sabbatical leave from Edinburgh's chair of moral philosophy, in order to study and work abroad for a year or two, leaving his post open to contest.

In their campaign to promote Beattie, Edinburgh's traditionalists could call upon powerful assistance from outside Scotland. The archbishop of York and the lord chief justice, Scotsmen by birth but Englishmen by upbringing, were both found, upon application, to have ideological sympathies with Beattie's cause, and political motives for advancing it. Through them, and through others in civil and ecclesiastical administration, Beattie's book was introduced at court. The king and queen both read it, and expressed their approval. It was passed about among senior government ministers. The book obviously chimed well with the current concerns of England's ruling circles, preoccupied as they were with the problems of reimposing order and authority in a world that seemed to be breaking loose from its moorings. For this was the age of Wilkite turbulence on the streets of the metropolis, of mounting defiance from the colonists of North America, of pronounced restlessness among dissenting and even among Anglican clergy. Beattie's *Essay* seemed to provide some explanation for these disparate but evidently interlocking phenomena by pointing to the influence of scepticism in under-mining people's faith in traditional values and the traditional institutions which embodied them.

Beattie was therefore sent for, to come to London in the summer of 1773. He was received graciously in private audience by their majesties, and granted a royal pension for life. He was interviewed by government ministers, welcomed by judges, and feted by bishops. He was carried down to Oxford and awarded an honorary degree at the ceremonial inauguration of Lord North as vice-chancellor of the university. At last he was sent back to Aberdeen with a fanfare of publicity and an aureole of glory. A year later Edinburgh's town council was confidentially but weightily advised that the king would be well pleased to see Beattie appointed in Adam Ferguson's place as professor of moral philosophy in their university.[1]

Several men occupied at that time those interesting borderlands between the worlds of Scotland and England. But the prime instrument of their interaction in this story was the deputy commander-in-chief of the armed forces in North Britain, General Sir James Adolphus Oughton. Beattie had been introduced to him during a visit to Edinburgh in July 1772 by Dr John Gregory, a moral philosopher and medical professor transplanted from Aberdeen to Edinburgh. And though Beattie's visit had been too short for Oughton, as he wrote to Beattie, 'to cultivate that acquaintance with you which I wished', the General began to promote Beattie's interest by dropping his name in conversations with the king's ministers during a visit to London in November of that year.[2] The following summer Beattie was ushered up to his royal reception by means of a strong letter of introduction from Oughton

[1] For the foregoing, see in general Ernest C. Mossner, *The Life of David Hume* (Edinburgh 1954) and Margaret Forbes, *Beattie and his friends* (London 1904).

[2] Sir William Forbes, *An Account of the Life and Writings of James Beattie* (Edinburgh 1806), I, 235-7. All subsequent references to Oughton's relations with Beattie, and to Forbes's account of Oughton, will be to these pages in this volume, unless otherwise specified.

o his old friend Lord Dartmouth, Secretary of State for the Colonies.[3] And in
774 it was Oughton who was directed by Dartmouth to convey to Edin-
urgh's town council the king's desire that Beattie should replace Ferguson in
he moral philosophy chair.[4] Oughton's origins, connections, pursuits, and
ttitudes will be investigated here to explain, as far as may be possible, that
etermined patronage of Beattie which might at first sight appear unusual in a
ife-long professional soldier.

Oughton was the illegitimate son of a man who had made a successful career
n the Duke of Marlborough's army; who had ended as colonel of a regiment
f dragoons, owner of an estate in Warwickshire, M.P. for Coventry, and a
aronet. His father was married; but, begetting no legitimate heirs, gave his
wn name to his illegitimate son, took care that he should receive the classical
ducation of an English gentleman, and dying in 1736, when his son was
ixteen years old, bequeathed him £1,500, invested for the promotion of his
areer. James Adolphus Oughton was at that time a scholarship boy at
Charterhouse school, whence he proceeded to Trinity College Dublin,
efore entering the army in 1741 as a lieutenant in what had been his father's
egiment. He first went to Scotland in 1746 in the army of the Duke of
Cumberland and fought at Culloden. He saw active service also in Flanders
nd in Germany, commanding a regiment distinguished for its bravery at
Minden in 1759. Thereafter he was lieutenant-governor of Antigua for
everal years before returning to Scotland, where he reappeared in 1767 as
deputy commander under Lord Lorne. There he remained, being sub-
equently appointed official commander-in-chief himself, until his departure
o die at Bath early in 1780.[5]

During the early 1750s Oughton's regiment had been stationed in
Minorca, and Oughton took advantage of the peaceful conditions then
prevailing on the Continent to make a prolonged tour of Italy. There he
ndulged both his love of classical antiquities and his taste for the fine arts. For
ome time thereafter he kept up a correspondence with Thomas Jenkins, an
rt dealer residing in Rome who long supplied a copious stream of paintings,
drawings, and sculptures to wealthy art-lovers in Britain.[6] The fruits of this

---

[3] Ralph S. Walker (ed.), *James Beattie's London Diary 1773* (Aberdeen 1946), 29-30. Stafford
County Record Office, Dartmouth MSS, D.1778/V/855: Oughton to Dartmouth, 30 April
1773. Among these Dartmouth MSS are eight letters from Oughton to Dartmouth, dated:
30 April 1773; 3 Nov. 1773; 1 Mar. 1774; 10 Mar. 1774; 7 Nov. 1774; 16 Nov. 1774; 25 Aug.
1775; 6 Nov. 1775; also a paper numbered D.1778/II/1634 and entitled 'Hints from Sir Adolphus
Oughton relative to carrying on the war in America', n.d. but 1775. There are also (a) a letter
from Oughton to Lord Cathcart, 6 Nov. 1775; (b) a copy of Dartmouth's letter to Oughton,
21 Feb. 1774; (c) a letter from George III to Dartmouth, 10 Mar. 1774, numbered D.1778/I/ii/
1767. All subsequent references to relations between Oughton and Dartmouth will be to one of
these 12 documents, and will not be footnoted separately when they can readily be identified
from the text. I am grateful to the Earl of Dartmouth for permission to consult and quote these
documents, and to the archivists of Stafford County Record Office for their assistance.
Oughton's letters to Dartmouth of 16 Nov. 1774 and 24 Aug. 1775 were partially printed in
Historical Manuscripts Commission reports cited below.
[4] Stafford CRO, Dartmouth MSS, D.1778/III/307.
[5] *Dictionary of National Biography* and Forbes, *Life of Beattie.*
[6] Historical Manuscripts Commission, 15th Report, Appendix, Part I (Dartmouth MSS, vol 3), 170.

interest were revealed in Oughton's election to membership of the Society of
Antiquaries of London on 9 April 1767, and in his collection of Roman
armour which was later to arouse the admiration of the antiquaries of
Edinburgh. It is very likely that Oughton was responsible for selecting
Alexander Runciman to paint the murals in the new episcopalian church
which was opened in Edinburgh in October 1774: for the English general was
one of the principal patrons of the new building; and indeed it was he who had
laid the first stone in a public ceremony on 3 April 1771.[7] Another aspect of
his cultivation may be glimpsed in his membership of the Musical Society at
Edinburgh, which organised and attended the lively series of concerts at Saint
Cecilia's Hall during the 1770s.[8]

The sprinkling of Latin tags in Oughton's letters reveals his pleasure in the
command of classical literature. He is said to have possessed an extraordinary
talent for languages: not only knowing Greek and Latin, French and Italian,
but having some knowledge even of oriental literature. At the age of fifty,
after he had settled in Edinburgh, he set himself seriously to study Gaelic and
attained remarkable proficiency.[9] Before his death he had transcribed into a
book 'a pretty large collection of Gaelic pieces' which he had rendered into
English verse. These translations he used occasionally to read aloud in private
to other literary gentlemen like Lord Monboddo and Sir James Foulis. But
they would never, he said, be published while he was alive: he not choosing
to appear in the role of a poet while he was acting as a general.[10] He read
notable new books as they were published, and engaged in literary controversies: not only about Beattie's *Essay on Truth*, but also as to the authenticity
of Macpherson's *Ossian*, and the credibility of Monboddo's philosophical
anthropology.[11] Pamphlets were dedicated to him even by men who had
never met him personally. To such publications as met his approval he could
be a useful patron. In March 1774 he sent on to Lord Dartmouth, as Secretary
of State for the Colonies, one on emigration which, he judged, 'allowing for
the attachment to clanship inseparable from an Highlander, seems to be
wrote with truth and candour'. On occasion Oughton took up the pen
himself to compose a tract for the times: in November 1775 he was circulating among his friends a short piece designed to pour ridicule on the
behaviour of the parliamentary opposition.[12] His interests extended also to
natural history: in November 1773, commenting on Dartmouth's recent
acquisition of a flamingo, he described its natural habitat, noted the species to
which it belonged, and gave its Latin appelation. Sir William Forbes, an
Aberdonian who had been bred a banker in Edinburgh, and who came to
know Oughton quite well, relates of him that 'from his great stock of
acquired knowledge, his conversation was uncommonly instructive and

[7] *Scots Magazine*, Oct. 1774, pp.505–6.
[8] David Fraser Harris, *Saint Cecilia's Hall in the Niddry Wynd* (Edinburgh 1899), Appendix III,
pp.290–4.
[9] Forbes, *Life of Beattie*.
[10] Edinburgh University Library, MS DK.2.12, pp.26–7: Sir James Foulis to Earl of Buchan,
1783, transcribed by Buchan into a commonplace book.
[11] James Boswell, *The Life of Samuel Johnson* (Oxford 1934), v, 45.
[12] Stafford CRO, Dartmouth MSS, DS.1778/V/368.

ntertaining'. To Boswell he was 'one of the most universal scholars I ever new'. And when an English major stationed at Fort George said Oughton knew a great deal for a military man', Johnson roundly declared: 'Sir, you vill find few men, of any profession, who know more. Sir Adolphus is a very xtraordinary man; a man of boundless curiosity and unwearied diligence.' [13]

On the surface, Oughton's character was that of a well-bred man of the vorld: 'extremely polite in his deportment', an adroit and good-tempered onversationalist, he enjoyed the pleasures of society, and entertained ompany frequently in his grand residence of Caroline Park, on the edge of he Firth of Forth three miles out from the centre of Edinburgh. [14] He was lways concerned to preserve the decencies: his entertainments were invariably restrained to what was temperate; his attendance at public worship vas punctiliously regular; and he constantly bore in mind the respect due to is public station. [15] Vigorous in supporting his own opinions in an argument, ne was able, when faced with a possibly damaging public contest with a ormidable antagonist, to sidestep gracefully and withdraw with his credit ntact. A playful wit seasoned the gentlemanly good humour which he nabitually maintained in company. Boswell noticed, after dining with Oughton one day at the house of a common friend, that in Oughton's presence he always felt himself 'inspirited'. [16]

Yet behind this lively, polite and even-tempered social front lived a man of leeply felt emotions, who held a threatening world at bay by a constant application to public duty. He was devoted to his personal friends, and was not at all embarrassed to let the intensity of his feelings shine through even etters on official business – a remarkable trait in a man who had spent all the hirty-odd years of his adult life as a professional soldier. Public business had o be seen to at all costs, however. So, when the Duke of Atholl died suddenly a week before his re-election as one of Scotland's sixteen representative peers, Oughton at once notified the government of the immediate need to select a replacement. But it was painful. As he wrote to Dartmouth, 'It is with great grief and agitation of mind I sit down to acquaint your Lordship with the loss of our most excellent friend the Duke of Atholl.'

While in Oughton's scale of values the private and domestic virtues rated very high in estimating a man's worth, he held it to be the duty of worthy men to hold fast to the performance of public duty, and not to consult their

[13] Boswell, *Life of Johnson*, v, 45, and v, 124-5.

[14] The house survives today, containing internally some few but fine relics of its original splendour, but miserably cramped in its patch of waste land between huge and hideous neighbours: elephantine tenements of awful monotony on the one hand, vast acres of malodorous gasometers on the other. For the first two centuries of its existence, see David Fraser Harris, *Caroline Park House and Roystoun Castle* (Edinburgh 1896).

[15] Characteristics drawn from Forbes, *Life of Beattie*; Boswell, *Life of Johnson*, v, 45; Charles Ryskamp and F. A. Pottle (eds), *Boswell: The Ominous Years, 1774-6*, p.9: Boswell's diary for 30 Sept. 1774; Stafford CRO, Dartmouth MSS, D.1778/II/844. See also Lady Anne Barnard's sketch of Oughton in Lord Lindsay's *Lives of the Lindsays; or a memoir of the houses of Crawford and Balcarres* (Wigan 1840), II, 184-7.

[16] Boswell, *Life of Johnson*, v, 45; and Ryskamp and Pottle (eds), *Boswell's Ominous Years*, 43: 10 Dec. 1774.

merely private comfort. In November 1775 he strenuously urged his old friend Lord Cathcart, who was to die only half a year later, not to retire from public affairs: 'men of intrinsic worth, sound judgment, political experience and persuasive oratory are too precious to be spared at such a crisis; when the events of a day may become decisive.'[17]

Oughton considered himself a practical man: one who could realistically assess what was possible to achieve, and what was not; and who could suppress his desire for the unreasonable. By early 1774 private subscriptions had fallen far short of the costs of building the new episcopal church in Edinburgh, which Oughton had much at heart. He therefore confided to Lord Dartmouth 'a little plan of mine for obtaining some assistance' from the Treasury. But having outlined this, he concluded: 'If your Lordship approves of my scheme, I shall flatter myself with your good offices: if you think it idle or impracticable, you will be so indulgent to me as to forget that I ever troubled you with it.' Eighteen months later, giving Dartmouth his assessment of the situation in the rebellious American colonies, Oughton again displayed the same awareness of the tension between the ideal and the practicable, and the same conviction that realists would always acquiesce however reluctantly at times, in the inherent limitations of the situation which they had inherited. Some of the American leaders had proclaimed their aspirations to an independent sovereignty: but 'sensible men, however fond of the idea, must see the absurdity of it, and that their Utopian state can never exist but in the interior wilds of that vast continent, while Britain is master of a fleet.'

Yet it seems likely that Oughton, in his fifties, retained some of this tension within himself; and that, when the choice confronted him personally, it was by an effort of will, derived from his experience in the regiment of life, that he resolved the tension in favour of accepting the conventional wisdom. For there is a persistent, if occasional, leakage into his letters of another, more youthful state of mind, in which unruly inclinations were less than perfectly matched by expectations severely restricted: it survived in his evident love of allusion to the literature of the picaresque and the fantastic. The horses of Lord Dartmouth's sons visiting him at Caroline Park were, for Oughton, the 'Rozinantes' of Don Quixote's adventures. When Dartmouth himself half-spoke of visiting them at Caroline Park, their hearts 'leapt with joy at the momentary idea of your appearance: but, as Bishop Wilkin's scheme has never yet been reduced to practice, and terrestrial angels are not furnished with wings, I will not give up hopes of your trusting to a post-chaise for the mode of conveyance, when the service of the public can spare you for a few days to the embraces of your Hyperborean friends.'[18]

If this analysis is correct, if Oughton's playfulness did in truth disguise a

---

[17] Stafford CRO, Dartmouth MSS, D.1778/V/368.

[18] Stafford CRO, Dartmouth MSS, D.1778/II/1462. Oughton referred here to John Wilkins's *The Discovery of the New World in the Moon* (1638), which portrayed a travelling machine capable of defying the earth's gravity by the speed of its projection.

personal sense of tension between what might be dreamed and what must be done, it may shed a little light on the psychological roots of his strong emotional commitment to the formal structures – the monarchy, the church – which embodied and sustained the traditional values of English gentry culture, and which were now called upon to contain the turbulent thrust of new developments. It may help to explain the outrage he felt at the rebellion of the American colonists against their mother-country, against their father the king; the 'anxiety' and 'alarm' he expressed at the collapse of so many of Scotland's financial institutions in 1772, with the attendant crumbling of the old social system in bankruptcies and emigrations;[19] his eagerness to put Beattie in the most favourable position for championing the cause of intellectual orthodoxy against the corrosive scepticism of Hume's philosophy.

Politically, socially and intellectually, the new forces of liberalism aroused in Oughton dismay, anger and a determination to do what in him lay to uphold the power of traditional authority. He might be prepared on occasion, and in public, to pay lip-service to the system of constitutional balances established at the Glorious Revolution.[20] But in practice, and in private, he deplored the modern diminution in the power of the monarchy. 'It is equally to be lamented that, from the nature of our constitution, and the violence of our parties, the king's power, even of doing good, should in many instances be limited, in most obstructed.' The concept of a parliamentary opposition to the king's government was anathema to him. The duty of members of parliament was to support and assist the ministers whom the king had appointed. Any criticism 'is justifiable that tends to rouse ministers to the most lively exertion of their faculties in this great and momentous crisis of public affairs: but those who first endeavour to tie a minister's legs, and then accuse him for not running, I must deem enemies of their country as well as of the minister.' He was 'grieved to see men of character capable of being so misled by the spirit of party as to labour to frustrate the measures of government in a matter of so great national importance; and lend their aid and respectable names to the support of rebels and subversion of the state.' The freedom of the press was a principle equally obnoxious. He deplored the 'impunity' with which the press, following recent legal developments, was able to 'spew out' what he considered to be 'seditious papers'.[21]

If political disagreements were not to be allowed within the body of the nation, how much less could Oughton tolerate opposition from subordinate parts of Britain's empire. He was not prepared to admit that the American colonists had any right whatsoever to question, let alone resist, any part of the policies of the British government – whose authority ought to be absolute.[22] In his letters there is no glimmer of comprehension of the process of historical change, by which new relationships might arise which it would be expedient

[19] Stafford CRO, Dartmouth MSS, D.1778/II/1462; D.1778/V/368; D.1778/II/854.
[20] *Scots Magazine*, Nov. 1773, p.613: report of Oughton's speech to Edinburgh Revolution Club, 15 Nov.
[21] Forbes, *Life of Beattie*; Stafford CRO, Dartmouth MSS, D.1778/V/368 and D.1778/II/1462.
[22] Stafford CRO, Dartmouth MSS, D.1778/II/1462 and D.1778/II/1634.

to recognise. The American colonies had been originally planted by authority of the English crown: for Oughton, that was enough to define the relationship for ever. For Oughton, as for Beattie, the pattern of truth was something laid down *ab initio*; thenceforth it was immutable.

Corresponding to his emphasis on the principle of authority in political affairs, Oughton's views on the structure of society were avowedly hierarchical. Of 'the people' in general he was contemptuous. 'The populace is very short-sighted, if not totally blind, and may be led to believe anything'; easily made 'the dupes of interested and designing men'; subject to fits of dangerous enthusiasm; soon ready, if distressed in their bellies, to turn against their own leaders, and plunder one another. In the American colonies, and especially in New York, the British government should exert 'all possible means' for 'recovering the power out of the hands of the populace', and for restoring it into the hands of 'the wise and well-disposed', who would then be able 'to bring order out of the confusion which has so long prevailed'. But the merchants, too, must be watched carefully, for among them were those 'interested and designing men': the non-importation scheme of the Philadelphia congress in 1774, for instance, was designed for 'throwing the whole commerce into the hands of a few artful monopolisers'. Strong government was necessary to hold down such unruly subjects and to compel them to do their duty to society and the state. The parliamentary opposition was playing with fire in seeking to ride to power on the backs of supporters like these: 'republicans and independents.' If the opposition did achieve power they would 'find too late that they have given themselves masters as well as the state, who will have as little mercy on their honours and estates as they have on the constitution'. The upper levels of society, Oughton said, ought to take their tone from the example set by a wise and good king: he regretted that they no longer did so.[23]

In the realm of ideas Oughton, as might be expected in a supporter of Beattie, laid great stress on the authority of cultural tradition as a criterion of objective truth: 'proverbial sayings, as resulting from the experience of mankind, and appealing to their common sense, have generally been received as axioms.'[24] Even Oughton's tactics in a controversy bear a remarkable resemblance to those of Beattie. In late 1775, when he wrote for private circulation a pamphlet which aimed to counteract the position taken on American affairs by the parliamentary opposition, he cast it in a satirical form: 'when tempers are soured by party one should endeavour to raise a laugh: and the *reductio ad absurdum* frequently succeeds where better argument fails.'[25]

---

[23] Stafford CRO, Dartmouth MSS, D.1778/II/1462; D.1778/II/1634; D.1778/V/368; Forbes, *Life of Beattie*.

[24] Forbes, *Life of Beattie*.

[25] Stafford CRO, Dartmouth MSS, D.1778/V/368: Oughton to Cathcart, 6 Nov. 1775. Thanks to Boswell one can observe Oughton applying this technique in an argument with that contentious bear Samuel Johnson over the authenticity of Ossian. Just when Boswell, in whose house they met, became alarmed that tempers were growing hot, Oughton changed the subject and began to poke fun at Lord Monboddo's anthropological theories, at which Johnson too could join in the general laugh. Boswell, *Life of Johnson*, v, 45.

But the recourse to arguments based on guile commonly has an effect upon the user as well as upon those against whom they are used. It can insinuate in the user's mind a propensity to believe that the arguments of those with whom he disagrees are not merely erroneous in fact or logic, but actually dishonest in intention: webs of fiction designed to throw a veil over ulterior motives. As with Beattie, so with Oughton; though the impact of one was literary, the other political. His suspicion of the Americans left no room for crediting good intentions, or even muddled intentions. The armed encounters at Lexington and Concord 'were the consequences of a long premeditated, regular, and well laid plan'. 'Those who believe them to be the result of chance or hasty resolutions are capable of believing anything. We hear much talk of conciliatory proposals from the Congress, and suspension of arms. The one must be fallacious, the other pernicious to the last degree: the purport of both to gain time.'

A conviction as to the moral iniquity of an opponent all too usually dissolves any scruples as to the mode of gaining the victory over him. Just as Beattie was prepared, as he admitted, to put on all the clothes in the wardrobe of rhetoric in the attempt to frighten people into rejecting Hume's philosophy; so Oughton disavowed all restraints in his desire to bludgeon the American colonists into obedience: no money should be spared in bribing their leaders; all the inhabitants of Boston should be turned out of the town; all colonial ships should be dismasted; the southern colonies should be threatened with a proclamation of freedom for negroes; and so on.[26] Such is the force of moral absolutism.

It seems very likely that Oughton's temper was sharpened at this time, and his view of the world jaundiced, as he experienced the pressure of severe financial difficulties. First his regiment's finances were disordered by the recklessness of its paymaster in America and the death of its agent in Britain. Then Oughton's personal funds were involved in the great crash of Douglas Heron and Company in June 1772. Small wonder that on 23 June 1772 one of Oughton's friends was shaking his head sympathetically over 'the intricate and distressful situation' of Oughton's financial affairs.[27] It was several years before the tangled affairs of Douglas Heron and Company were finally unravelled, and in the mean time all those connected with it suffered severely.

Money troubles may well, therefore, help to provide a partial and temporary explanation for Oughton's attitudes and behaviour in this period of his life. What is certain, however, is that in the shaping of those attitudes and behaviour a permanent and fundamental part was played by his sense of the importance of religion. Personal, social and political considerations each contributed their share to his commitment to upholding the cause of the sacred truths. Sir William Forbes remarked how Oughton 'united, in no

[26] Historical Manuscripts Commission, 14th Report, part X (Dartmouth MSS, vol. 2), 360–1; and Stafford CRO, Dartmouth MSS, D.1778/II/1634.

[27] B.L., Add. MSS. 21729, ff.164–5; P.R.O., WO 3/2/p.64, and WO 4/89/pp.164, 168, 358, 382; Edward William Harcourt, *The Harcourt Papers* (Oxford 1876–1905), XI, 162. See, too, Henry Hamilton, *An Economic History of Scotland in the Eighteenth Century* (Oxford 1963), 317–25.

common degree, the character of the man of piety with that of the man of the world'. What Forbes noticed most particularly about the nature of Oughton's religious practice was its combination of emotional and aesthetic sensibility on a personal level with a simultaneous concern for its use as a means of social control: 'I know not that I have ever felt more forcibly the power of devotion, than when on a Sunday evening at his house, in the neighbourhood of Edinburgh, collecting his guests around him, I have heard him read the church-service, from the English liturgy, with the utmost fervour, and most graceful elocution.'

A self-proclaimed true believer, Oughton felt that he was living amidst 'a deluded and dissipated people', whose eyes were blind and whose hearts were stubborn.[28] In Edinburgh David Hume had many friends, 'and I fear too many disciples'.[29] Describing his situation to a religious friend in England, he testified to the deplorable fact that the sceptical philosophers 'are a powerful body in this country both for abilities and connections'.[30]

One way in which Oughton could seek to reclaim his fellow subjects from the paths of error was by using his influence to promote the career of a professed author like Beattie who would 'dedicate as much of his time as possible to the defence of the sacred truths'.[31] But the chief recourse for a man in his public station was to set a high moral example himself. Forbes attested of Oughton that 'in his attention to all the external observances of religion, he was most exact'. The effect which this public example had upon the citizens of Edinburgh may be glimpsed in the diary of James Boswell – that chronicle of incessant fluctuation between 'infidelity' and belief, probity and temptation. Sauntering down the Canongate one Sunday morning in September 1774 and on the point of entering a club to lounge, drink tea and read the newspapers, instead of going to church, Boswell observed Sir Adolphus and Lady Oughton driving to the English chapel; felt a spark of envy for the 'uniform decency' of Oughton's life; and promptly experienced within himself 'a kind of bashfulness and unwillingness to be looked at'.[32]

The 'English chapel' to which Oughton was driving when Boswell saw him in late September of 1774 had been built during the previous three years, and owed much to Oughton's concern for the proper appearance of his public worship. The three existing episcopalian chapels in Edinburgh had been judged inadequate. When the expense of constructing a new church proved too great for private subscription, Oughton procured government support to the tune of £200, on the ground that although the commander-in-chief of the army in North Britain was generally an Englishman (belonging, of course, to the Anglican church), 'no provision has hitherto been made by government for the exercise of his religion': government assistance was therefore justified in order to ensure that a pew was purchased and properly furnished so that the commander-in-chief in Scotland could worship publicly in a style appropriate

[28] Forbes, *Life of Beattie*.
[29] Stafford CRO, Dartmouth MSS, D.1778/II/844.
[30] Stafford CRO, Dartmouth MSS, D.1778/II/854.
[31] Ibid.
[32] Ryskamp and Pottle (eds), *Boswell's Ominous Years*, 9: diary for 30 Sept. 1774.

to his high office.[33]

Religious ceremonies were, for Oughton, a principal means of enhancing the public's awareness of the importance of thinking right and acting right. Even so essentially secular an event as the revolution of 1688 was retrospectively to be accorded an ecclesiastical commemoration, symbolic of the alliance between church and state. At a general meeting of the Edinburgh Revolution Club in November 1773 Oughton successfully proposed that in future the annual gathering at the Assembly Hall should be preceded by a solemn procession of the club's members to church, where a sermon would be preached 'on purpose to retain and cherish in the minds of the people' a proper sense of the blessings of the British constitution.[34]

Whatever might be the personal origins of his own religious sentiments, Oughton undoubtedly always viewed religion socially as a bulwark of the establishment. Faced by the fact that in America 'factious preachers' (nonconformists, of course) were among those responsible for instigating the colonists to neglect their duty to the mother country, Oughton fell back on an attitude which, however characteristic of the eighteenth-century English gentleman, should not in strict logic have provided an explanation of such phenomena that would be attractive to one who himself felt, in some degree, the strength of religious motivation: the belief that religious 'enthusiasm' was something associated with the great unwashed, and not with 'the wise and well disposed'. 'The populace,' he declared, 'is very short-sighted, if not totally blind, and may be led to believe anything; and enthusiasm, whether religious or political, is capable of amazing efforts and productive of the most fatal catastrophes.'[35]

That he could speak in this manner about religious enthusiasm to his 'dearest friend' Lord Dartmouth, who was himself notoriously a patron of 'enthusiastic' field-preachers in England, reveals how easily Oughton's sense of a personal religion could be submerged by his preoccupation with social control. When he learned from Beattie that George III openly avowed his high esteem for Lord Dartmouth, Oughton wrote that he was filled with exultation: 'it may do the King much good – it may do the nation much good – and may establish his throne in righteousness, which I most earnestly pray for.' In the church, as in the state, Oughton sought for society's motivating spirit in the person of the king, 'who is so eminent a patron of piety and virtue'.[36]

Oughton's religion was thus genuine enough. But it was a religion strongly marked with the principles of authority, hierarchy, traditionalism and conformity. It was his religion which brought him into close contact with that circle of displaced Aberdonians who formed the leadership of the episcopalians of Edinburgh, and whose spirit of attenuated Jacobitism had much in common with Oughton's outlook. And it was through this episcopalian, Aberdonian

[33] *Scots Magazine*, Oct. 1774, pp.505-6. A contemporary account of this building may be found in Hugo Arnot's *History of Edinburgh* (Edinburgh 1779), 283-7 (the church survives today, converted to Roman Catholic use); Stafford CRO, Dartmouth MSS, D.1778/II/844 and D.1778/II/1462.
[34] *Scots Magazine*, Nov. 1773, p.613.
[35] Stafford CRO, Dartmouth MSS, D.1778/II/1462.
[36] Stafford CRO, Dartmouth MSS, D.1778/III/303 and D.1778/II/844.

circle in Edinburgh that Oughton was introduced to, and became the patron of, James Beattie.

It remains now to determine the extent of Oughton's influence in Edinburgh, to uncover the sources of that influence, and to examine the ways in which he used it. His office as deputy commander-in-chief of the army in Scotland, the charm and energy of his personality, and the circle of family relations and friends which he established for himself, all contributed something to build for him a position of considerable local weight. But far the most important source of influence was the fact that, by the early 1770s, the men with whom he had been longest and closest connected had themselves reached the very head of the government at Westminster.

Oughton had met Lord North and his step-brother Lord Dartmouth in Italy during their grand tour of 1752-4. The friendship begun then was firmly cemented during subsequent years.[37] In the early 1770s Oughton and Dartmouth were exchanging letters frequently; in November 1773 Dartmouth's sons Lord Lewisham and Mr Legge were staying with Oughton at Caroline Park; and when Oughton went to London he saw regularly both Dartmouth and North.[38] The relationship was by no means exclusively a personal friendship: the content of many of Oughton's letters and interviews was avowedly political. Writing in August 1775, not long before Dartmouth exchanged the hot seat of the Secretary of State for the Colonies for the less exposed position of Lord Privy Seal, Oughton gave him advice on how best to deal firmly and decisively with the rebellious Americans, referring by way of self-justification to his own 'anxious concern for whatever my dearest friend is interested in'. The sagacity of Oughton's judgment of individuals, and the absolute reliability of his support for government, led Lord North to place in the army's effective commander-in-chief in Scotland a considerable degree of responsibility for the political management of that country.

In the period of preparation for the general election of November 1774 Oughton was reporting to Dartmouth on the immense number of fictitious votes being made in Scotland; the state of feeling in the country about the forthcoming Linen Bill; and the general anxiety arising from the spate of bankruptcies and emigrations still issuing forth in the wake of the great financial crisis of the summer of 1772. But the part which Oughton played in the political management of Scotland for Lord North can be most appropriately illustrated by his activities in connection with the election of the sixteen peers who were to represent the Scottish nobility in the House of Lords. First, he recommended suitable candidates to fill up the vacancies on the government's list.[39] In 1774, however, recommendations were not enough. For the formal circular lists of the government's candidates sent out by Lord Suffolk as Secretary of State for the Northern Department appeared offensively arrogant to a substantial body of the peers; and the government

[37] Forbes, *Life of Beattie*; H.M.C. 15th Report, Part I (Dartmouth MSS, vol. 3), 170.
[38] Forbes, *Life of Beattie*; Stafford CRO, Dartmouth MSS, D.1778/II/854.
[39] Stafford CRO, Dartmouth MSS, D.1778/II/854.

was faced with the prospect of a vigorous, and potentially damaging public contest.[40] Oughton's personal supervision of the situation was required. He sent the government copies of pamphlets published by opposition peers like Lord Elibank; he was kept informed about the pre-election manoeuvres of the Duke of Buccleuch to bring the angry peers back into the fold; and he was personally present at the election itself: as a visible witness to the peers that their speeches and votes were being individually recorded and directly reported back to government.[41]

Other aspects of Oughton's influence in Edinburgh are occasionally visible: his leading role among episcopalians; his capacity to sway the Revolution Club; the fact that he was Grand Master Mason of Scotland in 1771; that he was elected to the management committee to sort out the affairs of Douglas Heron and Company;[42] that he was a director of the city's academy for riding and fencing.[43] Moreover, Oughton's own personality – his charm, his energy, his reputation as a man of honour and a patriot – were by no means negligible assets in his use of the arts of persuasion. As he wrote to Dartmouth, his arguments in favour of the appointment of Beattie to the Edinburgh professorship would strike the lord provost all the more forcibly 'from my well-known zeal for the honour and welfare of this country'.

Most of the professorships in the University of Edinburgh lay within the patronage of the town council, that small body elected out of the leading merchants and craftsmen of the city. Even within this very circumscribed circle it is possible to trace some of Oughton's connections, and occasionally to observe him in the act of exerting his influence. Boswell recorded in his diary on 10 December 1774 that he and his wife dined with Sir Adolphus and Lady Oughton at the house of James Hunter. James Hunter was the partner of Sir William Forbes in one of Edinburgh's most important banking houses: though not on the town council at this date, he was an active local politician, had been a member of council a few years previously, and a decade later was not only lord provost, but also M.P. for the city and a baronet. Boswell's diary entry for 30 January 1776 suggests why Edinburgh's politicians might well consider it highly desirable to cultivate Oughton's good will. The army sent a recruiting captain to enlist soldiers even in the centre of the city. The town council disliked this, but could not cite any legal privilege of exemption. The lord provost therefore appealed to Oughton to interpose by his authority as commander-in-chief. Deciding that this was an innovation which might produce a disturbance of public order, Oughton came down firmly on the lord provost's side, and flatly prohibited the recruiting party from operating within the city's limits.[44]

---

[40] These election missives to the peers of Scotland were often directed to them at Caroline Park under cover of the secretary of state's correspondence with Oughton. See P.R.O., SP/54/46, ff.417-18: Cathcart to Suffolk, 15 Nov. 1774.

[41] H.M.C., 11th Report, Part V, 369-70.

[42] *Scots Magazine* for Oct. 1774, pp.505-6; for Nov. 1773, p.613; and for Dec. 1773, p.668.

[43] John Anderson (ed.), *A Calendar of the Laing Charters belonging to the University of Edinburgh* (Edinburgh 1899), p.739, item 3248.

[44] Ryskamp and Pottle (eds), *Boswell's Ominous Years*, 43: diary for 10 Dec. 1774; and 226: diary for 30 Jan. 1776. The impression this last entry gives is misleading, and must be corrected by reference to a document in EUL, La. II. 509: copies of the letter Boswell wrote for recruiting captain Flint, and of the responses to it of Lord Provost Stoddart and Oughton, 23 and 25 Jan.

There was one substantial limitation on Oughton's influence in Edinburgh in the early 1770s. He was evidently not on good terms with the M.P. for the city, Sir Laurence Dundas: that overgrown merchant turned feudal lord, who had amassed a prodigious fortune out of contracts to supply Britain's armies on the Continent during the Seven Years War, when Oughton had been colonel of a regiment fighting in Germany. Sir Laurence spent his money lavishly and unscrupulously to achieve what was then an unchallengeable control over the political allegiance of the city of Edinburgh. When Oughton wrote to Beattie in February 1774 about the prospects of obtaining for him the appointment to the Edinburgh chair of moral philosophy, he told him that the town council was said to be entirely in the pocket of Sir Laurence Dundas: and that any recommendation from him to the town council would carry little weight if it did not coincide with the wishes of the great city boss.[45]

But Oughton was no defeatist, whatever his caution in not promising success. For a few days later he was writing to Dartmouth, and describing the tactics he proposed to use in order to secure the Edinburgh professorship for Beattie. Chief among these there figured a conversation with the lord provost over dinner at Caroline Park. He would then urge that as Beattie had received a government pension so recently as last summer it could no doubt be taken for granted that his appointment would be viewed with gratification in the highest circles. Oughton did not propose, at this first meeting, to name Lord North directly. But of all possible lord provosts of Edinburgh, Gilbert Laurie was the one least likely to mistake a hint like that. For he was not only a successful merchant; he was also a commissioner of the excise. Thus he would certainly know that government pensions were authorised by the first lord of the treasury himself.

It is time, finally, to trace the course of the relationship between Oughton and Beattie, which the foregoing pages have sought to explain. Oughton was obviously very favourably impressed by Beattie at their first meeting in July 1772, when Dr John Gregory took advantage of Beattie's brief visit to Edinburgh to introduce him to a powerful patron. For when Oughton wrote to Beattie from London a few months later he declared that 'as a lover of truth', despite the slenderness of their personal acquaintance, 'I cannot but be warmly interested in the honour and welfare of its ablest champion'. It was with 'real pleasure' that he told Beattie the story – elicited from Dartmouth no doubt by Oughton's own prompting – how 'our excellent Sovereign has read your *Essay* with the utmost attention and approbation, and expressed his intention of bestowing on you some mark of his royal favour, when a proper opportunity shall offer'. He urged Beattie to continue his labours 'for the true interests of mankind': 'pursue then the glorious task; open the eyes and amend the hearts of a deluded and dissipated people.' Beattie's writings would do good; and the reward which he deserved would be assured.

At the end of April Beattie spent two days in Edinburgh on his way to London, paid two visits to Oughton, and brought away a letter of introduction

[45] Aberdeen University Library, Beattie Papers, C.176.

from him to Lord Dartmouth.[46] In this letter Oughton proclaimed Beattie 'the ablest advocate for truth which this age has produced'; he attested the fact that Beattie's 'acknowledged merit as a man' was 'not inferior to what he has shewn as an author'; and indicated his desire that Dartmouth would help Beattie to obtain either an increase in his income as a professor at Aberdeen or an 'encouragement' to take orders in the Anglican church, 'in which he may be of eminent service to the cause of religion and virtue'.

Several times during that summer, which he spent entirely in England, Beattie wrote to Oughton: describing the warm welcome accorded him by Dartmouth, the interviews with other eminent and friendly Englishmen, and the satisfactory progress of the negotiations for a pension from the government. On his return to Scotland in late September, Beattie was invited to dine at Caroline Park.[47]

There Beattie repeated to Oughton his vows of eternal gratitude to Lord Dartmouth, recounted his gracious reception by their majesties and retailed the king's expression of the high esteem in which he held Dartmouth's personal character. On hearing this, as he wrote to Dartmouth, Oughton was overjoyed 'to an immoderate degree – embraced Beattie, would have kissed the King if I could have got at him; and hugged your Lordship to death if you had been within my reach.'

In the following February Oughton was informed by Dartmouth of the project to bring Beattie to Edinburgh as professor of moral philosophy in place of Adam Ferguson, whom a party on the town council were attempting to evict from his chair. Beattie's friends on the town council had written to 'some of the principal people' in the administration at London for their support.[48] Dartmouth responded by entrusting the government's backing for Beattie's candidature to the capable hands of Oughton.[49]

Oughton had not hitherto been informed either of the present, or of the previous attempts to provide a chair for Beattie in the University of Edinburgh.[50] He therefore wrote to Beattie directly with the assurance that he would most zealously do whatever he could for him. But he needed information as to what were the best channels to employ in Edinburgh, for his own personal influence was very limited in a matter such as the appointment to the chair of moral philosophy. 'As I understand it is at the disposal of the magistrates, and am told that they are entirely under the influence of Sir Laurence Dundas, I much fear that any application from me will have but small weight with them.'[51] While waiting for Beattie's reply he set to work, unravelling the details of the situation, and making a few preliminary moves. Beattie's chances, Oughton wrote to Dartmouth, depended initially on whether the town council could compel Ferguson either to resign the travelling tutorship with Lord Chesterfield which he had recently accepted, or to forfeit

[46] Walker (ed.), *Beattie's Diary 1773*, p.29.
[47] Ibid., 30, 57, 73, 85, 95.
[48] Forbes, *Beattie and his friends*, 104.
[49] Stafford CRO, Dartmouth MSS, D.1778/III/307.
[50] Stafford CRO, Dartmouth MSS, D.1778/II/844.
[51] AUL, Beattie Papers, C.176.

his chair if he were to absent himself from Edinburgh for more than one year. In the latter event, Oughton reported:

> Dr Beattie, I am told, stands very well with the Magistrates; but has created himself many enemies here by his attack on Mr Hume . . . I have thrown out some hints that it will be a great honour to the Magistrates and University if they can get a man of Dr Beattie's character to fill the moral chair; and that, from the marks that gentleman has received of royal favour, they may be well assured their nomination of him would be acceptable to their Sovereign, who is so eminent a patron of piety and virtue. I have asked the Lord Provost to dine with me that I may feel his pulse; and urge those reasons more strongly from my well known zeal for the honour and welfare of this country. But shall take care not to commit your Lordship or Lord North, without opposition from some other quarter should make it necessary, and your Lordship should empower me so to do.

The steps Oughton had taken were communicated by Dartmouth to the king, who approved them as seeming 'very judicious and most likely to be crowned with success'.[52]

Beattie, meanwhile, had replied to Oughton that, contrary to report, he was declining to appear as a candidate for Ferguson's chair, and that 'for private reasons I would not accept of it even if it were in my offer'. For details he referred Oughton to a letter he had written to his friend Sir William Forbes the banker the previous October: at which time friends had also been engaged in thrusting his name forward for a vacancy then expected at Edinburgh.[53] Forbes duly showed to Oughton Beattie's explanatory letter of the previous October, and transmitted simultaneously the regrets which Beattie was now expressing that the solicitations of his supporters in Edinburgh had, unbeknownst to him, instigated his highly-placed friends in England to take unnecessary trouble on his behalf. Oughton found Beattie's letter of explanation 'very judicious'. But, as he withdrew from this anticipated involvement in local Edinburgh politics, he was already manifesting his concern to preserve a face of dignity for the authority of the king's government. He told Forbes that he imagined 'it was a view of serving the worthy Doctor, and rendering him more diffusively useful to his fellow subjects, not any solicitations from hence, that induced his Majesty's confidential servants to wish he might fill the moral philosophy chair at Edinburgh'.[54]

Reporting finally to Dartmouth on the outcome of this *excursus*, Oughton summarised Beattie's reasons for declining the contest as founded 'chiefly on the experienced animosity of his literary antagonists, and his resolution to dedicate as much of his time as possible to the defence of the sacred truths against the sceptical philosophers, who are a powerful body in this country both for abilities and connections'.

Oughton's endeavours to promote Beattie ended there. Oughton remained at his post in Edinburgh, struggling with characteristic energy and devotion to cope with the rising tide of turbulence at home and abroad which marked

[52] Stafford CRO, Dartmouth MSS, D.1778/I/ii/1767.
[53] Forbes, *Beattie and his friends*, 104.
[54] Forbes, *Life of Beattie*, I, 305.

the second half of the 1770s, until, late in 1779, he finally collapsed under the pressure of his duties. He retired, a sick man, to Bath, where death overtook him in the following spring. A plaque commemorates him in Westminster Abbey.[55]

---

[55] A perceptive account of Oughton in the troubles of 1778-9 is given in the second section of John Prebble's most interesting and original work *Mutiny: Highland Regiments in Revolt 1743-1804* (London 1975), which also reproduces a portrait of him from the Scottish National Portrait Gallery.

20

Thermidor or the Retreat from Fantasy

Richard Cobb

From the start we are plunged, without explanation, into a fantasy world, drifting apparently outside time and space, *l'Embarquement pour Cythère*, and peopled by strange, hybrid creatures: a *Lycoperde*, a *Nerprum*, a *Sorgho*, all three perhaps in flight from the zealously proscribed *emblèmes féodaux*, the mark of iniquity, and attempting to earn their passage, like unicorns who, abandoning their side of the Royal Arms, and turning to republicanism, in the new institutions and in the purified vocabulary of Virtue, leave the lions in sole control. Or, perhaps, we have strayed, inadvertently, into a closed, scented and overheated *pensionnat*, a well organised finishing school of elaborate vice, run by Madame Janus or an Academy of Manners for the Instruction of Innocence, in the tender path of *Paul et Virginie*. Or judging from the names of those present, of the female company: a bit of both, the exciting ambivalence of Innocence and Vice. For here are the rather prissy *Guimauve*, the rather melancholy *Ancolie*, the quarrelsome and strident *Coriandre*, the intrepid *Sabine*, the gentle *Garence*, the tender *Carline*, the exotic *Cochléaria*, the sleepy *Gentiane*, the lachrymose *Armoise*, the virtuous, big-breasted *Romaine*, the pretty *Pimprenelle*, the dusky *Mandragore* (recruited from the Algiers slave market of Delacroix), the rustic *Pâquerette*, the mysterious *Orcanète*, the shameless *Jonquille*, the incorrigible *Roquette*, the insipid *Réglisse*, the jolly, southern-voiced *Pastèque*, her vowels wide open, the splendid, big-limbed *Bigarade*, full house at *les Contemporaines*, but hinting too at the crowded stage of the *Boulevard du Crime* and at the twilight fantasies of de Lautréamont, or, more banally, at the clinical, closely observed map of Paris prostitution of Parent-Duchâtelet, as if the *pensionnaires* had somehow escaped from the tight corset of the Year II of the French Republic, or as if, bored stiff and fed up with so much neo-classical posturing, with pretending to be Sabines, when in fact they were but laundresses and *plumassières* from the Faubourg Poissonnière, they had all at once stepped out of one of David's enormous set pieces, to return to the realities of the rue des Filles-Dieu, the most ill-named of all Parisian streets.

But, in this heavily perfumed and scantily clothed community, there are uggestions too of *la Belle Epoque*, of *Casque-d'Or*, and of the vulgar, nuscular bad girls of the Faubourg: of Belleville and Montmartre, the chosen or imposed terrain of *Belle-de-nuit*, *Garence*, *Corbeille-d'or*, *Verge-d'or*, and *Valérine*. As for *Pulmonaire*, she may be encountered in and around the *4me rrondissement* throughout the nineteenth century, just as she had stumped acques Roux's parish of the Gravilliers from the ancien régime through the Revolution, with thoughts only of l'Hôtel-Dieu and a bed on which finally to est. *Traînasse* too belongs to every age, though, in the revolutionary ontext, she is the most likely to frequent one of the ill-lit streets off the Palais-Egalité (ci-devant Royal) – rue Traversière-Honoré – or lurk in the dank, suppurating shadows of the old *Barrières*, on the northern perimeter of he city. Before long she too will find her way to Saint-Lazare. *Tubéreuse* is already there.

Charme, *Mélèze*, and *Pensée* – a jolly, giggly threesome; they know it is best to hunt in threes, as they drag their nets behind them off the Champs-Elysées on summer Sundays – are willing, though protesting *pour la forme*, volunteers for an outing down the Marne, with young men in striped vests and their partings in the middle, for a *partie de campagne* of the 1900s. Not for them David's stiff and frozen studio; they have walked out, pink, gently curved, and scantily clothed in pale blue, lilac, and cream, from one of Renoir's sunny canvases.

Myrte, *Silvye*, and *Rose* work with their sleeves rolled up and their large hands red with the *savon de Marseille* on the steaming laundry boats. *Angélique* has been pulled in, again and again, for soliciting, for *touching*, strategically and very actively, for indecency and insulting language of amazing coarseness and inventiveness, under the wooden gallery of the Palais-Egalité (ci-devant Royal).

Most are *filles-légères* who are hiding their natural, indeed enthusiastic, loudly proclaimed lack of virtue under deceptively pretty names, the pressed flowers of innocence. But *Héliotrope* gives herself airs, takes herself seriously, she is a *tragédienne*, employed in secondary parts, in the *troupe* of la Montansier.

We are better acquainted with the martial *Amaranthe* and with the vulgar, foul-mouthed *Bacchante*, in red dress, bare-foot and stockingless. *Réséda* is another model from the studio of Delacroix, in the place Furstembourg, again a slave girl in the slave market of Algiers, cowering imploringly at the feet of a cruel Moor. The sulky, sultry *Bithume* has her regular customers among those who have a taste for *la peau mate* and who patronise the establishments of the rue de la Lune: *descends, Bithume, il y en a pour toi*. *Balsamine* is not the sort of girl from whom to accept a drink, she has already disposed of three husbands and half-a-dozen male relatives, as if predestined to poisoning by a Christian name that seems to have soporific qualities. *Dentleraire* is the rather cruel nickname of an elderly prostitute of the quartier des Halles who has lost both teeth and hair as a result of venereal disease.

So far it has been a predominantly *female* world from which the occasional male is roughly jostled out, in a generally successful endeavour to remove his watch, but a world becoming *more* female in the summer, as the warm evenings bring them out in colourful clusters, while, at the same time, removing much of their clothing, baring their breasts and shoulders. A few men indeed do manage to intrude and to find a narrow ledge on this highly coloured *radeau du Méduse*: the handsome *Marceau*, with his military gait turning up a bit before his allotted time, as if he had jumped the queue and no heeded the whispers of the prompter; poor, stiff, overworked *Tomate*, exhibiting himself in a shop-window to draw attention to some product with his pointing finger; the Hellenic poet, *Salsifis*, living in poverty in one of the Marseille *îles* before dying of cholera in Alexandria; *Amarillis*, another elusive escaper, who has managed to get out of his residential Miltonian shade to find a sort of *droit de cité* and a dubious living in revolutionary Paris, strongly recommended by the London Corresponding Society. Poor silly *Citrouille*, wide-faced, open-eyed and open-mouthed, a country bumpkin if ever there was one, hanging about the *foire* Saint-Laurent, and a ready prey to the sharp Parisian; the doubtful *Macre*, a thin-faced, dank-haired, pale fellow, on the watch from a *câfé* rue Berger, to make sure that his *Genièvre* brings in the cash; *Olive* and *Narcisse* dark strangers, refugees from the massacres of the Midi; *Pignon*, on the other hand, a native-born Parisian, well-known and respected in his quarter, and with a reputed shop commanding a key position on a busy street; *Thlapsi* another Greek poet; *Thymélé*, a philosopher of similar origin, and likewise established in Marseille, where he shares a garret with *Mézéréon*. *Avelinier* is a dull fellow, self-taught, attending night classes at the *Université Populaire* of Kremlin-Bicêtre, and gravitating towards anarcho-syndicalism and the *bande à Bonnot*, before having his head removed from the rest of him, at dawn, boulevard Arago. *Tuffilage* is an incendiarist who has wandered out of an emblematic novel by Michel Tournier. *Cornouiller*, like the hero of *Bel-Ami*, has come from the suburbs of Rouen to seek his fortune in Paris. *Vélard* and *Corfeuil* are associates, predecessors of the *maison Borniol* in the decent disposal of the recently dead, in four classes. *Capillaire* is a learned professor, in the magic world of the court of King Baba. *Bourache*, a rough horse-dealer from the Perche, has come up to the Faubourg Saint-Marceau on professional business, accompanied by his cousin, *Buglose*. *Fromental*, the first cousin of Germinal and godfather to Prairial and Messidor, is a *blâtier* from the Beauce who, as a regular visitor to the Halle-au-bled, is an equally regular practitioner of the nearby Palais-Royal and the lover of *Hémérocale*. *Martagon, Serpolet* and *Bétoine, les Trois Mousquetaires*, as they are known on and off the Champs-Elysées and in the numerous *salles d'armes* of the rue Montmartre, are three swaggering *hussards* from the East who also hunt in threes and who are extremely ticklish on points of honour. *Sureau* and *Barbot* are *apaches* operating on the *boulevards extérieurs*, near the Buttes-Chaumont and in the rue de Lappe, both are handy with the knife. *Tanche*, second-in-command of the National Guard of the Section du Luxembourg, had performed a rather dubious rôle in the September Massacres of 1792.[1] The ridiculous and pretentious *Topinambour*, a correspondent of Bouvard and Pécuchet, is a leading figure in the *Société d'Emulation* of Rocamadour, and a *chevalier des palmes académiques*.

[1] See my article 'Tanche, commandant-en-second de la Section du Luxembourg et le Massacre des Carmes', *AHRF* (1949).

What a literary hotch-potch indeed! *Le monde balzacien*, but that too of Restif and Jarry, of Charles-Louis Philippe and of Louis-Ferdinand Céline, and with plenty of reminders too of *Alice*. The time-machine seems indeed to have broken down, probably from over-winding, so that figures from the 1770s and the 1790s are jostled by those of the 1830s, the 1880s, of *la Belle Epoque* and of the *Passage des Panoramas*, making of the chevalier Valmont a contemporary of Boni de Castellane. It is the sort of thing that is likely to happen when one starts fiddling about with the clock and the calendar, making the hour last a hundred minutes, thus adding a third on to the working day, and making the week stretch out to near-breaking point of nine days of work and one of leisure. What is more, people would be expected to distinguish between, and to memorise, 360 different names of the days of the week (or, rather, of the *décade*). It was presuming too much both of human memory and of individual zeal and industry. Who would have been fooled by the new definition of an hour? The rawest apprentice would have been quick to spot that it was an hour plus forty minutes. Who was likely to remember that *Balsamine* was the new disguise adopted by Friday 27 September 1793? Or to spot that under the attractive *Belle-de-nuit* lurked Monday 7 October of the same year? Or that *Dentelaire* fell on a Friday in November? Or that *Salicor* papered over a Wednesday in July? No wonder those who had started out so boldly on this vast array of new names for old days that were, however, now much longer working ones, or were intended to be, in the unlikely event of employers and employees procuring themselves new watches, after one year of such fantasy had reluctantly to fall back on the unimaginative, but at least understandable, *primidi, duodi, tridi,* and so on to *décadi*.

It was also too much to expect that, just out of homage to inspiring novelty, people would be willing to work a nine-day week, and an eighteen-hour day, when they had been in the habit of working a five-day week, and a day of no determined length and much interspersed with stolen snatches of leisure. It was too much to expect that people would even remember the *décadi*, close up shop, and respect the new official day of rest. In fact, as we know, they did nothing of the sort, and even in the Year VIII, in Central Paris, shop-keepers aver, when asked why they are open on a *décadi*, that they have only raised the shutters to *air* the shop, or that they had had to leave the shop-door *half* open to allow the fresh paint to dry in the interior, or that they had had to call in their assistants, because a new supply of stationery had just come in. Or they will argue that the shop may *appear* open, but that in fact it is not, that it is merely being swept out. Or they simply answer rudely that they will open when they feel like it. Most people did not live in a fantasy world of cardboard make-believe, and, for most people, Carnaval came round only once a year. However much they might have liked to have met *Angélique* or *Marceau* in the flesh, they were certainly not going to accept them masquerading as weekdays or Sundays, in their new guise as *the Girl who was Thursday*, or *the Man who was Tuesday*.

Well, yes, of course, the secret is out. I have been referring to the names of medicinal herbs and healing plants, of pretty flowers and nourishing vegetables, all drawn from my own copy of *l'Almanach National de France, l'an Deuxième de la République Française, Une et Indivisible* (chez Testu, successeur de la veuve d'Houry, rue Hautefeuille no 14). And so I must send this little army of attractive, impudent, wilting, shy, fainting, presumptuous, coarse, insolent, provocative, indecent, decaying girls and of martial young men, country bumpkins, *apaches*, provincial eccentrics and small-town *casse-pieds* back to the fantasy world from which I have briefly rescued them in order to put on a colourful and energetic *farandole* for our benefit. Alas, these were *never real* people: just liquids in the coloured jars of *apothicaires* and *herboristes*, just *useful* plants and nutritious vegetables. It is only I, a frivolous historian, who have endowed them with a brief vitality, human face and gesture, before sending them back to the box of revolutionary toys to which they belong. But then, those who invented them mobilised them in the service, if not of *l'An Deux Mille*, at least of *l'An Deux*, assigned to each 1/360th of a rôle – a pretty short appearance – had never *met* real people, did not even know about real people, thinking only in terms of Concepts, albeit Concepts with legs on (to use a wonderful phrase of Norman Hampson's[2]). I suspect that Robespierre, above all, marked out what were to be his last, hot days according to the new formula, so that his youngish life – he was only 36 – ran out through *Bélier, Prèle, Armoise, Carthame, Mûres*, to culminate, in the unspeakable, horrible fashion known to all on the *décadi*, in fact a Monday, *Arrosoir*, cutting him off for ever even of a glimpse of *Carline, Gentiane, Pastèque, Verge-d'or*, as the revolutionary year ran out without him, even though he may have marked them down – he marked down most things, well in advance, not trusting to his own, meagre powers of improvisation – as a subject for public soul-baring on this or that day (and he must still have had plenty of homilies in reserve): *Complot, Bonheur, Corruption, Vertu, Sacrifice, Innocence, Vieillesse, Récompense, l'Etranger, Maternité* (like that other childless French bore, Pétain, he was very keen on this theme), on his personal, illustrated (the illustrations would have been done, in pen and wash, by the girls) calendar hanging up in his salon, *chez Duplay*. Robespierre, more than anyone else, even Fabre, would have been quite at home in such a pretty flower and vegetable garden. He liked pretty things, pretty colours, pretty dresses (with pretty girls inside them, but not outside them), he felt secure in half-tones and muted shades: pale blue, pale pink, pale yellow. No doubt the flowers of Thermidor had been freshly provided each day in his study. He was one of those provincial poets who thought they understood the language of flowers: roses, daffodils, jonquils would have inspired him, behind his tinted glasses, to suitably restrained tears and to gently turned evocation. It is appropriate that what must have been the happiest day of his public and his private life (there had really been no division between the two since May 1789), or at least what had started out as such, 20 Prairial, the Feast of the Supreme Being, should have fallen both on a Sunday (Whit Sunday) and a *décadi* called, rather menacingly, *Fourche* – a warning perhaps not lost on a man so deeply concerned with

[2] Norman Hampson, *Danton* (1978). His actual phrase, applied to Danton, is: 'He liked to be liked and he saw people as people and not as principles on two legs . . .'

symbols and images, because they protected him from a reality that he might have found distasteful, or that, in his ignorance of the ways of the world, he might even have failed to recognise.

Robespierre had to be surrounded by symbols, because they cossetted him in the reassurance of a familiar interior. Not just objects, but also words. The tragic dimension of this unimaginative, unattractive, uninspiring, bookish man, is to be discovered in the gulf that separated his personal iconography and his personal vocabulary from the awful reality of what was going on down below, in the airless, sweaty streets, below his open windows (through which he never looked out) and from the appalling manner of his own death. He was a man who seems to have used words as screens. Thus, 4 Germinal, the day of the execution of the so-called *hébertistes*, was rendered almost bloodless under its label: *Tulipe*. If anyone was deceived by this kind of verbal sleight of hand, Robespierre would have been. On the 14th of that month, it was the turn of the so-called *dantonistes*, spirited away almost rustically under the harmless codeword *Hêtre*. What could apparently be more inoffensive than the hideous Law of 22 Prairial when packaged under the insipid label of *Camomille*? It is like having the murder rooms hygienically designed with washable tiles. It is like those jolly Soviet songs of the second half of the 1930s, full of health, muscle, optimism, and collective joy, in which every propeller would call out the words *Long Live Stalin*.

The Year II, as idealised and sanitised in the revolutionary calendar, resembled one of David's stage-managed papier-mâché collective festivals extended over a whole year. It was a carefully constructed edifice of fantasy and illusion. Even the new months – however pretty-sounding – had been the creations of poets who had never ploughed nor sown, who knew nothing of the burdens of the agricultural calendar, and who could in all comfort evoke the rigours of *Nivôse*, because they had fires laid for them at home, and travelled, well wrapped-up, in closed carriages, or who, in *Brumaire*, had torch-bearers walk before them. Apart from Jean-Bon Saint-André, would there have been a single Conventionnel to have experienced the realities of *Ventôse* at sea? And *Vendémiaire* could be joyfully evoked at the imbibing end by those who had not the first idea about the process of wine-making. *Thermidor* and *Fructidor* no doubt could incommode every city-dweller, but in very different proportions between those who slept alone or two in a bed, and those who slept in a room containing half-a-dozen mattresses on the floor. I have not encountered any Deputies on the river bank or swimming naked in the Seine. Novelty and invention represent the enjoyment of the privileged and the educated, those cognisant of the new codewords and of the fashionable analogies, because they serve to separate them from the mass of the population, so that the new months must have reinforced any exclusiveness that they were meant, theoretically, to combat. Their current use represented a parlour game for the elect. And by the Year XIII, even *Thermidor* failed to echo any *national* experience, whether of extreme heat and accompanying pestilence, or of *national* memory. It had become, it is true, along with *Messidor* and *Fructidor*, the hardy annual of south-eastern killing and vengeance, as well as of Parisian insult, but that was because they merely papered over the familiar June to September cycle of vengeance and bad temper, not because people consciously harked back to the political significance of the original *Thermidor* of the Year II. *Thermidor*, and its accompaniment, *Thermidorian*, dangerous words that have stalked through the political vocabulary of the nineteenth and twentieth centuries, and that have even now not quite lost their potency, remained the property only of the politically conscious and committed, of revolutionary minorities and their opponents.

Can one imagine a water-carrier or a *savetier*, a *décrotteur* or a horsedealer exclaiming: 'This is a warm day for *Frimaire*', or 'The leaves are turning late this *Fructidor*'? As if there had ever been any *other Fructidor*! Can one hear a countryman comment, on meeting a neighbour in the street, or a *portière*, shaking out her broom on the doorstep early in the morning: 'Le fond de l'air reste frais pour *Floréal*'? Popular indifference or rejection may also have owed something to the unfortunate way which the vagaries of the season had had, from the very start, of hitting back at the new calendar, and making it look, at best, very silly, at worst, positively baneful. *Messidor* was designed to spell out the golden ears of ripe corn waving in the gentle wind – a favourite sexual symbol in boring Swedish or Czech films of the 1930s – yet in *Messidor Year II*, the harvest was quite disastrous, the worst since 1789, only about a third of the usual annual yield; and that of *Messidor Year III* was even worse. If *Messidor*, *Thermidor* and *Fructidor* were supposed to suggest heat, as well as abundance, France got the heat all right, but not the abundance, the summers of 1794 and 1795 being the hottest of the century. And it was the same with the cold months of *Frimaire* and *Nivôse*, even colder in the Year III than in the Year II, as if out to prove their worth and the accuracy of their names. Deep frost and deep snow came as if to order, followed, in *Pluviôse*, of both these terrible years, by freezing rain and sleet.

Superstitious people had some reason to suggest that the new months brought bad luck, *portaient la guigne*. And, indeed, they went on making a fairly regular habit of doing so, in the various, odd corners in which they have managed to survive up to the present day. A submarine called *le Floréal* sank in shallow water off Calais, with the loss of all hands, in 1913. I do not know whether the French Navy had imprudently committed itself to a dozen submarines similarly named; but service on *le Nivôse* would hardly have been appealing, despite the obvious inaccuracy of the name. Nor do I know whether *le Vendémiaire*, the first of the series, and *le Fructidor*, the last, suffered similar fates, and sank, like stones, in shallow water, or whether, after the disappearance of *le Floréal*, the naval authorities, never known in any case for their attachment to the First French Revolution, decided on a crash programme of re-naming. But I recall the tragic fate of the Dieppe trawler, *le Vert Prairial*, smashed to bits on the rocks off Land's End some time in the 1950s, again with the loss of all hands: there was a photograph in *The Times* of the stricken ship, lying on its side, the trefoil on its funnel, the emblem of the trawler company, clearly visible. Again, whether there were sister ships called *le Vert Floréal* and *le Vert Messidor* – there could hardly be a *Vert Frimaire*

- I do not know. The company went into liquidation. A café with an orchestra on the boulevard Bonne-Nouvelle, *le Floréal*, a familiar landmark of the 1930s, went bankrupt in the 1950s, and was replaced by a café with a name less likely to tempt providence. The mine, in *Germinal*, as is well known, collapsed with a mighty roar, providing Zola with one of his finest *pièces montées*. Marx hardly contributed to the rehabilitation of *Brumaire*; and a Soviet friend of mine, Yakov Moissevich Zakher, owed to the fact that he had written a book in the 1920s entitled *9 Thermidora*,[3] a sojourn of twenty-six years in the area of the White Sea and far away from the French Revolution. After he had turned up at one of the Leningrad terminuses – I do not know whether it was the Finland Station – holding a brown paper parcel containing his possessions, and taken up his chair again, in 1956, he started to catch up on twenty-six years' reading. Stalin had been – rightly – sensitive to the sound and to the allegory of Thermidor, a word that carried with it the, to us, comforting suggestion – indeed the historical proof – that a revolutionary dictatorship could be brought to a sudden end, and that a process of revolutionising was not irreversible. *Ventôse*, it is true, has managed to survive, without any apparent damage, in the small and pretty town of Dourdan, in the form of the annual March fair, *la foire de Ventôse*. I do not know the fates of the poor mites who, in the Year II, even in the Year III – but not after that – parents and administrators of orphanages having no doubt learnt their lesson by then – were given the names of the revolutionary months in which they were born. There must surely have been some *Germinals* and *Floréals*, and *Vendémiaire* would have been quite a promising name for a girl; but *Ventôse* would have been liable to misinterpretation, or, on the contrary, to an interpretation too literal, and even the most ardent Jacobin would surely have thought twice about calling an infant *Messidor*. But, judging from the register of the Dijon foundling hospital, *les Bonnets Rouges* (nothing to do with the phrygian cap of the Jacobins), children with revolutionary names did not have long to bear them: poor little *Noisetier* lasted six weeks of the spring and summer of the Year II, *Probus* only three weeks, *Brutus* under a month, *Lin* only three weeks. *Espérance* lived just over a week, but it is arguable that her unfortunate name was not strictly revolutionary. It would be only fair to add that the more conventional Ursules, Sophies, Victoires, Adélaïdes, Jeans, Edmés, and Philiberts died almost as quickly.[4]

In terms of vocabulary, the Year II was a vast charade in which the official nomenclature and the official costumes contrasted quite horribly with the ugly realities that they may have been designed to disguise. Or perhaps this is rather a jaded view of the contemporary scene. Some people may have really believed in the charade and may have persuaded themselves that a vocabulary of hope, innocence, and utility would condition a new race of citizens distinguished by their optimism, their purity and their skills. It is easy to mock; and it may even have been fun to have been a child in such exciting

[3] Y. M. Zahker, *9 Thermidora* (Leningrad 1926).
[4] A. D. Côte-d'Or L 1216+: registre d'entrées aux Bonnets Rouges, 1790–an IV.

times. No school, and plenty of spectacles. Plenty of opportunity too for a new race of little *Emiles, Brutuses* and *Guillaume Tells* to denounce their parents, though goodness knows what happened to such little zealots of Virtue in the very different conditions of the Year III, when parents no longer had anything to fear from that quarter. There is certainly no evidence to suggest that people were any *better* in the Year II than in the years preceding such collective regeneration. In Paris, both murders and suicides were a little above the annual average; so were divorces (but there was a long backlog on which to catch up, and many of the divorces of the Year II concerned couples long since alienated). Banditry was down, but embezzlement was up.

Evidence, in terms of absenteeism, the declining attendance figures at clubs would suggest that, by the summer of 1794, by *Floréal*, more and more people, among the literate and the politically committed, had begun to turn their backs on the charade, on symbolism, myth and fantasy, had become *bored* with such insistent collective pressures, and had sought solace in more conventional refuges: the family, the *billard*, the enjoyments of leisure, the extreme privacy of love, the private world of greed and lust, even in *promenades solitaires* so oddly recommended by the originator of the charade, Rousseau. By the summer of the Year II, the fantasies had worn very thin, and a vocabulary of abundance could not conceal the visible and daily evidence of penury. What a derision to call a *décadi* CHEVAL, when there was not a horse to be had up and down the country, almost all having been requisitioned for the Army! To call a *quintidi* COCHON, when, in cities at least, all pigs and, indeed, most other livestock, had been slaughtered for sale on the black market! Why call a *décadi* CHARRUE, when the only hands to a plough were those of women and children and old men? Why give a *quintidi* to CHIEN when, all over the Republic, urban bow-wows had been put down, as providing bad sexual examples to young citizens, or had been eaten? Why award a *quintidi* to TRUITE at a time when rivers had been fished dry, generally at night, often with the help of explosives (one of the few articles of which there was no shortage)? And so why make mouths water at the mention of CARPE? Where would one encounter a DINDON or a PINTADE, other than in the pages of the revolutionary calendar? One could not eat the revolutionary calendar, a document that laid out a rich menu that did not exist. It is easy to see how people might turn away, in disgust and fury, from a fantasy that must have seemed a cruel provocation in existing conditions. One could not expect miracles such as those that occurred in Aymé's story in *le Vin de Paris*, when a painter of still life, during the Occupation, all at once discovered that his paintings of game, meat, fruit and vegetables were actually eatable.

The régime of the Year II was offering its citizens a whole range of objects that it could not provide, many of which had become little more than memories, *names*, thus lending to the new calendar and the new vocabulary a sort of ironical reality. It was all very well for Robespierre to ask why he should have to bother himself with 'vulgar groceries' when he had the Happiness of Mankind to work on; on his table, as we know, there appeared, regularly, *real* tomatoes and oranges, peaches, small birds and pastries. He might – and did – live in a fantasy world, but he did not have to eat his own fantasies, tasting as they would of cheap, coarse, yellowish revolutionary paper. His Golden City was not one conjured up by a delirious, starving man. But then, Robespierre kept away from the window, looked inwards, and only received the sort of people who talked his own language. It is doubtful if he ever even *noticed* the queues outside the shops in his own street, he had no eyes for that sort of thing, and, of course, he would not know about queueing, something that could be left to women and servants. By Thermidor – perhaps long before it – in Germinal or, at the latest, Floréal – people who took the trouble to read had got fed up with Virtue. It was not an edible commodity. They had got tired, too, of the endless reiteration of the words Unanimity and Indivisibility, because, like Abundance (illustrated in pretty pictures of cows, trees and farmyard animals, windmills, waterfalls, canals, bridges), they too flew in the face of evidence. Most people knew that the France of the Year II was endlessly divisible, whether into 83, or into 40,000 separate components; and Unanimity was like a game of Musical Chairs, with fewer and fewer players, as one rigged trial after another removed more and more of those who were *not* unanimous. By Thermidor it might indeed have seemed that it would all end with the Unanimity of one. That would remove the problem. It was the same with Plots; there had been too many of them, they had all followed the same recipe, they had all been served up several times, both hot and cold, according to a menu as repetitive and as improbable as that advertised in *l'Almanach National*. Nor could Supreme Beings contribute to the food shortage. Much of the execration heaped over the memory of the recently murdered Robespierre, in no way a really bad man, rather a boring, self-righteous one full of good intentions, was that reserved for someone who had been, rightly, shown up as a *marchand d'illusions*.

Robespierre had been the principal victim of his own fantasies, at least in the last month of his life, for, earlier, he had managed to combine Virtue, *le Bonheur Commun*, with a healthy sense of political realism. In this case, there had been a retreat into make-believe, provoked possibly by increasing despair. Saint-Just is a more complex case. In his missions to the Armies of the North and the East, he had shown quite remarkable qualities of military leadership and conciliation, had taken a sensible middle-of-the-road line, lashing out at the extremists, the out-and-outers, the impossibilities. Yet he had also contemplated putting the population – or at least the male half of it – into white, as worthy members of a new Sparta. All were to wear linen togas. What this would have meant in terms of the mud, dust and filth of the Paris streets and of the almost total lack of soap – the selfish city of Marseille taking care to hold on to this precious commodity – is not hard to imagine. It would certainly have made of the Year II a (somewhat shivering) Republic of *blanchisseuses, repasseuses*, and *amidonniers* and would have drawn on the brawny, watery support of the *garçons baigneurs* of the public baths – *Bains Chinois, Bains Poitevin*, and so on. Historically, there must be some lingering interest in such unpublished fantasies of Saint-Just, as perhaps the first revolutionary theorist to have equated political orthodoxy with personal cleanliness. Certainly an illusion as great as any of Robespierre's, as there is ample evidence to suggest that, the more a *sans-culotte* was orthodox, the more he smelt. But, unlike Robespierre's, Saint-Just's fantasies were only made known a number of years after his death, when his secretary, Gateau, published extracts from his *Fragments*.

Thermidor, the most accidental of all the revolutionary *journées*, the most unexpected, save by a narrow circle of politicians that included Robespierre himself and his most consistent enemies: Amar, Vadier, Rühl, Fouché, Châles, Thuriot, Bourdon de l'Oise, Léonard Bourdon, Lecointre de Versailles, Tallien, and the most widely and spontaneously welcomed, for once on a truly national scale, has not ceased to be an object of discussion among historians, both as to its causes and its consequences. The Thermidorians, a very mixed bag, are themselves not easy to define, even in the simple statement that they were all those who survived Thermidor, for some of these were to survive only to Germinal or Prairial of the following year; and the Thermidorian régime (should one not say régimes?) is so fragmented as to defy any simple analysis. But the most positive effect of this momentous *journée* was to bring a sense of physical relief and an end to fear; and, up and down the country, as the news of what had happened in Paris; in Rouen, on the 12th; in le Havre and Dieppe, on the 13th; in Dijon, on the 14th; in Lyon, on the 16th; in Marseille, on the 19th; in Toulouse, on the 22nd; in Perpignan, on the 24th; in Bayonne, on the 25th; in Nice, outside the month which had given its name to the *journée*, at the beginning of Fructidor, the same thing happened without any orders having been given by higher authority: the prisons were opened, and the prisoners, both political and criminal, poured out. There may have been some sort of chain reaction, the Narbonnais benefiting from the news of what had happened in Montpellier, the Perpignannais emulating the Toulousains, though there is no firm evidence for such transmission of news. It seems more likely that, everywhere, municipalities and National Guards bowed to irresistible and spontaneous public pressure. And those who expressed incredulity, or who suggested that it would be best to wait for further orders, were at once brushed aside. So Thermidor opened, as the First Restoration was to open in March 1814, as a day of national reconciliation and forgiveness, a mood, however, that was not to last, soon giving way to unrestrained vengeance. In this respect, Thermidor represented a return to the type of local initiative that had so much marked the early stages of the Revolution; and this was a process that rapidly proved irreversible. Thus Thermidor also represented the decisive defeat of Paris and of Parisian dictatorship, an event to which the *journées* of Germinal, Prairial, and Vendémiaire merely provided the epilogue.

But there is another aspect of Thermidor that has received scant attention. It represented a deliberate escape from fantasy and illusion, a rejection of boring and meaningless orthodoxies on such subjects as Indivisibility, Unanimity, Vigilance, a revolt against a public language that had become totally divorced from private discourse. So it signified a conscious attempt to out meaning back into words and to lessen the gap between intention and reality, and the rejection of a vocabulary weighed down and obscured by hints and allusions. For instance, whereas in the spring of 1794, at the time of the crisis of Ventôse-Germinal, the official line had been that there *was* no food shortage, denying the evidence of the queues, and that indeed there *would* be no food shortage, provided people did not talk about such a possibility (so that anyone who *did* talk about such a possibility could be seen as deliberately seeking to bring about a *disette factice*), *after* Thermidor, the authorities, both municipal and national (though the former were the more candid) referred openly to the existence of a famine crisis, which, by the autumn of 1794, was real enough, and suggested practical remedies by which it might be alleviated: the purchase of grain on the Baltic markets, of rice in the United States, public subscriptions for the relief of the starving, the expulsion from the cities of those who could not justify the proof of a year's residence. Thermidor brought to an end hints and silence, releasing a cacophony of dissent, discussion, denunciation and argument, giving momentary vigour to a quarrelsome press, and even raising hopes among ultra-revolutionaries. It also bridged the gap that had grown up between public and private language, to the advantage of the latter, in the same way that it represented the assertion of long-contained private aspirations, private enjoyments, and private pleasures (including every possible form of vice). Thermidor was a public assertion of privacy, both in language and in priorities.

Robespierre, in the last few tormented weeks of his life, had retreated so far into his closed vocabulary of rhetoric and hint as to fail even to name names, so that even the Enemies of the Republic – and these continued to turn up with distressing regularity, no sooner than the last lot had been cut down – had become little more than the other faceless, bodiless concepts that provided the Incorruptible's most malleable company, as opaque as Innocence, Virtue, Youth, and Age, so that they might be almost anybody at all, or at least anybody known by name to Robespierre; and, as he knew a great many people, probably as much as half his six hundred-odd colleagues in the Convention, a great many might be asking themselves if they were not the latest *promotion* from Robespierre's flourishing *Ecole Pratique pour la Formation des Ennemis de la République*. And this could be a very alarming thought, as the school continued to pour out successful candidates who had passed the course each month.

There was *one* area at least in which Robespierre, indeed to the very last, and increasingly so, as Messidor ran into Thermidor, retained a firm *hold* on reality. That was his insistence on *death*, and indeed – for he had to personalise everything, whether it were Virtue, or Moderation, or Sufficiency (*une honnête suffisance*, meaning what it would take to keep him in soap, starch, laundry, powder, and regular, if slight, meals, washed down with watered wine) – on his *own* death, almost as if this was his one remaining aim, in a world of imperfection, corruption, and compromise. No doubt, at first – and he had been evoking his own death, as a threat, should he not get his way in this matter or that, almost from the beginning of the Revolution, possibly as a reminder of what a terrible loss it would be to the people of France – this had been little more than a formal exercise in rhetoric, yet another example of his taking refuge in fantasy; but, by the summer of 1794, he seems to have envisaged his own premature death as a distinct, and even desirable, possibility. So many other things had by then eluded him, as he began to despair of the ultimate perfectibility of revolutionary man and of the emergence, here and now, of the Republic of Virtue. Robespierre, like de Gaulle, had soon come to the conclusion – by the summer of 1794 at any rate – that the French were *unworthy* of him and of the high purpose to which he had destined them. But, unlike de Gaulle, there was no comfortable line of retreat, no Colombey-les-Deux-Eglises, no Erménonville amidst grottoes, cascades, broken columns and artificial ruins, beneath the weeping willow, for him to go and sulk in, till the Call came. The fate of Danton had proved that it was impossible for a revolutionary of the first rank to pull out and retire to the country; and, in any case, Robespierre was much too conceited ever to have contemplated a return to Arras, something that would have been an admission of defeat and failure in the eyes of his compatriots, and he had always been particularly anxious to impress the Arrageois. He had remained a provincial scholarship boy. If he had never quite come to grips with the realities of life and with the existence of living people – and he was certainly not what might be described as a 'life-enhancing person' – he could at least make sure of a death of suitably emblematic significance.

I am not suggesting that he had actually stage-managed every detail of the truly horrible and cruel process that had taken him from the tribune of the Convention to the Louis XVI table in the Pavillon de Flore, and thence to the Place de la Révolution, though, such was his sense of self-importance, such was his concern for detail (death, like a speech, or a *journée*, could not be improvised, it had to be worked on, like a *devoir* in a lined notebook), the desire to be his own *entrepreneur de pompes funèbres* (after all, he had before him the examples of Brutus, Marat, Lepeletier and the poor little Ruined Boys of the revolutionary prize-givings, Bara, Viala, and so on. Ruined Girls, too, pierced with a thousand counter-revolutionary bayonets, as, dressed as soldiers, they had attempted to hold the bridge; and he would not have wanted a *discreet* departure), one would not have put it past him. When the time came, though previously he had given so much thought to the event, important to himself, and, as he saw it, to the Republic, he had in fact been overtaken by accident, a tiresome, disrespectful imp, his plans had gone awry, and he had been borne away on a stream that he had not conjured up, like that which had spewed forth from the mouth of the cardboard Virtue, at his touch, on the Feast of the Supreme Being. He had gone through all his usual meticulous ablutions on the morning of the 9th, had taken his usual care about his personal appearance, had put on his best clothes, as if in preparation for some big event. And it was to have *been* a big event: he was to appear at the tribune of the Convention, there would be a hush of respect, and then he would proceed, yet again, to 'unveil all' (*tout dévoîler*): the evidence of plots, much wickedness, Pitt-organised corruption, the cancer of the Republic, the blight on a rosy future. Certainly, it could never have occurred to him that, this time, he would be prevented from being *heard*. Such a shabby trick did not figure in the Classics: a dagger, a *thousand* daggers (*mille poignards*), a knife, a shot, a poisoned chalice (of only the best quality), an Infernal Machine (most flattering), *yes*. But *not* an unruly uproar, as if the Convention had transformed itself into one of the lower, rougher forms in the Collège Harcourt. So when it came, it did come as a surprise, so that all the diligent preparation in the lined notebooks proved a waste of time, quite uncalled for. Even so, the sheer horror of the business ensured Robespierre, dead at 36, nearly two hundred years of posthumous interest. His death assured him an importance that, owing to his inability to cope with life, he did not deserve.

Death had, of course, long occupied a place of honour, along with its accompaniments of willows, urns, and weeping vestals, in the impossible vocabulary of revolutionary orthodoxy – always concerned to impose a final choice – *this* or *that*: *Liberté ou la Mort* (when most people would have said: 'Neither, thank you very much, but could I have more mustard?'). And the morbid David had made sure that *perfect* death – at the hands of counter-revolutionary assassins – should be brought home, in pictorial form, to his colleagues, in his two huge pictures of the murdered Marat and the dead Lepeletier (the latter apparently mixed up with the bloody bedclothes). David had also taken a more practical interest in death, as a member of the Committee of General Security.)

Nor was this repetitive evocation of death merely an exercise in revolutionary symbolism and exaggeration (for any person of sense, that is almost anyone other than Robespierre, would know that a choice, say, between *Victory or Death* was just not on). Revolutions are primarily destroyers of life, human and animal, revolutionaries are haters of life, at least as it *is*, here and now, something that can be lightly discarded in order to ensure a golden future; they are unable or impatient to come to terms with its complexities, its doubts, and its contradictions; and the one thing that all revolutions have been successful at is death. The revolutionaries of the Year II had destroyed the crops, livestock, agricultural productivity, but, always, death they had over-produced. Revolutionaries such as Robespierre did not like corpses in the street – they would stay indoors till they had been cleared away – but they thought nothing of signing away thousands of lives, as long as they were just names on pieces of official paper (though it should be added, in fairness to Robespierre, that even this aspect of revolutionary productivity was beginning to worry him in the last weeks of his life). By the summer of 1794, France had had a surfeit of death, only a professional like Fouquier-Tinville had retained an appetite for still more. And the *early* Thermidorians at least had spoken from the heart when, after the 10th, they had suggested that it was now time to get back to the business of *living* and *enjoying* (after, it must be said, quite a bit of clearing up first). Not that death was banished from Thermidorian France. Rather was it stripped of its litanic, evocative pomp. No more invocations; no more packaged choices, more likely a cynical, flippant slogan such as Death *and* Dishonour. But plenty more lynchings on the basis of individual initiative (the Thermidorians believed in free enterprise). The symbols and trappings of death disappeared from the letterheads of official notepaper. And only a handful of Montagnards, like Robespierre the victims of a classical education, *les Martyrs de Prairial* – were sufficiently attached to a now dated revolutionary grandiloquence ostentatiously to have stabbed themselves on the steps of the Convention, a gesture both disgusting and inconsiderate that did not provoke a wave of emulation. It was a matter of taking revolutionary vocabulary too literally.

Thermidorian death was re-personalised, given names, stripped of the alarming anonymity of so many of the *robespierriste* invocations of the previous summer, principally in the form of vengeance, which, to be effective, had to be visible. The Thermidorian approach to death was a practical one: a dead terrorist was better than a living terrorist. And the *égorgeurs* of the Midi *enjoyed* killing their known and named (and often *tutoyés*) victims, generally their neighbours. So killing became more intimate and was deprived of its moral force. No one after Thermidor put forward the idea that killing was *good* for you, even, and especially, for the victims, that it was a purge that would make the Republic better. Killing became a private or semi-collective enjoyment, stripped of its medicinal qualities. Thermidor was a régime of enjoyment (at least for those who could afford it), in which random killing could be accompanied by over-eating, over-drinking, singing and dancing, though there do not seem to have been many instances of the *égorgeurs* actually *eating* their victims, an exercise in revolutionary symbolism carried a stage too far by some of the more simple-minded *septembriseurs* of 1792, who, like Robespierre, had been unable to distinguish between words and realities and who had apparently believed that, by eating various parts of the Princesse de Lamballe, they were making a major contribution to the destruction of aristocracy. The *septembriseurs* tended to take words rather literally.

In respect of death, as in so many other matters, Thermidor witnessed a return to private values. 1795, the Year III, *Nonante-Cinq*, was, indeed, a year of death, one almost as abundant as the Year II. But the dead of the Year III, in Paris at least, were discreet and often nameless: *cadavre masculin inconnu*, naked, with a grey beard, washed up from the Seine, *cadavre féminin inconnu*, clothed, but shoeless, lying in the snow, having died of cold or hunger. There seem to have been rather more suicides in the Year III than in Robespierre's golden year (or almost completed golden year); but these – and those that followed during the years of the Directory and the Consulate – often represented a backlog from the high tide of Terror and Revolution, the memory of terrible events, and the nagging fear of their return. Thus the Terror of 1793 and the Year II cast a long shadow over the years that followed. No one expected Robespierre to rise from the dead (though some of the silly *babouvistes* seem to have *hoped* that he would) but the Revolution had been such a fearful experience for so many ordinary, humble people, that the idle, imprudent boasts of some ex-terrorists that they would soon be back in the saddle and that the guillotine would be back in a central location, place des Terreaux, place de Grève, place de la Révolution, place de la Rougemare,

)lace des Quinconces, place de la Comédie, was enough to drive quite a
1umber of people to kill themselves, rather than risk witnessing it all over
gain (or, at least, this is what they often say in suicide notes left behind on the
nantelpiece, and there seems no reason to disbelieve them).⁵ The Year II was
ı year of fear, much more than the optimistic 1789. And the fear lingered on,
)ften into the next century. But at least the Thermidorian authorities, cynical
ınd hard-headed people, never attempted to make of death an act of state and
ın example of moral regeneration. They were more merciful – or merely
nore experienced – than their predecessors (in many parts of France, espe-
:ially the East, at local level they were in fact the same people)⁶ and, faced
vith the daily spread of massive desertion and *insoumission*, they had no need
o be reminded of the rapid decline of revolutionary spirit and enthusiasm. *La
République ou la Mort* was not a slogan of the Year III, most men, particularly
⁄oung men, not wanting either, indeed, actively rejecting both. *La trompette
ıuerrière* now blew very thin indeed, and young men showed no inclination to
•mulate Bara and Viala. They did not want to get killed, at least in the service
)f the Republic, even though they might be prepared to take to the road, to
he perilous highroad, of banditry, which, in many of the craggier parts of
·rance, offered quite a reasonable chance of survival, for a few years at least.⁷
n important matters – and none more important than life and death – the
Thermidorians were realistic people who had lived through and beyond the
⁄ears of enthusiasm – *le délire révolutionnaire* – and who had come to know
1ow little to expect of their compatriots. They were well aware, from the
ıummer of 1794 onwards, that *arbres de la liberté*, fragile saplings planted at a
ime when Liberty was non-existent – a typical example of revolutionary
ogic – tended to wither away and die, or met with accidents: sawn through,
ınapped by a cart or a carriage, teetering over. They did their rounds, as
)bedient *commissaires* or *juges de paix*, reported the dying or destroyed
.ymbols of the Year II, suggested, without enthusiasm, that *perhaps* they
night be replaced (they never were).⁸

It was now the same with the *décadi*; they went through the motions,
ıdmonished offenders, and seem to have been really surprised when they
ıctually found a shop closed on the official day of rest; (it would generally
urn out that it had been closed for some private reason: death, illness, a
;tock-taking, a removal). Death, too, had been demoted, it was now – as it
ıad been before the terrible Revolution – a *problème de voierie*, a matter of
ceeping the streets clean and tidy, and corpses hidden from public view.
?eople who live in post-revolutionary periods are exceedingly fortunate, if,
hat is, they manage to reach that happy stage. The Year III was pretty awful;
)ut things had been so much *worse*.

⁵ See my *Death in Paris* (1979).
⁶ See the unpublished D.Phil. thesis of the Hon. Justin Wigoder on the Courts of the Haute-
Marne during the revolutionary period.
⁷ See my *Reactions to the French Revolution* (1972), 181-211.
⁸ See my *Sociability and Neighbourhood in an Urban Environment: Paris and Rouen*, to be published
ın the near future.

Of course, Thermidor was not long in creating its own fantasies, its own vocabularies, not least the much-reiterated slogan of *le retour au règne des lois*, an intention both reasonable and sincere in July 1794, but which would look pretty odd in the conditions of local anarchy and vengeance, of banditry and lawlessness that were to prevail in much of France one year later. What the Thermidorians *most* wanted – and, just because they were such a mixed lot: moderates, former ultra-terrorists and dechristianisers, royalists, adventurers – they *had* to find some common platform – was a return to some semblance of legality and an end to random 'revolutionising' and to revolutionary justice operated through so-called peoples' courts. The *règne des lois* meant what it said: the re-establishment, in all their powers, of the normal courts: *tribunaux criminels de Département, tribunaux criminels de District*, and an end to parallel justice. In the Departments and the Districts, the leading, most zealous, and most influential Thermidorians were judges and public prosecutors, especially in the District courts. And these were the people who carried out the legal proscription of the former terrorists. Thermidor also represented a return to another sort of legality in that it re-established parliamentary government, as a result of the demotion of the two governing committees (though that of General Security retained some negative power throughout the Year III, as a check at least on full-scale anti-terrorism, and as a safeguard for some of the leading provincial terrorists) and a return of sovereign power to the Convention, or to what was left of it. This concern for a return to some form of legality – but from when to date legality, in a revolutionary period? the Thermidorians would have said: 1790–1, no doubt – was further expressed in the new importance, among governmental committees, of the *Comité de Législation*, which, in a period of extreme confusion, particularly at local level, is revealed, time and again, as the ultimate arbiter in points of law (like so many Thermidorian bodies, it was composed of professional men of law of considerable experience and ponderation).

With a return to parliamentary sovereignty came the renewed importance of the Departmental authorities, and, above all, of their representatives in Paris, the *députations*. Though central authority was maintained by the despatch, as in the previous year, of *représentants en mission* to specific areas, real power, both at local and national level, came to be increasingly monopolised by the 83 *députations*. Thus, in the Thermidorian Convention, the *députation* of the Seine-inférieure would be likely to get its way in all matters directly concerning that Department; and the powers of *députations* increased the further south one moved from Paris, so that those of the Bouches-du-Rhône, the Gard, the Ardèche, the Rhône, the Haute-Loire, notably, could generally succeed in limiting the interference of visiting *Représentants* sent from Paris. The autonomy of the *députations* and their identity of interests with the Departments that they represented brought about a devolution of authority that was to make Thermidorian France extraordinarily difficult to govern. Indeed, it can hardly be said to have been governed. But the longing for legitimacy was genuine enough, at least in the summer of 1794. And when the Thermidorians invoked the pressing desirability of *la concorde*, they were not being hypocritical, were not speaking in riddles. Thermidor was the one genuinely national *journée* of the revolutionary period; all the preceding ones had been received with mixed feelings at the local level. And the Thermidorians were well aware that they enjoyed the active support of a population fed up with orthodoxy, austerity, revolutionising and make-believe. *La concorde* would include everybody save the terrorists and the non-jurors; and as the terrorists represented a tiny minority – 40,000 at most – they could safely be left out: a very minor amputation compared to those carried out in the autumn and winter of 1793 and in the summer of 1794. The Thermidorians had neither the will nor the means to go to war with this or that area of France, as the Jacobins had done and the authorities of the Directory were to do. Even Lyon could find a rightful place in the Thermidorian scheme of things. So they meant what they said and did not attempt to hide their message in riddles.

They were equally candid in their reference to themselves: *les honnêtes gens*. This was not to be taken literally, for no contemporary would have suggested that a Barras, a Fréron, a Tallien, an Isabeau, or a Boisset, or scores of other Thermidorian luminaries, were honest. *Les honnêtes gens* meant respectable people, those with a stake in the country, wealthy *acquéreurs de biens nationaux*, property-holders, office-holders, members of the judicature, traders, men of substance, in fact the very opposite to the erstwhile *sans-culottes*. The Thermidorian régime was a class régime, and was not afraid of describing itself as one. The Jacobin dictatorship had also been a class régime; but it had been afraid of describing itself as such. Robespierre at least, so often the first victim of his own fantasies, may even have believed that it was *not* a class régime, and that it enjoyed popular support. So the Thermidorians at least had the virtue of candour; they said what they meant: that the Republic was to be made safe for men of substance, and they then proceeded to ensure that it would be.

In a régime bent on putting everyone back in his proper place, the shop-keeper in his shop, and so on, occupational professional and trade definitions re-acquired an accuracy that they had often lost in the course of the Year II, when a vast number of people had been pretending to be what they were not. In the Year III, a building-contractor would not be afraid of committing a sin against Equality by describing himself as such; but, in the previous year, he would, as often as not, have demoted himself to 'carpenter', might indeed even have put on a carpenter's clothes every time he went out.[9] In 1794, the number of people who dressed like *sans-culottes* far outnumbered the totality of that elusive and holy state, and neutral visitors to Paris might have been excused for coming away with the impression that Equality had indeed become personalised and was walking the streets and sitting in the cafés. A régime of make-believe will be given to dressing-up; and revolutionary conformism, at least up to the spring of 1794, would even have offered a premium to girls to dress up as men, thanks to the idealisation of those girls who are supposed to have got into the armies of the Republic and not to have

[9] See my *Police and the People* (1970), 49-81.

been spotted until they had been wounded or met a heroic death. In the Year III, the pretence and the clothing of Equality were abandoned, with alacrity, and in the interest of accuracy, recognition, and good policing. One can bemoan the fate of poor Duplay, but, with his two hundred-odd employees, he had himself participated in fashionable make-believe when he had allowed himself to be described, and had indeed described himself, as *le menuisier Duplay*. The Thermidorian régime was no doubt more selfish, less optimistic, but it was also more honest.

Of course new clichés, new riddles replaced those outmoded by Thermidor. Few can really have believed that *buveurs de sang* – the official epithet now applied collectively to the former terrorists, or, at least, to the lower ranks of the former terrorists (for no one would have suggested, in the Year III, that leading Thermidorians such as Fouché or Boisset could be so described) – was to be taken literally. At worst, it was meant to suggest that they had drunk a lot of wine and spirits – probably stolen – not blood. *La jeunesse dorée* was a very polite definition of very nasty, selfish, cowardly middle-class young men who were just over-dressed thugs. The guillotine continued to masquerade under half-a-dozen squeamish euphemisms – *glaive de la justice*, and that sort of thing – while the man who operated it, with an assistant, was still never called *le bourreau*, the word would have shocked Thermidorian susceptibilities, just as much as it had shocked Jacobin ones, as altogether too reminiscent of the elaborate executions of the ancien régime. It was only those – a closed corporation of fifty or so, all of them closely related, through direct descent or marraige, who practised that profession, who continued to insist on being called by an old name that they clearly felt honourable, while firmly rejecting the immensely pompous official designation of *executeur des hautes oeuvres*, as if they had been superior undertakers. What nonsense! They were nothing more than honest artisans, most of them carpenters by trade, who knew their job and who gloried in the fact that they had practised it, *de père en fils*, or from father-in-law to son-in-law, without a break since the later Valois.

But at least some words, designed to mislead or to frighten, disappeared altogether. The adjective *révolutionnaire* (which, in fact, meant 'arbitrary', as well as, even more sinisterly, 'expeditive') was the first to go, much to the general relief; and while *contre-révolutionnaires* still flourished, in real life as much as in the official vocabulary – the Thermidorians needed them as much as had the Jacobins, and they would have invented them, had they not existed, and multiplied in fact – their opposite numbers, *révolutionnaires*, went out of business, changed their clothing and their language, a silent and unspectacular process which had already begun several months *before* Thermidor, from the time, in December 1793, when Saint-Just had started to coin the expression: *ultra-révolutionnaires*. Officially, there were no revolutionaries any more in Thermidorian France. Nor was there a Revolution. The omission was deliberate, as indicating that the Revolution had been completed. This certainly was the image that the Thermidorians most wished to promote, both at home and abroad. At home, they were highly successful, only too successful, so that, in Lyon and most of the South-East, the genuine counter-revolutionaries were encouraged to believe that their moment had arrived. Abroad, on the other hand, they completely failed, fears of revolutionary France being even greater in 1795, in England and elsewhere, than they had been during the Jacobin period.

The dropping of *révolutionnaire* was not just an omission. It was meant to have a more positive constitutional significance, as proclaiming publicly the abrogation of the famous decree of Brumaire Year II stating that 'le gouvernement de la France sera révolutionnaire jusqu'à la paix', a characteristically oblique manner of indicating – and warning – that the Revolutionary Government (the Jacobin dictatorship) would go on indefinitely – for, in the autumn of 1793, the prospect of peace seemed pretty remote, and, indeed, the Committees of Government could be relied on to *keep* it remote, as the best means of prolonging their own power – and that there was no question, in the near future, of a return to parliamentary government. Well, through no fault of the leading Thermidorians in the Committee of Public Safety and in that of General Security, who, in toppling Robespierre and his alleged accomplices, had had no intention of dismantling the huge apparatus of centralist dictatorship, within six weeks of Thermidor, the Revolutionary Government was in ruins. The *true* Thermidorians – those who had been opposed to the Revolutionary Government from the autumn of 1793 – were concerned to get the message home and to proclaim that both the apparatus and the Revolution itself were over, and that power had now reverted to the legitimate authorities: *les autorités constituées*. Contemporaries were quick to interpret such subtle changes of language, such silent dropping of words. It is more difficult for ourselves, unused to such negative hints. In revolutionary and post-revolutionary language, the undramatic disappearance of a word previously much in use may provide evidence for a total change of the political climate.

Another adjective: *temporaire* (which, in fact, had meant just the opposite, at least in intention, for, in Revolutions, what is 'temporary' is pretty sure of becoming 'permanent'; it is just that 'temporary' sounds more reassuring, with the vague suggestion of an end that is not going to come; and it is thus a word likely to put people off their guard, in the mistaken belief that it is only a matter of sitting things out, when there will be light at the end of the tunnel) was likewise quietly dropped. The Thermidorians, in their optimism, were hoping for permanence and stability; but they were also aware of the sort of shudders that the evocation of the dreadful *Commission Temporaire de Commune-Affranchie*,[10] the authority entrusted with the carrying out of massive repression in Lyon, following the surrender of the Second City in the autumn of 1793, would send down the spines of those Lyonnais and Lyonnaises lucky enough merely to have survived into the Thermidorian period, a case of very fine timing for many, as guillotines, up and down the country, had been taking an increasingly heavy toll even on 8 Thermidor. The Thermidorians were themselves quite capable of setting up *ad hoc* bodies to try political offenders –

[10] See my *Terreur et Subsistances* (1970): 'La Commission Temporaire de Commune-Affranchie', 55–94.

as after Prairial – but they took care not to call them 'temporary', even though
that is what they were. Bluntly, and accurately, they would call them
Commissions militaires.

Another favourite of the Year II: *populaire*, was drummed out, as reminiscent
of the various *Commissions populaires* or *Commissions de justice populaire* that
had been the principal administrators of collective killings in provincial
France in 1793–4, killings, of course, in the name of the People, another
disembodied concept that would have appealed to Rousseau. The People
either were absent from such proceedings or provided its principal victims.
The logic would be that an *ouvrier en soie* or a *fileuse*, condemned to death by
such a body in Lyon, would readily *accept* their fate, as being self-imposed.
Populaire meant in practice: 'arbitrary', 'without appeal', in the absence of a
jury, rapid, political, allegedly class-motivated, in short, a mockery of justice,
delivered by amateurs, militants who had grown experienced in summary
repession in the back areas of the Vendée and Brittany in the summer of 1793.
It is an adjective that has made a sinister, and apparently permanent, return to
political vocabulary in the present century, in the equally mendacious form of
'Popular Democracies', a double misnomer.

'Populaire', in Thermidorian remembrance, evoked not just justice – or
injustice – but also power. The *sociétés populaires*, political clubs run by and
composed of tiny militant groups, had, at one time, laid claim to sovereignty,
before being definitively silenced by Robespierre and his colleagues in the
spring of 1794. The Thermidorians merely completed the process formally in
Ventôse Year III, when any surviving clubs were legally dissolved. Needless
to say that, in their hey-day, the *sociétés populaires* had included men of
substance, professional people, well-to-do merchants and tradesmen, whole-
salers, manufacturers, shopkeepers, independent artisans, schoolmasters,
publicans, but that the People had not gained an entry. In the *société populaire*
of le Havre-Marat (the Marat was dropped shortly after Thermidor, the bust
of the Martyr, on which two small Havrais had wickedly pencilled a mous-
tache, was ceremoniously smashed with a hammer, and the port became once
more le Havre-de-Grâce), dockworkers had been specifically excluded, as
being too ignorant to participate in discussions relating to the Public Good.[11]

Other words to fall into oblivion at this time were *électrique*, meaning much
the same as the adjective *révolutionnaire* and, like that adjective, calculated to
frighten into submission, and *choc électrique*, one of many euphemisms for a
really good, but quite unscientific and unhygienic, massacre. Out, too,
would be the verbs *révolutionner* and *électriser*. The Thermidorians were
themselves not averse to moving fast, particularly in the matter of prison
massacres, such as started to occur over much of the South-East from the
summer of 1795 (Prairial Year III) onwards, but they were less concerned
than their predecessors to place the emphasis on speed of action. They came
after a revolutionary process had run itself out, they felt that they had time on
their side, and that there was less need for haste (after Thermidor, one no

---

[11] See my *Terreur et Subsistances*: 'Politique et subsistances en l'an III: l'exemple du Havre',
221–55, and 'la société havraise', 95–120.

longer encounters the phrase, very much in vogue during the anarchical period of the Terror, in the autumn of 1793: *il faut frapper un grand coup*, as a way to impress, in the knowledge that one had little time in which *to* impress). They were probably right, because their mood and their priorities were much more in accordance with those of a population that had grown sick of constantly being whipped forward – faster, faster – verbally and even physically, and was only too anxious to resume a more comfortable, more traditional pattern of work and leisure, to sit on the step or at the open window, in order to enjoy the slow-moving spectacle and the varied noises of the street (something that poor Robespierre had never done, apparently even as a child).

As the Thermidorians, cynical in the awareness of their very diversity and fundamental disagreements, in their appreciation of pleasure, money, women, food, drink, never made any claim on Virtue and Purity – both notable victims of the famous *journée* – the equally menacing adjective: *épuratoire* (as in *scrutin épuratoire*, an operation of public breast-baring, conducted in the full glare of a club, generally at night, under the heat of blazing lights, a sort of revolutionary Quakerism by which the examinee owned up to all that he had done, or had *not* done, for the Revolution, where he had been at this or that crucial date, whether he had taken part in this or that killing: 'Where were you on the 10 August?' – 'I was fishing on the Petit Morin' – *Out* – 'I had gone to the funeral of my mother-in-law' – *fail* – 'I had drunk too much the night before and overslept, by the time I had got up, dressed, and put on my uniform and musket, it was all over, the killing had stopped, I was was very disappointed' – *fail* – 'What were you before the Revolution?' – 'A valet' – *fail* – 'Did you attend the feast of the Federation?' – 'I was not told about it' – *fail* – 'Did you turn out at the time of the Flight to Varennes?' – 'I was playing dominoes' – *fail* – 'Where were you on 31 May?' – 'I was in bed with a prostitute' – *fail* and *expulsion*) disappeared from the French vocabulary (only re-emerging in the sinister *Epuration* of the summer and autumn of 1944) along with the institutions that had made this sort of personal and public inquisition both possible and perilous.

Yet the Thermidorians occasionally fell into the same trap as their predecessors, in the belief that if you changed the name of something, you would change its nature. Predictably, after 9 Thermidor, *Section, sectionnaire* (a person) and *sectionnaire* (adjective) fell out of favour. The noun and the adjective disappeared, the topographical unit lingered on, very much in eclipse, until it was replaced, in 1796, by the apparently harmless word: *Division*. Paris had been divided into 48 *Sections*, it was now divided into 48 *Divisions* representing exactly the same aeas, though the names of some were changed: *Montagne*, back to *Butte-des-Moulins, Bonnet-rouge,* back to *Fontaine-de-Grenelle, Sansculottes,* back to *Jardin des Plantes, Unité,* back to *Thermes,* in all instances, a return to a name both more familiar, and, in a society largely illiterate, more meaningful, as depicting a recognisable topographical object: a hill, a fountain, a Roman ruin, a garden, an inn-sign, a hospital, a prison, a market. The Thermidorians, however, were not satisfied with eradicating the dangerous word: *Section*. They placed the unit itself under an entirely new administrative body, the twelve *arrondissements*, each one comprising four of the old *Sections*. Unhappily, the word – and the institution – *surveillance* survived Thermidor, though under entirely new management. The eye staring through the triangle likewise topped Thermidorian official note-paper, though it stared, balefully, in a different direction, and was on the look-out for those who, a year earlier, had been *surveillants*.

The revolutionary months and *décades* were retained, the former earning new significance, the latter almost universally ignored. Thus Germinal, associated in the Year II with the two great rigged trials, now became identified with the failure of a popular uprising; Prairial, linked with the terrible law of the 22nd Prairial, now marked the crushing defeat of the Faubourg (the two together providing the Soviet historian, Evgen Tarlé, with the title of his book, *Germinal i Prairial*). But both pretty Floréal and by no means innocent Prairial marked, in Year III parlance, the first round of the prison massacres in Lyon and Marseille and most of the other towns of the South-East, massacres that also added an equally sanguinary connotation to the following months of Messidor, Thermidor, and Fructidor, sultry months of vigorous killing in the same area. The winter months of the Year III, on the other hand, remained somewhat pale, as people in large numbers – 30,000 in Paris, a little more than in the previous year – died quietly of starvation and cold. There were few suicides in these pallid months, disease and want being the main agents of death. Ventôse this time witnessed a sudden and massive thaw, provoking all over the valley of the Seine and its tributaries disastrous floods, the predecessors of those painted by Sisley, in the same valleys, in the 1870s. [12]

The revolutionary months continued to lead a formal and rather bloodless existence for another nine years; and the longer they lasted, the weaker became their hold on popular awareness, not then like playing cards which grew limp, dirty and discoloured from constant use and replay, but more like a new pack hardly ever used. They merely became identified with a series of *coups d'état* that marked the troubled history of the Directory and the installation of the Consulate, and created new and barbarously-named groups to compete with the more familiar, almost respectable Thermidorians: Floréalists, Fructidorians, Brumairians. By the Year XIII, when the new calendar was interred without fuss, most people had probably lost count even of the new cycle of years. The resumption of the old calendar was as much a measure of common sense, as a conscious attempt to win over Catholic opinion. It was also a means of erasing the memory of a recent, and troublesome, past. At least then there could be no more Brumairians and their other bizarre partners or rivals.

At several stages in the subsequent revolutionary history of France, there were attempts, generally on the part of crackpots and backward-looking neo-jacobins and neo-*hébertistes*, to bring back to life the revolutionary months – it was more difficult for the years, with a gap of some fifty years: in 1848 and in 1871, efforts were briefly made to revive both, as if, by so doing,

[12] For the floods in the Ile-Saint-Denis and elsewhere, see my *Paris and its Provinces* (1900).

something of the vigour and the optimism of the Year II, in its early stages, not in its jaded state of Prairial, Messidor and Thermidor, would be injected into an evanescent régime. But new killings: *la Révolution de juillet, les journées de juin, le coup d'état de decembre, la semaine sanglante de mai,* made old revolutionary killing months seem irrelevant.

Thermidor is a suitable point at which to stop, to rest, and to observe: certainly no mountain, not even a *butte*, but rather the old, unspectacular marsh and plain, that had always been part of the landscape, but that, not being dramatic, had previously escaped attention, a landscape indeed favoured by those, the majority, whose prime concern had been to keep out of sight, well away from the tribune (how many Conventionnels *never* seem to have spoken at any time since their arrival in Paris in September 1792 and July 1794! though a number seem to have recovered speech after Thermidor), and so out of trouble, and so to survive, a perfectly respectable ambition in times of Revolution. In terms of the Convention, these were the nameless (though some regained their names as well as their tongues after July 1794, even adding lustre and originality to the much more lively debates of the rump Thermidorian assembly), but numerous, members of the old *Plaine* and the *Marais*, the true inheritors of Thermidor, men little concerned with pretty iridescent soap bubbles, golden, blue, red, and pink, and with gentle or fierce words recalling the soft breezes of spring, the dry *mistral* of the summer, the cruel winds of winter, the flowers of the field, the abundant cornucopia of well-tended garden and orchard, the golden corn, the contented Normandy cow, the powerful Percheron or Ardennais cart-horse, the snorting pig, and the shrill-voiced cock.

We should not make fun of Robespierre and those of his kind for their rather touching attachment to words and symbols; they probably believed in the regenerative power of both, and no doubt their greatest error was over-optimism, the naïve, but generous, belief that others would be willing to share their pretty dreams and to participate in their redeeming allegories. After Thermidor, the evocative months, Robespierre's cherished playthings, his brightly-coloured butterflies, lie like broken toys, or insects with their brilliant wings fading, adding to the bitter pathos of a life hardly lived, and then largely in fantasy, that had seen so little, neither the sea, nor the bright Midi, nor the Alps, nor the green Pyrenees, nor even very much of Paris, and terminated at 36. Of course, it should not have ended thus; he should have been allowed to wander on into old age, with his butterfly net and his water-colour pad, his chalks and his lined notebooks for delicately turned poems about bright flowers and rosy-cheeked girls with the pale blue eyes of the Pas-de-Calais. But here am I making the same mistake as he did, and giving metaphors and fancies the force of realities. 1794, the year of illusions, was followed by 1795, the year of the loss of illusions. After 1984, what of 1985?

21

Lord Holland

William Thomas

Henry Richard Fox, the third Lord Holland, would have been surprised to see his name in a list of Christ Church scholars and statesmen.[1] His tastes were scholarly, but dilettantish. He was born into the sort of milieu which produced statesmen, and many expected him to play a great part in politics; but his tenure of office was short and, it must be admitted, undistinguished. He was for six months, from October 1806 to March 1807, Lord Privy Seal in the shortlived Ministry of All the Talents, and then after a long gap, he served for eight years as Chancellor of the Duchy of Lancaster in the Whig ministries of Grey and Melbourne between 1830 and 1840. For thirty-six of his forty-four years in close touch with politics, he was associated with the opposition. Of course a man may still claim to be a statesman in such circumstances. Holland's volatile contemporary Henry Brougham enjoyed office for an even shorter period, yet he impressed himself vividly upon the politics of the time, and could well rank as one of the more remarkable statesmen of the early nineteenth century. But Holland was made of milder stuff. He was too placid and tolerant to make a good opposition politician, and in office he was too reasonable, too conscious of the many-sidedness of issues to have the influence which his excellent judgment and clear intellect deserved.

But Holland is worth studying, first, because he was an attractive figure in his own right; being more interesting than most politicians because more cultivated, more disinterested and more humane. Secondly, though he was not an important actor, he was an important, indeed an indispensable witness. One could write a history of English party politics from, say, 1784 to 1841 without making much mention of him. In fact it has been done more than once. But one could not do this without using the testimony he has left. He was, as I have said, a modest man; and, in some ways I shall come to, he was at odds with his time, and ineffectual in opposing certain tendencies of which he disapproved. But he was alert enough to see that he was living through momentous events in the company of some remarkable men and women, and he was modest enough to set his own ambitions aside and record those events and his impressions of those men and women, as fairly and veraciously

[1] The lecture which is reproduced here was delivered before the publication of Mr Leslie Mitchell's Holland House (1980), but in its published form it has benefited from his kind criticism.

as he could. So that, even if we feel inclined to discount him as a factor in the making of policy, we cannot discount him as a source. For those who cannot make history, the next best way to impress posterity is to collect it. That is what Holland did. Historians have found his *Foreign Reminiscences* too biased and opinionated, but they have used his *Memoirs of the Whig Party during my Time* and his *Further Memoirs of the Whig Party* a great deal.[2] Many are still working on the manuscripts he left and which are now in the British Museum. Recently an American scholar, Dr Kriegel, published an edition of the political diary which Holland kept between 1831 and his death, and which is a most important source for the Whig ministries in the decade of reform.[3] I think recent work on the Holland House papers is already revising our picture of the Whig party during Holland's lifetime.

Thirdly, Holland, being an unusually articulate and self-conscious specimen of his class and party, tells us much about the nature of Whiggism in the early nineteenth century, and saves us from a narrow conception of it as a mere political creed. I think Whiggism was more than this: it was also a culture, and a way of life; what Sir Keith Feiling in his essay on Holland called 'a temperament'.[4] Holland was a fine example of that temperament. Of course Whiggism had its faults and limitations. It represented a small and increasingly beleaguered class, not without its collective illusions and its arrogance of caste, and in a measure Holland shared these failings. But that is precisely what makes him so valuable. Because he recorded an outlook which other, more important men who shared it were too busy to record, we have to go to his work to appreciate what Whiggism was like, as it were, from the inside. But he did more than record an outlook. To an extent which is not I believe sufficiently recognised, he helped to shape and enrich that outlook. As I shall try to show presently, he presided over the social circle which more than any other in the early nineteenth century helped to keep the Whig outlook fresh and vigorous.

Holland was born into the Whig aristocracy just when its period of unchallenged supremacy was coming to an end. His grandfather was Henry Fox, the first Lord Holland, who had made his fortune as Paymaster General in the ministry of the Duke of Newcastle. That fortune had been greatly depleted by his death in July 1774; and if his heir Stephen Fox, the second Lord Holland, had lived for long, the third lord, my subject, would have come into a very wasted patrimony indeed, for Stephen's habits were still more spendthrift than his father's. But Stephen died only a few months after his father, in December 1774, leaving a widow who survived him by only four years, and two children, Caroline, born in 1767, and Henry Richard, born in 1773. Though orphaned so early, the two children had happy memories of childhood. The two dominant themes of Fox family life were intense domestic

---

[2] *Foreign Reminiscences* (1850); *Memoirs of the Whig Party during my Time* (2 vols, 1852-4), both edited by Henry, fourth Lord Holland; Lord Stavordale (ed.), *Further Memoirs of the Whig Party 1807-1821* (1905).

[3] A. D. Kriegel (ed.), *The Holland House Diaries 1831-1840. The Diary of Henry Richard Vassal Fox, Third Lord Holland, with extracts from the Diary of John Allen* (1977).

[4] K. Feiling, *In Christ Church Hall* (1960), 108.

affection and financial recklessness bordering on ruin. Henry must have heard enough of the latter in his father's life, and seen enough of its consequences at closer quarters in the career of his uncle Charles, to want to avoid it as much as he could. Throughout his life he was to experience financial difficulties of a sort, but they were not caused by his own thoughtlessness; he was never a compulsive gambler like Charles Fox, and save for one visit to the Derby, he avoided the turf.[5] Domestic affection on the other hand the two children had in abundance. Holland was brought up by his maternal grandfather, the Earl of Upper Ossory, and by his uncle Charles. Charles Fox's closest friend, Richard Fitzpatrick (whom he always called 'my uncle Dick') also took a close interest in his education. His mother's younger sister had become the second wife of Lord Shelburne, the first Marquis of Lansdowne, and on Lady Holland's death Caroline Fox was taken by her aunt into the Lansdowne household, where she became a sort of adopted daughter to the first Marquis and his prop and comfort in his old age. Lansdowne's third son, Henry Petty, who was to become the third Marquis on the death of his half-brother (the child of Lansdowne's first marriage) was therefore Holland's cousin, a fact of some importance in the later history of the Whig party. If the Whigs were, as Melbourne once called them, 'all cousins', Holland and his sister were born and brought up in the very centre of the cousinhood.

It would have been natural for Holland to follow in the footsteps of Fox and to be groomed for a political career. In an age when a famous name counted for much, and the name of Fox in particular helped bind together the divergent elements of the Whig party, Fox's favourite nephew must have had a head start on all his competitors. Many indeed looked to him as the inheritor of Fox's mantle, and expected him to assert himself as a leader of the Foxite Whigs of a later generation. But Holland never fulfilled this expectation.

There are obvious general reasons for this. Fox, for all his charm and ability, was a lazy politician, more inclined to retire from politics when he found men did not share his principles than to stand and fight tenaciously to enforce and extend them. Under his leadership, by turns nimbly opportunist and disastrously idealistic, his party became associated first with the fortunes of the unpopular Prince of Wales and then, with less justice but much more fatally, with the extremist supporters of the French Revolution. The Whig party was a loose aristocratic confederacy, united by family ties, obligations of office and the memory (increasingly remote) of an ancestral struggle with the Crown. Its leaders were grandees of great wealth and broad acres, whose political power was based on territorial influence in counties and the possession of numerous parliamentary boroughs. Below these were the rank and file of the party, men who drew their incomes from small estates, the law, or from trade, and who often depended on the grandees for their seats in Parliament. By connection Fox belonged to the aristocrats of the party, by intellect and sympathies with its rank and file. Few men were better situated for keeping the two sides in harmony. But the task needed assiduity, guile and an avoidance of divisive issues of principle, and in none of these (it is part of his charm) was

[5] Lord Ilchester, *Chronicles of Holland House 1820-1900* (1937), 270-1.

Fox particularly strong. He espoused the libertarian slogans of the French Revolution from sincere conviction, but when he had had plenty of warning of the excesses to which they might lead, he clung to them from an almost aristocratic sense of honour and consistency. The effect was to make him the object of the greatest suspicion among the propertied classes. He became the dark-jowled, Phrygian-capped revolutionary of Gillray's cartoons and, having done a good deal to provoke the caricature, he disdained to do anything to disown it. There is something touching in the way Fox clung to the hope that the French Revolution would come right in the end, that its excesses were caused by foreign threats of intervention, that only Pitt kept Europe from enjoying a general peace, and that Napoleon, even up to Ulm and Austerlitz, was anxious to avoid war. Those who condemn his stand as infatuated folly should perhaps consider why it has been possible in our own day for regimes ten times more oppressive and belligerent than Napoleon's to continue to retain the allegiance of the idealistic and the high-minded. But whatever Fox's motives for courting unpopularity by his French sympathies, the effect of his action was to split the Whigs. Many of the great landed magnates, faced with the choice of keeping their principles or preserving their order, with little hesitation decided on the latter. The Foxites saw many of their estwhile leaders gravitate to the party of Pitt, and many of their rank and file drawn to the Jacobinical radicalism of Horne Tooke and Godwin. As the war with France progressed their moderation had less and less appeal to a country experiencing an upsurge of crude patriotic feeling. When Holland made his political debut the prospects of the Foxites were very bleak. In 1797, despairing of their attempts to check Pitt's war policy, and disheartened by the experience of tiny parliamentary minorities, they were to take the almost suicidal course of seceding from Parliament in a block, a move Holland himself opposed.

Holland was not the sort of man to reverse the party's fortunes. In part this was a matter of temperament. Nearly everyone who has left recollections of him comments on his unfailing good nature. He had his uncle Charles's charm, as well as his genial tolerance of differences of opinion. Perhaps because he was an orphan, he treated his friends with the sort of unreserved intimacy more common between close relatives. He was genuinely distressed at the prospect of disagreement, and he hated bearing a grudge. Nothing illustrates this better than his relations with Canning, whom he had known at Eton and followed to Christ Church. Canning's political ambitions soon conflicted with his early Whig allegiance, and he not only joined Pitt, but became a savage critic of the Whigs. Some of them could never forgive the brilliant squibs which Canning wrote about them in the *Anti-Jacobin*. Grey's resentment was to be so long-lasting that he nearly forfeited the leadership of the Whigs rather than support Canning's ministry in 1827. But Holland's affection survived all the political vicissitudes.

There were other factors which diminished his political effectiveness. As a peer he had to sit in the House of Lords, where his uncle's followers were a tiny handful easily outvoted by the ministerial peers. Besides, he had received an education which in some ways unfitted him for political responsibility. It was assumed in the eighteenth century that a successful politician must be a good orator, and a good orator must be nurtured on the Greek and Latin classics. In this Christ Church offered little variation on the instruction at Eton. Holland later recalled that he had passed through both 'without disgrace and without distinction',[6] which probably means that he had no difficulty meeting the standards expected by his tutors but that those standards were not very high. He was a member neither of the dissipated, hard-drinking set of gentlemen commoners conspicuous in Oxford at the time, nor of the inner circle of Dean Jackson's favourites. In retrospect his verdict on the University was harsh. When in 1796 he heard that his cousin Lord Henry Petty was going to Edinburgh rather than to Oxford he commented:

> The more I think of the opinions of Oxford people, of the method of education there and the habits of a young man's life, the more I am convinced that there never was an institution so well calculated to damp the ambition of a young man & to direct it (if it should be too luxuriant to be entirely destroyed) to improper, ridiculous and trivial objects. The real end of the institution is to keep men children, and the way they do so is to hold cheap, nay more to represent as childish all that is manly or useful.[7]

He was twenty-three when he wrote this, old enough to have discovered the shortcomings of his equipment, but not so old as to be prepared to take some of the blame, and perhaps we should not take him too literally. The benefits of a university education are notoriously intangible and indirect, and the beneficiary's own verdict on the process is often the least reliable.

In one respect, Holland was a good advertisement for the formal instruction he had received. He was a good classic, and the fact stamps everything he wrote. He looked on the literature of ancient Rome and Greece as providing what he once called 'the foundation and models of all good taste'.[8] This was not mere lip-service to the prevailing intellectual fashion. He was to find Virgil and Horace, Cicero and Livy a never-failing source of pleasure to the end of his life. Possibly he was less at home with Greek authors. Whereas his love of Latin was the basis for his easy mastery of Italian and Spanish, he seems to have felt less affinity with Greek, and, perhaps for that reason, remained relatively unenthusiastic about the cause of Philhellenism into which so many classically-educated liberals threw themselves in the 1820s. His early training shaped his taste in English literature. He was fondest of the writers of our own Augustan age: Pope and Dryden in poetry; Addison, Bolingbroke and Johnson in prose. When he wrote verse, which he did shyly but compulsively all his life, it was in metres culled from the English poets of the pre-romantic era; heroic couplets for political themes, lyric measures for more tender sentiment. I should guess (though I cannot be sure) that he remained indifferent to the poetry of the great romantics with the exception

[6] *Memoirs of the Whig Party*, I, 3.

[7] British Library, Additional MS. (hereafter Add.MS.) 51,734, ff.46-7, Holland to Caroline Fox, 20 Sept. 1796.

[8] Add.MS. 51,731, f.206, to the same, 3 Mar. 1794.

of Byron. He thought the greatest poet of his day was Crabbe. This traditionalism eventually put him completely out of harmony with the romantic taste which prevailed in the latter half of his life. He was, for example, remarkably well read in Spanish literature, and in a three-year stay in Spain from 1802 to 1805 he made a close study of the work of the sixteenth-century Spanish dramatists Lope de Vega and Guillén de Castro, which he published on his return to England, in the form of two short literary biographies.[9] The style of these is evidently modelled on Johnson's *Lives of the Poets*, and though Holland has not Johnson's profundity, he has the same assumption that the standards of taste in his own age are superior to those of sixteenth-century Spain. It is manifestly the work of a man who thinks Dryden's *All for Love* a better play than Shakespeare's *Antony and Cleopatra* because it observes the unities. One critic, remarking on his translations from Spanish two years before his death, commented: 'How completely [it carries] us back to the days of rounded sentences and powdered hair, classical epigrams and shoe-buckles!'[10] The same might have been said of his prose. Even his letters and his journals, written unselfconsciously and often at the end of a tiring day, show that 'rounded sentences' and balanced antitheses were his natural mode of expression. His taste reflected the culture of the Age of Reason, the Whig world of what Burke once called 'classical elegance and honest agriculture', the restrained magnificence of Georgian country houses and mansions, sustained by broad acres scientifically farmed.

But in other respects this classical education had disadvantages which the political developments of Holland's early life made more and more serious. To begin with, it was politically naïve. The preoccupation with classical models encouraged the student to think of the ancient world as representing so high a point of civilised achievement that the intervening ages between it and his own day seemed by contrast only a long night of barbarism and superstition. He tended to undervalue the political and spiritual achievements of medieval and early modern Europe and to treat the institutions which embodied them merely as symptoms of a barbarism doomed to fade before the daylight of reason. The very completeness of the victory which classical culture had won encouraged the illusion, for eighteenth-century monarchs were eager to show themselves devotees of classical learning, and clergymen to teach it instead of Christian theology. It was very natural for a young man, educated as Holland had been, unacquainted with political responsibility, to be theoretically a republican, and it is easy to see that the enthusiasm which he and many other young men felt for the French Revolution had very little to do with sympathy for popular aspirations. In 1791, after he had taken his degree, Holland went on a European tour, and his political sympathies with the French Revolution were characteristically expressed in verses against the Duke of Brunswick:

[9] *Some Account of the Life and Writings of Lope Felix de Vega Carpio and Guillen de Castro* (2 vols, 1817).
[10] 'Poets of the Melbourne Ministry', *London and Westminster Review*, VII and XXXIX (Apr. 1838), 201.

> As long as tyrants indignation raise,
> As virtue gains involuntary praise,
> As long as nature steadfast to her plan
> Plants love of freedom in the soul of man,
> So long shall every friend to Human race
> Curse Brunswick's name, large Europe's sad disgrace
> So long shall he to infamy consigned
> Be stiled the scourge of God the pest of Humankind . . .[11]

When two years later the Reign of Terror dashed these hopes he could only adopt a proud Roman scorn for mankind's relapse into barbarism. In 1794 he wrote as follows to his sister:

> There seems to be a bound not only to the individual happiness and knowledge of man but to the improvement of society and the enlargement of the understanding. When the Romans attained a point of civilisation till then unknown, what with the effects of luxury, ambition, & of fanaticism they relapsed into a state little better than their original ignorance & superstition & barbarity. Within these last two hundred years we have been emerging from the darkness which succeeded Roman civilisation & certainly our advances have been most wonderful. Four years ago, one should have imagined that the doctrines of humanity, the spirit of true and candid liberty and the researches of science would have kept pace with one another and tended to increase the happiness . . . of Mankind. But alas! How different has it all turned out. Intolerance, persecution, superstition & enthusiasm seem once more to have deafened us to . . . reason & hardened us to pity and compassion.[12]

Other liberals, of course, felt the same disillusionment; but in Holland's case the cycle of hope and disappointment was expressed in a confining framework of classical precept and example.

This brings me to another gap in Holland's education. In his comments on the war with France (which hardly seems to have affected his travels through the European capitals or ruffled the gay, aristocratic society which welcomed him in each) he showed hardly any awareness of economic issues. His education had been liberal in the classical sense. Even at Christ Church he seems to have received only a course of Euclid and a smattering of trigonometry by way of a mathematical education. He was indifferent to business, and even in questions affecting his own income he was entirely in the hands of the various subordinate agents whom he employed. While he was abroad Holland House nearly collapsed through an accumulation of water around its foundations, and when his more practical sister Caroline urged him to a decision he handed the whole matter over to her discretion. This patrician distaste for money was of course common among the Whig aristocracy, and it partly explains why they were such ineffectual opponents of Pitt's fiscal measures. (Pitt received an education in which mathematics played a much larger part.) Fox once, in a letter to his nephew, called political economy 'that most nonsensical of all sciences',[13] and to the end of his life Holland remained

---

[11] Add.MS. 51,731, f.82, to Caroline Fox, ?4 Oct. 1792.

[12] Add.MS. 51,732, f.16, to the same, 30 May 1794.

[13] Lord John Russell (ed.), *Memorials and Correspondence of C. J. Fox* (4 vols, 1854), III, 242 (19 Mar. 1804).

true to this example. Even in the 1820s, when political economy had established itself as a subject which young aristocrats might study without demeaning themselves, and some understanding of it was essential if one was to follow the debates over the stability of the currency, the corn laws and the freeing of trade, Holland's comments are amazingly innocent. 'I have much less dislike to voting than to hearing, reading or saying anything on the subject of currency,' he wrote to Grey in 1826. 'I do not pretend to understand anything about these matters . . . Allen once made me comprehend the question between gold and silver as a standard & tho I have in some measure forgotten the reasons I still retain the conviction that silver should in all prudence be our standard.'[14]

The other matter which makes him conspicuously out of key with his time is religion. By this I do not mean the principles of belief, but the practice, and in particular its significance in the lives of Holland's countrymen. 'Our education,' Burke wrote in the *Reflections*, 'is in a manner wholly in the hands of ecclesiastics, and in all stages from infancy to manhood.' Burke goes on to say that the good thing about having clergymen around, 'as friends and companions of a graver character', is not merely that we thereby attach our gentlemen to the church, but also that 'we liberalise the church by an intercourse with the leading characters of the country'.[15] It was not so much that the nobility and gentry became religious, as that the clergy became laicised. Holland's education shows what Burke meant. In his youth he was surrounded by clergymen, but they were accommodating and obsequious men, much too conscious of their obligations to the laity and especially to the nobility in matters of preferment to insist upon the less comfortable aspects of the Christian faith. Already, however, there were signs of a change. The evangelical revival was beginning to affect even the upper echelons of the Church. The French Revolution brought a sharp reaction against the laxity of the eighteenth-century Church, and even in Whig families religion began to be taken more seriously. Holland's near-contemporary at Christ Church, Charles Jenkinson, was a portent of the change. Solemn and high-principled where Holland was cheerful and easy-going, deferential to authority where Holland was critical of it, Jenkinson was more in tune with the new mood. When, as Lord Liverpool, he became Prime Minister, he was to renounce the Whig practice of making bishops out of younger sons of the nobility and to insist on the appointment of men of piety and learning.

The religious revival affected all sorts of reforming causes, like the emancipation of the slaves, the education of the poor, and the softening of the harsher aspects of the new industrialism. One reason why the Whig party remained relatively untouched by these developments is that its aristocratic leadership had much the same attitude of aloof scepticism that we find in Holland. It was not that he was unmoved by the evils which the evangelicals pointed out. In the case of the slave trade he played an honourable part against his own interests, as we shall see. But he disliked the self-righteousness of

[14] Add.MS. 51,547, ff.132-3, Holland to Grey, 12 Feb. 1826.
[15] *Reflections on the Revolution in France* (third edn, 1790), 148.

reformers generally, and the meddlesome, interfering spirit of the evangelical variety in particular. He never understood the ardours of religious conviction. He was too fastidious and too tolerant to succumb to 'enthusiasm', a word he always used in a pejorative sense. So by the end of his life he had become a kind of relic; to pious Tories a hideous relic of Voltairean infidelity, but even to the rising generation of young Whig noblemen a relic of a frivolous world which was passing away. An amusing instance of this was recorded by Holland's cabinet colleague J. C. Hobhouse after the two men had dined together in March 1839. Holland told Hobhouse that he had never attended a church in London in his whole life, and he added, à propos 'the religious turn of our young men',[16] that he was almost afraid to talk in front of Howick and Morpeth. Howick's diary, with its high moral sentiments, its record of regular bible-reading and church attendance and its earnest analysis of each Sunday's sermon, gives us an idea what Holland meant.

Holland might have remained an ineffectual Whig nobleman, aimlessly travelling through Europe savouring antiquities, or pleasantly stagnating in some congenial foreign embassy, but for an event in 1794. In that year he met in Florence the beautiful Lady Elizabeth Webster and the two were soon deeply in love. She was the daughter of a rich Jamaica planter named Vassall, and at the tender age of fifteen had been married to a Sussex country gentleman named Sir Godfrey Webster. He was probably after her fortune, but what made things worse was that he had none of her tastes and was old enough to be her father. By 1794 she is referring to him in her journal as 'my tormentor'.[17] Actually, for a tormentor, he seems to have been remarkably complaisant, for he soon departed for England, obligingly leaving his wife and two little children behind in Italy with Holland as companion. For two years Holland dallied in Italy, parrying entreaties from home that he should come and take his seat in the Lords, but in 1796 he finally decided to return and go through with a divorce. By then Lady Webster was carrying his child, and his fear was not so much the scandal which a divorce would cause (for in the lax Whig world such things were taken very tolerantly) as that Webster might see that his interest lay in keeping the marriage intact, and with it control of his wife's money. In the event, the divorce cost Holland dear, though not as dear as he had feared. Webster's lawyers persuaded him to sue for divorce because he was still likely to enjoy her fortune during their joint lives. Holland, on the other hand, took comfort from the fact that Webster, being twenty years older than his wife, would not live so long, and that on his death the estate would revert to her and her children.[18] The event came even sooner than expected. Webster took to gambling and in 1800, apparently after incurring heavy debts, shot himself. His ex-wife, now Lady Holland, recovered her fortune, but not the custody of her children by her first marriage. One curious result was that Holland, the opponent of the slave trade, now became, through his wife, the owner of West-Indian estates

---

[16] Add.MS. 56,560, f.88, J. C. Hobhouse's diary, 2 Mar. 1839.
[17] Lord Ilchester (ed.), *The Journal of Elizabeth Lady Holland, 1791-1811* (2 vols, 1908), I, 129.
[18] Add.MS. 51,734, f.26, Holland to Caroline Fox, 20 July 1796.

worked by slaves. This did not prevent him, when a minister in the Talents Ministry, from voting and speaking in favour of the abolition of the trade.

Lady Holland had great force of character. She had had a wretched childhood and almost no formal education, but she had clearly a strong intellect which made up the deficiency, and being accustomed (probably well before she met Holland) to having men fall madly in love with her, she had developed a strategy of alternating meekness and aggression which usually got her her own way. Her journals show that she had less subtlety but much more practical sense than her husband. In questions of literature and ideas she betrays a patchy education in opinions which are eccentric and often downright ignorant. When she met Wordsworth for example she pronounced him 'much superior to his writings', and was less interested in his poetry than the fact that he was writing a guide to the Lakes.[19] But her everyday observations of people show an unerring eye for the telling detail, and she could express herself with great point and conciseness. If her conversation was anything like as vivid as her journal and letters she must have been fascinating, if rather disturbing company. Above all, she had a shrewd sense of what I would call political forces, which contrasts sharply with Holland's kindly acquiescence. She was a born manipulator, and having rapidly appreciated the hopeless political situation into which the Foxite Whigs had reduced themselves by the secession, she at once set about introducing a little common sense into their politics. As she was an outsider to the peculiar network of family alliances which made the Whig connection, she saw how irrelevant to national needs their loyalties had become. 'There is a bigotry in their adherence to their ineffectual principles that borders upon infatuation.'[20] No one suffered from this infatuation more than her husband, and she was soon weaning him away from his doctrinaire Foxite opinions.

Unfortunately the only way in which a woman could exercise political influence in those unliberated days was as a hostess, and here Lady Holland suffered from her status as a divorcee. She could not be received at Court, even though George III's sons were none of them models of domestic propriety; and many society ladies would not visit her because of what they regarded as her equivocal position. She undoubtedly felt this exclusion very keenly, and it partly accounts for her mania for foreign travel which she made her husband indulge during the early years of their marriage, and for her frequent expressions of dislike for the English climate and English travel. In 1802 they set out with Fox to Paris, to pay their respects to the First Consul, and thence travelled to Spain where they were to remain until 1805. After Fox's death and the dismissal of the Talents Ministry had released them from political life, they went again in 1808. This time the Spanish had risen against the French, and travel was much more dangerous. It was, incidentally, this second tour which led many of Holland's friends to remonstrate at the risk he was taking, both to himself and to his reputation in England. A man in his position, they felt, should be careful not to seem so attached to 'foreign

[19] *Journal*, II, 231.
[20] Ibid., I, 148-9.

notions' and manners.[21]

They need not have worried. In the course of his travels Holland made contact with many Spanish liberals, who saw the war of liberation as a chance of getting a constitution for their country; but he is unlikely to have imbibed any foreign notions from them. It was rather the other way about. He gave them the pure milk of the Whig political gospel. On his first stay he had taken with him as physician a staunch Scotch Whig, John Allen, whose great abilities soon made him a trusted companion and adviser in all sorts of other matters, economic, political and antiquarian. In 1809, as the result of his Spanish experiences, Allen drew up, no doubt under Lord Holland's eye, a pamphlet setting out suggestions for the composition of a Spanish parliament. It is called *Suggestions on the Cortes*.[22] I do not know whether the Spanish liberals took any notice of it, but it seems to me that it has some relevance to English history, for its provisions are strikingly like the Whig Reform Bill of 1831. When one considers that the chief architect of that Bill was Lord John Russell, and that he was travelling with the Hollands on this trip to Spain in 1808-9, would it really be too much to consider *Suggestions on the Cortes* as the germ of the English Reform Bill?

The Peninsular War ended the Hollands' habit of self-imposed exile. They were reconciled to a conflict which could be seen as aimed at the liberation of Spain, and though Tories continued to suspect them (not without some grounds) of a disloyal admiration for Napoleon, his wars effectively confined them to England. It was now that Lady Holland had her revenge upon the society that slighted her. She decided to make Holland House into the most sought-after salon in England. If people were so bigoted as not to want to call upon her, she would make them feel their self-imposed exclusion as a serious handicap. The ingredients were ideal. Holland House was a rambling Elizabethan house on the outskirts of London, far enough from the expanding suburb to offer country air, but near enough for politicians and MPs to ride out to it for dinner or for breakfast after a debate had ended in the small hours. In the parliamentary recess it was a country retreat; during the session it was more like a political club. It was large enough to accommodate many guests overnight (though this was a privilege given only to Cabinet ministers and regular guests particularly favoured) but not so large as to be a drain upon the Hollands' comparatively slender means. Its hospitality was comfortable, but not grandiose. Because prudish aristocratic ladies avoided it, the company was predominantly male. The Hollands' tastes ensured that it was also predominantly clever.

It is almost impossible to convey the flavour of the society which gathered there. For the physical setting (now that the house itself has gone) one has to go to Lord Ilchester's two books.[23] For the company, one has to make up a composite picture from the recollections of the many people who were entertained there. As host and hostess Lord and Lady Holland had com-

---

[21] S. H. Romilly (ed.), *Letters to 'Ivy' from the first Earl of Dudley* (1905), 58.
[22] 1809.
[23] *Home of the Hollands* (1937); and see above, n.5.

plementary qualities. He was good humoured, with a gift for setting his guests at their ease and drawing them out. She was more imperious, ordering her guests about, changing the topic of conversation, and issuing her own downright opinions. Macaulay, who was introduced to Holland House in 1831 when it was already a legend, and has left some of the most vivid descriptions of it, noted that

> The Centurion did not keep his soldiers in better order than she keeps her guests . . . 'Ring the bell, Mr Macaulay.' 'Lay down that screen, Lord Russell; – you will spoil it.' 'Mr Allen, take a candle and shew Mr Cradock the picture of Buonaparte' . . .[24]

Some guests did not take kindly to this treatment. When the great Irish orator Henry Grattan paid his first visit he was so stunned that he did not utter a word throughout dinner. Sydney Smith once assured Lady Ashburton that London apothecaries had a special draught which they gave to people who had been frightened at Holland House.[25] His own way of parrying Lady Holland's bullying was to turn the other cheek. 'Ring the bell, Sydney.' 'Oh, yes, and shall I sweep the floor?'[26]

But probably more formidable than Lady Holland's manner to her guests was the fact that they were expected to shine in conversation. Holland House was the resort of an extraordinary assortment of clever men. There were professional wits, like Luttrell and Alvanley and 'Conversation' Sharp, who have, alas, left no memorial that can convey the slightest idea of the conversation which made them such valued guests. There were distinguished foreigners like Talleyrand, who enthralled his hearers with his recollections of the French Revolution. There was a succession of less prepossessing foreign exiles, like the Spanish-Irish priest Joseph Blanco White, who came as tutor to Lord Holland's son and later became a Fellow of Oriel; or the Italian poet Ugo Foscolo. There were scholars like Porson and Samuel Parr. There were poets like Rogers and Byron and Tom Moore. And there were of course the Edinburgh reviewers, Francis Jeffrey, Sydney Smith, Henry Brougham, Francis Horner, and later Mackintosh and Macaulay and many others. All these ensured that the talk at Holland House was always lively, and often very taxing. Charles Greville the diarist, who was not a stupid man, once sat through an evening at Holland House, during which the flow of talk had been so clever that his spirits became quite depressed, and he wrote in his diary a sad confession of his own misspent youth.[27]

It was in the 1820s, when Holland House reached its apogee as a Whig salon, that Holland composed the volumes of *Memoirs* I have mentioned. They are essentially a valediction. The Whigs, after the unsuccessful negotiations at the start of the Regency had apparently destroyed their hopes of

[24] G. O. Trevelyan, *Life and Letters of Lord Macaulay* (2 vols, 1876), 209; and T. Pinney (ed.), *Letters of T. B. Macaulay*, II (1974), 22–3.

[25] N. C. Smith (ed.), *Letters of Sydney Smith* (2 vols, 1953), II, 647.

[26] Mr Alan Bell tells me this anecdote first appears in Princess Marie Liechtenstein's *Holland House* (2 vols, 1874), I, 157. It is repeated, with variants, in Ilchester, *Chronicles of Holland House*, 85, and in Hesketh Pearson's *The Smith of Smiths* (1948), 120.

[27] L. Strachey and R. Fulford (eds), *Greville Memoirs* (8 vols, 1938), III, 76–8.

returning to office, and after the 'trial' of Queen Caroline in 1820 had
underlined the barrenness of their political prospects, could find little to
comfort them but their memories. Holland decided to write his down. They
show very clearly the limitations of the Whig outlook as well as its strengths.
But they should be used cautiously as history. They were published after
Holland's death by his son, and they were immediately subjected to the most
searching criticisms by a Tory critic, in the *Quarterly Review*. The author was
John Wilson Croker, one of the most severe critics of an age which is
particularly rich in critical hatchet-men. Croker was seven years younger
than Holland, but he had been in politics longer, and as Secretary to the
Admiralty under Perceval and Liverpool he had enjoyed an inside knowledge
of politics right through the period when Holland and his party were in
opposition. His method was to take individual assertions from the *Memoirs*,
to check them against other available material and to find them wanting. By
compiling a catalogue of inaccuracies, he sought to show not merely that
Holland was careless and slipshod in his recollections of facts and dates, but
also that his mistakes taken together furnished a proof of complete political
bad faith.

For example, Holland gave an account in his first volume of the arrest of
Lord Edward Fitzgerald during the 1798 Irish rebellion. Fitzgerald was a
cousin of Fox, and his part in the rebellion was a great embarrassment to
Fox's friends. Holland's account softens the harsher features of the case. This
is how he describes Fitzgerald's arrest:

> He was for some time concealed in Dublin, and was at last discovered in his bed
> reading Gil Blas. After a forcible attack, and a spirited and bloody resistance, he was
> arrested on the 19th May, 1798 . . . His kindness of heart led him on his deathbed to
> acquit the officer who inflicted his wounds of all malice, and even to commend him
> for an honest discharge of his duty . . .[28]

Croker has no difficulty producing evidence to refute this. The picturesque
detail about *Gil Blas* he passes over, but from the testimony of the police he
proves that the first policeman sent to arrest Lord Edward was unarmed; that
the latter was first to draw a dagger and wounded the policeman, who then
called for help; that a second officer in the struggle that ensued was given
thirteen stab wounds from Fitzgerald's dagger before he expired; and that the
victim was finally disabled only by a pistol shot from a third policeman, who
succeeded in wounding him in his shoulder. In fact, he shows that there need
have been no bloodshed had Lord Edward 'come quietly'.[29] Croker goes on
to uncover many other similar mistakes, and his criticism does indeed build
up a serious charge of inaccuracy, not to say misrepresentation.

But we need not on that account avoid the *Memoirs of the Whig Party* as
totally without merit. For if we look at Holland's own introductory remarks
we find that they were not intended to be a history at all. Holland wrote
them, he says, to find out how far he had changed his principles, to remind

---

[28] *Memoirs of the Whig Party*, I, 110–11.
[29] *Quarterly Review*, CXI, no. 181 (June 1852), 243–8. This dealt only with the first volume of the
Memoirs. A further article (XCIV, no. 188 (March 1854), 384–422) dealt with the second volume.

himself of his reasons for holding those principles, and to refresh his memory. He adds:

> As the perusal of these pages will, in all probability, be confined during my life to the writer of them or to his nearest relations and dearest friends, I have no great reason to dread the severity of criticism, and I am too indolent voluntarily to impose on myself much attention to style or even to method. I shall write down what has come to my knowledge respecting publick events and publick characters . . . with little or no regard to the manner of relating it.[30]

If we compare the various recollections which have come down to us of the talk at Holland House, with the *Memoirs*, bearing this prefatory disclaimer in mind, it becomes clear what Holland was trying to do. He was making a collection, in a roughly chronological order, of his anecdotes. The inaccuracy which Croker proves with such eager partisanship turns out to have a much more innocent origin than political bad faith. It lies simply in the fact that anecdotes, when told again and again, have a way, like pebbles in the bed of a stream, of rubbing off their edges, until they are smooth and round and pleasingly unlike the stones on the highway. The *Memoirs of the Whig Party* may be poor as history, but they are fascinating as historiography. They represent an early stage in the making of the legend centred around Charles James Fox and the Whig party of his time.

Fortunately, Holland's valediction was premature. The party, so near to disintegration in the 1820s, saw a revival. The Tories, or what Holland in his old-fashioned way would have called the party of the Court, were also divided, between the old anti-Jacobin school of Lord Sidmouth and Lord Eldon, and the more liberal school of Holland's old friend Canning. In 1827, Liverpool, who had held them together more by a successful avoidance of contention than by any positive policy, suffered a stroke, and George IV appointed Canning as his successor. Canning may have alienated many Whigs, but he had also offended many of his own party, not least the Duke of Wellington, and he was suddenly faced by the mass-resignation of those who followed the Duke. Canning was forced to turn to the Whigs, and it was in his negotiations with their leader, Holland's cousin the Marquis of Lansdowne, that Holland was able to serve as the go-between, between his party and his old friend.[31] Canning died, and it may be that even if he had lived, his ministry, composed of such disparate elements, could not have lasted. But the important thing was that the Tory party under Wellington had been fatally weakened by the secession from his rival, while the Whigs at last added the prospect of office to their consciousness of their common principles. From then on they became once again a party with a prospect of office. When Wellington was finally obliged to pass Catholic Emancipation in 1829 he suffered much the same kind of ultra Tory revolt that he had encouraged against Canning two years before. The difference was that now the revolt was fatal. Public opinion, sensing in the emancipation of the Catholics an end to the old regime, began to demand parliamentary reform, and this the Whigs

[30] *Memoirs of the Whig Party*, I, 2–3.
[31] A. Aspinall (ed.), *The Formation of Canning's Ministry* (Camden Society 1937), 144–6.

were able to provide.

It is perfectly true that the Whig ministry of Grey was a coalition of Whigs and Tories. It is also true that it was hardly stronger than Wellington's ministry which preceded it. The Whigs had been so long in opposition that they knew very little about what was required of them, and the efficient posts in the ministry were manned by moderate Tories. As Mr Brock has said in his fine study of *The Great Reform Act*, 'They did not know much about their ship: they had not been on the bridge until recently.'[32] And yet the direction in which they now falteringly set that ship was a Whig direction: they determined on a reform which would embody all those cautious maxims of policy which they had evolved in the previous twenty years of hesitation between radical extremism and Tory stationariness. Moreover, in this hesitant and uncertain course, they probably owed as much to Holland as to Grey. Grey had more experience of office and he carried more prestige, but he had been an isolated figure in the years in the wilderness. Holland was not regarded as ministerial timber; he had neither the territorial weight of the great magnates nor the ministerial experience of the professional politician. But much more than Grey he had provided the party with a centre and a common social life. He had as Fox's nephew been the guardian of its memories; he had tried to preserve its principles and extend them to men born outside the aristocratic Whig pale. Thanks to him and his hospitality, men like Brougham and Jeffrey, Horner and Sydney Smith, Mackintosh and Macaulay, had been drawn into the Whig fold. It would not be too much to say that these men owed their Whiggism to Holland House. I do not mean that the views they expressed in their speeches and articles were first submitted to Holland for approval; or that they are likely to have taken literally or even seriously the sort of nostalgic Whiggism which he conveyed in his anecdotes. But I think it clear that there did grow up a Holland House view of politics, not so practical as to be a policy nor so rigid as to be an orthodoxy, but still distinctive enough to be marked out from the views of other political groups; and that when the Whigs came into office in 1830 this view formed an important part of the political opinions of the Whig rank and file. In that sense, Holland did more than merely preserve and propagate the legend of his uncle Fox. It would not be too much to say that he had kept alive his party's mind.

---

[32] M. G. Brock, *The Great Reform Act* (1973), 152.

22

Peter and the Wallah: from Kinsfolk to Competition

John Clive

There are at least two fortuitous links between John Gibson Lockhart and George Otto Trevelyan. Both produced justly admired and still eminently readable biographies of close and famous relations – Lockhart that of his father-in-law, Sir Walter Scott, Trevelyan that of his uncle, Thomas Babington Macaulay. And both while still in their mid-twenties wrote series of pseudonymous letters about aspects of British society, in Scotland and England respectively, which caused shock and amusement at the time, and are now largely, and undeservedly, forgotten. It is to their common role as epistolary authors that this essay addresses itself. Beneath their leisurely and often playful use of the epistolary genre lay serious concerns and polemical intentions.

Lockhart and Trevelyan were both twenty-five years old, bright young men, gently born, on the way up, when they published their fictitious letters – Lockhart his *Peter's Letters to his Kinsfolk* (1819) and Trevelyan (in 1863) his *The Competition Wallah*. Lockhart, a son of the manse on both sides of his parentage, had by then received his education at Glasgow University and at Balliol College, Oxford, where, like Adam Smith before him, he was awarded the Snell Exhibition. At Balliol he had immersed himself in German and Spanish literature as well as in the classics. He thought of joining the Spanish patriots who had risen against Napoleon, and offered to take Anglican orders if his father would allow him to serve as a chaplain in Wellington's army. His father would have none of it. Those who knew Lockhart at Oxford were struck by his satirical bent and by his ability to draw vivid and telling caricatures of his contemporaries. That was a habit he carried with him to Edinburgh, where he arrived in 1815 with the intention of pursuing a legal career. 'A mischievous Oxford puppy', is how his close friend James Hogg, the Ettrick Shepherd, described him, 'dancing after the young ladies, and drawing caricatures of everyone who came into contact with him'.

His real bent was literary, not legal. When he returned to Scotland after getting a first at Oxford, he thought of writing a novel in the style of Galt.

Later he was to write several novels; one of them, *Adam Blair*, is still in print.
For the moment, however, he was a willing recruit for the magazine founded
in 1817 by William Blackwood, whose aim it was to counteract from the
Tory side the triumphant reign of the *Edinburgh Review*. In the so-called
'Chaldee Manuscript', a satirical commentary in biblical idiom on some of
the leading Edinburgh literati, which appeared in an early number of *Blackwood's*, one verse read: 'There came also from a far country the Scorpion
which delighteth to sting the faces of men.' The scorpion was Lockhart, who
was then doing his best to live up (or down) to that sobriquet. Writing as
'Baron von Lauerwinkel', he reprimanded two prominent Scotch figures, the
theologian Dr Chalmers and the mathematician Professor Playfair, for their
association with the *Edinburgh Review*, and lambasted the 'Cockney School of
Poetry' and its guiding spirit, Leigh Hunt. Perhaps most notoriously, it was
Lockhart who wrote that scabrous and wrong-headed review of Keats's
Endymion – 'back to the shop Mr John, back to "plasters, pills, and ointment
boxes"' – which impelled the mortally ill poet to exclaim to a friend: 'If I die
you must ruin Lockhart.' Meanwhile, his interest in German literature and
philosophy remained unabated. He translated Friedrich von Schlegel's
Lectures on the History of Literature Ancient and Modern into English, and used
the publisher's advance to finance a visit to Germany, where he had a (for
him) ever memorable meeting with Goethe – 'the finest specimen of humanity
I ever beheld'.

George Otto Trevelyan was born in 1838. His father, Charles Edward, was a
prominent civil servant descended from an old and distinguished Cornish
family; his mother was Macaulay's beloved sister Hannah. They had met,
fallen in love, and married in Calcutta, where she had accompanied her
brother when he took up his post as legal member of Council in 1834, and
where Trevelyan was then secretary to the Bengal political department.
George attended Harrow under Vaughan, won all the prizes, and went on to
his uncle's Cambridge college, Trinity. There he gained a certain local fame
by his satirical verses; he shone at the Union; he became an 'apostle', as well as
a friend of the Prince of Wales; and he emerged from the Tripos as second
classic. But, much to his chagrin, he failed to get a Trinity fellowship. So he
tendered a 'non-fellowship dinner' to his friends and, at the end of 1862, took
ship for India with his father who was returning there in the role of financial
member of the Council. His son was to be his private secretary.
   The India to which they sailed was still under the impact of the mutiny of
1857. The cruelty and violence of the mutineers had been matched by the
cruelty and violence with which the mutiny had been put down. That had left
deep scars on both sides. In 1862, the year of G. O. Trevelyan's arrival in
India, panic was caused by a report that the assassination of all Europeans was
being planned: 'Even British officials became savage. The life of an Indian,
according to the Viceroy [Elgin], was estimated by most Europeans no higher
than that of a dog.'[1] The phrase 'even British officials' implies, correctly, that

[1] S. Gopal, *British Policy in India 1858-1905* (Cambridge 1965), 36.

t was not usually they who showed the greatest antagonism to Indians. It was, rather, the large body of traders and planters who, even before the mutiny, had felt that the East India Company did not sufficiently favour British commercial interests. Parliament had wanted to reassure them, by taking over direct control of the Company from 1858, that they were not forgotten. Now, less concerned with responsible government than with maximum profits, they had become the principal opponents of a 'soft' attitude towards the Indians. The result was tension between settlers and civil servants, or, as they were called, civilians. That tension was memorably recorded in the 'improving exercise of writing about what he has seen' which, according to his father, G. O. Trevelyan 'imposed upon himself' during his Indian sojourn, and which resulted in *The Competition Wallah*.[2]

'Competition wallahs', in Anglo-Indian usage, were those among the higher ranks of the Indian Civil Service who had received their posts since 1853, when Parliament had abolished patronage and had opened all appointments to competition. Macaulay, helped and advised by his brother-in-law, chaired the committee to implement the legislation. Until the mid-nineteenth century, directors of the East India Company could nominate candidates to 'writerships'. Those candidates then sat an examination and, if successful, spent two years at the Company's college at Haileybury, before proceeding to India. All that was now changed. Any student at Oxford or Cambridge could compete for an Indian Civil Service appointment. Haileybury was closed in 1857.

The impulse was reformist; but it was scarcely democratic. The new system was intended to produce civilians who conformed to the ideal of the gentleman. In the event, however, it failed to appeal to the higher social echelons. Those competitioners who got to India – where they had to take two more examinations, in Indian law and languages – were attacked as too bookish, as lacking in manners, and as weak in field sports.

'Henry Broughton', the ostensible author of *The Competition Wallah*, was one of those civilians selected under the system which resulted from the act of 1853. The letters he addressed to his Trinity (Cambridge) friend, 'Charles Simkins', were first published in England in successive numbers of *Macmillan's Magazine* between 24 January 1863 and 20 July 1864. They appeared in book form in the following year, with certain omissions. By that time all pretence of anonymity had been dropped, and Trevelyan's name was on the title page. *The Competition Wallah* describes life in British India as seen through the eyes of a young civilian, a former Trinity man, who has just arrived there after receiving his degree. It depicts the competitioners' way of life in India, their contacts with Anglo-Indian society, a railway journey, visits to a government school and an opium factory, conditions in Calcutta, a tiger hunt, a Hindu religious festival, and a sojourn in the interior. We are given vignettes of Anglo-Indian life which, in their descriptive power, are reminiscent of Kipling. At the same time, the letters discuss some of the major issues of contemporary controversy: the effects of the mutiny; the

[2] G. M. Trevelyan, *Sir George Otto Trevelyan: A Memoir* (London 1932), 66.

desirability of the law of contracts which, on pain of criminal penalties
prevented workers from leaving their jobs; the position of Christianity; and
above all, relations between English settlers and native Indians in the post-
mutiny period.

The narrative framework of the book is cleverly established at the
beginning, when 'Charles Simkins, B.A.' writes to *Macmillan's Magazine* in
order to introduce the letters addressed to him by 'Henry Broughton', his
closest friend at Radley and then at Cambridge. When they were at Trinity
Broughton was the man of action who rowed for the college and spoke at the
Union, while Simkins 'conversed with a few kindred souls' – presumably the
apostles – about the problems of existence. Both take the competitive examination for the Indian Civil Service. Broughton triumphs, coming third
Simkins – the very name seems to whisper failure – fails. The two friends had
agreed in advance that the 'survivor' of the examination should write a full
account of his Indian experience to the less fortunate competitor. That is the
ostensible origin of *The Competition Wallah*, where Broughton, in his letters
to Simkins, assumes an affectionate indulgence befitting a correspondence
between a pro-consul and a bookworm.

Peter's Letters to his Kinsfolk were published forty-four years before *The
Competition Wallah*. As well as the distances of time and of geography
between the two works, there is the distance of subject-matter. The chief
concern of Dr Peter Morris, the ostensible author of Lockhart's three
volumes, is with the prominent literati, lawyers, professors and judges of
Edinburgh, whose activities are held as a mirror to the intellectual and, so to
speak, the spiritual state of the city. As a reviewer for *Blackwood's*, Lockhart
had taken the Tory side in the war against the reigning Whig literary-legal
establishment. The *Letters* must be read in that context; although they also
contain much non-political, primarily descriptive material, and although, as
we shall see, their intellectual scope far transcends the battle between the
reviews. On one level, *Peter's Letters* may certainly be read as a cultural
gazetteer, with emphasis on the direct observation – and overhearing – of
leading civic and literary personages. Lockhart's descriptive powers, like
Trevelyan's, are considerable. He has a highly developed sense of the ludicrous, and an exact and delightful ear for the local argot. By courtesy of the
ostensible author, we attend dinner parties and university lectures in both
Edinburgh and Glasgow. We visit Jeffrey's house at Craigcrook and Walter
Scott's Abbotsford. We inspect bookshops, critically examine books and
paintings, meet bluestockings and dandies. We are present at the law courts
at a Burns dinner, and at a General Assembly of the Scotch Kirk.

Lockhart, whose characterisations are more subtle than Trevelyan's
employs the more complex narrative device. Many observations in *Peter's
Letters* are filtered through the eyes of two persons rather than one. The two
are Morris, a convivial and bibulous Welsh physician whose mother was
Scotch but who, himself educated at Oxford, is imbued with English rather
than Welsh or Scotch national feeling; and one Wastle, an episcopalian Scotch

aird who alternately resides in his Berwickshire castle and in lodgings in the old town of Edinburgh. A former contemporary of Peter Morris in Oxford, Wastle acts as a guide during the doctor's Edinburgh visit. He is said to be the keenest Tory in Scotland; his Toryism, approaching that of the old Cavalier school, was, Morris noted, 'far more keen and intolerant than that of any man of superior attainments I ever met with on either side of the Tweed'. Unlike Morris, who is impressed by the absence of party spirit in the social inter-course of the Edinburgh literati, Wastle is wholly intolerant of Whigs and Calvinists; being too great a bigot, Morris writes, to feel much happiness in the presence of men who differed from him on important points. Whereas Morris (who has a particular interest in phrenology) is keenly observant and prides himself in taking nothing on trust, Wastle lives almost wholly in the past, his head full of Gothic antiquities and of the history, the poetry and the romance of the middle ages.

Professor Francis Hart may well be right in viewing Morris and Wastle as the projections of a conflict in Lockhart's own mind and experience, between the unbending Toryism of *Blackwood's* and the less rigidly conservative outlook of Scott, whom Lockhart had first met during the summer of 1818, who had lost no time in inviting him to Abbotsford, and whom he already greatly admired.[3] The question of the relationship between Lockhart and his two fictitious protagonists is complicated by the appearance in *Peter's Letters* of the author *in propria persona*; described by Morris as a very young man who might soon find that there were better things in literature than satire. Morris-Wastle-Lockhart – perhaps we should not be surprised to find so solipsistic a preoccupation with the different facets of an author's own psyche and per-sonality in a Calvinist country, and in a city that within half-a-dozen years was to witness the publication of *The Confessions of a Justified Sinner* by Lockhart's friend James Hogg.

The general target of *Peter's Letters* is Scotch Whiggery. Its particular targets are the *Edinburgh Review* and its editor, Francis Jeffrey. In the Edin-burgh of 1819, Dr Morris observes, the Tories had all the political power, but the Whigs were still lords of public opinion. One reason for this, Morris argues, is that whereas in England important literary figures like Words-worth, Coleridge and Southey could be counted on the Tory side, in Scotland the leading literary lights – Scott, of course, was the exception – tended to be Whigs. And the leader of the pack, by virtue of his immense power as editor of the *Edinburgh Review*, was Jeffrey. Listening to 'the sharp, shrill, but deep-toned trumpet of [Jeffrey's] voice in court', Morris finds it impossible to conceive of a more fertile, towering intellect; but he adds: 'There cannot be a finer display of ingenuity than his mode of addressing a set of plain conscientious men [the jury], whom it is his business to bamboozle.' Jeffrey seemed to exert the same power over the jury that his journal exerted over Edinburgh opinion. And, in Morris's view, to much the same effect. He recognises the *Review*'s 'wonderful authority . . . although it never did anything to entitle it to much respect from English scholars, English patriots,

[3] Francis R. Hart, *Lockhart as Romantic Biographer* (Edinburgh 1971), 62.

and English Christians'.

As we learn in the course of *Peter's Letters*, English Christians were repelled by the *Edinburgh's* infidelity, English patriots by its defeatist posture during the Napoleonic wars, and English scholars by its lack of critical judgment. For the last, Morris holds Jeffrey altogether responsible. How, for example, could he have launched such a long, deliberate and elaborate attack on the character of Robert Burns? It was all too easy to rail against the dissipation of those who were poor, and in drudgery. An attack of that kind was a defeat both of nationality and of humanity of feeling. For Lockhart, who may have derived the idea from Schlegel, literary and national genius were, or ought to be, inextricably linked. A great national author, he proclaims through Morris (the author in question was William Robertson), 'connects himself for ever with all the better part of the nation, by the ties of an intellectual kinsmanship – ties which in his own age are scarcely less powerful than those of the kinsmanship of blood, and which, instead of evaporating and being forgotten in the course of a few generations, as the bonds of blood must inevitably be, are only riveted the faster by every year that passes over them'.

Morris thoroughly approved of the great Burns dinner which, with all the leading Edinburgh literati, he was privileged to attend, and at which the requisite national enthusiasm was displayed in honour of a lowborn peasant genius. But his hope that the dinner would be non-political was to be disappointed. The toasts has been prearranged by the Whig reviewers. Not one of them had the common candour or manliness, at a dinner which honoured poetical genius, to propose the health of Wordsworth, Southey or Coleridge; while Crabbe, Rogers and even Montgomery were duly toasted. The lack of respect shown by the *Edinburgh* for the Lake school, and for Wordsworth in particular, seemed to Lockhart unforgivable. In his eyes, Wordsworth was as much a great moral guide as he was a great poet. The finest introduction to any book of psychology or ethics in the world was the opening of the *Excursion*, that poem of which Jeffrey had written in a famous review that it would 'never do'. Lockhart himself was embarrassed by the fact that *Blackwood's* had only recently savaged Coleridge's *Biographia Literaria*, in an article filled with personal venom. So Peter Morris expresses shock at this 'sad offence', adding that 'if there be any man of grand and original genius alive at this moment in Europe, such a man is Mr Coleridge'.

Students of the conservative school of European romanticism in the early nineteenth century can have a field day with *Peter's Letters*. All the expected indicators are present, beginning with love of history, 'the only study which presents to all our endeavours and aspirations after higher intellectual cultivation, a fast middle-point and grappling place'. But history ought not to be a mere chronicle of names, years and external events. It ought to be a study which 'seizes and expands before us the spirit of great men, great times, and great actions'. Morris is stirred by his visits to cathedrals in South Germany and Spain, and laments the discontinuance of Gregorian chant by the Church of England. Lockhart's nostalgia is evident too in Morris's reaction to the roll-call of the venerable Henry Mackenzie's heroes and heroines of days gone by, which 'sounded in my ears like the echoes of some old romantic melody, too simple, and too beautiful, to have been framed in these degenerate over-scientific days'. Morris most sympathetically describes Mackenzie's loving evocation of Edinburgh life as it used to be, when all the genteel population lived in the tall citadels of the town, and when the general style of entertaining was less formal and at the same time heartier and friendlier. Lockhart's anti-mechanism emerges in the doctor's strictures against contemporary Scotch philosophers like Thomas Brown and Dugald Stewart, who favoured the investigation of human thoughts and feelings by mechanical modes of observation. That approach, Morris thought, was bound to fail: for human affections could never become an object of successful scientific inquiry. Anti-mechanism is associated with a revulsion against urban industrialism. During his visit to a Glasgow cotton factory, Morris's spirits are 'not a little depressed' by the eternal rack and buzz of wheels and spindles. He finds relief by quickly escaping for a walk in the fields.

Morris's values are starkly opposed to those held dear by Jeffrey and his colleagues on the *Edinburgh Review*. They aimed to bring Whiggery into touch with the forward-looking outlook of the middle classes and with the lessons and the values of political economy. Lockhart's romantic Toryism was repelled by most manifestations of modernity. But *Peter's Letters* give evidence of a philosophical conflict more fundamental than the contrast between past and present, one that cut more deeply than Lockhart's quarrel with Jeffrey over the appropriate responses to Burns and Wordsworth. From Lockhart's point of view, the *Edinburgh* reviewers were chiefly dangerous because they were the spiritual heirs of Hume who, with his pervasive scepticism, had spared no pains in 'convulsing the whole soil, wherein feelings both religious and national had taken root'.

Hume's writings on religion, Lockhart thought, had increased the prevalence of infidelity. Commenting in 1851 on a review of Cockburn's *Life* of Jeffrey, Lockhart remarked that 'I fancy the whole set [of *Edinburgh* reviewers] were really most thorough infidels and S[ydney Smith] at the top of them in this respect as in all others'.[4] But Hume's pernicious influence had done more than foster infidelity. The doctrine of trying everything by the standard of mere utility, set on foot by Hume, Adam Smith and the other philosophers of their sect, had undoubtedly been 'the most dangerous present ever conferred by men of high and powerful intellects upon the herd of the species'. Hume's Toryism was another matter, of course. But the Whigs contrived to dismiss that as 'David's one little foible'. At the same time, they fortified the influence of his deleterious philosophy by giving them prominence in the *Edinburgh*. Wastle, while recognising Jeffrey's intellect and his general rectitude of feeling and principle, 'regards the Scotch philosophers of the present day, and among them or above the rest, Mr Jeffrey and the Edinburgh Reviewers, as the legitimate progeny of the sceptical philosophers of the last age'. Morris agrees. It is particularly unfortunate, he thinks, that at the present time a thoroughgoing scepticism has no object on which the

[4] Marion Lochhead, *John Gibson Lockhart* (London 1954), 291.

disinterested affections might exercise themselves. Self-gratification, there-fore, had become the principal aim of common minds; and when there were no longer any earnest notions about what it meant to be loved and respected, the reading public easily fell in with the sceptical critic's tendency to despise everything and to admire nothing. Moreover, by not sufficiently em-phasising the study of the classics, the Scotch universities provided no barrier against the spirit of mockery. Only acquaintance with the great models of antiquity moves men to love and reverence the great authors of their own time, who are the intellectual kinsmen of the ancients and who 'seem to revive the greatness of the departed, and vindicate once more the innate greatness of our nature'.

There are connections between those concerns and Lockhart's political beliefs. On the one hand, there was the self-love of those conceited block-heads who, egged on by Jeffrey's sarcasm, were convinced that they them-selves were superior to anything the age could produce. On the other hand, there was the self-love that had characterised the worst periods of the French Revolution, one 'gratified with the downfall of so many kinds of distinction, that at last it grew to be a blind, infuriate, ungovernable impulse, which could not remain quiet, while any individual yet retained qualities which raised him above the multitude'. Here were two kinds of self-love that were closely linked. For both were inevitable results of religious scepticism, of sub-stituting the self-sufficing, self-satisfied reason of the speculative human intellect for divine wisdom.

Thus Lockhart's critique of the *Edinburgh Review* and its editor derives not merely from his stance as a romantic partisan, but also, and more significantly, from a congeries of ideas in which theology and politics are blended with literature and philosophy. The real enemy was not so much Jeffrey as the destructive influence of Hume which, seen from this point of view, resembled the 'Geist der stets verneint' of Lockhart's beloved Goethe. It was no accident that Jeffrey, when he pleaded before the Scottish bar, showed little sympathy for the simple and unadorned workings of the affections. Equally, as Professor Hart has argued, it was no accident that Dr Morris was so enamoured of phrenology, a branch of study which, because it threw light on the primitive or elementary faculties and feelings, was, like Lockhart's Germanism, a critical vantage-point against Scotch metaphysics.[5] Far more than the repu-tation of the Lake poets was at stake for Lockhart when, through Morris and Wastle, he took aim at Jeffrey and the *Edinburgh Review* in *Peter's Letters*.

G. O. Trevelyan's declared purpose in writing his *Competition Wallah* was to make Englishmen at home aware of the harshness and contempt with which so many European settlers in India, most of them English, treated the native population. Their slogan was 'a Criminal Contract Law, and damn the Niggers!'. Whereas, on the whole, people in England had soon repented of their enthusiasm for a severe and retributive policy, many of the settlers had, if anything, become even more firmly attached to the great principle of the

[5] Hart, *Lockhart*, 58.

debasement of the native, the domination of the 'Anglo-Saxons', and the development of the resources of British India for the benefit of English pockets.

The political creed of at least one of the English characters in Trevelyan's play 'The Dawk Bungalow: or "Is his Appointment Pucka?"', performed at the residence of the Lieutenant-Governor of Bengal on 21 December 1863, included the sentiment that 'when you hit a nigger, he dies on purpose to spite you'. At the Sanapore race meeting, Henry Broughton watches an incident which he reports to Simkins with a passion clearly derived from Trevelyan's own: 'I saw – with my own eyes I saw – a tall, raw-boned brute of a planter' rush at a number of well-dressed, well-to-do natives (respectable shop-keepers, men of business, gentlemen of rank) who had as good a right to be here as the Governor-General himself, 'and flay them with a double-thonged hunting-whip, until he had driven them in humiliating confusion and terror for the distance of many yards'. One or two civilians remarked to each other that it was a shame. But no one seemed astounded or horrified. No one interposed. No one prosecuted. 'No one objected to meet the blackguard at dinner, or to take the odds from him at the ordinary.'

Trevelyan was enough of a realist to understand that any hope of the complete amalgamation of rulers and ruled in India was utopian. But he saw no reason why the two races should not live side by side in amity. For that to happen, however, there would have to be a marked improvement in the 'tone' of the settlers. 'The intense Anglo–Saxon spirit of self-approbation, which, though dominant at home, is unpleasantly perceptible among vulgar Englishmen on the Continent, becomes rampant in India.' Enlightened opinion in England must keep a close watch on the non–official English in India. That was one theme, and by Trevelyan's own account the most important, of *The Competition Wallah*.

Another clearly enunciated theme is the sympathetic portrait of the life of the young civil servants who had come out to India under the new competitive system. There was no better company in the world, Broughton declared, than a rising civilian; for he altogether lacked 'that carping spirit of discontent' which was so painfully apparent in able men in England who found themselves kept in the background for want of interest or money. The competitioner and his colleagues were kept busy enough with practical problems in a dangerous setting where men had to help each other to survive and where tolerance was essential. 'In spite of Dr Pusey,' Broughton writes, 'I cannot help greeting as a brother Protestant the little Danish missionary who has changed those blackguard murderous villages of Kurnam into Christians and payers of rent. Flanagan rides twenty miles every fortnight to Dinagepur to hear mass; but I can remember when he rode as many leagues, through the September sun, with my baby in the saddle before him, a musket-ball in his shoulder, and his cheek laid open by a sabre cut.' Was not that sort of life better than the heart-sickness of briefs deferred, dreary chambers, or drumming Latin verses into dull English schoolboys?

It is not, I believe, merely coincidental that a work dealing with life in India contains references to briefs and chambers, Latin verses and Dr Pusey. *The*

Competition Wallah may have been written partly in condemnation of the racist attitudes of English settlers, partly in praise of the new civilian's mode of life. But it is as much a revelation of the general outlook of a young Whiggish Radical as it is an account of a sojourn in India. As such, it provides a fascinating counterpoint to the Tory views expressed in a very different context by the young Lockhart four and a half decades before. Broughton-Trevelyan welcomes the triumphs of technology. He rejoices that the entire Indian continent is now covered with a network of telephone wires and that railways connect all the chief cities, with light tramways branching out from the trunk lines. Never has he been so impressed by 'the triumph of progress, the march of mind', as during his first railway journey in Bengal: 'Those two thin strips of iron, representing as they do the mightiest and most fruitful conquest of science . . .' On and near the railway line there are signs of England's handiwork everywhere to be seen – viaducts, iron sheds, the refreshment room, even the true British station master. But a hundred yards from the embankment, one found oneself amidst 'scenes that Arrian might have witnessed': bullock litters, trains of pilgrims, filthy beggars – 'these are sights which have very little in common with Didcot or Crewe Junction'.

Trevelyan does more than point the obvious contrast between ancient and modern civilisation. When he takes us inside an Indian train and imagines Simkins asking how 'our countrymen manage to appropriate to themselves the first-class carriages without a special regulation to that effect', he uses a purely English class analogy to underline his outrage at one of those Anglo-Indian customs that impeded good race relations. How is it, Simkins is asked in return, 'that there are no tradesmen's sons at Eton or Harrow? There is no law, written or unwritten, which excludes them from those schools, and yet the boys take good care that if one comes he shall not stay there very long.'

Trevelyan does not idealise the Indians. He notes their lack of stamina, their indolence, their want of truthfulness, their litigiousness. But mendacious habits, however deeply engrained in the mysterious Hindu nature, could be corrected and modified in time, if only the English settlers would stop using their 'damned Nigger style' and try, by an act of imagination, to put themselves into the position of the Hindus, and to see themselves as they were seen. After all, Hindu civilisation went back to an ancient social order, 'with titles which were borne by his forefathers, when the ancestors of English dukes still paddled about in wicker canoes, when "wild in woods the noble marquis ran"'.

The Indian mind, Broughton points out, is bound to be outraged by much English behaviour. Imagine, for example, the horror with which a punctilious Brahmin must regard people who eat cow or pig flesh, and consume liquor. English energy and earnestness must strike the languid and voluptuous aristocracy of the East as oppressive and importunate. English honesty must appear contemptible to the tortuous Hindu mind. English disregard of *les convenances*, in matters of hygiene for example, must seem inexplicable and hateful. Add to that the mysterious awe in which Englishmen were shrouded in native eyes, 'and you will have some conception of the picture presented to he Hindu mind by an indefatigable, plain-spoken, beer-drinking, cigar-smoking, tiger-shooting collector'. To the Indians, the English probably seemed a species of quaint and somewhat objectionable demon, with a rare aptitude for fighting and for administration, but foul and degraded in their habits.

While Trevelyan is anxious that the English in India should learn to recognise the profound differences between the two races, he does not advocate a policy of cultural *laissez faire*. That would be expecting too much of Macaulay's nephew who, like his uncle, believed firmly that the rulers had a civilising role to fulfil. It is our duty, he writes, to educate and to enlighten, to strike off the fetters of custom and superstition. Schools and railroads had already done much to set 'the fresh air of European civilisation' circulating freely through every pore of the vast Indian community. But after sixty years of European missionary activity, the proportion of heathen to Christians was still a thousand to one; indeed, in Northern India, ten thousand to one. Why, under the very shadow of the Christian churches and colleges, do men cry aloud to Seeva, and cut themselves after their manner with knives and lancets, till the blood gushes out of them'?

The answer to that question elicited, once again, Trevelyan's awareness of cultural relativism, in this case his recognition that an elevated and philosophical religion, adapted to the needs of an enlightened and progressive society, could not achieve success as a proselytising creed in India; and that Protestant simplicity could not appeal to a people accustomed to elaborate ritual. If an English clergyman 'chose to stand for twenty years at a stretch on the top of the Ochterlony monument, or take up his abode under a cocoa-nut tree in the Sunderbunds, he would have thousands of worshippers and admirers; but the Bishop of Oxford or Dr Guthrie might preach through all the cities in the north of India without making two dozen proselytes.' To be effective in India, Christian missionaries would be well advised to abandon their European way of life; not to hesitate to sacrifice comfort, society, and respectability for the cause of Christ. Certain groups of German Lutherans, Broughton notes, had succeeded in this. They lived simply and austerely. They spoke Indian languages with fluency and precision. Their children ate rice and curried lentils. The Lutherans had retained their remarkable influence over the people in their territory.

Both of our authors came to regret the manner, if not the substance, of what they had written. Yet it may be worth pondering certain other similarities between these two epistolary works, published almost half a century apart, by men whose outlooks differed in so many ways. To begin with, both series of letters were, in a very real sense, footnotes to great political events; and both were violently attacked in certain quarters. In the case of *The Competition Wallah*, that is hardly surprising. The mutiny, so W. L. Burn has written, was like 'a red-hot poker thrust into the face of the Englishman'.[6] The desire for revenge, accompanied by undisguised hostility to Indians, was slow to evaporate. Trevelyan himself tells us that after the publication of his

[6] W. L. Burn, *The Age of Equipoise: A Study of the Mid-Victorian Generation* (London 1964), 84.

ninth letter, which condemned the bloodthirstiness of some of the 'Anglo-Saxons', the leading Calcutta journals which had hitherto spoken of the *Wallah* 'in terms of extravagant and unmerited eulogy' discovered that he was an ignorant, conceited coxcomb, fresh from college, 'whose effusions could only be received with silent contempt'.

But why did *Peter's Letters* give offence? Sir Walter Scott, who was in on the secret of the authorship from the start, had a ready answer. It was, he wrote, because 'few men, and least of all Scotchmen, can hear the actual truth in conversation, or in that which approaches nearest to conversation – a work like the Doctor's, published within the circle to which it refers'. In fact, Scott believed, Lockhart had been too gentle and had refrained from depicting Edinburgh's embattled and vindictive literary society in its true colours. After first reading the letters, in July 1819, he had told him that 'the general tone is perhaps too favourable to the state of public society and of individual character'. But Lockhart had been right to 'throw a Claude Lorraine tint over our Northern landscape', since Scotchmen could not tolerate the bare truth, either in conversation or in a work like *Peter's Letters*.

Coleridge informed Lockhart that the spleen and criticism provoked by the book had been exceptional. If that was so, Lockhart replied in a postscript to the third edition, the true reason for the anger of the Scotch Whigs went much deeper than annoyance at their sharp delineation by Dr Morris. Peter's real crime was to have declared himself 'an enemy to the pestilent genius of Scottish republicanism and Scottish infidelity'. It was not merely that Morris had exposed the Scotch Whigs' lack of patriotism, a deficiency exemplified, he observed, by the failure of the *Edinburgh Review* to have rendered steady support for the Spanish patriots who rose against Napoleon. Something more was at stake now. 1819, the year of the book's publication, was, after all, a year of domestic crisis for England. Afflictions beyond the reach of human aid were being fancifully interpreted by a suffering populace as symbols and consequences of oppression. And what had the Scotch Whigs been doing? Pouring oil on the kindling embers of disaffection, and, according to Morris-Lockhart, hailing England's internal enemies with the same fervour with which, for so many years, they had hailed Bonaparte. No wonder they were furious with Dr Morris, whose Tory loyalty to church and state matched his still evident joy at the triumph of English arms and honour over Napoleon.

Peter's Letters, then, are as much a by-product of Waterloo, and of the post-war social and economic dislocations that led to Peterloo, as *The Competition Wallah* is a belated by-product of the Indian Mutiny. Both works can be read, on one level, as polemical tracts, and they were certainly assailed as such. But there are deeper similarities between the two books than those to be found in their common membership of the epistolary genre and in the hostility which their publication aroused. In the first place, both Lockhart and Trevelyan were fervent English patriots. Lockhart's revenge for the attacks made on him by the Scotch Whigs consists, so he tells Coleridge, of taking special pleasure in every present and future assertion of English onour, and in every spectacle of English glory. Trevelyan, for his part, celebrates the heroic defence of 'the little house at Arrah' by the outnumbered English against the rebels with an eloquence that reminds us of his uncle's account of the siege of Londonderry. He rejoices that, in the mutiny, 'the blaze of Oriental fanaticism . . . at length yielded to the courageous perseverance, and the unconquerable energy of our race'. Trevelyan praises not only English heroism but the sacredness of the English marriage tie, the purity of Englsh literature, and his compatriots' capacity for charity and humanity. As for the English reputation for snobbery, 'what is the champagne from the public-house round the corner, and the greengrocer in white cotton gloves making off with a cold chicken in his umbrella, to the gigantic, ruinous pretension and display of a highborn Zemindar? I hate this ignorant abuse of everything English.'

Both Lockhart and Trevelyan valued classical learning – both had performed brilliantly in that subject at university – and their pages are studded with classical allusions and quotations. For Lockhart, a classical education, by making men acquainted with human nature displaying itself under the guise of manners very different from their own, makes it possible for them to understand their own manners and nature better than they could do otherwise. If there is an awareness of cultural relativism in Trevelyan, it is present in the romantic Tory Lockhart too. Trevelyan, for his part, turns to the classics to increase his understanding not so much of English as of Indian institutions, manners and customs; particularly when he discusses Indian religion. He observes that the introduction of Western learning has produced the same effect on that religion, that is to say a clandestine turning to deism, which the progress of civilisation had produced on the ancient classical creeds. What Trevelyan and Lockhart both valued in religion was authenticity. The Indians found it, Trevelyan believed, in elaborate oriental ritual: Lockhart found it in a simple rustic gathering which took the sacrament in a Scotch country kirk.

For all his praise of material progress, rationalism and tolerance, Trevelyan finds that there are times when an oppressive sense of the nineteenth century weighs heavily upon the soul –

> when we shudder to hear Mr Cobden pronounce that one number of the *Times* newspaper is worth the eight books of Thucydides. There are moments when we feel that locomotives and power-looms are not everything; that black care sits behind the stoker; that death knocks with equal foot at the door of the Turkey Red Yarn Establishment. Then it is good to turn from the perusal of the share-list; from pensive reflections on the steadiness of piece-goods, the languor of gunnycloths, and the want of animation evinced by muletwist, to the contemplation of qualities which are recognised and valued by all ages alike. It is good to know that trade, and luxury, and the march of science, have not unnerved our wrists, and dulled our eyes, and turned our blood to water. There is much in common with Leonidas dressing his hair before he went forth to his last fight, and Colvin [one of the defenders of the little house at Arrah] laughing over the rice and salt, while the bullets pattered on the wall like hail.

Those sentiments are not so far removed from Lockhart's suspicion of the test of mere utility, from his dread of uniformity in an age when 'so much oil is poured upon the whole surface of the ocean', or from his celebration of national heroes, whether of the past or in the shape of contemporaries like Wellington, Scott and Wordsworth.

Trevelyan, indeed, was no more a pure Utilitarian than his uncle, or, for that matter, the later John Stuart Mill. His literary tastes – though, to be sure, not his literary knowledge – ranged far more widely than Macaulay's. He liked not only Browning and Carlyle, but also Wordsworth and Ruskin. He was to call Goethe, in hyperbolic language that echoes Lockhart's, 'the greatest master who ever consciously made art out of literature'. That is not the only reminder of Lockhart to be found in *The Competition Wallah*. We notice, for example, Trevelyan's comment, during his comparison of the civilians of his own day with those of the eighteen-thirties, that while his contemporaries could certainly be said to be doing their duty on behalf of the Hindus, that task was no longer a labour of love. *The Competition Wallah* is, in large part, an appeal by an English patriot for a revival of that spirit as well as for an end to race hatred on the part of the English settlers; just as *Peter's Letters*, in their turn, are largely an appeal by an earlier English patriot – Lockhart's patriotism was as much English as Scotch – for the replacement of self-love, mechanism and artifice by genuine love of country and authentic depth of feeling. Hunting lions in Edinburgh was, perhaps, not all that different from hunting tigers in India.

Peter's Letters to his Kinsfolk and *The Competition Wallah* are youthful and idiosyncratic productions, *jeux d'esprit*, and it would no doubt be unwise to search too hard in them for broad conclusions about the intellectual history of the period. 'From Kinsfolk to Competition' is merely a conflation of the two titles, and thus less portentous than it may sound. Its evocation of echoes of 'from status to contract', 'from *Gemeinschaft* to *Gesellschaft*', is however not entirely accidental. Lockhart's 'kinsfolk' connotes community, history and hierarchy. Trevelyan's 'competition' is linked to science, reason and progress. Yet his *cri de coeur* against the 'oppressive sense of the nineteenth century' recalls Albert Hirschman's recent observation that 'as soon as capitalism was triumphant and "passions" seemed indeed to be restrained and perhaps even extinguished in the comparatively peaceful, tranquil, and business-minded Europe of the period after the Congress of Vienna, the world suddenly appeared empty, petty, and boring and the stage was set for the Romantic critique of the bourgeois order as incredibly impoverished in relation to earlier ages – the new world seemed to lack nobility, grandeur, mystery, and, above all, passion'.[7] Are we not mistaken if we think in terms of a rigid intellectual barrier between the old regime and the new world of capitalism and democracy?

Marx had an answer. 'The bourgeois viewpoint,' he declared in the *Grundrisse*, 'has never advanced beyond the antithesis between itself and the romantic viewpoint, and the latter will accompany it as its legitimate antithesis up to its

[7] Albert O. Hirschman, *The Passions and the Interests* (Princeton 1977), 132.

blessed end.' But that answer, though brilliantly suggestive, is not wholly satisfactory. Neither Lockhart or Trevelyan fits snugly into the 'bourgeois' pigeonhole. And the romantic viewpoint, to accommodate both, needs more stretching than Marx allows. Yet, in a very real sense, it does accommodate them. That is some measure of its triumph. One ends by hoping that there will soon appear more books like Raymond Williams's *Culture and Society*, broadly conceived studies of nineteenth-century ideas in their relation to politics and class. But one ends too with the conviction that such studies must concern themselves, not with England alone, but with Britain as a whole, including Scotland and Anglo-India. After all, those Utilitarian ideas which had their origins north of the border, and which Wastle and Dr Morris found so sinister, were to hold partial sway, in one form or another, over British India in the nineteenth century. And Macaulay, who had not a little to do with that, knew and loved his Scott almost as well as did Peter Morris. Reading provocative pseudonymous letters can be instructive as well as amusing. As for writing them – ah, but who, in (to recall Lockhart's phrase) 'these degenerate over-scientific days', would hazard that rash undertaking?

The Jameson Raid and 'The Missing Telegrams'

Robert Blake

The Jameson Raid, launched on 29 December 1895 and ending in a fiasco four days later, is one of the most controversial episodes in imperial history. Some fresh light is thrown on certain aspects of the controversy by papers which the Rhodes Trust recently inherited from Miss Georgia Rhodes, the last surviving niece of the 'Colossus', and which have not been previously available to historians. The most important is a letter of 22 May 1897 to Cecil Rhodes in Cape Town from Bourchier F. Hawksley in London. Hawksley acted as solicitor both for the British South Africa Company and for Rhodes and Jameson in their personal capacities. He was present throughout the hearings of the Select Committee of the House of Commons into the Raid, before which Rhodes gave evidence in February and March of that year. The letter touches upon two problems which have long vexed historians: the complicity of Joseph Chamberlain, and the disappearance of vital evidence – the question of the so-called 'missing telegrams'.

To understand Chamberlain's role it is necessary to analyse the explosive situation which he had faced in South Africa ever since he was appointed Colonial Secretary by Lord Salisbury in June 1895. Britain's interest in that area ultimately stemmed from the need to secure the route to India. The acquisition of Cape Colony had caused the Great Trek northwards of the more obdurate Afrikaners and the creation of the basically hostile Boer republics of the Transvaal and the Orange Free State. An attempt to conquer them failed at Majuba, but their ultimate peaceful absorption into Cape Colony seemed the most likely future development. They had little drawing power for the Afrikaners of the Cape who enjoyed a higher standard of living and far greater prosperity. It was the ambition of Cecil Rhodes who acquired Rhodesia for his British South Africa Company – 'the Chartered Company' – and became Premier of Cape Colony simultaneously in 1890 to bring about this union with the north under the British flag.

The position had, however, been transformed only a few years earlier by the discovery of gold on the Rand in 1886. The Transvaal was now a country of vast potential wealth, and immigrants, largely British subjects, poured in to exploit it. The republic, like the oil rich states of the Middle East in more recent times, faced all the problems of the impact of a single commodity economy upon an impoverished, pastoral, backward, devout 'people of the book', but it also became militarily much stronger. The Boers under President Kruger excluded the 'Uitlanders', as the immigrants were called, from the franchise, taxed them to the hilt and used the proceeds to construct a formi- dable engine of war and repression. Johannesburg was the centre of wealth, Pretoria of power. Each glared at the other. It was far from clear which would win. The struggle between Boer and Briton for supremacy in South Africa no longer seemed a foregone conclusion. The Afrikaners of the Cape attracted by the lure of gold might join with their compatriots in the north and create an independent state instead of the South African dominion under the Union Jack which had appeared to be the obvious development a few years earlier.

The Jameson Raid was an attempt to force the issue in favour of Britain. Throughout the autumn of 1895 Johannesburg seemed to be boiling up to a revolution against Kruger. If this occurred Chamberlain could legitimately intervene to restore law and order through the High Commissioner at Cape Town, Sir Hercules Robinson. What he could not legitimately do was to foment the revolution from outside or even connive at action to do so by other people based on British territory. Rhodes and Jameson, however, were encouraging the revolution not merely with words but with money and arms. Moreover, a force consisting largely of troopers of the British South Africa Police was stationed under Jameson at Pitsani on a narrow strip of Bechuanaland which had been ceded to the Chartered Company on 7 November 1895. This was the nearest place to Johannesburg from which to launch an expedition, and the plan was to do so as soon as the expected revolution broke out. But on 29 December Jameson, observing that Clive 'would have done it', took the bit between his teeth. Consulting no one and unauthorised by anyone he commenced the ignominious foray which ended on 2 January with the capture of his entire force.

Rhodes was taken by surprise and at once saw the danger. What he had intended was first an Uitlander revolution in Johannesburg which he and Beit were actively supporting. As soon as it broke out Jameson and his men were to move in from Pitsani to restore order and pave the way for mediation by Sir Hercules Robinson. Rhodes never contemplated the reverse order, a raid first with the object of stimulating a subsequent revolution. What he did contemplate was, however, equally illegal. The 'Jameson Plan' (which would be better described as the 'Rhodes Plan'), as opposed to the 'Jameson Raid', made better practical sense, but contravened the law just as clearly.

It is important to be clear about the nature of this illegality. It would not have been illegal to station a force on the border with instructions to move when ordered by the Crown, in the event of a spontaneous uprising in Johannesburg. This had indeed been the proposal of Robinson's predecessor, Sir Henry (later Lord) Loch, in 1894. The 'Loch Line', or 'position', as it came to be called, was rejected by the then Liberal Cabinet, but on grounds of expediency, not illegality. Rhodes's defenders were to argue that the 'Jameson Plan' did not differ fundamentally from the 'Loch Line'. But of course it did in two vital respects: first the force stationed at Pitsani took its orders not from the Crown, but the Company, i.e. in practice Rhodes, for the Chartered Board had no control at all; secondly, the revolution in Johannesburg was not spontaneous but was being financed and armed by Rhodes and his partner, Alfred Beit. If it could be shown that Chamberlain encouraged these arrangements or even that he merely knew about them and took no action to stop them, he too would have been acting illegally.

Rhodes was Prime Minister of Cape Colony and he at once offered his resignation, for he knew that legally he had not a leg to stand on as soon as the facts emerged about his plans for a revolution in Johannesburg. But, although he had not authorised the Raid, he was reluctant at once to repudiate Jameson. Indeed he strongly objected to the High Commissioner's immediate pro-clamation against the raiders. He was hoping against hope till 2 January that the *coup*, totally unauthorised as it was, might nevertheless come off.

Chamberlain's reaction was very different. The news of the raid was brought to him by special messenger on the evening of 30 December at Highbury where he was about to dress for dinner for the annual servants' ball. 'If this succeeds it will ruin me,' he said to some of his family present; 'I am going up to London to crush it.' He took the 12.50 from Birmingham and arrived at his London house at 4 a.m. At the Colonial Office next morning he instructed Sir Hercules Robinson to denounce the raid to Rhodes as 'an act of war or rather filibustering', and to warn him that, if the British South Africa Company was involved, it might well lose its charter. This instant action by Chamberlain was one of the main reasons why even the opponents of the Government who were on the Select Committee of Enquiry believed him to be innocent of any complicity over the Raid. What was never properly probed was a different question – the degree of foreknowledge that he possessed of the Jameson or Rhodes Plan.

Throughout the early months of 1896 rumours began to circulate in London that Chamberlain and the Colonial Office were deeply involved. The source of these rumours was the knowledge that there existed an allegedly damaging dossier of cablegrams exchanged between Rhodes and his agents in London. The agents were Dr Rutherfoord Harris, a brassy and somewhat 'bounderish' medico whose intimacy with Rhodes reflects little credit on the latter's judgment; and Rochfort Maguire, an urbane lawyer and Fellow of All Souls, who had married into the aristocracy. Rhodes handed the copies of the cables which were in his possession to Hawksley early in 1896. The cables could not in themselves establish Chamberlain's involve-ment since none of them were sent by him or on his authority. But, if they were correct records of discussions by Rutherfoord Harris and others with Chamberlain and some of his officials at the Colonial Office, they indicated a far greater degree of knowledge about the Plan than Chamberlain was willing to admit. If published in full they might have led to questions which would have been fatal to his survival as Colonial Secretary. Their precise number is uncertain. According to J. L. Garvin, Chamberlain's official biographer, and to Ethel Drus, whose valuable investigations of the Colonial Office and Chamberlain papers have been published in two learned journals,[1] there were fifty-one. According to Lady Longford (Elizabeth Pakenham), who follows the figure given by Sir Graham Bower in his long suppressed account of the Raid, there were fifty-four. It will be seen later that there is some reason to query both these figures. What is clear is that forty-six telegrams, whether or not all of them corresponded to items in Hawksley's dossier, were extracted from the Eastern and South African Telegraph Company and eventually published in the Report of the Select Committee. It is also clear that at least eight telegrams in the dossier were not published in the report. We know indirectly of their existence and of some of their contents, but with one exception[2] they have never seen the daylight of history in their original form. These are the famous so-called 'missing telegrams' (actually cablegrams, but the custom of using the words indiscriminately will be followed here).

Hawksley saw Edward Fairfield who was in charge of the South Africa Desk in the Colonial Office on 4 February 1896, the very day on which Rhodes arrived in England on a visit to see Chamberlain. He hinted that he had some damaging documents in his possession, and Chamberlain through Fairfield asked to see them. Hawksley refused, replying on 5 February: 'Mr. C. knows what I know and can shape his course with that knowledge. As I hope I made clear to you before, there is not the slightest intention to make any use whatever of confidential communications.'[3] There can be no doubt that, although at the subsequent Enquiry Chamberlain saw fit to treat the letter as being of no special significance,[4] it was one prong of a double attack on the Colonial Secretary. The other was the interview which took place next day between Chamberlain and Rhodes who did not, however, mention the telegrams. The object was to prevent both the holding of an enquiry and the abrogation of the Charter. Chamberlain, whom Garvin depicts as unperturbed, was more worried than he seemed to be,[5] and rumours gathered force during the next few months. On 6 June he insisted on seeing the telegrams, and Hawksley sent his dossier for 'confidential perusal and return'. We will never know exactly what it contained. At Rhodes's insistence it was not produced at the Enquiry, and it seems to have been destroyed after Hawksley's death. The Colonial Office took a copy,[6] but this too has sub-

---

[1] *Bulletin of the Institute of Historical Research*, XXV (1952), 33–61 (hereafter *Bulletin*), and *English Historical Review*, LXVIII (1953), 583–93.

[2] This was the first from Harris dated 2 August 1895. It only survives because the Secretary of the Chartered Company in London sent a confirmatory copy by post which was discovered among the Rhodes Papers by Mr C. M. Woodhouse in the process of completing the biography of Rhodes begun by Mr J. G. Lockhart – *Rhodes* (1963), Appendix I. See also a most interesting analysis of the telegrams and their decipherment in two articles by Mr Woodhouse in *History Today*, June and July 1962.

[3] J. L. Garvin, *Life of Joseph Chamberlain*, III (1934), 109.

[4] *Second Report from the Select Committee on British South Africa*, H.C. 311 (1897), 499–50 Q 9559. Henceforth cited as H.C. 311.

[5] Drus, *Bulletin*, 39, quoting Chamberlain Papers, Grey to Chamberlain, 21 March 1896.

[6] A point of some importance, for the Select Committee could have pressed for the production of this when blocked by Hawksley, or indeed Chamberlain might have offered to show it.

sequently disappeared. There are various versions of the circumstances in which these disappearances occurred, but they do not affect this narrative.

Chamberlain showed the dossier to Lord Salisbury and offered his resignation, which was promptly refused. On 12 June he wrote an important memorandum on the telegrams in the form of a despatch to Sir Hercules Robinson. It is a statement for the defence, for at the time Chamberlain must have regarded full publication of the telegrams as at least a strong possibility. Ironically it is now the only source of information about the contents, even existence, of some of the most compromising of them. But it only gives summaries or partial quotations because the Colonial Office's copy (now vanished) of the telegrams was attached to the memorandum[7] and so could be seen *in extenso* by those who read it. Lord Salisbury refused to let it be published[8] and it remained in the Colonial Office files. There is an abbreviated and garbled version in Garvin's *Chamberlain*,[9] but the significant passages were not published in full till 1952.[10] The cables were returned to Hawksley on 17 June with a sharp letter from Fairfield:

> Mr. Chamberlain feels the greatest surprise that such telegrams should ever have been sent – or that if sent – they should not have been submitted to him for confirmation or correction . . . If they should be made public – to which Mr. Chamberlain makes no personal objection whatever – he will be prepared to deal with them as they deserve.[11]

Hawksley considered that publication of the telegrams would be fatal to the Colonial Secretary. He detested Chamberlain, who, he believed, had grossly traduced him to Rhodes in his professional capacity as a lawyer and had spread malicious rumours about him to Sir William Harcourt.[12] Hawksley was a Liberal, as was Maguire; it is quite wrong to assume that Rhodes and his associates were on the Unionist side simply because that party is the one associated with 'Imperialism'. Rhodes was a 'Big-Englander' like Chamberlain, but he believed, unlike Chamberlain, in the 'Colonial' not the 'Imperial' Factor, and there was no love lost between them. Maguire had sat as an Irish Nationalist M.P. and he fought a seat in the Liberal interest in 1900 (although to the relief of at least one member of the Shadow Cabinet, Lord Ripon, he did not get in). Hawksley spoke on Liberal platforms in the same election, and eleven years later we find his name on the list of people to whom Asquith would have offered peerages, had it been necessary in order to carry the Parliament Act. Rhodes himself had on occasions contributed both to Parnell's and to the Liberal Party funds.

Hawksley was not, however, motivated only by dislike of Chamberlain. He also thought that publication of his dossier would help Jameson in his defence against criminal charges under the Foreign Enlistment Act and later that it would help Rhodes when the Select Committee made its report. He

[7] Drus, *Bulletin*, 45.
[8] Ibid., 51.
[9] III (1934), 110–11.
[10] Drus, *Bulletin*, 46–51.
[11] Garvin, III, 113.
[12] Rhodes Papers, MSS. Afr. s. 228 c11/1, Hawksley to Rhodes, 28 January 1897.

never understood why Rhodes refused at that stage to allow the telegrams to be produced, and he protested bitterly. We can now see that Rhodes and Chamberlain had a relationship of mutual blackmail. The blackmailer loses his power the moment he reveals the incriminating document. The bargain, tacit no doubt, was that Rhodes would refuse publication as long as Chamberlain made no move to abrogate the Charter. The blackmail worked both ways because Chamberlain made it quite clear that the Charter would not survive if the telegrams were published. Moreover, there were limits to the effectiveness of the telegrams as a weapon. Twice Rhodes and Hawksley tried to use them to prevent an enquiry altogether, but Chamberlain was adamant that it could not be avoided. Nor was he going to let Rhodes use them to veto the inclusion of his bitterest enemy, Labouchere, among the Select Committee.[13] The most he would do was to nominate, on Hawksley's suggestion, an ally of Rhodes, George Wyndham, as a counter-balance.

But Chamberlain was nevertheless extremely anxious to avoid publication. His avowed reason, as far as his officials and colleagues were concerned, was not of course that the telegrams proved anything against him. On the contrary, he claimed that they were either caused by misunderstanding or else framed deliberately to distort his real role and to provide material for blackmail. But he argued that their publication, although it would not damage him in Britain, might have an adverse effect in South Africa and Europe, where his defence would be received with engrained hostile prejudice: in the national interest it was better that they should not appear – at any rate not all of them.

Hawksley's hitherto unpublished letter was written on 22 May 1897 in the closing stages of the enquiry by the 'Select Committee on British South Africa' which for ineffectiveness (or worse) has only been surpassed in modern times by the Marconi Enquiry of 1913. It had been sitting since the middle of February and its first six sessions were devoted to examination of Rhodes. On 26 February, one of its shrewdest members, Edward Blake, an Irish Nationalist M.P., asked about the telegrams between Rhodes and Harris. Rhodes replied in an off-hand way that he had not got them with him:

986. Do you mean you have not brought them to England? – No

987. Did you keep copies or have copies kept of your communications with Dr Harris? – No

988. So the Cable Company would be the only means of getting them? – I do not say that . . .

990. Are you aware of any other means of getting your communications from Dr Harris than the Cable Company? – That I cannot answer

991. You do not know any other means? – I do not know; I cannot answer the question.[14]

Astonishingly, the matter was left at that. When Rhodes gave his final evidence

[13]Drus, *Bulletin*, 56, quoting Chamberlain to Earl Grey (Administrator of Southern Rhodesia), 13 October 1896. Grey had suggested that Rhodes's 'loyalty' in withholding the telegrams would be tried too far if this occurred.
[14]H.C. 311, 61.

on 5 March there was no suggestion that he might be recalled, and he departed to South Africa.

However, when Rutherfoord Harris came to be examined in May the Committee became more inquisitive. There seems to have been a sort of pert shiftiness about Harris which inspired dislike and distrust. His evasive answers determined the Committee to obtain copies from the Eastern and South African Telegraph Company whose manager obeyed the order after a strong protest made by his Counsel. Harris was examined on the telegrams on 18 May. It was obvious from references in them that some were missing. On 21 May after further examination of Harris, Labouchere moved that Hawksley should be called on to produce the telegrams he had shown to Chamberlain, and that Flora Shaw, head of the South African department of *The Times*, whose name was mentioned in the telegrams, should be summoned to give evidence. Hawksley wrote on 22 May:

> Just before the close of the day's proceedings, Mr. Jackson [Chairman of the Committee] asked me to go into the witness chair and then said the Committee had determined to call upon me to produce the copy cables I shewed to the Colonial Office in June last under circumstances which are familiar to you and which I may remind you arose out of the interview I had with the Colonial Office immediately on your arrival in London on the 4th February, 1896.
>
> You may remember that when the Colonial Office sent me back the copy cables with Fairfield's official letter of 17th June, I was enjoined by Fairfield to retain and not destroy the copy cables which had been before Mr. Chamberlain as they contained pencil notes made by people in the Colonial Office.
>
> I purposely explained this position yesterday in pursuance of our policy that if the cables are to be produced it must be at the instance of the Committee and/or the Government – indeed the unanimous demand by the Committee of course includes a demand by Mr. Chamberlain as Secretary of State . . .

Having explained at some length why he did not feel able to take the advice of Maguire and Harris 'to put these cable copies out of reach', he continued:

> As you know from my telegram the Cable Company have in the ordinary course destroyed all their copies or originals down to and including 31st October 1895. You will have seen Mr. Pender's [Manager of the Eastern Telegraph Company] evidence given on behalf of the Company. He was ordered to produce all cables in the Company's possession that passed between you and Harris in the month of November 1895. I enclose a print of those produced as recorded. You will notice that many are missing. We are all absolutely in the dark as to how and why this is. It is impossible that their absence is an accident as might have been assumed if one or two, important or unimportant, could not be produced, but when we find that the most important ones are consistently absent, it is impossible not to draw the inference that something has been done of which we are unaware. Whether this is through Sir Robert Herbert [former Permanent Head of Colonial Office, but retired in 1892] or not I do not know. I scarcely think he would have been party to any such step. On the other hand I do not see who else could have managed it even if he wished to do so and [*sc.* 'but'] I am certainly not going to suggest that it was Sir Robert Herbert. I enclose copies of the November ones that are thus missing.
>
> However, the facts being as they are and more compromising cables not having been produced, I do not feel entirely free to act upon the cable you sent saying that if some were produced all were to come out including particularly those from Maguire to Harris on 20th and 21st December 1895.

This last paragraph does not at first sight fit with the normal division of opinion between Rhodes and Hawksley; viz. that the latter did and the former did not want the telegrams to be published. Why should Rhodes have said that, if any were published, all ought to be? The answer is that his cable was probably sent off, like so many, on the spur of the moment, and certainly without any idea which telegrams from the Hawksley dossier would appear. As for Hawksley, he was the loyal solicitor who, no doubt, guessed that the order did not correspond to Rhodes's real wishes even if he personally thought that it corresponded to Rhodes's real interests. The whole matter had been settled by cable long before Hawksley's letter reached Cape Town. On 28 May he formally refused on Rhodes's behalf to produce the dossier. The Attorney General had stated that a Law Court could insist and that the Committee claimed no greater powers. Hawksley, after pointing out that Rhodes could have been, but was not, personally challenged on the matter, observed: 'I will only add with the deepest respect, that I think, with regard to what the Attorney General has said, that this can scarcely be described as a judicial tribunal.' No further action was taken and the Hawksley dossier was never produced.

What the Committee had before it on 18 May were thirty-three cables exchanged in November between Harris and Rhodes, and extracted from the Telegraph Company, later printed as Appendix 14 to the Report; also three cables of no great importance from the London Office of the British South Africa Company to 'Charter Cape Town' printed as Appendix 15 and produced by the Company's Assistant Secretary, J. F. Jones, who deciphered all thirty-six with the aid of the Company's code handed in by Hawksley. He did not, however, invariably get it right. Mr C. M. Woodhoue has shown that in one of the apparently more compromising – No. 7, dated 4 November from Harris, containing the expression 'I have spoken open E. Fairfield', the word 'open' was a mistake and should not have been there. It was not in the telegram which Rhodes saw (as we know from one of the few Cape Town deciphered versions which have survived in his papers) and it certainly would not have been in the Hawksley dossier which consisted of the telegraphese versions prepared for encipherment and despatch from London. At the Enquiry Harris either forgot that he had never written 'open', or deliberately led the Committee a dance. There is something almost comical about the evasions, prevarications and allegations – not to mention the amount of time wasted both by the Select Committee and subsequent historians – about the significance of a word which was conjured up by a cryptographical error, and could have been explained away by Chamberlain himself from his own copy of the Hawksley dossier, had he seen fit to do so.

Later, another ten telegrams exchanged during December 1895 between Flora Shaw, head of the South African department of *The Times*, and Rhodes or Harris (who arrived in Cape Town on 17 December) were extracted from the Eastern Telegraph Company, decoded and laid before the Committee on 29 June. Historians have treated these also as versions corresponding to telegrams in the Hawksley dossier. In fact they were not. Harcourt raised the point examining Flora Shaw on 2 July:

> Q.9719 It is very important to know these things because of what is said in Mr. Hawksley's letter referring to the telegrams which he reported to the Colonial Office, and I presume these of yours were among the number? – I think not so far as I am aware.
>
> Q.9720 None of them? – Not so far as I am aware.
>
> Mr. Secretary *Chamberlain*: To the best of my knowledge and belief, not one of them. [15]

Veracity was not the strong point of witnesses in the 'Lying in State', but there seems no reason to query this piece of evidence. If Flora Shaw and Chamberlain were right, some doubt is cast on the accepted figure of fifty-four telegrams in Hawksley's dossier. He never stated any number himself, and if the figure is derived by adding the forty-six telegrams printed in the Report to the eight 'missing telegrams', it evidently has no foundation. It is not even certain that the three telegrams from London Head Office to 'Charter Cape Town' should be counted either.

However this may be, Hawksley was mainly concerned in his letter with the telegrams exchanged between Rutherfoord Harris and Rhodes in November 1895. It was obvious from references in the published telegrams that others were missing. A telegram from Harris to Rhodes of 18 November [16] refers to telegrams received from Rhodes on 26 October and 3, 5 and 16 November. None of these was produced before the Committee. Given the Telegraph Company's routine destruction of all telegrams sent or received before 31 October 1895, one would expect the first to be missing, but not the November telegrams, [17] and it was for this reason that the Committee, at Labouchere's instance, summoned Hawksley to produce his dossier.

How many missing telegrams were there? The accepted view is eight – all of them from London to Cape Town. This is based on Chamberlain's memorandum of 12 June 1896. He actually deals with ten, but two (2 and 4 November) were in the event produced by the Telegraph Company. The remaining eight were not known about at all as far as the Committee was concerned. Five of them – 2, 13 and 21 August and 28 and 29 October – would have been destroyed under the Telegraph Company's rules, but three, those of 5 and 7 November and 20 December, ought to have been in the Company's files. If one adds to these the telegram of 21 December from Maguire (mentioned in Hawksley's letter, but nowhere else), and the four telegrams from Rhodes referred to in Harris's telegram of 18 November (i.e. those dated 26 October and 3, 5 and 16 November), we reach a minimum of thirteen of which five were sent in November.

It is hard to believe, in the light of the fourth paragraph of the extract from Hawksley's letter quoted above (p.332), that there were not more. He was, it should be remembered, dealing there with the November telegrams only.

[15] H.C. 311, 528. This point seems to have escaped the attention of historians.
[16] H.C. 311, 596.
[17] Ibid., 433 Q 8238.

We know of the two from Harris, discussed in Chamberlain's memorandum. Obviously those from London were likely to be more important and potentially compromising than those from Cape Town. We also know from internal evidence of three from Rhodes. Hawksley's language is scarcely compatible with these five being the only telegrams missing in November. 'You will notice that many are missing . . . It is impossible that their absence is an accident as might have been assumed if one or two, important or un-important, could not be produced, but when we find that the most important ones are consistently absent . . . ' etc. 'Many', 'most important', 'consistently absent' – these phrases suggest something more than two from Harris and three from Rhodes.

It is true that, as far as November was concerned, Chamberlain in his memorandum only commented upon the two missing telegrams from Harris; presumably these were the ones which he regarded as most damaging to the Colonial Office. But Hawksley's judgment about what was 'important' cannot be ignored. On any reasonable interpretation of his letter, he must have noticed a larger number than five missing cables of significance when he compared his own dossier with the list produced by the Telegraph Company.

There is a further point of importance in Hawksley's letter. In the last paragraph quoted above (p.332) he refers to 'the cable you sent saying that if some [cables] were produced all were to come out including particularly those from Maguire to Harris on 20th and 21st December'. Maguire was at that stage acting as Rhodes's London agent, since Harris was now in Cape Town. Chamberlain in his memorandum discusses without quoting it the telegram of 20 December. It must have been one of the most compromising of all, for it followed a talk between Maguire and Fairfield and its gist evidently was that Chamberlain would prefer a rising to occur sooner rather than later. Often described as the 'hurry up' telegram, though its actual words are unknown, it triggered off a message from Beit in Cape Town to Lionel Phillips, one of the leading Uitlanders: 'Our foreign supporters urge immediate flotation' – the conspirators' jargon for starting a revolution. But there is no reference in Chamberlain's memorandum or anywhere else to a second telegram from Maguire next day. In view of the importance attached to it by both Rhodes and Hawksley one can hardly doubt that it too was potentially compromising.

Who was responsible for tampering with the Telegraph Company's copies? Hawksley hints that Sir Robert Herbert might have been the man. It is not at first sight obvious why, for Sir Robert had retired as Permanent Head of the Colonial Office in 1892. But a glance at his obituary notice in *The Times* (8 May 1905) shows something not mentioned in the usual reference books. On his retirement he joined, as *The Times* puts it, 'the boards of various companies connected with the interests of Greater Britain' and one of these was the Eastern and South African Telegraph Company.

He might well, therefore, have been in a position to remove compromising cables. We know that the Colonial Office was determined to avoid the production of the Hawksley dossier. It is more than likely that Herbert kept in touch with his old friends and former subordinates, and he could have regarded it as a patriotic duty to prevent the publication of documents which he, with many others, believed capable of exacerbating British relations with the Transvaal and the Cape, and possibly leading to war. There is no proof that he did act in this way, but someone removed the copies. Who would be better placed to do it than an ex-Permanent Under Secretary at the Colonial Office who was now a Director of the Telegraph Company?

We are not likely to discover at this distance of time exactly how the 'missing telegrams' were caused to disappear. But it is obvious who had the motive. Chamberlain would not have survived a full disclosure, whatever the real facts about his involvement, and he could argue that more was involved than the fall of a prominent Minister. It was widely held by those in the know that publication of the full Hawksley dossier would be very damaging to the national interest. This was a reasonable view to take even if one believed or pretended to believe that the telegrams has been drafted with the deliberate purpose of 'framing' Chamberlain. In fact that theory, though frequently advanced, is almost certainly wrong. Harris may have been a clumsy reporter of delicate interviews, but there is no reason to think that he was engaged in a Machiavellian plot deliberately to falsify his talks with Chamberlain, Fairfield and others. What is clear is that those ministers or officials who had seen the telegrams had strong reasons to prevent their being published in full. Chamberlain had implied to Rhodes that, if they were, the Charter would not survive. He concealed his own copies of the dossier from the Select Committee. He was one of the most ruthless figures in British politics, and he would have stopped at nothing – or very little – to prevent them from appearing. There were only two sources from which they could come. One was Rhodes, and Chamberlain knew he was safe there. The other was the Telegraph Company. The Company's collaboration must have been secured somehow, and Hawksley's suggestion that the person who managed it was Sir Robert Herbert seems the most probable solution.

Herbert is historically a somewhat shadowy figure, as permanent officials, however able and eminent, often are. He was born in 1831, a grandson of the first Earl of Carnarvon. He had a brilliant academic career at Eton and Balliol, and obtained a Fellowship at All Souls which, since he never married, he held for life. He went to Australia in 1859 becoming the first Premier of the newly created colony of Queensland in 1860. He returned to England in 1867, and in 1871 became Permanent Under Secretary to the Colonial Office, a post which he held for twenty-one years. He was by all accounts a man of great business ability and much personal charm – very much a 'clubman' who included Grillions and 'The Club' among the societies he adorned. He was offered a directorship of the Chartered Company in 1898, but refused. He was briefly recalled to the Colonial Office in 1900, and he was very active up to his death in Chamberlain's Tariff Reform campaign.

As we saw, Hawksley himself took the view that the telegrams ought to be published. In a later passage in the letter of 22 May 1897 he wrote to Rhodes:

We told Mr. Chamberlain, you will remember, directly you came over last year, that the cables sent to South Africa by Harris in 1895, which of course contained true reports of what had passed [i.e. between Harris and Chamberlain or his officials], had influenced the action of those in South Africa, and we warned him that this being so it was impossible for him to take up a position based on any allegation or suggestion that the cables to you did not accurately represent what had passed . . . In my judgment we, having thus cited the cables as the ground for, or at least as supporting, certain action in South Africa, we cannot refuse to produce the cables to the tribunal appointed to investigate the action thus taken.

This was a perfectly logical legal view and one can understand Hawksley's exasperation with Rhodes, and also with Beit, Harris and Maguire who were cabling from London in the opposite sense. One can also see that they understood what it was all about much more clearly than Hawksley. To him, refusal was a perverse enigma. To them, knowing Rhodes's mind and something of his relations with Chamberlain, it was the salvation of the Charter. Hawksley's naïvety and also his honesty come out in the final passages of the letter:

I fear Mr. Chamberlain cannot politically survive the disclosure [of the cables], but this is no fault of yours, but entirely arises from the attitude, notwithstanding the warning we gave him, he has chosen to take up and I do not want you to be involved in his catastrophe as I am sure there is serious fear you would be if you declined to allow production.

Obtuseness could hardly go further. It was precisely to prevent the fall of Chamberlain that Rhodes was against disclosure, for no other Colonial Secretary was likely to preserve the Charter. Of course Chamberlain might not have fallen, but he would have been far less ready to resist the demand for its abrogation if Rhodes had gone back on their tacit bargain. Chamberlain's 'catastrophe' would indeed have involved Rhodes, and that was why Rhodes was determined to prevent it by declining to produce the cables. Hawksley ended his ten-page letter with one of the most explicit statements to have emerged so far of what the missing telegrams revealed:

Had Mr. Chamberlain had the courage to admit that he allowed the troops to be put on the border in connection with the anticipated rising in Johannesburg, the country would, I am satisfied, have accepted the position and then if he had to retire for a short time he would have come back stronger than ever. At present the real offence is, as of course you appreciate, that he has deceived the House of Commons and the country, if not also his colleagues in the Cabinet.
Believe me
very truly yours,
Bourchier Hawksley

Historians have long ago ceased to accept the defence of Chamberlain in Garvin's biography. The high probability of his involvement has been widely recognised as a result of the writings of Ethel Drus and Jean van der Poel.[18] Yet it has never been proved that he handed the Pitsani strip to the Chartered Company with the deliberate purpose of allowing the Company's troops to

---

[18] *The Jameson Raid* (1951).

be placed there for action in the event of the expected Uitlander revolution. Nor does Hawksley's letter finally settle the matter. None the less this statement from a man who had read all the telegrams goes a long way towards doing so. Although many people saw the whole dossier, no others have said what was in them. Moreover, if the inference made from the first section of Hawksley's letter quoted above is correct, there were more missing telegrams than the eight commented upon by Garvin (inadequately) and by Ethel Drus (fully and acutely). Hawksley may well have seen material of which we know nothing at all, and this gives the more weight to his verdict.

There can be no real doubt that Chamberlain was aware of what Rhodes intended to do and that he assisted him in his purpose. But Jameson's reckless act threw everything into confusion. Chamberlain had to fight for his political life. He knew well enough that politicians seldom retire and 'come back stronger than ever' – certainly not those as controversial and hated as he was. Whether or not he deceived his colleagues in the Cabinet, he certainly deceived the House of Commons and the Country about his role in the affair. He was not the first or last statesman to do this, and it is fair to say that other and greater matters were at stake than personal survival.

As a tail piece one is tempted to quote from the 'Apologia' written by Sir Graham Bower, the Imperial Secretary at Cape Town, who admitted his own knowledge of the Jameson Plan but denied passing it on and accepted the role of 'scapegoat' to cover up the complicity of both the High Commissioner and the Colonial Secretary. He was shabbily treated. He had to resign and the expectation held out to him of reinstatement at an appropriate level was never fulfilled. Although he remained loyally silent in public he wrote several accounts of the affair. His papers in accordance with the instructions in his will were not opened until 1946. When they were there was something of a sensation. Bower's papers were one of the most important sources used for the first time in Jean van der Poel's book on the Raid. What follows is taken from the version dated February 1901 presented to Rhodes House by Miss Bryce, daughter of Lord Bryce, the Liberal politician:

> If in a criminal trial a criminal were allowed to appoint nine of his own friends on a jury of fifteen and to finish off by taking a seat on the bench himself, the world would hesitate to say whether it was a joke or whether it was the act of a lunatic.
> But if he went further and calmly drew up his own indictment. That is to say if he was accused of sheep stealing and elected to take his trial on a charge of murder there would be no doubt in men's minds that the whole thing was a farce. This was the case with the South Africa Committee. The real criminal on trial was Chamberlain. He drew the indictment on the wrong charge and then packed the jury with nine of his own men who could be guaranteed by the party whips to vote that black was white.[19]

There was actually nothing odd in the political statistics. A Select Committee normally reflects party strengths, and in the end the Liberal members, apart from Labouchere, voted for the Report. But it was certainly odd – and an object of suspicion at the time – that Chamberlain should have been a

[19] MSS. Afr. s. 63.

member. It was even odder that the real charge against him was never probed. Moreover Bower could have added – and must have suspected – yet another irregularity: the 'criminal' not only sat on the bench, but tampered with the evidence for the prosecution. Perhaps the last word should be left with Chamberlain himself. Hawksley, on 20 August 1896, suggested to Fairfield 'that Mr. Chamberlain will recognise that reasons other than the ostensible ones were intimated to him why the acquisition by the Chartered Company of Bechuanaland Protectorate was urgently necessary'. Chamberlain, iron throughout his career, gave nothing away. When Fairfield forwarded Hawksley's observation to him, he replied: 'What is there in South Africa, I wonder, that makes blackguards of all who get involved in its politics?'

24

Empire, Race and War in pre-1914 Britain

Michael Howard

Among all the fiends in the liberal demonology today, Imperialism, Racism and Militarism reign supreme; an evil trinity at whose collective door most of the wrong-doing in the world can conveniently be laid. Yet little more than three generations ago, within the memory of people still alive, these words and the ideas associated with them evoked, even among professed Liberal thinkers, a very different response. Empire, Race and War: these were seen as facts of life to be accepted if not indeed welcomed; certainly ones that presented challenges to be met and problems to be solved if disaster was not to ensue. It was generally assumed in Britain at the turn of the century that the white races were inherently superior to the brown and the black and so had the right, indeed the duty, to govern them. It was assumed by all save a small dissident minority that the British Empire was the greatest force for good that the world had seen since the disintegration of the Roman Empire, and by bringing the benefits of peace, prosperity and civilisation to so vast an area of the world's surface was even more worthy of respect. And it was taken for granted – by all save a slightly larger minority – that the Empire, having been built up by war, might be legitimately extended by war, and would probably have one day to be defended by war. The military virtues were thus considered part of the essence of an Imperial Race.

For the inhabitants of these islands at the beginning of this century the British Empire was for better or worse what Lord Curzon described as 'a great historical and political and sociological fact which is one of the guiding factors in the history of mankind'.[1] Most of them (at least outside Ireland) seem to have thought it to be for the better. It was, in a term which came into very general use at this period, a 'Heritage', built up by the heroism and labour of past generations, to be handed on, intact or increased. Rudyard Kipling used the word as the title for the poem which he wrote to introduce a sumptuous volume which appeared in 1905 called *The Empire and the Century*:[2]

[1] George Nathaniel, Marquess of Curzon, *Subjects of the Day* (London 1915), 5.
[2] C. S. Goldman (ed.), *The Empire and the Century* (London 1905), 1.

> Dear-bought and clear, a thousand year
> Our fathers' title runs,
> Make we likewise our sacrifice,
> Defrauding not our sons.

One can perhaps trace in the consciousness of inherited responsibility so frequently reiterated in this period the beginnings of that loss of confidence which historians of a later generation were to discern among the late Victorians and Edwardians. But we must set these people in the context of their times. They had grown up at a time when Britain was at her apogee. Born at mid-century, they would in childhood have heard the talk of men and women who remembered the Napoleonic Wars. They would have been brought up in the nursery on the patriotic verse of Robert Southey and Thomas Campbell. At school their minds would have been moulded by men with the robust and simple-minded patriotism of Charles Kingsley and of William Johnson Cory, that vehement enthusiast who taught so many future members of the ruling class at Eton, not least among them Lord Rosebery and Lord Esher. From schools where they came under the influence of such teachers, this generation passed to universities where they came in contact with professors like John Ruskin: Ruskin, who told the audience at his Inaugural Lecture as Slade Professor of Fine Art at Oxford in 1870 that it must be the task of Englishmen 'still undegenerate in race; a race mingled of the best northern blood', to 'found colonies as fast and as far as she is able, formed of her most energetic and worthiest men; – seizing every piece of fruitful waste ground she can set her foot on, and there teaching these her colonists that their chief virtue is to be fidelity to their country, and that their first aim is to be to advance the power of England by land and sea.'[3] If they were historians, they would be introduced to the works of Carlyle and Froude, who spread the same message: the need for the British, who were so clearly marked out by their history and their culture as a master race, to extend their habitations and their principles throughout the world (this, be it noted, a good twenty years before the *economic* arguments for Empire became fashionable). They would have read Charles Dilke's *Greater Britain* which, published in 1867, had urged the British to people the empty spaces of the world with their stock and to raise up and educate the inferior races they found there.

And in the 1880s, when this generation was entering early middle age, all these vague aspirations towards settlement and extension of authority and enlargement of prestige and power would have come together in the concept of Empire; a concept first crystallised in the work, *The Expansion of England*, which Professor J. R. Seeley of the University of Cambridge published in 1883.

For Seeley the Empire did not consist, as had previous Empires, of the rule of a metropolis over alien peoples abroad. For him the Empire was the British nation itself, which had grown slowly but inexorably according to its own laws and was now spread all over the world; and which needed a new self-consciousness in order to realise the full potential of its greatness. The

---

[3] John Ruskin, *Lectures in Art delivered before the University of Oxford in Hilary Term 1870* (Oxford 1870).

world, he discerned, as had de Tocqueville before him, was moving from the age of European powers into that of global, or as we would today call them, Superpowers. 'Russia and the United States,' he prophesied, 'will surpass in power the states now called great as much as the great country-states of the sixteenth century surpassed Florence.' But the links which were building up the great continental states by land had in the case of the British to be created and maintained by sea. It was, and must be, an oceanic power. Its destiny lay beyond the seas, and there need be no limit to its natural growth.

So began, in Britain, the age of Imperialism. From being a sentiment, Imperialism became a programme, and one supported by politicians of all parties. In 1884 there was founded an Imperial Federation League, very largely in direct response to the challenge posed by Seeley. More effective than most such organisations, it convened an Imperial Exhibition in London in 1886, for which Lord Tennyson and Arthur Sullivan combined to write an anthem. It established a bricks-and-mortar shrine of Imperialism in the Imperial Institute at South Kensington, the tower of which remains, splendidly flamboyant among the utilitarian clutter of the (still) Imperial College of Science and Technology; and it convened in 1887 a Colonial Conference in London in the hope that this would lead to the creation of a great, unified Imperial Federation on the model of the United States. It did nothing of the kind, largely because the colonies of Australia, New Zealand, Canada and South Africa, having escaped from the tutelage of London, showed no enthusiasm to submit to it again. But the age of High Imperialism was ushered in by these celebrations, an age which found its Laureate in the facile talent of the young Rudyard Kipling. Ten years later the age reached its apogee with the Diamond Jubilee celebrations; an apogee from which, as a slightly more mature Rudyard Kipling pointed out in his *Recessional*, decline was, if not inevitable, at least all too likely.

Such a decline did not, however, lie within the horizon of that arch-priest of Empire, Cecil Rhodes; and it is worth recalling the original terms of the will which Rhodes drew up in 1877, at the age of twenty-four, since, fantastic as they seem today, there is little evidence that he ever seriously changed his mind about his ultimate objectives. His intention was to set up a trust

> To and for the establishment, promotion and development of a Secret Society, the true aim and object whereof shall be the extension of British rule throughout the world, the perfecting of a system of emigration from the United Kingdom, and of colonisation by British subjects of all lands where the means of livelihood are attainable by energy, labour and enterprise, and especially the occupation by British settlers of the entire Continent of Africa, the Holy Land, the Valley of the Euphrates, the Isles of Cyprus and Candia, the whole of South America, the Islands of the Pacific not heretofore possessed by Great Britain, the whole of the Malay Archipelago, the seaboard of China and Japan, the ultimate recovery of the United States of America as an integral part of the British Empire, the inauguration of a system of colonial representation in the Imperial Parliament which may tend to weld together the disjointed members of the Empire, and finally the foundation of so great a power as hereafter to render wars impossible and promote the best interests of humanity.[4]

[4] Lewis Michell, *The Life of the Rt. Hon. Cecil Rhodes* (London 1910), I, 68.

Few of Rhodes's contemporaries would have dared to spell out their secret hopes quite so explicitly, but those hopes were not untypical. Lord Rosebery, the President of the Imperial Federation League, stated in 1893 that it 'was part of our responsibility and our heritage to take care that the world, as far as it can be moulded by us, shall receive an Anglo-Saxon and not another character'.[5] A man of a slightly younger generation, Leopold Amery, who was born in 1873 in time to be influenced as a precocious schoolboy by the writings of Seeley and Froude, was to write in his memoirs that

> If the feeble control of the Manchu dynasty should break down entirely, as that of the dynasty had broken down in India, then presumably we might have to take on greater responsibilities . . . No one was clamouring to see Queen Victoria Empress of China as well as Empress of India. But none, at the time of her Diamond Jubilee would have dismissed the idea as inconceivable.[6]

Nor must we forget that it was to be Amery's generation which, in the aftermath of the First World War, actually did extend the frontiers of Empire to embrace, however briefly, the Holy Land and the valley of the Euphrates; and did not conceal its desire to extend them into regions of central Asia which not even Rhodes had thought about.

The Empire might thus have continued to grow, whether to create favourable conditions for British trade, as it did in West Africa and might have done in China; or to gain strategic security, as it did in Mesopotamia and might have done in Persia; or to obtain more land for white settlement, as it did in Southern Africa and conceivably might have done in South America; as well as from the general sense, which historians must neither underrate nor mock, that it was its destiny to continue to grow, and that Englishmen had the duty and responsibility to ensure its growth. It was this accumulated national and imperial dynamic which was to be concentrated on South Africa at the turn of the century, where Kruger and the Boers were seen as irritating and anachronistic obstructions in the path of a historical process as inevitable as it was necessary.

Necessary, certainly; for what would happen in the almost inconceivable eventuality of the British people betraying their trust and *not* showing themselves worthy of their destiny? There was the general feeling that what did not expand must shrink; what did not grow must decline. Seeley had prophesied the advent of the age of the Superpowers in the 1880s, and Halford Mackinder was to buttress his prophetic vision with geo-political analysis a quarter of a century later. The former Great Powers of Europe were dwindling, in historical perspective, to the scale of the Italian city-states. Big was now beautiful, in political as in economic organisation, where the great industrial cartels were forming, and with them the big unions. As one imperial publicist put it in 1905, 'The day of the individual and the small nation has gone for England with the advent of rivals. In any era of competition, Providence is on the side of the big battalions.'[7] The examples

[5] Quoted in R. Koerbner and H. D. Schmidt, *Imperialism* (Cambridge 1964), 192.
[6] L. S. Amery, *My Political Life* (London 1953), I, 145.
[7] C. S. Goldman, op. cit., xix.

admired and applauded, by Liberals and Conservatives alike, were those provided on the Continent by Bismarck and Cavour, who had so clearly led their nations towards their manifest destinies; and as they had forged the small particles of their communities into great nation-states, so must the British create their own yet greater world-state. The idea, if not the phrase, which was to become current in Germany, *Weltmacht oder Niedergang*, was no less prevalent in England; we must become a power on a global scale, or we shall go under.

This was the fear expressed by Joseph Chamberlain, the spokesman for those economic interests in the Midlands which were beginning to feel the blast of international competition. Chamberlain's Imperialism was frankly economic. 'Is there,' he demanded in 1888, 'any man in his senses who believes that the crowded population of these islands could exist for a single day if we were to cut adrift from us the great dependencies which now look to us for protection and assistance and which are the natural markets for our trade?'[8] The example of the German *Zollverein* was infectious, both as providing a solution in itself to Britain's economic problems and, as in Germany, as a step towards political unification of the Empire.

There might be disagreement about the details of the solution – whether the Empire should become an economically autarkic entity, or be sustained as it had been hitherto by the great and uninterrupted currents of free trade – but there was very general agreement about the nature of the problem. It was defined in a rough and ready way by Rhodes himself. 'I never lose an opportunity of pointing out to the people,' he said in 1892, 'that in view of the fact that these islands can only support six out of their thirty-six millions, and in view also of the action of the world in trying to exclude our goods, we cannot afford to part with one inch of the world's surface which affords a free and open market to the manufacture of our countrymen.'[9] There must be great new spaces in which to settle. For an increasingly explosive social situation at home, the Empire seemed to provide a simple and obvious answer. Instead of a restive proletariat remaining bottled up in the stinking cities of late-Victorian England, the industries in which they worked increasingly vulnerable to foreign competition, with unemployment and social squalor driving them to drink or, worse, to revolution, let there be massive emigration to the new lands of white settlement, where the emigrants could rediscover the good life, establish healthy pastoral communities, and provide secure markets for their brethren who remained at home.

Lord Rosebery declared in 1893 that 'An Empire such as ours requires as its first condition an imperial race – a race vigorous and industrious and intrepid. In the rookeries and slums which still survive, an imperial race cannot be reared.' 'A drink-sodden population,' he said a few years later, 'is not the true basis of a prosperous Empire.'[10] It had to be admitted that the urban population

[8] Quoted in Bernard Semmel, *Imperialism and Social Reform: English Social and Imperial Thought 1895-1914* (London 1960), 85.
[9] Lewis Michell, op. cit., II, 61.
[10] Quoted in Semmel, op. cit., 62-3.

of Britain in the first decade of the new century did not *look* very much like empire-builders; and writers educated in the classics, as so many of the university-trained population still were, began to discern alarming similarities with the later development of Imperial Rome. A classical scholar writing on the eve of the Great War found the analogies with Roman decline all too apparent. There was, it seemed,

> the same decay of agriculture; the same predominance of town over country life; the same deterioration of physique and general health; the same growth of luxury and desire for bodily comfort; the same increasing distaste for the burdens of married life; the same decline in the birth rate; the same excessive taxation, the same decadence in public morals; the same reaction towards morbid and monstrous superstitions; the same substitution of State gratuities for parental duties; the same love of display in social life; the same lust for gladiatorial exhibitions of athletic skills; the same decreasing sense of national responsibility and self-sacrificing patriotism.[11]

Much the same thought occurred to Lord Cromer, one of the greatest proconsuls of the High Imperialist era, when he reviewed Thomas Hodgkin's study of *Italy and her Invaders* in 1908. 'Are we so far deceived,' he asked, 'and are we so incapable of peering into the future as to be unable to see that many of the steps which now appear calculated to enhance and to stereotype Anglo-Saxon domination are but the precursors of a period of national decay and sterility?'[12]

The Edwardian era was thus one of growing doubts about the validity even of the imperial solution to the problems which were beginning to dominate Metropolitan Britain. Were the British really, as Joseph Chamberlain had termed them in 1895, 'the greatest Imperial Race the world has ever seen'?

At the time when Chamberlain had made this claim there were few who doubted it. The books and newspapers of the period are full of references to the Imperial Race, the Island Race, the Island Breed, British stock, and so on, without a shadow of apology or even of self-consciousness. This was the way it was. The white man *was* superior to the dark-skinned man; a position which gave him privileges and responsibilities, rights and duties. He *was* more civilised, and had to uphold and extend the standards of that civilisation. It was a burden which weighed on all white men alike (though people were never quite sure about the Russians) but upon the Anglo-Saxon races most of all. When at the end of the century the Americans at last plunged into colonial adventure and took over, with the best possible of intentions, the governance of the Philippines from the palsied hands of Spain, the general reaction in the British Press was well summed up in Kipling's poem, *The White Man's Burden*: about time too.

The term 'Race' was used at the time very loosely; not that we can claim that it is employed with any great precision today. Usually when people used the term they meant what today we would term 'cultures', and certainly any writer who allowed himself to be cross-examined about the actual composition

[11] H. B. Gray, *The Public Schools and the Empire* (London 1913), 3.
[12] Evelyn, Earl of Cromer, *Political and Literary Essays 1908-1913* (London 1913), 3.

of the so-called 'Anglo-Saxon Race' would have found himself in difficulties. But all recent ages have used jargon derived from a skimpy knowledge of one or more of the sciences. As we tend to think in ill-digested concepts drawn from economics, or sociology, or cybernetics, or, most fashionable of all, ecology, so at the end of the last century publicists of all kinds thought in terms of the anthropological and biological sciences, especially as popularised by Charles Darwin. Probably as few people had actually read Darwin as have, in more recent times, read Max Weber, or Maynard Keynes, or Lévi-Strauss; but all literate Europeans and Americans reckoned that they knew what he had said. Life had evolved, in popular Darwinian theory, by a process of adaptation of species to their surroundings; an adaptation which inevitably involved conflict. Those species which proved themselves best able to exploit and dominate their environment, including competition from rival species, were those which survived. Those which could not so adapt and prevail in the struggle for life disappeared.

   Into this framework there fitted very easily the work of early anthropologists on the development and distinctions between the various races of mankind, which naturally became of absorbing interest as the nineteenth century made global travel possible for more than a small number of traders, soldiers and adventurers. Further, such travel brought the West for the first time into continuous contact with a wider range of societies than the familiar high cultures of the East, Arab, Indian, Chinese, with whom the West had trafficked for centuries without any feeling of superiority other than the normal xenophobia of the ignorant. Even with those societies, where Europeans had until the eighteenth century interacted on a basis of cultural equality, the scientific and technical transformations of the early nineteenth century had now put the white man on a new footing of effective superiority. Their steamships, their railways, their manufacturing machinery, and not least their weapons, turned them from privileged traders exercising a loose political suzerainty into dominators and rulers, firmly imposing new cultural patterns. As for the black-skinned peoples with whom the Europeans only began to come into close and continuous contact when they began to open up the hinterland of Africa during the second half of the nineteenth century, the cultural difference was from the beginning so vast, so apparently unbridgeable that the concept of 'equality', except in the purely theological sense, seemed irrelevant and inapplicable. Marjorie Perham expressed the situation well in her Reith Lectures in 1961 dealing primarily with West Africa: 'The suddenness and strength of this penetration (which) meant taking over tribal Africa just as it was, almost intact, and then confronting it with twentieth-century Europe . . . (was) a cruel trick which history played on (the Africans) and . . . upon us Europeans.'[13]

   This kind of cultural confrontation was probably far more influential in shaping British attitudes about what they loosely called 'race' than any of the notorious works of Gobineau or Houston Stewart Chamberlain, which were probably read, if at all, only by a small number of cranks. We do know,

[13] Marjorie Perham, *The Colonial Reckoning* (London 1961), 32.

however, that an enormous number of people did read Benjamin Kidd. His book, *Social Evolution*, first published in 1893, sold so many copies and ran into so many editions that he was able to retire from the civil service and subsist for the remaining twenty-three years of his life as a freelance writer.

It is still worth reading *Social Evolution* to see how Social-Darwinian ideas were disseminated among a popular audience. The criterion of survival, wrote Kidd, was 'social efficiency', and survival had to be fought for in a highly competitive environment. 'Societies, like the individuals comprising them, are to be regarded as the product of the circumstances in which they exist, – the survival of the fittest in the rivalry which is constantly in progress . . . the resources of the individual are drawn upon to the fullest extent to keep the rivalry (of societies) to the highest pitch; the winning societies gradually extinguish their competitors, the weaker peoples disappear before the stronger, and the subordination or exclusion of the least efficient is still the prevailing feature of advancing humanity.'

According to Kidd, 'The wide interval between the people who have attained the highest social development and the lowest races is not mainly the result of a difference in intellectual, but of a difference in ethical development . . . Members of the inferior races . . . scarcely ever possess those qualities of intense application and of prolonged persevering effort, without which it is absolutely impossible to obtain high proficiency in any branch of learning . . . The lacking qualities are not intellectual qualities at all; they are precisely those which contribute in so high a degree to social efficiency and racial ascendancy and they are consequently, as might be expected, the invariable inheritance of those races which have reached a state of high social development and of those races only.' It was, said Kidd, 'the Teutonic peoples (who) possess . . . qualities, not in themselves intellectual, which contribute to a higher degree to social efficiency'; and this accounted for 'the . . . triumphant and overwhelming expansion of the peoples of Teutonic stock'.[14]

The Teutonic races, and the British race in particular, thus owed their pre-eminence to having developed, over the centuries, the correct blend of social and individual qualities which best enabled them to survive and defeat their rivals in a highly competitive environment. One need look no further for their right to rule.

That right was seen as carrying with it the positive duty of exercising authority in regions, such as India and Egypt, where conquest or trade had brought the British into contact with 'inferior' races; for their authority, in the words of Alfred Lord Milner, 'is the only one capable, under present circumstances, of ensuring to the peoples of these countries the primary blessings of order and justice'.[15] It never occurred to Milner and his contemporaries to doubt that 'order and justice', as the British understood it, was what these peoples needed, and when one considers the administrative confusion in which they found Egypt in the 1880s, and the situation which they confronted in West Africa a decade later, it would have been surprising if it

[14] Benjamin Kidd, *Social Evolution* (2nd edn, London 1896), 46, 70, 266, 295, 299.
[15] Vladimir Halperin, *Lord Milner and His Empire* (London 1952), 195.

had. The cultural relativism of the anthropologist did not come naturally to them. They felt they had duties, responsibilities. They moved into these areas with the tight-lipped determination of sanitary squads cleansing infected buildings, making them fit for human habitation.

Nowhere can one see this more clearly than in Egypt, where Milner first cut his imperial teeth. Milner's study, *England in Egypt*, became one of the text-books of Imperialism at the turn of the century. The British went into Egypt, according to Milner, simply to restore order, but this meant reforming the Egyptian administration root and branch. And they intended to stay there until the Egyptians could run their own affairs properly. There was nothing in it, economically, for Britain. Egypt's trade in the '80s and '90s was overwhelmingly with countries other than the British. But they had to stay until the Egyptians showed themselves capable of doing a decent job. Milner described an imaginary conversation between an Englishman and an Egyptian, with the former saying: 'We do not want to stay in your country for ever. We don't despair of your learning to manage decently your own affairs . . . You need to be shown what to do, but you also need to practise doing it. You need energy, initiative, self-reliance.'[16] Thus might the head of a house at a British public school exhort a rather unsatisfactory junior rugger team.

This consciousness of racial superiority, and of the responsibilities that went with it, inspired all the great British proconsuls. Lugard in West Africa described how, 'as Roman imperialism laid the foundations of modern civilisation and led the wild barbarians of these islands along the path of progress, so in Africa today we are repaying the debt, and bringing to the dark places of the earth, the abode of barbarism and cruelty, the torch of culture and progress, while ministering to the needs of our own civilisation'; and declared firmly, 'We hold these countries because it is the genius of our race to colonise, to trade, and to govern.'[17]

And in a very revealing article on 'The Government of Subject Races', originally printed in *The Edinburgh Review* for January 1908, Lord Cromer set out the views of what he called 'a sound but reasonable Imperialist'.[18] It was of course necessary, he wrote, to govern in the interests of the subject peoples. But he added, 'We need not always enquire too closely what these peoples, who are after all *in statu pupillari*, themselves think best in their own interests, although that is a point which deserves serious consideration. But it is essential that each special issue should be decided mainly with reference to what, by the light of Western knowledge and experience tempered by local considerations, we conscientiously think is best for the subject race, without any real or supposed advantage which may accrue to England as a nation or – as is more frequently the case – to the special interests represented by some one or more influential class of Englishman.' If the English pursued such a just and disinterested policy they might hope to gain, not the love of their

[16] Alfred, Viscount Milner, *England in Egypt* (London 1893), 40.
[17] Frederick, Lord Lugard, *The Dual Mandate in Tropical Africa* (London 1929), quoted in Philip D. Curtin, *Imperialism* (London 1972), 318.
[18] Cromer, op. cit., 12.

subjects, but 'some sort of cosmopolitan allegiance grounded on the respect always accorded to superior talents and unselfish conduct, and on the gratitude derived both from favours conferred and from those to come'.

What Cromer and his contemporaries preached in fact was enlightened despotism; always the most precarious and the shortest-lived of regimes. 'Do not let us for a moment believe,' Cromer warned, 'that the fatally simple idea of despotic rule will readily give way to the far more complex conception of ordered liberty. The transformation, if it takes place at all, will probably be the work, not of generations, but of centuries . . . Our primary duty is, not to introduce a system which under the specious cloak of free institutions, will enable a small minority of natives to misgovern their countrymen, but to establish one which will enable the mass of the population to be governed according to the code of Christian morality . . . Before Orientals can attain anything approaching to the British ideal of self-government, they will have to undergo very numerous transmigrations of political thought.'[19] It can be said that although the British governed the Egyptians for two generations on the whole very honourably and very justly, they did not begin to understand them; and though the Egyptians learned to respect certain qualities in their British rulers, they did not begin to like them. It was not a good formula for an enduring regime, and it was Milner himself who first recognised, after the war of 1914–18, that it had broken down, and that the Egyptians, whatever their lack of qualifications for the task, must be left to govern themselves. The capacity of the British race to govern the Egyptians better than they could themselves was still undoubted. What was in question was their continuing will to do so.

What, finally, of war? Compared with previous empires, the military element in the growth and maintenance of British rule was not large. The main impulse in British expansion had been one of trade and settlement, and the principal task of naval and military forces had been to eliminate Britain's European rivals from the scene. But in the second half of the nineteenth century the emphasis began to change. In India, the Mutiny transformed what had been basically a trading Empire into an explicitly military one, with an army of occupation whose primary duties were to assist the civil power in maintaining British rule. Simultaneously the advance of Russian power towards the Oxus gave Britain what she had not had in her history since the Act of Union with Scotland; a land frontier with another and potentially hostile State. The British Army for the first time had a permanent *raison d'être*, comparable to those of its great continental rivals, and began to emerge as a comparable factor in administration, if not in politics. It was of India that the British primarily thought when the Army was mentioned, and the work of Kipling did much to fix the stereotype in the popular mind. But most of the actual fighting occurred in Africa; against the Egyptians, against the Boers, against the Zulus, against the Ashantis, and finally against the Boers again. The generation of High Imperialists were very conscious of the military basis

[19] Ibid., 27–8.

of British expansion during their lifetime, and they saw that their children were as well. The works of G. A. Henty and of Rider Haggard were staple reading for boys in the Edwardian era, and there can have been few school libraries or schoolrooms which did not contain a lavishly illustrated edition of *Deeds that Won the Empire*.

At the level of what we might term High Culture, this emphasis on military matters was no less intense. From Darwin, on the one hand, and Hegel, on the other, the belief in the inevitability of, and the social necessity for, armed conflict in the development of mankind was deeply rooted in the minds of the late Victorians and the Edwardians; though the matter was discussed with much greater enthusiasm before rather than after the Boer War. Writing in *The Nineteenth Century* in 1899, Sidney Low pointed out that 'There is scarcely a nation in the world – certainly not in our high-strung, masterful, Caucasian world – that does not value itself chiefly for its martial achievements . . . A righteous and necessary war is no more brutal than a surgical operation. Better give the patient some pain, and make your own fingers unpleasantly red, than allow the disease to grow upon him until he becomes an offence to himself and the world and dies in lingering agony.'[20] That the war which broke out in South Africa a few months later was 'righteous and necessary' seemed to Low and most of his colleagues quite self-evident. Professor Cramb of London University welcomed it ecstatically. 'War,' he declared, 'is the supreme act in the life of the State, and it is the motives which impel, the ideal which is pursued, that determine the greatness or insignificance of that act . . . The War in South Africa . . . is the first event or series of events upon a great scale; the genesis lies in this force named Imperialism. It is the first conspicuous expression of this ideal in the world of action – of heroic action, which now as always implies heroic suffering.'[21] For the Social Darwinians it was part of the process by which the British people had to show themselves fit to survive. War, Karl Pearson warned his countrymen in 1900, involved 'suffering, intense suffering' but without wars progress would be impossible. 'The dependence of progress on the survival of the fitter race, terribly black as it may seem to some of you, gives the struggle for existence its redeeming features; it is the fiery crucible out of which comes the finest metal.' A nation, he said, had to be 'kept up to a high pitch of efficiency by contest, chiefly by war with inferior races, by the struggle for trade routes and for the sources of raw material and of food supply'.[22]

It was as Benjamin Kidd had written in *Social Evolution* in 1896: 'The law of life has always been the same from the beginning, – ceaseless and inevitable struggle and competition, ceaseless and inevitable progress.'[23] And what was so worrying about the Boer War was that the confusion and incompetence of its conduct made people wonder whether the British really were 'fit to survive'. It was something that worried the Fabians no less than it did the

[20] *The Nineteenth Century*, XLV (May 1899), 692.
[21] J. A. Cramb, *Reflections on the Origins and Destiny of Imperial Britain* (London 1915), 89.
[22] Quoted in Semmel, op. cit., 41.
[23] Benjamin Kidd, op. cit., 39.

Imperialists of the Right wing. In his pamphlet *Fabianism and the Empire* George Bernard Shaw demanded, as part of 'the effective social organisation of the whole Empire, and its rescue from the strife of classes and private interest', the transformation of the army into a citizen body based on national service for all, involving 'a combination of physical exercises, technical education, education in civil citizenship . . . and field training in the use of modern weapons'.[24] It led Kipling to his philippic against the established orders in *The Islanders*, with their 'flannelled fools at the wicket or the muddied oafs at the goal'; the indifferent landed gentry, the greedy and short-sighted commercial classes, the self-absorbed workers, the frivolous intellectuals; and to his vision, published in 1904, of *The Army of a Dream*; an elaborate fantasy in which compulsory military service dissolved all the class conflicts of the time and made England Merrie again.[25]

Writing in 1909 to a master at Eton, Lord Esher told him that his boys 'cannot begin too early to train to defend their country and Empire. It is not only physical training that is required, but they should acquire early the habit of thinking over the problems of National Defence . . . If our country is to maintain the place which our forefathers won for us, physical training is a vital part of the Englishman's equipment, and rational thinking men who watch the trend of events, not only in Europe but all over the world, begin to see that the use of arms is also an essential part of a sound educational curriculum.' In order to survive in the new, harsher world of the twentieth century, the young manhood of Britain, like its contemporaries on the Continent, had to be carefully and scientifically trained and indoctrinated for war. 'It is,' Esher added, 'most necessary that their minds as well as their bodies should be trained on military lines when they are young. It is just as important to be taught early to think correctly upon matters affecting the defence of our country and the Empire as to be taught the truths of history and science.'[26] It was also a consideration not far from the minds of the authorities of the University of Oxford when in 1909 they established a Chair in the History of War.[27]

What seemed particularly disturbing was the probability, increasingly accepted during the first decade of the new century, that in the very near future the British fitness to survive would be put to the test by an adversary even stronger and better armed than the Boers; and if the British military capacity could be stretched to breaking point by the Boers, how could it cope with the Germans – a nation among whom the teachings of Hegel and Darwin were taken even more seriously than they were in Britain? For those Edwardians who concerned themselves with such matters, the need to create a military organisation, and to evoke a military spirit to inspire it, became a matter of increasing concern; no longer to defend the frontiers of Empire, and to maintain order within them, but to save Britain herself from a national

[24] George Bernard Shaw, *Fabianism and the Empire* (London 1900), 41-2.
[25] Rudyard Kipling, *The Army of a Dream* (London 1904), passim.
[26] Reginald, Viscount Esher, to R. de Haviland Esq., 23 June 1909, Esher Papers, Churchill College, Cambridge.
[27] Spenser Wilkinson, *The University and the Study of War* (Oxford 1909).

humiliation far worse than Jena or Waterloo.

Confronted by a bombardment of German militaristic writings between 1904 and 1914, British writers showed themselves less inclined than were their Teutonic cousins to glorify war as the supreme act of the State, and adopted a more pragmatic and defensive approach to the military problems which confronted them. Not all did, however. In 1907 Colonel F. N. Maude brought out a book entitled *War and the World's Life*; probably in connection with the new edition of Clausewitz *On War* to which he contributed a foreword. Much of the work was a direct transcription of Benjamin Kidd; but whereas Kidd had evoked the ethical principle of character, hard work, and self-abnegation which subordinates the individual to the group as a feature of social life in general, for Colonel Maude it was applicable solely to war. 'Two Races,' he warned, 'may be equal in physical capacity, in intelligence and directing ability, but if the standard of self-sacrifice in the one is lower than in the other, the balance will infallibly turn against it in the final arbitrament on the field of Battle.' 'Races have survived in precise proportion to the purity of the conception of self-sacrifice embodied in their respective creeds,' he wrote; 'We are governed by the spirits of our dead; and I submit that this inherited instinct of self-sacrifice is so deeply ingrained in the race that the intellectual disturbances of the moment, whatever they may be from time to time, no more ruffle its foundation than the waves of a storm trouble the bed of the ocean.'

The British people he believed to be sound at heart; and 'If we succeed in imparting to the youth of the Nation the elementary concepts of religion and morality, together with a respect for the deeds of their forefathers, and a knowledge of all they have bequeathed to us, then I think that the training for the final act of battle can be well attained in the time available.' His final conclusion was inspiring or macabre, depending on the way one looks at it. 'Given a Leader who, conscious of the power latent in the Race and the means by which to develop it, applies all the means which science has now rendered available to the definite end of teaching men "to know how to die" – not how to avoid dying – and we shall soon find men as ready as ever were their ancestors to clamour for the right of rushing to what will appear to them to be certain death, when they know that thereby they will attain a great end.'[28]

One can by selective quotation from a narrow range of writers present an alarming picture of pre-1914 Britain as a proto-Fascist society, but in fact it was nothing of the kind. The ideas expressed by such writers as Maude existed generally in very mild solution. The pride in Empire, the belief in the superiority of Anglo-Saxon culture, the consciousness of military achievement in the past and the determination if necessary to parallel it in the future, all this was there, but without rancour or fanaticism; still underpinned by a strong Christian ethic and leavened by the values of Victorian liberalism. What could have happened if Britain had lost the war; whether these sentiments would have turned sour and fanatical and acquired the sinister power that they did elsewhere in Europe is, fortunately, no part of the historian's

[28] Colonel F. N. Maude, *War and the World's Life* (London 1907), vii, 244, 249, 252.

task to assess; but it would be realistic to assume that we would not have been immune to the disease.

As it was, although Edwardian Britain was conscious of the need for the martial virtues and spasmodic efforts were made to inculcate them, it cannot be called a militaristic society; indeed the lack of active interest in military matters and the low prestige enjoyed by the Army among the bulk of the population was a matter of repeated complaint. The flood of 'next war' literature which reached a climax with the 'Dreadnought Scare' of 1909 had as its almost constant theme the total unpreparedness of Britain to deal with the probable eventuality of a German invasion. The repeated official inquiries into the dangers posed by such an invasion all took as their starting point the assumption that it would have to be dealt with by the Navy and the Army in the context of an indifferent, certainly an unmobilised, population. The agitation for the introduction of National Service, though it mustered such impressive leaders as Lord Milner and Field Marshal Lord Roberts, never became a matter for serious discussion within the government. The Territorial Army was created as a second-line reserve, and found little difficulty in recruiting the enthusiastic amateurs who previously had founded the volunteer regiments in the towns or officered the Militia and Yeomanry in the country, but this was very far from being a People in Arms. H. G. Wells complained, in *Mr. Britling Sees it Through*, of this remoteness of the Armed Forces from the rest of the nation.

> The army had been a thing aloof, for a special end. It had developed all the characteristics of a caste. It had very high standards along the lines of its specialisation, but it was inadaptable and conservative. Its exclusiveness was not so much a deliberate culture as a consequence of its detached function . . . Directly one grasped how apart the army lived from the ordinary life of the community, from industrialism or from economic necessities, directly one understood how the great mass of Englishmen were simply 'outsiders' to the War Office mind, one began to realise the complete unfitness of either government or War Office for the conduct of so great a national effort as was now needed.[29]

The creation of a Nation in Arms thus remained no more than an aspiration of largely maverick politicians and publicists until the outbreak of war in 1914 took matters out of their hands.

The trouble was that the whole traditional apparatus of Empire, and the patterns of thought associated with it, could only with difficulty be adjusted to dealing with the type of continental threat offered by Germany. None of the stock responses, naval, military or civilian, were appropriate to it. Almost as a matter of habit publicists like Lord Esher and Spenser Wilkinson, in campaigning for the National Service League, continued to talk about 'the Defence of the Empire', but the defence of the Empire was no longer the principal problem. By 1909 Britain had made peace with her main imperial rivals, France and Russia. No one was now going to attack India or Egypt, let alone Canada, Australia or South Africa. Germany could not get at them. But Germany could get at Britain herself, if she defeated France on land and the

[29] H. G. Wells, *Mr. Britling Sees it Through* (London 1916), 237.

Royal Navy at sea; and when Esher declared, as he did in a speech to the Imperial Press Conference in 1909, that 'The basis of Imperial defence was the unity of the Empire under one flag', and that 'if we were to hold our own among the Imperial races of the world, the wealth and population of the Empire should be organised in peace with a view to the demands which would inevitably be made on them in war',[30] he was not really talking about the defence of the Empire as such. He was talking about the mobilising of imperial resources under British control for the defence of the United Kingdom, which was a different matter; as such statesmen as Deakin of Australia and Laurier of Canada realised very well.

Moreover the essence of Imperial Defence, as was generally recognised, was naval, not military. If Britain lost 'command of the sea' she would lose both her Empire and her own immunity from invasion. And command of the sea had to be fought for, not in the North Atlantic or the Indian Ocean, but in the North Sea, and it was there that the Admiralty wished to see the Imperial Fleet concentrated. Similarly the General Staff wished to see the military organisation and armament of the Empire standardised on the British model and integrated with the British staff organisation – to make it look better it was renamed the Imperial General Staff – to enable contingents from the Empire to take their place alongside British troops on the battlefields where the war would finally be decided; and the overwhelming probability was that this would be in Europe. As it happened, the entry of the Ottoman Empire into the war on the side of the Central Powers was to provide Imperial troops – Indian, Australian and New Zealanders – with imperial battlefields of their own, the Dardanelles, Palestine and Mesopotamia; but basically the Empire had to be defended in France and Flanders in a struggle the grimness and prolonged nature of which came as no surprise to a generation which had been brought up from boyhood to expect just such a test of the Nation's 'fitness to survive'.

Eventually the war was won, and the Imperial contribution was handsomely acknowledged. Cenotaphs everywhere commemorated the dead of the British Empire. An Imperial War Museum was established to record the struggle, an Imperial Defence College to study its lessons. But already the mood had changed. Within the Colonial Office the concept of Imperial Rule was increasingly seen as one of 'trusteeship'. How could it be otherwise, after a war allegedly fought in the name of democracy and self-determination? The work of Lugard and his colleagues had introduced ideas of cultural relativism that eroded the serene assumption of racial superiority. The diffusion of European ideas of self-government among indigenous elites could be contained only by violent repression of a kind that the newly-enlarged domestic electorate was unwilling to support. As for the defence of the Empire, this was beginning to present problems on so massive a scale that Britain's military leaders were foremost among those who, in the 1930s, wished to avoid or at least postpone war at almost any cost. The Empire was still a 'fact', but increasingly seen (except by Lord Beaverbrook) as an embarrassing

[30] *The Times*, 28 June 1909.

one. It was still certainly a Heritage, but one which, like so many estates inherited within Britain itself during this period, was too large to be kept up by a new and impoverished generation. The consciousness of being an 'Imperial Race' was not widespread among the British after 1918. After 1945 it disappeared altogether. The way was clear for a new, but no less moralistic, generation to castigate their forbears for ever having entertained such illusions.

History and Imagination*

Hugh Trevor-Roper

What does one say in a valedictory lecture, apart from the valediction which comes at the end? I am taking my leave, not of my subject, nor, I hope, of Oxford, nor of you, but of my chair. Perhaps I should add, as it were, an epilogue to the inaugural lecture which I gave on first adjusting myself to it twenty-three years ago. I then spoke of the need of history, though professional in its methods, to provide an education to the layman. I have decided now to say something of another non-professional aspect of historical study. Originally, as I was writing my lecture, I entitled it *History and Free-will*; and that perhaps you will think a more appropriate title to what I shall say. But free-will, the choice of alternatives, is in the actor: the historian's function is to discern those alternatives, and that, surely, is the function of imagination. Therefore I have entitled my lecture *History and Imagination*.

Any such discussion is necessarily somewhat subjective, and I hope that I shall be forgiven, especially in these circumstances, for a certain infusion of autobiography. Our views on history come from the impact of experience upon reading and of reading upon experience; and both reading and experience are personal. Objective science has its place in historical study, but it is a subordinate place: the heart of the subject is not in the method but in the motor, not in the technique but in the historian.

There are of course some people who believe that history itself is an objective science. They see it, I suppose, as the gradual refinement of scholarly technique until the past can be reconstructed with mathematical precision and total objectivity. However, I do not think that many historians subscribe to that belief today. We owe a great deal to the technicians of history, from the philologists of the Renaissance to the source-critics of the nineteenth century. Thanks to them, we approach the great problems of historical reconstruction in a more exact and useful manner than our predecessors could do; which does not, however, make us better historians. Even the most 'objective' of historians, we soon discover, are imprisoned, though they may not know it, in a philosophy which is conditioned by subjective experience. Even a computer has to be programmed. Objective theories, perfect instruments, do not exist. It is vain to suppose that they will be devised in the calm of the monastery or

*A Valedictory Lecture delivered before the University of Oxford on 20 May 1980.

the think-tank – what useful idea has ever come out of a think-tank? Ideas and skills are evolved under the pressure of the outer world: a pressure which varies from generation to generation, person to person, and can never be exactly the same.

We are all, at times, tempted to make history more scientific than we find it to be: to reduce it from its beginnings in literature, myth, or poetry, to a regular system, with iron laws. But in the end we have to admit that such a process, though it can be refined, can never be perfected. We refine away, reducing the ingredient of Fortune or human freedom, but if we should ever succeed in eliminating them altogether, behold! We have killed the subject. Our chemical distillations will be rejected in favour of less antiseptic water, fresh from the spring.

Why, I now wonder, was I drawn to the study of history – and of a particular kind of history – in my early years? Partly, I sometimes think, through an accident of birth. I was brought up in rural north Northumberland, with the symbols, or deposit, of age after age of history around me: not dead relics, to be scientifically dug up or patiently reconstructed, but visible, palpable, alive to the least sophisticated imagination. To the South was Hadrian's Wall, whose great tract, rising and falling with the contours of the hills and moors, so impressed Camden when he visited it nearly four centuries ago: surely the greatest monument of Roman Britain. To the North were the Cheviot hills, with their fortified houses and peel-towers, looking, through their narrow slit-eyes, with well-justified suspicion, towards the weasel Scots; and the city of Berwick, finally repossessed by Richard III (be that remembered to his credit) and made secure behind those splendid fortified walls built for Queen Elizabeth by two Italian refugees. In the West, waste empty moors saved us from thinking of the Welsh of Cumbria, psychologically as remote from us as the Antipodes; and in the East there was that marvellous coast of dolerite cliffs, tidal rocks, and sand, with its string of romantic castles: first the twin watch-towers of Lindisfarne and Bamburgh, still on their Saxon sites, looking at each other, like Sestos and Abydos, over the intervening arm of the sea; then, further south, the ruined medieval fortresses of Dunstanburgh, which Malory supposed might be Arthur's Joyous Garde, and Warkworth, still answering to Shakespeare's description of it as

this worm-eaten hold of ragged stone.

In that country – that island rather, bounded by hill and wall and moor and sea – layer after layer of English history lay visible to the eye of imagination; and I now think that perhaps it is not an accident that that underpopulated area has been or become the home of so many historians: Trevelyans at Wallington, conscious heirs and continuators of Macaulay, their uncle and great-uncle; two Hodgkins, the historians of Italy and her Invaders and of Anglo-Saxon England; Mandell Creighton writing his History of the Popes in the vicarage of Embleton; my predecessor Sir Maurice Powicke, born at Alnwick and Dame Veronica Wedgwood at Newcastle; my neighbour Sir Steven Runciman at Doxford.

Of course, this is not a very intellectual reason for studying history. Perhaps it is a very parochial reason too. But one has to start somewhere, and perhaps to start with the imagination is no bad thing. It can always be corrected afterwards, whereas to begin with correctitude may be to end with Dryasdust. When was it corrected for me? I would like to say that it was when I read the Oxford history school, but I am not sure that that was true. At best it was only partially true.

It was in my second year at Oxford, when I was reading the inexpressibly tedious Greek epic poem of Nonnus, that I decided to change my subject from classics to history. By now, I said to myself, I had read all classical literature worth reading, and much that was not. Why scrape the bottom of the barrel? Nonnus, it seemed to me, was very near the bottom.[1] So I decided that from now on the classics might be my relaxation but I would turn for sustenance to history, to which there was no bottom, no end. The tutors of Christ Church were then, as they no doubt still are, very tolerant. No discussion, no objection, no reasoning took place, and I turned to Modern History. My reading, from amateur, became, or began to become, professional. Almost immediately I discovered that history was not an art but a science.

There was at that time a young tutor in my college, now an ennobled ex-politician, who was determined to reform and modernise what he considered to be the somewhat traditional and old-fashioned teaching of the subject there. In my first term as a student of history, he invited me and my contemporaries to his rooms and there gave us a talk on the Marxist philosophy of history, which he had embraced with evident zeal. He explained that, theoretically, it should be possible to discover the objective laws of historical change, and that the way to test such laws, once discovered, was to see whether they enabled one to predict the next stage in the historical process. The Marxist interpretation, he assured us, had survived this test: it had predicted the course of events since Marx's own time with remarkable accuracy; and therefore it could now be regarded as scientifically valid: as another Marxist writer, from the Balliol school, put it, once it is accepted, 'everything suddenly falls into place'. No doubt our tutor said more than this; but this was what impressed me most. The vast pageant of history, hitherto so indeterminate, so formless, so mysterious, now had, as it seemed, a beautiful, mechanical regularity, and modern science had supplied a master-key which, with a satisfying click, would turn in every lock, open all its dark chambers, and reveal all its secret workings. This was very exciting. Unfortunately, when I began to apply the key, I soon encountered some difficulties. These difficulties lay not in the history of the past, that weak unresisting substance which is malleable at will, but in actual experience, which is not.

Historians of every generation, I believe, unless they are pure antiquaries, see history against the background – the controlling background – of current events. They call upon it to explain the problems of their own time, to give to those problems a philosophical context, a *continuum* in which they may be

---

[1] Though I must allow some redeeming virtue to a poet who was admired by Thomas Love Peacock and his epicurean clergyman Dr Folliott.

reduced to proportion and perhaps made intelligible. The historians of the Italian Renaissance sought to account for the revolutions which destroyed their world at its highest splendour, those of the Enlightenment to discover the mechanics of progress. In the nineteenth century, English historians looked into history for the sources of our institutional strength, while the Germans found that it justified the defeat of Napoleon and the unification of Germany under the Prussian monarchy: a view not entirely accepted by the French.

And what, we naturally asked, was the great problem of the 1930s? It was, of course, the sudden and apparently irresistible rise of aggressive dictatorships in a world which, we had always been told, had been made safe for democracy by the victory of 1918. How illusory those old promises now seemed! In Italy Mussolini had created a new form of power and was preparing to found a new Roman Empire in the Mediterranean and in Africa. In Germany, Hitler had ended democracy and was threatening to reorder Europe by force. Japanese imperialism was conquering China. These dynamic new dictators made the pace in world politics. They did not shrink from war. They were already fomenting civil war in Spain. And that civil war, which they would win, seemed to us the prelude, and the dress-rehearsal, for an even greater war which, given the reluctance and pacifism of the West, they might also win.

We all know how this problem obsessed that generation of undergraduates, and how, in the high-minded, solipsistic enclaves of certain Cambridge colleges, it led even intelligent young men into the most absurd positions, surrendering themselves, *perinde ac cadavera*, to Soviet Communism as the only force which would guarantee a liberal future for the world. In Oxford, such abject conclusions were not drawn. To me, one result was that I found it difficult to accept the authority of Marxist historical science.

For had Marx, or any Marxist tipster, prophesied the rise of Fascism? The answer was, No. All that could be said was that, after Fascism had appeared, the prophets had hastily updated their prophecies, explaining that Fascism was simply the last stage of imperialism. Just as the millenarian prophets of the seventeenth century met inconvenient objections to their scientific predictions by explaining that Antichrist must be loosed and have his last brief fling before the final reign of Christ and his saints could begin, so the modern Marxist thinkers dismissed Hitler and Mussolini as ephemeral phenomena, too unimportant to have been mentioned in the official blueprints: bubbles which would surface only to burst and be dissolved again into the majestic stream of history, rolling onward in its predetermined course. This, of course, had always been the official doctrine of the Russian Communist party. In 1933, Moscow had instructed the German Communists not to waste time in opposing the Nazis, who were doomed to fail, but to reserve their fire for use against the more dangerous 'Social Fascists' – i.e. the Social Democrats. Naturally the same doctrine was discovered to be true by the independent research of the objective Marxist intellectuals in the West.

In 1939 the expected European war drew near, and as it approached, these comforting rationalisations began to look very thin. Communist Russia, far from proving the only opponent of Nazi Germany, promptly became its ally and ensured its immediate success. By 1940, thanks to the co-operation of Stalin, Hitler was master of Europe, and at any time in the next year, an accident – yes, an accident – could have put him in a position to conquer the world. Fascism, that irrelevant bubble, would then have diverted the majestic stream of history into a completely new course. It is from that time that I date the strongest conviction that I hold as a historian: the belief in historical free-will.

You will say that I have begged some questions. So let me be a little more explicit. Objectively, in 1940, Hitler had won the war in the West and Britain's refusal to accept defeat was illogical, unrealistic, absurd. If only Britain had recognised this, and given up the struggle, Hitler would have been in the position of Bismarck in 1866. Having defeated his other rivals, he would have been free to concentrate his forces against the last enemy and, by its defeat in a third *Blitzkrieg*, to establish his new empire.[2] That, in such circumstances, he could have defeated Russia can hardly be denied. Even as it was, he very nearly did so. 'All that Lenin and we have sought to build is now lost!' exclaimed Stalin as he evacuated his government from a Moscow that seemed doomed to fall before that first shattering invasion. A final German victory in the West, had it been achieved, could have made all the difference.

And how easily, in that year, the German victory in the West might, by a mere accident, have been made final! I can think of at least four such hypothetical accidents, any one of which might have had that effect. First, no one could rationally have assumed that at the precise moment of the fall of France there would be, in Britain, a statesman able to unite all parties, and the people, in the will and confidence to continue what could easily have been represented as a pointless struggle. The crisis does not always produce the man; moments of vital decision quickly pass; and in a period of confusion the power to act may be irrevocably lost. Equally, no one could have predicted that, at that historic moment, we would possess the vital intelligence – 'the Ultra secret' – which, directly or indirectly, may have ensured the air victory over Britain.[3] Thirdly, it was not reasonable to suppose, or even to hope, that General Franco, who after all had been placed in power by our enemies, would resist the temptation to which Mussolini had so easily yielded, and would refuse to rush to the aid of the apparent victor. Had Franco agreed to allow an assault on Gibraltar, that assault – as the experiences of Crete and Singapore were to show – would probably have been successful. Then the Mediterranean sea would have been closed to Britain and a whole potential theatre of future war and victory would have been shut off. Finally, no one could have guessed that Mussolini would take it into his head to disrupt Hitler's plans for the invasion of Russia by a surprise invasion of Greece.

[2] Hitler himself made the comparison: 'So wie aus dem Jahre 1866 das Reich Bismarcks entstand', he said on 9 April 1940, 'so wird aus dem heutigen Tag das Grossgermanische Reich entstehen' (*Das Politische Tagebuch Alfred Rosenbergs* (Munich 1964), 81).

[3] Even if 'Ultra' did not directly turn the scales by its operational intelligence, it provided the clue thanks to which we were able, by 'bending the beam', to preserve our airfields from destruction.

Had any one of these conditions not been met, I believe that the whole history of the war might have been changed. Would Japan wantonly have attacked Pearl Harbor when defeated Britain and Russia offered an undefended prey? Would America have intervened in Europe, when there was no bridgehead left, in order to save Communist Russia? Is it not more likely that Hitler's dream would have been realised: that a German empire would have been established, dominating Europe and hither Asia: that, in Hitler's own phrase, the German age of the world would have begun?

Of course there are a hundred possible variations of detail, but they are irrelevant to my argument, which is, simply, that the political form of the world at any time is not logically deducible from previous history, that 'scientific' history is rendered impossible by human accident, and in particular (though this is now merely the occasion of the argument), that any science is ludicrous which has to 'save the phenomena' by desperate expedients. For surely it is a gesture of despair to dismiss as ephemeral a movement which, by a slight variation of fortune, might have dominated the history of a whole age.

And not only the history: also the historiography. Nothing succeeds like success, and if Hitler had founded his empire – that dreadful empire whose character he drew in his *Table Talk* – we can well imagine how later historians would have treated him. Historians in general are great toadies of power. Hitler was not more ruthless, or less intelligent, than Lenin or Stalin, and yet they, because they succeeded, have never lacked historical supporters. If Hitler had won his last gamble, as Bismarck won his, how would he have featured in the text-books? Would he not now appear as the founder of the last and greatest German Reich, the statesman of genius who – at some price indeed, but a price must always be paid in politics: greatness is not won by virtue alone, or perhaps at all – had realised the ambition of a century, the historical destiny of a nation? Would he not be acclaimed for having restored, on a larger, more permanent base, and by the same methods (which would thereby be doubly consecrated), the empire which Bismarck had founded but which had since – by miscalculation, not fundamental error – been allowed to fail? And yet objectively, he is the same person who, because he was narrowly defeated, has been dismissed by a succession of reputable historians as a mere 'mountebank dictator', a mindless, rootless adventurer, with no ideas except the pursuit of personal power.

Nor is it only an individual reputation that has been transformed by that narrow margin. In his fall, Hitler has dragged Bismarck down too. Bismarck's achievement, which seemed so solid in the 1890s, looks more fragile when viewed from this side of 1945. And with Bismarck there sinks also the distinctive historical philosophy which had been built up in nineteenth-century Germany, which his achievement had consolidated, and which was the orthodoxy of the German schools till our time.

What a liberating philosophy that was when it was first uttered, fresh from the inspiration of Herder and Goethe, when the dusk of the Enlightenment was merging into the first golden dawn of Romanticism: a philosophy which restored the autonomy of the past and gave us our whole concept of culture! In the course of a century, that philosophy pervaded all historical thinking. Outside Germany – in Switzerland, in Romania – it inspired some of the greatest of historians.[4] But in Germany, as state power assumed the rights of culture and as race then took over the rights already usurped by the state, it was gradually transformed; and yet, because it still clung to its old justification, it was still, in 1939, being advanced, not merely by vulgar propagandists, but by the greatest, most sophisticated historians of Germany, who would glory in Hitler's victorious war as the realisation of a historic mission and of their own historical philosophy.[5] If Hitler had won his war, can we doubt that that philosophy, which is now stone-dead, would have been reinvigorated, would have become the orthodoxy of the Continent?

Thus, I do not hesitate to say that in 1940-1 a mere accident, and one which might easily have occurred, could not only have reversed the outcome of the war, and transformed the subsequent shape of the world, but also have imposed upon the world a new synthesis of ideas and power, creating a new context for both politics and thought. Such a synthesis, once created, could have lasted for generations, as the Communist synthesis has done; which, by the same accident, would have suffered instead the fate of Nazism: it would have been totally dismantled, never to be reassembled in the same form. This is a very chastening thought, which cannot but affect our ideas of the historical process.

When Pascal wrote that, if the nose of Cleopatra had been a little longer, the face of the world would have been changed, he was indulging in un-documented rhetoric such as any exact historian must deplore. And yet I cannot but think that if General Franco, at Hendaye on 23 October 1940, had effectively substituted one monosyllable for another – if instead of *No* he had said *Yes* – our world would be quite different: the present, the future, and the past would all have been changed. But once they had been changed, no one would have dwelt on that little episode. The German victory would then have been ascribed not to such trivial causes but to historical necessity.

Of course, after 1945, the old orthodoxies re-established themselves. Once Hitler had lost the war, we were told that he could never have won it. Foolishly, madly, he had challenged the great powers of the future. He had attempted to halt the progress of mankind, to deflect the course of world history. Clearly he was a lunatic, foredoomed to failure; for world history, being what is afterwards known to have happened, must always, by definition, prevail.

This restored orthodoxy was expressed, in sophisticated and lapidary form, by a distinguished historian, Mr E. H. Carr, in a series of lectures

[4] I refer, of course, to Jacob Burckhardt and Nicolae Iorga whose historical work is inspired by the philosophy of the German *Aufklärung*, still undistorted (for they lived in small countries) by the marriage of culture with state-power and its offspring, *Staatsräson*.

[5] I refer here, in particular, to Friedrich Meinecke who, for all his reservations about 'the negative side' of Nazism, saw it as 'a great and necessary revolution' and welcomed the victories of 1940 with 'profound emotion, pride and joy'. See his letters of that period in his *Werke* (Munich 1962), VI.

which he gave at Cambridge in 1961 and published in the same year under the title *What is History?* According to Mr Carr, History is the record of what people did, not of what they failed to do; and he spoke somewhat contemptuously of those who show interest in the dead-ends and 'might-have-beens' of history. That this was not a mere *boutade* is clear from Mr Carr's own historical work, in which the doctrine of progress, and its identification with the cause which actually triumphed, is elegantly set out. There we see Napoleon sweeping away 'the millennial rubbish of feudalism', and the unsuccessful rivals of Lenin ignominiously consigned to the dustbin of history. 'The only proper way to the historian,' says Mr Carr defiantly, is to write 'as if what happened was in fact bound to happen, and as if it was his business simply to explain what happened and why.' Those who play 'parlour-games' with historical 'might-have-beens' cannot, he thinks, be serious historians, or even honest men. They may think that they are interested in the truth, but in fact they are seeking to compensate themselves for personal failure or disappointment. Indeed, they are already themselves in the historical dustbin, and dustbin is calling to dustbin with thin, plaintive voice. So let us not waste time over them, or strain our ears to catch those faint, dying syllables, choked with tears and circumjacent garbage. Or, as he more summarily puts it, 'let us get rid of this red herring once and for all'.

I suppose that no phrase was more of an affront to my own historical beliefs than that phrase about the might-have-beens of history. Of course I agree that some historical speculations are useless, and some may reflect personal nostalgia. But at any given moment of history there are real alternatives, and to dismiss them as unreal because they were not realised – because (in Mr Carr's phrase) they have been 'closed by the *fait accompli*' – is to take the reality out of the situation. How can we '*explain* what happened and *why*' if we only look at what happened and never consider the alternatives, the total pattern of forces whose pressure created the event?

Take the case of revolutions. We all know the revolutions which happened. But how can we 'explain' them unless we can compare them with the revolutions which have not happened – that is, with those moments in history when similar circumstances and similar forces existed and yet revolution did not break out? To assume that 'what happened was bound to happen' is to beg the question why it happened, and to deprive history, at one blow, both of its lessons and of its life.

In 1646 the English Parliament had won the war against Charles I, and its recently appointed official historian, the republican poet Tom May, expressed the view, which has been repeated by many later historians, that the revolution had always been bound to happen. It had been blowing up, he wrote, since the last years of Queen Elizabeth and was plainly visible, beneath the surface, in the outwardly peaceful time of Charles I. This view was confirmed by the fashionable puritan ideologues who had also, by now, entered the game. Conjuring with the mystical mathematics of the city of Heaven, they declared that the political struggles of England had been darkly foreshadowed by the prophets of Israel, and that the issue of the battle of

Marston Moor – a damned close-run thing in the view of those who had fought it – had been implicit in the enigmatology of Daniel and Revelation. But a greater historian than Tom May thought otherwise. 'I am not so sharp-sighted,' wrote the royalist Clarendon, 'as those who have discerned this rebellion contriving from, if not before, the death of Queen Elizabeth', and he insisted that at many moments, especially in 1641, prudent politics could have prevented 'this unnecessary rebellion'. Perhaps he was right. Who are we, three centuries later, to deny such a possibility? And then, perhaps, time would have worn out those millenarian fantasies, which would have remained buried in the obsolescent subculture of backward-looking puritan fundamentalists until, with the passage of a generation, they would have dropped, unnoticed, like so many other fond fancies, into the ever open historical dustbin.

Could revolution have been prevented in England in the 1640s, just as it was prevented – i.e. did not happen – in the 1840s? Were Charles I and James II bound to fail? Could not a wiser king than either of them have preserved or restored an authoritarian monarchy in England, as was done in so many European countries? If contemporaries thought that they could, why should we rule it out? In the 1630s England was becoming accustomed to conciliar rule. No doubt old parliament-men disliked it, just as the Estates had disliked the new centralised government in Bavaria or Austria; but a new generation accepted the change. In 1640, according to Messrs Brunton and Pennington, the opponents of Charles I were, on average, eleven years older than the royalist members in Parliament. A few more years, and the balance might have shifted decisively. And then, since power is a great magnet, would not the leaders of society have adjusted themselves to it and invested in its new form?

Similarly in the early 1680s. By then, an authoritarian monarchy, firmly based on the alliance of land, city, and Church, seemed almost a fact. If James II, like his brother, had set politics above religion – if he had not wantonly broken the consensus of Church and landed society – might not the 'Stuart reaction' have gathered momentum, taken root; and then would not the Whig grandees of England, like the Huguenot grandees of France, have turned to worship the risen sun? Instead of a 'whig ascendancy' we would have had an 'enlightened despotism'; and historians would have explained that it too was inevitable.

If we are to study history as a living subject, not merely as a coloured pageant, or an antiquarian chronicle, or a dogmatic scheme, we must not indeed lose ourselves in barren speculations, but we must leave some room for the imagination. History is not merely what happened: it is what happened in the context of what might have happened. Therefore it must incorporate, as a necessary element, the alternatives, the might-have-beens. They may be in the dustbin now; but so, after all, are those who put them there; and who is to say, with assurance, which is the 'dead-end'? Pilate, no doubt, after washing his hands, believed that a certain episode had been 'closed by the *fait accompli*' of the Crucifixion; and three centuries would pass before educated Romans would recognise that it was he, not Jesus, who had been the dead-end.

It is an error to confuse facts with causes, and to suppose that the historian can explain all by confining his interest to 'what happened'. Why should we assume that all the answers are contained within the facts? There are facts which are not causes and causes which are not facts. Ideas and myths are potent forces in history. So are mere moods: in two historical conjunctures the objective facts may be the same, but tempers may be different. And then there are those 'lost moments', those historical conjunctures in which great aspirations seem about to be realised, only to be overtaken – perhaps not inevitably, perhaps through accident or human folly – by a very different reality. I think of that summer of 1641 in England, when agreement seemed to have been achieved, a basis for a new peaceful reformation: when John Milton and Stephen Marshall hailed 'the very jubilee and resurrection of the State'; or of the beginning of the French Revolution, when Wordsworth thought it bliss to be alive; or of that moment in the history of the Netherlands, after the Pacification of Ghent, so brilliantly reconstructed by Dame Frances Yates.[6] All those moments of promise were lost; but were they necessarily lost? Are there not other such moments that have been won? To ignore such lost moments, to erase them impatiently from the page of history as mere non-events, is surely not only an error but a vulgar error: an error, because, even though abortive, they explain the motives of historical persons and contain a historical lesson; a vulgar error because they have a deeper reality which it is philistine and insensitive to ignore: though politically barren, they have contributed, more than any mere facts, to that art and literature which is the permanently valuable deposit of past history.

It is only if we place ourselves before the alternatives of the past, as of the present, only if we live for a moment, as the men of the time lived, in its still fluid context and among its still unresolved problems, if we see those problems coming upon us, as well as look back on them after they have gone away, that we can draw useful lessons from history. That is what was meant by the famous phrase of Ranke – of the young Ranke, still uncorrupted by the philosophical determinism of Berlin: the phrase which has been so often quoted, and almost as often misapplied, '*wie es eigentlich gewesen*'.

To restore to the past its lost uncertainties, to reopen, if only for an instant, the doors which the *fait accompli* has closed, this requires an effort of imagination. But surely it is a necessary effort if we are to see history as reality, not merely as a convenient scheme. For how often has real history mocked its 'scientific' prophets: how often has its actual course flowed not out of obvious events but from hidden and undetected springs! To those who state that the course of history can be predicted otherwise than in the most general or conditional way, I am inclined to put a very simple question. Let such people imagine themselves at some point of time, not too remote, still within human memory, and say honestly whether, at that point of time, they could have predicted what did in fact follow: the events of their own lifetime, their own experience.

[6] Frances Yates, *The Valois Tapestries* (1959), ch.5.

Take, as our point of time, the year 1945. In 1945 anyone might have predicted the rivalry of the two superpowers, the United States and Russia. That, after all, had been foreseen by de Tocqueville and others a century earlier. But could anyone have predicted that Germany, thirty-five years after its defeat, would still be divided; that Berlin would still be a subdivided island in a Communist sea; that there would be a Russian outpost off the coast of Florida; and that whole countries in Africa would be conquered by the armies of that Caribbean island?

Or again, to go a little further back, take 1910. Anyone, in 1910, might have predicted a European war provoked by German industrial and military power. But could anyone have foreseen the consequences of such a war: the collapse of three great empires, the Bolshevik revolution, the rise of Fascism? In retrospect, of course, we read the signs, select the evidence, and complacently predict what has already only too visibly happened; but at the time who foresaw such things, or would have believed them if foretold? A century ago, geopoliticians could have foreseen the continued colonisation by Russia and the United States of the empty lands to the East and the West; but who could have foreseen that far more astounding colonisation in the Eastern Mediterranean, the creation of the state of Israel? We may like it or not, we may admire it as the realisation of a romantic dream, a victory of human will power over the obstinate realities which are thought to limit it, or we may deplore it as the last Western crusade, the latest venture of Western imperialism, seeking not trade but settlement, *Lebensraum*; and in fact surely it is both these things. But we cannot deny that it is an extraordinary historical achievement. How little the British statesmen who listened to its early advocates foresaw the present consequences: the replacement of a Jewish 'national home' by a national state; the consequent transformation of the Middle East, the inflammation of the whole Muslim world; great powers, even superpowers, held to ransom by Islamic fundamentalists in Libya and whirling dervishes in Iran. But then who, at that time, could have foreseen the terrible holocaust in Europe which made it possible?

Twenty years ago I was myself in Iran, and I chanced to visit the holy city of Qum, the home of a then unknown Shi'ite mullah, the ayatollah Khomeini. A new oil-well had recently been opened near Qum, and there I was entertained by the engineer in charge of it, a genial, Western-educated Persian, who rejoiced in this new triumph of technological progress. With mounting enthusiasm he enumerated the thousands of barrels of oil that were now rolling and the tens of thousands that would soon roll, in daily sequence, out of his gushing well, and like the young Macaulay he gloried in his vision of the new modern society that would be created around it: pylon nodding to pylon in the Persian hills and the desert blossoming like the slag-heap. In twenty years' time, he said proudly, we shall have created a new Iran, a new Iranian man, and those old mullahs there – and he waved his hand contemptuously towards the holy city – will have withered away: they will have no place, they will not even be imaginable, in our brave new world . . . Today the twenty years are up. I wonder if that genial technologist is still alive in

Iran. If so, he must be very surprised.

He need not be ashamed. History is full of such surprises, and no men are more surprised than those who believe that they have discovered its secret: who think that they know, not intuitively but scientifically, the direction in which it is moving. The Calvinists of the sixteenth century were such men. They thought that they knew. They had built up, out of the two most certain sciences of the time, out of Scripture and mathematics, a great system of history whose operations they could project into the future; and in the early seventeenth century they looked confidently forward to the fulfilment of their dreams – or rather, as they imagined, of the divine purpose. How completely they were deceived! In the space of a few years, their great synthesis lay in ruins, like the wreck of some elaborate but ill-contrived flying-machine, whose still useful parts – clocks and compasses and casual fittings – have been pilfered for domestic use, but whose powerful theological engine and proud philosophical wings are left, crumpled and burnt out, to rust in a Bohemian ravine.

Such is generally the fate of great historical systems. The eighteenth-century Encyclopaedists were surprised by the French Revolution. The nineteenth-century Whigs were surprised by the rise of Socialism, the twentieth-century Marxists by that of Fascism. The Islamic Revolution of our day, like the development of the state of Israel, is a phenomenon which could have been predicted – and soon, no doubt, the text-books will be making it seem the most obvious thing in the world. But it was never predicted by those scientific historians who looked too confidently forward into the future because they had looked, with insufficient imagination, on the past.

Who then, among historians, has seen farthest into the future? Ironically, it is those who have made the least claim to rational prophecy: those who, in looking at past history, have admitted the limitations of human free-will but have been most careful to reserve its rights, and who, in order to leave some room for the operations of the imagination, have preferred to pose rather than to answer questions, to wonder rather than to 'explain why'. What has been called 'the mysterious wisdom of Thucydides' will continue to be read, though he offers no system and answers no question, while the 'universal histories' of the great philosophers follow each other into oblivion. Of the great 'philosophical' historians only Gibbon survives, and that not because he had a consistent philosophy (as indeed he had) but because his philosophy never forced the pace. It never denied the power of free-will. Above all, his imagination never slept.

Always, as his eye was fixed on one event, or one situation in history, Gibbon's mind was ranging over distant horizons, thinking of analogies, contrasts, possibilities, to envisage, or correct, a generalisation. Might the ancient classics have been more completely saved, in the Middle Ages, if the technique of printing, instead of the manufacture of silk, had been conveyed from China to Europe? Or should we 'tremble at the thought' that they might have been more completely lost by an earlier Turkish conquest of Byzantium? How narrowly Rome was saved, by the valour of a single pope, in the seventh century, from the oblivion that has enveloped Thebes and Babylon and Carthage! How injuriously the Goths – 'those innocent barbarians' – are accused of the ruin of antiquity! 'What a moment in the annals of science' was the preservation, by Alexander, of the Babylonian astronomical records, and their communication, at the request of Aristotle, to the astronomers of Greece![7] How well the Lombard barbarians of the Dark Ages stand comparison, in their treatment of witches, with the lawyers and clergy of the seventh century! How fatal have been the long-term effects of the Mongol conquest of Russia, 'the deep and perhaps indelible mark which the servitude of 200 years has imprinted on the character of the Russians!' And how can I resist, in this place, the temptation to quote that vision of the future if the outcome of the eighth-century battle of Poitiers had been different: the advance of Islam to the confines of Poland and the Highlands of Scotland. 'The Rhine is not more impassable than the Nile or Euphrates, and the Arabian fleet might have sailed without a naval combat into the mouth of the Thames. Perhaps the interpretation of the Koran would now be taught in the Schools of Oxford, and her pulpits might demonstrate to a circumcised people the sanctity and truth of the revelation of Mohammed.' Perhaps it still may.

For in the end, it is the imagination of the historian, not his scholarship or his method (necessary though these are), which will discern the hidden forces of change. This, I suppose, is what Theodore Mommsen meant when he spoke of the divinatory gift of the historian, and this is what Jacob Burck-hardt meant when he spoke of *Ahnung*, contemplation, the capacity 'to see the present lying in the past'. Burckhardt denied that history was scientific. He recognised no orderly *Weltgeschichte*, no 'world plan'. He refused to prophesy, as his German contemporaries prophesied. 'We would gladly know the waves which are to carry us out into the ocean' of the immediate future, he wrote in 1870; 'but we ourselves are those waves'. Yet by his marvellous combination of historical understanding and imagination he alone foresaw, what neither Ranke nor Marx nor any other contemporary could foresee: the emergence, out of the decaying body of liberal Europe, of the new industrial despotisms of the twentieth century, and, in particular, of twentieth-century Germany. Some years ago, in a published article, I touched lightly on this contrast, and was duly reproved by a Marxist historian who protested that Burckhardt merely scored a lucky shot: there was no science behind that accidental bull's-eye: he could not be compared with the 'scientific' Marx. Anyone who reads Burckhardt's writings, and can extract the profound philosophy which lies behind and sustains that deeply felt conviction, can dispose of that criticism. Altogether I do not regret that I have made most of you read some of Gibbon and some of you taste a little of Burckhardt.

Such is the imagination of which historical writing, and historical study, will always, I think, have need. To exercise such imagination may not be

[7] Gibbon wrote 'to the astronomer Hipparchus', which cannot be true; but the factual error does not affect the present point. He made a similar chronological error about the invention of printing in China.

within our power as historians; but to allow its importance, to recognise it when it is exercised, is, I believe, essential if we are to keep historical study among the humane subjects, to keep it alive.

With that last word I must prepare for my departure, always grateful to the university to which I owe my education over so long a period, and to the Faculty which has tolerated and sustained me, and happy that the chair which I am now to leave has not been frozen, or declared redundant, but is to be occupied by a historian of great distinction who happens also to be a fellow collegian, a former pupil, and an old friend.

I am glad also to observe, in the circumstances of my own departure, an instance of almost Burckhardtian historical prediction. Twenty-six years ago I was so unfortunate as to displease, by a historical *obiter dictum*, that great champion of the Catholic Church, the late Mr Evelyn Waugh. In the course of the public debate which followed, and which became at times somewhat tart, that vigorous writer, believing that he had gained some advantage over me, broke into a cry of triumph. 'One honourable course,' he wrote, 'is open to Mr Trevor-Roper. He should change his name and seek a livelihood at Cambridge.'[8] This little episode had long faded from my memory, when it was recalled to it, a few weeks ago, outside Blackwell's bookshop, by that accurate recorder of ancient history, Professor Momigliano. I am sorry that Mr Waugh is not alive to savour this little victory, which I would willingly concede to one who cared so much for 'our rich and delicate language', the necessary vehicle and sole preservative, for us, both of history and of imagination.

[8] *New Statesman*, 2 Jan. 1954.

Index

Abbas, Ali, on the spleen, 82
Abbot, Archbishop George, a Balliol man, 161
Abbotsford, Walter Scott's house at, 314–15
Aberdeen: opposes Enlightenment, 204–6, 258, 265–6, 269; Marischal College, 16
Abyssinia, Mussolini and, 359
Adams, Thomas, preaches on poor relief, 130
Addington, Henry, first Viscount Sidmouth, Toryism of, 309
Addison, John, admired by Lord Holland, 300
Africanus, Constantinus, translator, 82
Agrippa, Henry Cornelius, and neo-Platonism, 106–11, 114
Alais, Peace of, 79
Alasco, John, Polish prince, 105
Alberti, Salomon, and the spleen, 83
alehouses: in Laudian Oxford, 153–5, 159; see also Milton
Alençon, François Duc de, matched, 94
Alexander the Great, and Gibbon, 368
Alexander VI, Pope, and elevation of J. Morton, 58
Alfonsi, Petrus, Jewish convert to Christianity, 32–3
Allen, John, staunch Scotch Whig, 303, 306–7
almsgiving, 46–7, 59; see also poor relief
Alvanley, Lord, see Arden
Amar, André, enemy of Robespierre, 282
Amboise, placards in, 75
America, North, 8, 16, 283; pre-Columbian, 13; colonised, 207; in eighteenth century, 243–5, 247–8, 256, 260–2, 265–6; United States, 342, 361, 366; see also Canada
Amery, Leopold, and imperialism, 343
Ammonio, Antonio, and T. More, 63
Amsterdam, prosperity of, 80
Anabaptists, at Münster, 75
Andreas, Archbishop of Bari, 34
Andrew, St., Apostle, 238
Angle, Guichard d', Earl of Huntingdon, plain burial of, 51
Anglicus, Bartholomaeus, and the spleen, 82
Anne, Empress of Russia, and German party, 236
Antichrist, final fling of, 359
Antigua, 257
Antwerp: prosperity of, 80; printer of, 136

Aquinas, Thomas: on sin of curiosity, 38; T. More and, 61, 65; respected by G. Bruno, 111
Archilochus, and Homer, 28
Arden, Richard Pepper, second Lord Alvanley, at Holland House, 307
Aristides, A. Marvell compared to, 200
Aristotle: on Homer, 27; T. More and, 58; G. Bruno and, 111; T. Hobbes and, 183; and mathematics, 219–20, 368
Arminianism: and Archbishop Laud, 156–7; and republicanism, 195
Arnauld, Antoine, and Cartesianism, 225
Arthur, King, legend of, 357
Arundel Castle, prayers at, 46
Arundel, Archbishop Thomas, makes a self-deprecating will, 51
Arundel, Earl of, see Fitzalan, Richard
Ashburton, Lady, see Baring, Anne Louisa
Ashkenaz, son of Gomer and forebear of Teutons, 137
Asquith, Herbert Henry: his classical education, 8; his list of peerages, 330
Assyria, ancient barbarism of, 9
Athens, festival at, 19, 28
Atholl, Duke of, see Murray
Aubignac et de Meimec, Abbé François de, his low opinion of Homer, 15, 18
Aubrey, John, on his contemporaries, 184n, 191, 214
Augsburg, Peace of, 76
Augustine, St.: T. More on, 58; thought of, 68–9, 138–9, 143
Augustus Caesar, and Charles II, 194n
Aurelianus, Caelius, on the spleen, 83
Austerlitz, battle of, 299
Australia, 336, 353–4
Austria, centralised, 364
Axholme, Charterhouse of, 52
Aymé, Marcel, novelist, 280

Babylon, astronomical records of, 368
Bacon, Francis: in parliament, 98; on tongues, 133; a friendship of, 189; on foreign policy, 198n; admired by Voltaire, 221
Bacon, Roger, school of, 111
Baltic, grain from, 283
Balzac, 275